Chronicle of King Charles VII

OTHER BOOKS FROM BLUE KEY

Chronicle of King Charles VII: Part I: 1422 – 1448, by Jean Chartier, translated and edited by Derek R. Whaley (2024)

The Wilted Lily Representations of the Greater Capetian Dynasty within the Vernacular Tradition of Saint-Denis, 1274-1461, by Derek R. Whaley (2024)

Adaptations of Dune*: Frank Herbert's Story on Screen*, by Kara Kennedy (2024)

OTHER WORKS BY DEREK R. WHALEY

'From *a* Salic Law to *the* Salic Law: The Creation and Re-Creation of the Royal Succession System of Medieval France', in *The Routledge History of Monarchy* (Routledge, 2019)

'Jean Chartier and the End of the Vernacular Tradition of Saint-Denis', in *The Waxing of the Middle Ages: Revisiting Late Medieval France* (University of Delaware Press, 2023)

'The Queens' Reflection: French Consorts as a Mirror of French History', in *The Routledge Handbook of French History* (Routledge, 2023)

Chronicle of King Charles VII

PART II: 1449 – 1461

By Jean Chartier,
grand chanter and royal historiographer
at the Abbey of Saint-Denis in France

Translated and edited by
Derek R. Whaley

First published in 2026 by
BLUE KEY
Phoenix, Arizona

First edition, February 2026

Cover design by Derek R. Whaley

Library of Congress Control Number: 2026900091

ISBN 978-1-953609-95-3

Publisher's Cataloging-in-Publication data

Chartier, Jean, unknown–1464, author ; Whaley, Derek Ryan, 1983–, editor, translator
[Chronique du roy charles vii, English]
Chronicle of King Charles VII, Part II : 1449 – 1461 / Jean Chartier ; edited and translated by Derek R. Whaley.—1st ed.
xviii, 540 p. : ill. ; 20 cm.
ISBN 978-1-953609-95-3
1. Chartier, Jean. 2. Abbaye de Saint-Denis (Saint-Denis, France). 3. France—History—Medieval period, 987-1515—Sources. 4. Charles VII,—King of France, 1403-1461. 5. France—History—Charles VII, 1422-1461. I. Title.
DC102.A2 C5 2025
944.026 2026900091

Special thanks to the
Bibliographical Society
for providing funding in
support of this publication

Introduction

By Derek R. Whaley

In the late summer of 2014, I began work on my doctoral thesis at the University of Canterbury in Christchurch, New Zealand. My research focused on the vernacular chronicles produced at the Benedictine Abbey of Saint-Denis in France, a monastic institution where the bodies of the Frankish and French kings of the Merovingian, Carolingian, and Capetian dynasties were interred until the death of Louis XVIII in 1824. This research eventually resulted in my book, *The Wilted Lily: Representations of the Greater Capetian Dynasty within the Vernacular Tradition of Saint-Denis, 1274–1461*, as well as several chapters in edited collections.

From almost the moment I submitted the final version of my thesis to my supervisor in August 2017, I began work on a translation of Jean Chartier's *Chronicle of King Charles VII*. At first, it was intended to keep my knowledge of Middle French current and provide me with an initial academic project if my career went in that direction. Yet, although I ultimately chose a different path, my work on this translation continued as some lingering thread to a career unrealised. Eight years have now passed, and this book represents the second half of my transcription and translation of Chartier's most well-known text. On many occasions I have considered abandoning the project or been encouraged to do so by others, but by chipping away at a page or two a day, slow but steady

progress was made and I feel the results are of sufficient quality to justify publication even if the quality of the final translation is somewhat less than I had imagined.

Middle French in many ways is an easier language to read and translate than modern French. It sits as a continuation language in the evolution of Classical Latin into modern French and as such is heavily influenced by Latin to the exclusion of most other linguistic influences. The language arose in the thirteenth century out of Old French and became the most common language among European countries due to the Crusades, inter-dynastic marriages with French royals and aristocrats, and the spread of French-inspired chivalric culture. However, the literary culture of France was dominated by Church Latin despite the fact that few even amongst the elite could understand the language. Demand for vernacular texts generally went unanswered since the most literate in society—the clergy—were the very people ensuring the dominance of Latin. Nevertheless, vernacular texts began to emerge in this period.

By the 1200s, the French royal court itself began commissioning texts in the vernacular, probably to serve as textbooks to teach royal and aristocratic children morality, good governance, religion, and other matters related to leadership. As the protectors and purveyors of knowledge, monks working at scriptoriums such as that at the Benedictine Abbey of Saint-Denis decided it was better to accept commissions to write such works and remain in the good grace of the French king than to decline on principle and risk losing royal patronage. While earlier vernacular French texts have been found, the earliest produced at Saint-Denis was the *Roman des rois*,

compiled, adapted, and translated by the monk Primat and presented to King Philippe III in the year 1274. It was a long chronicle of French history beginning with the Siege of Troy as depicted in the *Aeneid* and concluding with the death of Philippe II Auguste in 1223.

Following Primat, other monks at Saint-Denis and elsewhere continued the tradition for nearly 200 more years. His immediate successors at the abbey were Guillaume de Nangis and Richard Lescot, who both concurrently wrote Latin and French language chronicles documenting the reigns of the kings to 1350. While Lescot and Michel Pintoin extended the Latin chronicle further to 1419, several government officials—Pierre d'Orgemont, Jean Juvénal des Ursins, and Gilles le Bouvier—oversaw the continuation of the French chronicle to the death of Charles VI in 1422. By this year, the French monarchy reached one of its lowest points, with northern France including Paris and Saint-Denis in the hands of the English and Burgundians and the new king, Charles VII, running his court out of Bourges in the south. The Latin and vernacular chronicle traditions fell into abeyance as the monks at Saint-Denis awaited either salvation or acceptance of their new place within Anglo-Burgundian society. It was in this environment that Jean Chartier first entered the pages of history.

The life of Jean Chartier has been much discussed over the past four centuries, and little is certain regarding the Benedictine monk outside of what he says in his works. Through careful analysis of dozens of primary and secondary sources, a concise biography has largely been agreed upon by historians; however, it still leaves much in doubt. Chartier's origins

remain mysterious and were long a point of debate among historians. For many centuries, he was named a brother of Guillaume Chartier, bishop of Paris, and Alain Chartier, a well-known poet and royal secretary, but these associations were disproven at the turn of the twentieth century by Gaston du Fresne de Beaucourt and Charles Samaran. The first verifiable fact about the monk is that he was provost of Garenne in 1430, a position responsible for the maintenance of multiple abbey properties, which suggests he was greatly respected by his colleagues at the abbey. He became provost of Mareuil for a year from 1433 and then became commander (treasurer) of Saint-Denis, placing him in rank directly below the abbot. This positioned him well in 1440 when the abbot died and he was appointed co-regent. While in this role, Chartier achieved his final promotion to the position of Grand Chanter, a title he likely accepted in November 1441 shortly after the incumbent, Hue Pain, passed away. Chartier was personally given the new position of Royal Historiographer by Charles VII on 8 November 1437. This role granted him a pension of 200 *livres parisis* annually and obliged him to accompany the court on royal processions and military campaigns. The accomplished chanter died on 9 February 1464 and was succeeded as Royal Historiographer by Jean Castel and as Grand Chanter by Jean Jaloux.

Historians agree that Chartier produced two chronicles, one in Latin and one in French, and most also acknowledge him as the author of the final three years of Pintoin's *Chronicorum Karoli Sexti*, the chronicle of Charles VI. However, the centuries of fabricated and erroneous history regarding the monk's biography have left a substantial impact on how

modern historians approach Chartier. One point of contention is when precisely the monk began writing his Latin chronicle, which all agree is his earlier work. When Michel Pintoin died in 1421—a year after Saint-Denis was given to the English in the Treaty of Troyes—it appears that no abbey historian replaced him. Chartier states this outright, explaining in the prologue to his Latin chronicle, "Necessity compels me to fill a fifteen-year gap. . . . Moreover, since this time [1422], the deeds have by no means been recorded, or [only] a small amount has been done to provide any record of events. It is for this reason that necessity compels me to recover the said time, piece by piece". It was only after Chartier was appointed historiographer in 1437 that literary output again issued from the abbey. Once installed, Chartier completed Pintoin's Latin chronicle, continuing it to 1450. He made the decision to end the *Chronique Latine* prematurely, not with the death of the king in 1461 but at the end of his Normandy campaign in August 1450. After recounting the French capture of Cherbourg, Chartier appends a short epilogue that states that the king's victory over the English serves as an appropriate conclusion to this work.

Chartier began writing his *Chronique du roi Charles VII* between 1441 and 1445, after he became chanter, the title that he calls himself in the prologue. Like the Latin text, it was produced under the sponsorship of the French king. In general, the vernacular chronicle serves as a direct translation of the *Chronique Latine*, but it also includes many extended and new chapters. Most of the narrative differences between the two texts revolve around political issues, especially those relating to Burgundy. Only the final eleven years of the text

are completely unique to the chronicle. Notably, material relating to four of those years is almost completely absent, as is any hint of the rehabilitation trial of Jeanne d'Arc, which is considered by historians to be an important capstone to Charles VII's reign. In 1476, printer Pasquier Bonhomme made Chartier's work the concluding piece in the *Chroniques de France*, which was the first French history published on a printing press. The subsequent diffusion of this work throughout northern France and the Low Countries rendered the vernacular chronicle more important than its Latin counterpart and it remains the better known of Chartier's works today.

This translation of Chartier's *Chronique du roi Charles VII* is derived from the second half of Bibliothèque nationale de France manuscrit français 5051 (BNF fr. 5051). It is written entirely by a single hand in a late medieval humanist miniscule style, which was a common style used by government officials at the time. Each chapter is adorned with a rubric written in red ink. Yellow stains around characters found throughout the book suggest residue from an adhesive that likely held gold leaf. Curiously, the book never advanced to its final stage of production; spaces for large decorated capitals at the start of each chapter remain vacant except for small reference letters. Only two large red capitals have been included—one at the beginning of the chronicle and a second near the middle—suggesting the text was abandoned not long after the primary text was written, before any decision regarding illumination was made.

It is important to emphasise that this is not the original text completed by Jean Chartier prior to his death in 1464. The original has either been lost or has not been identified. The

transcriber of this volume was clearly copying from another edition, possibly the original. As evidence for this assertion, the writing features numerous corrected and uncorrected mistakes (noted in this transcription with an underline or strikethrough), many the result of the copyist skipping ahead several words while transcribing. However, it is also probably the earliest surviving version of the text. The slightly later source used by Auguste Vallet de Viriville in his 1858 transcription includes several chapters and passages absent in this edition as well as a higher level of detail, suggesting editorial tinkering of the original text by Chartier. Notably some names, usually of Englishmen, included in later editions are left blank in this edition, suggesting the copyist or Chartier himself planned to input these names later but never did.

Stylistically, this edition uses Latin and Middle French shorthand irregularly, evidence that Chartier or the copyist may not have been entirely comfortable with this style of writing. Indeed, if this is the fault of Chartier, it may reflect a loss of knowledge of Latin shorthand during the fifteen years Saint-Denis was occupied by the English. In the transcription included in this book, all of the shorthand has been retained using modern typographical equivalents. The 'long s' (ſ), which was standard in French writing until the nineteenth century, is used throughout. The copyist also occasionally used the 'Tironian et' (⁊) in place of writing out 'et' (English: 'and'), and sometimes used the Latin shorthand character ꝯ as a prefix to replace 'con-' and its superscripted equivalent (ꝰ) as a suffix to replace '-us'. Other superscripted letters appear throughout the text in relation to dates, titles, and common words, but those are not detailed here since most are obvious

in their meaning from context.

In addition to employing shorthand characters, the copyist frequently used scribal abbreviation techniques to suppress specific letters from words, most frequently the letters s and n. In this transcription, these abbreviations are denoted with inverted (ˆ) and double-inverted (⁀) breves where they appear in the text. Medieval French was a more linguistically reflexive language than modern French. As such, it relied heavily on the word 'dit' (English: 'said') to refer to people, places, or events previously mentioned, often adding the word as a suffix to a pronoun or article, for example 'mondit' (English: 'my said') or 'leſdits' ('the saids'). The copyist, recognising the frequency of this adjective, in almost all cases reduced the 'dit' to the letter 'd' (e.g., 'mond' or 'leſd'), regardless of whether it was paired with a singular or plural noun or part of a compound noun. French at this time did not have separate characters for the letters J and V. Therefore, these letters do not or only rarely appear in the transcription and otherwise are rendered using the letters I and U. Lastly, the letters R and I are often capitalised by the copyist for unknown reasons—this style has been retained in the transcription where it appears in the original manuscript.

This translation is an attempt at a literal interpretation of BNF fr. 5051, whenever possible. This is not done out of some methodological desire for precision but rather is a practical decision made in order to make completing the task easier. Translating a Middle French chronicle over 500 pages long is difficult, especially for someone doing it as a hobby rather than as part of their profession. Thus, this translation has room for improvement in many different ways. Sentences

have been rearranged for readability and other quality-of-life compromises have been made, but there are other places in this translation where Chartier's meaning remains unclear. While all words have been translated, their meanings sometimes had to be gleaned from the context and may be incorrect. Such are the problems of translating a dead language where idioms and word definitions have been lost.

Chartier himself and Middle French in general are to blame for some of these issues. The chanter often replicated the style of his predecessors and it is clear that he did not always understand their style of writing. Furthermore, he relied on a variety of contemporary and near contemporary documents to compose his chronicle and sometimes misinterpreted, mistranscribed, mistranslated, or misunderstood these sources. And one must not forget that Middle French was a rapidly evolving language and grammatical rules were not yet standardised. Many sentences follow a Latin structure with the subject and object nouns gathered before or after a verb. This can cause confusion to the reader if the context does not clarify the correct order or leaves the subject ambiguous. Chartier also rarely used pronouns, forcing conjugated verbs to do all of the work and leaving open the possibility of subject–object confusion, especially if a sentence includes a subject, direct object, and indirect object that are arranged together. More broadly, a lack of punctuation, overuse of misleading gilded lettering, and inconsistent grammar leave some sentences without verbs or lacking other important grammatical features. These issues and others make the task of translating this manuscript all the more difficult.

Ultimately, one must draw the line somewhere. After a

full transcription and translation using Vallet de Viriville's transcription as a basis, two thorough revisions of this transcription to match it to the text of BNF fr. 5051, and two extensive revisions of the translations to ensure consistency and improve readability, this book and its predecessor are the results. This is by no means a perfect translation, but it is a well-intended one.

When this project first began, I had a vision that the transcription and translation could serve as a textbook for a Middle French language course. That dream has faded but the output remains. Perhaps this translation can still serve as an inspiration and guide for students encountering Middle French for the first time. Close attention has been paid to the transcription to bring it in line with the manuscript which, through this work and the generous financial support of the Bibliographical Society, has been made available digitally on the website of the Bibliothèque nationale de France. May students use this transcription and the original manuscript to attempt their own translations, compare them to this one, and improve upon it, all while learning about the calamitous times that Chartier witnessed in the concluding decades of the Hundred Years' War.

Chronicle of King Charles VII

Comment laville ⁊chaſteau defougr̃es furent p̊ns par les adherens aux angloiz les treves durât ent̃ les Roys defrance et dangleterre.

En ce meſme an veille denot̃ dame deMars fut laville ⁊chaſteau defougieres ſituez en laduchie debretaigne alentree deNormendie qui eſtoit tres Riche bien peupplee deNotables gens et demoult grant Renommee detoute anciennete prinſe ⁊pillee en enfraignat̃ les treves ⁊durat̃ Icelles. Ent̃ les Roys defrance ⁊dangleterre. Ceſt aſſavoir par meſſire francois deſuirenne dit larragonnoiz delordre delaIairtiere dud Roy danglet̃re ⁊grant capitaine es marches defrâce obeiſſans auſd angloiz accompaignie deſix aſept cens combatans tant delalangue defrancecom̃ dud anglet̃re. Et tellement quilz tueret̃ en Icelle ville aucunes gens les aut̃s prindrent priſõniers viollerent egliſes ⁊femmes Ravirent to⁹ les biens qui yeſtoien. Et firent to^s les maulx donc Ilz ſepeurent adviſer. Et non contens encore delad prinſe allerent courir en laduche debretaigne prendre priſonniers appatiſſier lepays tuerent gens. Et generallement firent tous exploitz acouſtumes aufait deguerre laquelle prinſe ⁊aut̃s choſes deſſſd venues alacongnoeſſance demonſ^r francois duc de bretaigne comme fort Indigne et ſoy ſentant dicelle prinſe fort greve. Envoya devers leRoy defrance achinon leveſque deRegnes leſire dekarmene et leſire deguymene ſon chancellr̃ ⁊aut̃s lui Remonſtr̃ côme ſoubz latreve en laquelle Il avoit eſte comp̃is ſoy confiant ⁊aſſeurant en Icelle les angloiz avoient prins les chaſteau ⁊ville defougiere. En lui Rq̃rant comme ſon treſhumble parent ⁊ſerviteur quil lui pleuſt aider ſecourir ⁊conforter en ſoy deſclairant

How the town of Fougières was captured by the adherents to the English during the period of truce between the kings of France and of England

In this same year [1449], on the eve of Notre-Dame in March, the town and castle of Fougières, situated in the duchy of Brittany at the entrance to Normandy, which was very wealthy, well-peopled by notable men, and very greatly renowned from ancient days, was captured and pillaged, infracting upon the truces and during those [truces] between the kings of France and of England. It was done by messire Francis de Surienne, called the Aragonese, of the Order of the Garter of the said king of England, and a great captain in the marches of France obedient to the said English, accompanied by 600 to 700 soldiers, both of the language of France and of the said England. And such that they killed several men in this town, the others being imprisoned, violated churches and women, ravaged all the goods that were there. And they did all the evil things that they could. And, still not content with the said sacking, they went into the duchy of Brittany, captured prisoners, razed the country, killed men, and generally made all exploits accustomed to the deeds of war, which captures and other abovesaid things came to the knowledge of monseigneur François, duke of Brittany, who was very indignant and felt himself to be very aggrieved by this seizure. He sent to the king of France at Chinon the bishop of Rennes, the sire de Charmène and the sire of Guéménée, his chancellor, and others to show him under the truce in which he had agreed, himself confident and assured in this, the English had captured the castle and town of Fougières. By asking him, as his very humble relative and servant, that

en laguerre cont̂ Iceulx angloiz. Car desapart Il estoit ainssi prest delefr sans yRiens espargner. Aquoy leRoy lui Respondit quil ne labandonneroit point ⁊quil feroit desacause lasienne comme bien Rais estoit. Maiz pour mieulx ~~d~~ mettre desapart et le~~dame~~ tort ases ennemys Il envoya p̊mierement sommer leRoy dangleterre deReparer led excepz et leduc desômrecet son lieutenant ⁊gouverneur pour lui desalamer es pays obess alui. Et lequel apres povoir defaire Remparer toutes choses qui seferoient cont̂ et en p̊iudice de latreve. Et feroit bien Ioyeulx q̂ Icellui Roy dangleťre ⁊leduc desombrecet feissent Reparacion dud cas advenu pour evitter to⁹Inconveniens qui alocasion dece pourroient advenir tant par guerre q̂ autment. Et pour ce fr envoya devr̂s led Roy dangleťre son varlet trenchant nôme Iehan havart et maistre guillaume cousinot lun des maistres des Requestes deson hostel. Et devers led duc desombrecet pierre de fontaines son escuier descuyerie lesquelz Raporteret̂ Responce tant dud Roy dangleťre comme dud duc desombrecet que Ilz desadvouoient led messire frâcois desurienne dece quil avoit fait Iasoit ceque lad prinse avoit este faicte par lecon mandemen exortacion etordonnance diceulx Roy et sombrecet. Leduc debretaigne pareillement qui avoit grant In̂tests en laprinse envoya sommer led duc par son herault Roy darmes defaire Rendre ⁊Remparer lad ville defougieres et Restituer les deniers biens meubles comme Ioyaulx ⁊autr̂s marchandises qui dedens avoiet̂ este prinses. Estimees alavalleur desaize Cens mille escuz. Auquel fut Respondu quil nadvouoit en Riens lad prinse. Apres ledepartement desquelz ambassadeurs et herault led duc desombrecet considerant lafaulte qui avoit este fctê en ceste partie par led

he would aid, help, and comfort him, in declaring himself in a state of war against these English. Because on his part, he was already ready to do it without losing anything. To which the king responded to him that he would no longer abandon him and that he would make his cause his own, as is good policy. But to better place himself for his part and the wrongdoing of his enemies, he sent first to summon the king of England and the duke of Somerset, his lieutenant and governor for him in the lands obedient to him over the sea, to repair the said error, and who had power to repair all the things that he had done against and in prejudice of the truce. And it would show faithfulness if this king of England and the duke of Somerset would make reparations for the said incident to avoid all inconveniences which in the event of this could occur both by war and otherwise. And for this, he sent to the said king of England his servant, named Jean Havart, and master Guillaume Cousinot, one of the masters of the requests of his hotel, and to the duke of Somerset, Pierre de Fontaines, his squire of the squirery, who reported the response of both the said king of England and the said duke of Somerset, who disavowed the said messire François de Surienne for that which he had done, insomuch as the said capture had been made by the command, exortation, and order of those of the king and Somerset. The duke of Brittany likewise, who had great interest in the capture, sent to summon the said duke by his herald king at arms to make, render, and repair the said town of Fougières and restore the monies, goods, such as jewelry and other merchandise that had been taken, estimated at a value of 600,000 écus, to which he responded that he had nothing from the said capture. After the departure of these ambassadors and herald, the said duke of

deſurienne envoya devr̃s le Roy ſes ambaſſadeurs pour plus plainement le excuſer dud fait defougieres. Ceſt aſſavoir meſſire Ieh͡ haneford chlr̃ angloiz et maiſtre Iehan lenffant En deſadvouant ~~tu~~ touſiours led meſſire francois et diſant Icelle prinſe eſtre alui moult deſplaiſans qui ſont ⁊eſtoient parolles frivolles. Et quant de faire offre aucune deReparer lecas torciônairem͡et advenu ne parlerent en Rien ne nedonneret̂ ĉtainete Maiz ſeullemet̂ Requeroient auſurplus pour leur advantaige que tout demouraſt en ſeurete tant dun coſte que daut̂. Aquoy leur fut Reſpondu par leRoy que ce led duc deſombreſet eſtoit deſplaiſat̂ delad prinſe quil feiſt ſon devoir comme celui qui en avoit lepovoir que Reſtitucion fuſt faicte delad place. Avec Reparacion des biens qui dedens avoient eſte prins furtivement ⁊cont̂ Raiſon. Et que parce moien latreve leur ſeroit cont̂tenue. Et aucontraire pareillement ſe ainſſi ne le faiſoient fuſſent ſceurs ⁊ĉtains quil ſouſtiendroit ſon beau nepveu debretaigne avoit degrans ſ^rs deſon Royaulme ſes parens. Et yavoit pluſſieurs chiefz. Et quant deleur baillr̃ des places ſceurte eſtans es mains diceulx angloiz Il nen bailleroit point diſant que ſon beau nepveu debretaigne avoit degrans ſeigneurs deſon Royaulme ſes parens et yavoit pluſſieurs chiefz deguerre et cappitaines en Icellui delanacion debretaigne qui eſtoient fort Indignez delad prinſe defoug͡ers. Et eſtoit acroire que Ilz mettroient paine deſẽ Revenge ⁊Recôqueſtr̃ ſur Iceulx angloiz ſilz povoiet̂. Et pource gardaſſent bien leurs places ſibon leur ſembloit car deſapart mettroit paine abien garder les ſiennes. Laquelle Rêce ouye ſupplierent au Roy les deſſſd haneford et lenffant quil luy pleuſt envoyer ſes ambaſſadeurs alouviers fondez depovoir ſouffiſant. Et q̂ eulx

Somerset, considering the error that had been made in this part by the said de Surienne, sent to the king his ambassadors to more plainly excuse himself for the said deeds at Fougières, it is known messire John Haneford, an English knight, and master John Lenffant, disavowing everything by the said messire François and saying this capture was very displeasing to him, which are and were frivolous words. And when he offered to repair what accidentally happened, they said nothing [and] gave no guarantees, but they would only ask for the surplus of their advantage that all would remain as surety, both on one side and the other. To which it was said to them by the king that if the said duke of Somerset was displeased by the said capture, that he would do his duty, as much as he had the power, so that restitution was made for the said place, with reparation of goods that had been taken furtively and against reason. And that, by this means, the truce between them would be continued. And if not, likewise, he did not do so, they were sure and certain that he would support his good nephew of Brittany. And when for them to give of the places surety, being in the hands of these Englishmen, he would no longer release it, saying that his good nephew of Brittany had of great lords of his kingdom, his relatives, and there were several war leaders and captains of the nation of Brittany who were very indignant due to the said capture of Fougères. And it was believed that they took pain to avenge themselves and reconquer it from these Englishmen, if they could. And for this they guarded well their places as it seemed good to them, because on his part it would be difficult to guard his things. Which response being heard, the abovesaid Haneford and Lenffant begged the king that he could send his ambassadors to Louviers in search of sufficient

Rtournez aRouen Ilz fairoient bien q̂ leconte deſombrecet conmettroit deſes gens po^{r} aſſembler avec eulx. Affin deparvenir aquelq̂ bon appôtemet̂ et acord laquelle choſe par leRoy deſirant touſiou^{s} ladoulce voye et eviter effuſion deſangc humain leur fut adcordee ⁊furent commis deſapart le ſire deculant et maiſtre guillaume couſinot maiſtre des Requeſtes deſon hoſtel. Et atant ſe departirent leſd angloiz et ſen Rtournerent devers led duc deſombrecet ~~Aufs~~ Auquel Ilz narrerent ce quilz avoient fait avecques le Roy de france et lappoinctement quilz avoient prins ꝑquoy en briefve eſpace detemps Il envoya deſes gens ~~audur~~ audit lieu delouviers pour convenir avecq͡z les ambaſſadeurs dud Roy defrance ſur lamatiere deſſſd. Ainſſi com̂ promis ⁊appoinctie avoit eſte.

Du diſcord et diviſion meu en Royaulme dangleterre.

En ce meſmes temps ⁊oud an environ lafin dekareſme commenca grant cômocion de peuple en laville ⁊cite delondres duquel peuple eſtoit ducteur ⁊conduiſeur lemaire deladcite leſquelz par linſtigacion delennemy eſmeuz dele^{r} voullente deſraiſonnable tuerent Inhumainement leveſque deceleſte garde duprive ſeel duRoy danglet̂re qui eſtoit ſimple bonne perſonne ⁊fonde en ſcience. Et avecques ce prindrent lemarquis deſufford qui eſtoit grant ſeigneur et lemirent en priſon en la groſſe tour delondres. Ced maire amoult grat̂ puiſſance en Icelle ville. Et porte len leſpee devat̂ luy quant Il va parmy laville. En cetemps eſte leRoy danglet̂re atrois lieues delondres ſur laRivrê detamiſe le-

power. And that [when] they returned to Rouen, they would make good that the earl of Somerset would commit his men to assemble with them. So that he could reach such a good agreement and accord, which thing by the king, desiring always the gentle path and to avoid the effusion of human blood, agreed with them, and the sire de Culant and master Guillaume Cousinot, master of the requests of his hotel, commited [to this goal] on his part. And many of the said Englishmen departed and returned to the said duke of Somerset, to whom they described what they had done with the king of France and the agreement that they had made, during which brief space of time, he send some of his men to the said place of Louviers to discuss with the ambassadors of the said king of France on the abovesaid matter, as was promised and had been agreed.

Of the discord and divisions moving in the kingdom of England

In this same time and in the said year, around the end of Lent, there arose a great commotion amongst the people in the town and city of London, over which people was commander and leader the mayor of the said city, which, by the instigation of the enemy, moved by their unreasonable will, inhumainly killed the bishop of Gloucester, guardian of the privy seal of the king of England, who was a simple, good person, and student of science. And with him, they seized the marquis of Suffolk, who was a great lord, and they put him in prison in the largest tower [in the Tower of] London. This said mayor had very great power in this town. And he carried the sword before him when he went about the town. In this time, the king of England was three leagues

quel fut moult eſbahy quāt Il ouyt ſes nouvelles. Et Incontinent manda le lieutenāt delad groſſe tour quil veniſt devers lui. Aquoy Il obbait treſdilliganment comme aſon ſouverain ſeigneur. Et apres quil ouyt lamaniere ⁊lefait tel comme Il eſtoit advenu ouy ⁊ſceu au vray luy fiſt commandement que ſans delay aucun quil envoyaſt querir led marquis deſuffford et amenſaſt ſauvement ou autment Il leferoit mourir en ſaprce. Et pource trouva maniere delamener devrs leRoy ſans le ſceu dud maire ⁊peuple. Et aps que led Roy leut ouy parlr̃ lefiſt monter achl et ſen fuyt droit aupays dunort ou Il ſemiſt en mer pour venir en france. Et fut Rencontre de c̃taines gens qui eſtoient auduc deſombrecet Leſquelz leprindrent ⁊lui coupperēt lateſte la quelle Ilz envoyerent avecques lecorps en lad ville delondres. Et adonc manderent au Roy leſd maire ⁊hâtans dicelle ville quilz eſtoient treſmal contens dece quil avoit fait delivrer led marquis. En lui Requerant quil leur envoyaſt aucuns deſon conſeil qui avoient pourchaſſe lad delibrance. Lequel doubtant fureur depeuple et linconvenient delamort les leur envoya. Et tantoſt leur firēt tranchr̃ les teſtes. Et Ainſſi ceulx delondres apres c̃taine eſpace detemps furent appaiſez devers leRoy.

Dame fême pandus aparis et Iugee par lecourt deparlemēt Sans aucune appellacion.

Lan mille CCCC quarante neuf leſamedy dixhucitieſme Iour davril furēt Iugez parlacour deparlement deux coquins ⁊une conquine aeſtre pendus ⁊eſtranglez. Et pource furent levees une potences deboys pour plus man-

from London on the River Thames, who was very disturbed when he heard this news. And angered, he ordered the lieutenant of the said Tower to come to him. For which he obeyed very diligently as his sovereign lord. And after he heard the manner and the facts as it had heard it and knew the truth, he ordered without delay several that he sent to fetch the said marquis of Suffolk and bring him safely to him, or otherwise he would be killed in his presence. And for this, he found the manner to bring him to the king without the knowledge of the said mayor and people. And after the said king had spoken to him, he mounted a horse and went straight to the lands of the North, where he set out to sea in order to come to France. And he encountered certain men who were of the duke of Somerset, who took him and beheaded him, whom they sent, with the body, to the said town of London. And then the said mayor and inhabitants of this town told the king that they were very displeased that he had released the said marquis, asking him that he would send to them any member of his council who had assisted in the said escape. Who, fearing the furor of the people and the inconvenience of the death, sent them to them. And soon they had beheaded them. And, thus, those of London, after a certain space of time, were appeased by the king.

A lady condemned at Paris and judged by the court of parlement without any summons

The year 1449, Saturday, the 28th day of April, two scoundrels and one mischievious woman were judged by the court of parlement to be hanged and strangled. And for this, a gallows of wood was raised in order to execute their sen-

ifefter leurs cas qui eftoient maulvaiz et dampnable Comme davoir creve les deux yeulx aung enffant pupille eftant lors en laage de deux ans et avoient fait cedelit defpingles qui eftoit grant tirannee. Et auffi deftre larrons ⁊actaints depluffieurs auťs malefices par eulx Recongnus lune defquelles potences fut mefr hors delaporte fainct Iacques en laquelle fut pendu lung defd deux hommes. Et lauť fut mife hors de laporte fainct denis enť lachapelle et lemolin avent. Alaquelle furent penduz lautre hôme qui eftoit Ioueur devielle et avecques lui lad fême. Et combien quilz fuffent mariez to⁹ deux. Neantmoins Il la maintenoit. Or eft vray que to⁹ les trois furet̂ livrez aubourreau aux prifons delaconciergerie. Et yeftoient acheval pour les convoyer laplufgrat̂ partie des huiffiers deparlement pource q lafentce avoit efte donnee fur lefd malfacteurs par lad cour. Et eft affavoir que grant multitude de peuple affluet detoutes pars. Et par efpecial femmes ⁊filles pour lavois lagrande nouveaulte que cetoit devoir pendre en Royaulme defrance une fême car oncques ou fut veu oud Roy[me]. Et fut lad femme pendue toute defchevelee en une longue Robe fainte dune corde les deux Iambes enfemble audeffoubz des genoulx. Et defoient aucuns quielle Requift eftre auffi executee et q̂ lacouftume defon pays eftoit telle en telcas. Et les autres difoient que lafentence fut donnee telle affin quil en fuft plus longue memoire aux autres femmes et auffi ledelict eftoit fienorme quil yappartenoit bien plus grande pugnicion quelle ne fut. Et yen et pluffieurs auťs pendus ⁊pluff[rs] auťs to⁹ coquins qui eftoient encores et prifons en chaftellet que on gardoit pour ĉtains caufes. Et par efpecial Iucques ace ~~en euft~~ q̂on preuft prendre ĉtains auťs coquins qui eftoient de leur bande ⁊li-

tence, which was evil and damnable, since, having punctured the two eyes of a small child who was then aged two years and having done this deed with pins, which was a great tyranny, and also to be a thief and tainted person of several other bad things proven by them and recognised, one of the gallows was built outside the gate of Saint James, on which was hanged one of the said two men, and the other was put outside the gate of Saint Denis, between the chapel and the windmill on which was hanged the other man, who was an old entertainer, and with him the said woman. And, although they were both married, nonetheless, he kept her. It is true that all three were handed to the executioner in the prisons of the caretaker of the palace. And there they were [placed] on horses to convey them [by] the greater part of the ballifs of parlement, by whom the sentence had been given on the said misdeeds by the said court. And it is known that the great multitude of people hastened from all parts. And especially women and girls, for the great novelty that it was to hang a woman in the kingdom of France, because until now, this had never been seen in the said kingdom. And the said woman was hanged all dishevelled, in a long holy robe with her two legs tied together below the knees. And they said that she requested not to be executed and that the custom of her country was such the case. And the others said that the sentence was given as such in order to give a longer memory to the other women and also the crime was so enormous that it deserved a much greater punishment than she had. And they and several others, all thiefs who were still in prison at the Châtellet who were guarded for certain reasons, were all hanged there. And especially those who one had stolen certain other thieves who were of their band and in

gue. Et ſuyuorient les pardons en pluſſieurs et divers lieux dece Royaume côme aladedicaſſe deſaint denis alaſaint mor alaſainct fiacre aſainct mathulin ⁊ailluers et ſetenoient es grans chemins des boys ou Ilz faiſoient de grans ſuiſſes ſoubz umbre dedemander laumoſne deſquelz en oult eſte prins les aucuns par les gens ⁊officiers duRoy apres pou dallarion detemps.

Laprinſe dupont delarche. par les francois.

Audit an xv^me^Iour dud moys de May les ambaſſadeurs du Roy ⁊ceulx duduc de ſombrecet eſtans aſſemblez en laville de louviers pour lefait delaville defougeres côm appoincte eſtoit enſ̂ leſd parties et des gens et alyez duduc debretagne Ceſt aſſavoir demeſſire Iehan debreze chlr̂ ⁊cap^ne^ delouviers Leſire demauny Robert deflocques dit flocquet bailly devreux et Iacques declermont trouverent facon ⁊manê deprend lechaſtel ⁊ville du pont delarche eſtans ſur laRiviere deſeine aquatre lieues deRouen. Et eſt vray q̂ ung voicturier delouviers eſtoit deIour aauſ̂ et ſouventeſſois Rencontre pas les angloiz en paſſant parmy led pont et veoit quil yavoit petite garde. Et pource ſe tranſporta devers leſd capitaine ſiegneur demauny Iacques declermoſ̂ et bailly devreux. Auſquelz traicta delui baillr̂ gens pour unes avecques lui et leur expoſa ĉtain moyen quil leur deſclara pour prendre lad place lequel leur ſembla bien poſſible. Et fut prins Iour decomparoir en loſtel dun tav̂nier demourant es faulxbourgs. Et ace Iour vindreſ̂ pluſſieurs des gens dicellui bailly ⁊leſire de maugny les ungz apres les auſ̂s affin q̂on ne ſaperceuſt

league. And they would seek alms in several and diverse places of this kingdom, such as at the dedicated of Saint-Denis, at Saint-Mor, at Saint-Fiacre, at Saint-Mathurin, and elsewhere, and they would stick to the great roads in the woods, where they would do bad things under the guise of asking for alms, several of whom were arrested by the men and officers of the king shortly afterwards.

The capture of Pont-de-l'Arche by the French

In the said year, fifteenth day of the month of May, the ambassadors of the king and those of the duke of Somerset were assembled in the town of Louviers to discuss the matter of the town of Fougères, since it had been agreed between the two said parties and some of the men and allies of the duke of Brittany—it is known messire Jean de Brezée, knight and captain of Louviers, the sire de Maulny, Robert de Flocques, called Flouquet, balliff of Évreux, and Jacques de Clermont—found a means and manner of capturing the castle and town of Pont-de-l'Arche on the river Seine four leagues from Rouen. And it is true that a goods hauler from Louviers passed frequently and often encountered the English in passing near the said bridge, and he saw that a very small guard was kept there. And because of this, he transported to this place the said captains: the seigneur de Maulny, Jacques de Clermont, and the bailly of Évreux. Through which agreement, men were exchanged for ones with him, and he revealed to them certain means by which he planned to capture the said place, which seemed very possible to them. And it took a day to prepare, staying in a hotel of a tavern in the suburbs. And on this day, there came several of the

deRien. Ent̂ leſquels on en avoit deux habillez en facon decharpentiers chc͡n ſa hache ſur lecol. Et auſſi aRivatantoſt apres led charoeties charrant aucue͡s denrees. Et apres que chc͡n fut loge environ lanuytant p̊rdret̂ Icelliu tavernier et ſes gens ⁊les ſarrerent en une chambre affin que leur ent̂prinſe ne fuſt deſcouverte. Et adonc ſedecouvrirent aud tav̂nier apres quil fut bien tant lequel en fut moult Ioyeaulx côme Il diſoit pource q̂ aucuns delagarniſon dicelle ville lavoient frappe denouvel. Et adonc ung led ſ[r] debreze ⁊ĉtaine gens depie avecques eulx embuſches pres dud lieu ducoſte dedevers lepont ſaint ouen. Et led bailly devreux quatre ou cinq cens combatans acheval en ſacompaigne auplus pres delad ville dedans leboys ducoſte dud louviers. Et auſſi led Iacques dechermot̂ Et led voicturier ung pou devant le Iour ſa voiture charge vint devant Icelluy pont priant auportier que Il peuſt paſſer pource q̂ Il avoit haſte. Et Il paieroit treſbien vin. En lacompaignie duquel eſtoient ſeullement leſd deux charpentiers. Pour lepaſſage deſquelz Reſpondit Icellui voicturier. Et tantoſt led portier pour convoitiſe davoir argent print ung aut̂ angloiz avec lui ⁊vindrent avaller lepont. Et quant led voicturier fut ſus le p̊rimier pont atout ſacharretier Il tira deſa bource deux bretons ⁊une placque pour paier led angloiz. Et laiſſa cheoir deſongre ~~une~~ ung breton pour lequel lever ſebaiſſa led angloiz portier. Et en ſebaiſſant led voiturier tira ſadague et letua. Et pareillemet̂ les deux charpentiers qui Ia eſtoient ſur leſecond pont tueret̂ laut̂ angloiz. Et adonc ſaillirent ceux delambuſche tant depie que decheval. Et entreret̂ dedens laville ⁊pont en criant ſaint ~~deux~~ yves bretaigne. Et eſtoient to⁹ les angloiz encores couche et furet̂ to⁹ prins Iuques au nombre decent aSix vingtz angloiz. Ent̂ leſquelz

men of this bailiff and sire de Maulny, one after another, so that one would notice nothing. Amongst whom there were two dressed in the guise of carpenters, each wearing his axe lapel on the collar, and also, soon afterwards, the said vallet arrived with several carts of merchandise. And after each was lodged, around midnight, they took this tavern-keeper and all his men and squeezed them into a room, so that their attack was not discovered. And so they discovered themselves at the said tavern afterwards he was well as long as he was very loyal, it is said, because none of the garrison of this town had struck him again. And thus the said sire de Breezé and certain footmen with him lay in ambush near the said place, on the side towards the gate of Saint-Ouen, and the said bailiff of Évreux, [with] 400 or 500 on horseback near to the said town, within the forest on the side of the said Louviers, and also the abovesaid Jacques de Clermont, and the said valet, a little before daybreak, having his cart loaded before this bridge, begging to the porter that he could pass, because he was in a very great haste. And he paid him very willingly with wine. In the company of whom was only the said two carpenters. And soon the said porter, for lust of money, took another Englishman with him and went downsteam of the bridge. And when the valet was on the first bridge with all of his carts, he took out of his purse two Bretons coins and a plate to pay the Englishman. And he allowed a Breton coin to fall in order for the said English porter to lean down. And while leaning, the said valet stabbed him with a dagger and killed him. And at the same time, the two carpenters, who were already at the second bridge, killed the other Englishman. And thus, those of the ambush sallied out, both on foot and on horseback. And they entered into the town and bridge crying: 'Saint-Yves! Brittany!' And all the Englishmen who were still hiding inside were captured, until the number was

eſtoit leſr defouquenberge chevallier angloiz qui eſtoit vieu leſon bon priſonnier pour vingt mille eſcuz lequel fut mene alouviers pour plus grant ſeurte. Et demourerēt aucuns deſd conqueſteurs gardes delad place Iuſques ace q̂ auītment en fuſt ordonne. laquelle p̊nſe venue alacôgnoiſſance deſd angloiz furēt fort deſoufortiz ⁊troublez et prindrent lachoſe a moult grant deſplaiſe. Et auſſi cevenu alacognoiſſance du-Roŷ defrance deſirant lebien ⁊prouffilt deſon beau nepveu leduc debretaigne Apres pluſſieurs Iournees Ia tenues. Et aſſemblees aud lieu delouviers fut contant q̂ tout fuſt Repare tant dun coſte q̂ dauī. Ceſt aſſavoir led fougeres aud duc avec les biens qui eſtoiēt dedans eſtimez aſeize cent [mille] eſcuz côme dit eſt. Et lad ville dupont delarche aleſd angloiz avec led ſr defaucquanberge qui dedans avoit eſte prins. Alaquelle choſe les angloiz ne vouldrent entendre qui eſtoit alle directe-mēt conī Raiſon ſicomme Il ſembloit. Et pource deRechief prn̂s ĉtains notaires apoſtolicques ⁊Imperieaux firēt leſd am-baſſadeurs du Roy aucunes proteſtactions et en Requirent lecrîs et Instrumens des offres par eulx faictes aud ~~auf~~ an-gloiz. En Remonſtrāt comme dieu ⁊lemonde pouvoient aſſez côgnoiſtre et appercevoir que leRoy ceſtoit moult grâdemēt cas en ſon devoir. Et q̂ par ſacoulpe laguerre aguirre ſille advenoit que dieu ne vouſiſt eſtoit point parlie. Et auſſi ſed-partirent les angloiz et ſen Rtournrēt devers leduc de ſom-brecet lui narrer et faire ſavoir cequi avoit eſte pourparle et fait enī leſd paſtus. Et ce pend pour proced plus ſeurement ⁊ſaigement LeRoy envoya devers ſon nepveu debretaigne avec grant ⁊ample povoir Monſr leconte de dunoiz Les ſires deRaiz et decoitivy admiral defrance et meſſire bertram de-beauvau ſr depreſigny Leſquelz firent appoinctement Apres

100 to 120 Englishmen. Amongst whom was Lord Faukenburg, an English knight, who was a good prisoner worth 20,000 *écus*, who was captured at Louviers during a great sortie. And several of the said conquerers remained to guard the said place, until they were ordered otherwise. When this capture came to the knowledge of the said Englishmen, they were very angered and troubled, and took the matter with great displeasure. And it also came to the knowledge of the king of France, who desired good and profit for his good nephew, the duke of Brittany, after several days already waiting. And meeting at the said place of Louviers, he was happy that all was repaired, on one side and the other. It is known, that the said Fougères [would be rendered] to the said duke, with the goods that were within, estimated at the sum of 600,000 *écus*, as it is said. And the said town of Pont-de-l'Arche with the said Englishmen, with the said Lord Faukenburg, who had been captured. To which thing the said English would not hear anything, which was directly against reason, so it seemed. And because of that, certain apostolic and imperial notairies being present, the said ambassadors of the king made several protestations and requested letters and instruments of the offers made by them to the said English, in protesting how God and the world could know enough and perceive that the king had put himself greatly in his debt. And that by his fault, the war (if it happened, then God no longer wants it!) was caused. And so the said Englishmen left and they returned to the said duke of Somerset to narrate to him and make known that which had happened and was discussed between the said ambassadors. And, however, in order to proceed more surely and wisely, the king sent to his said nephew of Brittany, with great and ample power, monseigneur the count of Dunois, the sires de Rais and de Coïtivy, admiral of France, and messire Bertram de Beauvau, seigneur de Présigny,

pluſſieurs narracions avec leduc debret[gne] luy eſtant en laville deRennes ou Il avoit aſſemble lapluſpart deſes parens prelatz barons ⁊chr̃s deſon pays que led duc promectoit deleſervir con les angloiz deſaperſonne ⁊puiſſance par mer et par terre. Ne Iamaiz aceulx neſeroit tractie ne paix que ce ne fuſt duconſentemet̃ congie et bon plaiſir du Roy. Et dece en bailla ſes lectres patentes ſignees deſamain. Eſquelles lectres eſtoient les ſeaulx ⁊ſeingz manuelz deſond pays. Et out̃ ſes parens ⁊barons lepromiſdrent deleur mains atouchre acelle dud contre dedunoiz de faire et tenir depoint en point ſans Iaunaz aller alencont̃ anul Iour lecontenu eſd lect̃s. Et de lapart duRoy en baillant leurs lec̃s quilz feroient Ratifier par leRoy led appoinctemet̃ cõme depuis Il a fait ⁊baille ſes lectres aud duc promectat̃ deleporter ⁊ſouſtenir et faire deſacauſe laſienne propre Ne nefera paix ne ault̃ appoinctemet̃ aux angloiz ſans lui comprend. Et ſes pays et q̃ Il fuſt Reſtitue p̊mierement dece que les angloiz tendroient duſien. Et encas q̂ lad place defougeres neluiſeroit Rendue leRoy ſedeſclairoit alaguerre out̃vertemet̃ ⁊applain cont̃ les angloiz dedans laffin du moys de Iuillet prochainement enſ.

Laprinſse de Gerberoys

En ce meſme an ⁊temps fut prinse laplace de gerberoys en beauvoiſin deſchelle par leſire demouy gouverneur dupays. Et lafuret̃ tuez tous les angloiz qui dedans eſtoient Nombrez trente perſonnes donc eſtoit chef et capitaine Nomme Jehan harpe qui ce Iour eſtoit alle agournay. Et auſſi fut Reduitte lad ville en lobbaiſſance duRoy defrance.

who were appointed after several discussions with the duke of Brittany, he being in his town of Rennes, where he had the better part of his relatives, prelates, barons, and knights of his country, which the said duke promised to serve him against the English personally and by the power of sea and land. Never would he treat for peace without the consent, leave, and good pleasure of the king. And for this, he released his letters patent, signed by his hand, in which letters were the seals and signatures of the barons of his said country. And in addition, his relatives and barons would promise by delivering their hands to that of my said lord of Dunois, to hold point-by-point without going against any of the content in the said letters. And on the part of the king, by delivered letters to them, that they would by the king ratify the said agreement, which had been done and he delivered his letters to the said duke, promising to carry and sustain him, and to make his cause his own, to not make peace nor other agreement with the English without his knowledge. And that he would first restore his lands, that which the English held of his. And in the case of the said place of Fougères, if it would not render itself, the king would declare himself in open and full war against the English by the end of the month of the following July.

The capture of Gerberoy

In the said year and time, the place of Gerberoy in Beauvoisin was captured by scaling by the sire de Mouy, governor of the land. And all the Englishmen who were within were killed, totalling thirty people, over whom was leader and captain one named John Harpe, who had arrived that day from Gournay. And thus the said town was reduced into the obedience of the king of France.

Lap̊riſe deconches par les francois.

En ce meſmes temps et bien pou apres fut p̊rſe laville deconches Par robert deflocques dit flocquet bailly devreulx.

Lap̊rſe decognat et deSaint maulgrin. en pays debourdellaiz par les francois.

En ce meſmes temps et an ung gentil hôme nôme verdin du pays de gaſcongne alaveu et duconſentement dud duc debretaigne print deſchelles ⁊emble les places deCoſnac et deſaint magrin aſſiſes au pays et deſſus les marches debordelaiz deſquelles eſtoit garde ⁊cap[ne] pour leRoy dangleт̂re ung eſcuier nomme mondeth delauſal lequel fut prins pres dud coſnac en venant debordaulx car Il cuidoit q̂ lad place fuſt encore en lobbeiſſance dud Roy dangleт̂re et en ſagarde côme ꝑdevant eſtoit. Et auſſi ~~apertit~~ apprit q̂ les bien veullans et allyez dud duc debretaigne veillent ⁊travailleт̂ fort pour grever ſes ennemys. Eſquelles deux places fureт̂ prins pluſſieurs priſonniers. Et quant les angloiz ſceureт̂ les nouvelles larceveſq̂ debôdeaulx et ceulx delacite envoyerent ung pourſuivant de chinon devers leRoy defrance lui Requrant quil fiſt Rendre leſd places deCoſnac et deſaint magrin et quil leur donnaſt ſaufconduit feignans venir devers luy dont detout on ne fiſt Rien pô ĉtaines cauſes mouvans leRoy ⁊ſon conſeil. Et pareillemeт̂ envoyerent leſd ducz deſombrecet et leſire de tallebot devers leRoy aud lieu dechinon. Maiſtre Iehan lenfant et ung auт̂ dangleт̂re po[r] Requerir que on ne

The capture of Conches by the French

In this same time and a little while afterwards, the town of Conches was captured by Robert de Flocques, called Flocquet, bailiff of Évreux.

The capture of Cognat and of Saint-Maigrin in the land of the Bordelais by the French

In this same time and year, a gentleman named Verdin of the land of Gascony, with the knowledge and consent of the said duke of Brittany, captured by scaling and pillaging the places of Cognac and Saint-Maigrin, situated in the lands and below the marches of Bordeaux, over whom was guardian and captain for the English a squire named Modeth de Lauzac, who was captured near the said Cognac while travelling to Bordeaux, because he thought the said place was still in the obedience of the said king of England and under his guardianship, as it was before. And also he learned that the good peasants and allies of the said duke of Brittany kept guard and worked hard to aggrieve his enemies. In which two places were captured several prisoners. And when the English learned the news, the archbishop of Bordeaux and those of the city sent a runner to Chinon to the king of France, requesting that he render to them the said places of Cognac and Saint-Maigrin, and that he give them safe conduct, feigning that they wanted to come to him, for which nothing was done, for certain reasons moving within the king and his council. And equally, the said duke of Somerset and Lord Talbot sent to the king in this place of Chinon master John l'Enfant and

leur donnaſt les places dupont delarche deconches deCoſnac deſaint magrin ⁊deĝbrez. A quoy leRoy leur Reſpondit q̂ cilz voulloieт̂ Rend fougieres aſon beau nepveu debretaigne. Et Reſtituer les biens qui avoient eſte prins dedans Il ſefaiſoit fort deleur faire Rend les places quilz demandoient par Icelluy duc debretaigne ou par ceulx qui aſon adveu les avoient prinſes. Cela Reſpondirent leſd ambaſſadeurs quilz navoient aucune puiſſance detouches aufait defougieres. Et pource ſen Retournerent aRouen deṽrs led duc deſombrecet ſans autre choſe faire.

Comment leRoy et pourquoy. Il ſedeſclaira alaguerre. contre les anglois ~~~~

Tantoſt apres ſe Raſſemblement les ambaſſ deurs deſd deux parties aune convencion qui fut en labbaye debon port ou les gens duRoys firent aucunes offres aux angloiz que ſe Ilz voulloieт̂ Rendre les chaſteau ⁊ville defougieres dedens ung Iour qui fut nomme lequel eſtoit convenable et Raiſonnable es mains demonſr leduc de bretaigne ſoubz lobeiſſance duRoy et les biens qui avoient eſte prins dedens eſtimez com̂ dit ot Il Laſomme dexvi^c mille eſcuz on leur Rendroit coſnac Saint magrin gerberoye Conches et lepont delarche. Et meſmement laperſonne dud ~~me~~ſſire defaquêberge chevallier angloiz qui avoit eſte prins dedens led pont. Et que tous atemptas fuſſent Repparez dun coſte ⁊dant̂. Laquelle choſe Ilz Reffuſzant et convint Retourner les ſaurcois devers leRoy en ceſt eſtat comme devant. ~ Lequel ouye laRelacion deſeſd ambaſſadeurs Iuſtifiee ⁊agre-

another of England to request that one return to them the said places of Pont-de-l'Arche, Conches, Cognac, Saint-Maigrin, and Gerberoy. On which topic the king responded to them that if they would render Fougères to his good nephew of Brittany and restore the goods that had been taken within, he would make every effort to render to them the places that they asked from this duke of Brittany or by those who, by his leave, had taken them. To which the said ambassadors responded that they had no power regarding Fougères. And because of this, they returned to Rouen to the said duke of Somerset without doing anything else.

How the king and why he declared himself at war against the English

Soon afterwards, the ambassadors assembled themselves from the said two parties at a convention which was held in the abbey of Bon-Port where the men of the king made several offers to the English that if they would render the castle and town of Fougères on a day that would be named that was good and reasonable into the hands of monseigneur the duke of Brittany under the obedience of the king, and goods that were taken within, which was estimated, as it is said, the sum of 160,000 *écus,* one would render to them Cognac, Saint-Maigrin, Gerberoy, Conches, and Pont-de-l'Arche. And also the person of the said Lord Fucqueburg, an English knight, who had been captured within the said Pont-de-l'Arche. And that all the damage by one side and the other would be repaired. Which thing they refused, and they decided to return the knowledge to to the king in the same state as before, who, hearing what the said ambas-

ment par beaulx Inſtrumens apl̂icques faiſans mencion delacongnoiſſance et devoir en quoy Il ſeſtoit mis et delafaulte qui procedoit delapart deſd angloiz ledommage quilz portorent et qui pourroient avoir ſes ſubgectz. Auſquelz Il doit garder leurs action. Auſſi laRompture deſd treves ſans Rien voulloir Repparer par leſd angloiz. Et meſmement conſidere quilz lui voulloient oſter ung tel ſubget comme leduc debretaigne et lefruſtrer deſon pays. Pargrande ⁊mure et deliberacion deſon conſeil et en acquitant ſacôciêce leRoy ſedelibera et fut delibere apres les premonicions et offices. Iaſoit ce quilz ſufficent ſi meſtes et Raiſonables que faire ſepouvoit et pl⁹ nul ne devoit comme Il appert et appra ſe meſtier eſt deleur faire guerre ⁊Recouvrer ſa ſeigneurie par toutes voyes licites ⁊poſſibles laquelle leſd angloiz avoient occuppe Indeuemet̂ et uſurpe par longue eſpace detemps. Parquoy lui fut conseille que ſelon dieu Raiſon ⁊côcience Il ledevoit aiſſi faire et que autrement Il ne faiſoit † pas ſon devoir. En executant la quelle choſe fut conclud quil envoyeroit devr̂s Leduc debretaigne pour ſur letout prendre concluſion et appoinctement.

Une eſcarmouche danglois ⁊de bretons.

En ce meſmes an LeRoy defrance fut deuement Informe delaguerre que les angloiz faiſoient eu Royaulme deſcoſſe lequel eſtoit comprins eſd treves. Et auſſi delaguerre quilz faiſoient par mar au roy desſaigne ſon alye qui eſtoit eſmes treves. Et paraillement aſes ſubgectz delaRochelle dedieppe ⁊dailleurs depuis lecommencement deſd treves continuellement ſans Rendre ne Repparer choſe quilz eu-

sadors related, justified and approved by the good apostolic instruments, making mention of the offer and of the duty in which he was and of the fault which proceeded on the part of the said English, the damage which they wrought and which they could be done to his subjects, to which he ought to guard their actions. Also, the breaking of the said truces without wanting to repair anything by the said English. And even considering that they wanted to remove such a subject as was the duke of Brittany and to vex him in his lands. By great and careful deliberation by his council, and by clearing his conscience, the king deliberated and decided after the warnings and offers. He knew that they were sufficient, so fair and reasonable, that it could be done and more than it ought to be, as it appears and needs to be to make war and recover his lordships by all laws and obligations, that the said English had occupied illegally and usurped for a long period of time. For which he was advised that according to God, reason, and conscience, he ought to have it done and that otherwise he would not fulfil his duty. In executing this thing, it was concluded that he would send to the duke of Brittany in order to resolve everything and come to an agreement.

A skirmish between Englishmen and Bretons

In this same year, the king was duly informed of the war that the English conducted in the kingdom of Scotland, which was included in the said truces. And also the war which they conducted by sea with the king of Spain, his ally, who was similarly included in the same truces. And even with his subjects in La Rochelle, Dieppe, and elsewhere, since the beginning of the said truces, continued, without restoring or repairing anything that

ſſent faicte conт̂ Icelles treves ne par mar ne par terre. Combien que par pluſſieurs ⁊diṽſes foiz et meſmement po[r] lad ville defougieres Il avoit fait ſommer et Rquerir par ſes ambaſſadeurs ⁊ceulx dud duc debretaigne leRoy dangleт̂re en ſon pays et ceulx qui depar lui avoient legouvê-ment en normandie que Ilz Reparaſſent ou feiſſent Reparer les mallefiſſes ⁊dommaiges par eulx et leurs ſubgectz faiz ⁊perpetrez durant leſd treves deſquelles choſes acomplir Ilz auroient eſte Reffuſans. Et pource delibera leRoy en ſon grant conſeil voyant ce que dit eſt quil ceſtoit mis en ſon devoir deſon coſte de<u>ſoy</u> entênener leſd treves. Leur faire guerre par terre et par mer. Car tant que les treves avoieт̂ dure les angloiz deMante deverneul et delongnie alloient ſur les chemins dorleans et deparis po[r] deſRouber et couppes les gorges et mardur <u>les</u> gentilz hommes en leurs les qui eſtoient delobbeiſſ duRoy. Comme leſeigneurs demaillebois leſeigne[r] deſainct Remy olivier denoirequerque ⁊pluſſieurs auт̂ et deRechief pluſſieurs marchands laboureus ⁊auт̂s gens demeſtier du pays denormendie qui ceſtoient Retirez en lobeiſſance duRoy pour les griefs quilz ſouffroient durant leſd treves don̑n et eulx confians dicelles eſtoient Retournez en leurs maiſons pour faire leurs labours et m̂châdiſes. Maiz leſd angloiz les fut venuz tuer en les appellaт̂ faulx traictres armignatz. Ce ſont ⁊eſtoient les beaulx exploitz que ont fait Iceulx angloiz durant leſd treves. Et ſenommoient ⁊faiſoieт̂ appellr̂ ſes malfacteurs les faulx viſaiges po[r]ce que en faiſant ces choſes Ilz ſeveſtoient et deſguiſoient dabiz et diſſoulz et eſpouvantables afin que on ne les congeuſt. Et pource pour obeir atous mallefices et ſubugnes leſd angloiz qui auſſi gre-voient lepeuple fraudellerſement et traiterſſement fiſt leRoy

they had done against these truces, neither on sea nor on land. Such that several and various times, and even on the said town of Fougères, he had summoned and commanded, via his ambassadors and those of the said duke of Brittany, the king of England in his lands, and those who through him had the government of Normandy, that they restore or make repairs for the bad deeds and damages done and perpetuated by them or their subjects during the said truces, for doing which things, they would be refused. And because of this, the king discussed in his great council, seeing that which was said, that he had to put himself in his duty on his side to maintain the said truces, to make war on them by land and by sea. Because, as long as the truces endured, the Englishmen of Mantes, of Vernuel, and of Longy took their trains on the roads of Orléans and Paris in order to steal and cut the throats of and murder gentlemen in their homes who were under the obedience of the king, such as the seigneur de Maillebois, the seigneur de Saint-Remy, Olivier de Noirequerque, and several others, and again several merchants, labourers, and other men working in the land of Normandy, who had withdrawn their obedience to the king, because of the griefs that they had suffered during the said truces given, and those confiding in these returned to their houses in order to do their labours and sell wares. But the said Englishmen came to kill several of them, calling them false, traitorous, [and] armagnacs. These are and were the good exploits that these Englishmen had done during the said truces. And these malfactors named themselves and were named the false visions, because, while doing these things, they clothed and disguised themselves overindulgently and appallingly, so that one did not know them. And so in order to obviate such wickedness and subject the said English, who also aggrieved the people fraudulently

defrance grant aſſemblee degens deguerre dunpart. Et led duc debretaigne pareillement pour leurs ſrontũ cont̂ Iceulx angloiz. Et eſt vray que ceulx de lagarniſon defougeres firent une ſaillye ſur les gens dicellui duc leſquelz les Rebouteret̂ ſidoulement et ſus eulx firent ſivaillenmet̂ quilz yfurent que mors que prins. Six vingtz dangloiz.

Laprinſe. delaville. deverneul. par. les. francoiz.

En ce temps meſmes et oud an ung Monnier delaville deverneul fut batu dun angloiz et faiſant leguet pource quil dormoit. Et en deſpit dece alla devers lebailly devreux. Et promiſt ap̊r ĉtraines convenances faictes ent̂ eulx lebouter dedens lad ville. Parqouy ſaſſemblerent meſſ^r pierre debreze ſeneſchal depoitou led bailly ~ devreux Iacques declermont ⁊aut̂s ⁊chevaucheret̂ tant et ſidilligemment que to⁹ enſemble ſe trouverent lexix Iour deIuillet aupoint duIour pres des murs delad ville. Led monnier qui faiſ leguet ceIour fiſt deſſendre les aut̂s qui eſtoient auguet plus matin quilz navoient acouſtume pource quil eſtoit dimenche et ſehaſterent daller alameſſe pour deſunner. Adonc les francois alaide que leur fiſtoit led monnier dreſſeret̂ leur eſchelles audroit du mollin et ent̂rent en lad ville ſans ce que nul ſen aperceuſt. Et yavoit dedans vi^xx angloiz donc les aucuns furet̂ mors ⁊prins et les aut̂s ſe Ranirent auchaſtel agrant haſte lelendemain led monnier oſta ⁊tollit une partie deleau des foſſez dud chaſteau lequel fut aſſally moult vaillenment et deffendre. Maiz en laffin fut prins daſſault auquel eult moult

and treasonously, the king of France made a great assembly of men of war on one side, and the said duke of Brittany equally did so on the other side against these Englishmen. And it is true that those of the said garrison of Fougères made a sally on the men of this duke, whom they routed there completely and they did so bravely that they killed and captured there 120 Englishmen.

The capture of the town of Verneul by the French

In this same time and in the said year, a miller of the town of Verneul was beaten up by an Englishman while taking the watch because he was sleeping. And, in spite of this, he went to the bailly of Évreux. And he promised to do certain things afterwards between them to eject them from the said town. For which the said messire Pierre de Bresay, seneschal of Poitou, the said bailly of Évreux, Jacques de Clermont, and others assembled themselves and rode out such and so diligently that all together they found themselves on the nineteenth day of July, at the break of day, outside the walls of the said town. The said miller, who had the watch this day, sent the others who were on watch later in the morning than they had been accustomed, because it was Sunday, and so they hastened to go to mass for breakfast. Thus, the Frenchmen, with the aid that the said miller gave to them, pitched their ladders to the right of the said windmill and entered the said town, without anybody noticing anything. And there were in this garrison around 120 Englishmen, for which some were killed and captured and the others retreated into the castle with great haste; the next day, the said miller removed and destroyed a part of the moat of this castle, which afterwards was assaulted and defended

debelles armes faites. En eſpecial parled ſeneſchal qui y acquiſt moult grant honneur. Et meſmement ~~de~~tous les auťs. Car Il ny eult point degroſſe artillerye ducoſte des aſſaill̅. Et lafuret̂ pluſſieurs angloiz mors et prins. Et les aut̂s ſeRetayrent alatour griſe agrand haſte Laquelle eſt moult forte et Imprenable tant quil yait dedens que manger. Car elle eſt haute ⁊groſſe ſeparee dud chaſteau treſbn garnie et environnee defoſſez plains deaue.

Commet̂. monſr. dedunoiz. de nouvel. Inſtitue. lieutenant general. du roy en ſes guerres. miſt. leſiege. devant la groſſe. tour. de. vernoil.

Ce Iour aRiva monſr leconte dedunoiz de nouvel ~~Inftue~~ Inſtuie lieutenant gnal du Roy defrance en ſes guerres acompagne du ſire deculant auſſi de nouvellement fait grant maiſtre doſtel demeſſire florans de Illiers et depluſſieurs aut̂s chevalliers ⁊eſcuiers gens darmes et detrait leſquelz miſdrent leſiege deto⁹ coſtez contra lad tour. Puis ouyrent nouvell̅ que leſire detallebot eſtoit venu Iuſques a verneul pour aider et ſecourir les aſſiegez ~ qui eſtoient dedens Icelle tour. Et ſeptirent to⁹ ~~tof~~ Reſerve led meſſire florant qui demoura pour gouverner lad ſiege atout huit cent combatans. Et chevaucharent tant quilz Ra conſeurent ⁊Ratagnerent led ſire detallebot pres deharcourt lequel quant Il les aperceult ſefortiffia etferma dehayes et deſes chariotz quil avoit amenez pour portier ſes vivres en tellemainze com ne lepouvoit

very bravely. But in the end, it was taken by assault, for which there were many beautiful feats of arms, especially by the said seneschal, who acquired there great honour, and also all the others, because there was no large artillery on the side of the assailants. And there were several Englishmen killed and captured. And the others fled to the grey tower with great haste, which tower was very strong and impregnable, so long as they had enough to eat inside. Because it was high and large, separated from the said castle, very well supplied, and surrounded by a moat filled with water.

How monseigneur de Dunois, newly instituted lieutenant general of the king in his wars, laid siege before the great tower of Verneul

This day, monseigneur the count of Dunois, newly instituted lieutenant general of the king of France in his wars, arrived accompanied by the sire de Culant, also newly made grand master of the hotel, by messire Florent d'Illiers, and by several other knights and squires, men-at-arms, and conscripts, who laid siege before all sides of the said tower. Then news came that Lord Talbot was coming to Vernuel to aide and rescue the besieged who were within this tower. And they all departed except the said messire Florant, who remained to govern the said siege with around 800 soldiers. And they rode so that they caught up with and reached the said Talbot near Harcourt, who, when he saw them, fortified himself and arranged the mules and his carts that he had brought to resupply them in such a manner that nobody could attack it. And when night fell, he

grever. Et quant vint ſur lanuyt Il ſeRetrait haſtivement dud ſire deharcourt. Leſd ſeigneurs francois qui furent tout ce Iour en bataille devant ledit tallebot. Cuidans lacombatre. Maiz Il ne~~vzt~~voult oncques ſaillir hors deſafortifficacion qui fut grant deſhonneur pour lui et grant hommes pour les francois. Et furent faiz chevalliers leſire deherbault ſire Iehan debar seigneur de laigny et Iehan daillon eſcuier deſcuierie du Roy. Et ce fait leſdits francois voyans led ſire detallebot Retrait aud harecourt ſen vindrent aumoulx ſeſons. Et le vi-meIour daouſt oud an LeRoy defrance tus aambroiſe pour paſſer laRiviere deloire et mettre ſes gens deguerre en ſon pays denormandie. Et por ſecourir conforter et aider ceulx qui tenoient led ſiege devant lad tour deverneul. Et monſr leconte dedunoiz avec toute ſa compagnee ſes ala amoureux ou Il fut deux Iours.

Comment Lechaſteau denogent fut prins. et depuis ans par les francois.

LE vendredy viiimIour du moys daouſt Lan que deſſus Leconte deu et deſaĩt pol atout quatre mille chevaulx ou environ vindrent courrir devant lechaſteau deNogen deſquelz yot trente ou environ des plus vaill̃ delavantgarde qui ſevindrent fourrer de plaine eſcouſſe dedans labaſſecourt et gagnerent labarriere. Et pource quilz ~ gagnoient fort les canons ſeRetrairent 7Retarderẽt pour actendre leurs gens. Et laiſſerent leſd ~ angloiz couller laharche ſi haſtivement q̊l demoura deux des francoiz dedans qui furẽt prins priſonniers. Pourquoy lacompaigne venue ſans delay au-

retreated quickly into the castle of the said Harcourt, which said French lords, who were arranged in batallions all day before the said Talbot, intending to fight him, but he would not sally out of the fortress, which was a great dishonour for him and many men for the French. And there were made knights: the sire de Herbault; Sir Jean de Bar, seigneur de Laigny; and Jean d'Aulon, squire of the squirery of the king. And this being done, the said French, seeing the said Lord Talbot retreated into the said Harcourt, went to wherever it seemed good to them. And the sixth of August in the said year, the king of France advanced to Amboise in order to cross the river Loire and bring his men of war into his land of Normandy. And in order to help, comfort, and aid those who held the said siege before the said tower of Verneul. And monseigneur the count of Dunois with all his company [went] to Évreux, where he remained for two days.

How the castle of Nogent was captured and held by the French

THE Friday, eighth day of the month of August, in the year abovesaid, the count of Eu and of Saint-Pol, with around 4,000 horsemen or therearound went to ride before the castle of Nogent-Pré, for which there were 30 or therearound of the bravest in the avantgarde, who came full of zeal into the rear courtyard and overtook the barrier. And because they seized strong cannons, they retreated and stopped to wait for their men. And the said Englishmen left to lower the portcullis so quickly that there remained two of the Frenchmen within, who were taken prisoner, for which the company came without delay; sev-

cun fut Icelle place aſſaillye ducoſte des coſtes prez bien aſprement ⁊vaillanmeт̂. Et yen ot grant puiſſon de navrez dun coſte ⁊dauт̂. Et en eſtoit cappitaine et garde pour les angloiz ung nôme Iehan lefevre natif dampres louviers. Lequel avoit aveques lui trente compaignons deguerre or environ. Et leſamedy ſeRndirent enт̂ xi ⁊xii heures pas telle compoſicion quilz ſen allerent leurs tous ⁊leurs corps ſaufz ſans touteffoiz emporter aulgui habillement deguerre excepter lecap[ne] on emporta une eſpee. Et midrent to⁹ leurs biens acelle heure dedens lemouſtr̂ ſainct pierre. Leſquelz depuis vindrent querir ⁊emporter ou bon leur ſembla. Et le dymanche enſuivaт̂ leſd contes voyans lad place neſtre point du tenable ſedeſſogerent et audepartir bouterет̂ leurs gens lefeu dedens tant quelle fut toute arſe et deſemparee.

Commeт̂ leponteaudemer fut p̊ns daſſault.

CE meſme Iour levendredy viii[me]Iour dud ~ moys deſſſd Ce partit devreux Led conte dedunoiz legrant maiſtre doſtel Les ſires deblainville debreze demaugny Lebailly devreux ⁊pluſſieurs autres chevalliers et eſcuiers Iuſques aunombre dedeux mille cinq cents combatans dun coſte. Et dauт̂ coſte partirent ⁊paſſerent environ deux Iours ap̊s aupont delarche Les contes deu ⁊deſainct pol Les ſires deſaveuſe deRaiz. demouy deRambures ⁊pluſſieurs auт̂s Iucques au nombre detrois cens lances et dexiiii axv[C] archiers qui to⁹ chevauchoient dun coſte ⁊auт̂ pour eulx aſſembler. Et tant q̂ lexii[me]Iour dud moys ſetrouverent to⁹ devant lad ville duponteaudemer. Ceſt aſſavoir led ſ[r] de dunoiz lieuten̂ gn̄ral duRoy côme dit eſt ducoſte dedevers

eral assailed this place from the side nearest in good hope and bravery. And a great many were wounded there on one side and the other. And the captain and guardian for the English was one named Jean le Fevre, native of Louviers, who had with him thirty companions of war or therearound. And the Saturday, they rendered themselves between 9:00 and 12:00 o'clock by such an agreement that all their goods and bodies could go safely, without taking any equipment of war except the captain, who took a sword. And they put all their goods at this hour into the mill of Saint-Pierre, which they could come to seek and take wherever it seemed good to them. And the following Sunday, the said counts, seeing the said place was no longer tenable, dislodged and, in order to depart, they pushed their men to light a fire within, such that it was all burned and destroyed.

How Pont-Audemer was captured by assault

This same day of Friday, eighth of the said month abovesaid, the said count de Dunois, the grand master of the hotel, the sires of Blainville, of Brezée, of Maulny, the baliff of Évreux, and several other knights and squires, totalling 2,500 soldiers of their side, left from Évreux. And on the other side, the counts of Eu and of Saint-Pol, the sires of Saveuses, of Rais, of Mouy, of Rambures, and several others, totalling 300 lances and 1,400 to 1,500 archers, left and went about two days afterwards from Pont-de-l'Arche, [and they] all rode on one side and the other to assemble themselves. And such that the twelfth day of the said month, they found themselves all before the town of Ponteau-de-Mer. It is known, the said seigneur de Dunois, lieutenant general of the king, as it is

Rouen. Et lefd contes deu et defainct pol atoute leur compaignie ducofte dedevers honnefleu delaut̂ cofte delaRiviere deRuille qui paffe encont̂ Icelle ville et la meft chc͡n feigneur fon tout que alieu aptr̂ fes gens en ordonnance pour affailles lad ville. Et p̊rmierement ducofte dud conte defainct pol fut affailly fe vigoreufement ⁊tellement quilz emporterent daffaut lad ville Iafoitce q̂ lefd angloiz qui eftoient dedens firent bien et grandement leur devoir delagardes et deffendre. Et ducofte demond f^r dedunoiz yot demoult belles armes faictes dutant ou pl⁹ quil yot ducofte par ou Ilz entreret̂ p̊mieremet̂. Et entrerent dedens Icelle ville daffault autant dun cofte q̂ daut̂. Mone͡n auffi et par lefire qui yfut mis et defufees Igers. Et eft chofe bien anoter qui les aucuns des affaillans febouterent dedens les foffez ou Ilz eftoient en leaue Iufques aucol qui eftoit une belle proueffe. Et fe Retraient les angloiz Iuques aubout delaville en une maifon fort et eftoient au nombre iv^C xx angloiz donc eftoient chefz ⁊capitaines montfort treforier de normandie et foulques eton lefquelz feRendirent to⁹ prifonniers aufd contes dedunoiz et defainct pol. Et acelle befongne furet̂ faiz chevalliers les feigneurs deRaiz. deMouy. Lefilz du videfme damyens lefilz dufire deRambures ⁊pluff^s aut̂s du pays depicardie. Et Iucques au nombre dexxii deauffii demoura lad place en lobbeiffance duRoy defrance. Et fut commons alagarde Et ce Iour aRiva leRoy avandofme. Et le lundy fe partit pour allr̂ achartres ou Il aRiva lexxii^me Io^r enf.

said, on the side toward Rouen. And the said counts of Eu and Saint-Pol, with all their company, on the side toward Honfleur on the other side of the river Ruille, which passes around this town, and each lord put there at this place all his men in order to assault the said town. And firstly on the side of the said count of Saint-Pol was so vigourously and assaulted such that they won by assault the said town despite the fact that the said Englishmen who were within were very greatly dutybound to guard and defend it. And on the side of monseigneur de Dunois, there were many beautiful feats performed, as many or more than were done there as on the side where they first entered. And they entered within this town by assault from one side and the other. Even also and by the aid of fire, which was brought there and used as flaming fireballs. And it is a good thing to note that several of the assailants pushed into the moat where they were in the water up to their armpits, which was a brave feat. And the Englishmen retreated to the end of the town, into a fortified house, and they numbered 420 Englishmen, of whom was chief and captain Montfort, treasurer of Normandy, and Fouques Ethon, who rendered all prisoners to the abovesaid counts of Dunois and of Saint-Pol. And at this siege were made knights the lords of Rais and of Mouy, the sons of the Vidame of Amiens, the sons of the sire de Rambures, and several others of the land of Picardy, and until the number was twenty-two; and so the said place remained in the obedience of the king of France. And [Mauny] was given the guardianship. And this day, the king arrived at Vendôme. And Monday, he left in order to go to Chartres, where he arrived on the twenty-second day following.

Commet̃ les anglois furet̃ deſconfitz en pays deſcoce. Lequel eſtoit comprins es tienes deſd deux Roẏs de france et dangleterre.

Pour monſtrer evidemment lavertu divine eſt contre les angloiz et comê choſe meritoire eſt vray que voiſins xpiens tant auRoyaume defrance comê deſcoce. Et es ſ^ries de Irlande galles et ailleurs. Et tellement qui par eulx ont eſte faiz ſans maulx ⁊promes par voye defait viollentemet̃ et ſans Raiſon. Et nont point eu devant les yeulx les parolles denoſ̃ſeineur Ihêcriſt ou Il diſt Reddite que ſunt ceſaris ceſari et que ſunt dei deo. En eſt adonc Renduz aceſas ce qui eſt deſon pays de afaire. Et auſſi ce qui appartirent adonc Rendus luy. Ent̂ leſquelz maulx ⁊extorcions par eulx faiz en pluſſ et divers lieux ont fait une ent̃prinſe axercion po^r aller courir au Royaume deſcoce. Et envoya leconte deſallebry angloiz pour mener guerre auſd eſcoſſoẏs deux ſeigneurs degrant Renom natifz dud pays danglet̂re. Ceſt aſſavoir meſſire thomas de harnitoune chevallier et leſeigneur duparcy filz du conte demontoberlant acompaignez dexv^m angloiz au nombre dupays. Et paſſerent une Rivê appellee ſallonnoiſe pour entrer aud Royaume deſoce ouquel Ilz furent par leſpace detrois Iours entiers et Iucqz aſix^m oud pays qui vallent trois lieues defrance Naz cevenu alacognoiſſance duduc duglas eſcocoys print tantoſt et ſans delay en ſacôpaignie vi^m eſcoſſoys et vintrent aſſaillir aplaine heure de Iour et en plain champs led angloiz. En laquelle bataille fut fort combatu dune part ⁊daut̂. Et tell-

How the English were defeated in the land of Scotland, which was understood as held by the said two kings of France and England

To show that divine virtue is evidentally against the English and as something meritorious, it is true that Christian neighbours, both of the kingdom of France as of Scotland, and to the lordships of Ireland, Wales, and elsewhere, and such that by those, he had done without evil and promised by sight of deeds violently and without reason. And he no longer had before the eyes the words of the Our Lord Jesus Christ where he said: "Give to Caesar what is Caesar's and to God what is God's." In that it is thus rendered that which is of the lands under his control. And also that which they belong thus renders to him. Among which bad deeds and exortations by them made in several and diverse places, he had made a plan of attack to go campaign through the kingdom of Scotland. And the earl of Salisbury, an Englishman, sent to make war against the said Scots two lords of great renown, natives of the lands of England, it is known messire Thomas Harnitoune, a knight, and the lord of Percy, son of the earl of Northumberland, accompanied by 15,000 Englishmen of the region. And they crossed a river named Sallonnoise in order to enter into the said kingdom of Scotland, at which place they were for the space of three whole days and six miles within the said land, which is three leagues in the land of France, and when this came to the knowledge of duke of Douglas, a Scot, he took immediately and without delay into his company 6,000 Scotsman and went to assail within the hour of the day and in

ement quil en yot moult demoys dechc̃n coſte ⁊pluſſieurs priſonniers deſd angloiz. Et fut Ia laIournee cont̂ eulx et lechamp demooura auſd eſcoſſoys. Delaquelle Iournee furet̂ prins leſd ſeigneurs deharontoune et de perſy. Et ceulx qui peuret̂ eſchapper porterent leurs piteuſes nouvelles aud conte deſalbury les quel fut moult dollent ⁊cource decelles et non pas ſans cauſe. Et tantoſt fiſt plus grant manderent que devant. Et aſſembla bien quarante mille angloiz au nombre q̂ deſſus pour cuider aller tout deſtruire au Royaulme deſcoſſe. Et tantoſt quilz oulrent paſſes laRiviere deſſſd ſadeſſendue vint alacognoiſſance dud duc duglas et duconte doremont ſon frere eulx ayans deux devant les yeulx et voyans leſd angloiz Impor tunement et ſans quelconque droit venir gaſter leur pays en concordant auſd dethatomat maner peine de Reſiſter. Car Il eſt licte aung chc̃n de combatre pour ſon pays. Et pource tantoſt ⁊ſans delay firent leurs armee leſd ſeigneurs deſcoſſe et ſetrouverent bien en nombre xxxii mille eſcoſſoys bons ⁊ſubtilz en garoi[c]. Leſquelz vindret̂ ung matin frapper ſur les logis diceulx angloiz et les prindrent en deſaroy. Et tellement furet̂ aſſalliz quil leur en faillut fuyz ⁊deſplaices et ſen ot grant nombre demors et denavrez ⁊deprins. Et furet̂ chaſſez etpourſuiviz deſi pres Iuſques aIcelle Riviere que en yot grant fouiſſon denoyez. Et aurcq͡z a en ya bien eu que mors que prins aſs deux Iournees de xx axxvi mille angloiz au nôbre du pays. Et depuis leſd eſcoſſoys atribuans led deſtrouſſe alagrace dedivine et non pas ala puiſſance humaine. Et ace que leſd angloiz ne fuſſent plus ſi oultrageulx deconquerrir ce quil neſtoit pas leur. En pourſuivat̂ leſd angloiz paſſerent lad

open field the said Englishmen, in which battle was fought one part and the other and such that many were killed there on each side and several of the said English were captured. And finally, the day turned against them and the field remained with the said Scotsmen. On which day, the said lords of Harnitoune and of Percy were captured. And those who could escape took their piteous news to the said earl of Salisbury, who was very angry and enraged by this, and not without cause. And soon he made a greater order than before and he assembled around 40,000 Englishmen in order as before in order to go destroy everything in the kingdom of Scotland. And as soon as they heard the abovesaid river was crossed, this descent came to the knowledge of the duke of Douglas and the earl of Ormont, his brother; both having before the eyes and seeing the said Englishmen, importunely and without any right to come spoil their lands agreed with the said Harnitourne, manœuvering for full resistance, because it is lawful for anyone to fight for their lands. And for this, soon and without delay, the said Scottish lords sent their army and they found it numbered 32,000 Scotsmen, well and fully armed, who went one morning to attack the lodgings of these Englishmen and take them in disarray. And they were assailed such that it was necessary for them to flee and decamp, and a great number were killed, wounded, and captured. And they were chased and pursued until a great many drowned at this river. And with them, there had been killed or captured across these two days between 20,000 and 26,000 Englishmen from the land. And then the said Scotsmen attributed the said destruction to divine grace and not to human power. And so much that the English were no longer so audacious as to conquer that which was not theirs. In pursuing the said Englishmen, they crossed the said river in order to

Riviere pour entrers pays dagletre desgasterent bien vingt lieues delong et six lieues delarge des lieues defrance. Et Iucques aune place forte nômme leneufchastel. Et nelaissiret Iucques ville ne maison que forte nefust ars en leur chacun ou aucunes laplusgrant partie dela Icelle chasse fut mort ung chlr escossoys degrat auctorite nomme messire Iehan Wouailles. Et aussi Retournerent Iceulx escossoy seurement et sauvement en leurd pays. Lesd batailles Relactees asaint denis en france par trois prestres dupays descosse du drocese dedoublemaince donc lui estoit chanoine et bien autentique personne p semblâce qui les affirmerent fait devant les precieulx corps monseigneur saint denis et ses compaignons et en parolle deprestre estre et avoit este vrayes par laforme que dit est Iceulx examinez par le croniquer defrance en laprce deplussieurs Relig dicelle eglise.

Laprinse desaint lame debuvron.

Ledit xiimIour dud moys daoust ou environ lan que dessus aRiva avendosme leRoy de france grandement d acompagne degens deguerre tant seigneurs chlrs escuiers archers côe autres. Et la fut Iucques aulundy ens xviiimIour dud moys. Et cepend lesire deloheac lemareschal debretane messire guiffroy decouvren et Ioachim Rouault avecques plussieurs auts. Assailles laville desait Iame debuvron siduremet ⁊aspremement que lassalt dura depuis neuf heures dematin Iucques alanuyt. Et fut fort tire cont Icelle tant degrosse artillerie que demenues fort assailly et aussi fort deffendu. Et lendemain sen allerent pas composicion les angloiz qui dedens estoient leurs corps et leurs

enter the land of England, where they ravaged twenty leagues long and six leagues deep, in the measurement of France. And until a strong place named Newscastle-upon-Tyne. And they did not leave until no town nor house was entirely burned or at least for the most part; on which raid was killed a Scottish knight of great authority named messire John Wales. And so these Scotsmen returned surely and safely into their land. The said battles were related to Saint-Denis in France by three presbyters of the land of Scotland, who recounted to him since he was a chanter and a very authoritative person, as it seemed, who by affirmation before the precious body of monseigneur Saint-Denis and his companions and in speaking for the priest to be and it had been true by the form which he said, these were examined by the chronicler of France in the presence of several of the monks of this church.

The capture of Saint-Jaime de Bouvron

The said twelfth day of the said month of August or therearound, the year above, the king of France arrived, greatly accompanied by men-at-arms, both lords, knights, squires, archers, and others. And he was there until the following Monday, eighteenth day of the said month. And, however, the sire de Lohéac, the marshal of Brittany, messire Geoffroi de Couvren, and Joachim Roualt, with several others, assailed the town of Saint-Jaime-de-Bouvron so strongly and so long that this assault endured from nine in the morning until almost nightfall. And it was strongly pressed against this place, both by large pieces of artillery and smaller; it was strongly assaulted and also strongly defended. And the next morning, these Englishmen went out by agreement, which was such that

biens ſaufz. Et ainſſi fut Redduite Icelle place et miſe en lobbeiſſance duRoy defrance.

LaReducion delaville et groſſe tour devernoil.

Le xxiim Iour dud moys aud an entra leRoy en ſa cite dechartres. Et lelendemain ſeRendireẽ ceulx delatour deverneul ſes priſonniers qui neſtoieẽ que xxx donc laplus part eſtoient francois Renoyez. Car peu devant eſtoient eſchappez pluſſieurs deulx et avoient emporte tout lavoir ⁊cheauce qui de dens eſtoit pas lafaulte deceux qui faiſoient le guet Icelle nuyt. Led meſſire florent devant nomme en fut fort blaſeme. Car peu pas avant leRoy lui avoit mande pas ung deſes heraulx qui ces gardaſt bien. Et apres ledepartemeẽ deceulx leRoy fut content defaire donnes bon appoinctemeẽ ceulx qui eſtoient demourez. Et ce pour ĉtaines conſideracions quil avoit Pourquoy firent letraite dicelle tour leſire deſpreſigny et debaugy. Par auſſi que venu que lad place eſtoit Imprenable ſinon par deffault devivres. Ilz paierent ĝraciuſe Rancon. Et auſſi ſedepartirent en baillant laplace auRoy donc chc̃n eſtoit et fut bien Ioyeaulx.

Laprinſe deſaint guille̾ de mortaing par les francois.

En ce temps ou peu apres print Ioachin Rouault ſainct guillaume demortaing avec partie des ſeigneurs qui avoient prins Sainct Iames debuvron. Et deva laſſault deprins dix heures Iuſques auſoir.

they would safely have their bodies and their goods. And so this place was reduced and put into the obedience of the king of France.

The reduction of the town and great tower of Verneul

The twenty-second day of the said month in the said year, the king entered into his city of Chartres. And the next day, those of the tower of Verneul rendered themselves as their prisoners, who were only thirty, the most part were French renegades, because a little earlier, several of them escaped and they took nearly everything they had and the money, which was inside; this was the fault of those who were the guards this night. The said messire Florent before named was blamed [for this]. Because shortly before, the king had sent to him via one of his heralds to set a good guard. And after the departure of these men, the king was happy to make a good agrement with those who remained and for certain considerations that he had, for which the sires de Presigny and Baughy made the said treaty for this tower considering also that the said place was impregnable, if not for lack of food. And they payed only a gracious ransom. And then they departed after delivering the place to the king, for which each had been and was very joyous.

The capture of Saint-Guillaume de Mortain by the French

In this same time or a little after, Joachim Rouault captured Saint-Guillaume-de-Mortain, with part of his lords who were near Saint-Jaime-de-Bouvron. And the above assault lasted ten hours until the evening.

La Redducion de liſieux au roy de france.

En ce meſme temps et an led conte dedunoiz liuten general duRoy comme dit eſt le conte deſainct pol et autſ qui avoient eſte alapnſe duponteaudemer ſepartirent 7chevaucheret tous enſemble en grant ordonnance et multitude de gens deguerre Iuſques devant lacite deliſieux pour ymettre leſiege Maiz quant ceulx delad ville aperceuret ſigrant nombre degens conſiderâs que lad ville ne pouvoit pas longuemet tenir ne Reſiſter acelle puiſſance doubtans auſſi gamble ne fuſt prinſe daſſault et parce perye pillye et deſtruite. Apres pluſſieurs parolles et parlemens faiz enteulx lamirent en lobbeiſſ duRoy defrance es mains deſon lieutan par laduadviſement 7conſeil deleur eveſque qui ſi gouverna grandement 7honorablement et ny eult en Icelle fait aucun dommaige ou parpetie Maiz demoureret to⁹ et ung chen en droit ſoy maiſtres 7ſrs deleurs biens 7Revenues donc Ilz poſſedoient aupavant dela Reduction. Et Rendirent avec ce pluſſieurs menues places eſtans alentons dud deliſieux.

Laprinſe demante ſur les angloiz.

LE xxvi^m Iour dud moys daouſt oud an le lendemain defeſte monſiegneur ſaint loys. Ce partit leRoy dechartres et alla augiſte amoult belle notable et grant compaignie a chaſteau neuf en thimerais. Et deue envoya ſommer ceulx demante par ung deſes heraulx delui Rendre

The reduction of Lisieux to the king of France

In this same time and year, the said count of Dunois, lieutenant general of the king, as it is said, the count of Saint-Pol, and others who had been at the capture of Ponteau-de-Mer left and rode all together in a large and well-organised suite of men of war until they were before the city of Lisieux in order to lay siege there. But when those of the said town perceived so great a number of men, considering that the said town could not hold out for long resisting such power, fearing also to be captured by assault and by this be burned, pillaged, and destroyed, after many words and discussions made between them, they put themselves into the obedience of the king of France via the hands of his lieutenant, by the good advice and council of their bishop, who governed grandly and honourably, and in this deed there was no damage or pillaging done there, but they all remained there and each in right were masters and lords of all their goods and revenues that they had possessed before the said submission. And they rendered with this several small places which were around the said Lisieux.

The capture of Mantes by the English

The twenty-sixth day of the said month of August in the said year, the day after the feast of monseigneur Saint Louis, the king departed from Chartres and went to rest in a very good, notable, and large company at Châteauneuf in Thimerais. And from there, he sent to summon those of Mantes via one of his heralds to

lad ville laquelle Ilz tenoient et occupoient oultȓ ſon gre et par deſſus ſavolle9te. Et cepend que led herault eſtoit allefaire ſa legacion leconte dedunoiz les contes deu et de ſainct pol et ceulx deſacompaignie deſſſ nomz qui eſtoient deCinq aSix mille combatans aRivereȓ led Iour xxvi^m^Iour daouſt devant lad ville demante pour ſommer les gens deguerre manans ⁊hâtans Icelle deville delaRend Reſtiuer ⁊remettre en lobbeiſſ duRoy defrance. Auquel elle appartenoit deſon propre hȓitage. Aquoy furent aucunemeȓ Reffez les deſſ moiz pour lameus des gens deguerre qui eſtoient dedans combien q̂ les francois manans ⁊ĉtains dicelle avoieȓ bonne voullête deſȓ ſoubz leRoy defrance ⁊en ſaſubection. Adoĉ led lieutan et ſacompaignie ſeprepareȓ pour aſſallȓ lad ville. Et cevoyant leſd hâtans doubtans fort les angloiz qui eſtoient dedans en garniſon Iucques au nombre dedeux cens Soixante hômes deguerre deſquelz eſtoit cap^me^ en Icelle ville meſſ^re^ thas hos chlȓ chancellȓ des angloiz en leur party lequel neſtoit pas lad ville. Maiz ſon lieutenaȓ nôme Thas deSainte-barbe lequel yeſtoit bailly dicelle. Et voulloit atoutes fins tenir ⁊deffendre Icelle place conȓ toute lacompaignie des francois. Pourquoy Iceulx manans ⁊hâtans voyans ence faiſſ lapdicion dicelle ville. Apres laſommation aeulx faicte fireȓ dire aud bailly que ce Il neprenoit auſd ſeigneurs et en prenoit compoſicion q ĉtainement Ilz prendroieȓ compoſicion eulx meſmes. Cequilz neuſſeȓ Iamaiz dit ne oſe enȓprendre ſe Ilz ne ſefuſſeȓ ſentuz les plus fors. Et defait pour mieux ſubuguer Iceulx angloiz leſd hâtans gaignerent latour ⁊portal appelle laporte auſaint aveques ung quartȓ dicelle ville et les montees. Affin q̂ les angloiz meſe

render to him the said town, which they held and occupied against his desire and against his will. And, however, while the said herald went to do his task, the count of Dunois, the counts of Eu and of Saint-Pol, and those of their company abovenamed, which was 5,000 to 6,000 soldiers in size, arrived on the said twenty-sixth day of August before the said town of Mantes to summon the men of war, labourers, and inhabitants of this town to render, restore, and return themselves into the obedience of the king of France, to whom it beloned by his rightful heritage: to which several refused the above due to pressure from the men of war who were within, even though the French labourers and certain of those who had good will to submit to the king of France and be under his subjugation. Thus, the said lieutenant and his company prepared themselves to assault this town. And, seeing this, the said inhabitants feared strongly the Englishmen who were within the garrison—amounting to 260 men of war, over whom was captain in this town messire Thomas Hoo, a knight and chancellor of the English in their party, who was not then in the said town. But his lieutenant, named Thomas de Saint-Barbe, who was bailiff of this place. And he wanted in the end to hold and defend this place against all this company of Frenchmen. For which these labourers and inhabitants saw in this action the ruin of this town. After the summons that was made, they made to say to the said baliff that if he did not meet with the said lords and make an agreement that certainly they would make an agreement themselves. This they would never have dared to say if they did not feel themselves to be the stronger. And, in order to better subjugate these Englishmen, the said inhabitants seized the tower and gate, named the Port-au-Saint, with a quarter of this town, and the staircases, so that the Englishmen could not move against them. And then several sallied out of this town, and they went before the

meuſſent cont̂ eulx. Et adonc yſſirais aucuns dicelle ville ⁊alleret̂ dev̂s led lieuten̅ et les ſ[rs] eſtans en ſacompaignie et firet̂ appointment enſamble depuis lequel ſevouldret̂ eſmouvoir Iceulx angloiz et defait ſefuſſet̂ eſmeuz ſe neuſt eſte latour ⁊leſd montees q̂ leſd hâtans tenoiet̂ ⁊occupoiet̂. Et pource furet̂ envoyez apres lacompoſicion Reſtee ent̂ Iceulx ſeigneurs ⁊hâtans environ quat̂ heures apres none ung herault du Roy et aveques cinquâte hômes darmes etvindret̂ en lad ville. Et furet̂ Receuz par leſd hâtans et mis leſd portail et tour pour Icelle deffendre cont̂ Iceulx angloiz ſe meſtr̂ eſtoit. Combien que led bailly et lieuten̅ ducap[ne] avoit Ia accepte pour lui ⁊ſes compaignons letra-ictie fait ⁊paſſe côme deſſoiz pluſapplein ſera couche. Et furet̂ to⁹ les gens darmes devant Icelle tour ⁊ville oud Iour deprins lematin Iucques auſoir q̂ led lieuten̅ entra avec ĉtain gens darmes po[r] garder leſd hâtans depillerye ou aut̂s oppreſſions q̂ gens darmes ont acouſtu̅e defaire en tel cas. Et pour conſſuers ⁊garder lappoinctemet̂ tel quil avoit eſte fait aveques leſd habitans et capitaine par laReddition dicelle ville en lobbeiſſſ duRoyauê ſouzerain ſeigneur. Et delapartie de meſſ[rs] les conte dedunoiz lieuten̅ gnâl côme dit eſt deu et deſaint pol leſeneſchal depoictou et deculant grant maiſtre doſtel et maiſtre guillaume couſinot bailly deRouen dune part. Et thomas deSainctebarbe eſcuier bailly et lieuten̅ ducap[ne] dud lieu demante et lemaire de-lad ville pour et ou nom des gens degliſe nobles officiers gens deguerre ⁊bourgeois marchands et hâtans delad ville dautre part duquel appoîtemet̂ et acord Lateneur ſenſuyt.

said lieutenant and the lords who were in his company, and they made an agreement together, since these Englishmen wanted to move and, in fact, they would have moved if it had not been for the tower and the said stairs, which the said inhabitants had taken and occupied. And for this, they sent, after the agreement between these lords and the inhabitants, around four o'clock in the afternoon, one of the heralds of the king, and with him fifty men-at-arms, and they came into the said town. And they were received by the inhabitants and put into the said gate and tower, in order to defend this place against the English who were besieging it, such that the said bailiff and lieutenant of the captain had already accepted for himself and his companions the agreement made and passed as below will be detailed at length. And all the men-at-arms were before this tower and town on the said day, outside from morning until evening, for which the said lieutenant entered with certain men-at-arms in order to guard the said inhabitants from pillaging or other oppressions that the men-at-arms were accustomed to do in such a case, and to better maintain and protect the agreement such that had been made with the inhabitants and captain for the reduction of this town into the obedience of the kingdom's lord suzerain. And of the party of messires the count of Dunois, lieutenant general, it is said, [the counts] of Eu and of Saint-Pol, the seneschal of Poitou and of Culant, grand master of the hotel and master Guillaume Cousinot, baliff of Rouen on one part, and Thomas de Saint-Barbe, squire, baliff, and lieutenant of the captain of the said place of Mantes, and the mayor of the town for and in the name of the men of the church, nobles, officers, men of war, and citizens, merchants, and inhabitants of the said town on the other part, for which agreement and accord the wording was as follows:

Appointement.

Premierement aeſte 7app adcord et appoincte que tous les gens deguerre ou auts̃ quelzconques ſoient hommes fẽmes ou enffs eſtans en lad ville dequelle nacion ou condicion quilz ſoient ſen pouront aller ou bon leur ſẽblera es leur party pourveu q̃Iceulx gens deguerre napporcherot̃ dune lieue pres daucun oſt ou ſiege qui ſeroit tenu par les gens delobbeſſance duRoy noſtr̃. C Item que Iceulx gens deguerre et auts̃ deſſſd pourront emporter aveques eulx to⁹ leurs biens meubles quelz quilz ſoient par eaue ou par ter̃ ou Iceulx biens faire emmener ou emporter par auts̃ perſonnes ainſſi que bon leur ſemblera par une ou pluſſieurs foiz durat̃ letemps dela ſeurete qui leur ſera pource faire baillee donc cy apres eſt faicte mencion. C Item et leſquels lectres deſeurete faictes qui ſeront baillees auſd gens deguerre 7auts̃ deſſſd pour eulx en allr̃ durerot̃ letemps 7terme dehuit Iours et pour eulx en allr̃ et pour emporter leurſd biens letemps 7terme dexv Iours. C Item et leſquelles ſeuretez ſeront vallables pour eulx 7aut̃ en leur abſeñ portans leſd ſeurtez letemps 7terme dicelles durat̃ pour faire 7accomplir les choſes deſſſd. C Item et q̃ leſd gens deguerre 7auts̃ qui ſen voudrot̃ allr̃ pourront letemps 7terme deſſſd durat̃ vendr̃ et adiener ſibon leur ſemble to⁹ les biens quilz ont en lad place et en ~~deſſus~~ diſpoſer aleur pofit et plaiſir aucas que nemporter ou fr̃ emporter en levouldroiet̃. C Item et quat̃ aux gens degliſe nobles bourgoiz manans 7hâtans en lad ville demante eſt appoincte 7adcorde quilz Ioyront et leur demoureront ceſt aſſavoir aux gens degliſe

Agreement

Firstly, it is agreed and accorded that all the men of war or others whatsoever, being men, women, or children, being in the said town of which nation or condition that they are in, can go wherever it seems good to them in their party, provided that these men of war do not approach near a place of any army or siege that is being held by men under the obedience of the king, our lord. C Item, that those men of war and others abovesaid will be able to take with them all their moveable goods whatever they are, by sea or by land, wherever these goods are able to be taken or carried by other persons, such that it seems good to them, once or several times, during the time of the surety that will be granted to them to do this, for which above is made mention. C Item, and which letters of surety being made, which are released to the said men of war and others abovesaid for them to go, endure for the time and term of eight days, and, in order to go and take away their said goods, the time and term of fifteen days. C Item, and that these sureties will be valid for them and others, in their absence, carrying the said sureties for the time and term in which they endure, in order to make and accomplish the abovesaid things. C Item, and that the said men of war and others who want to go can in the abovesaid time and term, sell and alienate, if it seems good to them, all their goods that they had in the said place, and dispose to their profit and pleasure, in case they do not want to take or have them taken away. C Item and regarding the men of the church, nobles, citizens, workers, and inhabitants of the said town of Mantes, it is agreed and accorded that they will enjoy and remain theirs, it is known, to the men of the church their benefices, of which

leurs bn̂fices doĉ deprî Ilz ſont poceſſeurs aquelque tiltre que ceſoit ſauf pas privacion deceulx qui auroient tenu ou ſeſeroient Rendus en lobbeiſſance du Royaû deſr̃. Et quat̂ aux aut̂s ⁊aIceulx gens degliſe ento⁹ leurs hr̂tages ⁊poſſeſſions biens ⁊Immeubles quel que part quilz ſoient ſituez ⁊aſſis et auſſi avecˢ meubles eſtans en lad ville. C Item et auront Iceulx gens degliſe nobles bourgoiz officiers marchans manans ⁊hâtans delad ville dequelque eſtat naſcion ou condicion quilz ſoiet̂. Et du Retrait ⁊chaſtellenie dicelle abolicion generalle deto⁹ cas crimes et offences quilz pourrot̂ avoir faitz ditz ou pourpencez alencont̂ duRoy nor̂d ſeigneur deſaſeigneurie et ſubgectz en bône forme ⁊vallable. Et tellement quilz devront eſtre contens. Et ſeaucun des manans ou hat̂ans delad ville ou chaſtellenie dequelq̂ eſtat cod̂icion ou nacion quilz ſoient eſtans abſens leſquelz veilleſ̂ Retourner dix au xxiiiiᵐIour deſeptembre prochainement ~~auf~~ venant faire lepourront ſans aucune Reprehencion ne quilz ſeront tenus prend aut̂ ſeurete ou ſaufconduit fors ſes pr̂tes ou vidimus dicelles. Et Ioyront deto⁹ leurs biens meubles et Immeubles aiſſi q̂ les auſs deſſſd. C Item eſt entendu que ceulx qui ſenvouldront allr̂ leſquelz peuveſ̂ emporter leurs biens par letraicte deſſſd en Iceulx biens ſont comprins toutes manieres demeubles ſauf canoſ̂ qualevrines arbaleſtes ⁊auſ̂ ſemblable artillerie ſi non q̂ ſeſoient les ars ⁊trouſſes aux compaignoſ̂ et aux arbaleſtriers leurs arbaleſtes. C Item et parmy cetraicte faiſ̂ Rendront ⁊deliveroſ̂ leſd bailly maire et officiers manans et hat̂ans lad ville deMantes es depputiz demeſdſſᵉˢ deſſſd oualeurs cŏmis et depputtez pour et au nom du Royaûd ſʳ dedens demain ħ douze heures deIoʳ. Et pour ſeurete dece

at present they possess, in whatever capacity they know it, save those who took at the deprivation of the people, who should have held or should have rendered themselves into the obedience of the king of France. And as for the others and those men of the church, the enjoyment of all their heritages and possessions, permanent and moveable, wherever they are located and situated, remain theirs, and also with the moveable goods in the said town. C Item, and these men of the church, nobles, citizens, officers, merchants, labourers, and inhabitants of the said town, from whatever state, nation, or condition who are there, and of [every] jurisdication and castellany of those, have a general abolition from all cases, crimes, and offenses that they could have done, said, or planned against the king, our lord, and his lordship and subjects, in good and valid form. And such that they will be happy. And any of the labourers or inhabitants of the said town or castellany of any state, condition, or nation, whoever they are, being absent, who want to return ten days to the forthcoming twenty-fourth day of September, they can do so, without any apprehension that they will be required to take any surety or safe conduct, apart from these present or copies of them. And they will enjoy all their moveable and immoveable goods, as with the others abovesaid. C Item. It is understood that those who want to leave, they can take their goods by the abovesaid treaty, which goods are comprised of all manner of moveables, except cannon, coulevrines, ballistas, and other similar artillery devices, except those that are the bows and kits to the companions and to the crossbowmen, their crossbows. C Item and upon completion of this treaty, the said bailiff, mayor and officers, labourers, and inhabitants will render and deliver the said town of Mantes to the deputies of my said lords abovesaid, clerks commissioned and deputised for and in the name of the kingdom

des led Iourduy appoĩtemeƭ ſigne ſelle ⁊groſſoye et trois ſauf-conduitz po[r] la ſeurete deceulx qui ſen vouldront aller bailliz bailleront et mettront mains demeſd ſ[rs] ou de leurs commis ⁊depputtiz latour et et portal appelle laporte au ſainct. Laquelle Ilz pouront faire mettre Iucques au nombre de cinquante hommes et audeſſoubz. Et auſſi eſt promis par cepnƭ appoinctemeƭ aux deſſſd que Iucques aleure limitee delaReddicion delad ville nulz auƭs que ceulx qui ſeront dedens leportail nentreront en lad ville ſinon q̂ ſeſont du conſentemeƭ deſdeſſſd ne ne leur ſera fait ou porte aucun grief p̊udice ou dōmaige en aucē manreƭ. C Item et adcorde auſd gens degliſe bourgeois marchands manans ⁊hãtans delad ville demante quilz ſeront maintenuz ⁊gr̃dez en leurs franchiſers libertez p̊vileges p̊rogativs̃ p̊eminences ainſſi quilz eſtoient en paravaƭ deladeſſente du Roy henry dan-gleƭre dRenier treſpaſſe. Toutes leſquelles choſ deſſſd ont eſte par leſd parties eſte adcordees le tout ſans fraulde barat ou mal engin. Et que auvidimus deces pr̃tes fait ſoubs ſeel Royal ſoy ſoit ⁊ſeroit adiouſtee cōme aceprƭ original fait aSainct ladre pres lad ville de mante lexxvi[me]Iour daouſt lan mil cccc quarante neuf deſſſd. Ainſſi ſigne Chr̃les Loys Iehan P. breze culant G couſinot avec leſquelz ſeingtz ma-nuelz aung chcn̄ mis ſon ſeel en double queue et en cire-vr̊meille pour grandemus ſeurete. Et avecqẑ ce ont promis les ſ[rs] deſſſd defaire Ratiffier confirmer et approver par le-Roy lappoinctement les que dit eſt ce qui depuis aeſte fait. Et par Ainſſi ſdepartit lad lieutenant et toute la compaigne. Et laiſſaiont cappitaine et garde en ladite ville.

the next day at two o'clock, and for surety on the said day, appointed signed, sealed, and notarised, and granted three safe conducts for the safety of those who would go deliver and put into the hands of my said lords or of their commissioned and deputised the tower and gate named Porte-au-Saint, which they can do to install until the number is fifty men or fewer. And also it is promised by this present agreement, to the abovesaid, that, until the specified time of the reduction of the said town, no one other than those who were within the said gates can enter into the said town without the consent of the abovesaid, nor will there be done to them at the gate any grief, prejudice, or damage in any manner. C Item and it is agreed to the said men of the church, citizens, merchants, labourers, and inhabitants of the said town of Mantes that their franchises, liberties, priviledges, prerogatives, and preeminences will be maintained and protected as they were before the arrival of king Henry of England, lately passed. All which things abovesaid had by the said parties been agreed without fraud, deception, or ill will. And that we agree to these present, made under the royal seal, it is and will be added as in this present original, made at Saint-Ladre near the said town of Mantes, twenty-sixth day of August, the year 1449 abovesaid. So signed: Charles, Louis, John, P[ierre de] Bresay, Culant, G[uillaume] Cousinot, with which signings by hand each has placed his seal in duplicate and with vermillion for greater insurance. And with this, the abovesaid lords promised to have ratified, confirmed, and approved by the king the agreements that are said, which has since been done. And by this also, the said lieutenant and all his company departed. And they left as captain and guardian in the said town [Pierre de Bresay].

Lentree du Roy aVernoil et ce pendant fut p̊rs lechaſteau de Longny par les francois.

Le xxviimeIour dud moys oud an entra le Roy en ſaville deverneul en moult grant eſtat et noblement acompaigne lequel fut honnorablement Receu et agrant Ioye deceulx delaville qui furent aux champs audevant de lui atoutes les proceſſions faiſans les feux en cryant noel deIoye. Parmy laville en laquelle Il fut pas c̑tains eſpace detemps Auquil lieu vindrent devers lui les eveſques deliſieux et celui dauxerre lui faiſant hommaige. Et cepend fut faicte une ent̂priſe par leſenal depoitou pour allr̂ prend lechaſteau deloigny que tenoit et occupoit ung eſcuier denormandie nomme leſire deſaincte marie capne dud chaſteau ſoubz meſſire francois deſurienne dit laragônoiz ſeigur ~~dud~~ delad place qui avoit marie ſafille aud eſcuier. Et combien q̂ lad ſenal ny fuſt poit̑ en perſonne. Neantmoins Il avoit fait lappoîtemet̂ avec led capne qui avoit en ſacompaignie deux cens combatans logez en labaſſecourt. Et eſt vray que les francois comparans devat̂ lad place furet̂ boutez dedens Icelle par ledonIon moyena͡ dud capitaine ſans leſceu des gens deguerre qui avoient eſte envoyez par led meſſire francois pour lagarde dud chaſteau et deſafemme qui eſtoit dedens leſquelz quant Ilz aperceuret̂ les francois ſecuiderent mettre en deffen~~de~~ce. Maiz pource quilz eſtoient trop foibles aleur advis Ilz ſedepporterent atant. Et furet̂ prins en Icelle baſſecourt to⁹ leurs chevaulx ⁊autres biens. Et demourerent to⁹ priſonniers alavoulête du Roy excepte lafemme demeſſire

The entrance of the king at Verneuil and how during this the castle of Longny was captured by the French

The twenty-seventh day of the said month in the said year, the king entered into his town of Verneuil, in very great state and nobly accompanied, who was received honourably and with great joy by those of the said town, who were on the fields before him all in processions, making fires while crying Noël in joy. While at the town in which he remained for a space of time, at which place came before him the bishops of Lisieux and those of Avranches to make homage to him. And, however, an expeditionary force was made by the seneschal of Poitou to go take the castle of Loigny that was held and occupied by a squire of Normandy named the sire de Sainte-Marie, captain of the said castle, under messire Francis de Surienne, called the Aragonnais, lord of the said place, who had married his daughter to the said squire. And although the said seneschal could not go in person, nonetheless he had made an agreement and treaty with the said captain, who had in his company 200 soldiers lodged in the inner courtyard. And it is true that the Frenchmen encamped before the said place struck within this place by the dungeon by means of the said captain, without the knowledge of the said men of war, who had been sent by the said Francis in order to guard the said castle and his wife, who was inside, which men, when they perceived the Frenchmen, thought to put up a defense. But because their council was very weak, they wavered. And they were captured in the lower court with all the horses and other goods. And all remained prisoners at the will of the king, except the wife of messire Francis, who went with all

francois. Laquelle ſen alla atout ſes biens treſmal contente deſon gêdre. Et demoura Icellui ſ^r deſaincte marie pour cap^ne et garde dicellui chaſteau auſſy que paravant.

Laprinſe devernon et vernonnet.

Cedit Iour et an fut envoye devant vernon lepourſuivant deRobert deflocques bailly de evreulx et cap^ne decˆtain nombre degens deguerre ſommer les angloiz ⁊aulꞇ̂s hâtans delad ville de vernon pour Icelle Rend et mecꞇ̂ en en lobeiſſâce du Roy defrance en lui baillant pour Icelle ſ^rs les clefz des portes. A quoy fut Reſpondu par Iean dormont eſcuier filz duconte dormont ⁊dillande cap^ne dud lieu que treſvoullentiers leferoit et pource en ſigne dedeſriſion et democquerie ala en loſtel des ſerruciers et amaſſa toutes les vielles clefs quil peult trouvr̂ dont ⁊deſquelles Il fuſt prnt̂ aud pourſuivant lequel Reſpondit quelles eſtoient trop vulles pour ſervir ala fermeture dune telle ville. Et atant se departit pour aller faire ſaRelacion et Rapport aux gens du Roy deſquelz eſtoit chef comme lieuten̂ general du-Roy monſ^r leconte dedunoiz que neſtoit gueres loing delad ville. Et lelendemain aumatin xxviiime vindrent led lieutan̂ et meſſ^rs les conte deu et deſaint pol avecques eulx monſ^r leſen^al depoitou et pluſſieurs aulꞇs cap^nes agrant nombre degens deguerre pour mecꞇ leſiege devaꞇ lad ville et aRriverent ducoſte dederˆs Rouen et devaꞇ lechaſteau devernonnet aſſiege vindrent de monſ^r demouy guillaume chenu ⁊pluſſ^rs aulꞇs cap^ns avec grant nombre degens deguerre francois mis et Inſtituez denouvel en france qui gaigneꞇ aſſortes pluſſieurs cauſes combien quilz ne gectoireꞇ̂

her goods, very discontented at her said son-in-law. And this place retained the seigneur de Saint-Marie as captain and guardian of this castle, as he had previously been.

The capture of Vernon and Vernonnet

This said day and year, a courier of Robert de Flocques, called Floquet, baliff of Évreux and captain of a certain number of men of war, was sent before Vernon to call upon the English and other inhabitants of the said town of Vernon in order to render this place and put it into the obedience of the king of France, delivering to him from this place the keys of the gates. To whom responded John of Ormond, squire, son of the earl of Ormond and Ireland, captain of this place, that he would very willingly do so, and for this, as a sign of derision and mockery, he went to the house of the blacksmith and collected all the old keys that he could find, so that and for which he sent to make a present to this courier, who responded that they were too rusted to serve to lock up such a city. And having done this, he departed to make his account and report to the men of the king, over whom was leader as lieutenant general of the king, monseigneur the count of Dunois, who was not far from the said city. And the next day, the twenty-eighth, in the morning, the said lieutenant and messieurs, the counts of Eu and Saint-Pol, having with them monseigneur the seneschal of Poitou and several other captains, with a great number of men of war, went to lay siege before the said town, and they arrived on the side toward Rouen, and besieging before the castle of Vernonnet came monseigneur de Mouy, Guillaume Chanu, and several other captains, with a great number of French men of war, newly made and instituted in France, who won sev-

point. Maiz fut eſcarmoche atrait et tellemeт̂ q̂ lepont fut gaigne ſur les angloiz et yfut lecapne dicelle ville perche dune fleche pas les deux Ioues depart en part qui fort les eſbahy. Pôquoy eux conſiderans lagrant puiſſance qui eſtoit devaſ eulx et les acquiſicions antecedentes Requireт̂ Iceulx habitans ⁊angloiz aud conte dedunoiz lieutan̑ general cône dit eſt ſeurete pour quaſ ou cinq perſonnes affin dallr̃ parlr̃ alui touch̃ lefait de pr̊ſommation aeulx faite ce qui leur fut adcore. Et pource parlordon̑n ducapne et haı̃tans furent eſleuz et envoyez. Ceſt aſſavoir Iehan abaron angloiz mareſchal des gens deguerre dicelle ville Maiſtre guillaume aaguenet advocat duRoy plus extreme en laquerelle des angloiz que nul auſ Regnaud debourdeaulx ⁊c̃tains aulſs. Et fut ordonne led daguenet por porter laparole. Lequel ſalutacion pr̊nſe aud lieutenant deſes et propoſa en audience telles parolles qui ſenſ ou en ſubſtance. Monſr vo⁹ no⁹ avez envoyes ſommer depar voſſ foy delui Rendre ceſte ville devernon dictes no⁹ qui vo⁹ moult ace ne que nous demandez. Adonc mond ſr dedunoiz côme froit et atrempe ſeigneur Repreſentant lap̑rs duRoy leur commẽca adire ⁊expoſer en beaulx ⁊haulx termes et comme ung des beaulx pleurs en francois qui ſoit delalangue defrance q̃ lad ville ⁊chaſteau tant dededens que dedehors competoient ⁊appartenoient auRoy ſon ſouverain ſeigneur et leleur. Pour Raiſon deſon droit domaine et heritage leſquelz avoient eſte ſoubſtraiz afeu debonne memoire ſon pere aveq̃s auſ grant partie deſon Royaulme et plus par viollance q̃ auſment. Et leur Recita en beau ſtille et auſſi prudemment que euſt ſceu faire ung maiſtre en theologie lefait delaguerre qui avoit eſte enſ leRoy defrance ⁊leRoy

eral sorties though they did not accomplish anything. But it was fought with conscripts and such that the bridge was won by the English, and there, the captain of this town was pierced by two arrows on one side and the other, which greatly shocked them. For which, considering the great power which was before them and the previous conquests, these inhabitants and Englishmen asked the said count of Dunois, lieutenant general it is said, for the safe conduct of four or six people to go to him to discuss the fate of the said summons made to them, which they were granted. And for this, it is known, John Habaron, an Englishman, marshal of the men of war of this town; master William Daguenet, lawyer of the king [and] more extremely interested in the quarrel with the English than anyone else; Regnaud de Bourdeaux, and certain others were elected and sent by order of the captain and the inhabitants. And the said Daguenet was made the spokesperson, who, making salutations to the said lieutenant, said and proposed in his presence such words that follow or in substance: 'Monseigneur, you are sent to summon us by your liege to render to him this town of Vernon—tell us what moves you to this, not what you ask of us'. Thus, my said seigneur of Dunois, as a severe and hardened lord, representing the presence of the king, began to tell and to expose to them in good and high terms and as several of the beautiful words in French which are in the language of France, that the said town and castle, both within and without, are under the jurisdiction of and belong to the king, his sovereign lord and theirs. By reason of his right, possession, and heritage, which had been reduced under his father of good memory with another part of his kingdom, and moreso by violence than otherwise. And he recited to him in good style and also prudently in a way that could only be done by a master in theology the facts of the war which had been

dangleˆ donc eſtoient deſRenduz maus maulx Inomm rables ⁊grans Inconveniens qui ſeroit longue choſe aReciter. Pour laquelle guerre pacifier leRoy meu degrant charite paciemment avoit voulu ꝼ conſentu ⁊adcorde c̃taines treves pour durant Icelles trouver aucune bonne expedition dappoinctement. Et que ce non obſtant les angloiz deleur voullente deſordonnee avoient prins damblee Laville defougeres appartenant au duc debretaigne lequel eſt parent ⁊ſubject du Roy et nomme leſd treves. Et leur fut Recite toutes les alteracions qui en ceſte matreˆ avoieƭ eſte ainſſi par laforme et maniere deſſus deſclaree. Et conſidere leRoy par meure deliberacion deſes parens prouchains ⁊aufs ſeigneurs chevalliers capitaines conſeillers ⁊bien veullans voyans linfidelite diceulx angloiz amis ſon armee ſus pour conquerir ce que lui appartient deſon droict demaine. Ace ſr ma com̃is ſon lieutenant. P̲quoy Il vo⁹ ay envoyez ſommer et encores deRechef vo⁹ ſomme demoy Rendre lad ville pour leRoy afin que cil vo⁹ en vient aucun Inconvenient par Rebellion ou Inobediance que vo⁹ nelatribuiz pas au Roy voſ̃ ſouverain ſeigneur et lemien ne amoy que deſa begnigne grace ma Inſtitue ſon lieutenant en ceſte partie. Apres le propos duquel ſeigneurs ſeRetrayrent appart leſd angloiz et hab̃tans pour parler enſemble delamateˆ etſavoir quilz avoient affaire. En traitant delaquelle chryrant en grand diſcord et contravſſion. Car les francois conſidrans leRoy de france eſtre leur natural ſr. Et tout ce que par led lieutenant aeſte expoſe fondre enRaiſ ſevoullorent bien Rendre et les aufs angloiznon. Toutesſfoiz apres pluſſieurs parolles deus et altercacions fut dit conclud ⁊ordonne par leſd habitans quilz ſe Rendroient vouſiſſent les angloiz ou

between the king of France and the king of England, from which was derived innumerable bad things and great inconveniences, that it would be a very long thing to recite. In order to pacify which war, the king, moved to great charity, patiently had wanted, consented, and agreed to certain truces, in order, during these, to find any good expedition and manner of agreement. And that this notwithstanding, the English, ordered by their will, had taken with ease the town of Fougères, belonging to the duke of Brittany, who was a relative and subject of the king, and was named in the said treaties. And he recited to them all the altercations which, in this matter, had occurred such in the form and manner above declared. And the king considered, moved by the deliberation of his nearest relatives and other lords, knights, captains, councillors, and good citizens, seeing the infidelity of these Englishmen, prepared his army to conquer that which belonged to him by his rightful heritage. For this, he commissioned me as his lieutenant. For which you have been sent sommons and again I summon you to render to me the said town for the king so that no inconvenience comes to you by rebellion or disobedience that you attribute no fault to the king, your sovereign lord and mine, nor to me, who, of his benign grace, has instituted me his lieutenancy in this region'. After the completion of which the lords retreated to go to the said Englishmen and inhabitants in order to discuss together the matter, and to know what they had to do. During which discussion, there were cries of great discord and controversy, because the Frenchmen considered the king of France to be their rightful lord. And everything that the said lieutenant had revealed to them, they very much wanted to render to him, and the Englishmen did not. However, after several words and altercations, it was said, concluded, and ordered by the said inhabitants that they would render themselves,

non en faiſant aucun bon traictie pour tous Iceulx hâtans enquel ſeroient leſd angloiz adointz ſe bon leur ſembloit. Et adonc Iceulx angloiz voyans quilz ne pouvoient Reſiſter alintencion deſd ha͂tans promlguer Requirant avoir lectres ſeellees duſeau dicelle ville faiſant mencion que lad Reduction neſtoit point faicte deleur conſentement et adcord cequi leur fut acord. Et auiſſi Retournereſ dev̄s mondſr dedunoiz avecques lequel Ilz firent traicte ⁊appoĩtement par leconſeil des ſeigneurs eſtans en ſacōpaignie en laurauene et pas laforme qui ſuiſuy.

Comment Vernon fut francois

EN faiſant lequel traicte ⁊appoinctement les angloiz vuyderent leurs main duchaſteau devernonnet aſſis dehors laville duquel eſtoit cap^ne ung angloiz nōme ſcandit et fut mis en lagarde duconte deu pour leRoy defrance ⁊en baillant pas les francois trois cauxcions Ceſt aſſavoir ung nōme Jehan depuiſieux ung auſ nomme ~~lamaie~~ Iavequin Retous ſerviteur dud conte. Et ung eſcuier nōme corguillery leſquelz furent baillez es mains deſd angloiz. Et Iceulx capitaines et habitans delaville bailleref pour hoſtage es mains des francois Leſd mareſchal Daguenet et debourdeaulx pour Rend lad ville au Roy ou aſon lieuteſ leſamedy proch̄ enſ heure demidy aucas quilz neſeronent ſecouruz. Et ſe ſecourus eſtoient aud Iour tout ſedevoit Reparer tant dune partu que dauſ. Et lappointement eſtre dit nul. Auquel Iour ne comparureſ aucuns pour les ſecourir. Car Ilz noſoient deſemparer la ville deRouen depaour daucune cōmocion. Touteffoiz larmee deſd

whether the English wanted to or not, by making any treaty for all those inhabitants in which the said Englishmen would be allowed to go wherever it seemed good to them. And so these Englishmen, seeing that they could not resist the intention of the said inhabitants, requested to have letters sealed from this town making mention that the said submission was not done by their consent or according to that which they had agreed. And thus, they returned to monseigneur de Dunois with what they had treated and agreed by the council of the lords who were in his company in Lorraine and in the form that follows:

How Vernon became French

In making which treaty and agreement, the English relinquished their control over the castle of Vernonnet, situated within the town, over which was captain an Englishman named Standish, and it was put under the guardianship of the count of Eu for the king of France, and in delivering this, the French gave three squires as hostages: it is known, one named Jean de Puisieux, another named Ravequin Retono, servant to the said count, and a squire named Corguillery, which three were entrusted into the hands of the said Englishmen. And these captains and inhabitants of the town delivered as hostages into the hands of the Frenchmen the said marshal, Daguenet, and de Bourdeaux, in order to render the said town to the king or to his lieutenant, the next Saturday, at the hour of midday, in the event that they were not relieved. And if rescue came on the said day, everybody would return to one side and the other. And the agreements would be declared null. On which day, nobody appeared to relieve them, because they had not dared to leave the town of Rouen, out of fear of some commotion. Thus,

deſd francois compararet̂ en belle bataille. Et ſeprt̃erent enſ vernon et ung vilaige nomme longueville. Et adonc ſeptirent to⁹ les angloiz eſtans en lad ville devernon eſtimez aVIXX hommes deguerre leſquelz firent grant diligence leIeundy et levendredy pour emporter toutes leurs bagues Ainſſi que portoit letraicte par eaue et par t̃re ou bon leur ſembloit aRouen ouailleurs. Et leſamedy environ midy print mond ſ dedunoiz lapoceſſion dicelle ville en dentant to⁹ officiers Iucques ace q̃ leRoy yeuſt auſment pourveu. Et laiſſa pour garde et capitaine tant delaville q̃ duchaſteau ung chlr̃ nomme meſſre Rignault defontaines ſoubz lequel demoureref les hãtans ⁊ceulx des villages qui eſtoient Retraiz dedens ſans ce quilz euſſef aucun dommaige en corps ne en Biens. Et de puis aleRoy donne lad ville ⁊chaſteau avecq̃z leurs appartenances aud conte dedunoiz pour les ſ grans ſervices quil luy avoit faitz. Et avoit ferme eſperance quil luy firoit en la conqeuſte deſon pays denormandie ⁊ailleurs en ſes affaires et neceſſitez.

Levirtue duRoy aemoulx. et alouviers. ~~~

Environ laffin daouſt ſu partit leRoẙ de france deſaville deverneul. Et entra not̃lement et grandement acompaigne et en grant appareil en ſa cite devreulx ou Il fut Receu treſſumptueuſement des hâtans delad ville en allant audevant delui en faiſ fieux et cryant noel et les Rues tendues. Et coucha en Icelle ville une nuyt ſeullemet̂. Et lelendemain ſepartit pour allr̂ en ſaville de louviers ou Il fut ſemblablement Receu agrat̂ Ioye et avoit en

the army of the said French appeared in organised batallions. And they departed from Vernon and a town named Longueville. And so, all the English within the said town of Vernon, estimated to 120 men of war, who made great efforts from Monday until Friday to sell all of their goods, departed according to the treaty, by water and land, wherever it seemed good to them, to Rouen or elsewhere. And the Saturday after miday, the possession of this town was taken by my said lord the count of Dunois, relieving all the officers except those whom the king had otherwise provided. And he left as guardian and captain, both for the town and the castle, a knight named messire Rigault de Fontaines, under whom remained the inhabitants and those of the villages who had retreated within, without which they would suffered damage to their bodies or goods. And then the king gave the said town and castle with their aputrements to the count of Dunois, for the great services which he had done for him. And he held a firm hope that he would do [more] for him in the conquest of his land of Normandy and elsewhere in his affairs and necessities.

The welcome of the king at Évreux and at Louviers

Around the end of August, the king of France left from his town of Verneul and he entered, notably and grandly accompanied and in great fashion, into his city of Évreux, where he was very sumptuously received by the inhabitants of the said town, who came before him in making the fires and crying noel, and the streets were filled. And he remained in this town only one night. And the next day, he departed in order to go to his town of Louviers, where he was similarly received with great joy, and he

ſacompagnie monſ^r leconte du maine frere duRoy deSecille et delaRoyne defrance monſ^r leconte declermont filz aiſne duduc debourbon Monſ^r leviconte delongmaigne aiſne filz duconte darmaignac Monſ^r leconte decaſtres filz duconte delamarche Monſ^r le cadit dalbreth Iehan monſ^r deloraine Monſ^r lemontgaſcon monſ^r detraynel chancellr̃ de france Monſ^r deculant grant maiſtre doſtel duRoy Monſ^r leconte detanquerville Monſ^r delafaiette mareſchal defrance Monſ^r de gaucourt Monſ^r deblainville Monſ^r de precigny leconte dedampmâtin grant panetier Monſ^r delaRochette maiſtre doſtel Monſ^r demalicorne Meſſire Iehan duſingne Monſ^r demonteil Monſ^r debaugy general defrâce monſ^r depruilly monſ^r deham en champagne meſſire theaulde devalpergne Monſ^r dela boiſſiere meſſire denis dechailly bailly de meaulx monſ^r dechepeaulx monſ^r dumouſtet monſ^r degraville meſſire Iehan decourtenay monſ^r deſaint briſſon meſſire Ieh̑ dechallon bailly detonnerre Meſſire Robinet deſtampes Et pluſſieurs auẗs chevallr̃s et eſcuiers en grat̂ et exceſſif nombre. Et avecques ce avoit pour lagarde deſon corps deux cens lances et les archr̃s dedens lad ville Sans en ce comprend quatre armees qui eſtoient ſur les champs. Ceſt aſſavoir larmee duduc debretaigne larmee duconte de dunoiz lieutan̑ general larmee des contes deu et deſaint pol. Et celle duduc dallencon. Et faiſoit leRoy grant dilligence depourvoir leſd armees dece quil leur eſtoit meſtr̃ tant argent bombards artillerie comme auẗs choſ. Et venoient detoutes pars gens normaulx po^r partes auRoy et auſd armees.

had in his company monseigneur the count of Maine, brother of the king of Sicily and the queen of France; monseigneur the count of Clermont, eldest son of the duke of Bourbon; monseigneur the viscount of Lomagne, eldest son of the count of Armagnac; monsiegneur the count of Castres, son of the count of la Marche; monseigneur the cadet of Albret; Jean, monseigneur of Lorraine; monseigneur le Montgascon; monseigneur de Traignel, chancellor of France, chancellor of France; monseigneur de Culant, grand master of the hotel of the king; monseigneur the count of Tancarville; monseigneur de la Fayette, marschal of France; monseigneur de Gaucourt; monseigneur de Blainville; monseigneur de Precigny; the count of Dammartin, grand quartermaster; monseigneur de Rochète, master of the hotel; monseigneur de Malicorne; messire Jean du Singne; monseigneur de Monteil; monseigneur de Baugy, general of France; monseigneur de Pruilly; monseigneur de Ham in Champagne; messire Théodore de Valpergue; monseigneur de la Boissière; messire Denis de Chailly, bailiff of Meaux; monseigneur de Chepeaux; monseigneur du Moustet; monseigneur de Graville; messire Jean de Courtenay; monseigneur de Saint-Brisson; messire Jean de Chalon, bailiff of Tonnerre; messire Robinet d'Étampes; and several other knights and squires in great and excessive numbers. And accompanying this, to protect his body, were 200 lances and the archers within the said town, without including four armies that were in the field. Those being the army of the duke of Brittany; the army of the count of Dunois, lieutenant general of the king; the army of the counts of Eu and of Saint-Pol; and that of the duke of Alençon. And the king made a great effort to provide for the said armies that which they needed, both money, bombards, artillery, and other things. And from all parts, average people came to parties of the king and to the said armies.

Laprinſe duchaſteau de dangu par les francois.

Led Iour deſamedy oud an guillaume chenu capitaine depontoiſe avec certain nombre degens deguerre alla courir devant lechaſteau et laſomma depar leRoy defrance portugal capitaine dud leur deRendre lad place et mettre en lobbeiſſance duRoy. Aquoy led capitaine oyant nouvelles deIour enIour commeť lepays ſe Rendoit au Roy defrance et laRecognoiſſoient les hâtans dicellui pays leur ſouverain ſeigneur voullans aIcellui obair et ſachant levray lui eſtre Impoſſible Reſiſter auRoy ne aſapuiſſance afait compoſicion avecq̄z Icellui chenu en lui Rendant Icelle place. Ceſt aſavoir que led cap^ne et to⁹ ſes compaignons de guerre eſtuez a ſen yroient francs et quictes et emporteroient tous leurs biens ou bon leur ſembleroit. Et ainſſi ſedepartirent et meant lad place en lamain dud chenu parmy ce q̂ Il promîſt quil ne ſeroit ou pôchaſ aucun dommage es corps ne es biens des gens learms Retirez. Et pource que leſd angloiz ne pouvoient pas bien emporter leurs biens les out vindres et debetiz ſus leleur. Ala garde duquel chaſteau aceſte commis et ordonne pour leRoy.

La Reddicion des ville et chaſteau degournay.

Le dimenche enſ Se partit meſſire Iehan deluxembourg conte deſaint pol dud vernon eſpriant mettre leſiege devant gournay. Et [...] lui aRive vindrent au-

The capture of the castle of Dangu by the French

The said day of Saturday in the said year, Guillaume Chanu, captain of Pontoise, with a certain number of men of war, went to run before the castle and summon there, in the name of the king of France, Portugal, captain of the said [place], to render to them the said place and put it into the obedience of the king. To which the said captain heard news from day to day concerning the lands rendering themselves to the king of France and the inhabitants of this country recognized him as their sovereign lord, desiring them to obey and knowing the truth that it is impossible to resist the king nor his power made an agreement with this Chenu regarding rendering this place to him. It is known, that the said captain and all his companions of war would be free to go from there and leave and take all their goods wherever it seemed good to them. And so they departed and they put the said place into the hands of the said Chenu for the king, for which thing he promised that he would not do nor inflict any damage to the bodies nor to the goods of the people who left. And because the said Englishmen could not well bring their goods, they sold and debited what they could. For the guardianship of which castle, he was committed and ordained by the king.

The reduction of the town and castle of Gournay

The following Sunday, messire Jean de Luxembourg, count of Saint-Pol, departed from the said Vernon hoping to lay siege before Gournay. And [when] he arrived, several of the citizens of the

cuns des bourgois delad ville degournay donc estoit garde guillaume hepe soubz guillaume couronan duquel afin debaillr̃ et liverer aud conte lad place. Et pource que led lieutenant doubtoient fort que Il ne venast mettre lesiege devãt eulx sachant aussi ledemene delaguerre. Et comment leurs voisins cestoient portes en tels cas cõsiderãs aussi les parolles du~~sieg~~ saige or Il dit belle doctrine prant en luy qui sechastie par autruy. Pourquoy led conte aRome vint lesd guillaume hape et avec lui lun des hâtans dicelle ville nomme Raoullet pillaoutne ou avecques auts pour enttenir letraite fait avecques auts pour enttener le traicte fait avecques led conte desaint pol lequel avoit este fait aud lieu delongueville. Et fut lappoinctement que lad ville lui seroit Rendue. Cest assavoir ville ⁊chasteau et par ainssi sen devoient aller ou bon leur sembla et emporter toutes leurs bagues. Et qui voulloit demeurer en faisant leserment faire lepouvoit. Combien q̂ monsr demouy et guillaume chanu Ignorans lenťprinse dicelle conte desainct pol laborerent fort et incesammet pour cuider prendre lad ville demblee. Maiz ce venu aleur congnoissance sedepporter pour lonneur dicellui conte. Ainssi lad ville et chasteau estoient batuz dedeux verges la [...] leRoy adonna aud conte savie durant avec toutes les appartenances pour laquelle garde des ville ⁊chasteau. Aeste cõmis par led conte messire georges decroix sr debaissel. Et en pendant q̂ les appoinctemens se faisoient monsr leconte deu sestoit Retrait Aandely sur seine avecq̂z lui monsr deculant grant maistre dostel poston grant escuier descuierie et monsr dorval filz deconte dalbreth. Et led conte desaint pol sen Retourna logr̃ aupont Saint pierre ou Il faite trois Iours. Avecques lequel allerent lesd conte

said town of Gournay came to him, over whom was guardian William Hepe, under William Couronon, for which to hand over and deliver the said place to the said count. And because of this, the said lieutenant strongly feared that he would not go lay the siege before them, knowing also the struggle of the war. And how their neighbours were carried themselves in such case, considering also the words of the sage, where it is said: Good doctrine is found in he who chastises himself. Because the said count arrived, the said William Hepe came and with him one of the inhabitants of this town named Raoullet Pillaountne and with others to negotiate the treaty made with others in order to negotiation the treaty made with the count of Saint-Pol, which had been made at the said place of Longueville. And it was agreed that the the said town would be rendered to him. It is known the town and the castle, and so they must go wherever it seemed good to them, and to take with them all their goods. And whoever wanted to remain, by making the oath could do so. However, monseigneur de Mouy and Guillaume de Chanu, ignorant of the capture of this count of Saint-Pol, laboured strongly and incessantly, thinking to take the said town by assault. But when this came to their knowledge, they stood their ground for the honour of this count. And so the said town and castle were struck from two sides, the [...] the king gave to the said count for the duration of his life, with all the apputrements, with which to guard this town and castle, the said count commissioned messire Georges de la Croix, seigneur de Baissel. And while these appointments were being made, monseigneur the count of Eu returned to Andely-sur-Seine alongside monseigneur de Culant, grand master of the hotel; Poton, grand squire of the squirie; and monseigneur d'Orval, son of monseigneur d'Albret. And the said count of Saint-Pol returned to lodge at Pont-de-Saint-Pierre, where he remained three days. With whom went the said

deu et lemareſchal deIalongnes et leſd de cullant poſton et dorval allerent mettre leſiege devant harcourt et Repaſſerent ſeine pource faire.

Laprinſe delaroche guiôn par les francois. ~~~~

LE lundy enſuivant xxix[me]Iour dud moys daouſt ſepartirent to9les ſeigneurs qui avoient eſte alaprinſe devernon et tirerent to9 pour allr̃ devers leRoy alouviers pour conclure [*two pages missing—text taken from Vallet de Viriville's transcription*] etadviſer enſemble cômént on procederoit out̂ ou fait delacôqueſte. Pendant quilz furent enſemble monſ[r] deIalongnes mareſchal defrance etmonſ[r] delaRoche guyon ayans grant compaignie degens deguerre adviſerent voie etmaniere deconquerir etReduire lechaſteau delaRoche guyon etpour ce faire envoierent trente compaignons ou environ par eaue bien abilles detrait etdecanons leſquelz vindrent devant lad place faignans yvouloir mettre leſiege devant. Ilz faiſoient une ſigrande huee etbruit que quant Ilz euſſent eſte deux cens Ilz nen auroient pu faire davantaige. Et ſeIournerent devant led lundi lemardi et lemercredi touſiours eſcarmochant et combien quilz fuſſent dedens lad place lvi hommes angloiz ou au deſſus aut̂s diſoient ſeulement xlv neantmoins Ilz ne conqueſterent Riens ſur leſd francois. Or leIeudi troiſieſme Iour deſeptembre vindrent leſdits ſeigneurs deIalongnes etdelaRoche guyon devant lad place. Ce que voyant Iehan houel angloiz cap[ne] dud lieu etque telle compaignie venoit laſſallir alaquelle lui eſtoit fort Impoſſible deReſiſter conſid-

count of Eu and the marshal of Jalongnes, and the saids de Culant, Poton, and d'Orval went to lay siege before Harcourt and recrossed the Seine in order to do this.

The capture of La Roche Guion by the French

THE following Monday, the twenty-nineth day of the said month of August, all the lords who had been at the capture of Vernon departed and they all went straight to the king at Louviers to conclude and advise together how to procede further and conduct the conquest. While they were together, monseigneur of Jalongnes, marshal of France, and monseigneur de la Roche-Guyon, having a large company of men of war, advised the means and manner of the conquest and reduction of the castle of Roche-Guyon, and in order to do this, they sent thirty companions or therearound by water, well supplied with arrows and cannon, who went before the said place, feigning that they wanted to lay siege before it. They made so great a ruckus and sound that had they been 200 people, they could not have made more. And they remained before the said place Monday, Tuesday, and Wednesday, always skirmishing, and so much so that those within the said place, fifty-six Englishmen or more—others said only fifty-five—nonetheless, they did not conquer anything from the said French. Now, Thursday, the third day of September, the said lords of Jalongnes and of Roche-Guyon came before the said place. This was seen by John Houel, an Englishman, captain of the said place, and that such company came to assail it, which was almost impossible to resist, considering also all the good right that the king had

erans auſſi aucunement lebon droit quavoit leRoy en Reconquerant ſon Royaume. Et meſmement voyant leſr delad place yeſtre en perſonne avec les auťs Il traita avecques leſd ſeigneurs en lamaniere qui ſenſuit ceſt aſſavoir que ſilz neſtoient ſecourus duRoy dangleterre ou de ſon lieuteñ dedens leterme dexv Iours prochainement enſuivans en ce cas Il Rendroit lad place. Et auſſi ſen devoient aller lui et ſes compaignons deguerre en leur party ou bon leur ſembleroit. Et emporter avecques eux to⁹ leurs biens meubles quelconques ſans en ſecomprendre canons et coulevrines. Lequel projet detraictie Il fit ſavoir auduc deſombrecet gouverneur denormendie pour leRoy dangleterre qui eſtoit lors aRouen. En ſuite dequoi celui qui avoit porte leſd nouvelles ace duc deſombrecet trouva moien avec xxiv auťs angloiz de eux venir bouter dedens lad place ou Ilz avoient machine etReſolu detuer led Iehan houel gouverneur. Lequel meſſager tant toſt quil fut de Retour aud lieu delaRoche guyon cuida actraire aucuns delagarniſon por bouter dedens leſd xxiv angloiz afin depouvoir executer ſon maudit et dampnable propos et enťprinſe maiz tout cela eſtant venu alacongnoiſſance dud houel par ĉtaines congectures envoya haſtivement en advertir et querir led ſieur delaRoche guyon lequel ſeſtoit Retraict en actendant leſuſd xvme Iour qui eſtoit prins par appoinctement comme deſſus eſt dit auquel decelle heure delivra et bailla lad place. Et apres ſepartirent Iceulx angloiz delagarniſon et ſen allerent avecquez bon ſauf conduit en toute ſeurete apres avoir diſpoſe deleurs biens ou bon leur ſembla ainſſi que par led traictie et appoinctement fait avecques eux avoit eſte accorde. Et ydemoura led Iehan houel qui print lors leparti des francois en leur faiſant leſer-

in reconquering his kingdom. And even seeing the lord of the said place there in person with the others, he negotiated with the said lords in the manner which followed: it is known that if they were not rescued by the king of England or by his lieutenant within the term of fifteen days following, in this case he would render the said place. And also they must leave, he and his companions of war in their party, wherever it seemed good to them, and take with them all of their moveable goods, except taking cannon and culverins. Which proposed treaty he made known to the duke of Somerset, governor of Normandy for the king of England, who was then at Rouen. As a consequence of which, the one who had brought the said news to this duke found means with twenty-four other Englishmen to come strike within the said place, where they plotted and resolved to kill the said John Houel, governor. Which messenger, soon after he had returned to the said place of Roche-Guyon, thought to attract several of the garrison to fight against the said twenty-four Englishmen, so that he could execute his evil and damnable intention and plot, but when all of this came to the knowledge of the said Houel by certain conjectures, he sent quickly to warn and seek the said lord of Roche-Guyon, who withdrew to await the abovesaid fifteenth day which was set for the agreement, as is above said, which, at that hour, he would deliver and hand over the said place. And after these Englishmen of the garrison had left and went with good safe conduct in all safety, after having disposed of their goods, wherever it seemed good to them, according to the said treaty and agreement made with them having been agreed. And the said John Houel remained there, who then took to the party of the French, making oaths to them amongst whon he would enjoy

ment parmi quil devoit Ioir des terres que ſafemme poſſedoit eſtans en lobeiſſance duRoy car Icelle eſtoit natifve defrance et ordonna led ſr delaRoche guyon lemeſme deſſus dit gouverneur por lagarde deſon chaſteau lequel par ainſſi demoura ſous lauthorite et laſuIetion duRoy.

Laprinſe faicte par les francois. duneufchaſtel denicourt.

Environ lamiſeptembre Il fut adviſe et conclu alouviers que veu lagrande ſeigneurie et chevalerie defrancois qui eſtoit alors aſſemblee Il eſtoit expedient por faciliter et abbreger laconqueſte ſuſ mentionnee deſeparer et mettre enii parties lad armee ceſt aſſavoir que charles dartois conte deu Iehan deluxembourg conte deſainct pol et Iehan deſaveuſe leſquelz avoient en leur compaignie deiiim a ivm combatans yroient mettre le [*original text resumes*] ſiege devant leneufchaſtel denicourt duquel eſtoit capitaine adam heton angloiz. Et pŏr ſepartirent pour allers mettre led ſiege et aRivereȇ lemardy xximIour deſeptembre et leIeuſdy enſ fut priſe daſſault. Et lechaſteau demoura aſſeige lequel ~~demoura~~ ſerendit aubout dexv Iours par compoſicion. Ceſt aſſavoir que en laiſſant laplace led capitaine et ſept vingtz angloiz ſes compaignons deguerre ſon devoient allȓ en leur party ou bon leur ſembleroit et emporter to9 leurs biens meubles fuſt acallaiz Rouen et ailleurs. Et oulȇ plus fut acorde par lappoinctement que qui vouldroit demourer et faire leſerment auRoy de france faire en leportoit. Et ainſſi laplace fut deſemparee par leſd ꞙ angloiz fut commis ala garde dicelle pour leRoy.

the lands that his wife possed, being under the obedience of the king, because she was a native of France, and the said lord of la Roche-Guyon was ordained the same abovesaid governor as guardian of his castle, which thus remained under the authority and subjection of the king.

The capture made by the French of Neufchâtel-de-Nicourt

Around mid-September, it was advised and concluded at Louviers that, seeing the great lordship and cavalry of Frenchmen who were then assembled, it would be expedient, in order to facilitate and shorten the conquest above mentioned, to separate and establish in two parts the said army: it is known, that Charles d'Artois, count of Eu; Jean de Luxembourg, count of Saint-Pol; and Jean de Saveuse, who had in their company from 3,000 to 4,000 soldiers, would go lay siege before Neufchâtel-de-Nicourt, over whom Adam Heton, an Englishman, was captain. And for this, they went to go lay the said siege, and they arrived Tuesday, the twenty-first day of September, and the Thursday following this town was taken by assault. And the castle remained besieged, which rendered itself at the end of fifteen days by agreement. It is known, that in leaving the place, the said captain and the 140 Englishmen, his companions of war, must go to places in their party or wherever it seemed good to them, and to take all their moveable goods, to Calais, Rouen, or wherever. And otherwise it was agreed by this agreement that whoever wanted to remain, by making an oath to the king of France, he could do so. And thus the place was emptied by the said Englishmen and it was committed into the guardianship of this place for the king.

Lap̊nſe du chaſteau dechâbroys par les francois.

Pour lautre armee fut ordonne monſ le conte dedunoiz lieutenant general duRoy comme dit eſt Avecquel lequel eſtoient le conte declermont et de Nevers les ſeigneurs dorval de Ialongnes mareſchal defrance Chr̃les deculant grant maiſtre doſtel meſſire pierre debreze ſeneſchal depoitou celui deblainville maſt̃ des arbaleſtriers du bueil degaucourt et les baillifz deberry devreux atout detrois aquatre mille gens deguerre et bons combatans leſquelz apres ledepartement delouviers allerent metr̃ leſiege devant lechaſteau dechambrays lexviii^me Iour deſeptembre duquel eſtoit cap^ne guillaume harniton angloiz acompaigne dedeux cens hômes de guerre devant lequel chaſtel Ilz furet̃ par leſpace dehuit Iours ou environ. Et apres ſeRendirent par celle compoſicion leconte declermont aud cap^ne et adeux cens hommes deguerre eſtans en lad place. Ainſſi demoura lad chaſteau en lobbeiſſ duRoy Io^r lagarde duquel fut commis et ordonne.

Laprinſe duchaſteau deharcourt. par les francois.

Depuis et ſans Int̃valle alla monſ^r dedunoiz et toute ſacompaignie devant lechaſteau deharcourt qui eſt bel et fort duquel eſtoit cap^ne meſſire Richard frougneral angloiz lequel avoit avec lui vii^xx angloiz ou environ. Et

The capture of the castle de Chambrais by the French

For the other army was commanded by monseigneur the count of Dunois, lieutenant general of the king, it is said, with whom were monseigneur the count of Clermont and of Nevers; the seigneurs d'Orval [and] of Jalongnes, marshal of France; Charles de Culant, grand master of the hotel; messire Pierre de Brezée, seneschal of Poitou; the same de Blainville, master of the crossbowmen; du Bueil; de Gaucourt; and the baliffs of Berry [and] of Évreux, with 3,000 to 4,000 men of war and good soldiers, who, after their departure from Louviers, went to lay siege before the castle of Chambrais the twenty-eighth day of September, over which was captain William Harniton, an Englishman, accompanied by 200 men of war, before which castle they were there for the space of eight days or therearound. And afterwards, they rendered themselves by this agreement [between] the count of Clermont with the said captain and with the 200 men-of-war who were in the said place. Thus, the said castle remained in the obedience of the king, over which [Jalongnes] was commissioned and ordained as guardian.

The capture of the castle of Harcourt by the French

Then, and without interruption, monseigneur de Dunois and all his company went before the castle of Harcourt, which was strong and fortified, over which was captain messire Richard Frognall, an English knight, who had with him 140 English-

furet̃ aſſeigez par mond ſr dedunoiz lequel ſiege yfut pas leſpace dexv Iours en eſcarmouchant leſd angloiz par ~ eſpace de xv Iours chûn Iour et firent de grans aprouches eſquelles fut tue dun canon ung vaill̃ hôme darmes francois delagarniſon delouviers. Et ung angloiz fut pareillement tue dune coulevrine ſur leportail delaſbaſſecourt. Et eſtoit lors led frogneval deſhonore et pendu par les piez daporte dud louviers. Et adonc les francois qui devant eulx eſtoient voyant leurs Rebellion firet̃ aſſortir et gecter decanons et tellement q̃ du premier coup Ilz percherent tout oult̃ les murs delabaſſe court. Et alors leſd angloiz doubtans fort leſd canons compoſerent aRendre led chaſteau aucas quilz ne ſeroient les plus fors en champ aung Iour dit que fut levendredy. Et dece baillerent hoſtage. Auquel Iour Il ne ſetrouvant point. Et pource Rendirent led chaſteau lequel Ilz avoient tenu par leſpace dexv Iours et ſen allerent leurs corps et leurs biens ſaufs comme firent ceulx dechambrays. Et par ainſſi demeura led chaſteau en lobbeiſſance du Roy.

Comme ceulx duchaſteau deſſsay firent prins et par lemon lechaſteau Rendu aux francois.

En ce temps les angloiz delagarniſon dela ville etchaſteau deſſay allerent peſchr̃ ung eſtanc aſſez loing deladville. Et venue alacognoiſſance duduc dalencon lequel ~ Incontinent monta acheval. Et print gens aveq̃ lui pour yallr̃ leplus ſegrettement q̃ faire le pouroit. Et tellement et ſi ſaigrement ybeſoig̃ quilz furent tous prins. Et aupluſtoſt

men or therearound. And they were besieged by my said lord of Dunois, which siege lasted there for the space of fifteen days, the said English skirmishing each day for the space of fifteen days, and there were great attacks during which a brave man-at-arms, a Frenchman, from the garrison of Louviers was killed by a cannon. And an Englishman was similarly killed by a culverin under the gate of the lower court. And then the said Frognall was very dishonoured, and he was hanged by the feet at the gate of the said Louviers. And then, the Frenchmen who before them, seeing their resistence, made to set up and launch cannon, such that on the first hit, they destroyed all the walls of the lower court. And then the said Englishmen, fearing strongly the said cannon, decided to render the said castle since they were not strong enough in the field on the said day, which was Wednesday, and they gave hostages. On which day, they [the relieving army] were not found. And because of this, they rendered the said castle, which they had held for the space of fifteen days, and they went, their bodies and goods safely, as they had at Chambrais. And so the said castle remained in the obedience of the king.

How those of the castle of Essay were captured and by the means the castle was rendered to the French

In this time, the Englishmen of the garrison of the town and castle of Essay went to fish in a pond far from the said town. And this came to the knowledge of the duke of Alençon, who immediately mounted a horse. And he took men with him to go there as secretly as he could do it. And such and so cautiously did they work, that they captured everyone. And soon afterwards, he

les mena devant lad ville deſſay laquelle lui fut Rendre ou auſ̃ment Il lieus euſt fait tranchẽ les teſtes. Et ainſſi demoura lad ville en lobbeiſſance du Roy. Pour lagarde deſquelle ville et chaſteau fut commis.

Laprinſe delabbaye de. feſcamp par les francois.

CE pendant ceulx delagarniſon dedieppe pour leRoy defrance ſceurent quil yavoit pou dangloiz en labbaye defeſcamp qui eſt ung port demer yallerent ſegrettement et la prindrent demblee. Et tantoſt apres yaRiva une nef qui venoit dangleẗre en laquelle yavoit quatre vingtz dixſept angloiz gens deguerre qui venoient pour entre en garniſon en lad Abbaye ~ Cuidans quelle fuſt encore en leur obbaiſſance Maiz les francois tout degre les laiſſerent deſcend Leſquelz furent tout prins et demourerent p̃ſonniers auſd francois.

Commeȇ francois duc debretaigne entra ~ En normendie et print lacite decôſtances

EN ce meſme temps et oud an iiii^c xlix tres haulx et treſpuiſſans princes Monſeigne^r francois duc debretaigne et monſ^r artus de bretaigne conte deRichemont ⁊conneſtable defrance en leur compaignie monſ^r Iacques deluxembourg monſ^r leconte delaval monſ^r deloheac mareſchal defrance monſ^r decotiny baron etRaiz admiral defrance Monſ^r deſtouteville monſ^r debricquebec ſon filz Monſ^r debouſſac monſ^r demaleſtroit ~ monſ^r delahaynauldaye Monſ^r dedorval Joachim Rouault Meſſire guiffroy

led them before the said town of Essay, which rendered itself to him, threatening that otherwise he would cut off the heads. And so the said town remained in the obedience of the king. For the guardianship of which town and castle it was committed.

The capture of the abbey of Fécamp by the French

During this, those of the garrison of Dieppe for the king of France, learning that there were a few Englishmen in the abbey of Fécamp, which was a seaport, they went there secretly and took to plundering. And soon, a ship arrived there, which came from England, in which there were ninety-seven English men of war, who came to enter into the garrison in the said abbey, thinking that it was still in their obedience. But the French all willingly let them descend, who were all captured and remained prisoners of the said Frenchmen.

How the French duke of Brittany entered into Normandy and captured the city of Coutances

IN this same time and in the said year 1449, the very high and very powerful princes monseigneur François, duke of Brittany, and monseigneur Arthur of Brittany, earl of Richmond and constable of France, having in their company monseigneur Jacques de Luxembourg, monseigneur the count of Laval, monseigneur the count of Lohéac, marshal of France, monseigneur de Coitivy, baron de Rais and admiral of France, monseigneur d'Étouteville, monseigneur de Briquebec, his son, monseigneur de Boussac, monseigneur de Malestroit, monseigneur de la Hunaudaye, monseigneur d'Orval, Joachim

decouvran Olivier — debron et guillaume deRoſenyinem avec monſ^{r} demontauban mareſchal debretaigne Et pluſ^{rs} aut̂s chevalliers et esſcuiers dupays debretiagne eſtans en nombre ^{de} mil axii^{c} combatans entrerent enlabaſſe normendie pour Redduire et mettre en lobbeiſſance duRoy ~~d~~ led pays que les angloiz anciens ennemys du Royaume avoient uſurpe ettenu cont̂ Raiſon xxxii ans avoit ou environ. Et vindrent augiſte aumont ſaint michel leſd princes ſeigneurs et leurs gens logier et paroiſſ des pas ardemon hault et bas courtiz Saint geor en gayne portblanc et Illec environ. Et aupartir debretaigne laiſſa ſon frere meſſire pierre debretaigne ſur les marches defougeres et davranches pour lagarde dupays atout iii^{c} lances. Et lelendemain meſſ^{r} leduc ⁊côneſtable furent leur avantgarde laquelle Ilz envoyerent devant couſtanſtes couſtances en laquelle eſt mond ſ^{r} Iacques deluxembourg lieute͡n dud conneſtable. Leſd mareſchal ⁊admiral defrance Leſd deſtouteville et debriquebec debouſſac Ioachim et leſd decouvran debron et deRoſêvinin eſtans enſemble dequat̂ acinq cens lances que ce lui Iour allerent couchr̂ devat̂ lad ville de couſtances. Et meſd ſeigneurs leduc ⁊côneſtable en leur compaignie leconte delaval etleſurplus deſd ſ^{rs} pour labataille eſtoient enſemble de v avi^{C} lances. Et demourerent celle nuyt agrantville et Icelleenviron. Et lelendemain meſd ſ^{rs} ~~y~~ leduc ⁊conneſtable avecques lad ~~balte~~ bataille allerent aud lieu decouſtances et aRiverent devr̂s loſtel dieu. Et depuis le armee aRiva devant lad ville deconſtances ne tant que ung Iour dequirer et ſen allerent les angloiz leurs biens ſaufz et les bourgeois manans ⁊hâtants delad ville demourerent en leurs biens meubles et heritages.

Rouault, messire Geoffroi de Couvran, Olivier de Bron, and Giillaume de Rosenvinem, with monseigneur de Montauban, marshal of Brittany, and several other knights and squires of the land of Brittany, being in number 1,000 to 1,200 soldiers, entered Lower Normandy in order to reduce and put the said land into the obedience of the king, the said land which the English, ancient enemies of the kingdom, had usurped and held against reason for thirty-two years or therearound. And the said princes and lords came to rest at Mont-Saint-Michael and their men camped and lodged in the parishes of Pas-Ardemon, upper and lower Courtils, Saint-Georges-en-Gaine, Pont-Blanc, and the surrounding area. And at the departure from Brittany, messire Pierre of Brittany left his brother on the marches of Fougères and Avranches to guard the land with around 300 lances. And the next day, messire the duke and constable got up and made their avantgarde, which they sent before Coutances, in which avantgarde was the said monseigneur Jacques, Jacques de Luxembourg, lieutenant of the said constable, the saids marshal and admiral of France, the said d'Étouteville and de Briquebec, de Boussac, Joachim. and the said de Couvran, de Bron, and de Rosenivinin, together making 400 to 500 lances, which the said day they went to camp before the said town of Coutances. And the said monseigneurs the duke and constable, having in their company the count of Laval, and the remainder of the said lords remaining in the batallion were together comprised of about 600 lances. And they remained this night at Granville and around this area. And the next day, the said monseigneurs, the duke and the constable, with the said batallion, went to the place of Coutances and arrived before the house of God. And since army arrived before the said town of Coutances only one day earlier, the English went from the place with their goods safely and the citizens, workers, and inhabitants of the said town remained in the possession of their moveable goods and possessions.

Laprinſe deSaintlo par les francois.

Tantoſt apres ala leduc debretaigne mettre leſiege devant Sainct lo. Et yenvoya Premierement ſadicte avantgarde qui ſelogea dun coſte. Et lelendemain yarriverent meſd ſ^rs leduc et conneſtable avec leur bataille dautre coſte. Auquel lieu eſtoient deux cens combatans donc eſtoit capitaine meſſ^r guillaume poitou. Et combien quilz fuſſent belle compaignie Neantmoins ne firent aucune Reſiſtance. Maiz firēt compoſicion avecques led duc par laquelle Ilz ſen devoient aller franchement en leur party ou bon leur ſembleroit et emporter to⁹ leurs biens. Et ainſſi ſedepartirent dud lieu lexvii^me Iour dud moys deſeptembre. Et demoura lad place en lobbeiſſance duRoy defrance et meſdſ^rs et conſtable eulx eſtans aud Saint lo furent gagnees par ~~les~~ leurs gens les places qui ſenſ. Ceſt aſſavoir lehommel neufville torigny beuſeville hambye lamottelleveſque labbaye dupuys chantelou laune et pluſſieurs autres petites places alautour dud Saint lo. Et nuſt gades en chac͡n pour leRoy defrance. Et dud lieu deSaint lo meſdſ^r leduc ⁊conneſtable ēvoyerēt lad avantgarde devant laville decarentan et lelendemain yarriverent meſdſ^rs et leurs bataille. Et ne tindrent ceulx dededans lad place que trois Iours deguerre. Et ſen allerent les angloiz po^r toutes e̊ſpous ung baſton en leur main ſeullement. Et les bourgeois manans ⁊hâtans demourerēt en la gracieuſe mercy demeſdſ^rs leduc ⁊conneſtable. Leſquelz apres leur firent grace et les Reſtituerēt en leurs biens meubles ⁊hêtages. Et dela leſd mareſhal et admiral

The capture of Saint-Lô by the French

Soon after the duke of Brittany went to lay siege before Saint-Lô. And he sent there first his said avant-garde, which lodged themselves on one side. And the next day, the said monseigneurs, the duke and constable of France, arrived there with their batallion on the other side. In which place were 200 soldiers, over whom was captain messire William Poitou. And those within were a very great company. Nonetheless they gave no resistence. But they made an agreement with the said duke, by which they were able to go freely in their party or wherever it seemed good to them, and they took all their goods. And thus they left from the said place, the seventeenth day of the said month of September. And the said place remained in the obedience of the king of France, and the said monseigneurs and constable being at the said Saint-Lô won via their men the places that follow: it is known: le Hommel, Neuville, Torigny, Beuseville, Hambre, Motte-l'Évesque, the abbey of Puys, Chantelou, l'Aune, and several other small places in the area around the said Saint-Lô. And guardians were put into each for the king of France. And from the said place of Saint-Lô, the said monseigneurs, the duke and the constable, sent the said avant-garde before the town of Carentan, and the next day the said monseigneurs and their batallion arrived there. And those within held the said place for only three days of war. And the Englishmen left, all of them having only a stick in their hand. And the citizens, labourers, and inhabitants remained in the gracious mercy of the said monseigneurs, the duke and the constable, who afterwards were gracious and restored to them their goods, both moveable and hereditary. And from there, the said marshal and admiral of France, the said siege being at the said

defrance led ſiege eſtant aud carentan allerent devant lepont donc lequel Ilz prindrent daſſault et ſans Iuſ̂talle toute lad avantgarde alla courir Iucques auclos deconſtantin et ſeRendit aceux laplace laquelle fut baillee agarde aIoachim Rouault et dud lieu decarentan les ſeigneurs deſſuſd ſen Retournereſ̂ acouſtances. Et dela en moys doctobre envoyerent meſdſ[rs] Iacques debriquebec demaleſtroit debouſſac dedernal ⁊delahunaudaye et Iamet deillay bailly devermandoiz devant gauray et lelendemain yaRiva ~~ylad ce~~ mondſ[rs] leconneſtable et devoir Leduc celui Iour aud lieu decouſtances. Et auſ̂ lavenue dud conneſtable avoit eſte prins et daſſault laboullevert dud gauray. Et le lendemain meſ[re] guiffroy decouvren qui faiſoit leguet myna et fiſt aproches telles q̂ celui Iour lad gauray fut aſailly bien ⁊vaillammeſ̂ et tellement q̂ les angloiz qui eſtoient dedans devi a vii [XX] combatans demandereſ̂ aparler aud coneſtable pour faire leur compoſicion. Leſquelz par compoſicion ſen allerent eulx et leurs biens ſaufz.

Lap̂nſe dalencon par les francois.

Durant cetemps leduc dalencon ſe tranſporta aupoint deIour devant la ville dalencon par leconſentemeſ̂ des bourgeoiz et habitans dicelle ville et par lemoyen ~ deſquelz led duc print et entra dedens ſad ville. Et ſeRetirerent les angloiz dedens lechaſteau lequel Incontinent fut aſſiege par led duc lequel avoit en ſacompaignie huit vingtz lances et les archers ou environ. Et eſtoient grant nombre dangloiz dedans lad place qui oulrent tous leceur failly car Ilz firent petite Reſiſtance. Et ſe Rendirent aud duc dalencon au-

Carentan, went before Pont-d'One, which they captured by assault and without losing any time, the said avant-garde went to march until the cloister of Constantin, and those of the place rendered itself to them, which was given in guardianship to Joachim Raoualt, and from the said place of Caretan the abovesaid lords returned to Coutances. And from there, in the month of October, the said monseigneurs Jacques de Briquebec, de Malestroit, de Boussac, de Dernal, and de Hunaudaye, and Jamet du Tillay, balliff of Vermandois, were sent before Gauray, and the said monseigneure the constable arrived the next day and the duke remained this day at the said place of Coutances. And after the arrival of the said constable, the bulwark of the said Gauray was captured by assault. And the next day, messire Geoffroy de Couvren, who had the watch, sacked the place and made such incursions that this day the said Gauray was assailed very bravely and such that the Englishmen, who numbered 100 to 120 soldiers, asked to speak to the said constable in order to make their surrender. By which agreement they left, both themselves and their goods, safely.

The capture of Alençon by the French

During this time, the duke of Alençon went at daybreak before the town of Alençon by the consent of the citizens and inhabitants of this town, and by the means of this, the said duke captured it and entered into his town. And the English retired into the castle, which was immediately besieged by the said duke, who had in his company eighty lances and archers, or therearound. And there were a great number of the Englishmen within the said place who had all lost hope because they had little resistance. And they rendered themselves to the said duke of Alençon, who

quel competoit et appartenoit lad ville deſon propre hêtage alayde duquel vint meſſire loys debeaumont gouv̂ne[r] dumans atout lx ~~au~~ lances et les archers et pour lors eſtoit encores leRoy alouviers.

Lap̂nſe des ville ⁊chaſteau demauleon ſur les anglois.

En ce meſme temps environ lafin du moys de ſeptembre leconte defourz acompaigne des contes decomminges et deſtrac duviconte delautrac ſon frere et depluſſieurs auſs ſeigneurs barons chlr̃s eſcuiers des pays defourlz decomminge deſtrac debigoree et debearn Iucques au nombre de~~fix~~ cinq. aſix cens lances et dix milles arbaleſtriers. Et partit deſon pays debearne et chevaucha ainſi que dit eſt acompagne par les pays des baſques Iuques devant laville demauleon et deſolle ou Il miſt le ſiege. Et tantoſt apres led ſiege mis ceulx delad ville doubtans quilz meſuſſet̂ p̊ns daſſault meſmement veu ⁊conſidere lagrant compaignie des gens deguerre qui eſtoient devat̂ eulx pour eviter to[9] Inconveniens qui aloccaſion dud ſiege leur pourroient advenir ſeRendiret̂ par compoſicion. Ceſt aſſavoir quilz nedômageroiet̂ en corps ne en biens Iceulx hâtans delad ville. Et cors ſeRetrayrent les anglaiz dedans lachaſteau qui eſt leplus fort deladuche deguienne car Il eſt merveilleuſement hault aſſis ſur ung Roc led conte defourlz ſarchant quil ẙavoit peu devivres dedens Icellui chaſteau. Et pource yeuſt leſiege deto[9] coſtez. Aquoy leRoy denavarre ces nouvelles venues aſacognoiſſance ſy y voult obvier et pour baillr̃ ſecours auſd aſſiegez et pour lever led

had jurisdiction and to whom the said town belonged by rightful heritage, to the aid of whom came messire Louis de Beaumont, governor of Le Mans, with around sixty lances and archers, and during this time the king was still in Louviers.

The capture of the town and castle of Maulin from the English

In this same time, around the end of the month of September, the count of Foix, accompanied by the counts of Commings and Étrac, the viscount of Lautrac, his brother, and several other lords, barons, knights, and squires of the lands of Foix, Commings, Étrac, Bigore, and Béarn, until the number was 500 to 600 lances and 10,000 crossbowmen. And he left from his land of Béarn and rode so accompanied, it is said, among the lands of the Basques, until before the town of Mauléon, where he laid siege. And soon after the said siege was lain, those of the said town, fearing that they would be captured by assault, also seeing and considering the large company of the men of war who were before them, to avoid all inconveniences which the occasion of the said siege would cause to them, went to render themselves by agreement. It is known that they would not injure these inhabitants of the said town in body nor in their goods. And then the Englishmen retreated into the castle, which was the strongest in the duchy of Guyenne because it was extremely high, seated atop a rock, the said count of Foix, knowing that there had few supplies within this castle. And because of this, he laid siege to it on all sides. Which news came to the knowledge of the king of Navarre, who, wanting to obviate and in order to delivery supplies to the said besieged and to lift the said siege, mobilized his forces

ſiege ſon mandement de toutes parts. Et chevaucha acompaigne de ſix mille arragonnoys gaſcongs angloiz et navarroiz Iucques adeux lieues pres dud ſiege lecuidant lever. Maiz quant Il ſceut laforteſ ⁊puiſſance deceulx qui tirorent led ſiege fiſt Reculler ſes gens ⁊Retraire puis envoya ~~ſiege~~ meſſagiers devers led conte defourlz lui faire aſſavoir quil deſiroit deparler alui. Parquoy lui envoya ſeurete devenir devers lui atoute telle compaignie q̂ bon lui ſembleroit. Et ung led Roy denavarre atout petite compaignie aung quart delieue pres dud ſiege atoute ſa ſeurete ou eſtoit led conte defourlz. Auquel apres laſalutacion faite Il diſt aud conte que veu quil avoit eſpouſe ſafille donc Il avoit belle lignee ⁊auſſi laffinite qui par ce devoit eſtre ent̂ eulx deux ſedomoit grant marvaille comme Il avoit voulu aſſieger lad place ſoubz ſa ſauvegarde. Et meſmement veu que ſon coneſtable en eſtoit capitaine de par lui pour Roy danglet̂re Auquel Il avoit promis lafaire garder ſeurement encont̂ to[9] led conte defourlz ſon gendre gracieuſement et en portant tout honneur lui diſt quil eſtoit lieutenant general du Roy defrance es parties dent̂ gironde et les mons eſpiraulx ſon parent et ſon ſubjet et par ſon commandement et ordonnace avoit prins lad ville et mis leſiege devant le chaſteau. Et pource pour ſon honne[r] garder et affin q̂ au temps advenir ne lui fuſt Impute aucun crime ou Reprouche ne ahomme deſon lignaige Iamais pour homme ne ſen leveroit et ne ſen deſplaceroit ~~ne~~ en lui en ſon oſt cil neſtoit combatu et vaincu Iucques ace q̂ led chaſteau fuſt Redduit en lobbeiſſance du Roy maiz en toutes choſes alui poſſibles Il aideroit ſeconforteroit et ſerviroit led Roy deNavarre pere deſafemme Reſerve touteſſoiz cont̂ leRoy defrance

from all parts. And he rode out accompanied by 6,000 Aragonese, Gascons, Englishmen, and Navarrese to within two leagues of the said siege, thinking to lift it. But when he learned of the great strength and power of those who held the said siege, his men turned around and retreated; then, he sent messengers to the said count of Foix, making it known to him that he desired to speak to him, for which he sent to him promises of safe passage to come to him with all such company as seemed good to him. And the said king of Navarre with a small company [came] within a quarter league of the said siege where the said count of Foix was in full safety, who after greeting him said to the said count that, seeing that he had married his daughter, thus he had good lineage, and also the affinitity which, by this means, ought to be between them both, he was astounded how he had wanted to besiege the said place under his safeguard. And even seeing that his constable, who was captain for him by the king of England, to whom he had promised to keep it firmly against all, the said count of Foix, his relative, graciously, and showing all honour, responded to him that he was lieutenant general of the king of France for the areas between the Gironde and the Pyrenees Mountains, his relative and his subject, and by his command and order he had captured the said town and laid the siege before the castle. And for this, it was his honour to guard it, and to do this until the time to come, he was would not allow any opposition nor reproche from a man of his lineage, never for a man would he lift it and he would not remove himself nor his army unless he was fought and defeated, until this said castle was reduced into the obedience of the king; but in all other things it was possible he would bring help to him, comfort him, and serve him, the said king of Navarre, father to his wife, excepting only against the king of France, his subjects and allies,

ſes ſubgetz et allyez en tant q̂ touche lefait delacouronne defrance. Et ainſſi ſen Retourna led Roy denavarre et ſon oſt en ſon pays et quant ceulx duchaſteau virient quilz ne pouvoiet̂ eſtre en Rien ſecourus actendre lanereſſite quilz avoient devenois Rendirent lad chaſteau aud conte defourlz par compoſicion. Et ainſſi demoura lad chaſteau ⁊ville en lobbeiſſance duRoy defrance. Et tantoſt apres leſire deluce a compaigne devi^C combatans portans tous les croix Rouges lequel eſt homme duRoy defrance a cauſe duchaſteau demauleon alui competant et appartenat̂ ala faire auRoy homaige en la main dud conte defourlz ſon lieuten̂ general es marches et pays qui dit eſt. Et Incontinet̂ apres leſerment par lui et ſes gens fait ſen Retourna atout ſacompaignie en ſa maiſon portans tous les croix blanche donc lepeuple hommes ſires et enffans firent moult eſbahis. Et defait ſen alla led conte defourlz et ſes gens en ſon pays apres garde ſouffiſante ⁊cap^ne mis aud mauleon.

Lapr̂nſe. detouques. par les francois.

LE xxviime Iour du moys deſeptembre alla monſeigneur deblainville agrant cồpaignie degens darmes devant lechaſteau detoucque qui eſt treſſort chaſteau aſſis ~~ung~~ ſur ung Roc Ioignant de lamer auquel eſtoient en garniſon ſoixante angloiz pour lagarde dicellui leſquelz voyans ſi grant compaignie eſtre devant eulx ne firent gueres deReſiſtance. Maiz pr̂drent compoſicion avec led ſeigneur par laquelle Ilz ſen allerent to⁹ leurs corps et leurs biens ſaufz. Et eurent bon ſaufconduit pour eulx en allr̂ en leur party ou bon leur ſembla.

due to the obligations he made to the crown of France. And thus, the said king of Navarre and his army returned into his lands, and when those of the castle learned that they could not be in any way rescued, waiting the agreed time that they had been given to come, they rendered the said castle to the count of Foix by agreement. And so the said castle and town remained in the said obedience of the king of France. And soon afterwards, the sire of Lucé with a company of 600 soldiers, all carrying the red cross, who were men of the king of France, because the castle of Mauléon were under his jurisdiction and belonged to him, went to make homage in the hands of the said count of Foix, his lieutenant general, it is said, for the marches and lands. And immediately after making the oath by him and his men, he went to return with all his company in his house, carrying all white banners, for which the people, men, lords, and landowners were very astonished. And this deed done, the said count of Foix and his men went into his lands, after guarding sufficiently and installing a captain at Mauléon.

The capture of Touques by the French

THE twenty-seventh day of the month of September, monseigneur de Blainville with a large company of men-at-arms went before the castle of Touques, which was a very strong castle sitting on a rock adjoining the sea, within which was garrisoned sixty Englishmen for the guardianship of this place; whom, seeing so great a company before them, put up no resistence. But it was captured by agreement with the said lord, by which they left safely with all their bodies and their goods. And they had safe conduct in order to go into the places of their party, wherever seemed good to them.

Laꝑ̊nſe dẙemmes ꝑ les francois.

EN ce meſme an led ſixieme Iour dumois deSeptembre leſd contes dedunoiz de clermont et de Nevers et pluſſieurs auts̃ deleʳ compaignie devantdicte menant leſiege devat̃ lechaſteau dyemmes. Lequel Rendirent Incôtinet̃ les angloiz qui dedans eſtoient et ſen allerent ſeurement et franchement leurs corps et leurs biens ſaufz. Et ainſſi demoura lad place en lobeiſſance du Roy. Alaquelle gandes fut commes et ordonne pour leRoẙ par led conte dedunoiz.

Laprinſe delaville et chaſteau dargentain par les francois

APRES ledepartement dyennes ſen alla lad armee avec led conte dedunoiz lieutenant general devant laville ⁊lechaſteau dargentan Ilz mirent leſiege. Et tantoſt les angloiz qui dedens eſtoient fautement commencerent a parlementer. Combien quilz navoient aucune voulente deux Rendre. Et quant les bourgeois et hâtans delad ville virent ⁊congneret̃ les angloiz auſſi abuſer les francois aparlementer Recognoiſſ que leur voullente eſtoit deulx tenir cont̃ lapuiſſance deſd francois et quilz diſoient auplus loing deleur penſees Iceulx bourgois et hâtans delad ville appellerent aucuns deſd francois ducoſte ou Ilz ne parlementoit point et leur dirent leur voullente et ce q̂ les angloiz avoient Intencion defaire Pourqouy leur demanderent eſtendart bannere ou panôceau pour enſeigne. Et leur dirent que la ou Ilz mettroient lad enſeigne quilz vineſſent ſeuremet̃ et Ilz les

The capture of Dyemmes by the French

IN this same year, the said sixteenth day of the month of September, the said counts of Dunois, of Clermont, and of Nevers, and several others of their aforementioned company laid siege before the castle of Dyemmes, which the Englishmen who were inside rendered immediately, and they left safely and freely, their bodies and goods safe. And so the said place returned into the obedience of the king, the guardianship for which was done and organised for the king by the said count of Dunois.

The capture of the town and castle of Argentain by the French

AFTER the capture of Yennes, the said army went with the said count of Dunois, lieutenant general, before the town and castle of Argentain, where they laid siege. And soon afterwards, the Englishmen who were inside began to talk, even though they had no desire to render themselves. And when the citizens and inhabitants of the said town saw and learned that the Englishmen also abused the Frenchmen with whom they wanted to speak, recognizing that their desire was to hold themselves against the power of the said Frenchmen and that they said as much as their thoughts, these citizens and inhabitants of the said town called several of the said Frenchmen on a side where there was no longer talk, and said to them their will and what the Englishmen intended to do. For which they requested some banner or insignia in order to serve as a sign. And they said to them that when they placed the said sign there, that they would surely come and they would

boutiroient dedens lad ville. Et ainſſi la firent. Et quant les angloiz les apperceuref̃ leurs Ilz ſeRetrahirent haſtivement oud chaſteau. Et Incontenef̃ on tous conf̃ lamuraille dicelle ou groſſe bombarde qui yfuſt ung grant trou aſſez grant pour paſſer une charrette. Et lors les francoiz voyans lemur eſtre ainſſi abatu Ilz aſſallirent Icellui chaſteau et entrerent dedens parmy led trou. Maiz les angloiz ſeRetirerent en donIon dilligement lequel auplus toſt Ilz Rendirent depaour deſtre prins daſſault. Et combien quilz demandaſſent composicion nean emporterent que chc͡n ung baſton en ſon poing tant ſeullement. Non obſtant quilz eſtoient grant nombre dangloiz dedans leſquelz eſtoient to⁹ honteulx deulx en aller ſipouvrement et ſemeſchau. Et ainſſi demoura lad place en lobbeiſſance duRoy defrance. Pour laquelle garder fut cômis et ordonne par de conte dedunoiz lieutenant general.

Commef̃ leſiege fut mis devant gaillard par les francois.

EN ce meſme temps 7ſaiſon vint leRoy deCecile devers leRoy defrance aud louviers lequel fut Receu amoult grant chere. Et auſſi la eſtoient leconte dumaine ſon frere leviconte delomaigne Levicomte decaſtres Lecadet dalbreth lebaron de traynel chancellr̃ defrance leſire deculant graf̃ maiſtre doſtel les contes detancarville et de dampmâtin lemareſchal delapirte feroy Monſ[re] deloraine Iehan monſ[re] ſon frere les ſeigneurs deblainville demontgaſcon depreci-gny degaucourt depreilly delabaiſſiere demontart debrion de beauvaiz dehan champaigne degraville et demalicorne. Meſſire theaulde devalperne meſſire Iehan duſigne meſſire

allow them within the said town. And so they did. And when the Englishmen learned this from them, they quickly retreated into the said castle. And against the wall of this [castle], a projectile from a large catapult was launched immediately, by which was made a hole large enough for a cart to pass through. And then the Frenchmen, seeing the wall to be so destroyed, they assailed this strong castle and entered within the said hole. But, retreating diligently to the dungeon, the Englishmen soon rendered themselves, fearing to be captured by assault, and such that they requested an agreement; however, they each carried only one stick from this place. Nonetheless, there were a great number of Englishmen within, who were all ashamed of themselves for going so poorly and unhappily. And so the said place remained in the obedience of the king of France. For which the guardianship was committed and organised by the count of Dunois, lieutenant general.

How the siege was lain before Gaillart by the French

IN this same time and season, the king of Sicily went before the king of France at the said Louviers, who was received with great cheer. And also there were the count of Maine, his brother; the viscount of Lomagne; the count of Castres; the cadet of Albret; the baron de Traignal, chancellor of France; the sire de Culant, grand master of the hotel; the counts of Tancarville and of Dammartin, the marshal de Lafayette; Ferry, monseigneur de Lorraine; Jean, monseigneur his brother; the seigneurs de Blainville, de Montgascon, de Précigny, de Gaucourt, de Preuilly, de Bessiere, de Monteil, de Brion, de Beauvais, de Laon in Champagne, de Graville, and de Malicorne; messire Théaude de

loys delaRochette maiſtre Robert deſtampes et pluſſieurs auťs chlřs 7eſcuiers qui ſeroit longue choſe aReciter et Iuſques au nombre dedeux cens lances 7les archiers ſans en ce comprendre ~~lar~~ larmee 7compaignie duduc dalencon celle duduc debretaigne celle duconte dedunoiz lieutenant et celle duconte declermont. Et ſans celles des contes deu et deſainct pol eſquelles quatre armees yavoit grant compaignie et notable comme deſſ eſt dit et deſclare. Et pource voyant ſi noble chevallerie ſi conclud et delibera deprocedř oulť alaconqueſte 7Recouvrauce deſon pays et duchie denormendie. Parquoy fiſt mettre leſiege aung lundy devant lechaſteau gaillard qui eſt mout fort et Imprenable ſinon par famine et neſtpas poſſible deprandre par force led chaſteau tant quil yait vivres dedens laplace car Il eſt aſſis pres delaRiviere deſaine ſur ung Roc et en tel lieu que nulz engins ne lepourroient grever. Et yfut mis led ſiege par leſeneſchal depoictou leſire deIalongnes mareſchal defrance meſſire Iehan debreze meſſire denis dechailly 7pluſſrs auťs leſquelz alimeť ſigouvernerent grandemeť et vaillamment. Et yeſtoit leRoy en perſonne.

Laprinſe defreſnay. p les francois.

EN ce meſme temps monſr leduc dalencon miſt leſiege devant laville 7chaſteau defreſnay ou Il avoit grant quantite dangloiz leſquelz ne ſeRebellerent en Rien. Pource quilz voient les gens duRoy ainſſi proſperer. Maiz Rendirent laplace aud duc dalencon par compoſicion auſſi demoura lad place en lobeiſſance duRoy vous laquelle garder cômſt et ordonna.

Valpergue; messire Jean du Signe; messire Louis de la Rochète; master Robert d'Étampes; and several other knights and squires, which would be long to recite, until the number was 200 lances and the archers, without counting the army and company of the duke of Alençon, that of the duke of Brittany, that of the count of Dunois, lieutenant, and that of the count of Clermont. And without those of the counts of Eu and Saint-Pol, in which were four armies there, being great and notable, as has above been said and declared. And for this, seeing so noble a cavalry, he concluded and decided to proceed immediately with the conquest and recovery of his land and duchy of Normandy, for which he laid siege on a Monday before Castle Gaillard, which was very strong and impregnable, except by starvation, and the castle was impossible to take by force as long as there was food within the place, because it was situated near the river Seine on a rock, and in such place that no artillery could aggrieve it. And the said siege there was established by the seneschal of Poitou, the sire de Jallognes, marshal of France, messire Jean de Bréze, messire Denis de Chailly, and several others, who governed themselves there grandly and bravely. And the king was there in person.

The capture of Fresnay by the French

IN this same time, monseigneur the duke of Alençon laid siege before the town and castle of Fresnay, where there was a very large quantity of Englishmen, who did not resist at all, because they saw that the men of the king were very successful. But they rendered the place to the said duke of Alençon by an agreement; thus, the said place returned to the obedience of the king, in whom he [Alençon] was committed and ordained guardian.

Traite. fait ſus laReddicion degiſors.

CE pendant que leſiege eſtoit aud gaillard avant laReddicion dicellui avant deux ou trois Iours led ſeneſchal depoitou et ung des des eſcuiers deſcuierie duRoẏ̊ Nomme paryot et ung aut nomme pierre decourcelles parent dela femme meſſire Richard marbury chlr̃ angloiz et capitaine degiſors aveques led capitaine et fait compoſicion pour laReddicion dicelle ville ⁊chaſteau degiſors et Iceulx mettre en lobeiſſance du Roy defrance. Et pource led capitaine traict et promiſt Rendre lad place lexvi[ii]Iour du moys deſeptiembre enſ. Et defait ſeRendit francois et fiſt leſerement en tel cas acouſtume parmy ce q̂ on lui delivraſt puremet̂ nectemet̂ et ſans deſpens deux deſes enffans nommez Iehan et emond leſquelz avoient eſte prins auponteaudemer. Et aveques celui fut acorde quil Ioyroit des ſes deſd femme q̂ les francois tenoient ⁊occupoient fuſt par don duRoy ou ault̂ment. Et out̂plus alaRequeſte des parens delad femme et pour les agreables ſervices q̂ leRoy eſperoit q̂ lui et ſes enffans lui firoient ou temps advenir lefiſt capitaine deſaint germain en laye et lui donna ſavie durant ſeullemet̂ to⁹ les profits et emoulumens apparten̂ alad capitainerie. Et demoura capitaine par ledon duRoy de lad ville ⁊chaſteau degiſors monſ[r] degaucourt lequel agrandement travaille ſon corps au ſervice du Roy. Et tellement q̂ veu ſon age qui eſt deiv[xx] ans ou meaulx Il a acqueſta ung grant honneur et afait comme vaillant chlr̃ bon ⁊vray ſubgect aſon ſouverain ſeigne[r] doit faire.

Treaty made for the surrender of Gisors

WHILE the siege was held at the said Gaillard, two or three days before the reduction of this place, the said seneschal of Poitou and one of the squires of the squirie of the king named Pariot and another named Pierre de Courcelles, relatives of the wife of messire Richard de Marbury, an English knight and captain of Gisors, went with the said captain and made an agreement for the reduction of this town and castle of Gisors and to put this place into the obedience of the king of France. And for this, the said captain agreed and promised to render the said place the sixteenth day of the following month of September. And to do this, the Frenchman rendered himself and made the oath in such case is accustomed, that he would deliver to him purely, naturally, and without any cost two of his children, named Jean and Edmund, who had been captured at Ponteau-de-Mer. And wirh this, it was agreed that he would enjoy the abovesaid lands of his wife that the French held and occupied by the gift of the king or otherwise. And in addition, at the request of the relatives of the said wife and for the agreeable services that the king hoped he and his children would do for him in the time to come, he made him captain of Saint-Germain-en-Laye and gave him for the duration of his life all the profits and emuluments belonging to the said captaincy. And monseigneur de Gaucourt, who had greatly worked his body in service to the king, remained captain by the gift of the king in the said town and castle of Gisors. And such that, seeing his old age, which was eighty years or more, he granted him a great honour and treated him as a brave knight as a good and true subject to his sovereign lord ought to do.

OU moẙs doctobre oud an LeRoy defrance manda auconte dedunoiz ⁊aux aufs ſʳ deſacompaignie tenans les champs qui avoient mis dargentan en ſon obbeiſſance. Et pareillement mande aux contes deu et deſaint pol ⁊aut̂s deſacompaignie quilz vinſſent devers lui pource quil voulloit mett̂ leſiege devant laville deRouen et laRedduire en ſon obbaiſſance. Et vindrent to⁹ haſtivemet̂ aſon mandement et chevaucherent tant q̂ les compaignie dud conte dedunoiz ſetrouveref̂ en champaigne du neuf bourg et ceulx deſd conte deu ⁊deſaint pol. Et ſaſemblerent delauf̂ coſte devers Rouen. Et tantoſt apres ſepartit leRoy deſaville delouviers acompaigne du Roy deSecille ⁊aut̂s devant nomẑ et chevaucha Iucques devant lepot̂ delarche ou ceulx delaville vindrent audevaf̂ delui aux champs faiſans grant Ioye deſon ~ advenement. Et lors envoya ſommer ſans quelq̂ delay ceulx delaville et cite deRouen par ſes heraulx. Affin que ſans oppreſſion Ilz lui vouliſſent Rendre et mettre en ſon obbeiſſance ſad ville ⁊cite deRouen. Maiz les anglois qui de dens eſtoient conſiderans aſſez lacauſe pourquoy leſd heraulx venoient ne les vouldrent point laiſſer aprouchr̂ delad ville ne baillr̂ leur ſommacion ains leurs Reſpondirent quilz ſen Retournaſſef̂ agraf̂ dangier heſte et ainſſi firent Ilz cas Ilz furent en grant pol ⁊dangr̂ demort. Et Rapport fait leRoy voyant lamanẽ que les angloiz avoient tenue aſeſd heraulx fiſt paſſer tous ſes gens darmes aud pont delarche deſquelz eſtoit conduiſeur led conte dedunoiz cōme lieutenant general et les envoya devant lacite deRouen ou Ilz furef̂ trois Iours en grant multitude ⁊puiſſance degens pendans leſquelz trois Iours Iceulx ~~trois Io~~ Iceulx gens deguerre

IN the month of October in the said year, the king of France summoned the count of Dunois and the other lords of his company holding the field, who had newly put Argentan under his obedience, and he also summoned the counts of Eu and of Saint-Pol and others of their company, who came to him because he wanted to lay siege before the town of Rouen and to reduce it into his obedience. And everyone came quickly to his summons and rode such that the company of the said count of Dunois found themselves in Champagne at Neubourg and those of the said counts of Eu and Saint-Pol. And they assembled on the other side toward Rouen. And soon afterwards, the king left from his town of Louviers accompanied by the king of Sicily and others above named, and he rode until he was before Pont-de-l'Arche, where those of the town came before him to the field expressing great joy at his arrival. And then he sent summons without any delay to those of the town and city of Rouen by his heralds. So that without fighting, they would want to come to him to render and put into his obedience his said town and city of Rouen. But the English who were within, considering also the cause for which the said heralds came, no longer wanting to allow them to approach the said town nor deliver their summons, thus they responded to them that they must return, with great danger, hastily, and so they were in great risk and danger of death. And delivering the report, the king, seeing the manner that the Englishmen had directed toward his said heralds, prepared all his men-at-arms at the said Pont-de-l'Arche, over whom was leader the said count of Dunois, as lieutenant general, and he sent them before the city of Rouen, where for three days, there was a great multitude and power of men, during which three days, those men of war, both great and small, underwent much suffering and endured a downpour of

tant legrant que lepetit ourent moult aſouffrir et endurer par lorage depluye quil faiſoit. Et apou eſtoit tout loſt perdu delord chemin ⁊plus quil faiſoit. Et ce non obſtant ceulx dededens firent degrans ſaillies ou Il yoult demoult belles proueſſes et armee faictes. Et yoult ung eſcuier francois nomme lebaſtard ſorbier par ſon cheval qui ſt cheut ſoubz lui leſd ſeigneurs et gens darmes quelq̃ temps quil fiſt ſemidrent en bataille devant lad cite et les envoyerent laſegonde foiz ſommer par leſd heraultx du Roy. Maiz les angloiz ne vouldreƈ ſouffrir quilz approuchaſſent lad ville me quils parlaſſerent lepeuple. Et ainſſi ſen Retoũreƈ ſans Rien faire côme Ilz avoieƈ fait lapm̊iere foiz qui eſt conƈ tout ordre deſ^re^ie ⁊chevalerie. Car heraulx ſedoiveƈ aller ⁊venir ſauvement et ſeurement pour ſ^e^ ce aquoy Ilz ſont envoyez pourveu quil ny ait en leurs fait aucuẽ traiſon. Et ſe leſd angloiz euſſent eſte telz et dutelle naturel quilz deuſſent avoir eſte Ilz deuſſent avoir actrait leſd heraulx et ouis laſommacion telle quilz lavoulloient faire. Et apres leur porter aboire et amenger pour lonneur dup̊rce pour lequel Ilz eſtoient lavenus. Et apres le^r^ baillr̃ Reſponce telle que lecas leRequeroiet pour Icelle Rapporter aleurd prince. Et lors leſd heraulx Retournez et leur Rapport fait aud conte de dunoiz Icellui conte voyant q̃ nul delacite ne faiſoit ſemblant ne maniere delavoulloir Rendre lad ville. Conſiderant letemps et laſaiſon qui eſtoit ſus hyver et lepluye quil faiſoit ſen Retoũna autiers Iour aupont delarche les gens deguerre ſelogerent alentour dicellui pont par les villages. Et meſmement ced Iour eſtoit venu leRoy de france et leRoy deCecille Iucques aune abbaye dedames aune lieue ⁊demye deRouen lequel ſen Retourna

rain. And a little of all of the army was lost from the train and more that it should have been. And this notwithstanding, those of the town made very great sallies, where there were feats of very good prowess and feats of arms. And a French squire named the bastard Sorbier [was captured because of] his horse, who fell under him, the said lords and men-at-arms, for some time, fought in battle before the said city and they sent to them for the second time summons by the said heralds of the king. But the Englishmen would not allow them to approach the said town so that they could speak to the people. And, thus, they returned without doing anything, just as they had done the first time, which was against all expectations of lordship and chivalry, because heralds ought to go and come safely and security in order to do that which they were sent, provided that in their task they conducted no treason. And if the said English had been such and of such nature as they ought to have been, they would have received the said heralds and heard their summons such that they would do it. And after they would have brought them drink and food for the honour of the prince for which they had gone there. And afterwards giving the response to them such as the case required, for these people to report to their said prince. And so, the said heralds returned and, their report being made to the said count of Dunois, this count saw that none of the said city seemed to make a move toward wanting to render the said town. Considering the time and the season, which was approaching winter, and the rain that they had, he went back on the said third day to Pont-de-l'Arche, the men of war camped around this said bridge near the villages. And even this said day, the king of France and the king of Sicily came to an abbey of women one and a half leagues from Rouen, who then returned to the said Pont-de-'Arche to camp. And the said king of

aud pont delarche augiſte. Et demoura led Roy deCecille deſriere Iucques ace que toutes les compaignies ſefuſſent Retraictes aud pont delarche et es marches denviron. Pou ap̊s vindrent nouvelles aud Roy defrance que aucuŝ gens delad ville deRouen ſemettoient ſur la muraille delad ville dedens deux tours. Et lagardoient ung par devers en manier q̂ les francois pourroient bien entrer par la en Icelle ville. Et fut envoye dicelle part led conte dedunoiz avec larmee deſſſd pour enſprand Icelle beſongne leſquelz partoient to⁹ enſble leIeuſdy xvi^me^Iour dud moys doctobre et ſemiroiт̂ en moult belle ordonnant ſur les champs puis chevaucherent tant quilz arriveref devant la ville deRouen et ſe mirent en bataille ducoſte dedevs̃ leneufchaſtel delaquelle firent leſd ſ^rs^ deux parties donc lune eſtoit enſ laporte des chartreux et laporte beauvoiſine. Et en eſtoient conduiſeurs monſ^re^ leconte dedunoiz lieutenant general duRoy leconte deNevers leconte deu leconte deSainct pol monſ^re^ dorval monſ^re^ leſeneſchal depoictou monſ^re^ lemareſchal delafayete monſ^re^ degaucourt lebailly devreux et pluſſieurs aufs chevallr̃s et eſcuiers. Et lauf bataille eſtoit enſ laIuſtice deRouen et lacite ou eſtoient meſſ^rs^ les contes declermont decaſtres levicomte deloumaigne monſ^r^ deculaf grant maiſtre doſtel duRoy meſſire phlê deculaf ſon frere mareſchal defrance monſ^r^ deblainville maiſtre des arbaleſtriers monſ^r^ debueil pierre de louvain et pluſſieurs aufs chevalliers ⁊eſcuiers. Et furef to⁹ en bataille Iucques adeux heures apres midy. Et acelle heure ſe ſaillit ung hm̂ delad cite ~~qui~~ acheval qui vint dire auſd ſ^rs^ ten̄ ~~de~~ leſd batailles quil yavoit des gens de lad ville qui tenoient defait et deforce deux tours pour bouter les gens duRoy pour boutr̂ dedens. Et Incontinent led

Sicily remained behind until all the companies had withdrawn to the said Pont-de-l'Arche and the marches around it. Shortly after, news came to the king of France that several people of the said town of Rouen were put on the wall of the said town atop two towers. And they would guard one in a manner that the French could well enter by there into this town. And he sent to this place the said count of Dunois with the abovesaid army to attempt this attack, which left altogether Friday, the seventheenth day of the month of October, and it put itself together in very good order on the field, then they rode such that they arrived before the said town of Rouen and put themselves in batallions on the side toward Neufchâtel, for which the said lords organised two groups; thus, one was between the Chartreux gate and Beauvoisine gate, and the leaders were monseigneur the count of Dunois, lieutenant general of the king; the count of Nevers; the count of Eu; the count of Saint-Pol; monseigneur d'Orval; monseigneur the seneschal of Poitou; monseigneur the marshal de Lafayère; monseigneur de Gaucourt; the bailiff of Évreux; and several other knights and squires. And the other batallion was between the justice precinct of Rouen and the city [offices], where were messires the counts of Clermont [and] of Castres; the viscount of Lomagne; monseigneur de Culant, grand master of the hotel of the king; messire Philippe de Culant, his brother, marshal of France; monseigneur de Blainville, master of the crossbowmen; monseigneur de Bueil; Pierre de Louvain; and several other knights and squires. And they were all there in batallions until two hours after midday. And at this hour, a man from the said town sallied out on horseback, who came to say to the said lords commanding the said batallions that there were some men of the said town who held by combat and by force two towers in order to allow the men of the

conte dedunoiz et les auſs ſeigneurs teñ labataille devant la porte des chartreux firent marcher appartimet̂ les gens detrait pour venir Ioindre aung pu demur enſ leſd deux tours. Et lors deſce͠dit apie led conte dedunoiz et ceulx deſacompaignie et marcheroient Iucques alamuraille deladitville ou Ilz dreſſerent tant peu deſchelles quilz avoient enſ leſd deux tours et faiſoit ung chcñ grat̂ diligence pour monter conſmont lamur. La furet̂ faiz chevalliers leconte deNevers le ſire deconcreſſault brunet delongchamp leſire deplemartin pierre delafayette leſire de greville maiſtre guillaume couſinot Iaqz͠ delaRiviere bailly dyernois Robert deherenville et pluſſieurs auſs qui to⁹ faiſoient grandement leur devoir demonter ſur lad muraille. Et tellement quilz eſtoient dexxx axl fr͠coiz tant deſſus lemur que dedens laville. Sur leſquelz vint chr͠ger moult vaillamet̂ leſire detallebot atout trois cent angloiz en ſaco͠paignie. Lequel vint planter ſabanniere ſur lamur ſa. Afin deRebouter leſd angloiz qui Iaeſtoient en partie dedens laville co͠me dit eſt. En ſe entrecombatant moult vaillamment Iceulx francois. Et tellement que lapluſgrande partie ſe ſauva aReſſailler dedens les foſſez. Et furet contraints an faire par laforce dutrait que les angloiz tirant et ceulx qui ne ſepeureſ Retraier fureſ mors ou prins dedens lad ville et chargerent ſi aprement ſus leſd francois quilz furet̂ maiſtres detoute lamuraille et deſd deux tours. Et la furet̂ q̂ mors que prins oud aſſault de. l.alx. hommes tant defrancois que deceulx delad ville qui leur aidoient et favoriſoient et les aut̂s pour eulx cuider ſauver ſe tuereſ et les auſs eſchapperent. Et meſmement aucuns deceulx qui eſtoient dedens leſd tours et [ſe] Rompirent ~~leſd~~ Iambes et les auſs fureſ ſ prins par les

king to get inside. And immediately the said count of Dunois and the other lords holding the batallion before the Chartreux gate marched promptly, the conscripts to come join them at a small section of wall between the said two towers. And then, the said count of Dunois and those of his company descended on foot and advanced until the wall of the town, where they leaned a few ladders that they had between the said two towers, and each one of them made great diligence to scale the wall. The count of Nevers, the sire de Concressault, Brunet de Longchamps, the sire de Plemartin, Pierre de Lafayète, the sire de la Graville, master Guillaume Cousinot, Jacques de la Rivière, baliff of Nivernois, Robert de Herenville, and several others were made knights there, who all grandly did their best to scale the said wall. And such that there were also 30 to 40 Frenchmen, both those who scaled the above wall and those inside the town, for which came charging very bravely the sire de Talbot with around 300 Englishmen in his company, who came to plant his banner on the wall of the place so as to encourage the said Englishmen who were on his side within the said town, it is said, in fighting these Frenchmen very bravely. And such that the greater part saved themselves while retreating within the trenches. And they were constrained in their deed by the force of the arrows that the Englishmen shot, and those who could not retreat were killed or captured within the said town, and the said Frenchmen charged so hopefully that they were masters of all the wall and of the said two towers. And more than fifty to sixty men, both from the French and from those of the said town who had helped and favoured them there were killed and captured at the said assault, and others, thinking to save them, were killed, and the others escaped, and even several of those who were inside the said tower, and they broke their arms [and]

angloiz et meurdoiz moult Inhumainemeſ. Et eſtoit grant abhominacion deveoir leſange qui eſtoit enť Icelles tours. En prend aRiverent aderneſtal leſd Roys afrance ⁊deCecille. Et leſquilz quant Ilz virient lachoſe ainſſi allř. Et ǭ ceulx delacite et delaville neſtoient pas bien voys enſemble ſen Retourneref lexvi^me^ Iour doctobre aud pont delarche. Et toutes les gens deguerre ſen allerent logr̃ les villages delaRiviere deſeine ou Ilz avoief le^rs^ ordonnâces.

Lareddicion. degiſors au Roy. defrance.

LE xxvii^me^Iour dumoys doctobre meſſire Richard marbury chevallř angloiz deſſus nommez en accompliſſant ſes promeſſes bailla et delivra les chaſteau ⁊ville degiſors. et Iceulx miſt es mains degaucourt pour leRoy defrance. Et par ainſi lui furet̂ Renduz ſes deux enffas̑ qui eſtoient priſonniers. Et aveques ce toutes auťs promeſſes alui faictes enťtenues. Et par ainſſi ſedepartit et fiſt partir ung capitaine angloiz nôme Regne ford qui ſoubz lui avoit lacharge ⁊garde des gens darmes auparvat̂ ce contract ordonne alagâde diceulx ville ⁊chaſteau.

Siege mis devant fougeres. par leduc debrataigne.

En ce temps ſepartit leduc debretaigne delabaſſe normandie ou Il avoit prins moult deplaces comme dit eſt deſſ. Et ſen Retourna mettre leſiege afougeres ǭ tenoit meſſire francois deſurenne dit laragonnois.

legs, and others were captured by the English and killed very inhumainely. And it was a great abomination to see the blood which was between these towers. During the capture, the said kings of France and of Sicily arrived at Darenetal, who, when they saw the thing, also left. And that those of the city and of the town not seeing eye to eye, they returned the sixteenth day of October to the said Pont-de-l'Arche. And all the men of war went to lodge in the villages beside the River Seine, where they kept their supplies.

The reduction of Gisors to the king of France

The twenty-seventh day the month of October, messire Richard Marbury, an English knight above named, in completing his promises, gave and delivered the castle and town of Gisors and put these into the hands of de Gaucourt for the king of France. And thus, his two children, who were prisoners, were returned to him. And in addition, all other promises made to him were maintained. And then he left, and he left an English captain named Regnefort, who previously had under him the charge and guardianship of the men-at-arms who were ordered to guard this town and this castle.

The seige before Fougières by the duke of Brittany

IN this time, the duke of Brittany left from Lower Normandy, where he had captured many places, as it is said, and he returned to lay siege to Fougières, which was held by François de Surienne, called the Arragonais.

Laprinſs duchaſteau de conde par les francois

En ce meſmes temps fut prins par les francois lachaſteau deconde ſur noireau par laporte par deffaulte degarde. Et la fut prinſe lafemme demeſſire francois larragonnoiz qui autffoiz avoit eſte deſuchie et deprins Rouen dedens led chaſteau deconde. Et oulret led francois to⁹ les biens eſtans en lad place avecques ce que leſd angloiz demourerent leurs priſonniers.

Ambaſſade des bourgoiz delaville de Rouen. envoya devans leRoy pour cautre deliu Rendue ladicte ville

LE xvi[me]Iour dud moys doctobre les manans et habitans delad ville deRouen pour la grant paour ⁊fraieur quilz avoient eue dud aſſault doubtans q̂ lad ville nefuſt prinſe en paouil cas et par ce moyen pillee deſoller et deſtruite et auſſi pour eviter leffuſion de ſange humain qui pourroit advenir par Icelle prinſe ſe aſſemblerent dun acord avecques larceveſq̄ deRouen leſquelz eſtoient eſmeuz et deſplaiſans delamort daucuns delad ville qui avoient eſte tuez et muerdiz aud aſſault. Et ſe Ilz euſſent Rencontre acelle heure et en lacolle ou Ilz eſtoient Leſire detallebot ſelon le commun langaige Ilz leuſſent occiz côme Il avoit fait aucuns leurs parens. Si Rencõtreref leduc deſombrecet et lui dirent quil eſtoit tres expedient ⁊choſe neceſſaire quilz euſſef traictie avec leRoy defrance car auſment Ilz eſtoient perduz et

The capture of the castle of Condé by the French

IN this same time, the castle of Condé-sur-Noireau was captured by the French via the gate by fault of the guard. And the wife of messire François the Aragonais, who previously had been at the capture Rouen, was captured there within the said castle of Condé. And the said François took all the goods that were in the said place with him, the said Englishmen remaining their prisoners.

Ambassador of the townspeople of the town of Rouen sent before the king to discuss the rendering of the said town

THE seventeenth day of the said month of October, the laborers and inhabitants of the said town of Rouen, for the great fear and dread that they had had by the said rude assault, fearing that the said town would finally be captured in such a case, and by this means pillaged, robbed, and totally destroyed, as well as to avoid the spilling of human blood that could happen by this capture, assembled themselves by mutual agreement with the archbishop of Rouen, who was moved and displeased by the death of many of the said city who had been killed and murdered at the said assault. And so they had met at this hour and in this place where they were, Lord Talbot, according to rumour, they would kill as he had done to their relatives. Thus, they met the duke of Somerset and they told him that it was very expedient and necessary that they negotiate with the king of France, because other-

affamez. Et quil yavoit plus deſix ſepmaines quil neſtoit entre en lad ville boys ble chas en vin. Leſquelles parolles ne furent gueres plaiſantes aud duc Parquoy commenca aRegarder autour delui et vit quil navoit en ſacompaignie q̃ cinquāte ou ſoixante angloiz. Et ceulx deRouen eſtoient bien dehuit cens amille. Sans ledruievant delad ville qui eſtoient en armes parmy les Rues donc fut moult eſbahy led duc. Et adonc commenca fort ahumilier. Et Reſpondit alarceveſque et aupeuple Illec aſſiſtant eſtoit preſt deſſ̃ tout ce que ceulx delaville vouldroient. Et adonc vint pour appaiſer le peuple aloſtel delaville ou les aſſemblees ont acouſtome defaire et lapourparlerent enſemble et tant que apres pluſſieurs allegacions et collacions fut conclud que led arceveſque aucuns chevaliers angloiz et aufs bourgois delad ville yroient auport ſaint ouen pour parler au Roy et aux ſeigneurs deſon grant conſeil pour lebien et utilite delad cite et dubien publicque. Et pource fut envoye lofficial delad ville deRouen aupont delarche devers leRoy pour avoir ung ſaufconduit pour aucuns dicelle tant degliſe gens dequizos marchans cōme aufs affin de trouver aucun bon traictie ou appoinctemeſ̃. Sileur fut octroye baille dehus. Et led official Retōrna devers larceveſque leduc et les cytouens delad ville fureſ̃ ordonnez larceveſque avecques ~ pluſſieurs aufs notables et aucuns chevalliers et eſcuiers delapart duduc deſombrecet pour aller auport ſaint ouen aune lieue pres dedit pont delarche ou Ilz trouvereſ̃ pour leRoy de france led conte dedunoiz liuteñ lechancelr̃ defrance et leſeneſchal depoictou meſſire guillaẽ couſinot et pluſſieurs auſ̂s avecquez les ~~auts~~ quilz Ilz parlementerent longuement et Requerans tres Inſtamment que abollicion

wise they would be lost and famished and that it had been more than six weeks since wood, wheat, meat, or wine had entered into the said town, which words were not pleasing to the said duke of Somerset, who began to look around him and saw that he had in his company fifty or sixty Englishmen and those of Rouen were nearly 800 to 1,000, not counting the rest of the said town, who were in arms along the streets, for which the said duke was very afraid. And so he began to strongly humble himself. And he responded to the archbishop and to the people that he was ready to do anything that those of the city wanted. And then he came to appease the people at the hotel of the town, where the assemblies were accustomed to meeting and they talked together and such that, after several conversations and discourses, it was concluded that the said archbishop, several English knights, and other citizens of the said town would go to Port-Saint-Ouen to speak to the king and to the other lords of his grand council for the good and benefit of the said city, and for the common good. And for this, the official of the said town of Rouen was sent to Pont-de-l'Arche to the king to receive a safeconduct for several people of this place, both men of the church, citizens, merchants, and others, in order to find any good treaty or agreement. So it was granted to release them to him. And the said official returned to the said archbishop, duke, and citizens of the said town; the archbishop with several other notable people and several knights and squires, on the part of this duke of Somerset, were ordered to go to the said gate of Saint-Ouen, to one league near Pont-de-l'Arche, where they found for the king of France the count of Dunois, lieutenant general, the chancellor of France, and the seneschal of Poitou, messire Guillaume Cousinot, and several others, with whom they spoke for a long time and requested very strongly that a general

generalle leur fuſt baille. Et ce que ceulx qui ſen vouldroient aller eu party des angloiz ſen allaſſent et ceulx qui vouldroient demourer demouraſſent ſans quelq̃ perdicion ou arreſt deleurs biens. Et avecques ce q̃ les angloiz ſen yroient en leur party et leur ſeroit baille bon et loyal ſaufconduit pour eulx et pour le[rs] biens. Leſquelles leur furent adcordees par led conte de dunoiz et auſs dugrant conſeil duRoy deſſ nomz̃ par ainſſi led arceveſque et ſes conſorts pro mettroient demettre lad ville et cite en lobbeiſſ duRoy defrance. Et atant ſedepartit led arceveſq̃ et ſes conſorts pour aller faire leur Rapport tant aux angloiz cōme aceulx delad cite. Maiz pōce quilz arriverent tart et denuyt nepeurẽt dire en faire leur Rapport ced Iour ſamedy vii[me]Iour dud moys auplus matin alla led arceveſque et ceulx qui avoient eſte avec lui aud ſaint ouen. en lamaiſon delad cite pour Renter devaſ les angloiz et les entoures lappointemẽt et les parolles quilz avoient eues avecques les gens decellui Roy defrance leſquelles parolles et appoinctement fureſ treſagreables aceulx delad ville. et treſdeſplaiſantes auſd angloiz leſquelz quant Ilz virent et apperceurent lavoullente et grant deſir que lepeuple avoit auRoy defrance firẽt moult eſbahes et par eſpecial led duc et leſire detallebot leſquelz ſe partirent mal cōtens deloſtel delaville et ſemirent to⁹ en armes puis ſeRetrayerent aupallaiz ſus lepont ⁊portaulx et auchaſteau delad ville. Et adonc quant ceulx delacite cogneurent leur contenance ſedoubterent fort. Et pource ſemirent paraiſſ en armes et firent grant guet et grant garde tout ce Iour deſamedy et lanuyt ſemblablamẽt. Et auſſi faiſoient Iceulx angloiz deleur party celle meſme nuyt les etours delad ville defrancs

absolution be granted to them. And that those who would like to go to the party of the English would go freely, and those who would want to remain could remain, without any punishment or seizure of their goods. And with this, that the Englishmen would go to places in their party and he would grant them good and loyal safeconduct for then and for their goods, which was agreeable to them by the said count of Dunois and others abovenamed of the great council of the king; also, the said archbishop and his companions promised to render the said town and city into the obedience of the king of France. And so the said archbishop and his companions left to go make their report, both to the English and to those of the said city. But because they arrived very late and at night, they could not make their report this said day; Saturday, the seventeenth day of the said month, very early in the morning, the said archbishop and those who had been with him at the said gate of Saint-Ouen went to the house of the said city to report before the Englishmen and those around the agreement and the words that they had had with the men of this king of France, which words and agreements were very agreeable to those of the said town and very displeasing to the said Englishmen, who when they came and perceived the will and great desire that the people had toward thc king of Francc, thcy wcrc very worried and especially the said duke and the Lord Talbot, who retreated very discontented from the hotel of the town and all put themselves in arms [and] then left from the palace via the bridge and gates and to the castle of the said town. And then, when those of the city knew their countenance, they were very afraid. And for this, they put themselves equally in arms and fortified themselves and made [a] tall watchtower and set a large guard all this day of Saturday and similarly the following night. And also these Englishmen made

⁊pillers les angloiz qui detraictie nevoulloient point. Pour laquelle choſe enoyverent ung hom̃ aupont delarche Lequel yarivaa aupoint duIour pour notiffier et faire aſſavoir auRoy q̃ Il venſy aleurs ſecours et Ilz lemettroient en lad ville. Et cedymanche qui fut lexix^me^ Iour dud moys doctobre ahuit heures dematin ſeſmeult les peuple que ſetenoit ſur ſagarde et vit leſd angloiz armez. Auſquilz Ilz commencant ſus et les chaſſerent ſi durement et ſi aſprement q̃ agrande paine peurent Ilz gaigner leſd pallaiz et le chaſteau. Et yen ot en lad chaſſe deſd angloiz mors deſept ahuit [personnes] ∞. Pendant laquelle chaſſe ceulx delad ville gaignerent les murs portaux et tours. Pour lequel ſecours donner promptement et en grant diligence led conte dedunoys lieuteñ duRoy monta acheval et avecques lui grande compaignie degens darmes pour Iceux ſecourir. Enť leſquelz eſtoit bailly devreulx lequel fut frappe dun cheval deſacompaignie tellement quil lui Rompue Iambe pource quil navoit pas eu loiſir deprendre ſon harnoiz de Iambe. Et fut porte aud pont delarche ~~apres~~ po^r^ garde apres quil ot baille legoveȓmment deſes gens amonſ^r^ demangny. Et quant lad cōpaignie fut aRivee devant Rouen ſommerent les gens deguerre eſtans dedens ſainte katherine de Rendre laplace au Roy lequel prend lad ſōmacion ſepartit dupont delarche grandement acōmpaigne degens darmes et detrait pour allȓ devant Rouen et fiſt chargȓ ſon artillerie pour faire aſſailles ſainte katherine. Combien q̃ decene fuſt aucun beſoing. car lecapitaine delad place lequel avoit en ſacompagnie vi^xx^ angloiz voyant ſi grande et ſi noble compaignie eſtre devant eulx ſachant auſſi lavenue

one for their side this same night around the said town of Frenchmen and the Englishmen, who no longer wanted to negotiate, pillaged. For which thing, a man was sent to Pont-de-l'Arche, who arrived at the bridge on the day to notify and make known to the king that he come to help them and that they would get him into the said town. And this Sunday, which was the nineteenth day of the said month of October, at eight o'clock in the morning, the people who held the watch moved themselves and saw the said Englishmen armed, for which they began to overrun them, and they pursued them so aggressively and so hopefully that with great pain they could capture the said palace and castle. And seventy to eighty of the said Englishmen were killed in the said chase. During which chase, those of the said town won the walls, gates, and towers. In response to which, in order to give help promptly and with great diligence, the said count of Dunois, lieutenant of the king, mounted a horse and with him a great company of men-at-arms to help these people. Amongst whom was [the] bailiff of Évreux, who was struck by a horse of his company such that he had a broken leg, because he did not have the time to put his leg in the stirrup. And he was taken to the said Pont-de-l'Arche, to guard it, after which he gave the governance of his men to monseigneur de Mauny. And when the said company arrived before Rouen, they summoned the men of war who were inside Saint-Katherine to render the place to the king, who, taking the said summons, departed from Pont-de-l'Arche grandly accompanied by men-at-arms and conscripts in order to go before Rouen and he charged his artillery to make an assault on Saint-Katherine, until it was no longer necessary, because the captain of the said place, who had in his company 120 Englishmen, seeing so great and so noble a company before him, learning also of the coming

duRoy et ſedoubtant fort Icellui Rendirent lad place aud conte dedunoiz et ſen allerent leſd angloiz en leur party ou bon leur ſembla . Et furent ordonnez a lagarde deicelle place Iucques alavenue du Roy les gens dubailly devreux pour laſeurete deſquilz angloiz leur fut baille ung herault duRoy pour les conduire et faire paſſer auport ſaint ouen avec ſon ſaufconduit. Et ainſſi quilz ſen alloient trouveret̂ et Recvoiteret̂ le Roy lequel leur diſt quilz ne priſſent Rien ſus lepays ſans paier. Et Ilz Reſpondirent quilz navoient point dargent ne quoy paier. Lors leur donna leRoy pour faire leur deſpens laſomme deCent frans. Et ainſſi allerent leurs corps et leurs biens ſaufz donc Ilz navoient gueres ahonnfleu ou allerens en leur party ou bon leur ſembla. Et leRoy ſen vint loger lanuyt aud lieu deſaincte katherine en pourſuivant touſiours lent̂prinſe davoir Rouen et vindrent monſʳ leconte dedunoiz leconte denevers monſʳ dorval monſʳ deblainville et monſʳ de maugny avec toutes les compaignies des ſeigneuʳᵉ leſd alaporte deRouen ducoſte dedevers paris nômee martinville atout les bannieres du Roy deſplayes. Et laſemirent to⁹ en bataille au plus pres duboullevart delad porte ou vindret̂ les bourgeois delad ville eux prêter et apporter les clefz aud conte dedunoiz en diſant quil lui pleuſt bouter dedens lad cite tel et ſi grant nombre degens darmes quil lui plairoit. Auquoy [*verso of page 148 and front of page 149 missing—the following text is taken from Vallet de Viriville's transcription*] leur Reſpondit que aleur gre et voullente ſe feroit.

of the king and fearing strongly, rendered the said place to the said count of Dunois and the said Englishmen went wherever in their party it seemed good to them. And the guardianship of this place until the coming of the king was granted to the men of the bailiff of Évreux; for the safety of which Englishmen, a herald of the king was appointed to conduct and ensure the passage to the bridge of Saint Ouen with their safe conduct. And as they went away, the king told them that they could not take anything from the land without paying. And they reponded that they no longer had any money with which to pay. And they responded that they no long had anything to pay with. Then the king gave them in order to settle their accounts the sum of 100 francs. And so they left, their bodies and their goods safe, so they could hardly go anywhere but Honfleur or wherever in their party it seemed good to them. And the king went to camp the night at the said place of Saint-Katherine, pursuing always the capture of Rouen, and monseigneur the count of Dunois, the count of Nevers, monseigneur d'Orval, monseigneur de Blainville, and monseigneur de Mauny, with all the companies of the lords came to the said gate of Rouen on the side facing Paris, named the gate of Martinville, with all the banners of the king of France displayed. And there they all set out all in batallions close to the bulwark of the said gate, where the leaders of the said town came to present and deliver to them the keys to the said count of Dunois, saying to him that it is pleasing to him to install within the said town such and so great a number of men-at-arms that he would like. To which he responded to them that, at their leave and will, he would do it.

Cõment leduc deſomrecet ſerendait deparler aleRoy defrance.

CE que voyant ce duc de Sombrecet qui eſtoit fort deſplaiſant dans lecoeur et marry de voir une ſi grande puiſſance que leRoy avoit contre luy Il le Requiſt de pouvoir parler a luy. Ce qui eſtant venu a la cognoiſſance du Roy Il fut tres content et auſſitoſt acorda que ce duc vint parler a luy diſant que tres voulentiers Il entendroit ce quil luy vouloit dire pourquoy ſe partit Icelluy duc dud palais leſixieſme Iour enſuivant acompaigne decertain nombre de ſes gens et daulcuns des heraultx du Roy leſquelz leconvoyerent pour plus grande ſeurete de ſaperſonne Iuſques aSaincte Katherine dumont de Rouen ou eſtoit lors logie le Roy avec le Roy de Cecille le conte de dunoiz et aulcuns autres de ſon conſeil et des ſeigneurs de ſon ſang larceveſque de Rouen et le patriarche dantioche celui de Ieruſalem et divers aultres prelats. Et apres que led duc eut ſalue et fait la Reverence au Roy lui Requiſt quil luy pleuſt leur octroier que lui leſire detalbot et les autres angloiz de ſa compaignie ſen peuſſent en aller ſeurement en Ioiſſant de labolicion ſuſmentionnee ainſſi que ceulx de lad ville et cite de Rouen lavoient faicte et paſſee avec lui ou avecques ceulx de ſon grant conſeil. Sur laquelle propoſicion leRoy lui Reſpondit tres modeſtement et avecques douceur et ſageſſe que ſa Requeſte neſtoit pas bien Iuſte ne fondee en Raiſon pour autant quil navoit pas voulu accepter aſſez a temps le traictie ny tenir et obſerver lappoinctement de labolicion deſſuſd ne adherer a Icelle maiz ou contempt dud appoinctement et contre la teneur et lexecucion dicelui avoit

How the duke of Somerset rendered himself to speak to the king of France

THIS being observed, this duke of Somerset, who was very displeased without heart and merriment to see such great power that the king had against him, requested if he could speak to him. This coming to the knowledge of the king, he was very happy and soon agreed for this duke to come speak with him, saying that he very willingly would hear that which he would say to him; for which this duke departed from the said palace the sixteenth day following, accompanied by a certain number of his men and several of the heralds of the king, who conveyed him for greater security of his person until Saint-Katherine-du-Mont-de-Rouen, where the king was then lodged with the king of Sicily, the count of Dunois, and several of his council, and of the lords of his blood, the archbishop of Rouen, and the patriarch of Antioch, that of Jerusalem, and several other prelats. And after the said duke had given his regards and made reverence to the king, he asked him if he could release to them people that he held—Lord Talbot and the other Englishmen of his company—so they could go safely, enjoying the abovementioned abolition, so that those of the said town and city of Rouen had made and passed with them or with those of his great council. For which proposition the king responded to him very modestly and with gentleness and wisdom that his request was not very just nor based on reason, since he had not wanted to accept at any time the treaty nor hold and observe the abovesaid agreement of abolution nor adhered to it, but out of contempt for the said agreement and against the tenor and the execution of this, he had de-

detenu et occupe et encore de preſent detenoit et occupoit lui et ſes conſorts les ſuſd palaiz et chaſtel dicelle ville de Rouen contre ſon gre et ſa voulente et navoit voulu que ceulx de Rouen lui Rendiſſent lad ville maiz y avoit donne empeſchement nuy et Reſiſte tant quil avoit peu pour leſquelles cauſes Il devoit eſtre fruſtre dicelle abolicion et avecques ce avant quil obtint liberte de pouvoir partir de ce palaiz falloit quil lui Rendit et fiſt mettre en pleine delivrance leſd places et villes de honnefleur et de harfleur avecques toutes les autres du pays decaulx eſtans encore entre les mains duRoy dangleterre. Sur ces paroles print congie du Roy led duc et ſen Retourna au ſuſd palaiz Regardant et conſiderant parmy les Rues tout le peuple portant alors la croix blanche de quoy Il neſtoit gueres Ioyeux. Et fut Reconvoie par meſſeigneurs les contes deu et declermont.

Comment leſiege fut mis devant lepalaiz et chaſteaux deRouen par les francois.

[Original text resumes]

LE mergredy xxii[me]Iour dud moys fiſt leRoy mettre leſiege devant led pallaiz par devers les champs et pareillement devant lachaſteau. Ceſt aſſavoir par les ſeigneurs decullant grant maiſtre doſtel dorval lemareſchal deIalongnes les gens duconte declermont ceulx duconte deNevers ceulx duſeigneurs decaſtres ceulx duſeigne[s] debueil Robert deconingan laquelle compaignie eſtoit nôbree aſix cens lances ⁊les archiers. Et leſquels firent degrands trenches tout autour dicellui pallaiz tant aux champs côme en laville. Et furent miſes et aſſiſes atoutes diligences bombardes et canons audevant delaporte dud pallaiz qui ou-

tained and occupied and still at present detained and occupied, himself and his companions, the abovesaid palace and castle of this town of Rouen, against his desire and his will, and he had not wanted those of Rouen to render to him the said town, but he had given obstacles, and resisted as much as he could, for which reasons he ought to be frustrated at this abolition, and with this person, since he obtained freedom to be able to leave from this palace, he would have to give it back to him and put into full deliverance the said places and towns of Honfleur and of Harfleur, with all the rest of the Pays de Caux that was still in the hands of the king of England. At these words, the said duke took leave of the king and returned to the abovesaid palace, observing and considering amongst the streets all the people carrying the white cross, for which he was not happy. And he was met by messeigneurs the counts of Eu and Clermont.

How the siege was laid before the palace and castle of Rouen by the French

THE Wednesday, twenty-second day of the said month, the king laid siege before the palace toward the fields and equally before the castle. It is known, by the seigneurs de Culant, grand master of the hotel, d'Orval, the marshal of Jalongnes, the men of the count of Clermont, those of the count of Nevers, those of the lords of Castres, those of the lords de Bueil, Robert de Conigam, which company was numbered 600 lances and the archers. And which were greatly entrenched all around this palace, both in the fields and in the town. And there were installed and situated in great diligence catapults and cannon before the gate of the said palace, which opened over the town and equally before that which

vre ſur laville et pareillement devant celle quid donne ſur les champs. Adonc quant led duc de ſombrecet vit et apperceult leſd approuches fut moult eſbay meſmement quil yavoit pou de vivres aud pallaiz et beaucoup gens conſiderant auſſi quil ny pouvoit aucunement eſtre ſecouru. Parquoy Requiſt ou fiſt Requerir le Ieudy xxiiime au Roy Icellui duc quil lui pleuſt que Ie allaſt parles alui. Se lui octroia leRoy treſbenignement. Et lors ſepartit dud pallaiz acompaigne dechlr̃s et eſcuiers angloyz ceſt aſſavoir demeſſire thôs hou chancellr̃ denormendie pour leRoy dangletr̂e. Lefilz duſeigneur deRaiz et deladucheſſe de ſombrecet ſafemme lefilz duconte dormont dIrlâ meſſire thomas Reddeford Nagueres bailly deRôn Meſſire thomas fourquenal et pluſſieurs aut̂s qui eſtoient principaulx deſacompaignie Iucques au nombre de xl ou environ. Et eſtoit led duc veſtu dune longue Robe develloux bleu figure fourree dunes martres ſubelines. Et ſus ſateſte avoit ung chappeau develloux vermeil fourre depareilles martres. Et paſſa parmy laville conveye ⁊conduit des heraulx duRoy. Et alaſaillye delaporte de lad ville vint monſ[r] leconte declermont aiſne fil deduc debourbon et pluſſieurs auts ſeigneurs chevalliers et eſcuiers leſquelz conduiſirent Iucques aſaincte katherine ou leRoy eſtoit logie lequel leReceut treſbenignement en une chambre treſRichement paree. Et eſtoient avecques lui alad Recepcion leRoy deCecille meſſ[rs] les contes dumaine et dedunoiz denevers led declermoſ deſaint pol. decaſtres detancarville. etleviconte delomaigne. Eſtoient auſſi avecques leRoy le ſire decullant detraynol chancellr̂ defrance de precigny et lepatriarche dantioche eveſque de poictiers Larceveſque deRouen les eveſques de liſieux de-

emptied from the fields. Thus, when the said duke of Somerset saw and perceived the said arrangement, he was very amazed since there were few supplies in the said palace and many people, considering also that it could no longer be relieved. For which this duke requested or signalled to request to the king, Thursday the twenty-third, that could go to speak with him, which the king granted to him very graciously. And thus he departed from the said palace, accompanied by several English knights and squires, it is known messire Thomas Hoo, chancellor of Normandy for the king of England, the sons of the lord of Rais and the duchess of Somerset, his wife, the sons of the Earl of Ormund in Ireland, messire Thomas Bedford, recent bailiff of Rouen, messire Thomas Fourquenal, and several others, who were the principal members of his company, until the number was forty or thereabout. And the said duke wore a long robe of sequined blue velvet, covered with sabled martens. And he wore on his head a cap of sequined green velvet, similarly covered with martens. And he passed through the town, conveyed and conducted by the heralds of the king. And at the sallyport of the said town, monseigneur the count of Clermont, eldest son of the duke of Bourbon, and several other lords, knights, and squires, came, who escorted [him] to Saint Katherine, where the king was still lodged, who received him very benignly in a richly adorned room. And with him at the said reception were the king of Sicily, messeigneurs the counts of Maine and Dunois, of Nevers, the said of Clermont, of Saint-Pol, of Castres, of Tancarville, and the viscount of Lomagne. Also with the king were the sire de Culant, de Traignel, chancellor of France, de Précigny, and the patriarch of Antioch, bishop of Poitiers, the archbishop of Rouen, the bishops of Lisieux, de Magallonne, and several other great lords, knights, and squires, which thing would

maguelonne et pluſſieurs aufs grans ſeigneurs chevalliers et eſcuiers qui feroit choſe tres proliye auarmes et aRacomptes. Et apres laſalutacion faicte auRoy par led duc lui ſupplia treſhumblement et Requiſt quil lui pleuſt donnez et aux angloiz pareillement qui eſtoient dedens la chaſteau et pallaiz delad ville telle cõpoſicion que avoient eu ceulx delad ville et cite. Aquoy lui fiſt Reſponſe et lui diſt en beaulx termes haulx et notables que par letraictie fait aud port ſaint ouen lui avoit eſte octroyé lacompoſicion telle que a ceulx de Rouen Maiz Il ne ſes adherans ⁊complices angloiz comme mal adviſz ne lavoient point voulu tenir. Parquoy ſaRequeſte neſtoit point Raiſõnable et pource Il non avoit point. Et par ainſſi print congie duRoy et ſen Retourna et ceulx deſa compaignie aud pallaiz pour laſeurete deſquilz furent conduitz par meſſ^s les contes declermont deu ⁊decaſtres. Et lors ordonna leRoy aux conte dedunoiz ſon lieutenant general quil fiſt faire autour dud pallaiz trenchees fouſſez et approuchemeт̃ pluſſors que par avant et tant ducoſte delaville que des champs. Aquoy led lieuteñ ſexhiba et fiſt degrans dilligences et ſemonſtra vaillať ⁊prudent chlr̃ en guerre et miſt laplace en telle diſpoſicion q̃ leſd angloiz ne pouvoient entrer neyſſes detous coſtes deſd pallaiz ⁊chaſteau. Etce voyans leſd angloiz Requidrent lexxiiii^me Iour dud moys doctobre aparlementer avec led conte dedunoiz lieuteñ duRoy et pource fr̃ furent treves donnes des deux coſtez. Et ainſſi leconte deu. lemareſhal delafayette et autres dugrant conſeil duRoy. Appellez avec led lieuteñ gnãl commencerent leſd parties aparelementer. Et fureť leſd treves continuees deIour a auf par leſpace dexii Iours et tout parce q̂ Iceulx angloiz ne voul-

be very long to narrate by hand and to recount. And after the greetings made to the king by the said duke, he supplicated himself very humbly and requested that he should give him, and equally to the Englishmen who were inside the castle and palace of the said town such agreement as had been made with those of the said town and city. To which he responded and said to him in very high and notable terms that by the treaty made at the gate of Saint-Ouen, he had been offered and granted an agreement such to the inhabitants of Rouen, but he, his adherents and English accomplices, through bad advice, had no longer wanted to accept this nor hold to it any longer. And for such, he took leave of the king and returned with those of his company to the said palace, and for their greater security, they were conducted by messeigneurs the counts of Clermont, Eu, and Castres. And then the king ordered to the count of Dunois, his lieutenant general, that he make around the said palace trenches, ditches, and approaches stronger than before, both on the side of the town and the fields. To which the said lieutenant exhibited and made great dilligences and showed himself bravely and prudently a knight in war, and he put this place in such disposition that the said Englishmen could no longer enter nor go out from any side of the said palace and castle. And seeing this, the said Englishmen requested the twenty-fourth day of the said month of October to speak with the said count of Dunois, lieutenant of the king, and in order to do this, truces were agreed between the two sides. And so the count of Eu, the marshal de Lafayète, and others of the great council of the king named with the said lieutenant general, began to speak with the said parties. And the said truces were continued from one day to another for the space of twelve days and all because these Englishmen would no longer agree while making the said treaty to leave as a hostage

loient point laiſſes en faiſant led traictie ꝉen hoſtage led ſire detallebot. Et apres pluſſieurs allegacions et parlemens faiz dun coſte ⁊dauſ finablement appoinctereſ enſemble conſentireſ et fureſ dacord led lieuteñ et ceulx dugrant conſeil duRoy que eſtoient pres̑ que led duc deſombrecet gouvernans pour leRoy danglefre ſafemme ſes enffans et to⁹ les auſs angloiz eſtans eſd pallaiz ⁊chaſteau ſen yroient ou bon leur ſembleroit en leur party leurs corps et leurs biens ſaufz Reſerve priſonniers et groſſe artillerie. Et parmy ce quilz paieroient au Roy dedens ung an Laſomme decinquante mille eſcus. Et aceulx qui avoient fait letraictie ſix mille. Et avecques ce promiſdrent paier tout ce quilz devoient loyaument aceulx delad cite tant hoſtelliers bourgeois m̃chans q̃ autres devoient oulſplus et promrent leſdeſſuſd deſombrecet mettre aplaine delivrance. les chaſteau darcques. laville decaudebec lechaſteau detancarville et liſlebonne. laville dehõnefleu et laville demonſtr̃villiers et Icelles baillr̃ au Roy ou aſes cõmis pour lui. Pour lacompliſſemeſ deſquelles choſes deſſſd et pour plus grant ſeurete dicelle bailla led duc deſombrecet ſes lectres patentes. Et avecques en demourerent en loſtage led ſire detallebot les filz duſeigne^r debargueny lefilz duſ^r deRozer deladucheſſe deſombrecet lefilz duconte dormont. diſlande et deux auſs ſeigneurs angloiz. Et par auſſi parmy ce traicte faiſant ſeparty dud pallaiz Le mardy xivme Iour du moys deNovembre led duc deſombrecet et ſen alla lui et ſes autres angloiz tant par eaue que par terre droit a harfleu et acaen. Et demourerent les hoſtages es mains duRoy defrance oudeſes cõmis dedens Rouen. Et depuis led duc voullant tenir ſes promeſſes commiſt et ordonna meſſire thas̃hou et fourques

the said Lord Talbot. And after several allegations and discussions made on one side and the other, finally an agreement was consented to and agreed together: the said lieutenant and those of the great council of the king who were present there, that the said duke of Somerset, governor for the king of England, his wife, their children, and all the other Englishmen who were in the palace and castle would go wherever it seemed good to them in the places in their party, their bodies and their goods safe, reserving prisoners and large artillary. And for this, they would pay to the king within a year the sum of 50,000 écus. And to those who had made the treaty 6,000 écus. And with this, they promised to pay loyally all that they could to those of the said city, both to the hotelliers, city-folk, merchants, and others; in addition, the abovesaid Somerset [and others] must and promise to put in full deliverance the castle of Arques, the town of Caudebec, the castle of Tancarville and Îlebonne, the town of Honfleur and the town of Monstiervilliers, and these to be delivered to the king or to those commissioned by him. For the accomplishment of the abovesaid things and for the greater security of this, the said duke of Somerset gave his letters patent. And with it they left as hostages the said Lord Talbot, the sons of Lord Bargueny, the sons of Lord Ros by the duchess of Somerset, the sons of the earl of Ormond in Ireland, and two other English lords. And also during this treaty-making, the said duke of Somerset left from the said palace Tuesday, the fourteenth day of the month of November, and he went and his other Englishmen, both by water and by land, straight to Harfleur and Caen. And the hostages remained in the hands of the king of France or his agents within Rouen. And thus the said duke, wanting to hold to his promises, committed and ordered messire Thomas Hou and Fulk Éthon to render to the king all the abovesaid and declared

ethon pour faire Rendre auRoy toutes les places deſſuſd ⁊deſclarees ce quilz firent Reſerve dicelles led honnefleu donc eſtoit capitaine ung nomme maiſtre courſſon qui ne lavoullut Rendre. Et pour ceſte cauſe demoura led ſeigneur detallebot priſonnier duRoy. Et lelundy x^me^Iour dud moys vielle Saint martin monſ^r^ leconte dedunoiz et lebailly deRouen firent mett̃ les baneres duRoy deſſus leſd chaſteau et pallaiz et des portes delad cite par ung des heraulx du Roy et en lapâce de plus notables bourgois delad ville et cite.

Commet̂ Le Roy entra en ſacite. et bonne ville deRouen.

Pendans leſd appoinctement faiz ent̂ leſd gens duRoy et leſd angloiz ſolempniſa leRoẙ lafeſte detouſſains aud lieu deSaincte katherine en grant Ioye et lieſſe dece quil voioit ainſſi ſes ennemys ſubcoumbez et touſiors en Remerciant dieu deſabonne fortune que lui envoyoit deIour en Iour. Lequel po^r^ venir en ſabonne ville deRouen apres ce que en Icelle fait mis police et gouv̂nement par led conte dedunoiz ſon lieutenant. En partit lelundy devat̂ dit dud lieu deSaincte katherine environ une heure apres midy acompaigne duRoy deCecille et dautŝ pluſſieurs autŝ grans ſeigneurs tant deſon ſange que dautŝ cy deſſoubz deſclares. Et miſt ſes gens en moult belle ordonnance. Premierement eſtoient tous les prommes les archiers du Roẙ defrance veſtuz de Iacquettes de coulleurs blanches Rouges deverd ſemees dorſaveries Avecques leſquelz les archiers duRoy deCecille du conte du maine et depluſſieurs autŝ ſeigne^rs^ Iucques aunombre

places, which they did, except for the said Honfleur, over which was captain one named Master Courson, who would not render it to them. And because of this, the said Lord Talbot remained a prisoner of the king. And Monday, tenth day of the said month, the eve of Saint-Martin, monseigneur the count of Dunois and the bailiff of Rouen set up flags of the king above the said castle and palace, and from the gates of the said city, by one of the heralds of the king, and in the presence of the most notable townsfolk of the said town and city.

How the king entered into the city and good town of Rouen

During the said agreement made between the said men of the king and the said Englishmen, the king celebrated the feast of All Saints at the said place of Saint-Catherine, in great joy and jubilation for which he saw also his enemies succumb and always thanking God for the good fortune that he sent him from day to day, who, in order to come into his good town of Rouen, afterwards, he placed in this place police and governance by the said count of Dunois, his lieutenant. Leaving the Monday from the said place of Saint-Catherine at around one in the afternoon, accompanied by the king of Sicily and several other great lords, both of his blood and others above declared, and he put his men in very good order. First of all walked the archers of the king of France, vested in jackets of the colours white, red, green, sown with gold sequins, amongst whom were the archers of the king of Sicily, of the count of Maine, and of several other lords, until the number was 600

deviC archiers bien montez to⁹ ayans brigandines et Iacquettes deſſus depluſſrs et diverſes facons harnoiz de Iambes eſpees et dagues et ſallades bien Richement garnes dargēt. Pour gouvernement et conduite deſquelz furēt commis et ordonnez depar leRoy les ſeigneurs depruilly et declere Meſſeigneurs theaulde devalpergue et aucuns auts qui to⁹ avoient lers chevaulx couvers deſatin dediverſes manieres et coulleurs. Apres leſd archiers eſtoient les heraulx duRoy defrance duRoy deCecille et dauts princes et ſeigneurs eſtans en ſacompaignie to⁹ veſtus deleurs cottes darmes. Et avecques eulx yavoit pluſſieurs pourſuvans. Et apres eſtoient les trompettes et clarons qui ſouvieēt le treſſort que ceſtoit grant melodre et ville choſe arms. Et eſtoient les trompettes du Roy veſtuz devermeil et les manches couvtes dorfevrerye. En apres eſtoit meſſire guillaume Iuvenel des urſins chevallier ſeigneur detraynel ⁊chancellr defrance veſtu en habit Royal. Ceſt aſſavoir Robe manteau et chapperon deſcarlacte fourre de menu vizy. Et ſur chune deſes ~~eſpal~~ eſpaulles trois Rubans dor et trois prouffilz delaitices devant lequel avoit deux varletz depie qui menoient une hacquenee blanche par labride Icelle couverte dedrap develloux bleu ſeme de fleurs deliz dor tiſſu ſur lacouverture duquel avoit ung petit coffre couvert auſſi develloux azur ſeme defleurs deliz dor dorfevrerie ouquel eſtre les grans ſeaulx duRoy defrance. Et en apres chevauchoit ung nomme pierre defontenil eſcuier deſcuierie arme tout aublanc ſur ung grant deſtrier couvert et enharneiche develloux azur agrant affiches dargent dore ſur ſateſte

archers, well mounted, all wearing coats of mail and jackets as above, of several and many fashions, leg harnesses, swords and daggers and sallets, very richly decorated with silver. For the governance and conduct of which were commissioned and ordered by the king the seigneurs de Pruilly and de Cleré, messire Théaulde de Valpergue, and some others, who all had their horses covered in satin of different materials and colours. After the said archers were the heralds of the king of France, of the king of Sicily, and of other princes and lords who were in the company, all vested in their coats of arms. And with them were several poursuivans. And after were the trumpeteers and clairons, who played so loudly that it was a great melody, and the town's guardsmen. And the trumpets of the king were vested in vermillion and the mounts covered in plated gold. Afterwards was messire Guillaume Juvénal des Ursins, knight, seigneur of Traignel, and chancellor of France, vested in royal clothing. It is known, the robe and hat of vermillion, covered with fine fur. And carrying on each of his shoulders three ribbons of gold, and three narrow strips of ermine, before whom were two varlets on foot, who held a white hackney by the bridle, covered in a cloth of blue velvet, sown with gold fleur-de-lis fabric, on which covering was a small chest covered also with azure velvet sown with fleurs-de-lis of gold plate, in which was the great seals of the king of France. And with him rode one named Pierre de Fontenil, squire of the squiry, armed all in white on a great destrier covered and decorated with azure velvet, with great placards of golden silver, having on his head a pointed hat in front of vermillion velvet stuffed with ermine,

ung chappeau pointu devant develloux vermeil fourre dermines lequel portoit en eſcharppe ung manteau deſ-carlatte pourpre fourre auſſi darmines. Apres led fontenil et ſans moyen devant leRoy eſtoit leſire deſaintrailles gran̂ eſcuier deſcuirie duRoy et bailly deberry lequel eſtoit tout arme ablanc et monte ſur ung deſtrier et pareil-lement couvert et enharneiche develloux azur agrans af-fices dargent dore côme led fôtenil. Lequel portoit en eſcharppe lagrant eſpee de Roy ~~en p~~ deparement donc lepômeau lacroix laboucle lemordant et labouterolle eſtoient dor. Et laſainture avecques la~~gaigne~~ gaine eſtoient couvertes develloux azur et par deſſſ ſemes de fleurs deliz dor. En apres leRoy arme detoutes pieces monte ſur ung courſſier ~~d~~ couvert Iucq̂z aux piez dedrap develloux azur ſeme defleurs deliz dor debroderie. Sur lateſte ung chappeau debievre double develloux vermeil ſur lequel avoit aubout une hoppe defil dor. Apres lui eſtoient ſes pages veſtuz devermeil leurs mâches cou-vertes toute dorfavrerye blanche. Et eſtoient les harnoiz des teſtes deleurs chevaulx couvers defin or dediverſes facons dorfavrerye et plumes dauſtruche depluſſieurs coulleurs. Aladextre duRoy chevauchoit leRoy deCe-cille. Et aſeneſtr̂ leconte ~~dem~~ duMaine ſon frere armez tout au blanc leurs chevaulx Richement couvers de couvertures develloux pareilles aux croix blâches et leurs deviſes parmy ſemees dehouppettes de fil or et les chevaulx et pages enharneches tout pareil delacouver-ture. Et eſtoient les harnoiz deteſte deſd ſeigneurs cou-vers dorfevrerie defin or aleurs deviſes. Et apres eſtoient meſſ^{rs} les contes deNevers deſaint pol et declermont.

who carried in a scarf a cloak of scarlet [and] purple, also stuffed with ermine. After the said Fontenil and without means before the king and bailiff of Berry, who was all armored in white and mounted atop a great destrier, equally covered and decorated with azure velvet with great placards of golden silver, like the said Fontenil, who carried on a sheet the great sword of the king, on which the head, the cross, the buckle, the blade, and the sheath was of gold. And the sword with shealth were covered in azure velvet and, as above, sown with fleurs-de-lis of gold. And afterwards, the king came armed in all pieces, mounted on a corsair covered to the feet in cloth of azure velvet, sown with fleurs-de-lis of gold embroidery, on the head, a cap of beaver crossed with vermillion velvet, on which was a tassel made of gold string. After him were his pages, vested in vermillion, their sleeves covered all in gold-embroidered white. And the harness of the heads of their horses were covered with fine gold of various styles of embroidery and ostrich feathers of several colours. At the right hand of the king rode the king of Sicily and at the left hand the count of Maine, his brother, armed all in white, their horses richly covered with cloth of similar velvet, with white crosses, and their devices among them, sown with tassels of gold string, their horses and pages decorated all similarly by the covering. And the harnesses at the heads of the said lords were covered with gold embroidery of gold string on their devices. And afterwards were messeigneurs the counts of Nevers, of Saint-Pol, and of Clermont. Those of Nevers were equally arrayed all in white, mounted on a corsair covered in green velvet, woven with gold string. And after

Celui deNevers eſtoit paraillement arme tout ablanc monte ſur ung courſſier couvert develloux verd broche defil dor. Et apres lui trois pages veſtuz deviollet et denoir et avoit en ſacompaignie xii gentilz hommes armes auſſi tout aublanc montez ſur chevaulx ꝑ couvers deſatin viollet et ſur chune couverture une croix blanche blanche Excepte lun diceulx lacouvêture eſtoit deſatin vert. Celui deSaint pol eſtoit paraill tout arme ablanc monte ſur ung deſtrier enharnache deſatin noir ſeme dorfavrerie et debroderie. Et apres lui cinq pages veſtuz deſatin noir decouppe par les bras. Icelles de couppeures couvertes dorfavrerie et les harnoiz des chevaulx demeſme lacouvêture lun deſd pages portoit une lance couvête develloux vêmeil lauť une couverte dedrap dor figure lauť portoit ung armeret en ſateſte tout defin or Richement ouvre et deſriere leſd pages eſtoient ſon palfrôner veſtu et habille et ſon cheval enharnache de pareille livree que dit eſt lequel menoit ung grant deſtȓ en ſamain. Et celui declermont eſtoit pareillement arme tout ablanc môte ſur ung courſſier couvert et ſes pages veſtuz deſalivree leſire decullant grant maiſtre doſtel duRoy ayant lacharge et gouveȓement delabataille ou avoit vi^c lances et en chacue ung panoncel deſatin vermeil aung ſoleil dor venoit apres les pages au duRoy arme detoutes pieces ung chappeau ſus ſateſte monte ſur ung courſſier Richement couvert develloux bleu et Rouge par bandes et deſſus aucunes deſd ꝑ bandes eſtoient atachees grandes feuilles dargent dores. et ſur les auťs dargent blanc et les harnoiz deſon chevaulx pareilz alad couvêture. Et avoit aſon col une eſcharpe defin or pendant Iucques alacrouppe deſon che-

him were three pages vested in violet and black sections, and he had in his company twelve gentlemen armed also all in white, mounted on horses covered in violet satin, and on each cover a white cross, except one for which the covering was green satin. This count of Saint-Pol was similarly all armed in white, mounted on a destrier decorated in black satin, sown with gold and embroidered. And after him, five pages vested in black satin cut off at the arms, these cut-offs covered in gold embroidery and the harnesses of the horses of the same covering; one of the said pages carried a lance covered in vermillion velvet, another one covered with embellished gold cloth, and another one an helmet on his head all of fine gold and richely worked, and behind the said pages was his groom, vested and dressed, and his horse decorated with equal livery as is said; he held a great destrier in his hand. And this of Clermont was equally armed all in white, mounted upon a covered corsair, and his pages vested in his livery; the sire de Culant, grand master of the hotel of the king, having the charge and governance of the batallion, where he had 600 lances, and in each a penoncel of vermillion satin with a gold sun, coming after the pages of the king, armed all with a hat on his head, mounted on a corsair richly covered in blue- and red-striped velvet, and to several of the abovesaid stripes were attached large sheets of gilded silver, and on the others white silver, and the harness of his horse equally of the said coverings. And he had on his collar a scarf of fine gold until the rump of his horse; with the said sire de Culant, behind the king, was a squire named Rogerin Blosset, squire of the squiry of the king, who carried the standard of the king, which was made

val Avecques led ſire decullant deſriere leRoy eſtoit ung eſcuier nomme Rogerin bloſſet eſcuier deſcuyerie du Roy lequel portoit leſtendart duRoy lequel eſtoit deſatin v̊-meil cramoyſy aung Saint michel dedens led eſtendart. Et eſtoit ſeme tout aulong deſolleux dor. Avecques cederere leRoy eſtoit Iehan de ſaceâville dit havart bailly decaux varlet trenchant duRoy lequel portoit lepanon qui eſtoit develloux azur atrois fleurs deliz dor debroderie. Et eſtoient leſd fleurs deliz brodes degroſſes perles. Et en lad côpaignie eſtoient pluſſieurs ſeigneurs. Ceſt aſſavoir le viconte delomaigne. leconte decaſtres. ferry monſ^r^ delorraine. Iehan monſ^r^ ſon frere. leſ^r^ dorval. Leconte detancarville. leſeigneur de montgaſcon filz duconte deboullongne ⁊dauvêgne leſeigneur deIalongnes mareſchal defrance le ſeigneur debeauvau et pluſſieurs autŝ gras̑ ſeigneurs chevalliers et eſcuires leſquelz eſtoient to⁹ armez aublanc et leurs chevaulx couvers develloux oudedrap deſoye et ſur chun̑ cheval lacroix blanche. Et ainſſi en ordonance en lamaniere que dit eſt chevaucha leRoy. Iucques aung trait darc pres delaporte beauvoiſine ducoſte des chartreux. Et la vint audevant monſ^r^ lecomte dedunoiz ſon lieutenant general monte ſur ung deſtrier couvert develloux vermeil veſtu dune Iacquette develloux vermeil fourre demartres. Et avoit ſante une moult Riche eſpee garnye depieries dedyamans Rubiz ⁊ballaiz priſee aquinze mille eſcuz eſtoient ainſſi leſeneſchal depotou et Iacques cuer argentr̂ du Roy montez ſur deſtriers veſtuz et couvers côme led lieuten̑. Avecques led lieutenant pareillemeт̂ eſtoieт̂ monſ^r^ leconte devreux et maiſtre guillaume couſinot led conte devreux eſtoit mon-

of vermillion-crimson satin, with [an emblem of] Saint Michael within the said standard. And it was sewn all along with suns of gold. With this, behind the king was Jean de Saceauville, called Havart, ballif of Caux, attendant to the king, who carried the pennon, which was made of azure velvet with three fleurs-de-lis of gold embroidered. And the said fleurs-de-lis were bordered by three large pearls. And in the said company were several lords, it is known, the viscount of Lomagne; the count of Castres; Ferry, monseigneur de Lorraine; Jehan, monseigneur his brother; the seigneur d'Orval; the count of Tancarville; the seigneur de Montgascon, son of the count of Boulongne and d'Auvergne; the seigneur de Jallongnes, marshal of France; the seigneur de Beauvau; and several other great lords, knights, and squires, who were all armed in white, and their horses covered in velvet or of cloth of silk, and on each horse the white cross. And so, in the order in the manner that is said, the king rode until reaching the arch near the Beauvoisine gate, on the side toward Chartreux. And there monseigneur the count of Dunois, his lieutenant general, came before him mounted on a destrier covered in vermillion velvet, vested in a jacket of vermillion velvet stuffed with martens. And he wore a very rich sword, garnished in jewels of diamonds, rubies, and spinels, worth 15,000 écus; there were also the seneschal of Poitou and Jacques Cœur, treasurer of the king, mounted on destriers vested and covered as the said lieutenant. With the said lieutenant equally was monseigneur the count d'Évreux and master Guillaume Cousinot, the said count d'Évreux was mounted on a courser covered with vermillion velvet in a jacket of similar cloth.

te ſur ung courſſier couvert develloux vermeil veſtu donc Iacquette depareil drap. Et led bailly Inſtitue denouvel eſtoit veſtu develloux bleu agrans affiches dargent dores et ſon cheval enharnache demeſmes. Et amena led lieutẽn devers leRoy pour lui faire laReverence et obbeiſſance leſarcheveſque deRouen et eveſq̃s deliſieux. debayeulx. decouſtances avecques les citoiens de ſabonne ville et cite deRouen. Et Incontinent que leſd prelatz oulrent fait leur devoir. Ainſſi que tenus ſont et eſtoient ſen Retournerent dedens lad cite et laiſſerent leſd citoiens qui eſtoient en grant nombre toꝰ veſtuz debleu etchapperons Rouges Avec led lieutenant lequel les prêta auRoy. Et apres humble Reverence et les clefz delad ville et cite baillers en lamain duRoy côme aleur ſouverain ſeigneur. Apres pluſſieurs choſes par eulx propoſees en beaulx termes et doulx langaiges les Receut treſbenignemet̂ et bailla Icelles clefz aud ſeneſchal qui lors fut Inſtitue capitaine dicelle cite ⁊ville. Et adonc leRoy et ſacompaignie commêceret̂ achevauchr̂ pour entrer en lad ville en lordônâce quilz eſtoient ſur les champs et comme cy deſſ eſt declaire. Et la au moumenant duRoy vindrent en ~~poſſeſſion~~ proceſſion ~~les~~ audevant delui les prelatz en habits ponthificaulx et toutes aut̂s gens degliſe tant Regulliers que ſeculiers en chappes portans Ioyaulx ⁊Reliques. Et meſmement les quatre ordres des mendians toꝰ chantans. Tedeum laudamus Pour la Iouyaulx advenement duRoy defrance leur ſouverain ſeigneur. Et ſemidrent devant ledit chancellier defrance leſr delafayette mareſchal defrance monſr degaucourt premier chambellain duRoẙ monſeigneur de precigny et Iacques cuer

And the said bailiff, newly-instituted, was vested in blue velvet with large emblems of golden silver and his horse decorated the same. And the said lieutenant brought to the king to make reverence and obedience to him the said archbishop of Rouen and the bishops of Lisieux, Bayeux, and Coustances, with the citizens of his good town and city of Rouen. And immediately, the said prelats made their oaths, as was required, and they returned within the said city and the said citizens, who were in great number, all vested in blue and wearing red hats, left with the said lieutenant, who presented them to the king. And after humble reverence, the keys of the said town and city were delivered into the hand of the king, as their sovereign lord. After several things were also proposed by them in handsome terms and honest language, he received them very benignly and gave these keys to the said seneschal, who then was instituted captain of this city and town. And then the king and his company began to ride to enter into the said town in the order that they had come on the fields, and as is above declared. And at the movement of the king, the prelats in pontifical habits and all other men of the church, both religious and secular came in procession before him, in cloaks, carrying jewels and relics, and even the four orders of the mendicants, all chanting Te Deum laudamus for the joyous coming of the king of France, their sovereign lord. And before the said chancellor of France were the seigneur de Lafayete, marshal of France; monseigneur de Gaucourt, first chamberlain of the king; monseigneur de Présigny; and Jacques Cœur, treasurer of the king, who all had their horses covered in velvet and satin and jackets of the same, with

argentř duRoy qui to⁹ avoient leurs chevaulx couvers develloux et deſatin et Iacquettes pareilles acroix blanches. Et devant leRoy ſemiſt ſond lieutenant conte dedunoiz enpres leſcuier deſcuyrie. Et eſt choſe ĉtaine quil neſt point en memoire que ouques hôme veiſ Roy pour une foiz ſibelle chevallerie et ſi Richement habillee ne ſi grant nombre degens deguerre côme leRoy avoit en ſaRecouvrance delad cite. Alentree delad ville fut fait chevallř par led ſeneſchal depoictou ung Ieune enffant aage de xii a xiii ans ou environ filz duſire deprecigny. Et yavoit alaporte duboullevart quaŝ bôgois deplus notables delad ville qui tenoient ung chiel treſbel et treſRiche lequel Ilz porterеŝ ſur lateſte duRoy Iucques aegliſe nrêdame deRouen. Ced boullevart laporte lentree fireŝ tenduz dedraps alalivree duRoy et ſes armes au milieu. Et toutes les Rues par ou Il paſſoit coûrtes aciel et garmes depeuple cryans noel pour ſon Ioyeaulx advenement par les carrefours avoit perſonnaiges. Ceſt aſſavoir enune place une fontaine aux armes dela ville qui ſont angnes dei gectant bruvages par les cornes. Ailleurs avoit ung tigre et les petitz qui ſemiroient en ung mirouers et auplus pres denořdame avoit ung ſerf vollaŝ moult bien et ſomptueuſtement fait aſon col Une couronne lequel ſe agenouilla par miſtrere devant leRoy quant Il paſſa par la pour allř en lad egliſe. La endroit eſtoit laſêres dud conte dedunoiz pour voir lemiſtere avecques ~~lequel eſtoit~~ laquelle eſtoit leſeignеř detalbot et les auŝs angloiz oſtages moult penſiz et maris en cuer et comme ceulx aqui lachoſe ne plaiſoit gueres leRoy aRive devaŝ legliſe noê

white crosses. And before the king was placed his said lieutenant, count of Dunois, and after, the squire of the squirey. And it is a certain thing that never in memory of men, the king came for one time such beautiful chivalry and so richly-clothed, nor a greater number of men-at-arms as the king had for the recovery of the said city. At the entry of the said town, a young child aged twelve or thirteen years or thereabout, son of the sire de Présigny, was made knight by the said seneschal of Poitou. And there was at the gate of the bulwark four of the most notable bougeois of the said town, who had a very beautiful and very rich canopy, which they carried over the head of the king, until the church of Notre-Dame-de-Rouen. This bulwark, the gate, [and] the entryway were held by sheets in the livery of the king, and the arms in the middle. And all the roads where he passed were covered overhead and filled with people crying noël for his joyous coming; by the crossroads, they had characters. It is known, in one place a fountain with the arms of the town, which were the *Angus Dei* throwing water at the corners. Elsewhere there was a tiger and its cubs which were reflected in mirrors, and closer to Notre-Dame there was a well-made and sumptuously-constructed kite, on his collar a crown which knelt down by the mystery before the king when he passed by to go into the said church. The place was the windows of the said count of Dunois in order to see the mystery, with whom was the Lord Talbot and the other English hostages, who were very thoughtful and saddened in their hearts, and like those to whom nothing can please; the king having arrived before the church of Notre-Dame, he descended on foot where he was received at the entrance

dame deſſendit apie ou Il fut Receu par led arceveſq̂ et lacolleige Richement Reveſtuz en chappes et entra dedens lad egliſe ou Il fut en oratoire en oraiſons et prieres par c̃taine eſpace detp̂s. Puis ſen alla en loſtel dud arceveſq̂ ou Il ſon logie et ainſſi ſedepartit ung chûn et ſen alla en ſon hoſtel ceulx delad ville degrant Ioye quilz avoient firent les feux par toute laville. Et lelendemain firent proceſſions generalles et ſolempnelles oufut led arceveſque. Et garderent laIournee detoutes ouvres t̃iênes côme ledymenche. Pareillement lemercredy et Ieudy enſ eſtoient les tables miſes parmy les Rues vins et viandes en habondance deſſus pour tout vians et tout aux deſprins des hâtans dicelle ville leſquelz firent avecques ce pluſſieurs grans dons au Roy ſes officiers ſes heraultx et pourſuivans qui la eſtoient depuis leRoy eſtant en loſtel dud arceveſq̂. Les gens degliſe manans et hâtans lui Requiret̂ eſtre ouys en c̃taines Requeſts quilz lui voulloiet̂ faire ce qui leur fut adcorde. Pourquoy ~ ~~veſtu et habille et ſon cheval en harnache depareille luine que dit eſt. lequel menoit ung grant deſtr̂ enſaman~~ entrerent en laſalle ou leRoy eſtoit aſſis en ſachaiere Richement aomene et paree de draps dor ceulx deſon conſeil avec lui. Et la propoſerent pluſſieurs choſes et ent̂ autres lui Remonſtrerent en ſuppliant treſhumblement qui les voulſiſt avoir en ſabonne grace et quil nelaiſſaſt point apourſuivre et faire guerre a ſes anciens ennemis les angloiz car par lemoyen des villes quilz tenant encores en normendie pouvoient encores faires pluſſieurs enormes maulx aupais. Et ace faire comme bons vrays ⁊loyaulx ſubgectz lui offrirent aider decorps et dechevance delaquelle

by the said archbishop and the college, richly vested in cloaks, and he entered into the said church where he was in the oratory for prayers and devotions for a certain period of time. Then he went into the hotel of the said archbishop, where [were] his lodgings, and thus each one departed and went to his house, those of the said town, [and] for the great joy that they had, they made fires all over the town. And the next day, general and solemn processions were made where the said archbishop was. And they guarded the day of all earthly deeds, since it was Sunday. Equally, the following Wednesday and Thursday tables were set among the streets with wines and meats in abundance, as above, for all peasants and all at the expense of the inhabitants of this town, during which several great gifts [were given] to the king, his officers, his heralds, and followers who were there; then, the king, being still in the home of the said archbishop, the men of the church and inhabitants asked that he hear certain requests that they wanted to make to him, which he accorded to them. For which they entered into the room where the king was seated in his chair, richly adorned and decorated with gold cloth, those of his council with him. And there they proposed several things and amongst others they showed to him, by begging him very humbly that he wanted to have them in his good grace, and that he would no longer pursue and wage war against his ancient enemies, the English, because by the means of the towns that they still occupied in Normandy, they could still do several great and enormous ill deeds in the country. And to do that, as good and loyal subjects, they offered to aid him in body and horses, to which proposition, promise, and

propoſicion promeſſe ⁊octroy leRoy fut tres content. Et leur fiſt faire Reſponce par ſon chancellr̃ telle que ſur to⁹ les pointz par eulx propoſez oulrent Icelle Reſponce bien a greable. Et ainſſi prindrent congie et ſen alleret̃ chun̑ en ſon lieu. depuis ſetint leRoy aud lieu deRouen pour mettre police ⁊officiers depar lui aagouverãnce Icelle ville. Et cependant auſſi Rendiret̂ le angloiz et mirent en lamain et obbeiſſance du Roy côme promis avoiet̂ et baille hoſtaiges pource faire lechaſteau darcques tancarville ~~lebonne~~ liſlebonne monſtr̃villr̃ et caudebec. Et combien quilz euſſent promis pareillement laville dehonnefleu. Neantmoins elle ne fut point Rendue pour que lecapitaine dud lieu ne les gens deguerre ne vouldrent obbair aud duc deſombrecet. Parquoy leſire detallebot et autres hoſtages demourerent priſonniers du Roy defrance. Et fut cômis et ordonne meſſire pierre debreze qui eſtoit ſeneſchal depoictou par lagrant vaillance qui eſtoit en lui cap[ne] dud Rouen.

Commet̂ Lechaſteau degaillard fut Rendu aux. francois

LE dimanche xxiii[me]Iour deNovembre ſe Rendit en lobbeiſſance du Roy lechaſteau degaillard qui eſt place Imprenable côme dit eſt. devant lequel fut leſiege par leſpace deſix ſemaines. Et ſeRendirent les angloiz eſtais dedens Iucques au numbre decens ou ſix vingtz par telle compoſicion quilz ſen devoient aller leurs corps et leurs biens ſaufz aharfleu ou ailleurs en lieu party ou bon leur ſembloit.

grant the king was very content. And he made to them in response via his chancellor such that all the points that were proposed by them were heard, this response being very agreeable. And so they took leave and went each to his place, then the king remained still at the said place of Rouen in order to install police and officers for the governance of this town. And, however, the English also rendered and placed into the hand and obedience of the king, as was promised, and delivered hostages in order to do this, the castle of Arcques, Tancarville, Île-bonne, Monstier-Villiers, and Caudebec. And so they had promised equally the town of Honfleur. Nonetheless, it was no longer rendered since the captain of the said place and the men of war would not obey the said duke of Somerset. For which the said Lord Talbot and other hostages remained prisoners by the king of France. And messire Pierre de Brézé, who was seneschal of Poitou, was made and ordained, for the great bravery that he had, captain of the said Rouen.

How the castle de Gaillart was rendered to the French

Sunday, the twenty-third day of November, Castle Gaillard, which was a nearly impregnable place, so it is said, before which was held a siege for the space of six weeks, rendered itself into the obedience of the king. And the Englishmen who were within, who numbered 100 to 120 people, rendered themselves by such agreement that they ought to go with their bodies and their goods safely to Harfleur or anywhere in their party that seemed good to them.

Comment les chaſteau ⁊ville de fougières furent Rendus au duc debretaigne ꝑ les angloiz

EN ce meſmes temps leduc debretaigne print laville ⁊chaſteau defougeres ou Il avoit tenu leſiege par leſpace dun moys ou environ pendant lequel ƚ temps Il fiſt faire telles aprouches et tellemeƭ batre lamuraille decanons et debombardes que lad ville eſtoit preſte daſſallis. Et lors voyans les anglois ledangier ou Ilz eſtoient et quilz avoient peu vivres veu quilz eſtoient decinq aSix cents doĉ eſtoit capitaine led meſſire francois deſurienne dit laragonnoiz ſe Rendit par compoſicion par laquelle ſen alleroient leurs chevaulx ⁊harnoiz ſaufz. Et chcn porant ung pet fardellet devant ſoy seullement. Et depuis ſeconnertit led meſſire francois et demour en lobbeiſſance duRoy defrance. Combien quil avoit prins paravant lad ville defougieres ſur leduc de bretaigne. Et aceſte occaſion furent Rompues les treves denƭ les Roys defrance ⁊dangleƭre comme deſſ eſt dit et deſclare led duc debretaigne avoit en ſacompaignie des ſeigneurs deſſ nommez huit mille combatans. Ceſt aſſavoir monſʳ le conte deRichemont conneſtable defrance monſʳ laduval debretaigne ſʳ degyemene Monſʳ preguy decoitivẙ admiral defrance les vicontes deRohan et delabilliere leſʳ delahaynaudan leſʳ deRothelant et dupont labbe. leſire dequintin Leſire demontauban mareſchal debretaigne Leſire decombours leſire depauchet et pluſſʳˢ auƭs chevalliers ⁊eſcuiers leſquilz apres ladicte prinſe ſen Retourneret̂ tous en leurs maiſons poʳ

How the castle and town of Fougères were taken by the duke of Brittany by the English

IN this same time, the duke of Brittany captured the town and castle of Fougères, where he held a siege for the space of a month or therearound, during which time he made such approaches and such bombardments against the walls by cannon and bombards that the said town was ready for assault. And then, the Englishmen, seeing the danger they were in and that they had few supplies, seeing that there were from 500 to 600 [soldiers], the captain of whom was the said messire François de Surienne, called the Aragonais, he rendered himself by agreement, by which they could leave safely with their horses and equipment. And each only carried a small bag before him. And afterwards, the said messire François switched sides and remained in the obedience of the king of France. So the said town of Fougères was captured as before by the duke of Brittany. And on this occasion, the truces between the kings of France and of England were broken, as is said and reported above, the said duke of Brittany having in his company the abovesaid lords [and] 8,000 soldiers, including monseigneur the earl of Richemont, constable of France; monseigneur the duke of Brittany; seigneur de Guémené; monseigneur Prégent de Coitivy, admiral of France; the viscounts of Rohan and of Bélière; the seigneur de la Hunaudaye; the seigneur de Rothelet and of Pont-l'Abbé; the sire de Quentin; the sire de Montauban, marshal of Brittany; the sire de Combours; the sire de Pauchet; and several other knights and squires, who after the said capture all

lamortalite qui eſtoit frappee en ſon oſt ouquel ſemoront grant nombre degens. Et enť les auťs mourult le filz duconte deRohan qui fut ung grant dommaige. Et parce ſen Retourna led duc en ſon pays apres quil ot laiſſe bonne garniſon es places par lui conqueſtees.

Laprinſe des ville et chaſteau debelleſme par les francois

EN ce meſme temps environ laffin denovembre miſt monſr leduc dalencon leſiege devant lachaſteau ⁊ville debeleſme alui appťent occupe par les angloiz conť Raiſon et ſavoullente. Et eſtoit en ſacompaignie leſire demontenay meſſire Raoulteſſon leſire deſaintrailles bailly de berry. et pluſſieurs auťs chevalliers et eſcuiers Iucques au nombre detrois cens lances et les archiers ſans ence comprendre pluſſieurs gens dedeffence deſes pays delaconte du maine et de vandoſme. qui eſtoient eſtimez trois mille côbatâs. Et apres pluſſieurs eſcarmoches ⁊ſaillies faictes les ungz ſur les auťs leſd angloiz voyans avoir peu depuiſſance aReſiſter conť Icellui duc — commencereť aparlementer. Et tantoſt apres compoſerent et promiſdrent par lad compoſicion facte de ceulx Rend lexx^{m} Iour dud moys dedex oucas que led Iour neſecurent ſecouruz des gens deleur party. et quilz au firoient leſplus fors en champ debataille. Pourquoy ſefortiffierent les deſſ ſeigneurs treſvaillameť en ung champ pour actendre lapuiſſance des angloiz leſquelz eſtoient en chemin cuidant venir lever led ſiege. Et firent deux mille angloiz ou environ Iucques atorigny ou Ilz boutterent lefeu et delavindreť athury duquel lieu oul-

returned to their houses due to the plague that had struck in his army, in which a great number of men died. And amongst the others, the son of the count of Rohan died, which was a great loss. And the said duke then returned into his country, after he had left several good garrisons in places he had conquered.

The capture of the town and castle of Bellême by the French

IN this same time, around the end of November, monseigneur the duke of Alençon laid siege before the castle and town of Bellême, which belonged to him, occupied by the English against reason and his will. And he had in his company the sire de Montenay, messire Raoul-Tesson, the sire de Saintrailles, bailiff of Berry, and several other knights and squires until the number was 300 lances and the archers, without counting several men of the defense of his lands from the county of Maine and of Vendôme, which were estimated at 3,000 soldiers. And after several skirmishes and sallies made one side against the other, the said Englishmen, seeing that they had little power to resist against this duke, opened negotiations. And soon afterwards, they composed and promised by the said agreement made by them, that they would render themselves on the twentieth day of the said month of December in the event that they were not rescued by men of their party and that they would not remain the strongest on the field of battle. For which the abovesaid lords fortified themselves very bravely on the field to await the power of the English, who were en route, thinking to come to relieve the said siege. And 2,000 Englishmen or thereabout advanced until Torigny, which they set aflame, and from there they went to Tury, where they

reȇ ĉtaines nouvelles delapuiſſance et ordonnance dudit duc dalencon. Parquoy ſen Retourneret̂ en leurs places et comme coznans meſirent allr̂ plus avant. Et auiſſi ced Iour xxme Iour dud moys leſiege eſtat̂ Ia aharfleu les angloiz eſtans dedens led bleſme Iucques au nombre dedeux cens côbatas donc eſtoit capitaine ung nomme mathago Rendirent lad place aud duc. Et ſen allerent par compoſicion leurs corps et leurs biens ſaufz es leur party ou bon leur ſembla led duc dalencon ſe governa honorablement et vaillamment Car Il tint laIournee lui et le ſire deſantrailles apeu degens pour actendre lapuiſſance des angloiz Iucques ace que leure ordonnee fuſt paſſee.

Une deſtronſſee ſen les angloiz.

Audit an environ noel les angloz dela garniſon devire. Iucques au nombre de xii^cc eſtoient allez courir aleur advantaige et furet̂ Rencontrez pres delacroix devamoux par aucuns des gens demonſ^r leconneſtable qui eſtoient en garniſon agauray. Ceſt aſſav̂ par meſſire guiffroy decouvren Ioachim Rouault et auťs. Et lafut fort combatu. Et en laffin furent les angloiz deſcoufilz les ungz mors les auťs pres et peu ſen eſchappirent.

Le ſiege deharf eu mis par les francois.

Tantoſt apres ſepartit leRoy defrance de ſacite deRouen arme dunes brigandines et par deſſus une Iacquette dedrap dor acômpagne duRoy deCecille et des

received certain news of the power and order of the said duke of Alençon. For which they returned to their places and did not dare to march any further. And thus this said day, twentiety of the said month, the siege being already at Harfleur, the Englishmen within the said castle of Belême, until the number was 200 soldiers, over which was captain, one named Matthew Gough, rendered this place to the said duke. And they went by agreement, their bodies and their goods safe, into places of their party, wherever it seemed good to them, the said duke of Alençon governing himself honorably and bravely, because he held the field, he and the sire de Santrailles, with few men, to face the power of the English, until the agreed upon hour had passed.

A destruction of the English

In the said year, around Christmas, the Englishmen of the garrison of Vire, about 1,200 in number, left to campaign to their advantage, and they were met near the crossroads of Vaujoux by several of the men of monseigneur the constable, who was in the garrison at Gauray—it is known, by messire Geoffroi de Couvren, Joachim Rouault, and others. And they fought hard there. And in the end, these Englishmen were defeated, some killed, the others captured, and a few escaped.

The siege of Harfleur laid by the French

Soon after, the king of France left from his city of Rouen, armed with a coat of armor, and over this with a jacquet of gold cloth, accompied by the king of Sicily and several other

autres deſon ſang en grans habillemens et Riches. Et par eſpecial Leconte deSainct pol lequel avoit ung chanfrain aſon cheval priſe trente mille eſcuz. Et chevaucha leRoy ainſſi acompaigne Iucques en laville de caudebec ou Il fut conclud dallr̃ mettre leſiege aharfleu. Pourquoy ſeprepara dallr̃ amonſtr̃vilir̃s qui eſt ademye lieue pres. Et envoya mettre led ſiege par ſon lieutan̂ general. leconte de dunoiz. Et auſſi par les contes deu declermont deNevers. decaſtres. lemareſchal deIalongnes Leſeigneur dorval. leſr dubueil. leſr debeauvau Leſr decullant. leſr deblainville maiſtre des arbaleſtriers Et pluſſieurs aut̂s chevalliers eſcuiers capitaines gens darmes et detraict tant de francs archiers q̂ daut̂s. Lacompaignie eſtimee aſix mille combatans et les francs archiers atrois mille. Sans ence comprend canonniers mr̃chands manouvriers gens demeſtier et mariniers. Et ſans les gens deguerre qui gardoient lamer en xxv. gros vaiſſeaulx. Et ſans ceulx qui tenoient laſiege auchef decaux en laville degraville eſtans tant degens darmes que francs archiers Iucques au nombre demille. Et yfut mis leſiege lelundy viii^m Iour dedex lequel fut moult grevable amettre pource quil ny avoit nulles maiſons prez ne boys ne arbres. Et ſi faiſoit ung treſgrant froit de greſles et deglaces et plus grant que Il navoit fait longe temps avoit. Et aiſſi pareillement une eſpace detemps fiſt grâdes pluyes qui eſtoient bien contraires aceulx duſiege. Pareillement oulrent braurons aſouffrir les aucuns pour lamer qui ſourdoit et venoit ſouvet̂ en pluſſieurs logez pource quilz eſtoient to⁹ en terre couvers ſeullemet̂ depaille et degeneres. devant lad ville furet̂ aſſorties ſaize groſſes bombardes. leſquelles leRoy qui eſtoit loge amonſtr̃villr̃ vint les faire gecter. Et yavoit

lords of his blood, greatly and richly clothed. And epecially the count of Saint-Pol, who had a chamfron on his horse valued at 30,000 écus. And the king rode so accompanied to the town of Caudebec, where it was agreed to go lay siege before Harfleur. For which he prepared to go to Monstiervilliers, which was half a league closer. And he sent his lieutenant general, the count of Dunois, to lay the said siege, and also the counts of Eu, of Clermont, of Nevers, and of Castres; the marshal of Jalongnes; the seigneur d'Orval; the seigneur de Bueil; the seigneur de Beauvais; the seigneur de Culant; the seigneur de Blainville, master of the crossbowmen, and several other knights, squires, captains, men-at-arms, and treaty men, both free archers and otherwise. The company estimated at 6,000 soldiers and the free archers at 3,000, without counting cannoniers, merchants, journeymen, tradesmen, and mariners, and without the men of war who protected the coasts on twenty-five large vessels, and without those who held the siege at the seat of Caux in the town of Graville, totalling, both the men-at-arms and the free archers, up to 1,000. And the said siege there was laid on Monday, the eighth day of December, which was very difficult to lay, because there were no houses nearby, nor woods, nor trees. And there was a very great freeze and frost and greater than had occurred in a long time. And also, after another space of time, there were great rains, which worked much against those of the siege. Similarly, some of them suffered greatly because of the sea, which welled up, and it came often into several lodgings, which were all on the land, covered only in straw and dilapidated; before the said town were arranged sixteen large bombards, which the king, who was lodged at Monstier-Villiers, came himself to fire. And there were great trenches and tunnels, in order to move more safely. And

grandes tranchees et parfondes pour allr̃ plus ſeurement. Et ſabandonna fort leRoy avenir voir batre les murs delad ville. Et fut en perſonne es foſſez et mynes arme ſaſallade en ſateſte et ſon pavoiz en ſamain. Et pouvoit on allr̃ par les mynes faictes Iucques aux moins dechaſteau. deſquilz canons et mynes eſtoit gouvr̃er̃ maiſtre Iehan bureau treſor̃ defrance. lequel eſt moult ſubtil et engegneulx en telles matieres et en pluſſieurs aut̂s. Avecques lui eſtoit auſſi Iaſpar bureau ſon frere qui eſtoit maiſtre delar tillerye du-Roy. Et voyant thomas oringan cap^ne^. delad ville deharfleu et aut̂s angloiz eſtans. avecques lui Iucques au nombre deſaize cens prenans gaiges. Et voyans lepuiſſance duRoy xxiiii^m^ Iour dud moys dedecembre veille denoel commencerent aparlementer avecques led conte dedunoiz lieuten̄ general duRoy. Et traicterêt lamatr̃ ced Iour deulx Rendre. Et lelendemain Iourdual furet̂ concluz deulx Rendre et mettre es mains duRoy. par ainſſi quilz ſen devoient allr̃ ou bon leur ſembleroit en leur party et pouvoient emporter to⁹ leurs biens ou par eaue ou par terre. Et pource fr̃ oulrent terme e̊ſx Iucques aup̊mier Iour delan. Et fut ſelle lapoîtement deſix ſeaulx duparty duRoy. Ceſt aſſr̃ demeſſeigneurs. leſeneſchal decullant. lemareſchal delalongnes. deblainville et maiſt̂ Iehan Bureau. Et duparty deſd angloiz furent baillez viii. oſtaiges gentilz hommes pour et affin dent̂tenir led appoinctement Leſquelz furent menes en gr̃de amonſtiervilliers.

the king put himself at serious risk to come see the bombardment of the walls of the said town. And he was pesonally in the trenches and mines, armed with his burnet on his head and his shield in his hand. And one could go via the mines until a little distance from the castle, over which the cannons and mines were governed by master Jean Bureau, treasurer of France, who was in such matters very subtle and ingenious, and in several other things. With him was also Gaspar Bureau, his brother, who was master of the artillery of the king. And seeing Thomas Oringan, captain of the said town of Harfleur, and the other Englishmen who were with him, totalling in number 1,600 mercenaries. And, seeing the power of the king, the twenty-fourth day of the said month of December, Christmas Eve, they began to speak with the said count of Dunois, lieutenant general of the king. And they negotiated the matter this said day of rendering themselves. And the next day, Christmas Day, it was concluded to render this place and put it into the hands of the king, for which they ought to go wherever it seemed good to them in their party, and they could take with them all their goods by water or by sea. And in order to do this, they had until the first day of the year. And the agreement was sealed by six notaries of the party of the king—it is known, my lords the seneschal, de Culant; the marshal, de Jalongnes; de Blainville; and master Jean Bureau. And from the party of the said English were delivered eight gentlemen as hostages for and to otherwise observe the said agreement, who were handed under guard at Montivilliers.

La Reddicion deharfleu au Roy defrance.

LE premier Iour deIanvier furẽt leſd angloiz menes aud lieu deharfleu pour fournir lappoinctemẽt tel q̃ dit eſt. Et ce Iour environ heure deveſpres led thomas aurignan angloiz et capitaine dud lieu bailla les clefz delad ville et des tours aud conte dedunoiz lieutān general en ſoy agenoullant et en grant Reveřce en laprêce de to⁹ les auťs angloiz. Et meſmement dung nomme maiſtre ſance qui avoit ammene aud lieu cinq cens angloiz to⁹ normaulx eu pas avant dud ſiege. Apres laRecepcion deſquelles clefz fut envoye par led lieutēn de ſes gens dedens les deux tours du hable et oſter labanniere des angloiz qui eſtoit ſur lune dicelles tours labanniers duRoy defrance. En laquelle mettant yavoit grant crie et grť Reſomſſiment depeuple. Et ainſſi furẽt garnies des gens dud lieutenant des tours dedevers Rouen. Et ced Iour ſepartit laplus partie deceulx angloiz par baſteaulx. Et pource quilz ne peurẽt to⁹ eſtre preſtz pour lamer qui ſeRetrait led lieutēn ouye humilite Requeſte et ſupplicacion diceux les permiſt demourer levendredy et leſamedy. Iucq̄z amidy. Et leur bailla garde affin quil ne leur fuſt Rien meffait. Et apres ledepartement diceulx DeleRoy donna lacapitainerie dud harfleu aſond lieutēn lequel ya commit ſoubz lui monſr demouy atout cent lances et les archiers pour lagarde dicelle ville. led ſiege avoit eſte ainſſi conduit par les ſeigneurs que dit eſt. IE frere Iehan charoitier chantre dud Saint denis et croniqueuer defrance. ĉtifie ce avoir veu et eſte prť en grans froidrans et vexation. Combn

The reduction of Harfleur by the King of France

THE first day of January, the said English hostages were released at the said place of Harfleur in accordance with the agreement, of which has been said. And this day, around the hour of vespers, the said Thomas Aurignan, an Englishman and captain of the said place, delivered the keys of the said town and of the towers to the said count of Dunois, lieutenant general, kneeling and in great reverence to him in the presence of all the other Englishmen. And even one named master Saince, who had newly come to the said place with 500 Englishmen, all regulars, a little before the said siege. After the reception of which keys, he was sent by the said lieutenant via his men within the two towers of the harbour and to replace the flag of the English, which was on one of these towers, with the banner of the king of France. At which raising there arose a great cry and great cheer by the people. And so, the towers toward Rouen were garrisoned by the men of the said lieutenant. And this said day, the greater part of the Englishmen left by boats. And since they could not all be ready, because of low tide, the said lieutenant, hearing the humble request and supplication of them, allowed them to remain the Friday and Saturday until noon. And he provided guards for them so that they did no misdeeds. And after the departure of these people, the king gave the captaincy of the said Harfleur to his said lieutenant, who placed it under him to monseigneur de Mouy with around one hundred lances and archers for the guardianship of this town; the said siege was thus conducted by the lords who are described. I, brother Jean Chartier, chanter of the

que Ieſtroya et ſuz ſallarie des deſprins demoy et demis
chevaulx par lordonnance du Roy comme dtoꝰ temps eſtoit
et eſt acouſtume pour plus grant ~~charete~~ ſeurete dupays.
Anſſi fuſte ordonne capitaine dud monſtr̃villr̃ et garde daut̂s
fortereſſes Iacques declermont eſcuier Auquel fut ordonne
pareilemet̂ cent lances et les archiers. Et ainſſi ſepartit le-
Roy demonſtr̃villr̃ apres ſes ordonnances faictes lev^{m} Iour
deIanvier. Et fiſt paſſer tantoſt apres lacompaignie. Les
ungz par Rouen. Les aut̂s par caudebec et les aucuns par
tancarville pour allr̃ mettre leſiege devant honnefleu. Et
ſeRetrait ſus la Reine deſauce en une abbaye deReligieux
nomme ~~Iumie~~ Iumeiges qui eſt cinq lieues audeſſoubz deR-
ouen. Et la ſeRefraichit une eſpace detemps pendant que
on faiſoit les ordonnances et preparacions pour aller mettre
leſiege aud lieu dehonnefleu. Et Icelle abbaye trouva leRoy
une damoiſelle nommee labelle agnez. qui la eſtoit venue com̂ elle diſoit pour adv̂tir leRoy et lui dire q̂ aucuns
deſes gens levoulloient trahir. Et livrer es mains deſes anciens ennemys les angloiz. dequoy leRoy ne tint gueres de-
compte et neſen fiſt que Rire. Et pource q̂ lad agnez avoit
eſte ou ſervice delaRoygne par leſpace decinq ans ou en ouquel elle avoit eu toutes plaiſances môdaines. Ceſt aſſavoir
deporter grans ⁊exceſſifz atours comme Iolye deRobbes.
fourrures colliers dor et depierres. Et toꝰ ſes aut̂s ꝼ deſirs.
Par quoẙ fut une commune Renommee q̂ leRoy. lamaîtenoit
en concubinage. Car au Iourduy lepeuple eſt plus enclin
amal dire que bien. Pourquoy. Ie croniqueur deſſſ nomme
deſirant eſtcripir levray me ſuys duement Informe deſavoir
laveritie et conduite ducas et ay trouve tant par chevallr̃s
eſcuiers conſeillers fuſecues cuerguins côme aut̂s dedivers

said Saint-Denis and chronicler of France, certify this, having seen and been present in great cold and vexation, such that I was and am salaried for the costs of myself and my horses by the order of the king, as at all times was and is acustomed, for the greater security of the country. Thus, Jacques de Clermont, a squire, was ordered captain of the said Montivilliers and guardian of other fortresses, to whom was assigned one hundred lances and archers. And so the king left from Montivilliers, after making his orders, the fifth day of January. And he soon afterwards gathered all his company, those of Rouen, others from Caudebec, and others from Tancarville, in order to go lay siege before Honfleur. And the queen retired in an abbey of monks named Jumièges, which was five leagues away from the town of Rouen. And there she retired for a space of time, during which one made orders and preparations to go lay siege to the said place of Honfleur. And [in] this abbey of Jumièges, the king found a damsel named the good Agnès, who came there, as it is said, in order to warn the king and tell him that some of his men wanted to betray and deliver him into the hands of his ancient enemies, the English, for which the king took little account and did not smile. And because the said Agnès had been in the service of the queen for the space of five years or there around, in which she had all kinds of worldly pleasantries—it is known, to wear great and excessive fineries such as pretty dresses, furs, collars of gold, and jewellery, and everything else she desired, for it was a common knowledge that the king held her in concubinage, because today people are more inclined to say bad things than good. For which I, the above-named chronicler, desiring to write the truth, am well duly informed by knowledge of the truth and conduct of the case and have found such by knights, squires,

eſtatz examinez par ſerment côme amon office appartient. Affin doſter labuz dupeuple que pendans leſd cinq. ans que lad damoiſelle ademoura avecques laRoyne oncques leRoy nelaiſſa acouchr̃ avecques lad Royne et acie debeaulx enf-fans delle. Et eſtoit contre ſavoullente q̂ lad agnes portoit ſi grand eſtat. Maiz pource que ceſtoit lebon plaiſir dicelle Roẙne Il temporiſoit au meulx quil pouvoit. Combien quil apercevoit et cognoiſſoit bien que cela lui Redondoit en oprobre. dient en oulť les Inťroguez ſur ceſte matrê que quant leRoy alloit voir les dames et damoiſelles et meſme-ment en labſence delaRoyne ou que labelle agnes le venoit veoir Il yavoit touſiours grať multitude degens pres͡ et que oncques ne lavirent touchr̃ par leRoy audeſſoubz. maiz ſen Retournoit apres les eſbatemens licites et honneſtes. faitz comme aRoy appartent en ~~chūn Iour par ſon~~ ſon logis par chūn ſus ſen Rtournoit et lad agnez auſien. Et lamour que leRoy avoit en elle comme chūn apie ap̱revous eſtoit pour les follies eſbatemens Ioyeuſetez et langaige bien polly qui eſtoient en elle. Et auſſi que entre les belles ceſt laplus belle du monde tenue. Il neſt pas auſſi vray ſemblable que leRoy fiſt ou ait eſte detel gouvernement. Car led tp͡s durant Il amis Iuſtice en nature qui eſtoit perye delonguemain. Aoſte toute pilleries ~~en~~ eſtans en ſon Royaume apourveu aladi-viſion delegliſe ~ tellement que paix et bonne concorde par ſon bon moyen et pourchaz yont eſte mis et pourquoy dieu lavoulu Remunerer en laRecoucrance departu de ſonpays denormandie occupez par les eſtrangers angloiz ſes anciens enemys. Et ſur Iceux exploite conte autant en deux ans quilz avoieť côqueſte en xxx. ans. Durant en oulť leſd dep-poſans q̂ lad agnes atouſiours eſte devie charitable et large

counsellors, relatives, and others of diverse estates, examined by oaths, as my office allows, in order to remove the abuse of the people, that, during the said five years that the said damsel remained with the queen, the king never stopped sleeping with the said queen and he had several beautiful children with her. And it was against her will that the said Agnès held so grand an estate. But, because this was the good pleasure of this queen, he controlled himself as best he could, even though he perceived and knew well that doing this reduced her in reproach, the interrogators saying in addition on this matter that, when the king went to see the ladies and damsels, and similarly in the absence of the queen, that it was this belle Agnès he came to see, he had always a great multitude of men present, and that never did the king come to touch her below the chin; but she returned after the legal and honest fun, making as if the king came into his home each evening, returning to himself and the said Agnès to herself. And the love that the king had in her as each a step before was for the follies, fun, joyousness, and good polite language which she had. And also that amongst the beautiful, she is held to be the most beautiful in the world. It also does not seem true that the king made or had been of such government, because during the said time, he had put justice in nature, which perished after good labour. He had removed all pillaging in his kingdom; had provided for the division of the church, such that peace and good concord by his means and purchase had been put there and for which God had wanted to remunerate him in the recovery of his lands of Normandy, occupied by English foreigners, his ancient enemies. And on this he had done in two years what they had conquered in thirty years. Throughout which, the said donations of the said Agnès had always been charitable and large in alms

en aumoſnes tant quilz lont cogneue. Et diſtribuoit duſien largement aux povres egliſes. aux mêdiens. Et que ſe aucune choſe en copullacion charnelle elle acommiſe avecque leRoy donc on ſe ſait pu appercevoir. Si avoit ce eſte cautement elle eſtant au ſervice delaRoyne deSicile et au par avant quelle fuſt Reſidente. Avecques laRoyne defrance. Bien eſt vray que lad agnes ot une fille qui ne veſquit gueres. Laquelle elle diſoit eſtre auRoy. Et lalui donna côme au mieulx aparent. Maiz leRoy ceſt touſiours fort excuſe ne ny clama oncques Rien. Et auſſi yavoit grâs ſeigneuries avecques lad Royne deSicile parquoy elle lepouvoit bien avoir emprunte ailleurs ces proclamations demal exemple Ainſſi mal publees venues alacognoiſſance delad agnes appellee mademoiſelle debeaulte par deſplaiſance côm Il eſt apreſuppoſer avecques autˆs couroux et diverſes ymaginacions. print leflue duventre donc elle fut malade par longue eſpace detp͡s devant laquelle maladie comme Ieporte par ladeppoſicion demaiſtre denis … auguſtin maiſtre en theologie ſon confeſſeur elle oult moult belle contriction et Repentance deſes pechez. Et lui ſouvint demarie magdeleine qui fut grant une peche delachair. et Invocquoit dieu devotemeˆt et lavierge marie aſon ayde. Et côme bonne catholique apres laRecepcion deſes ſacremens demanda ſes heures pour dire les vers ſaint bernard quelle avoit eſcriptz deſapropre main. Et dapres fiſt pluſſieurs vieux. leſquelz furent mis par eſcript Affin deles acomplis par ſe executeurs Avecques ſon treſtannant qui ſe povoit bien montre tant pour omoſuis comme Iome panes ſes ſemtreus. lx^{m} eſcuz. Et fiſt ſes excecutenans noble homme Iacques cuer conſeillˆr et argentier du Roy. Et honourables ⁊ſaiges

for those who had known her. And she distributed her estate largely to the poor churches and to the mendicants. And that if anything in carnal copulation she had committed with the king, of which one cannot perceive, it had been cautious, she being then in the service of the queen of Sicily and before she was resident with the queen of France. While it is true that the said Agnès had a daughter, who only lived briefly, who it is said was with the king, and she gave it to him as to a parent, but the king was always very apologetic and never claimed anything. And also, there were other great lordships with the said queen of Sicily, for which she could well have borrowed elsewhere these proclamations of bad examples, of cruelly bad publications that came to the knowledge of the said Agnès, named Mademoiselle of Beauty, with displeasure as it is to presume, with other angers and diverse imaginations, she developed stomach pains, for which she became sick for a long space of time, before which sickness as carried by the disposition to Master Denis..., Augustin, master in theology, her confessor, she had very beautiful remorse and repentance for her sins. And it reminded him of Mary Magdalene, who was a great sinner of the flesh and invoked God most devotedly and the virgin Mary ro her aide. And as a good catholic, after the reception of her sacraments, she asked for her Hours, in order to say the verse of Saint Bernard, which she had written in her own hand. And afterwards, she made several vows, which were put in writing, in order to accomplish this by her executors, with her testimony, which she could well show, both in order to give alms and to pay the servants, to 60,000 *écus*. And she appointed her executers a noble man, Jacques Cuer, councillor and treasurer of the king, and honourable and wise persons, Master Robert Poitevin, physician, and Master

prſonnes maiſtre Robert poitevin fuſicien. et maiſtre eſtienne chlr̃ treſorier auſſi duRoy. Et ordonna au leRoy ſeul et pour letout fuſt par deſſus les trois. Et depuis lad agnez voyant et ſachant ſa maladie engreger deplus en plus. diſt amonſr detancarville et amadame laſenſthalle de poitou. et alun des eſcuiers du Roy nomme gouffier et atoutes ſes damoiſelles que ceſtoit peu dechoſe et orde denor̃ fragilite. Et adonc Requiſt aud maiſtre denis ſon confeſſeur quil lavouſluſt abſouldre depaine et decoulpe par vertu dune abſolucion Laquelle eſtoit aloches comme elle diſoit. Ce que lad confeſſeur aſaRelacion fiſt. Et apres quelle ot fait ung hault cry en Reclamant dieu et labenoiſte vierge marie. ſeſepara ſon ame dacecques lecorps. Le xm Iour defevrier Lan mil cccc ~~xx~~ xlix. environ ſix heures ap̊s midy. Et pres fut depuis ouverte et ſon cuer mis en t̂re en lad abbaye. pourqouy fiſt degrans dons en Icelle. Et lecorps mene et ſepulture aloches honnourablement en egliſe collegial denêdaê ou elle avoit fait pluſſieurs belles fondacions et donacions. dieu lui face mercy alame et la mette en paradis. Amen.

Comment lechaſteau deguichen. fut prins par leconte defoix.

EN. ce meſmes temps. Leconte defoulz fiſt une groſſe armee. et aſſemblee degens et fiſt mettre leſiege par leſire delautret ſon frere. Et par lebaſtard defoulz devant lechaſteau deguiſchen qui eſt treſfort aſſis aquat̂ lieues pres debayonne. Et quant les angloiz leſceurent Ilz ſemirent ſur les champs Iucques atrois ~~cent~~ mille combatans donc eſtoit chef leconneſtable deNavarre et avec lui eſtoient le-

Étienne Chevalier, also treasurer of the king. And she ordered that the king alone and for all was as above the three. And then the said Agnès, seeing and knowing her sickness was getting worse and worse, said to Monseigneur of Tancarville and to madame the seneschal of Poitou, and to one of the squires of the king, named Gouffier, and to all her maids, that it was a little thing and ordained by our fragility. And so she requested to the said Master Denis, her confessor, that he would give her absolution of sin and of guilt, by virtue of an indulgence, who then was at Loches, as she said. This the said confessor did as she had related. And afterwards, she had made a very high cry in reclaiming God and the benevolent Virgin Mary, separating her soul from her body, the eighth day of February, the year 1449, around six in the afternoon. And then the chest was opened and her heart interred in the said abbey, for which she had made a very large donation. And the body was taken and interred at Loche honourably in the collegial church of Notre Dame, where she had made several wonderful commissions and donations—May God have mercy on her soul and put her in Paradise. Amen.

How the castle of Guischen was captured by the count of Foix

IN this same time, the count of Foix gathered a large army and assembly of men, and he laid siege via the sire de Lautrec, his brother, and by the bastard of Foix before the castle of Guissen, which was a very strong place, situated near Bayonne. And when the English learned this, they gathered on the field until they numbered 3,000 soldiers, over which was leader the constable of Navarre and with him was the mayor of Bayonne,

maire debayonne. george ſalteriton et pluſſieurs auťs angloiz leſquelz ſebouterȇt ⁊chargerent en vaiſſiaulx pour mettre ſur une Riviere qui paſſe parmy baionne. Et vindrent deſſendre pres dud chaſteau. Laquelle deſſente venue ala congnoiſſance deceulx qui tenoient led ſiege ſepartirent leplus ſegrettemeȇ q̂ faire peureȇ et allerent audevant deſd angloiz et les aſſailireȇ dureureȇ et ſi aprement que Ilz les deſconfirent et mirent en fuite Iucques aleurs ſd bateaux. Et cy furent que mors que prins en lad chaſſe xii^C^. angloiz. Et quant led ſalteriton vit Icelle deſtrouſſe doubta foruent q̂ Il ne peuſt Recouvȓ leſd navires. Et pource paſſa parmy leſiege atout lx. Lances. et ſeſauva treſvaillament pour Icelle heure dedens leboullevert dud chaſteau. Puis Regarda que leans ne pouvoit bonnement eſtre ſecouru. Parquoy ſiꝑtit denuyt lui et ſacompaignie cuidans Retôuner aud lieu debayonne. Maiz led baſtard defoix ſachant aucunement ſon partiment lepôſment et atagnit. Et tellement que lad ſaltinton fut laprins et laplus part deſes gens. Et lelendemain ſe Rendtit led chaſteau et tout lepays auȓ lamer et Bayo. et bayonne ouquel pays avoit xv. ou xvi. places fortes qui toutes ſe Rendirent aud conte de foulz. Et apres garniſons miſes eſd places ſouffiſãns ſen Retournerant les gens dud conte defoulz en leurs pays.

Leſiege deſhonnefleu mis ꝑ les francois

LE. xviime Iour deIanvier oud an fut mis le ſiege ahonnefleu. leRoy eſtant aIumeiges par monſ[r] leconte dedunoiz ſon lieuteñ general et auťs ſeigneurs deſſſ nommez leſquelz ſi gouv̂nereȇ moult vaillement et chaleureſement.

Georges Salteriton, and several other Englishmen, who loaded themselves onto and took charge of ships on a river that passes alongside Bayonne. And they came to descend near to the said castle. Which descent, [when it] came to the knowledge of those who held the said siege, they left as secretly as they could and went before the said Englishmen and they assailed them and so roughly that they defeated them and put them to flight to their said boats. And there were killed and captured in the said chase 1,200 Englishmen. And when the said Salteriton saw this destruction, he feared very strongly that he could not recover the said ships. And because of this, he crossed the siegelines with around forty lances and saved himself very valiantly at this hour within the bulwark of the said castle. Then, considering that those within could not likely save themselves. So he left by night, he and his company, thinking to return to the said place of Bayonne. But the bastard of Foix learned anyway of his departure and attacked him, and such that the said Salteriton was captured and the greater part of his men. And the next day, the said castle rendered itself and all the land around the sea and Bayonne, in which land were fiftteen or sixteen strong places, which all rendered themselves to the said count of Foix. And after sufficient garrisons were put into the said places, the men of the said count of Foix returned into their lands.

The siege of Honfleur laid by the French

THE seventeenth day of January in the said year, siege was lain before Honfleur, the king being at Jumièges, by monseigneur the count of Dunois, his lieutenant general, and the other lords abovenamed, who governed so very bravely and passionately. And

Et mefmement les francs archiers qui avoient efte logez pres dud honnefleu par lefpace dex. ou xii. Iours avant q̂ lafñe yunefift po' efcarmuchr̂ fus Iceulx angloiz. et apres que led fiege eult efte ferme fepartit leRoy dud Iumieges et alla loger en une abbaye nômee gretain adeux lieues dud honnefleu. Et tantoft ceulx qui eftoient aud fiege firent grans approches foffez et mynes et affortement bombardes canons et engins vollas̑ que moult efbahiment ceulx delad place donc eftoit capitaine ung nomme maiftre courffon qui avoit en facompaignie detrois aquat̂ cens angloiz Lefquelz faifoient grant devoir deulx deffend et detirer canons et autre trait fur les francois defquels fut tue ung efcuier nomme Regnault guill̑ bourguignon qui lors eftoit bailly demontargis dôc fut grant dommaige car Il eftoit vaillant homme defon corps. Et apres furent tellement ap-preffez lefd angloiz que paour et neceffite les contraigny deulx Rendre et prendre appoinctemet̂. Pourquoy fut faicte compoficion quilz Renderent lad place lxviii^m Iour defevrier prochain enf eucas quilz ne fecourent fecouruz. Et dece baillerent oftages par auiffi quilz fen yroient leurs corps et leurs biens faufz. Et pour combatre aud Iour firent lefd francois grans dilligences de ordonner et clorre lechamp ou Ilz eftoient. Maiz lefd angloiz ne vindrent point ne ny comparurent aucunement. Car leduc defombrecet nefoit defemparer la ville decaen. Et auffi neftoit pas affez fort fans avoir aut̂ fecours dangletr̂e. Et ainffi Rendirent laplace aud Iour et fen allerent en angleterre ou ailleurs en leur party avecques leurfd biens comme promis leur eftoit.

even the free archers, who had been lodged near to the said Honfleur for the space of ten or twelve days before the army laid siege there, in order to skirmish these Englishmen and, after the said siege had been set up, the king left from the said place of Jumièges and went to lodge in an abbey named Gretain two leagues from the said Honfleur. And soon, those who were at the said siege made large ditches, trenches, and mines, and set up large bombards, cannon, and other war engines, which was very astounding to those within the said place, over whom was captain one named master Courson, who had in his company around 300 to 400 Englishmen, who did great work to defend themselves and to fire cannon and other projectiles at the French, amongst whom was killed a squire named Renaud Guillaume, a Burgundian, who then was baliff of Montargis, which was a great loss because he was a very brave man of his body. And afterwards, the said Englishmen were in such a hurry that fear and necessity compelled them to render themselves and take a compromise. For which an agreement was made that they would render the said place the eighteenth day of the following February, in the event that they could find no help. And for this they delivered hostages, by means of which they also would leave there safely with their bodies and their goods. And in order to fight on the said day, the said Frenchmen made great dilligence to organise and close the field where they were. But the said Englishmen no longer came there nor appeared in any way, because the duke of Somerset did not dare decamp from the town of Caen. And also, he was not strong enough without receiving any relief from England. And thus, the said place was rendered on the said day and they went into England or wherever in their party, with their said goods as had been promised to them.

Siege mis afreſnaẙ. le. viconte par les francois.

Tantoſt. apres que laville dehonnefleu fut Redduite ſepartit leRoy delad abbaye degreſtain. et ſen alla abernay de la aeſſay et aalencon. Et envoya aucuns deſaſſie et meſmement les francs archiers pour mettre le ſiege devant freſnay duquel eſtoiẽt capitaines capitaines et gouverneurs deux angloiz. Lun nôme andey ~~trof~~ trollot. et laut̂ Iancquin baſquier Leſquelz avoient en leur compaignie dequat̂ acinq cens angloiz et normans appellez francois Regnez. Et chevauchorent leſd francois en moult belle ordonnance et en grant nombre. Parquoy Incontinent ceulx vienes devant lad place leſd angloiz commencerent atraicter delaReddicion deville. Et apres pluſſieurs parolles finablement fut appoincte q̂ en Rendant lad ville en lobbeiſſance duRoy defrance et en baillant. X.m ſaluz on leur delivreroit apur et aplain leur capitaine nôme montfort qui avoit eſte prins auponteaudemer et ſen yroient leurs corps et leurs biens saufz. Et ainſſi fut fait. Et ſepartirent lexxiim Iour de mars pour eulx en aller acaen ou afallaiſe ou bien leur ſembleroit.

Commet̂ leſiege fut mis devat̂ vallongnes par les angloiz.

Oudit an en laſaiſon decareſme deſſendiret̂ acherebourg trois mille angloiz qui venoiet̂ dupays danglet̂re donc eſtoit chief ⁊conduiſieur ung chlr̂ degrant Renom. Nomme

Siege lain before Fresnay-le-Vicomte by the French

Soon after the said town of Honfleur was reduced, the king left from the said abbey of Grestain and went to Bernay, from there to Essay, and then to Alençon. And he sent several of his seigneurie and even the free archers to lay siege before Fresnay, over which were captain and governor two Englishmen, one named Andrew Trollot and the other Pasquin Basguier, who had in their company from 400 to 500 Englishmen and Normans, called the French Renegades. And the said Frenchmen advanced in very good order and were in great number. For which, immediately after they arrived before the said place, the said Englishmen began to negotiate for the capitulation of the town. And after several discussions, it was finally agreed that they would render the said town into the obedience of the king of France, and in giving him 10,000 *salus*, pure and in full, their captain, named Montfort, who had been captured at Ponteau-de-Mer, would be delivered to them and they would go safely with their bodies and their goods. And so this was done. And they left the twenty-second day of March in order to go to Caen or to wherever it seemed good to them.

How the siege was lain before Vallongnes by the English

In the said year, in the season of Lent, 3,000 Englishmen who had newly come from the land of England descended upon Cherbourg, over whom was captain and leader a knight of great

meſſire thās kiriel. lequel et ſacomapignie chevaucherent fait quilz vindrent logier es faulxbourcs de vollongnes ou Ilz mirent leſiege et en eſtoit garde et capitaine pour le-Roy defrance ung eſcuier depoitou nomme abel Rouault lequel latint vaillamment et longuement au nom de ſon frere Ioachim Rouault ſans eſtre aucunement ſecouru. Parquoy lui convint Rend ~~kyriel~~ laplace aud kyriel apres quil leult tireme trois ſepmaines. Et ſepartit par compoſicion faicte led capitaine et ſes gens leurs corps chevaulx ⁊autˆ biens ſaufz. Combien que les gens duRoy ceſtoient aſſembles pour venir lever led ſiege. Et auſſi eſtoient les angloiz deleurs garniſons pour temps les champs. Ceſt aſſavoir meſſire Robert ver delaville decaen atout Six cens combatans Mathago delaville debayeulx atout viii^c^. côbatans henrẙ marbery delaville devire atout iiii^c^. combatans ou environ. Et eſtoient to⁹ nombre deſix aſept mille combatans. comprins led kyriel et ſacompaignie. Et ce voyans les francois ~ laiſſerent Rend lad ville car pource Ilz ne prenant point eſtre preſtz atemps pour Icelle ville ſecourer meſmement veu ⁊conſidere q̂ larmee du Roy neſtoit pas enſamble. Maiz eſtoit en diverſes parties pour plus dilligemeˆt Recouvrer Icelle duchie deNormandie qui eſt du propre domaine et hr̄itage du Roy^me^. defrance.

LaJournee defourmignẙ. pour les francois

Lan. mil CCCC. Cinquante. Lexii^m^ Iour davril. Apres paſques ſe deſlogerent dedevant laville devallongnes led kyriel et ſes gens. avecques ceulx des garniſons de

renown named Sir Thomas Kyriell, who with his company rode such that they came to lodge in the suburbs of Vallongnes, where they laid siege, and a squire of Poitou named Abel Rouault was the governor and captain for the king of France, who held it bravely and for a long time in the name of his brother, Joachim Rouault, without having any help, for which he was convinced to render the place to the said Kyriel, after he had sustained the siege for three weeks. And the said captain and his men left by an agreement made, their bodies, horses, and other goods safe. However, the men of the king were assembled to come to lift the said siege, and also the Englishmen from their garrisons were arranged on the field; it is known, messire Robert Ver of the town of Caen with around 600 soldiers; Matthew Gough of the town of Bayeux with around 800 soldiers; Henry Marbury of the town of Vire with about 400 soldiers, or therearound. And they were estimated to be around 6,000 to 7,000 soldiers including the said Kyriel and his company. And seeing the French, they left to render the said town, because they could no longer be captured with time to rescue this town, still seeing and considering that the army of the king was not assembled But was in diverse parts in order to more diligently recover this duchy of Normandy, which is the rightful domain and heritage of the king of France.

The campaign of Formigny by the French

The year 1450, the twelfth day of April, after Easter, the said Kyriell and his men, with those of the garrisons of Caen, Bayeux, and Vire, dislodged from above the town of Vallongnes

caen bayeulx etvire etpaſſirent to⁹ enſemble les guez ſaint clement pour tirer vers bayeulx et vers caen. Laquelle choſe venue alacognoiſſ des gens duRoy defrance qui ceſtoient mis ſur les champs pour les trouver les pourſuivirent. Combn quilz fuſſent aupetit nombre et chevaucherent fort tant que en laffin les actignirent. Et fut côme depar leRoy afaire ceſte pourſuitte et eſtre ſon lieuten. Leconte decleremont avecques lequel eſtoient Leconte decaſtres. leſeneſchal depoitou. les ſeigneurs demontgaſcon etdeRaiz Admiral defrance. leſeneſchal debourbonnoiz les ſ^rs^. demauny et demouy. Robert counigan — meſſire guiffroy decouvran. Ioachim Rouault olivier debron. et pluſſieurs auts Iucques au nôbre decinq. aſix cens lances et les archiers. dela quelle compaignie ſeſeparerent Leſd meſſire guiffroy decouvran et Iouachim Rouault pour querrir deto⁹ coſtez leurs advantages ſur leſd angloiz. Et tant chevaucherent quilz trouverent leur eſtrac. Et combien quil yeuſt peu degens avecques eulx. Neantmoins côme preux ⁊hardiz Ilz allerent bandement ⁊vaillamment ~~freres~~ ferir ſur leur arriere garde et en tuerent et manieret pluſieurs eſtans en lad arrieregarde puis ſe Retrayrent ung peu eſpace detemps. et manderent led conte declermont qui neſtoit pas loing. Lequel acompaigne côme dit eſt fiſt grat diligence detirer apres leſd angloiz. Et les pourſuivy aupres dun villaige nomme fourmigny ent carentan et bayeux. Et quant les angloiz les appercurent ſemerent en bataille et manderent diligemment querir ung capitaine deleur party nomme mathago lequel ceſtoit party deulx au matin ceIour propre xv^m^ Iour du moys davril po^r^

and all together crossed the Saint-Clement fords in order to head straight to the towns of Bayeux and Caen. Which came to the knowledge of the men of the king of France, who had put himself on the field to find them, pursuing them English since they were so small in number, and they rode so strongly that they eventually caught up to them. And it was commanded by the king to make this pursuit and the count of Clermont was his lieutenant, with whom was the count of Castres, the seneschal of Poitou, the seigneurs of Montgascon, and of Rais, admiral of France, the seneschal of the Bourbonnais, the seigneurs of Mauny and of Mouy, Robert Cunningham, messire Geoffroy de Couvran, Joachim Rouault, Olivier de Bron, and several others until the number was 500 to 600 lances and the archers, from which company the said messires Geoffroi de Couvran and Joachim Rouault split off to go seek on all sides their advantage against the said Englishmen. And so they rode until they found their tracks. And although they had few men with them; nonetheless, as brave and hardy men, they went bravely to strike their rear guard and they killed and mutilated several being in the said rear guard, then they retreated for a short period of time, and the said count of Clermont ordered that they not go far away, who accompanied, as it is said, made great diligence to strike against the said Englishmen. And to pursue them near a village named Formigny, between Carentan and Bayeux. And when the Englishmen perceived them, they arranged themselves in batallions and diligently ordered a captain of their party named Matthew Gough to be sought, who had left them this same day in the morning, the fifteenth day of April, in order to go to Bayeux. And for this, he returned to the aide of his companions. And the

ſen aller aud bayeulx. Et pource Retourna alayde deſes compaignons. Et lafuret̃ les angloiz et les francois les ung devant les auts̃ par leſpace detrois heures. Et touſiours en eſcarmouches. Et cepend firent leſd angloiz grans trous et foſſez en terre dedagues et deſpees devant eulx affin que ceulx qui les aſſauldroient pruſſent tôber eulx et leurs chevaulx leſd angloiz ceſtoient mis fort alavantage. Car Ilz avoient deſriere leurs dos ~~en~~ environ ung grant trait dauc ung petite Riviere. et ent̃ deux grant quantite des Iardinages plains depoviers pômes preriers ou et auts̃ devers abres affin con neleurs pueſt con ſes par defrance. Et pource q̂ led conte decleremont Inſtitute lieutenant pour leRoy en lapourſuite diceulx angloiz ſi avoit pou degens avecques lui. Envoya ~~ha~~ haſtivement aSaint lo devers leconte deRichemont conneſtable defrance Affin quil veniſt auſecours dud decleremont ou auſ̃met̃ lui et ſes gens eſtoient bien tailles davoir fort affaire vue que leſd angloiz excedoient en nombre degens deguerre par deſſſ les francois. Et tantoſt ce venu aſacognoiſſance ſeparty lemercredy. xv-[m]Iour davril environ trois heures du matin et vint haſtivement pour ſecourir labeſoigne. Combien quil venoit debretaigne ou detune et chevaucha Iucques aulieu detremeres a compaignie. demonſ[r] Iacques deluxembourg duconte de laval duſire deloheac mareſhal defrance. leſire deorval. lemareſchal debretaigne. leſire deſaincte ſevere et debouſſac et depluſſieurs auts̃ Iucques au nôbre deii[C]. axii[XX]. lances et viii[C]. archiers. ſepartit duvillage celieu eſtremeres ou Il avoit couche leſoir. et che vaucha treſdiligemment. Combien q̂ leſd angloiz avoient Iapaſſez les guez. et tant quil vint a compaigne côme dit eſt. Iucques aung moullin avent

English and the French, one before the other, were there for the space of three hours. And always engaging in skirmishes. And, however, the said Englishmen made big holes and ditches in the ground around them, and had swords before them so that those who would assault them would fall back with their horses—the said Englishmen were strongly at an advantage because at their backs, about an arrowshot's distance, there was a small river and between them a large number of gardens, full of pear trees, apple trees, plum trees, and other various trees, as is common in France, so that no one could approach them. And because of this, the said count of Clermont, instituted lieutenant of the king in the pursuit of these Englishmen, having few men with him, sent hastily to Saint-Lo to the earl of Richmond, constable of France, in order that he come to the rescue of the said of Clermont or otherwise he and his men, being very trapped for having strongly fought, seeing that the said Englishmen exceeded in number of men-of-war the abovesaid Frenchmen, and as soon as this came to his knowledge, he left Wednesday, the fifteenth day of April at around three in the morning, and he came quickly to rescue the besieged, such that he came from Brittany or from around and rode until a place called Tremères with a company of monseigneur Jacques de Luxembourg; of the count of Leval; of the sire de Lohéac, marshal of France; the sire of Orval, the marshal of Brittany; the sire de Saint-Sévère; and of de Boussac, and several others until the number was 200 to 240 lances and 800 archers; he left for the village, the place where he had rested the night, and he rode very diligently. Although the said Englishmen had already crossed the fords and such that he came with his company, as it is said, to a windmill above the abovesaid Formigny and within sight of these Englishmen, he put all his men into

audeſſus dud formigny. Et alaveue diceulx angloiz ſemerent to^s en bataille et eſtoient deſſenduz au des gens auconte decleremont devant lavenue dud conneſtable mil et cinq cens archiers Leſquelz firent Reboutez moult aſprement par leſd angloiz. Et avoient gaigne ĉtaines coulevrines ſur Iceulx francois. Et adonc monſ^r leconneſtable fiſt marchr̂ meſſire gilles deſainct ſimon. meſſire Iehan demal eſtroit et phlê demaleſtroit freres meſſire anceau gaudin. et lebaſtard delatremouille avecſes archr̂s droit aung pont. Et Incontinet̂ q̂ les angloiz aperceurent lavenue dud conneſtable mathago et maiſtre ver. et bien mil angloiz en leur compaignie ſen fuyrent acaen et abayeulx. Et led kyriel Il ſabataille ſeRetourent pour gaigner ung Ruſſiau et levillage qui la eſtoit. Et aubout dud pont deſſenerent apie partie des archiers dud côneſtable qui combatirent en leſle dembas delabataille deſd angloiz ou Il yen ot pluſſieurs demors ⁊deſconfilz deſd angloiz. Lors paſſa ledconneſtable led Ruiſeau et ſeIoignint avec led conte declermont apres. que lad eſle dembas fut deſconfite. Et Incontinent legrant ſenſchal denormandie demanda congie aud conneſtable defaire deſſend ſon enſaigne aleille damont. Et que led côneſtable lui acorda en laquelle Ilz combatirent fort et yfurent leſd angloiz mors et deſconfilz. Et tantoſt marcheret̂ les grans dud conneſtable en belle ordonance tant quilz furet̂ pres dud villaige ou paſſerent lad Riviere ſur legrant chemin. Et lors leſd angloiz doubtenant fort pourquoy laiſſerent lechamp et ſeRecullerent ſus lad Riviere ſur legrant chemin. Et lafurent aſſalliz deſd francois et fut baiſ͡le. combatu dunepart et daut̂. Et combien q̂ leſd francois ne fuſſent en tout par leRapport des heraultx q̂ trois mille combatans et

batallions and the men of the count of Clermont sent ahead before the arrival of the said constable 1,500 archers, who were pushed back very bitterly by the said Englishmen. And they had captured certain culevrines from these Frenchmen. And then monseigneur the constable marched [with] messire Gilles de Saint-Simon; messire Jean de Malestroit and Philippe de Malestroit, brothers; messire Anceau Gaudin; and the bastard de la Trémoïlle, with several archers straight to a bridge. And immediately after the Englishmen perceived the arrival of the said constable, Mathew Gough and master Vir, with around 1,000 Englishmen in their company, entrenched themselves at Caen and Bayeux. And the said Kyriell, he retreated to capture a brook and the town that was there. And around the said bridge, a party of archers of the said constable descended on foot, who fought on an island below the batallion of the said English, where several were killed and captured of the said English. Then the constable crossed the said small river and joined with the said count of Clermont, after the said island below was defeated. And immediately, the grand seneschal of Normandy requested leave of the said constable to lower his banner from above the island. And the said constable granted him that, in which they fought strongly and the said Engishmen were killed and defeated there. And soon the men of the said constable marched in good order such that they were near the said village where they crossed the said river in the great train. And then the said Englishmen feared strongly, for which they left the field and retreated across the said river in the great train. And there they were assaulted by the said French and combat was fought one side against the other. And such that the said Frenchmen were not more than, by the report of the heralds, 3,000 soldiers, and the said Englishmen

leſd angloiz eſtouant deſix aſept mille. Neantmoins par lagrace dedieu les francois deſconfirent leſd angloiz. Leſquelz par leRapport des heraulx des pbre͡s et des bonnes gens qui la eſtoient furent mors et enterois en laplace en xiiii foſſez. iii^{m}. vii^{c}. lxxiiii. Et yfurent prins priſonniers meſſire thomas kyriel meſſ^{re} henry norbery meſſ^{re} thomas driuc meſſire tha͡s cuqueby ~ xriſtofle auberchon. Jehan arpel. helix alangour Ianequin baſquner. godebert calleville et pluſſ aut̂s capitaines et gentilz hommes angloiz portans cottes darmes. Et en confermant en langaige vulgaire qui dit que mieulx vault une bonne fuitte que une mauvaiſe actente ſen fuyrent et habandonnerent leurs compaignons cõme gens ayans leceur failly. Ceſt aſſavoir matago Asire Robert ver. Henrẙ lours maiſtre meillan et ung aut̂ capitaine qui avoit charge de xxx. lances et cinq cens ~~angloiz~~ archiers. Et furent eſtimez les priſonniers angloiz prins en lad bataille dexii. axiiii^{C}. Et ſen alla led mathago abayeulx et led meſſire Robert acaen. Et ainſſi furent par lavirtu divine les angloiz deſconfitz. Et ſe porterent treſvaillamment et cheualeureuſement ſans aultruy blaſmer monſ^{r}. demontgaſcon et monſ^{r}. deſaincte ſevere. Et meſmement meſſ^{r} pierre debreze ſeneſchal depoictou ent̂ to^{9} fiſt bien vaillemment. Car leſd angloiz chargerent treſfort ſur ſes gens et ſur ceulx dubailly devreulx que gouvernoit leſire demaugny et tellement quilz gaignerent ducoſte ou Ilz eſtoient en bataille deux coulevrines ſur eulx. Et lors led ſeneſchal deſſendit apie et fiſt deſſendre ſes gens puis chargerent ſur leſd angloiz ſi durement quilz les Rebouteret̂ par ung des boutz deleur bataille delalongueu^{r} dequatre lances ou environ et Recouvra leſd coullevrines. Et aceſt aſſault yeult

were 6,000 to 7,000. Nonetheless, by the grace of God, the French defeated the said English, which, by the report of the heralds, of the priests, and the good men who were there, 3,774 were killed and enterred in the place in fourteen mass graves. And messire Thomas Kyriell, messire Henry Norbury, messire Thomas Driuc, messire Thomas Kirkeby, Christopher Auberchon, Jean Arpel, Helix Alangour, Janequin Basquier, Gobert Calleville, and several other English captains and gentlemen carrying coats of arms were taken prisoner there. And in confirming in vulgar language who said what better, wanting a good escape more than to do a bad act, they fled and abandoned their companions as men having a failing heart—it is known Matthew Gough, messire Robert Ver, Henry Lours, master Meillan, and another captain who had the charge of thirty lances and 500 archers. And the English prisoners captured in the said battle were estimated to be around 1,400. And the said Matthew Gough went to Bayeux and the said messire Robert to Caen. And so, by divine virtue, the English were defeated. And monseigneur de Montgascon and monseigneur de Saint-Sévère carried themselves very bravely and very chivalrously, without any blame. And so too did messire Pierre de Brézée, seneschal of Poitou, who amongst others was very brave. But the said Englishmen charged so strongly against his men and those of the bailiff of Évreux, which monseigneur de Mauny governed, and such that they captured on the side where they were in battle two culevrines for themselves. And so the said seneschal descended on foot and had his men descend, then they charged against the said Englishmen so mightily that they rebutted them by one of the ends of their battalion by the length of four lances, or thereabout, and he recovered the said culevrines. And at this assault, he

deux cens angloiz mors ou environ. Et lafuret̃ faiz chevallr̃s led conte decaſtres filz duconte delamarche. Goddefroy deboullongne filz duconte deboullõgne et dauvergne. Leſire devauvert filz duconte de villars. leſire deſaincte ſevere. Leſr. decharenton et pluſſieurs aut̃s. Et alad Iournee duparty des francois nemourut auplus q̃ huit perſonnes ſeul̃l. Et ainſſi ſedepartit loſt deſd francois. et ſen allerent to⁹ enſemble mettre leſiege devant Vire. Apres lequel departement ſemeult altr̃cacion ent̃ aucuns gens deguerre. diſant les unz que le louenge delaIournee devoit eſtre atribuee aud cõneſtable cõme lieutenant du Roy partout le-Royaulme defrance. Les aut̃s diſouant devoit eſtre lonneur aud conte decleremont cõme cõmis et lieuten̄ affaire celle pourſuite et deſaict que leſpiaciaulte deſrogoit alageneralite. Et combien q̃ led conneſtable ſoit lieutenant general du Roy partout le Royaume defrance Neantmoins veu ce que dit eſt leconte de clermont doit deplein droit emporter lonneur. Ce diſpute et argue pour les deux parties par pluſſieurs ſeigneurs. Et meſmemet̃ du conſentement du Roy fut Rlade amoy croniqueur que led conte declermont devoit emporter louanus. combien que par lemoyen dud conneſtable lachoſe proſpera en bien.

Une proceſſion fct̃e aparis aSat̃ Innocet̃.

Ceſt gracieuſe Iournee fut tantoſt de dunegee partout le-Royaulme defrance. Et en eſpecial vint alacongoiſſance deReverend pere en dieu maiſtre guillaume chartier eveſque departis. lequel pour Rem̃cier dieu deſagrace avoit voulu lad virtue eſtre obli[...] pour letreſxpien̄ Roy defrance. Alencontre

killed there 200 Englishmen or therearound. And there were made knights the count of Castres, son of the count of la Marche; Goddefroy de Boulogne, son of the count of Boulogne and Auvergne; the sire de Vauvert, son of the count of Vilars; the sire of Saint-Sévère; the sire de Charenton; and several others. At the said battle, only eight people of the party of the French were killed. And so the army of the said French left and went all together to lay siege before Vire. After which departure, an altercation between several men of war occurred, with one side saying that the praise of this battle ought to be attributed to the said constable, as lieutenant of the king for all the kingdom of France, the others saying that the honnour ought to be go to the said count of Clermont, as commissioned and lieutenant for making this pursuit and defeat since speciality disregards geneality. And even though the said constable was lieutenant general of the king for all the kingdom of France; nonetheless, seeing what was said above, the count of Clermont ought to be, by full right, given the honour. This was disputed and argued for the two parties by several lords. And finally, by the consent of the king, it was reported to me—chronicler—that the said count of Clermont ought to be lauded, even though by the means of the said constable the affair prospered well.

A procession made to Paris from Saint-Innocent

This gracious battle was soon recounted across the kingdom of France. And especially it came to the knowledge of the reverend father of God, master Guillaume Chartier, bishop of Paris, who, in order to thank God for his grace, had wanted the said virtue to be [*text garbled*] for the very Christian king of

de ſes anciens ennemys. en conſonant aux dire du pſalmite ou Ie dit. Ex ore Infantium et latemimˆperfeceſti laudem. Ordonna une proceſſ legliſe noȓ dame deparis. Et ny avoit en Icelle to⁹ ~~ef~~ enffans allans aux eſcholles. hors delacite delage deſept ans et Iucques axl ans tant maſles que femelle et meſmement enffans mendians des quatre ordre deparis avecques toˢ les maiſtres Iceulx enffans. Et eſtoit eſtimee lad congre gacion dexii. axiiiiᵐ. enffans deleage deſſſd. Leſquelz ſedepartirent delad egliſe deſainct Innocent ou lad congregacion avoit eſte fctê. Et portant chcn ung cierge ou auȋ luminaire ou ſamain. Et avec eulx eſtoient les chaportans dud ſaint Innocent qui portoient ung Reliquaire appelle innocent. Et duroit lad proceſſion depuis lad egliſe deSaint Innocent iucques en legliſe noȓ dame qui eſtoit moult belle choſe avoir et grant honneur pour led eveſque. Apres que lad compaignie fut arrivee en lad egliſe fut chante ſen meſſe Retournerent et Icelle chanter ſen Retournerent deux adeux comme Ilz eſtoient aller pour Reconner led ~~Rq̂~~ Relicquaire Iucques alad egliſe deSaiȋ Innoceȋ. Et delaſedepartirent et ſen allerent chcn en ſon eſcolle.

Commeȋ Laville devire fut. Reduic aux francois.

Tantoſt apres badeſconfiture deſſſd et ſans Inȋvalle alla toute lacompaignie mettre leſiege devant laville devire en la quelle avoit en garniſon atrois aquatre cens combatans angloiz donc eſtoit cappitaine led meſſire henry norbery°. lequel eſtoit priſonniers et avoit eſtre prins alaIournee dud formigny. Lequel ſiege ny fut my longuement pouvir que led capitaine la fiſt Rendre par com-

France at the encounter with his ancient enemies conforming to the sayings of the Psalmist, where he said: *out of the mouth of babes and sucklings, thou hath perfect praise*, ordering a processession [to] the church of Notre-Dame-de-Paris. And in this, they were all children going to the schools out of the city of the age of seven years until eleven years, both males and females, and even mendicant children of the four orders of Paris, with all the masters of these children. And the said congregation was estimated at 12,00 to 14,000 children of the abovesaid ages. Who departed from the said church of Saint-Innocent, where the said congregation had been made. And each carried a lit candle or other light in their hand from the said Saint-Innocent, which held a reliquery named Innocent. And the said procession went from the said church of Saint-Innocent until the church of Notre-Dame, which was a very beautiful thing to see and a great honour for the said bishop. After the said company arrived in the said church, it sang, [and then] they returned two-by-two as they had come to return the said reliquery to the said church of Saint Innocent. And they departed and went each into their school.

How the town of Vire was reduced to the French

Soon after the abovesaid defeat and without any interval, all of the company went to lay siege before the town of Vire, in which was garrisoned 300 to 400 English soldiers, over whom was captain the said messire Henry Norbury, who was a prisoner and had been captured at the said battle of the said Frémigny. Which siege was not held long before it, since the said captain made to render it by agreement such that

poſicion telle que ceulx qui eſtoient dedens ſen allerent acaen leurs biens et leurs corp et ainſſi Remirent laville. Pour lagarde delaquelle fut commis et ordonne capitaine deparleRoy. Et dela ſepartit toute larmee. Et ſeſepara en deux parties. Ceſt aſſavoir monſr. leconte clermont et ſacompaignie tirerent et aller vers bayeulx. Et led conneſtable et ſacôpaignie tirerent aallr̃ vers leduc debretagne por aller mettre leſiege. Davranches.

Siège mis Davranches par. leduc debretaigne.

Larmee duduc debretaigne Retournee devers lui apres quilz furent ung peu Icelle freſchez fiſt faire ſes monſtres. Et apres ſans aucune dillacion ſeprint bien garny decanos bombardes et toute aut̃ artillerie et alla mettre leſiege devant laville davranches en laquelle avoit garniſon dequat̃ acinq cens angloiz. donc eſtoit capne ung nomme lampet les gens dud duc aaſſeoir đ lad ſiege ſe porterent moult vaillament. Et yot degrans eſcarmoches dunepart ⁊daut̂. Et yfut led duc et ſon oſt par leſpace detrois ſepmaines. Pendant lequel temps firent degranes approches et baterent lad ville dengins et tellement que neceſſite contraignit lad capitaine et ſes gens de Rendre lad place auduc. Et quelque compoſicon que leſd angloiz demandaſſent Neantmoins ne peurent obtenir que deulx en allr̃ leurs corps ſaufz ſeulement. Et ainſſi Rendirent laplace. Et ſen allerent chcn ung baſton en leur poing tant capne. les auts̃. Et fut laiſſe et ordonne capitaine a lagarde delad place.

those who were within could go to Caen with their bodies and their goods, and so, the town returned. For the guardianship of which was committed and ordered captain by word of the king. And he departed from there with all the army and it separated into two parts—it is known, monseigneur the count of Clermont—and his company left and went toward Bayeux. And the said constable and his company left and went to the duke of Brittany in order to go lay siege to Avranches.

Siege laid before Avranches by the duke of Brittany

The army of the duke of Brittany returned to him, after which it was a little refreshed, he making his reviews. And afterwards, without any delay, it left well supplied with cannon, bombards, and all other artillery, and it went to lay siege before the town of Avranches, in which was garrisoned 400 to 500 Englishmen, over whom was captain one named [John] Lampet, the men of the said duke, overseeing the said siege, showed themselves to be very brave. And there were great skirmishes on one part and the other. And the said duke and his army were there for the space of three weeks. During which time they made great advances and bombarded the said town with siege engines, and such that necessity constrained the said captain and his men to render the said place. And the said Englishmen asked for some agreement. Nonetheless, they could only obtain from them going with their bodies safe. And so, they rendered the place. And they each went to a bastion under their control, both the captain and others. And a captain was left and ordained the guardian of the said place.

Comme laplace. detombellaine fut Rendue. aux francois

Apres. laReddicion dud avranches alla led duc debretaigne et ſon oſt devant la place detombellaine qui eſt une treſſforte place et Imprenable tant quil yait vivres dedans Icelle car elle eſt toute aſſiſe ſur Roc en leurs et pres du mont Saint michiel. En laquelle avoit pour garniſon. deiiii^{xx}. acent angloiz leſquelz voyans ſi groſſe puiſſance devant eulx ſe Rendirent par compoſicion telle quilz ſen devoiẽt aller leurs corps et biens ſaufz. Ainſſi ſen allerẽt cherebourc et Rendirent Icelle place. Aquoy fut cômes et ordonne pour lagarde decelle.

Audit an xvi Iour dud moys deMay. fiſt le Roy mettre leſiege devant lacite et ville ~~devreux~~ debayeulx. et yvint monſ^{r}. leconte dedunois lieutenant general duRoy. les contes de nevers et deu. Legrant maiſtre. doſtel meſſire phlẽs decullant mareſchal defrance Monſ^{r} dorval. Monſ^{r}. dubueil et pluſſieurs autẽs capitaines chevalliers et eſcuiers. Et fut logie led lieutenant et ſacompaignie es faulxbours ~~deveres~~ dedevers carentan firẽt logez les contes declermont et decaſtres et ceulx deleur com paignie qui avec eulx avoient eſte en labataille defromygny et alaprinſe devire. Et es faulxbours ducoſte des cordelliers eſtoient logiez monſ^{r} demontenay conduiſeur des gens duduc dalencon pierre louvain. Robert connigan avec grant nôbre defrancs archiers. Et tindrent leſiege leſd ſ^{r} devant lad ville par leſpace dexvi. Iours pendant lequel temps firent les francois grans approches defoſſez et demynes. Et tellement batuz de canons et de-

How the place of Tombelaine was rendered to the French

After the reduction of the said Avranches, the said duke of Brittany and his army went before the place of Tombelaine, which was a very strong place and nearly impenetrable, such that it had supplies within because it was situated on a rock, like mount Saint-Michael. In which place there was a garrison of 80 to 100 Englishmen, who, seeing so great power before them, rendered themselves by agreement such that they ought to leave safely with their bodies and their goods. Thus, they went to Cherbourg and rendered this place. To which was committed and ordered for the guardianship of this place.

In the said year, the sixteenth day of the said month of May, the king laid siege before the city and town of Bayeux, and monseigneur the count of Dunois, lieutenant general of the king; the counts of Nevers and Eu; the grand master of the hotel; messire Philippe de Culant, marshal of France; monseigneur d'Orval; monseigneur de Bueil, and several other captains, knights, and squires, went there. And the said lieutenant and his company camped in the suburbs near Carentan, [and] the counts of Clermont and Castres and those of their company who, with them, had been at the battle of Frémigny and at the capture of Vire were encamped. And in the suburbs, on the side toward Cordeliers, were lodged monseigneur de Montenay, leader of the men of the duke of Alençon; Pierre Louvain; and Robert Connigan, with a great number of free archers. And the said lords held the siege before the said town for the space of sixteen days, during which time the French made great approaches by tunnels and mines.

trait donc eſtoient gouvr̃neurs et conduiſeurs Maiſtre Iehan bureau treſorier defrance et Iaſpar bureau ſon frere maiſtre delartillerye que toute lamuraille eſtoit pr̃ce et abatue. Et tellement quil ne falloit pl⁹ que aſſallir. Et dece faire furẽt Requis leſd lieutenant ⁊aut̂ ſeigneurs et capitaines. Leſquelz conſiderans lagrant effuſion deſang ladeſolacion delad ville et autres maulx grans et Immurables qui ſen pouroient enſ ſi elle eſte prinſe daſſault ne levouldrent conſentr̃. Maiz ce non obſtant ſans congie ou autorite et ſans ordonance delagrant ardeur et convoitiſe q̂ avoient les gens deguerre degaigner aſſalliret̂ lad cite deux foiz en ung meſme Iour. Et oult moult belles armes faictes tant den coſte q̂ daut̂ deſquelles deux parties en yot pluſſieurs demors detrait et decoulevrines et convint aux francois eulx Retraire ſans aut̂ choſe faire pource que laſſault neſtoit que dun coſte. Et ſeladville euſt eſte aſſallye par lordonnance deſd ſeigne[rs] et capitaines ſans quelq̂ difficulte lad cite euſt eſte emportee daſſault. led mathago cap[ne] dedans Icelle fut fort eſpouvante delavallans [...] avoit venue es francois qui avoient aſſailly car [...] fut tue devaillans duparty deſd angloiz. Et [...] commenca aparlementer avec led conte dedunoiz et aut̂s ſeigneurs eſtans en ſacompaigne. Et apres pluſſieurs parolles dictes ent̂eulx led mathago et ſes gens tracterent ⁊compoſerent en lamanr̃e que enſ. Et quelq̂ compoſicion quilz demandaſſent ne peuret̂ obtenir pour [...] productions que deulx en allr̃ ung baſton chacun ſamain ſeullement. Et ainſſi ſen alleret̂ et ſaillirent dicelle ~~de~~ cite par laporte duchaſteau [...] leſd angloiz nombrez aneuf cens Renounes les plus vaillans gens deleur party pour [...] en aller acherbourg. Maiz combien fut telle q̂ dit eſt. Neantmoins leſd francois po[r] lonneur de-

And they bombarded with canons and arrows, which was overseen and conducted by master Jean Bureau, treasurer of France, and Gaspar Bureau, his brother, master of the artillery, that all the wall was pierced and battered, and such that it was no longer necessary to assault. And the said lieutenant and other lords and captains asked to do this. Who, considering the great loss of blood, the desolation of the said town, and other great and innumerable ills which would have followed if it had been taken by assault, would not consent. But this notwithstanding, without leave nor authority and without orders, for the great passion and desire which the men of war had to win, they assaulted the said city twice on the same day. And there were many beautiful feats of arms, both on one side and the other, of which two parties there were several killed by arrowfire and gunfire, and the French convinced them to retreat without doing anything else, for which the assault was only on one side. And the said town had been assailed by order of the said lords and captains; without any difficulty, the said city had been captured by assault; the said Matthew Gough, captain within, who was very terrified of the bravery [that] had come to the French, who had assaulted, because […] there were killed brave men of the party of the said English. And […] he spoke with the said count of Dunois and other lords who were in his company. And after several words said between them, the said Matthew Gough and his soldiers negotiated and composed in the manner which follows. And whatever agreement that they requested, they could obtain by […] productions that those in going each to a bastion in his hand alone. And thus, they went and sallied from this city by the gate of the castle, […] the said Englishmen numbering 900, reputed to be the most valliant of their party, in order […] to go to Cherbourg. But such was as

gentilleſſe leur laiſſerent partie deleurs chevaulx pour porter les damoiſelles et gentilz femmes. Et avecques ce leurs firent delivrer des charettes pour porter aucuns aut̂s pour porter aucuns des plus notables femmes deceulx angloiz qui ſen alloient avecques leurs mariz leſquelles Il faiſoit piteux veoir car Ilz partirent dicelle cite detrois aquatre cens femmes ſans les enffans donc Ilz avoit grant nombre les unes portoient les petits enffans en barſſeaulx ſur leurs teſtes les aut̂s ſur leur colz. les unes en avoient de penduz entour leurs corps en bandeaulx de toille et les aut̂s quilz tenoient par les mains et lemieux quilz pouvoient. Et ainſſi demoura lad cite en lobbeiſſance du Roy defrance. Ala~~go~~ quelle gouvr̂ner miſt pro viſion et officiers pour leRoy led conte de dunoiz ſon lieutenant gnal̂. Et cefait pâſ lui leconte declermont et leurs compaignies et tout loſt laRiviere dorne. Et mirent leurs gens vivre ſur ~~lepys en~~ lepays. en actendant lavenue duconte deRichemont conneſtable defrance. Et laiſſa aud bayeaux canons coulevrines et toute aut̂ artillerie pour allr̂ mettre leſiege acaen. Et deſe puis cetraicte fait yot pluſſieurs granes donnes et faictes par led conte dedunoiz aud mattre et ſes adherans. Pourquoy led traicte eſtre Iurire et mis par eſcript en laforme ⁊mannier qui ſenſuyt.

La traicte debayeulx.

Appoinctement fait par monſr. leconte dedunoiz lieutenant general duRoy. ſur lefait deſaguerre et les aut̂s ſeigneurs duſang Royal et gens duconſeil eſtans en ſiege devant bayeulx avecques mathago capitaine des gens darmes et detrait eſtans dedens lad ville pour et au nom

it was said. Nonetheless, the said Frenchmen, for the honour of gentility, allowed them to keep some of their horses to carry the damsels and gentlewomen. And with this, they had carts brought in to transport some of the more notable women of these Englishmen, who had been with their husbands, which was pitiful to see, because 300 to 400 women left from this city, without the children, although they had a great number; some carried the small children in cradles on their heads, others around their necks, some had taken them around their bodies in cloth wraps, and others held them by the hand and did the best they could. And so, the said city remained in the obedience of the king of France, for which governance the said count of Dunois, his lieutenant general, made provisions and officers for the king. And this being done, the count of Clermont and their companies and all the army crossed the River Orne. And they dispersed their men to forage in the land, waiting for the coming of the earl of Richmond, constable of France. And he left in the said Bayeux cannon, culverines, and all the other artillery, in order to lay siege to Caen. And for this then, this treaty made there had several great words and deeds by the said count of Dunois to the said Matthew and his adherents. For which the said treaty being composed and put in writing in the form and manner that follows.

The treaty of Bayeux

Agreement made by monseigneur the count of Dunois, lieutenant general of the king for the course of the war, and the other lords of royal blood and men of the council who were at the siege before Bayeux, with Matthew Gough, captain of the men-at-arms and conscript being within the said town, for and

deux et des gens degliſe nobles bourgois et hâtans dicelle en lamaniere qui ſenſ Premierement. que led capitaine hommes darmes archiers et autͣs gens deguerre eſtans en lad garniſon bailleront amonſʳ leconte dedunoiz pour et en nom duRoy lad ville et chaſteau debayeulx Rallement et defait dedens lemardy prochainement venant ahuit heures dumatin. Et pour ſeurete dece baillerôt hoſtages bons ⁊ſuffiſans Iucques au nombre de xii. Ceſt aſſavoir ſix deſd gens deguerre et ſix des bourgeois delad ville. C Item de dens ceIour demardy finy. ſedepartiront et en yront ceulx delad ville tēn leparty du Roy. dangleterre decelle ville ⁊chaſteau debayeulx apie ung baſton ſeullement en leur poing. Et ne pourront porter aucuns deleurs biens or ne argent avecques eulx. Maiz ſeront tenuz deles laiſſer en lad ville et les baillr̃ par Inventoire aceulx qui ace fr̃ ſeront cômis de par mond ſʳ ſauf et Reſerve que degrace et courtoiſie. Aeſte promis auſdeſſſd gens deguerre delagarniſon depouvoir emporter avecques eulx pour faire leurs deſpens ſur les champs. Ceſt aſſavoir chc̄n homme darmes Iucques adix eſcuz et chc̄n des autͣs. v. eſcuz avec leur veſture decorps autͣ q̂habillemens deguerre. Ceſt aſſavoir une Robe ou Iacquette chc̄n chapperon chauſſes ſoulliers et chemiſe tant ſeullement. C Item et ſen yront leſdeſſſd en angletͤre ou es Iſles par laville decherbourg ſans entrer acaen garniz debon ſaufconduit qui pource faire leur ſera baille et ne pourront demourer en aucunes villes ou place tenues par aucuns deleur party ne faire guerre durãt letemps deleur ſaufconduit. Et cilz ſont trouvez faiſans lecontraire Ilz ſeront exceptez ⁊forcloz detous traitez et compoſicions durant led tp̄s. C Item aeſte promis auſdeſſſd degrace et courtoiſie q̂ toꝰ ceulx qui vouldront de-

in the name of those [people] and the people of the church, nobles, citizens, and inhabitants of this place, in the manner that follows: Firstly, that the said captain, men-at-arms, archers, and other men of war being in the said garrison release to monseigneur the count of Dunois, for and in the name of the king, the said town and castle of Bayeux in reality and in fact, by the following Tuesday, at eight in the morning. And for surety of this, good and sufficient hostages will be delivered until the number is twelve; it is known, six of the said men of war and six of the citizens of the said town. Item, by this day of Tuesday, those of the said town holding to the party of the king of England will leave and go from this town and castle of Bayeux, on foot, with only a stick in their hand. And they cannot take any of their goods or money with them, but they will be required to leave them in the said town, and give them to be inventoried by those who will be commissioned for this by said monseigneur safely and save only by the grace and courtesy that has been promised to the abovesaid men of war of the garrison to be able to take with them in order to pay their expenses on the field—it is known, each man of arms up to ten *écus* and each of the other five *écus* with their clothes except for war clothing; it is known, each a robe or jacket, cape, shoes, breeches, and shirt, but only these. Item, and the abovesaid would go to England, or the islands, by way of the town of Cherbourg, without entering Caen, carrying [letters] of good safe conduct, which would be delivered to them, and they would not remain in any of the towns or places held by any of their party, nor make war during the time of their said safe conduct. And if they were found doing the contrary, they would be exempted and left out from all treaties and agreements during the said time. Item it has been promised to the abovesaid, by

mouȓ en lad ville dequelq̂ eſtat pays nacion ou condicion quilz ſoient faire lepourront dedens letemps et tȓme dedeux moys et ſeront Receus aſerment deſtre bons ⁊loyaulx gens leRoy de france et leur ſeront Reſtituez leurs heritages poceſſions et biens quelzconques. Et ſi ſen pourront allȓ ſibon leur ſemble en lamaniere deſſſd comme les gens deguerre et ſemploieront leſd ſ[rs] devers leRoy. deRecevoir to⁹ les hâtans delad ville qui demourer vouldront en ſabonne grace et deleur en faire avoir lectres. ℭ Item et ne pourront ceulx delad ne autȇs qui demôrerot̂ en Icelle ne autȇs advouer aeulx appartenir aucuns des biens deceulx qui ſen yront neles Receler. Maiz ſeront tenus deles denôcer ſi aucuns en ont aceulx qui ace fȓ ſeront cômis ſur paine deperdre leurs biens et depaier lamende. ℭ Item ſeront Reſtituez par ceulx delad gȓniſon to⁹ priſonniers et ſcellez qui ont deceulx duparty du Roy et demoureront quictes envȓs eulx tous ceulx dud party detoutes foy et promeſſes quilz leur pouroient avoir faictes acanſe delaguerre et aut̂ment. ℭ Item ſeront Reſtituez et Reſtabliz depar ceulx delad garniſon to⁹ les Ioyaulx et ornemens degliſe qui pourroient par eulx avoir eſte prinſes es egliſes delad ville et ceulx bourgs dicelle. ℭ Item que toutes dames damoiſelles et femmes eſtat mariees auront degrace don et courtoiſie tous les Ioyaulx a elles appartenans. ℭ Item que to⁹ les gens qui ſeront blacez ou en enfermete decorps qui ſont gens deguerre pourront demourer en lad ville pour eulx faire garer Iucques aung moys. Et ſe Ilz ſeveullent partir leur ſera baille ſaufcôduit bon et vallable pour eulx en allȓ en Royaulme dangletȇre. Toutes leſquelles choſes devant dictes et chacūe dicelles. No⁹ conte dedunoiz lieutenat̂ devant nomme promettons par la foy

grace and courtesy, that all those who would remain in the said town, from any state, country, nation, or condition that they had been, they will be able to do so for the time and length of two months, and would be received by oaths to be good and loyal men to the king of France, and they would be restored to their priviledges, possessions, and any goods. And they can go if they wish wherever they want in the manner abovesaid, as the men of war, and the said lords will work for the king to receive all the inhabitants of the said town who would remain in his good grace and to have letters made for them. Item and neither those of the said place, nor others who remain in this place can hold onto that which belonged to them any of the goods of those who will leave nor conceal them, but they will be required to denounce them, if none have, to those who will do this, under threat of losing their goods and paying amends. Item all prisoners and seals that they had by those of the party of the king will be restituted by those of the said garrison, and all those of the said party will remain quit of all oaths and promises that they could have made for the cause of the war or otherwise. Item all jewelry and ornaments of the church that could have been taken by them from the church of the said town and those suburbs of this place will be restituted and restored by those of the said garrison. Item that all ladies, damsels, and women in a state of marriage should have, by grace, donation, and courtesy, all the jewelry and clothing that belongs to them. Item that all the people who were wounded or were otherwise infirm in the body, who were men of war, would remain in the said town, in order for them to be healed, for a month. And if they wanted to leave, they would be released with good and valuable safe conduct in order to go to the kingdom of England. All of which things before said and each of

et ſerment denoſ̃ corps et ſur noſ̃ honneur detenir. enſ̃tener et acomplir depoint en point ſans fraulde barat ne mal engin. Et en teſmoing dece no⁹ avons ſigne ſes prêtes de noſ̃ main. et fait ſceller duſeau denoz armes Le xviᵐ Iour de Maẙ Lan mil CCCC Cinquâte. Et laconcluſion demathago eſt Toutes leſquelles choſes devant dictes No⁹ mathago capitaine devant nomme tant pour no⁹. comme prenant en main ~~par~~ pour to⁹ les gens deguerre et autres eſtans en lad ville debayeulx. Promettons par lafoy et ſerment denoſ̃ corps et ſur noſ̃ honneur tenir anſ̃tere et acomplir depoint en point Lecontenu ence peſ̃ traicte ſans fraulde barat ou mal engin. Et en teſmoin dece no⁹ avons ſigne ces prêtes denoſ̃ main et fait ſeller duſeau denoz armes. lexviᵐIour de May Lan mille CCCC Cinquante. Ainſſi ſigne. Mathago.

Laprinſe debriquebec p̲ les francois.

EN ce meſme temps leconeſtable defrance. Et ceulx deſacompaignie Ceſt aſſavoir Les gens demonſʳ delaval Lemareſchal de loheac. les gens deladmiral delamer. Et monſʳ deſtouteville prindrent laville de bricquebec et lamirent en lamain duRoy parmy ce quilz ſen alleret̃ leurs bes⁀ 7corps ſaufz.

Leſiege devallongnes mis p̲ les francois.

Apres laReddicion dud bricquebec ſen alla led coneſtable mettre leſiege devant laville devallongnes qui nagueres avoit eſte prinſe des angloiz ſur les francois devat̃ laquelle ne fut guerres. Maiz ſeRendirent toſt apres

them we, count of Dunois, lieutenant abovenamed, promise by the faith and oath of our body and on our honour, to hold, attend to, and accomplish precisely, without deceit, trickery, or evil intent. And in witness for this, we have signed these letters in our hand and made to seal it with the seal of our arms, the sixth day of May, the year 1450. And the conclusion by Matthew Gough was: all these things before said, we, Mathew Gough, captain before named, as much for us as taking into account all the men of war and others in the said town of Bayeux, we promise by the faith and the oath of our body and on our honour, to hold, attend, and accomplish point-by-point the contents presented in this treaty, without deceit, trickery, or evil intent, and in witness for this, we have sealed with the seal of our arms, the sixteenth day of May [in] the year 1450. Thus signed: Matthew Gough.

The capture of Bricquebec by the French

In this same time, the constable of France. And those of his company—it is known: the men of monseigneur de Laval, the marshal of Lohéac, the men of the admiral of the sea, and monseigneur d'Estouteville, captured the town of Bricquebec and they put it into the hand of the king, for which they went safely, their goods and bodies.

The siege of Vallongnes laid by the French

After the reduction of the said Bricquebec, the said constable went to lay siege before the town of Vallongnes, which not long ago had been captured by the English from the French, before there was war. But they rendered themselves soon after-

pource que lelieutenant dicelle place qui en avoit lagarde depar leRoy ~ dangleťre ceſtoit fait francois. Et pource trouva facon avec led conneſtable que les angloiz eſtans en lad ville Iucques au nombre devi.^{XX} angloiz ſen yroient acherbourg leurs corps et ~~vens~~ biens ſaufz. Ainſſi parce moyen ſepartireť Iceulx angloiz. Et laiſſirent lad ville en lobbeiſſance du Roy defrance.

Leſiege deSaint Sauve^r. Leviconte mis par les francois

APRES. ledepartirent duduc debretaigne led coneſtable defrance ſetira abayeulx. Et envoya Iacques deluxembourc ſon lieuteñ Et oudet daidye en ſacompaignie avec XXX. lances devant Saint ſauveur leviconte qui eſt moult belle place. Et lune des plus fortes deNormendie affin deymettre leſiege ou Ilz demourerent trois Iours en actendant lavenue des mareſchaulx defrance et debretaigne des ſeigneurs deſtouteville debouſſac ⁊autres delaquelle eſtoit capitaine. leſire deRobeſſac ung baron dehaynault qui avoit en lad place en garniſon II^{C}. combatans. leſd mareſchaulx et auťs acenttre led ſiege firent moult vaillammeť et grandement leur devoirs. Et firent degrans approuches et trenchees en faiſant leſquelles fit tue dun rauon ung vaillant eſcuier dupays deberry. nomme Iehan b^lancheford qui fut moult plaine. Et tantoſt apres les voyans leſd angloiz eſtre ſi oppreſſez ſans ce quilz fuſſent grevez decanons ne dautres engins car Ilz eſtoient to⁹ chargez pour meure acaen comme dit eſt Commencerent aparlementer. Et comme gens ayans leceur failly Rendirent lad place par comp^on telle quilz ſen devoient allř leurs corps et leurs biens

wards because the lieutenant of this place, who had the guardianship on behalf of the king of England, switched sides to the French. And for this, he found means with the said constable for the Englishmen who were in the said town, the number of which was 120 Englishmen, to go to Cherbourg, their bodies and goods safe. Thus, by this means, these Englishmen left. And they left the said town in the obedience of the king of France.

The siege of Saint-Saint-Sauveur-le-Viconte laid by the French

After the departure of the duke of Brittany, the said constable of France went to Bayeux. And he sent Jacques of Luxembourg, his lieutenant, and Odet d'Aidie in his company with thirty lances before Saint-Sauveur-le-Viconte, which was a very great place. And one of the strongest in Normandy, in order to lay siege there, where they remained for three days, preparing for the coming of the marshals of France and Brittany, of the seigneurs d'Estouteville, of Boussac, and others, over whom was captain the sire de Robessac, a baron of Hainault, who had garrisoned in this place 200 soldiers; the said marshals and others performed their work very bravely and grandly at the said siege. And they made approaches and trenches, a brave squire of the land of Berry named Jean Blanchefort, was killed while doing this, which was very sad. And soon afterwards, the Englishmen, seeing themselves to be so hard pressed, without which they still were afraid of cannon and other artillery, because they were all going to Caen, it is said, they began to speak. And as people having feeble hearts, they rendered the said place by agreement such that they must go, their bodies and goods safe, in eight

ſaufz ahuit Iours devvdange. Ainſſi par ce moyen fut Rendue lad ville deſaint ſauve^{r} leviconte etmiſe en lobeiſſance du-Roy. Et ce fait ſepartirent leſd mareſchaulx et chevaucherent Iucques adeux lieues pres de caen en ~~ung~~ ung village nomme ceux. ou eſtoit logiez led conneſtable et ſacompaigne. Et menoient avant eulx leſd mareſchalz les hoſtages que leſd angloiz avoient baillez po^{r} fereus lappoinctement q̂ dit eſt pource quilz ſepartirent et natendirent point les huit Iours devvydange q̂ les angloiz devoient avoir avvyder leurs biens dededens lad place. Avec led conneſtable eſtoient leconte delaval leſire deloheac ſon frere mareſchal defrance leſ^{r} deRaiz. Decoitivy. admiral defrance. leſire demontauban mareſchal debretaigne Le ſeneſchal depoitou. meſſire Iacques deluxembourg Leſire demaleſtroit. Leſire deſaincte ſevere et debouſſac et pluſſieurs autres chevalliers et eſcuiers.

Siege mis acaen par les francois.

LE. cinquieſme Iour deIuing aud an ſedeſloga led conneſtable et ſacôpaignie deſſuſd dud lieu deceux. Et ſen ala logier es faulxbours delaville decaen ducoſte dedevr̂s bayeulx dedens labbaẙe Saint Eſtienne pres delamuraille dicelle ville. Et ce Iour meſmes ſe partit devernueil. monſ^{r}. leconte deRichemont avecques lequel eſtoient leconte decaſtres le ſ^{r} demontgaſcon. leſ.^{r} demouy en beauvoiſin Robert coningan. Robert deflocques bailly devreulx pierre louvain. meſſ^{r} guiffroy decouvran meſſ^{r} charles delafayette et pluſſ^{rs}. aut̂s ſ^{rs} chevaliers et eſcuiers qui ſevindrent tous logier avecques led conneſtable aud lieu deſaint eſtienne. Et eſtoient en nombre avecq͡z leſdits deux ſ.^{rs} xii.^{C} lances.

days to vacate [the place]. Thus, by this means, the said town of Saint-Sauveur-le-Viconte was rendered into the obedience of the king. And this being done, the said marshals left and rode until two leagues near Caen, in a village named Cheux, where the constable and his company were camped. And the said marshals, taking with them the hostages that the said English had released in order to accomplish the agreement that is said, for which they left and no longer waited the eight days to leave, that the English are required to leave their goods within this place. With the said constable were then the count of Laval; the sire de Lohéac, his brother, marshal of France; the sire de Rais, of Coïtivy, admiral of France; the sire de Montauban, marshal of Brittany; the seneschal of Poitou; messire Jacques de Luxembourg; the sire of Malestroit; le sire of Saint-Sevère, and Boussac; and several other knights and squires.

Siege laid at Caen by the French

The fifth day of June in the said year, the said constable and his company decamped from the said place of Cheux. And they went to camp in the suburbs of the town of Caen on the side toward Bayeux, within the abbey of Saint-Étienne, near the wall of this town. And this same day, monseigneur the earl of Richmond left from Vernueil, with whom were the count of Castres; the seigneur de Montgascon; the seigneur de Mouy-en-Beauvoisin; Robert Coningan; Robert de Floques, bailiff of Évreux; Pierre Louvain; messire Geoffroi de Couvran; messire Charles de Lafayète; and several other lords, knights, and squires, who were all camped with the said constable in this place of Saint-Étienne. And with the said two lords, there were around 1,200 lanc-

et. Iiii.M et v.M archiers guiſarmiers et couſtilliers. et ii.C francs archiers apie. Et monſr leconte dedunoiz lieutēn gn̄rl du Roy ſedeſloga dedemye lemire pres de lad ville decheu. Et ſe vint logier es faulxbours devaucelles ducoſte dediveres pars. Et avoit et ſacompaignie monſr lagrant maiſtre doſtel ſe decullant. leſ.r dormal. meſſ.r phl̄s decullāt ſe delalongnes et mareſchal defrance. monſr dumontenay gouv̂neur des gens darmes du duc dalencon. leſr dmy provoſt deparis. le ſe deviammont ſon frevor et pluſſ.rs aut̂s Iucq̄z au nombre dev.C lances et de. Ii.M v.C archers guſarmes couſtillers archival. et de ii.M frans archers apie. Ainſſi fut aſſiegee lad ville des deux coſtez puis firent faire diligemmet̂ ung pont audeſſus delad ville pour paſſer la Riviere dun coſte ⁊daut̂. Pardeſſus lequel paſſerent leiiiine Iour apres. Les contes de Nevers et deu. leſire dubueil. leſ.r demontenay Ioachim Rouault. et avecques eulx grant compaignie degens darmes et detraict. leſquelz ſen allerent logr̂ es faulxbours delad ville ducoſte dedevers lamer et en une abbaye dedames nômee latrinite. Et ſitoſt que leſd francois furet̂ aRrivez fut aſſaillx leboullevart delaporte par ou len va abayeulx. Lequel fut moult vaillemmet̂ deffendu. Et yot demoult belles armes faites tant dun coſte q̂ daut̂. Et neant moins en laffin fut prins daſſault par les frâcois Leſquelz lelaiſſerent depuis pource quil eſtoit ouvert ducoſte dedevers lamuraille dicelle ville et ſemblablement demoura deſampare et fut habandonne par les angloiz pource quilz firent murer leur porte pour venir aud ſiege Cepartit leRoy defrance delaville dargentain en ſacompaignie leRoy deCecille leduc de calabre ſon filz leduc dalencon. les contes du maine ſaint pol. et detancarville le viconte delomaigne ferry monſr deloraine Iehan ſon

es and 4,000 to 5,000 archers, pikemen, and swordsmen, with 200 free archers on foot. And monseigneur the count of Dunois, lieutenant general of the king, decamped half a league away near the said town of Cheux. And they went to camp in the suburbs of Vaucelles on different sides. And he had in his company monseigneur the grand master of the hotel, the sire de Culant, the seigneur d'Orval, monseigneur Philippe de Culant, sire de Jalongnes, and marshal of France, monseigneur du Montenau, governor of the men-at-arms of the duke of Alencon, the seigneur de Muy, provost of Paris, the sire de Viammont, his servant, and several others until the number was 500 lances and 2,500 archers, pikemen, and swordsmen on horseback, and 2,000 free archers on foot. So the said town was besieged on two sides, then they made diligent effort at a bridge below the said town to cross the river on one side and the other, the above which was crossed on the fourth day afterwards by the counts of Nevers and Eu, the sire of Bueil, the seigneur of Montenay, Joachim Rouault, and with them a great company of men-at-arms and treaty men, who went to camp in the suburbs of the said town, on the side toward the sea, and in an abbey of ladies named La Trinité. And as soon as the said Frenchmen had arrived, the bulwerk of the gate was assaulted by those on the side toward Bayeux, which was very villigently defended. And then there were many great feats both on one side and the other. And nonetheless, at the end it was captured by assault by the French, which they then left, because it was open on the side toward the wall of this town, and similarly, it remained disabled and was abandoned by the English, because they walled off their gate in order to come to the said siege. The king left from the town of Argentain in the company of the king of Sicily; the duke of Calabria, his son; the duke of Alençon; the counts of Maine, of Saint-Pol, and of Tancarville; the viscount of

frere. lebaron detraynel chancelr̃ defrance les ſeigneurs deblainville et de prully. les baillifz deberry et delyon. Et pluſſieurs autſ̃ chevalliers eſcuiers gens darmes et detrait Iucques au nombre devi^{C} lances et les archiers. et alacoucher aſaint pere ſur yve. Et lelendemain aargences. Et le tres^{me} Iour vint diſgner auxfaulxbours devaucelles puis ſepartit Incontinent et paſſa laRiviere par deſſus led pont. Et ſen alla logier dedans une abbaye nommee ardenne ouIl fut duraт̂ led ſiege đ fors une nuyt quil fut logie en paſſant en lad abbaye delatrinite ou demoureret̂ leRoy deCecille leduc decalabre ſon filz et les autres ſeigneurs qui eſtoient venus avecques leRoy atout mille lances. deux mille archiers acheval. mille guiſarmiers et couſtilleurs a cheval. et deux cens francs archiers apie doĉ laplus part eſtoient logez es villages denviron. Et entre les chaſteau et abbaye dud Saint etienne eſtoient logiez les ſ^{rs} debeavoiz et debourbonnoiz qui avoient <u>moult bien fait leur devoir</u> trente lances. et mil. et cinq cens frans archiers. Tantoſt apres lavenue duRoy furent faites grandes diligences demynez et defoſſouier autour delad ville. Et faiſoit ung chu͡n endroit ſoy grant devoir. Et commêca premierement led conte dedunoiz lieutenant duRoy. afaire aſſallir les boullevers devaue͡ll qui eſtoient ſur lad Riviere dorne. leſquelz ſetindret̂ longuement et yfut combatu et deffendu treſvaillemment dun coſte et dautre. Maiz en laffin apres pluſſieurs beaulx faitz devers furet̂ leſd boullevars par leſd francois. Et yfurent prins mors et navrez grant foiſon dangloiz qui moult eſbahit leurs compaignons. Et en ch͡cn deſd logis dud ſiege avoit myn̊es Iucques dedens les foſſez delad ville. Et par eſpecial ducoſte dedevers led conneſtable ſes gens darmes mynerent ducoſte dedevers Saint eſtienne. Et

Lomagne; Ferry, monseigneur de Lorraine; Jean, his brother; the baron of Traignel, chancellor of France; the seigneurs de Blainville and de Prailly; the bailliffs of Berry and Lyon, and several other knights and squires, men-at-arms and conscripts, until the number was 600 lances and the archers, and he went to rest at Saint-Père-sur-Yve, and the next day at Argences. And the third day he went to dine at the suburbs of Vaucelles, then he left immediately and crossed the river by the abovesaid bridge, and he went to lodge within an abbey named Ardannes, where he stayed during the said siege; then, one night he lodged in passing in the said abbey of La Trinité, where the king of Sicily, the duke of Calabria, his son, and the other lords who had come with the king were situated—in all about 1,000 lances, 2,000 archers on horseback, 1,000 pikemen and swordsmen on horseback, and 2,000 free archers on foot, of whom the majority were camped in the surrounding villages. And between the castle and the said abbey of Saint-Étienne the seigneurs of Beauvais and of Bourbonnais were camped, who had well over thirty lances and 1,500 free archers. Soon after the coming of the king, great attempts were made to mine and dig trenches around the said town. And each one of them did his great duty. And the said count of Dunois, lieutenant of the king, began firstly to make an assault on the bulwerks of Vausselles, which were on the said River Orne, which held out for a long time and they fought and defended very bravely by one side and the other. But in the end, after several great feats, the said bulwerks were captured by the French. And a great amount of Englishmen were captured, killed, and wounded there, which greatly upset their companies. And in each of the said camps of the said siege were mines as far as the moats of the said town. And especially toward the side of the said constable, [because] his men-at-arms mined on the side toward Saint-Éti-

tellement que tout trabucha et cheut aŧre. Et pouvoient combatre les francois et les angloiz par Icellui lieu main amain. Et quant leſd angloiz ſevirent ainſſi fort oppreſſez et approuchez detoutes pars doubtans quilz ne fuſſent prins daſſault demanderent et Requirent aavoir traitie. Aquoy le-Roy de france meu depitie et decompaſſion qui ne demande pas lamort des pechenersm. Maiz lui ſuffiſt quilz ſecomêtiſſant en mettant dieu devaŧ lui. Conſiderant auſſi lagrant pirie et dommage q̂ ceuſt eſte dedeſtruire une telle ville. devioller les egliſes et piller les egliſes fammes et filles deſpuceler. Conſiderans auſſi leffuſion duſangt humaine qui euſt peu eſtre fait dedens lad ville. Ce ~~contit~~ conſentit voult et octroya q̂on print lad ville par compoſicion. Et en verite elle eſtoit p̊enable daſſault veu les ouv̂tures et Romptiens qui Ia eſtoient faites es murailles dicelle. Et quant auRegard duchaſteau et du donIon leſd angloiz les pouvoient bien tenir parlongue eſpace detep̄s cilz euſſeŧ eu couraige def[r]. Combien que enfin laffin veu lachevallerie et compaignie qui devant eulx eſtoit Il leur euſt fallu Rendre. Et pour monſtr̂ quil eſtoit tenable aceux qui nẙont point eſte. vray eſt que led chaſteau eſt ung des plus fors deNormendie garny dehaulx et grans boullevers de moult dure pierre et aſſiz ſur Roc. Lequel contient deſtendue par eſtimacion autant q̂ laville de corbueil. Et ya ung treſſort donIon fait dune large et haulte tour cacore entretenere fut autour dequatre groſſez tours maſſives depuis lepie du foſſe Iucques auhault alegal delaŧre. Leſquelles ſont moult haultes. et eſt fermee de haultes murailles et forte tout atour ſelon la quallite deſd tour. et degrans et parfous foſſez et tout aſſiz ſur Roc. dedens led chaſteau ſe tenoit leduc deſombrecet et ſafemme et enffans.

enne and such that everything fell and crumbled to the ground. And the Frenchmen and the Englishmen had to fight at this place hand-to-hand. And when the said Englishmen saw that they were so overwhelmed and surrounded on all sides, fearing that they would be captured by assault, they asked and requested to have a treaty. For which the king of France showed pity and compassion that he did not demand the death of his enemies. But he offered to them that they commit to putting God before them, considering also the great tragedy and damage that they caused to be destroyed such a town, to violate the churches and pillage the churches and deflower the women and girls. Considering also the effusion of human blood that could have been made within the said town. Consenting to this, he wanted and granted that one take the said town by agreement. And in truth, it was very easy to assault, considering the openings and breaches that were already made on the walls of this place. And upon looking at the castle and the moat, the English could very well hold them for a long space of time if they had had courage to do it. Such that, in the end, seeing the knighthood and company which was before them, he would have needed to render to them. And in order to show that it was tenable to those who had no longer been true was that the said castle is one of the most fortified in Normandy, supported by high and great bulwerks of very strong stone and seated on a rock, which contained by extent as an estimation the space of the town of Corbeil. And there is a very strong keep, composed of a large and high tower, sustained all around by four massive towers, masoned from the bottom of the trench to the top, equal to what comes closest to the earth, which towers were very high, and it is enclosed by high and strong walls all around, according to the quality of the said towers, and by large and deep trenches, and all situated on a rock, within the said castle, the duke of Som-

Et en lad ville eſtoient logiez. meſſire Robert veer. frere duconte deſufford. meſſ^re^ henry Ra defort. meſſ^re^ expencier. henry ſtandy. guil͡e cournon. guillaume loquet. fourques eton. henry lois et pluſſieurs autȿ leſquilz eſtoient côduiſ.^rs^ pour leduc deſombrecet de.iiii^m^ angloiz eſtans dedens lad ville pour lagarde decelle pour entrer doncques en lamatiere delad compoſicion ſaſſemblerent et convêſerent pluſſieurs foiz les angloiz et francois. Ceſt aſſavoir pour le Roy defrance led conte dedunoiz ſeneſchal depoitou ſ^r^ Iehan bureau treſorier defrance ⁊aucûs autȿ. Pour les angloiz. meſſire Richard hereſſon bailly decaen. Robert parges et aucuns autȿ. Et po^r^ lad ville. Euſtache gaumet lieutenant dud bailly et labbe dud Saint eſtienne. leſquelz parlamenterent et alleguerent pluſſieurs choſes en fortiffiant ch͡cn ſon fait. Et apres pluſſieurs parolles dictes ent̂ eulx compoſerent lelendemain delafeſte monſ^r^ ſainct Iehan baptiſte. Et promedroit̂ led angloiz mettre lad ville et chaſteau donIon es mains et obbeiſſance du Roy defrance dedans lepremier Iour deIuillet prouchain enſuivant ou cas quilz necombatroient leRoy et ſapuiſſance dedens led Iour parmy ce que led duc deſombrecet ſafemme et ſes enffans et autȿ angloiz qui ſen vouldroient en aller ſen yroient eulx leurs leurs femmes et enffans. Et emporteroient to⁹ leurs biens meubles. Et ſen yroient leurs corps chevaulx et harnoiz ſaufz. et porter et mener leurſd biens ou leur bailleroit vaiſſeaulx ⁊charoy et ce qui ſeroit deneceſſite pour paſſer en anglet̂re et non ailleurs aleurs deſpens et non aut̂ment. Pourveu toutefſoiz que Iceulx angloiz delivreroient to⁹ priſonniers Rendroient to⁹ ſcellez et quiteroiet̂ to⁹ ceulx delad ville tant degliſe bourgois côme autȿ qui leur devoient ou pouvoient devoir aucune choſe. Et ſans que

erset and his wife and children held themselves. And in the said town were lodged Sir Robert de Vere, brother of the earl of Suffolk; Sir Henry Radford; Sir Spencer; Henry Standish; William Couran; William Locke; Fulk Ethon; Henry Lewis; and several others, who were conducted by the duke of Somerset by 4,000 Englishmen within the said town for the guardianship of this place; in order to enter, thus, in the matter of the said agreement, the French and the English assembled and conversed several times—it is known, for the king of France, the said count of Dunois; seneschal of Poitou; seigneur Jean Bureau, treasurer of France; and some others. For the English, Sir Richard Harrison, bailiff of Caen; Robert Parges; and several others. And for the said town, Eustace Gaumet, lieutenant of the said bailiff, and the abbot of the said Saint-Étienne, who spoke and alleged several things, in strengthening each of his cases. And after several words said between them, they made an agreement the next day on the feast of monseigneur Saint John the Baptist. And the said English promised to put the said town and castle keep into the hands and obedience of the king of France by the first day of the next July following, in the event that they would not fight, the king and his power within the said day, amongst whom were the said duke of Somerset, his wife and his children, and other Englishmen who wanted to go, could go from there freely, themselves, their women and children, and take with them all their moveable goods. And they could go with their bodies, horses, and harnesses safely, and carry and take their said goods, for which they gave to them vessels and wagons and that which was necessary for them to pass into England and not elsewhere, at their expense and not otherwise, provided always that these Englishmen would deliver all prisoners, render all seals, and abandon all those of the said town, both of the church, cityfolk, and others, who owed them or

pource audeppartir peuſſent Riens duleur. Et avecque ce quilz laiſſeroient toute artillerye groſſe et menue Reſerve ars arbaleſtes et coullevrines amain. Pour lequel appoinctement contên les choſes deſſſd entenir baillerent leſd angloiz pour hoſtages xii. angloiz dangletre. deux chevalliers dangletre et quatre bourgois delad ville. Et pource quilz nefurent ſecouruz en aucune manerê led premier Iour deIuillet côme lacompoſicion porte ce Iour Rendirent lad ville chaſteau et donIon. Et porta les clefz aux champs par Icellui donIon le bailly deſſſnomme et les miſt en lamain de conneſtable defrance en la prêce dud conte dedunoiz lieutenant general. Auquel Incontinat les delivra Icellui conneſtable comme capitaine et gouvneur dicelle ville et chaſteau pour leRoy defrance. Et demoura led conneſtable aux champs pour faire tirer lechacun deſd angloiz droit aeſtreham. Et tantoſt apres leur departemet deleconte dedunoiz acompaigne dud mareſchal de Ialongnes devant lui deux cens archiers apie. et les trompettes et heraulx du Roy. ~ Et deſriere lui trois des eſcuires deſcuirie ~ portans les baniers du Roy. Et deſriere dicelles cent hommes darmes apie. Entra par led donIon dedens Icelle ville et chaſteau et fiſt mettre—leſd banieres ſur led donIon et portes.

Entrepinſe fcte acaen. p leRoy defrance

LE. ſixieſme Iour deIuillet ſepartit leRoy defrance delabbaye dardane pour entrer laville decaen et eſtoient en ſacompaignie to⁹ les ſeigneurs qui avoient eſte auſiege Excepte ſon lieutenant. et leſr deIalongnes que Ia eſtoient dedens laville. leſquelz eſtoient to⁹ grandemet et Richement

could owe them anything. And without which they could leave without delay. And with this, they would leave all the artillery, large or small, except bows, crossbows, and culverins by hand. For which agreement, containing the things abovesaid, to accomplish them, the said English released as hostages twelve Englishmen from England, two knights of England, and four cityfolk of the said town. And because there was no rescue in any matter, the said first day of July, according to the agreement, this day they rendered the said town, castle, and keep. And the above-named bailiff took the keys onto the fields by the keep and put them in the hands of the constable of France in the presence of the said count of Dunois, lieutenant general. To whom this constable immediately delivered them, as captain and governor of this town and castle for the king of France. And the said constable remained on the field in order to make each of the said Englishmen go straight to Étréham. And soon after their departure, the count of Dunois, accompanied by the said marshal of Jalongnes, having before him 200 archers on foot and trumpeters and heralds of the king, and behind him three of the squires of the squiriery carrying the banners of the king, and behind them 100 men-at-arms on foot, entered by the said keep into this town and castle, and he put the said banners on the keep and gates.

Entry made into Caen by the king of France

The sixth day of July, the king departed from the abbey of Ardenne in order to enter in the town of Caen, and there was in his company all the lords who had been at the siege, except his lieutenant and the seigneur de Jalongnes, who were already in the town, who were all greatly and richly clothed. And also 200

habillez. Et auſſi vint Iucques pres delad ville ii.c archiers marchans lui ſes heraulx et trompettes. Et deſriê delui avoit cent lances. lavindrent audevans delui hors delaville. Leconte dedunoiz qui yamena les bourgois delad ville en grant m͡ltitude degens leſquelz apres quilz oulrent fait laRev͡ce auRoy lui prêterent les ~~ch~~ clefs et Il les Receult Lagengnement. Apres cevindrent les gens de legliſe Reveſtuz aproceſſons auſſi quil eſt en tel cas acouſtume defaire puis entra en lad ville. Sur lequel quatre gentilz hommes chevalliers et eſcuires demourans en Icelle porterent ung ciel. Et eſtoient toutes les Rues par ou Il paſſoit tendues et couvertes aciel grandemet̂. Eſquelles avoit grant foiſſon peuple cryant noel. Et ainſſi chevaucha leRoy Iucques devant legliſe deSaint pierre. Et deſſendit alaporte pour aller faire ſon oroiſon et priere. laquelle faicte Il monta acheval. et ſen ala logier en lamaiſon dun bourgois delaville en la quelle Il demoura par ĉtaine eſpace detemps ſon lieuten͡ et conſeil avec lui pour mettre officiers police et gouvernement en lad ville. Et vindrent alaprinſe dud caen devers leRoy. monſr decroy. meſſire Iehan decroy ſon frere et monſr darcy Leſquelz eſtoient envoyez depar monſeigneur leduc debourgongne ~~le~~ pour traicter du mariage delafille duRoy. et monſ.r chr̄ls filz dud duc. Et pour pluſſieurs aut̂s groſſes choſes donc Ilz eſtoiet̂ chr̄ges depar mondſr leduc.

Comment LeSiege fut mis adallaiſe par les francois.

LE dit ſixieſme Iour fut mis leſiege de fallaiſe et ſe trouva lepremier poſton deſaintrailles bailly deberry. Et lelun-

archers came near to the said town, marching before him with his heralds and trumpets. And behind him were 100 lances; there came before him then in the town the count of Dunois, who took the cityfolk of the said town there in great number of men, who, after they had made reverence to the king, presented to him the keys and he received them very benignly. After this, the men of the church came, vested in profession, such that it was in such cases accustomed to do; then he entered into the said town. For which four gentlemen, knights, and squires remained in this gate with a canopy. And all the roads where he passed were raised and covered with a great canopy, under which was a great abundance of people crying Noël. And so the king rode until the church of Saint-Pierre. And he descended to the gate in order to go make his prayers and confessions, which he made. He mounted the horse and went to lodge in the house of a citizen of the town, in which he remained for a certain space of time, his lieutenant and his council with him, in order to assign officers, police, and government in the said town. And before the king came to this seizure of the said Caen monseigneur de Croy; messire Jean de Croy, his brother; and monseigneur d'Arcy, who were sent by monseigneur the duke of Burgundy in order to negotiate the marriage of the daughter of the king and monseigneur Charles, son of the said duke. And for several other large things of which they were charged by monseigneur the said duke.

How the siege was laid at Falaise by the French

The abovesaid sixth day, the siege was laid before the town of Falaise, and the first found there was Poton de Xaintrailles,

dy apres. ſus Iehan bureau treſorier defrance avecques lequel eſtoient les frans archiers pour conduire lartillerie donc Il eſtoit gouv̂neur. Et tantoſt q̂ les angloiz delaplace les apperceurent Ilz allerent audevant et les aſſaillirent treſaſprement. A Icellui aſſault ſegouv̂na led treſorier treſvaillemment. en ſoy deffendant conr̂ leſd angloiz. Etcependant vint led ſeigneur deſaintrailles aſon ſecours. Et tellemet̂ fut deffendue lad artillerye que leſd angloiz furet̂ Reboutez aux portes deleur forterreſſe. Et ence vint acques leſd bailly et treſorier treſgrant hône^r^. Puis ſepartit leRoy deſaville decaen pour allr̂ oud ſiege. et alaſoir augiſte aSaint Sauve^r^. Et lelendemain ſeloga ducoſte dedevers argentan aune lieue pres dud fallaiſe aune abbaye nômee Saint andrieu. Avec lui eſtoit leRoy deCecille le duc decalabre ſon filz. les contes du maine de Saint pol et detancarville. levicomte delomaigne et pluſſieurs aut̂s. Et leduc dalencon fut loge aSainte marguerite ducoſte dedevers paris ademye lieue pres delad abbaye. En ung lieu que on dit laguibray fut logie leconte dedunoiz et auplus pres delui leſire delaforeſt gouv̂neur des gens duconte dumaine. Audeſſoubz dela guibray en une abbaye eſtoient logiez deux mille francs archiers. ducoſte dedev̂s lemaine. Audroit delaporte pres duchaſteau furent logiez. leſire debeauvau. leſire debeauvaiz. Iehan monſ^r^ de lorraine et led bailly deberry. Et delaut̂ coſte dedevers caen furent logiez. les contes deNevers et deu. leſire decullant grant maiſtre doſtel Leſire dorval. Leſire deblainville. leſire demôtenay et pluſſieurs aut̂s. Et ainſſi fut mis leſiege to⁹ autour delad ville ~~doſt~~ defallaiſe. Et pource que leRoy avoit grant ſeigneurie avec lui et plus quil ne lui falloit pour tenir led ſiege et furent les contes deRichemont côneſtable defrance et declermont ordonnez depar leRoy

bailiff of Berry. And the Monday after, Jean Bureau, treasurer of France, arrived, with whom were free archers in order to conduct the artillery, over which he was leader. And soon after the Englishmen of this place learned of them, they went before them and assailed them very swiftly. At this attack, the said treasurer governed himself very bravely in defending himself against the said English. And, however, the said seigneur de Xaintrailles came to his rescue. And he defended the said artillery such that the said Englishmen were chased to the gates of their fortress. And in doing this the said bailiff and treasurer acquired very great honour. Then the king left from his town of Caen in order to come to the said siege, and to accomplish this, he went to Saint-Sauveur. And the next day, he lodged on the side toward Argentan, within a league of the said place of Falaise, in an abbey named Saint-Andrew. With him were the king of Sicily; the duke of Calabria, his brother; the counts of Maine, of Saint-Pol, and of Tancarville; the viscount of Lomagne; and several others. And the duke of Alençon was camped at Sainte-Marguerite, on the side toward Paris, a half league from the said abbey. In a place that one called La Guibray was lodged the count of Dunois, and closer to him the sire de La Forêt, principal governor of the men of the count of Maine. Below La Guibray in an abbey were lodged 2,000 free archers on the side toward Maine. To the right of the gate, near Chastel, were lodged the sire de Beauvau; the sire de Beauvais; Jean, monseigneur of Lorraine; and the said bailiff of Berry. And on the other side toward Caen were lodged the counts of Nevers and Eu; the sire de Culant, grand master of the hotel of the king; the sire d'Orval; the sire de Blainville; the sire de Montenay; and several others. And so the siege was laid all around the said town of Falaise. And because the king had the great seigneurie with him, and more than he needed to hold the said siege, the earl of

pour aller mettre lefiege devant cherbourc. Et avoient en leur compaignie leconte delaval. lefire de loheac. lefire de-Raiz. et decoitie. admiral de France. lefire demontgafcon. meffr phle de cullant marefchal defrance. lefenefchal de poitou. lefr demontaubain marefchal debretaigne Les f.rs deftouteville et demauny. lefenefchal debourbonnoiz. meffr guiffroy decouvran pierre de louvain. Robert deconigam. Iames detillay bailly devermandoiz. les gens duf.r deSaint fevere et deux mille francs archiers. Et toute le Refedu des gens darmes demoureret aud fiege defallaife avecques le-Roy lefquelz fegouvneret moult grandement en eulx fortif-fiant contre lad ville degrans trenchees et foffez. Et auffi fi-rent grans preparacions degecter bombardes et canons pour affallir lad ville en laquelle avoit en garnifon. mil et cinq cens angloiz les mieulx en point qui fuffent en normend-ie des gens deleur nacion donc eftoiet conduifers et cap-itaines foubz lefire detalbot deux gentil hommes angloiz lun nomme andre trollot. et lautre thomas cathon. lefquelz voyans telle et fi haulte feigneurie. et grant multitude de-gens darmes archiers et arbaleftriers devant eulx Requirent aparlamenter avec leconte dedunoiz. lequel par lecom-mandement et ordonnance du Roy leur bailla feurete pour aucuns denteulx pour venir aexpofer ce quilz voudroient dire. Et adonc Requirent aavoir compoficion avec leRoy defrance. Et pource quil leRoy atoufiours defire lafaluacion de lefang humain leur acorda. Et depres appoitemet avec led conte dedunoiz. lexii Iour deIuillet enf ou cas quilz meferoient fecourouz dedens ced Iour. pourveu que lefire detallebot qui eftoit feigneur delad place dudon du Roy dangletre foubz qui Ilz eftoient et font. lequel eftoit prifon-niers duRoy defrance enchafteau dedreux feroit delivre et

Richmond, constable of France, and [the count] of Clermont were ordered by the king to lay siege before Cherbourg. And they had in their company the count of Laval; the sire de Lohéac; the sire de Rais and de Coitivy, admiral of France; the sire de Montgascon; messire Philippe de Culant, marshal of France; the seneschal of Poitou; the sire de Mont-Aubain, marshal of Brittany; the seigneurs of Estouteville and Mauny; the seneschal of the Bourbonnais; messire Geoffroi de Couvran; Pierre de Louvain; Robert de Conigam; James de Tillay, bailiff of Vermandois; the men of the lord of Saint-Sévère; and 2,000 free archers. And all the surplus of the men-at-arms remained at the siege of Falaise with the king, who governed themselves very grandly in fortifying themselves against the said town with large ditches and trenches. And also they made great preparations to launch catapults and cannon in order to assail the said town, in which were in the garrison 1,500 Englishmen, the majority of whom were in Normandy of the men of their nation, of whom were the conductors and captains under Lord Talbot two English gentlemen: one named André Trollot, and the other Thomas Ethan, who seeing such and so much lordliness and so great a multitude of men-at-arms, archers, and crossbowmen before them, asked to speak with the count of Dunois, who, by the comandment and order of the king, gave safe passage for several of them to come to them in order to expose that which they wanted to say. And so they asked to have an agreement with the king of France. And because the king always desired to avoid the effusion of human blood, he agreed with them. And thus they agreed with the count of Dunois the tenth day of July following, in case they were rescued within the said day, provided that Lord Talbot, who was lord of the said place by the gift of the king of England, under whom there are and are those who were prisoners of the king of France in the castle of Dreux, were released and

mis en ſafranche liberte. Moiennant ĉtaines promeſſes q̂ led tallebot devoit avecques ceſaire auRoy. Et fureȇ baillers tenans enȇ leſd parties duraŝ depuis lex^m Iours Iucques au xxi^m deſſuſd. Et pour entretenir ce que dit eſt baillerent xii hoſtages. Et ſen devoient allȓ leſd angloiz en angleȓre leurs corps et leurs bieŝ ſaufz. encas quilz ne ſecourus ſecouruz dedens led mardy xxi^m Iour dud moys. Auquel Iour necomparant aucun ſecours. Pour quoy ſen allerent franchement ainſſi que promis avoieȇ. Et laiſſerent lad ville en lamain et obbeiſſ duRoy defrance. Alaquelle garder depar lui ordonna capitaine poton deſantrailles ſon graȇ eſcuier deſcuerie et bailly deberry.

Commeȇ. leSiege fut mis devaȇ les chaſteau et ville dedampfroȇ

LE. xxiii^m. Iour dud moys de Iuillet apres laReddiction defallaiſe. Separtirent delacompaignie duRoy meſſire chȓles decullaȇ grant maiſtre. doſtel. leſire deblainville. ſire Iehan bureau treſorier defrance ayant touſio^rs legouv̂nemeȇ delartillerie mil et v^c. frans archiers. Et allerent mettre devant laville et chaſteau dedampfront. En laquelle yavoit en garniſon devii. aviii^c. angloiz. leſquelz ſarchant legrant nombre des gens darmes et lagrant ſ^rie deux en laduchie deNormandie Rendirent leſd ville ⁊chaſteau et menant en lamain du Roy defrance. leſegond Iour daouſt enſ oud an par tell compoſicion quilz ſen alleȇ en angleȓre leurs corps et biens ſaufz. Ainſſi que avoient fait pluſſiuers ſouldoiers deleur party eſtans dedeus les villes ⁊chaſteau cẙ deſſus eſcripz. Et ydemoura cap^ne. pour leRoy.

put into their free liberty. Meaning certain promises that the said Talbot had to do with the king. And truces were held between the said parties lasting from the tenth day until the twenty-first day abovesaid. And in order to enter into that which was said, they handed over a dozen hostages. And the said Englishmen must go into England, their bodies and their goods safely, in the event that they were not rescued by the said Tuesday the twenty-first day of the said month. On which day, no help was given to them. So they went freely, such as had been promised to them. And they left the said town in the hand and obedience of the king of France. For the guardianship of which was ordained as captain Poton de Xaintrailles, his grand squire of the squirie and bailiff of Berry.

How siege was laid before the castle and town of Dampfront

The twenty-third day of the said month of July, after the reduction of Falaise, messire Charles de Culant, grand master of the hotel; the sire de Blainville; the sire Jean Bureau, treasurer of France, having also the management of the artillery, departed from the company of the king with 1,500 free archers. And they went to lay siege before the town and castle of Dampfront, in which there were in the garrison 700-800 Englishmen, who, learning of the great number of men-at-arms and the great lordship within the duchy of Normandy, rendered the said town and castle and put into the hand of the king of France the second day of August in the said year, by means of such agreement that they would go to England, their bodies and goods safe. [And] there had been several soldiers of their party being amongst the towns and castle as above written. And the captain remained there for the king.

Lamort du duc debritai[gne]. nomme francois.

Oudit an environ lafin dud moys deJIillet mourut demort naturelle treſhault et treſpuiſſant prince meſſire francois duc de bretaigne. nepveu duRoy defrance qui fut ung treſgrant dommaige pource Royaume que pleuſt adieu quil euſt veſqu pl[9] longue ment. Car Il eſtoit ung notable prince prud Ieune et vaillant hôme deſon corps. Et ceſtoit grandement travaille deſaperſonne et employa ſes gens et grant finance en ſervice duRoy alaconqueſte dupays de-Normandie côme cy devant eſt dit et deſclare. dieu par ſa ſancte enſecorde donit q̂ ſon aux ſort concorde alabeatitude deparades. avec ~~Iehs~~ Iheſus lefilz dedieu. Ced prince en ſon vivant aymoit leRoy defrance naturellement comme Il eſt aſſez apparu. Car Il aporte guerre ato[9] ceulx qui ſavoit eſtre cont̂ ſa maieſte Royalle. Et meſmement cont̂ ung deſes propres freres nomme meſſire gilles debretaigne. lequel au preudice duRoy defrance et ſans quelconque adveu delui avoit Receu lordre duRoy danglet̂re q̂on appelle laIartiere. Et accepte loffice deconneſtable dud Royaulme danglet̂re. Pourquoy tantoſt apres que cecy fut venu aſa cognoiſſance et notire. lefiſt prendre et mettre en aucuns deſes chaſteaulx fors ou Il fut par longue eſpace detemps diligemmet̂ garde. Et ſouvêteſſoiz eſtoit exorte et admôeſte par led duc ſes parens et ſubgetz et aut̂s [les] ~~ſes~~ bien vuaillans du Royaume de delaiſſer la querelle des angloiz qui ſouſtenoit cont̂ Raiſon Iuſtice et ordre dedroit. Et apres quil eult eſte traicte par doulces parolles fut traictie par parolles Rigoureuſes. Maiz oncques po[r] choſe com lui ſceuſt dire ne ſevoult Retraire

The death of the duke of Brittany, named François

In the said year, around the end of the said month of July, the very high and very powerful prince messire François, duke of Brittany, nephew of the king of France, died of natural causes, which was a great tragedy for the kingdom, which cried to God that he had lived longer. Because he was a notable prince, a prudent, youthful, and brave man of his body. And he had personally worked greatly and employed his men and great finances in the service of the king in the conquest of the land of Normandy, as it has been above said and declared. May God, through His holy mercy, grant that his soul be in concord with the bliss of Paradise, with Jesus, the son of God. This said prince, in his life, naturally loved the king of France, as was so apparent, because he went to war against all those who had been against his royal majesty. And even against one of his full brothers, named messire Giles of Brittany, who, at the prejudice of the king of France and without any thought of himself, had received the order of the king of England, which one called the Garter. And he accepted the office of constable of the said kingdom of England. For which, soon after this came to his knowledge, he made to take and capture several of his strong castles, which he had for a long space of time diligently guarded. And he was many times exhorted and admonished by the said duke, his relatives, and subjects, and other very brave people of the kingdom, to leave the quarrel on the side of English, which he sustained without reason, justice, and order of right. And after it had been negotiated through painful words, it was agreed by rigorous ones. But for reasons known only to him, he would not retreat from his purpose, for which the said duke of Brittany, his brother, conceived mortal hate against him and such

defon propos. Parquoy led duc debretaigne fon frere conceult hayne mortelle conť lui et telle quil lefift mourir. Et fut led duc plufieurs et diverfes foiz fomme du Roy dan gleterre par fes heraulx delui nevoyer fon con[ble] Lequel Il tenoit prifonnier. duquel en avoit lagarde artus demontaubran. Et defait pour leReffuz q̂ en fift led duc deleRendre. lefd angloiz lui envoyeret lectres dedeffiance qui Rengrega fon fait pez par avant. Et print led duc de une telle defplaifir en foy que comme lacommune Renommee ou Il aefte prifonnier et Il fut en une nuyt par lors dud duc eftrangle dedeux touailles torffes. Et ainffi finit fes Iours led meffire gilles mifera blement et pauvrfement qui eft grat exemple atous autres.

Comment meffire gilles frere auduc debretaigne fut tue.

DE. cefte mort auffi pitieufe on en ont parle bien aut̂ment en bretaigne. Car ainffi depuis. Ian ouy dire y Il yot dupoil dulou envers led montauban et fes complices qui legardoiť avec lui Pourtant quilz lefirent mourir ainfi que dit eft par faulx donne auctendre afon frere pour cuider admeans aaucunes chofes et Il eftoit content deRenoncer atoutes promeffes par lui faictes aux angloiz et defaire tout ceq̂ leRoy et fond frere euffent voulu. Maiz on le[r] eftrepuoint tout aucontraire comme on a affez fceu par aucuns deceulx que on apie prendre qui lacontent fait mourer. Lefquelz en ont des laverite. Et trefreullement en ont efte executez par Iuftice et les autres qui en ont peu efchaper me fe ofconent trouver eu pays et pour caufes.

that he ordered that he put him to death. And the said duke was several and diverse times summoned on the part of the king of England via his heralds, to send to him the said constable, whom he held prisoner, for which he had the guardianship of Arthur de Montaubran. And for the deed, for the refusal that he did to the said duke to render the said Englishmen, he sent him letters of defiance, which re-engendered his deed even more than before. And the said duke, as one such displeasure in faith that, as is commonly known, he took where he had been prisoner and he was in one night by those of the said duke strangled by two twisted ropes. And so the said messire Giles ended his days, miserably, poorly, and very piteously, which was a great example for all others.

How messire Giles, brother of the duke of Brittany, was killed

OF this death, so piteable, having otherwise spoken of it in Brittany, because, also since the year, I had heard said that there was some hair of the wolf toward the said of Montaubon and his accomplices, whom they guarded with him. Knowing that they killed him, as it is said, by falsehoods given within earshot of his brother, thinking by this means to achieve several things, and he was happy to renounce all the promises that he had made to the English, and to do all that the king and his said brother had wanted. But one gave them the opposite information, as one has seen enough, since by some of those whom one can take little, which they had done to kill him, which the the content made to die, which was the truth of it, and very rigorously he had been executed by justice and the others who had barely escaped, they have never dared to find in this country and for causes.

Commet̂ lefiege decherbourg fut vaillement tenu par les francois.

LE. fiege eftant devant cherebourg lequel avoit efte mis par leconte deRichemont con.ble defrance et par aut̂ groffe puiffance des feigne.rs chevaliers et ecuiers eftans en facompaignie côme Il efte defclare en laffin duchapittre delaReddicion defallaife fut et aefte grandement gouv̂ne et vaillamment par les francois eftans oud fiege et eftoient ceulx dededens fort appreffez detâches mynes et autŝ aprochements. Combien quil yot une chevallier et ung efcuier dupays debretaigne que firent tuez. Ceft affavoir meffire pregent decoitivi feigneur deRaiz et decoitivi. Lequel fut tue dun canon qui fut ung exceffif ~~de~~ et grant dommage pour leRoy. Car Il eftoit ung des vaillans chevalliers et bien Renome du Royaume defrance prudent homme et debon aage. Lautre fut tue dun bonhomme nomme tuddual lebourgois efcuier debien. Et bailly detrois. Lequel eftoit vaill̂ homme defon corps apie et acheval et degrant con duite et bien congnoiffant lafubtilite delaguerre. Lad ville fut fort batue decanons et debombardes et leplus fubtillement que oncques homme vit. Et mefmement ducofte delamer. Car Il yavoit bôbardes affes en lamer fus lagrane ou celle venoit par chun̂ Iour. Et eftoient lefd bombards chargees depierres. Et combien que lefd bombards fuffet̂ toutes covertes deau. quant leflo venoit. Ne antmoins par lemoyen deĉtaines peaulx engraiffes donc Ilz eftoient veftues. oncques lamer ne porta dommaige alad pouldre. Maiz aupluftoft que lamer eftoit Retraite les canonniers levoient les manteaulx et

How the siege of Cherbourg was bravely held by the French

THE siege, being before the castle of Cherbourg, which had been laid by the earl of Richmond, constable of France, and by other very powerful lords, knights, and squires who were in his company, as has been discussed at the end of the chapter on the reduction of Falaise, was conducted and had been greatly and bravely governed by the Frenchmen who were at this siege, and those within were hard pressed by the trenches, mines, and other approaches of the French, such that there was one knight and one squire from the land of Brittany who were killed—it is known messire Prégent de Coitivy, seigneur de Rais et Coitivy, who was killed by a cannon, which was an excessive and great sadness for the king, because he was one of the brave knights and well renowned throughout the kingdom of France, prudent man and of good age. The other killed was a gentleman named Tuddual the Citizen, a squire of good means and bailiff of Troyes, who was a very brave man of his body, on foot, and on horseback, and of great conduct, and well-known in the subtleties of warfare. The said town was strongly battered by cannon and by bombards, and more subtly than any man who lived, and even by the coast of the sea, because there were bombards arranged on the shore of the sea, notwithstanding that it rose twice each day. And the said bombards were supplied with rocks, and such that the said bombards were all covered by water when the tide came in. Nonetheless, by the means of certain greased skins which they used to clothe them, the sea never did any damage to the said powder, but as soon as the sea retreated, the cannoniers lifted the sheets and fired against the

gectroient couſt lad place donc les angloiz eſtoient moult eſbahis. Car oncqz navoient en congnoiſſance detel miſteres. Toutefois Il en yot trois bombardes et ung canon Ronpuz devant Icelle ville et yfurent faictes degrand et belles armes tant ſur terre que ſur mer et plus auprendree des angloiz que aleur profit. Parquoy thomas gouel eſcuier angloiz cap.ne dud lieu. lequel avoit en ſacompaignie de dens lad place mille combatans ſoubz lui Re quiſt aamors compoſicion avec led conneſtable. Laquelle Il obtint et aobtenne. Et fut apres pluſſieurs dictes compoſe et traicte entre leſd parties que led gouel laiſſeroit lad ville et chaſteau. en lobbeiſſance duRoy defrance. Parmy ce que on liu delivreroit ung ſein filz que eſtoit en oſtage. pour ſapart et porcion delargent deu au Roy defrance et aceulx deRouen. par lacompoſicion q̂ avoit faicte leduc deſombrecet lui eſtant aRouen. Et amiſſe que ſond filz lui fut Rendu franc chement et quicte Rendit lad ville et chaſteau decherbourc en lobbeiſſance duRoy defrance Lexxiime Iour dud moys daouſt oud an mille CCCC. cinquante. Et ſen allerent lui ſond filz et tous les ſouldoyers en angletre. leurs biens et leurs corps ſaufz. Puis en fut fait capitaine pour leRoy. leſire debueil atout iiii.xx. lances. et les archiers. Lequel avoit eſte fait et cree admiral defrance pour letreſpas dud coitivy. qui en ſon vivant eſtoit capitaine degranville. donc fut fait capitaine apres ſamort Iehan monſeigneur delorrraine. Atout cinquante lances. et les archiers. et ainſſi fut conqueſtee toute laduchie denormendie et toutes les citez villes et chaſteaulx dicelle mi ſe en obbaiſſance duRoy defrance. en ung an et ung Iours. qui eſt une grant merveille. Et peut bien que noſſr ya eſtendu ſagrace. Car Iamais ſi grant pays ne fut conquis en ſipeu

said place, for which the Englishmen were very amazed, because they never had known such mysteries. However, there were three bombards and a cannon that blast into this town and there were made great and beautiful [feats of] arms, both on the land and on the sea, more to the prejudice of the English than to their profit. For which Thomas Gouel, an English squire, captain of the said place, who had in his company within the said place 1,000 soldiers under him, requested due to deaths an agreement with the said constable, which he obtained and was granted. And afterwards, several words were said, composed, and agreed between the said parties that the said Gouel would leave the said town and castle in the obedience of the king of France by means that one would release to him his son, who was a hostage, for his sake and a portion of the gold owed to the king of France and to those of Rouen by the agreement that the duke of Somerset had made when he was at Rouen. And by the means of this, his said son was rendered to him freely and completely, and he rendered the said town and castle of Cherbourg into the obedience of the king of France the twenty-second day of the said month of August in the year 1450. And they went, he, his said son, and all his soldiers, into England, their bodies and their goods safe. Then the sire de Bueil was made captain for the king, with around eighty lances, and the archers, who had been newly made and created admiral of France by the passing of the said Coitivy, who in his life was captain of Granville, for which was made captain in his place, after his death, Jean, monseigneur de Lorraine, with around fifty lances and the archers, and, thus, was all the duchy of Normandy conquered and all the cities, towns, and castles of this land put into the obedience of the king of France in one year and one day, which was a great marvel. And it appeared well that Our Lord extended there his grace,

de temps ne amoins deciſion depeuple et degens ne amoins dedommage qui eſt ung grant honneur au Roy defrance. aux princes et aux autres ſeigneurs devant nommez et atous autres qui lont acompaigne. Au Recouvremeт̂ delad duchie premierement et par eſpecial doit on Rendre graces adieu gloire et louâge pource que ainſſi ya voulu eſtendre ſagrace pour Rendre au Roy defrance ce que eſt et doit etac Iuin et monſtrer les miracles. letemps le devoit ainſſi en partie car ceſt~~o~~[it] lannee dugraт̂ pardon general deRomme que len appelle lan du Iubilee. Cedit pays deNormendie contient ſix groſſez. Iournees delonge et dequaree te delarge et dedens ya ſix ~~arcevef~~ eveſques et ung archeveſque. et cent que villes q̂ chaſteaulx ſans ceulx qui ont eſte abatuz etdemoliz par la fortune delaguerre. Apres [ce] fait ordonna leRoy. vi[C] lances et les archiers. leſquelz Il laiſſa en lad duchie pour lagarde dicelle et envoya. les autres gens deguerre en guyenne. Puis ſepartit pour yaller et arriva en lacite detours en moys deSeptembre prochain enſuivant oud an. Et la par deliberacion deſon grant conſeil pour Rend graces adieu et leRemercier dicelle conqueſte. commanda celebrer proceſſions generales par toutes les egliſes deſon Royaulme Lexiiii[me] Iour doctobre enſuivant et dela en avant par chc͡n an lexii[me] Iour daouſt.

Laprinſe commeт̂ les francois eſtoient habillez alacongueſte deNormandie.

Qui. vouldroit faire mencion detous les vaillans hommes et des vaillances qui ont eſte faites durant le Recouvrement delad duchie denormend ce ſeroit trop longue choſe

because never so great a land was conquered in so little space of time except with a great loss of people and of men, nor with little damage, which was a great honour to the king of France, to the princes, and to the other lords above named, and to all others who had accompanied them. In the recovery of the said duchy, first and foremost one must render thanks to God, and to him because he had wanted thus to extend his grace to render to the king of France that which was and ought to be his, and to show the miracles, the time must also in part because it is the year of the great general pardon in Rome, which is named the year of Jubilee. This said land of Normandy is six days' journey long and four wide, and within there are six bishoprics and one archbishopric, and a hundred towns with castles, without those which had been destroyed and demolished by the fortunes of war. After this was done, the king gave 600 lances and the archers, which he left in the said duchy for the guardianship of this place, and he sent the other men of war into Guyenne. Then he departed in order to go there, and he arrrived in the city of Tours in the following month of September in the said year. And there, by the deliberation of his grand council, in order to render thanks to God and to thank him for this conquest, he commanded general procession celebrations by all the churches of his kingdom the fourteenth day of October following, and from then onwards each year on the twelfth day of August.

The capture—how the French were clothed in the conquest of Normandy

Who would want to make mention of all the brave men and their prowess, which had been displayed during the recovery of the said duchy of Normandy—it would be too

aeſcripre. Maiz neantmoins en fault Il aucunement faire memoire po[r] ceulx qui en temps advenir pouroient lire et ouir lafacon delaRecouvrance dicelle duchie. Premierement leRoy defrance amis en ſon armee et en ſaguerre ſi bon ordre aufait deſes gens darmes que ceſt belle choſe aſavoir. Car Il afait mettre tous leſd gens darmes et detrait en bons et ſeurs habillemens. Ceſt aſſavoir les hommes darmes to⁹ armez decuiraſſis harnoiz deIambes ſallades et eſpees toutes yarmes toutes garnies et lances que portoient les pages. dechc͡n hommes darmes montree detrois chevaulx pour lui ſon page et ſon varlet. lequel varlet eſt arme deſallade debrigadine Iacquette ou hogueton harche ou guiſarme. Et avoit chc͡n hommes darmes deux archiers achaval armez leplus debrigâdines harnois deIambes et ſallades donc laplus eſtoient garnis dargent. Et atout lemoins avoient tous Iacques ou bons haubergeons. Iceulx gens deguerre eſtoient tous paiez pour chc͡n moys ſans cequilz avent eſte ſi oſez ne ſi hardis deprendre durant lad guerre denormendie aucun͡s gens priſonniers ne Ranchonner cheval ne beſtes quilz conques. poſe ores quelle fuſt en lobbeiſſance des angloiz et aceulx deleur party. ne les venes et quelq̂ lieu que cefuſt fors ſeullement ſus ~ Icelux angloiz et gens tenans leur party qui eſtoit̂ trouvez faiſans guerre. Leſquelz Ilz pouvent prend licitement et leurs eſtoit permis et non auſ̂met̂. Lad guerre durant ſi gouverna vaillemment grandement et honorablement led conte de dunoiz lieutenant general duRoy. Et auſſi firent pareillement les contes denevers decaſtres deu. deſaint pol. leſire decullant grant maiſtre doſtel. Les ſeigneurs dorval. deſtouteville. de blainville. debeauvau. debeauvoiz. et demouy en beauvoiſin. Lemareſchal deIalongnes. Le ſeneſchal depoitou. Iehan monſ[r] delorraine

long a thing to write. But, nonetheless, it is necessary anyway to make a record for those who in the future would like to read and hear the method of the recovery of this duchy. Firstly, the king of France put in his army and in his war such good order on the matter of his men-at-arms that it was a beautiful thing to know, because he had had put all these said men-at-arms and conscripts in good and secure clothing—it is known: the men-at-arms were all armed with cuirasses, leg harnesses, helmets, and swords, arms all covered and lances, which the pages carried, each armed man mounted on three horses for himself, his page, and his attendant, which attendant was armed with helmet, brigadine, jacket, or polearm, hauberk, or axe. And each of the said men-at-arms had two archers per horse, most armed with brigadines, leg harnesses, and helmets, the majority of whom were wearing silver. And at least some had jackets or good hauberks. These men of war were all paid each month, who were so daring and so hardy to capture during the said war of Normandy any prisoners or horses or beasts that they captured to ransom, considering that it was in the obedience of the English and the men holding to their party who were found fighting, which they could take lawfully and were allowed to them and not otherwise. The said war was governed so bravely, greatly, and honourably by the said count of Dunois, lieutenant general of the king. And also the counts of Nevers, of Castres, of Eu, and of Saint-Pol; the sire de Culant, grand master of the hotel; the seigneurs d'Orval, d'Éstouteville, of Blainville, of Beauveau, of Beauvais, and of Müy-en-Beauvoisin; the marshal of Jallongnes, the seneschal of Poitou; Jean, monseigneur de Lorraine; Poton de Xaintrailles, bailiff of Berry; Robert de Flocques, called Flocquet, bailiff of Évreux; Pierre

poton deſaintrailles bailly deberry. Robert deflocques dit flocquet bailly devreux. pierre louvain Robert coningam et pluſſieurs auſ̂s grans ſ.[rs] chevalliers et eſcuiers qui to⁹ notablement et grandement ſiſont gouvernez agrans travaulx dangiers meſaiſes peines et perilz deleurs corps pareillement laproviſion que leRoy avoit miſe en fait deſon artillerie pour lefait deſaguerre ou Il avait leplus grant nombre debombardes groſſes degens canons veuglaires ſerpentines et paudins coulevrines et Ribaudequins qui neſt memoire domme qui Iamais veuſt aRoy xrien̄ ſagrant artillerie en ſi bien garnie depouldres manteaulx et detoutes autres choſes po.[r] aprouches aprendre chaſteaulx et villes. et qui euſt plus grant foiſon decharroy ales mener ne meneu.[rs] pour les gouverner quil avoit. leſquelz eſtoient paiez et ſouldoues deIour enIour. Et fureſ̂ gouverneurs et conduiſeurs delad artillerie ſire Iehan bureau. treſorier defrance. et Iaſpar bureau ſon frere maiſtre delad artillerye. leſquelz durant lad guerre en ont en degrans paines et perilz. car Ilz ont fait grant diligences et bien leur devoir. Ceſtoit choſe merveilleuſe aveoir les boullevers aprouchemens foſſez trenches et mynes que les deſſuſd faiſoient faire devaſ̂ toutes les villes et chaſteaulx qui fureſ̂ aſſiegez durant Icelle guerre. Car deverite Il nya Rendue place que ceſoit par compoſicion ou auſ̂ment qui neuſt eſte prinſe daſſault et par force darmes et par lavaillance et ſubtillete des gens deguerre qui la eſtoient. Maiz touſiours quant leſd places eſtoieſ̂ approuchees et preſtes aprendre et daſſault. Le Roy de ſa benignite voulloit que on les prinſſt par compoſicion pour obvier aeffuſion duſangc et aladeſtruction deſon pays et du people qui eſtoit encloz leſd fortereſſes.

Louvain; Robert Cunningham; and several other great lords, knights, and squires, who all notably and grandly governed himself with great labours, work, danger, illnesses, pains, and perils of their bodies; similarly was the provision that the king had done in making his artillery for the purpose of the war, where he had the greatest number of large bombards, large cannon, veuglaires, serpentines, and paudins, culverins and ribauldequins, which never in memory had ever a Christian king had so numerous artillery, nor furnished with such gunpowder and of all other things in order to make attacks and capture castles and towns, and who had so great abundance of wagons to take them, or leaders to govern them, than he had, which leaders were paid and compensated daily. And the leaders and conductors of the said artillery were sire Jean Bureau, treasurer of France, and Jaspar Bureau, his brother, master of the said artillery, who during the said war had suffered great pains and perils because they had made great diligence and well acquitted themselves. It was a marvellous thing to see the bulwerks, approaches, ditches, trenches, and mines that the abovesaid had made before all the towns and castles that were besieged during this war, because for truth there was no place rendered by agreement or otherwise that had not been captured by assault and by force of arms, and through bravery and subtlety by the men of war who were there. But always when the said places were strongly battered and ready to be captured and assaulted, the king, by his benign will, wanted always that it be captured by agreement in order to obviate the effusion of blood and the destruction of his land, and for the people who were enclosed in the said fortresses.

Ceſtoient ceulx qui ont travaille ala. cõqueſte denormend ou ꝑtie deceulx.

A la conqueſte delabaſſe Normendie donc eſtoit chief en ſon vivant led duc de bretaigne travaillirent et pererõt grandement Follin duc tant quil veſquid. Et par eſpecial le conte deRichemont conneſtable defrance ſon oncle led feu pregent decoitivie. que dieu abſolle et to⁹ autres qui alad conquiſte et Recouvremẽt fut treſpaſſez. lequel en ſon vivant eſtoit ſeigne[r] de Raiz et decoitivie et admiral defrance Ilz. travaillerent moult auſſi. leconte delaval le ſeigneur deloheac mareſchal defrance ſon frere leſeigneur demontauban mareſchal debretai.[gne] guiffray decouvran Iamet detillay. bailly de vermandoiz. et auſſi fiſt led tudual lebourgois tant quil veſquid. lequel eſtoit lors bailly de troyes pour entretenir lefait et charge delad mirre tant ſus lefait delaIuſtice qui des finances. et pour conſeillers bien et loyalemẽt lefait et entretenemẽt ~~lefait~~ des gens darmes et leRecouvrement delad duchie ſegouv̂nerẽt bien et labourerent grandement. leſ[r] detraynel chancellier defrance. leſ.[r] degaucourt. meſſ[re] theaulde de~~vaf~~ valpergue bailly delyon. Qui Iacques cueur conſeiller et argentier du Roy. le quel fiſt et trouva les manieres et toutes ſubtilitez alui poſſibles davoir finances et argent detoutes pars pour entretenir lad armee et ſouldoyez les gens deguerre donc Il fallut grans nombre. Et auſſi firent meſſire Iehan du bar ſeigneur debaugy. et ſire Iehan ~~har donyn~~ hardouin treſorier defrance qui leur fuſt grant honneur et atous les autres qui ont travaille et labonne en ceſte partie en ſervice du Roẙ. Auſquilz dieu dont par ſon plaiſir lou generent venue et bien mourir. Amen.

These were those who had worked for the conquest of Normandy or parts of this place

In the conquest of Lower Normandy, over whom the leader in his life was the said duke of Brittany, they worked and struggled greatly such that he was rewarded, especially the earl of Richmond, constable of France, his uncle; the said late Prégent-de Coitivy, whom God pardon, and all others who had died in the said conquest and recovery, who in his life was lord of Rais and Coitivy and admiral of France. Also working strongly were the count of Laval; the seigneur de Lohéac, marshal of France, his brother; the seigneur de Montauban, marshal of Brittany; Geoffroi de Couvran; Jamet de Tillay, bailiff of Vermandois; and also the said Tudual the Bourgois, as long as he lived, who was then bailiff of Troyes in order to maintain the affairs and charge of the said war, both in matters of justice and of finance, and to council well and loyally the work and maintenance of the men-at-arms and the recovery of the said duchy. The said de Traignel, chancellor of France; the seigneur de Gaucourt; messire Théaude de Valepergue, bailiff de Lyon governed well and laboured greatly. Jacques Cueur, councillor and treasurer of the king, who made and found the manners and all subtleties that were possible to him to have finances and money from all parts to maintain the said armies and train the men of war, by which he made a great amount. And also there were messire Jean du Bar, seigneur de Baugy, and sire Jean Hardouin, treasurer of France, which was a great honour to them and to all the others who had worked and contributed in this party in service to the king. To which God by his magnanimous pleasure came and died well. Amen.

Commet̂ leRoy ſe delibera deſoy en ~ aller conquiſter laduchie deguyenne. et ſaprinſe debergerac.

APRES. ceque leRoy treſxtien̄. Charles Sept.eme dece nom. au moien et conduitte delagrace divine principallement et deſa tres noble et puiſſant chevallerie ſes conſeillers et autŝ ſouldoyers dedivers eſtatz. Aeu côqueſte ſaduchie deNormendie qui avoit eſte occuppe par les angloiz ſes anciens ennemys leſpace deXXX ans ou envoiron ait ſebuigie tout lepays et en Icellui mis promiſion Regime et police nouvelle. Et meſmement gardes degens de guerre aladeffence tant des citez villes fermees comme chaſteaulx et autres fortereſſes lui touſ confiant en lagrace et miſericorde de~~Jhs~~ Roy des Roys. Lequel veult aung chc̄n garder ſon droit comme Il eſt eſcript en une ourlye de Saint mathieu. Ou Il dit en parlant aux phariſnes. Reddite. que ſunt. ceſaris. ceſon que ſunt de. deo. Qui eſt actendre que on doit Rendre aung chc̄n ce qui eſt ſien. Ceſt diſpoſa et delibere et delibere en voullente daller es pays deguyenne et debordellois occupez pas les angloiz deſi longe temps quil neſt memoire ducintraire en allant directement cont̂ Raiſon et lomelye deſſus deſalavoir. Et tout touſiours les nobles et popullanes decellui pays eſte faulx et Rebelles alacouronne defrance ou aumoîs puis deux cens ans qui eſt grant lapz detemps combien que led pays eſt et atouſiours eſte du demain ducellui Royaulme defrance ~ Pourquoy lui voullant uſer deconſeil et faire meurement ſes entreprinſes comme ſaige ſobtil et vaillant Roy. vint en ſaville detours

How the king decided by himself to go conquer the duchy of Guyenne, and his capture of Bergerac

Afterwards, the very Christian king Charles, seventh of this name, by means and conducted principally by divine grace, and by his very noble and powerful knights, his councillors, and other soldiers of various estates, he had conquered his duchy of Normandy, which had been occupied by the English, his ancient enemies, for the space of thirty years or therearound, having subdued all the lands, and in this place installed a regime and new policy. And even guards [composed of] of men of war for the defense, both for the cities, walled towns, castles, and other fortresses, always confiding himself in the grace and mercy of the King of Kings, who wants for each one to guard his right, as it is written in the sayings of Saint Matthew, who says to the Pharises: render that [which] is Caesar's, [and] that which is God's, which is to mean one ought to render to each what is his. Then he disposed and deliberated and decided to move into the lands of Guyenne and the Bordelais, occupied by the English for so long that it was hardly remembered otherwise, going directly against reason and honor, as mentioned above. And always all the nobles and the populace of this land had been false and rebellious to the crown of France, for at least two hundred years, which was a great passage of time, such that the said land was and had always been of the domain of this kingdom of France, because he, wanting to use by council and improve his enterprises, as a wise, subtle, and valiant king, went into his town of Tours in the month of September, the year 1450, where he

ou moys deSeptembre. Lan mil CCCC.Cinquāte ou Il convoqua et fiſt aſſembler grant et noble chevallerie et lafut delibere par ſon ꝯſeil darmes deſon ſang prelatz et autres ſes con ſeillers et capitaines de envoyer aud pays deguyenne apres proviſion et garde miſt oud pays deNormendie. Pour laquelle garde fut adonne treſhault et treſpuiſſant ſeigneur monſeigneur artus debretaigne et avecques lui les barons chevalliers et eſcuiers dud pays deNormendie. Avecques. v.[c] lances et les archr̃s paiz chc̄n moys et grant nombre defrancs archiers ordonnez depar leRoy. Et ainſſi fut baillee lagarde delacite deRouen et du pays decaux. meſſire pierre debreze grant ſen.[cal] deNormendie. Puis ordonna leRoy en ce meſme conſeil de entrer en Icellui pays deguyenne. Et aller mettre leſiege devant laville deber cezac aſſiſe ond pays en laconte depierregot ſur laRiviere dedourdaine. Et pource fiſt ſon lieutenant. hault et puiſſant ſeigneur le conte depenthievre et deperigort viconte de limoges Lequel ~~achepta~~ accepta lacharge dud ſiege. Et partirent en ſacompaignie Meſſire charles decullant ſeigneu.[r] deIalongnes et mareſchal defrance. poton deſaintrailles bailly deberry et grant eſcuier deſcuyerie duRoy guioffroy deſaint bellin. Ioachim Rouault pierre louvain. et pluſſieurs autr̂s ſeigneurs chevallr̂s eſcuiers et autres gens deguerre nombres v.[c] lances et les archiers. leſquelz mirent le ſiege hardiment et treſvaillemment et tel̄le que par leur puiſſance proueſſe et bon gouv̂ nement apres lartillerie venue et conduitte par maiſtre Iehan bureau treſorier defrance. Lequel eſt treſdiligent et actif en fait de guerre fut Rendue lad ville debergerac en lobbeiſſance du Roy puis ſen Retournerent leſd ſeigneurs et leurs gens eulx yverner es logez par eulx

convoked and made assemble a great and notable knighthood, and there it was debated by his council, soldiers, [members] of his blood, prelates, and others of his councillors and captains, to send into the said land of Guyenne, after good provision and after guardians had been placed in the said land of Normandy. For which the guardianship was granted to the very high and powerful lord monseigneur Arthur of Brittany, and with him the barons, knights, and squires of the said land of Normandy, with 600 lances and the archers, paid each month, and a great number of free archers ordered by the king. And also messire Pierre de Brézée, grand seneschal of Normandy, was given the guardianship of the city of Rouen and the lands of Caux. Then, the king ordered in this same council to enter into this land of Guyenne and to go lay siege before the town of Bergerac, a keep in the said land in the county of Périgord on the River Dourdaine. And for this, he made his lieutenant the high and powerful count of Penthièvre and of Périgord, viscount of Limoges, who accepted and took charge of the said siege. And departing in his company were messire Charles de Culant, seigneur de Jallongnes and marshal of France; Poton de Xaintrailles, bailiff of Berry and grand squire of the squirerie of the king; Geoffroi de Saint-Belin; Joachim Rouault; Pierre Louvain; and several other lords, knights, squires, and other men of war, numbering 500 lances and the archers, who hardily and very bravely laid siege and such that, by their power, prowess, and good governance, after the artillery came and was conducted by master Jean Bureau, treasurer of France, who was very diligent and active in the deeds of war, the said town of Bergerac was rendered to the obedience of the king; then the said lords and their men returned to winter in the lodgings ordered to them. And as captain and

ordonnez. Et demoura pour capitaine et garde dud bergerac mefˢʳᵉ phl̂e decullant deſſuſd et en ſacompaignie Cent lances et les archiers. Et ainſſi les angloiz ſen aller leurs chevaulx et biens ſaufz côme lacompoſicion avoit eſte faicte. Et auſſi devoient demeurer les hâtans cilz voulloiet̂ en faiſant leſer-ment. Et faire leurs labeurs et meſtiers comme par avant.

Laprinſe delanſac et montferant par les francois.

EN. ce meſmes temps et an leſd ſeigneurs et leur compaignie allerent devant ung chaſteau nomme Ianſac eſperans ymettre leſiege lequel eſt ſitue ſur lad Riviere de dordongne Lequel fut prins daſſault et yot des aſſāil ſept ou huit denavrez et des angloiz. Xxxv. mors ou environ et ledemourant furent prins priſonnier et demoura lad place en lobbeiſſance du Roy defrance. Puis apres ſediviſa lar-mee donc Il alla partie amontferrant ou Ilz tindrent leſiege par ĉtaine eſpace detemps. Auquel fut fort aſſailly et pou deffendu. Car leſeigneur dud lieu voyant lagroſſe aſſem-blee degens devat̂ lui ot paour et ſeRendit et demoura p̊ſonner en lad place en lobbeiſſance du Roy defrance. Et fut laiſſe alagarde decelle place.

Laprinſe deSaintefoy.

DEpuis et ſans Intervalle detemps ſen ala lad armee devant une ville nommee Saincte foy aſſiſe ſur lad Riviere qui ſeRendit pareillement ſans contredit. Et fut laiſſe cap.ⁿᵉ pour leRoy. alagarde decelle.

guardian of the said Bergerac remained the abovesaid messire Philippe de Culant, and in his company 100 lances and the archers. And so the Englishmen left, their horses and goods safe, as had been set out in the agreement. And also, the inhabitants could remain there, if they wanted, in making oaths and to do their labours and jobs as before.

The capture of Jonzac and Montferrant by the French

In this same time and year, the said lords and their company went before a castle named Jansac, hoping to lay siege to it, which castle was situated on the said River Dordogne, which was captured by assault, and seven or eight of the assailants were wounded there, and of the English, thirty-five or therearound were killed and the rest were taken prisoner, and the said place remained in the obedience of the king of France. Then afterwards, the army divided itself, where it partly went to Montferrant, where they held siege for a certain period of time. For which it was heavily assailed and poorly defended, because the lord of the said place, seeing so great an assembly of men before him, was afraid, and he rendered himself as a prisoner and put the said place in the obedience of the king of France. And a garrison was left in this place.

The capture of Saint-Foy

Then and without any interval of time, the said army went before a town named Saint-Foi, seated on the said river, which rendered itself likewise without a fight. And a captain was left by the king to guard this place.

Laprinſe decalaiz

EN. Apres lad armee en pourſuivant touſio.^{rs} leur bonne fortune ſen alla devant une place appeller calaiz. et lafut tenu leſiege par certaine eſpace detemps. Apres lequel les angloiz eſtans dedens. Iucques au nombre decinquante lances ayans leceur failly par ce quilz voioient telle compaignie devant eulx ſe Rendirent par telle compoſicion quilz ſen allerẽt leurs corps et biens ſaufz. Et mirent ladicte place en lamain du Roẙ. Pour laquelle gardz fut commis. pierre louvain.

Empriſonnement demaiſtre. Iehan dexancoings.

LE xvi^{m} Iour doctobre ou ~~envo~~ environ oud an mille CCCC. Cinquante fut areſte priſonnier. Maiſtre Iehan dexaincoins Receveur general des finances du Roy. et fut mis eu chaſteau detours pource quil avoit mauvaiſe ment diſtribue et employe les deniers deſa Recepte. Et tellement que leRoẙ aſon grat̂ beſoing ne povoit finer dargent pour payer les ſouldours et gens deguerre eſtans en ſon ſervice aufait deſaguerre deguyenne. Maiz lui convint trouver autres moiens merveilleux pour avoir finances. Car autrement ſon fait euſt eſte mal pour parvenir aſon Intencion. Et eſt vray que depuis que Icellui Recepue^{r} fut aud chaſteau en priſon enferme Il fut queſtionne par aucuns dugrant conſeil duRoy et aut̂s voyans et bien cognoiſſans en matiere definances. Et fut trouve par ſa confſſion avoir encouru

The capture of Chalais

Afterwards, the army, in pursuing always their good fortune, went before a place named Chalais, and siege was held there for a certain period of time. After which the Englishmen within, up to the number of fifty lances, having frail hearts because they saw such a company before them, rendered themselves by an agreement such that they would go, their bodies and goods safely. And the said place was put into the hand of the king. For the guardianship of which was commissioned Pierre de Louvain.

Imprisonment of master Jean de Xaincoins

The sixteenth day of October or therearound, in the year 1450, master Jean de Xaincoins, receiver general of the finances of the king, was arrested and was put in the castle of Tours because he had badly distributed and used the money under his receipt. And such that the king, in his great need, could not find money to pay the soldiers and the men of war who were in his service to make war in Guyenne. But he convinced him to find other marvellous means in order to have money, because otherwise his situation had been poor in order to achieve his intentions. And it is true that since this receiver was in the said castle in prison, he was questioned by several of the great council of the king and others, perceptive and knowledgeable in matters of finance. And he was found by his own confession to have incurred in his offense the crime

en offence decrime delezemageſte. Ceſt aſſavoir tant pour les deniers du Roy quil avoit deſrobez en grant et exceſſive ſomme comme pour c̃taines Ratures. Parquoy fut Repute fauſſaire qui ſout cauſes depaine cappitalle qui lui euſt voulu grandes Iuſtice. Maiz leRoy qui eſt doulx et miſericors lui afait du ammeil emil en conſonant ace quil eſt eſcript denr̃ ſauveur xhr̃riſt ou Ie dit. Nolo mortem pecatoris Sed. Nt. Mattis. Connertatus. Et. venat. Ceſt adire Il ne vueil point lamort dupurchans maiz quil ſeconnerteſſe et bien. Et pource ſes par grans et enormes par lui confeſſez conſiderez fut condampne par labouche duchancellier de france atenir priſon fermee certaine eſpace detemps avecques confiſcacion detous ſes biens deſquelz leRoy donna ung hoſtel quil avoit fait faire atours. Atreſhault et treſpuiſſ^t^ leconte dedunoiz et delongueville. Et oulẗplus fut led xaincoins condampne depaier etReſtituer au Roy. laſomme delx^m^ eſcuz dor qui ſembloit eſtre bien peu dechoſe au Regard dece quil lui avoit pillie comme ſaconfeſſion leporte. Et pour ſes plaiſances mondaines faire. Avecques lequel fut mis priſonnier ung nomme Iacques charrier clerc dud Receveur en priſon ſeparee. Lequel par lecommandement deſon maiſtre et comme complice dud criſme avoit Raſe et gratte par luſtegarcion delomeny denature pluſſieurs ſommes dedeniers pour Icelles con vertus au dommaige du Roy et aleur prouffiſt. Pourquoy avoit encouru ſentence cappitalle. Si lagrace et miſericorde duRoy neſefuſt pareillement eſtendue ſur lui et eſt ce chap.^ne^ bien anotter pour donner exemple aux autres.

of lèse-majesté—it is known, both for the money of the king that he had stolen in great and excessive sums, and for certain erasures. For which he was reputed to be a forger, which incurred a capital sentence, which he wanted to show him great justice. But the king, who was gentle and merciful, in accord with that which was written of Our Savoir, Christ, where he said: 'I do not desire the death of the sinner, but that he may be converted and live', which is to say that he no longer wanted the death of the sinner, but rather that he repent and do well. And because, by the great and enormous things confessed and considered by him, he was condemned by the mouth of the chancellor of France, to stay in prison for a certain space of time, with the confiscation of all his goods, for which the king gave a house, which he had had built in Tours to a very great and very powerful lord, monseigneur the count of Dunois and of Longueville. And in addition, the said Xaincoins was condemned to pay and restore to the king the sum of 60,000 *écus* of gold, which seemed to be a very little thing in view of what he had looted and stolen, as his confession stated, and in order to make his worldly treasures. With him was also made prisoner one named Jaques Charrier, clerk of the said receiver, in a separate prison, who, by thc command of his master and as an accomplice to the said crime, had erased and scratched out several sums of money, at the instigation of the man of wicked nature, in order to convert it, to the damage of the king and to their profit. For which he had incurred a capital sentence. If the grace and mercy of the king had not equally extended to him, and this chapter is good to note to give an example to others.

Rencontre de francois et. angloiz pres bourdeaulx.

Oudit an ledeſrnier Iour doctobre veille defeſte detouſſains. leſeigneur dorval tres filz duconte dalbreth fut logier en ſa compaignie en lacite debazas. et ſepartirent pour aller courir lepays debordelloys. Et eſtoient en ſacompaignie eſtienne detollereſſe dit de vignolles. Robin petit lou. capitaine des eſcoſſois ung cap.[ne] nomme leſpinace et pluſſieurs aut̂ gens deguerre Iucques au nombre dequatre acinq cens combatans deſirans deIuſulter les anciens ennemys duRoy defrance eſtans abordeaulx et eu pays denviron ſemirent en chemin pour aller en liſle demadoc ſur lequel chemin Repeurent et boys en ung lieu eſtant adeux lieues pres dud bordeaulx. Et lelendemain premier Iour denovembre Iour detouſſains auplus matin quilz furent montez acheval cuidans entrer en lad Iſle leur ſairent nouvelles eulx eſtans en lad cite debourdeaulx tant gens deguerre côme poppullaires eſtoient ſur les champs eu nombre dehuit aneuf mil tant depie que decheval pour comabtre led ſ.[r] dorval et ſacompaignie. Et neantmains ne laiſſa point ſon entrepriſe Icellui ſ.[r] maiz meu defranc courage et tenant ferme propos miſt ſes gens en belle et notable ordon̂n en actendant bataille combien quilz fuſſet̂ en moindre nombre que les angloiz acom pagnez des habitans dud bourdeaulx et du pays denviron. deſquelz eſtoit conduiſeur les maire dud lieu. Et adonc commencerent les cou reus dud ſeigneur dorval aleur aller faire barbe et bon viſage. leſd ſeigneur et ſes gens ~ marchant en bataille par belle ordonnance

Encounter by the French and English near Bordeaux

In the said year, the last day of October, eve of the feast of All Saints, the seigneur d'Orval, third son of the count of Albret, was lodged with his company in the city of Basas and they left to go campaign in the land of the Bordelais. And there were in his company Étienne de Tholeresse, called Vignoles; Robin Petit-Loup, captain of the Scots; a captain named the Épinasse; and several other men of war, until the number was 400 to 500 soldiers, hoping to defeat the ancient enemies of the king of France, being at Bordeaux and in the areas around; they organised themselves in a train in order to go to the isle of Madoc, in which train they recuperated and [collected] wood, in a place within two leagues of the said Bordeaux. And the next day, first day of November, the day of All Saints, the earliest in the morning that they could mount a horse, thinking to enter the said island, news came to them that those in the said city of Bordeaux, both the men of war and the populace, were in the fields totalling 8,000 to 9,000, both on foot and horseback, in order to fight the said seigneur d'Orval and his company. And nonetheless, this lord would no longer pursue his attack, but moved by free courage and holding a firm resolution, he set his men in good and notable order, in arranging batallions, even though they were fewer in number than the Englishmen, accompanied by the inhabitants of the said Bordeaux and of the surrounding land, over whom was leader the mayor of the said place. And then the runners of the said seigneur d'Orval began to shave their faces and put on a good face, the said lord and his men marching in batallions by such good or-

Lesquelz coureus prindrent ung gentil homme dud bordeaulx pris dun borage. Et la fut et vaillemment combatu par les gens du Roy quil mourut. Xviii.[c] hommes tant dangloiz que debordellays que sus lechamp que alasante aceulx qui sen fuyoirent donc fut leprincipal sen finte led maire debourdeaulx qui estoit de cheval. et habandonna to⁹ lesd gens depie lesquelz Il avoit mis devant pour faire fron tiere deleur bataille. Et oult̂ et par dessus les mors furent prins et demourerent p̊sonniers aulesd francois xii.[c] hommes qui fut grant honneur et prouffit ausd conquerans. mesme ment veu lepetit nombre des gens qui estoiet̂ au Regard deleurs ennemys. Et en devoient bien Regracier dieu et to⁹ les sains deparades donc Il estoit leur feste et sollempmite ce Iour.

Hommaige fait au Roẙ par. pierre. duc debretaigne.

Audit. an Lendemain du Iour des mors pierre duc debretaigne vint devers leRoy son souverain seigneur pour faire hommaige de saduchie debretaigne. et lui fist faire lesermet̂ en tel cas acoustume. Monseigneur leconte dedunoiz et delongueville. Et comme grant chambellan duRoy print sa sainture lespee et lebouclier comme alui appartenant. Et apres led serment fait led chancellier defrance lui dist quil estoit liege homme du Roy acause desad duchie. Aquoy fut Respondu par lechancellier decellui duc que sauf ~~sa~~ [la]Reverence duRoy et decellui nestoit pas liege acause dicelle duchie. Et surce furent en altercation pour aucune espace detemps. finablement leRoy leReceult en foy aux vz et coustumes ainssi comme ses predecesseurs

der; the said runners captured a gentleman of the said Bordeaux, taken by his hair. And there was and bravely fought the men of the king, and 1,800 men died, both Englishmen and Bourdelais, both on the field and from their wounds as they fled; the principal of whom in flight was the said mayor of Bordeaux, who was on horseback and abandoned all his said footmen, whom he had put in front in order to make a front for their batallion. And otherwise, and in addition to the dead, 1,200 men were captured and remained prisoners of the said French, which was a great honour and profit to the said conquerers, especially considering the small number of men who were there in comparison to their enemies. And they must have had good grace to God and all the departed saints, for which it was their feast and solemnity this day.

Homage made to the king by Pierre, duc of Brittany

In the said year, the day after the day of the dead, Pierre, duke of Brittany, came before the king, his sovereign lord, in order to make homage to him for his duchy of Brittany and he made the oath in such case as accustomed to monseigneur the count of Dunois and of Longueville, and, as grand chamberlain of the king, he took the belt, sword, and shield as to him it belonged. And after the said oath was made, the chancellor of France said to him that he was a liegeman of the king because of his said duchy. To which was responded by the chancellor of this duke that, except for the reverence of the king and for this, he was not a liegeman because of this duchy. And for this, they was an altercation for a space of time; finally, the king received him into the faith according to laws and customs, like his predecessor

ducz debretaigne avoient fait. Et apres Intvalle fiſt au-Roy ung hômage pour ſa conte demontfort pour laquelle Il con feſſa eſtre ſon liege homme et vaſſal. Et ace fut Receu agrant chere. duRoy et deſachevalerie et fut une petite ville et chaſteau appelle monbaſon ou leRoy ſetenoit pour lors Auquel lieu fut led duc grandement feſtoye des daes et damoiſelles. Et auſſi Il ſe acqueta gran dement envers elles. Monſ devillequier ~ eſcuier et mademoiſelle ſafemme eſtoient lors en grant auctorite en lacour du Roy. Et yot groſſes lettes et auts eſbatemens ~ durant xv. Iours ou environ que led duc fut devers le Roy. Icelliu duc vint bien en point et en bila compaigne et eſtoit avecqz lui leconte deRichemont conneſtable defrance et pluſſieurs auts ſeigneurs chevalliers et eſcuiers. Eſtimez Iucques au nombre dequat acinq. cens chevaulx.

EN. Lan enſuivant mil CCCC. Cinquante et ung. leRoy eſtant en ſacite detours ordonna leconte dedunoiz et delongueville ſon lieutenant general pour aller en ſaduchie de guyenne pour Icelle Redduire et mettre en ſon obbaiſſance. Et pource vint aud lieu detours au commencement du moys demay. puis manda leRoy apluſſieurs ſeigneurs chevallrs et eſcuiers que chcn ſepreparaſt pour aller alaconqueſte deſond pays deguyenne. Et pource ſepartit led lieutenant aſon grant et notable compaignie degens deguerre et alla mettre leſiege devant ung chaſtel nom mont guyon. Auquel lieu vint au ſervice du Roy. leconte dengouleſme frere legitime du duc dorleans. maiſtre Iehan bureau treſorier defrance. pierre louvain et pluſſieurs autres chevalliers eſcuiers et auts Iucques n au nombre de iiii.[c] lances et les

dukes of Brittany had made. And after a break, he made another homage to the king for his county of Montfort, for which he confessed to be his man and vassal. And it was received with great cheer by the king and by all his knighthood, and he [went to] a small town and castle named Monbason, where the king remained for the time, at which place the said duke feasted greatly [with] the ladies and the damsels, and also he aquitted himself greatly towards them. Monseigneur of Villequier, a squire, and mademoiselle his wife were then in great authority in the court of the king. And there were held great jousts and other entertainment during the fifteen days or therearound that the said duke was with the king, this duke came well appointed and in good company and with him was the earl of Richmond, constable of France, and several other lords, knights, and squires, estimated at around 400 to 500 knights.

IN the following year, 1451, the king being in the city of Tours, he ordered the count of Dunois and of Longueville, his lieutenant general, to go into his duchy of Guyenne to reduce this place and put it into his obedience. And for this, he came to the said place of Tours at the beginning of the month of May, then the king ordered several lords, knights, and squires, that each would prepare himself in order to go to the conquest of his said land of Guyenne. And for this, his said lieutenant departed with a great and notable company of men of war, and he went to lay siege before a castle named Mont-guyon, at which place came to the service of the king the count of Angoulême, legitimate brother of the duke of Orléans; master Jean Bureau, treasurer of France; Pierre de Louvain; and several other knights, squires, and others, until the number was 400 lances

archiers et guiſ armiers. avec iii.m francs archers qui tindrent le ſiege vaillemment en actendant touſiours pluſgrant ſ'ie qui devoit venir. lequel ſiege yfut par leſpace dehuit Iours ou environ. Et eſtoit capitaine dud chaſteau pour les angloiz. Regnauld deſainct Iehan eſcuier gaſcon et ſerviteur du captan des buchz avec ĉtain nombre degens darmes lequel voyant non pouvoir alapuiſſance qui devant lui eſtoit Re ſiſtes fiſt certain appoinctement avec les ſ.rs deſſuſd en lamaniere qui ſenſ.

Traicte deplace demontguyon

Appoinctement fait ent̂ meſſ.rs deRochouart delaRoche foucault et maiſtre Iehan bureau conſeiller du Roy nore ſ're et treſorier defrance pour et au nom demeſſeigneurs les contes dangoleſme et dedunoiz lieuten̂ du Roy dunepart. Et arnoul deſaint Iehan eſcuier capne delaplace et chaſteau demontguy pour la Reddicion dicelle place daut̂ part. Premierement led arnoul baillera lad place ameſd ſ.rs les contes ou atelle perſonne qui ler plaira ordonner. dedens leIour demardy neuf heures dematin proĉh ven̂ oucas que dedens Icellui Iour et heure ceulx duparty dud arnoul neſe Rendronent ſi fors devant Icelle place que par puiſſance darmes ny peuſſent faire departir meſdſ.rs les contes du lieu quilz prendront et tiendront devant lad place. Et auſſi ſependant ne po'ront Recevoir priſonner ne mettre dedens Icelle place. C Item et ſen pourra aller led arnoul led Iour demardy dedens lad heure deneuf heures. Et ceulx eſtans dedens lad place avec to9 leurs biens et habillemens deguerre. deſquelz homme ſepeult aider et porters en guerre apie et acheval. C

and the archers and pikemen, with 3,000 free archers, who held the said siege bravely, attending always with a very great seigneurie, who ought to come, which siege was held there for the space of eight days or therearound. And the captain of the said castle for the English was Regnaud de Saint-Jean, a Gascon squire and servant of the captal du Buch, with a certain number of men-at-arms, who, seeing that they could not [resist] the power that was laid out before them, made a certain agreement with the abovesaid lords in the manner which follows:

Treaty of the place of Montguyon

Agreement made between messeigneurs de Rochechouart, de la Roche Foucault, and master Jean Bureau, councillor of the king, our lord, and treasurer of France, for and in the name of messeigneurs the counts of Angoulême and of Dunois, lieutenant of the king, on one part, and Arnould de Saint-Jean, squire and captain of the place and the castle of Mont-Guyon, for the reduction of this place, on the other part. Firstly, the said Arnould will deliver the said place to my said lords the counts or to such person that they appoint by the next day of Tuesday, nine in the morning, or in case that by this day and hour those of the party of the said Arnould do not find themselves as strong before this place, neither by the power of arms nor power to make my said lords, the counts, leave from the place, that they will take and will have this place. And also, however, he will not receive prisoners nor admit anyone into this place. C Item and so the said Arnould can leave the said day of Tuesday at the said hour of nine. And those being within the said place, with all their goods and tools of war, for which men can help and carry in war on foot and on

Item et laiſſeront ceulx dededens lad place tout artillerie quelconque eſtant en Icelle place. excepte celle deſſſd que on porte apie et acheval donc hommes ſepeult aidz alamain. Et ne ladegaſteront ou dômage Ront en aucune maniere. Maiz labailleront par deſclaracion et par eſcript avant partir. C Item et demeureront en Icelle place tous priſonniers et ſcellez quilz peuvent avoir et quicteront toutes debtes et promeſſes quilz ont aulcuns eſtans duparty duRoy excepte des debtes qui ſont dues aud arnoul pour Reſponces de priſonniers et auſſi quicteront to[9] appactiz et les arrorages. C Item et cil ya aucuns en lad place qui ~~auſ̂ſfoo~~ autreffoiz aient eſte duparty du Roy Ilz demoureront alavoulente demeſditſ.[rs]. C Item et cil ya aucuns en lad place qui veuillent demourer afaire leſerment deſtre bons et loyaulx au Roy Ilz yſeront Receuz. et avo͡t leurs biens et heritaiges quelzconques. C Item et cil en ya aucuns dicelle place ou environ. qui depnt̂ ne furent en Icelle et Ilz veullent Retourner et faire leſerment comme deſſus faire lepourront et yſeront Receuz par lecap[ne] dud lieu en faiſant leſerment. et auront t̂me pource faire xv. Iours entiers acompter le dacte duIourduy. C Item et avoir led arnoul et ceulx dicelle place qui aller ſen vouldront bon et loyal ſaufconduit pour aller ou bon le[r] ſemblera en leur party avecques leurſd biens. Et auront voitures ou beſtes pour les emporter aleurs deſpens Iucques aillborne en baillant bonne ſeurete deles Renvoyer au party duRoy. C Item et pour faire et acomplir les choſes deſſſd delapart dud arnoul Il baillera quatre hoſtages deceulx eſtans en lad place en la main deſdeſſſd Iucque ace que lad place ſoit Rendue. C Item et pendant led temps de mardy. Ix. heures ch͡cn poura beſongner deſon coſte. ceſt

horseback. C Item and those within the said place will leave all artillery that is in this place, except the abovesaid that one carries on foot and on horseback that men can use by hand. And the said will not destroy or damage them in any manner, but they will deliver it by declaration and by writing before leaving. C Item and all the prisoners and seals that they had will remain in this place, and they will discharge all debts and promisses that they had to anyone of the party of the king, except for debts which are due to the abovesaid Arnould in regard to prisoners, and also they will abandon all interest and arrears for them. C Item and if there are any in the said place who otherwise had been of the party of the king, they will remain at the will of my said lords. C Item and if there are any in the said place who want to remain to take the oath to be good and loyal to the king, they will be received there, and they will have their goods and heritage whatever. C Item and if there are any of this place or nearby who at present are not in this place and they want to return and make the oath as above, they can do so, and they will be received by the captain of the said place, in making the oath, and they will have a term in order to do this of fifteen days from today. C Item and the said Arnould and those of this place who want to go will have good and loyal safe conduct in order to go wherever it seems good to them in their said party with their said goods. And they will have vehicles or beasts in order to carry them at their expense until Liborne, granting good surety for the return to the party of the king. C Item and in order to make and accomplish the abovesaid things on the part of the said Arnould, he will deliver four hostages of those being inside the said place into the hands of the abovesaid until the said place is rendered. C Item and at the said time of nine in the morning, each can work on his side, it is known those holding the

aſſavoir ceulx eſtans au ſiege dedens lepays quilz terment et ceulx delad place devant leur place et foſſez ainſſi que bon leur ſemblera. Eſquelz appoinctemens les deſſd nommez cômis delapart demeſd ſ.[rs] les contes dune part et led arnoul daut̂ ont Iure et promis entretenir depoint en point ſans enfraindre. Teſmoingz leurs ſaingz et ſeaulx manuelz mis oud appoinctement levi[m] Iour dumay Lan mil CCCC cinquante ⁊ung. Et pource que led arnoul neuſt aucuns ſecours des gens deſon party en accompliſſant ſapromeſſe Rendit lad place. et miſt en lamain du Roy lan et Iour deſſd. Et demoura cappitaine en Icelle place pour leRoy defrance.

Siege mis amontguyon ꝑles francois.

Oudit an mil CCCC. Cinquante ⁊ung le xvi[me] Iour dud moys demay. dapres la Reddicion dud montguyon alla led conte de dunoiz lieutenant et les autres ſeigneurs deſſd mettre leſiege devant lune des portes delaville deblaye. Et ſeIoignit avecques lui meſſire pierre debeauvau ſeigneur delabeſſiere et lieutenant duconte dumaine gouverneur deſes gens darmes. Et guiffroy deSaint belin Leſquelz avoient en leur compaignie viii.[xx] lâces et les archiers et guiſarmiers. Et latrouverent Meſſire Iacques dechabanes grant maiſtre doſtel du Roy et Ioachim Rouault Leſquelz avecques leur compaignie ſemirent ducoſte dedevers le chaſteau. et ſe logerent alamalladrie. Et avoiēt deux cens lances avecques les archiers. et deux mille francs archiers. Et la aRiva par mer grās foiſon deNavires donc eſtoit chief et gouvr̂nr̂ Meſſire Iehan lebourſſier general defrance. eſquelz navires avoit grant multitude degens darmes et detrait et grant garniſon

said siege within the lands that they occupy, and those of the said place before their place and the moats, however it seems good to them. Which agreements articles the above named commited on the part of my said lords, the counts, on one part, and the said Arnould on the other, were sworn and promised to maintain point by point, without any infraction. Witnessed, their seals and sigantures placed on the said agreement, the sixth day of May 1451. And because the said Arnould had no help from the men of his party to accomplish his promiss, he rendered the said place and put it into the hands of the king in the year and the day abovesaid. And he remained captain in this place for the king of France.

Siege laid at Mont-Guyon by the French

In the said year 1451, the sixteenth day of the said month of May, after the reduction of the said Mont-Guyon, the said count of Dunois, lieutenant, and the other abovesaid lords went to lay siege before one of the gates of the town of Blaye. And joining with him was messire Pierre de Beauvau, seigneur de la Bessière and lieutenant of the count of Maine, governor of his men-at-arms, and Geoffroi de Saint-Belin, who had in their company 160 lances and the archers and polemen. And messire Jacques de Chabannes, grand master of the hotel of the king, and Joachim Rouault were found there, who, with their company, laid [siege on the side] toward the castle, and they camped at Malladerie. And they had with them 200 lances and the archers, and 2,000 free archers. And a great abundance of ships arrived by sea there, over whom was leader and governor messire Jean Le Boursier, general of France, in which ships was a great multitude of men-at-arms and treatymen, and a good,

diverſes pour admittaillr̃ loſt qui eſtoit auſiege delad ville deblaye. Leſquelz navires en approuchant dud oſt trouverent devat̂ leport dicelle ville cinq gros vaiſſeaulx bien armez. Leſquelz eſtoient venus debourdeaulx po^{r} advitailler ſecourir et aider ceulx delad ville deblaye. Et fut combatu treſvaillamment et tellement que les navires et francois ~~et~~ mirent en fuite les angloiz. deſquelz en yot pluſſieurs mors et navrez. et leur convint deſancrer leurs vaiſſ eulx pour eulx enfuir droit abordaulx. Et les chaſſerent leſd francois Iucques auport. Et ence ſe gouverna meſſire Iehan lebourchier vaillemmet̑ et ſagement. Et pareillement firent ceulx de ſacompaignie. Puis ſen Retourna atout ſes navires devant leport deblayes affin que ſecours ne vivres ne peuſſent entrer par mer en lad ville. Et auſſi fut aſſiegee par mer et par terre detoutes pars. Et environ deux Iours apres cefait aRiva leconte depenthievre atout Cent lances et trois cens ~~archiers~~ arbaleſtriers. Et ſeloga auſiege aud conte dedunoiz. et adonc devant lad ville furent faictes degrans vaillances approuchemens defoſſez demynes et detrenches. et fut tirorblemet̂ batue degroſſes bombardes et decanons et tellemet̂ que lamuraille fut abatue en pluſſieurs lieux. Et eſtoient dedens lad ville pour ladeffence dicelle lapluſgrant part des plus vaillans hômes deguerre deladuchie deguienne tenans leparty du Roy dangleterre. Et environ lexx^{me} Iour dud moys demay ung peu ſouleil couchant aleure que on forne leguet. Aucuns francs archiers de lacompaignie deIehan demeauſe nomme leſ.^{re} demaugouverne capitaine des francs archiers de touraine et les gens depierre louvain monteret̂ ſur lamuralle delad ville et adonc commenca laſſault detoutes pars tellement que lad ville fut prinſe. Et yfut bien aud aſſault que mors que prins deux

diverse larder, in order to revitalise the army that was at this siege of the said town of Blaye. Which ships, in approaching the said army, found before the port of this town five large, well-armed vessels, who had come from Bordeaux in order to assist, help, and aide those of the said town of Blaye. And there was very brave combat and such that the ships and French put the English in flight, of whom several were killed or injured, and they convinced them to flee straight to Bordeaux. And the said French chased them to the port. And in doing this, messire Jean Le Boursier governed himself bravely and wisely, and equally did those of his company. Then he returned with all his ships before the port of Blaye, after which no rescue nor resupply could enter by sea in the said town. And so, it was besieged by sea and by land from all parts. And around two days after this was done, the count of Penthièvre arrived with around 100 lances and 300 crossbowmen. And he camped at the siege with the said count of Dunois and so before the said town were made great deeds, approaches, mines, and trenches, and it was battered furiously by large bombards and cannon, and such that the wall was demolished in several places. And within the said town were, for the defense of this place, the majority of the bravest men of war of the duchy of Guyenne holding to the party of the king of England. And around the twentieth day of the said month of May, a little before sunset, at the hour that one changes the guard, several of the free archers of the company of Jean de Meause, named the seigneur de Maugouverne, captain of the free archers of Touvaine, and the men of Pierre de Louvain, appeared before the walls of the said town, and then the assault began on all sides, such that the said town was captured. And at the said assault there were amongst the dead

cens angloiz. Et ſeRetrayner agrant haſte dedens lechaſteau lemaire et ſoubzmaire debourdeaulx. leſeigneur deleſparre Leſeigneur demontferant et pluſſieurs autẽ ſeigneurs et gens deguerre Iucques au nombre dedeux cens hommes. Et quant ceulx dud chſ vivent les approuchemens contre eulx et quilz nepouorent eſvader par faulte deſecours ne par mer ne par terre traictement deulx Rendre et mettre lechaſteau en lamain du Roy de france. Et auſſi leur fut faicte par les ſeigneurs francois leſiege gracieuſe compoſicion et traicte ſelon laforme et maniere qui ſenſ.

Traicte du chaſteau ⁊donlon deblaye.

Traicte et appoinctement fait Entẽ meſſeigneurs les grant maiſtre doſtel. leſeigneur deleſcars maiſtre Iehan bureau conſeiller du Roẙ treſorier defrance. monſr deſternay general defrance et Iouachim Rouault ſeigneur duboys menart cômis par monſ.r leconte dedunoiz lieutenant general du Roy ſur lefait deſaguerre dune part. Et meſſire gadifier chartreuſe chevallr̃ Maire debourdeaulx. pierre demonferrant ſoubz dit de Latrau et ſeigneur deleſparre. thomas gaciet ſoubz maire deBourdeaulx. et Rolland charnau eſleu to9 eſtans en garniſon eu chaſteau deblaye pour le Roy dangleterre dautẽ part. pour laReddiction dud chaſteau et donIon en lamaniere qui ſenſ. Pre mierement aeſte appoincte et acorde entre leſdeſſd ſrs led maire debourdeaulx et autres delagarniſon dud chaſteau deblaye mettront et Rendront Rallemẽt et defait leſd chaſteau et donIon es mains demondſr leconte dedunoiz ou deſes commis pour le Roymẽ deſſd dedens leIourhuẙ. C Item et delaiſſeront en Icellui chaſteau et don-

and captured around 200. And they retreated with great haste within the castle of the mayor and submayor of Bordeaux, the seigenur de la Parre, the seigneur de Montferrant, and several other lords and men of war, until the number was 200 men. And when those of the said leader saw the attacks against them and that they could not evade except by rescue, neither by sea nor land, they negotiated with them to render and put this castle into the hand of the king of France. And so a gracious agreement and treaty was made by the French lords [holding] the siege, according to the form and manner which follows:

Treaty of the castle and keep of Blaye

Treaty and agreement made between messeigneurs the grand master of the hotel, the seigneur d'Estrac; master Jean Bureau, councillor of the king, treasurer of France; monseigneur d'Esternay, general of France; and Joachim Rouault, seigneur du Boys, commissioned by monseigneur the count of Dunois, lieutenant general of the king for the matter of his war, on one part. And messier Gadifer Chartreuses, a knight, mayor of Bordeaux; Pierre de Montferrant, called Latreau; and seigneur de Lesparre, Thomas Gaciet, undermayor of Bordeaux; and Roland Charnau, elector; all being in the garrison of the castle of Blaye for the king of England, on the other part, for the reduction of the said castle and kee0, in the manner that follows: Firstly, to be appointed and agreed between the abovesaid lords, the said mayor of Bordeaux and others of the garrison of the said castle of Blaye will put and render genuinely and place the said castle and keep into the hands of my said lord, the count of Dunois, or to his commissioners, for the abovesaid king within this same day. C

Ion tous leurs biens quelzconq͡z or argent artillerie eſtant en Icellui chaſteau et donIon. Et Iceulx metront ou feront mettre par bonne et loyalle ~~memoire~~ Inventoire avant quilz choſe. C Item et demouront tous en Icellui chaſteau et donIon eſtans dedens Icellui. priſonniers alavoulête du Roy ſauvez leurs vies. Et cil plaiſt au Roẙ ou amond ſ^{r} leconte dedelivrer leſdiſſd ou les aucuns deulx plus toſt que letemps et terme de quatre moys prochains venans ſoubz les moyens et traictez qui ſeront adviſez cilz pouront eulx venues. alencontre du Roẙ ne aucun tenant ſon party pluſtoſt que leſd quat̂ moys prouchainement ve͡n ſoient paſſez et acompliz. C Item et cil ya aucuns qui autreffois avent tenu leparty duRoẙ Ilz demouront aſaplaine voullente. C Item et avant que leſdeſſd ne aucuns deulx ſoient delivrez ne mis affinance. Ilz ſeront tenus debailler Reallement et defait es mains demondſ.^{r} leconte dedunoiz. ~~et~~ ou deſes commis toutes les places quilz ~~troient~~ tenoient et occupent eu pays deguyenne. C Item et demouront tous priſonniers et ſcellez ſi aucuns en ont quictes et delivrez. et auſſi toutes promeſſes et obligacions quelzconques aeulx duparty duRoy defrance et apparte͡ns auſdeſſd et Rendront les oſtages quilz tiennent francs et quictes. C Item. et ſe les aucuns deceulx eſtans en lad place veullent demourer euparty du Roẙ. et faire leſerment deſtre doreſinant bons et loyaulx envers leRoy donc Ilz Ioiſſoient par avait. Toutes leſquelles choſes et chu͡ne dicelles leſdeſſſnommez et chu͡n deux ont Iure et promis chu͡n deſapart faire tenir et ac~~ordes~~ complir depoint en point ſelon leur forme et teneur ſans enfraindre en aucune maniere. Teſmoing leurs ſceaux et ſeingz manuelz cy mis aud blaye Lexxiiii^{me} Iour deMay. Lan mil CCCC Cinquante ⁊ung.

Item and they will leave in this castle and keep all their goods whatsoever, gold, money, and artillery being within this castle and keep. And they will make or prepare a good and accurate inventory before this thing is done. C Item and all those within this castle and keep will remain prisoners at the will of the king, save their lives. And if it is pleasing to the king or to monseigneur the count to release the abovesaid or several of them before the time and term of four months following coming, under the means and agreement which will be advised, they can never come against the king, nor any holding to his party, until the said four months have passed, elapsed, and been accomplished. C Item and if there are any who had otherwise held to the party of the king, they will remain at his full will. C Item and having the abovesaid or several of them released or put to ransom, they will be held to deliver in reality and in fact into the hands of my said lord, the count of Dunois, or one of his commissioners, all the places that they hold and occupy in the land of Guyenne. C Item and all the remaining prisoners and seals, if they have not been released and delivered, and also all promises and obligations whatsoever to those of the party of the king and belonging to the abovesaid, and the hostages that they hold will be released, freed, and quit. C Item and if any of those in the said place want to remain with the party of the king and make the oath to be in the future good and loyal toward him, then they will be received. All of which things and each of these the abovenamed and each of them had sworn and promised each one on his part to do, to hold, and to accomplish point-by-point, according to their form and tenor, without infringing in any manner. Witnessed their seals and manual signatures so affixed at the said Blaye the twenty-fourth day of May. The year 1451.

Ladelivrance depierre demôtferât p̊ſonnier.

Tractie et appoinctement fait. Entre Iehan baſtard dorleans. conte dedunoiz ⁊delongueville Lieutenant general duRoẙ. Meſſire Iacques decha banes chevallier grant maiſtre doſtel du Roẙ Et maiſre Iehan bureau treſorier defrance dune part. Et pierre demontferant ſoubz dit delatrau priſonniers deſuſſd nommez ſur lamaniere dela delivrance deſaperſonne. Premierement que led pierre demontferant baillera et paira po[r] ſaRanchon auſdeſſſ nommez laſomme dedix mille eſcuz dor dedens lexv[me] Iour deIuillet proch enſuivant ou alun deulx pour les trois. C Item et pour laſeurete diceulx dix mille eſcuz baillera les ſcellez demonſ[r] demontferant et demonſ[r] deduras. Et ſi baillera ſon aiſne filz hoſtage et ſon nepveu Ihaut defrans es mains dud grant maiſtre doſtel qui tiendront bonne et loyalle priſon et hoſtages Iucques aplein paiemet delad ſomme dedix mille eſcuz. C Item et a eſte promis par leſdeſſſd aud ſoubz dit que ſe Il lui plaiſt dedens letemps deſix ſemaines faire leſerment deſtre bon et loyal ſubget et obbeiſſant auRoẙ. defrance faire lepourra ⁊mettre cinq. places es mains deſdeſſſd ſeigneurs pour et eu nom duRoy defrance et deſon obbaiſſance. Et euce faiſant demoura quicte delad ſomme deſix mille eſcuz. Et pour ſeurete dentretenir ſond ſerment bien et loyamment delaiſſera en hoſtage et baillera deux deſes principalles places. Leſquelles leſdeſſd vouldront choiſir ou lun deulx. Touteſſoiz Il Ioyrades Revenus dicelles places. C Item et lmaiſtre adcorde et promis que tantoſt et Incontinant que la ville debordaulx ſera Redduicte et

The release of Pierre de Montferrant, prisoner

Treaty and agreement made between Jean, bastard of Orléans, count of Dunois and of Longueville, lieutenant general of the king; messire Jacques de Chabannes, knight, grand master of the hotel of the king; and messire Jean Bureau, treasurer of France; on one part. And Pierre de Montferrant, surnamed de la Trau, prisoner of the abovenamed, on the manner of the release of his person. Firstly, that the said Pierre de Montferrant will be released and pay for his ransom to the abovenamed the sum of 10,000 écus of gold by the fifteenth day of the following July, or to one of them a third. C Item and for the surety of this 10,000 écus, the seals of messire Bernard de Montferrant and of monseigneur de Duras will be delivered. And so he will give his eldest son and his nephew, Jaunet de France, into the hands of the said grand master of the hotel, who will hold them safely and loyally as prisoners and hostages, until the full payment of the abovesaid sum of the said 10,000 écus. C Item and it has been promised by the abovesaid to the undernamed that, if it pleases him within the time of six weeks to make the oath to be a good and loyal subject and vassal of the king of France, he can do so and put five places into the hands of the abovesaid lords for and in the name of the king of France and for his obeissance. And in doing which, he will be relieved of the said sum of 6,000 écus. And as surety for saying his said oath well and loyally, he will leave as hostages and deliver two of his principal places, which the abovesaid will want to chose or one of them. Furthermore, he will enjoy the revenues of these places. C Item and the master agreed and promissed that as soon as and immediately after the

miſe en lobbeiſſance du Roy defrance leſd deux places quil avoit ainſſi Renduiz lui feront Rebaillers et Reſtitures pour en Iouis par lui comme deſapropre choſe. Et pareillement lui demouront ſes autres places. Et ſe lui donnera leRoy ſaſ^re^ie debarat Iucques alavalleur decent livres tournoiz deRente. Et oult̂ plus lui donera leRoy en Recompenſaſſion dequatre mille francs deRente q̂ leRoy dangletr̂e lui avoit donnez eu pays deguyenne. Leſquelz Ia pn̂t habandonne pour lui et ſeſd places mettre en lobbeiſſance du Roy defrance. laſomme detrois mille eſcuz dor.

LaReddicion duchaſteau ~~duch~~ debourg.

Oudit. an ſans Intervalle apres laReddicion delad ville deblaye Separtit led conte dedunoiz avecques to⁹ les ſeigneurs et armee deſacompaignie. et alla mettre leſiege devât laville et lechaſteau debourg. tant par mer que par terre. et ny fut led ſiege que v. ou vi. Iours. Car quant ceulx qui eſtoient dedens virent ſigrant puiſſance et belle ordon̂ vyrent auſſi bombardes et canons aſſortes. vyret̂ auſſi mynes aprouchemens et trenches Ilz Requerent eulx Rendre leurs corps et biens ſaufs. Et eſtoient dedens Icelle place dequatre acinq cens combatans donc eſtoit cap^ne^ meſſire pierre berard demontferant. Alaquelle Requeſte les ſeigneurs deſſſd oulrent enſemble côſultans. Et apres leurs fut adcorde aprointement et traicte en lamaniere qui ſenſuyt.

town of Bordeaux is reduced and put into the obedience of the king of France, that the said two places that he had so delivered would be handed over and restored to him for his enjoyment as a rightful thing to him. And also, he retained his other places. And the king gave him the lordshop of Barat, totalling a value of 100 *livres tournois* of rent. And more, the king will give him, in compensation for 4,000 francs of rent that the king of England had given him in the lands of Guyenne, which he had already given up for himself and his said places put into the obedience of the king of France, the sum of 3,000 *écus* of gold.

The reduction of the castle of Bourg

In the said year, after the reduction of the said town of Blaye, the said count of Dunois left with all the lords and army of his company and went to lay siege before the town and the castle of Bourg, both by sea and by land, and the said siege was held there for only five or six days, because when those who were within saw so great power and such order also with the bombards and cannon assembled before them, in addition to the mines, approaches, and trenches, they asked to render themselves, their bodies and goods safely. And there were within this place 400 to 500 soldiers, over whom was captain messire Bernard de Montferrant, at whose request the abovesaid lords held council together. And afterwards, there was a concensus, agreement, and treaty made amongst them in the manner which follows.

Traicte et appoinctement.

Traicte. et appointement fait Enẗ meſſ.re Iehan lebourſſier chevallier ſeigner deſternay meſſire gaultier deperuce ſeigneur des eſcacs et maiſtre Iehan bureau treſorier defrance pour et eu nom demeſd ſ.rs Les contes dangoleſme et deponthieve et monſr leconte dedunoiz et de longueville lieuteñ general duRoy dunepart Et les maire gens degliſe nobles bourgois et hâtans delaville debourg dautrepart pour Raiſon delad ville aſſieger dautrepart par meſd ſ.rs Icellui appoîtemeẗ fait comme Il ſenſuyt. Premierement led maire gens degliſe nobles bourgois et habitans delad ville des mains demeſd ſ.rs les contes debourg mettront dedens leIourduy Rallement et defait lad ville es mains demeſd ſ.rs les contes ou deleurs cômis pour et eu nom du Roy defrance. C Item ſera donne ſaufconduit amonſr demontferant monſr delancas et ung nomme clemens et ceulx deleur compaignie et ato9 les auẗs eſtans en lad ville dequelque eſtat ou condicion quilz ſoient qui ſen vouldront aller et conduit degens ſi meſtȓ eſt. C Item et to9 ceulx qui vouldront demouȓ en lad ville dequelque eſtat ou condicion quilz ſoient faire lepourront en faiſ leſerment deſtre bons et vrays loyaulx auRoy et obbaiſſans ſubgetz et ence faiſant avoient to9 leurs biens et hȓtaiges quelzconques ou quilz ſoient ſituez et aſſis et auront abolicion generalle deto9 cas et choſes quelzconques. C Item et demoureront to9 leſd hîtans enleurs franchiſes privilegez et libertez ancienes aeulx donnez par les predeceſſeurs ducz de guyenne. Et ſe obligeront meſd ſrs les contes aler faire

Treaty and Agreement

Treaty and agreement made between messire Jean le Boursier, knight, seigneur d'Esternay; messire Gautier de Perrusse, lord of Escacs; and master Jean Bureau, treasurer of France, for and in the name of my said lords the counts of Angoulême and Penthièvre and monseigneur the count of Dunois and of Longueville, lieutenant genral of the king, on one part. And the mayor, men of the church, nobles, cityfolk, and inhabitants of the town of Bourg, on the other part, by reason of the said siege of the town by the other part by my said lords, which agreement made is as follows. Firstly, the said mayor, men of the church, nobles, cityfolk, and inhabitants of the said town of Bourg, by the hands of my said lords, the counts, will put within the day, completely and by deeds, the said town into the hands of my said lords, the counts, or their commissioners, for and in the name of the king of France. C Item, safe conduct will be given to monseigneur de Montferrant, monseigneur de Lancas, and one named Clement, and to those of their company, and to all the others who are in the said town, of whatever state or condition that they are, who want to go, and guided, if it is needed. C Item and all those who want to remain in the said town, of whichever state or condition that they are, they can do so by making the oath to be good, true, loyal, and obedient subjects of the king, in which case they will have all their goods and heritages whatsoever, wherever they were situated and seated, and will have a general pardon in all cases and things whatever. C Item and all of the said inhabitants will remain in their franchises, priviledges, and ancient liberties given to them by the previous dukes of Guyenne. And my said lords, the counts, will oblige

confermer par leRoy Iceulx privileges. C Item et auront ceulx qui ſen vouldront allr̃ to⁹ leurs biens chevaulx et harnoiz et avecques ce bon ſaufconduit. C Item et cil ya aucuns qui prête ment veuillet̂ faire leſerment et veuillet̂ aller faire leurs beſoignes et querer leurs biens ⁊debtes Ilz yſeront Receuz aceulx deſclares defaire francois Iucques anoel proch̃ veñ. Et ce pendant pourront Retourner ſibon leur ſemble en lad ville et faire leſerment et Ilz yſeront Receuz et auront tous leurs biens et heritage quelzconques. C Item et pend led temps denoel leſdeſſſd qui ſen yrot̂ pouront laiſſer en garde en lad ville to⁹ leurs biens ou aucuns diceulx ſibon leur ſemble et les envoyer querir ſibon leur ſemble pend Icellui temps ou les vendre et ne leur ſera donne en Iceulx biens quilz laiſſeront en lad ville aucun deſtroubier ou empeſchement. C Item et pôront demander leſd hâtains et arquirer eulx faire paier detoutes leurs debtes bonnes et loyalles de to⁹ ceulx qui aucune choſe leur devront ou pôront devoir aquelle cauſe ou coulleur que ceſoit non obſtant quilz ſen aillent auparty contraire. Item et ſi les hâtans decelle ville ou aucuns diceulx ont deleurs biens eu party contraire Ilz les pourront aller ou envoyer querir par lecongie deleur cap.ⁿᵉ ſans aucune Reprehencion. Leſquelles choſes les deſſ nommez commis deleur part promettront et Iureront tenir faire tenir et acomplir depoint en point ſelon leur forme et teneur ſans enfraindre en aucune maniere ci prt̂ traicte et appoinctement fait et paſſe leſamedy. xxixᵐᵉ Iour deMay. Lan mil CCCC Cinquante ⁊ung Apres lequel appoinctement auſſi fait fut baillee lad place en garde par meſd ſ.ʳˢ ameſſire Iacques dechabanes grant maiſtre doſtel du Roy.

themselves to confirm to them by the king these priviledges. C Item and those who want to leave will have all their goods, horses, and equipment, and with this good safe conduct. C Item and if there is anyone who presently wants to make the oath and wants to go to do their duties and request their goods and debts, they will be received to those declared free to do so until the following Christmas arrives. And during which time, they can return, if it seems good to them, into the said town and make the oath and they will be received there and will have all their goods and heritages whatsoever. C Item and during the said time of Christmas, the abovesaid who will go can leave as guardians in the said town all their goods or anything of theirs, if it seems good to them, and send them to seek requests if it seems good to them, taking this time or selling them, and they will not give them in these goods that were left in the said town any destruction or impediment. C Item and the said inhabitants can ask and require them to make payments of all their good and loyal debts to all those who have anything owed to them or may have, of whichever purpose or nature that it is, regardless of them being in the opposite party. Item and if the inhabitants of this town or any of them have their goods [in the possession of] the opposite party, they will go or send to look for them by leave of their captain, without any punishment. Which things the abovenamed commissioners of their party promise and swear to do, to hold, and to accomplish point-by-point, according to the form and the tenor without infracting in any manner; this preceding treaty and agreement made and passed Saturday, the twenty-ninth day of May [in] the year 1451, after which agreement thus made, the said place was delivered into the guardianship by my said lords to messire Jacques de Chabannes, grand master of the hotel of the king.

La Reddicion. delacite darquis.

EN. cemeſme an eu moys deMay. lecôte dalbreth. avecques les ſ.[rs] detartas ⁊dorval ſes filz. lequel avoit en ſacompaignie trois cens lances et II.[M] arbaleſtriers vint mettre leſiege devant lacite darques devant lacite debordeaulx aucoſte dedevers bordeaulx aubout dupont de devers laRiviere dedous. Et environ. x ou xii. heures apres q̂ led ſiege fut mis vint leconte defouclz. avec leviconte delautrec ſon frere legitiê Meſſire bernard deverne ſon frere naturel Illegitiê Les barons deNavailles. Delaurdin. deRos. et de caraye. Meſſire martin gracien cap.[ne] des eſpaignolz Robin petit lot. Cap.[ne] des eſcoſſoys. et pluſſ[rs] autŝ ſeigneurs eſcuiers et gens deguerre Iucques au nombre decinq cens lances et les archiers et deux mille arbaleſtriers mirent leſiege ducoſte de devers navarre et Debierne. lequel ſiege fut vaillemmet̂ tenu et yot fait pluſſieurs et beaulx faiz darmes. et auſſi treſvaillamment tenu par ceulx delacite. Et Iucques ace quil vint aleurs cognoiſſance que ceulx debordeaulx faiſoient ou avoient Intencion defaire aucun tractie avecqẑ led lieuten̂ ou ſes commis pour et eu nom du Roy defrance. Parquoy les aſſiegez alaRequeſte dud conte defouclz furent comprins alappoinctemet̂ que feroient ceulx debordeaulx. Et ainſſi fut miſe en lamaine et obbaiſſance du Roy defrance auquel dedroit elle appartient. Et fut commis alagarde decelle ville et chaſteau par les contes defouclz et dalbreth. aquarte barôs dupays debierne.

The reduction of the city of Arques

IN this same year in the month of May, the count of Albret, with the seigneurs of Tartas and of Orval, his sons, who had in his company 300 lances and 2,000 crossbowmen, went to lay siege before the city of Arques on the side toward Bordeaux, at a bridge over the River Adour. And around ten or twelve hours after the said siege was laid, the count of Foix came, [and] with him the viscount of Lautrec, his legitimate brother; messire Bernard of Béarn, his illegitimate natural brother; the barons of Navailles, of Loudrin, of Ros, and of Coarase; messire Martin Gration, captain of the Spaniards; Robin Petit-Loup, captain of the Scotsmen; and several other lords, squires, and men of war totalling 500 lances and the archers, and 2,000 crossbowmen, who similarly laid siege on the side toward Navarre and Béarn, which siege was bravely held, and there were several beautiful feats of arms and also it was very bravely held by those of the city. And so it was until it came to their knowledge that those of Bordeaux made or had the intention to make some treaty with the said lieutenant and his commissioners for and in the name of the king of France. For which the besiegers, at the request of the said count of Foix, committed to an agreement that was made with those of Bordeaux. And so, it was placed in the hand and obedience of the king of France, to whom by right it belonged. And the guardianship for this town and castles was committed by the counts of Foix and Albret to four barons of the land of Béarn.

Siege mis devat̂ Rionz. par les francois.

EN ce mesmes temps et moys separtit le conte darmignac de son pays et estoit avecq̂z lui. lesire desaintrailles et les quatre seneschaulx dethoulouse. deRouergue. dagoues. decrey. et le seneschal deguyenne. Et avoit led conte en sacompaignie tant des seigneurs dessſd comme des gens deson pays cinq cens lances et les archiers. Et vint mettre lesiege devant laplace nommee Ryous. ou Il fut par aucere espace detemps en portant forte guerre aux ennemis du Roy. Et cepend quil tenoit led siege lestait fort pourparle defaire appoinctement aceulx debordeaulx combien quilz portoient tousiours forte guerre les ungz cont̂ les autŝ et Iucques alappoinctement fait dud bordeaulx donc on esperont ~~Iour~~ ouir ĉtaines bonnes nouvell̂ deIo[r] en Io[r].

Siege mis devat̂ castillon. en peregort par les francois.

En. ce mesme temps et ~~an~~ moys fut mis le siege devant castillon en pierregort par monſ[r] leconte depontievre. monſ[r] deIalongnes mareschal defrance. et maistre Iehan bureau tresorier defrance. Et avoient en leur compaignie trois cens lances et les archiers. et deux mille francs archiers avec lartillerie grosse et menue qui fort les espovanta et aussi avecques lagrant vaillance quilz veoient aux assaillans. Et considerans q̂ leRoy estoit si puissant degens quil faisoit mettre plussieurs sieges ensemble et aunefoiz. trouveret̂ faron detraictez et faire composicion par laquelle to⁹

Siege laid before Rions by the French

IN this same time and month, the count of Armagnac departed from his lands and the sire de Xaintrailles and the four seneshals of Toulouse, Rouergue, Agenès, [and] Quercy, and the seneschal of Guyenne were with him. And the said count had in his company, both from the lords abovesaid and from the men of his land, 500 lances and the archers. And they went to lay siege before a place named Rions, where he, for the space of a certain time, led a strong war against the enemies of the king. And while he held the said siege, it was strongly discussed to make an agreement with those of Bordeaux, such that they made still stronger war one against the other, and until the agreement was made at the said Bordeaux, they hoped day-by-day to hear certain good news.

Siege laid before Châtillon in Pieregord by the French

In this same time and month, siege was laid before Châtillon in Pieregord by monseigneur the count of Penthièvre; monseigneur de Jallongnes, marshal of France; and master Jean Bureau, treasurer of France. And they had in their company 300 lances and the archers, and 2,000 free archers, with artillery both great and small, which freightened them and moreso with the great bravery that they saw amongst the assailants. And considering that the king was so powerful with men that he had laid several sieges together and at one time, they found the manner to obtain a treaty and make an arrangement, by which all those

ceulx de lad place ſen allerent abordeaulx et oubon leur ſembla en leur party leurs corps et leurs biens ſaufz. Et demoura Icelle place alamain du Roy. alaquelle place garder fut cômis et ordonne et fut fait cap.[ne] led maiſtre Iehan bureau treſorier defrance.

LaRiddicion delaville. deSaiᷓt melion.

EN. ce temps ſe Rendirent au Roy. ceulx de laville de-Saint melion car Ilz veonent quil ne pouvoient aller ne Reſiſter conᷓt ſapuiſſ et fut baillee lad ville [en garde] auconte depontievre en cas conqueſtes et acquiſicions ou au moins en aucuns ne ſepreneᷓt par bonnement gardes lordre des Iournees pource que aucuns ſieges ont eſte mis enſemble par divers ſ.[rs] et non pas ſucceſſivemeᷓt.

Siege mis des francois devaᷓt fronſſac

EN. pourſuivant lagrant felicite que leRoy par lagrace dedieu obtenoit deIour en Iour mond ſ.[re] leconte dedunoiz envoya mettre leſiege par mer et par terre devant une place nômee fronſac. et fut leſecond Iour de Iuing. Et demoura led lieuteñ en lad ville debourg par aucune eſpace detemps pour faire certaines ordonnances et mettre Regime et police aubien et prouffit duRoy. Et cefait vint perſonnellemeᷓt aud ſiege defronſac. Et envoya led ſ.[r] ung herault du-Roy po[r] ſommer ceulx delaville deliborne de eulx Rendre. Apres leſquelles normalles ouyes ordonnereᷓt des principaulx une quantite pour allers avecques Icellui herault devᷓs

of the said place would go to Bordeaux and wherever it seemed good to them in their party, their bodies and goods safe. And this place remained in the hands of the king, the guardianship for which place was committed and ordained, and master Jean Bureau, treasurer of France, was made captain.

The reduction of the town of Saint-Mélion

IN this time, those of the town of Saint-Mélion rendered themselves to the king, for they saw that they could neither escape nor resist against his power, and the said town was given into the guardianship of the count of Penthièvre; in the event of conquests and acquisitions or at least in certain cases, so that blame would not unjustly fall on the rightful guardians according to the schedule of campaigns, because some of these sieges had occurred simultaneously by different lords, and not successively.

Siege laid by the French before Fronsac

IN pursuing the great fortune that the king, by the grace of God, obtained from day-to-day, my said lord, the count of Dunois, sent to lay siege by sea and by land before a place named Fronsac, and it was the second day of June. And the said lieutenant remained in the said town of Bourg for some space of time, in order to make certain ordinances there and organise the regime and police for the good and profit of the king. And this being done, he went in person to the said siege of Fronsac. And the said lord sent a herald of the king in order to summon those of the town of Liborne to render themselves. After which summons were made of the principal people, a quantity went with

Icellui ſ.re pour ſre tracte et appointement pour to9 les hâtans eſtans en Icelle ville. Et led appoinctemet̂ fait et adcorde fut baille depar leRoy laville aumond ſr danIou leſire. Et quant aufait duchaſteau dud fronſac vray eſt que ceſt leplus fort chaſteau des mâches deguyenne. Et lequel atouſiours eſte garde dangloiz natifz dupays dangletr̂e. pource q̂ ceſt chambre Royalle et clef deguyenne et de bourdelloiz. pourrquoy eſtoit deneceſſite auſd angloiz detenir fort lamain ce quilz. ont fait au mieulx quilz ont peu. Et aceſte led chaſteau fort aſſailly par aucun temps et auſſi par les adverſaires fort deffendu. Et apres q̂ lad ſiege ot eſte environ xv. Iours devant lad place defronſac. Les angloiz qui dedens eſtoient voyans legrant nobeſſe et grant multitude degens de guerre devant eulx qui neſtoit pas lamontie delapuiſſance duRoẙ. Non pas lequart voyas auiſſi les bombardes canons etaut̂s artilleries qui aut̂s deulx et les approuchemens comme foſſez et mynes et lavaillante chevallierie que leRoy avoit par toute ſaduchie deguyenne et q̂ les francs archiers tenoiet̂ leſiege en iiii. lances pour celle heure leſquilz ſieges nepovouit̂ ſecourus les ungz aux aut̂s pour les groſſes Rivieres degaronne et dedôdon̂e qui eſtoient treſgroſſes pour les naiges qui foundoiet̂ es montagnes en ceſte ſaiſon. Et auiſſi conſidrout̂ bien les angloiz quil ny avoit ſiege tenu par les francois. Combien quilz fuſſent en divers lieux qui en fuſſent aſſez fors pour actendre et combatre toute lapuiſſance du Roy dangletr̂e quil avoit pour lors en guienne. Ces choſ conſideres ceulx delad place ~~Requere~~ defronſſac Requirent aplemêter avecques led conte dedunoiz lieuten̂ general du Roy. et tracterent en ceſte maner̂e q̂ ſi dedans laveille deſaint Iehan baptiſte procĥ ven̂

this herald to this lord to make a treaty and agreement for all the inhabitants being in this town. And the said agreement made and agreed was delivered on behalf of the king [to] the town by monseigneur d'Angoulême. And regarding the fate of the castle of Fronsac, it is true that it was very strong on the marches of Guyenne, and that it had always been guarded by Englishmen, natives of the land of England, because it was a royal chamber and the key to Guyenne and the Bordealais, for which it was of necessity to the said English to hold strongly the hand, which they had at the best that they had little. And the said castle was strongly assailed several times, and also strongly defended by the adversaries. And after the said siege had been going about fifteen days before the said place of Fronsac, nobles and a great magnitude of men of war before them [who] lacked the means of the power of the king. Not a quarter seeing also the bombards, cannon, being artillery that others of those and the approaches such as trenches and mines and the brave chivalry that the king had throughout all his duchy of Guyenne, and that the free archers held sieges in four places at this hour, which sieges could not help one another because of the Rivers Garonne and Dordogne, which were then very wide because the snows that fell in the mountains in this season. And considering well also the English who were at none of these four sieges held by the French, such that they were in several places that were strong enough to wait and fight all the power of the king of England that he had then in Guyenne. These things considered, those of the said place of Fronsac requested to speak with the said count of Dunois, lieutenant general of the king, and negotiate in this manner: that if by the eve of the upcoming [feast of] Saint John the Baptist, the French had not been engaged in battle before

les francois neſtoient combatuz devant lad place par les angloiz quilz ſe Rendroient et mettroient ladite place en lamain du Roy defrance. Et pareil feroient ceulx debordeaulx et les barons dupays eulx faiſans fors defaire Rendre toutes les places deladuchie deguienne eſtans en lobbeiſſ du Roy dangleťre. Pourquoy et agrangne^r ſeurete bailleront ceulx eſtans dedens lad place defronſſac ĉtains hoſtages affin dentĩtenir ce q̂ dit eſt avecques aucuns condicions faiſans tracte et appoinctemeť donc lateneur ſenſuyt.

Traicte delaville defronſſac

Traicte. et appoinctement fait Enť meſſ^r Iacqz dechabanes grant maiſtre doſtel du Roynrêſſ.^re meſſire theaulde devalpergue bailly delyon meſſ^re Iehan bureau chlř. leſ.^r deſternay general ſur lefait des finances du Roy. ace commis par monſ^r leconte dedunoiz et delongueville lieutenant general du Royauñd ſ.^r ſur lefait deſaguerre dunepart. Et leprieur defronſſac et lecure dud lieu. lecure devilleboſin. guille ormeſby maiſtre thonmas bon temps. thonmas legay. thâs delagarde et guille pelleetez. delapart deIeſ frangbays cap.^ne dud chaſteau dauťpart pour Raiſ delaReddicion dud chaſteau defronſſac qui ſe doit fř es mains du Roy dedens letps et Cuir en laforme et maniê cy apres deſclaree. Premierement leſd cappitaines et auťs deſſſ nomz. pour et aunom deto⁹ les gens deglife nobles bourgoiz et hâtans dicelle ville defronſſac bailleront Icelle place Rallement et defait es mains demond ſ.^r leconte ou deſes commis pour et ou nom du Roy. dedens leIour demardy xv Iour dece peť moys deIuing oucas touteſſois que

the said place by the English, that they will render themselves and put the said place into the hands of the king of France. And similarly, those of Bordeaux and the barons of the land would do the same, rendering all the places of the duchy of Guyenne that were under the obedience of the king of England. For which and for greater surety, those being within the said place of Fronsac will release certain hostages in order to ensure that said is done, with several conditions making a treaty and agreement, of which the tenor follows:

Treaty of the town of Fronsac

Treaty and agreement made between messire Jacques de Chabannes, grand master of the hotel of the king, our lord; messire Théaude de Valpergue, balliff of Lyon; messire Jean Bureau, knight, seigneur d'Esternay, general for the matter of the finances of the king; for this commissioned by monseigneur the count of Dunois and Longueville, lieutenant general of the king, our lord, for the matter of his war, on one part. And the prior of Fronsac and the priest of the said place; the priest of Villebousin, Guilluame Ormesby; master Thomas Bontemps; Thomas le Gay; Thomas de la Garde; and Guillaume Pelléctez, of the party of Fronsadais, captain of the said castle, on the other part, by reason of the reduction of the said castle of Fronsac, which ought to placed into the hands of the king within the time and term, and in the form and manner so afterwards declared. Firstly, the said captains and others abovenamed, for and in the name of all the people of the church, nobles, cityfolk, and inhabitants of this town of Fronsac, deliver this place by deed and fact into the hands of my said lord, the count or others he commissions for and in the

dedens led Iour les gens duparty des deſſſnom̂z eſtans en lad place defronſac ne viendront cependant fors que par puiſſance darmes. Ilz peuſſent debontes mond ſ.r leconte dedunoiz et ceulx deſon party delaplace q̂ ce pendant Il prendra devat̂ led chaſteau de fronſſac ouquel cas q̂ mond ſ.r leconte dedunoiz ſeroit deboute deſad place par lui prinſe et que lechamp demouroit aux angloiz mond ſ.r leconte dedunoiz ou ſes commis ſeront tenus de Rendre aud capne. defronſſac les oſtages quilz aurōt pource baillez francs et quictes. C Item et ne pouront cependant leſdſſnom̃z delad place de fronſſac aider aceulx deleur party neleur. donner aucun ſecours confort ou aide en quelq̂ maniere que ce ſoit pend les xv. Iour dece moys. C Item et en baillant lad place par leſdeſſſnom̃z aud xv Iour dece moys ~~monſ~~ mond ſr dedunoiz ſera tenu debaillr̂ atoꝰ ceulx eſtans en Icelle place qui aller ſen vouldront dequelq̂ eſtat ou côdicion quilz ſoient ſaufconduit et conduicte por eulx ſouffiſans pour eulx en aller ſeuremet̂ avecq̃z toꝰ leurs biens quilzconques en leur party ou bon leur ſemblera. Et pource ſre leur ſera ~~ball~~ bailler bateaulx et voictures ~~en b~~ aleurs deſpens en baillant par eulx bonne cauxion deles Renvoyer ou par eulx auront eſte prins et les gens qui les auront ~~d~~conduitz et menez. C Item et pourront leſdeſſnom̃z decelle garniſon emmener avecques eulx leurs chevaulx harnoiz et toꝰ habillemens deguerre donc hôme ſepeult aider deſon corps avecques toꝰ leurs biens meubles quelz conques. C Item et delaiſſeront en lad place leſdeſſſnom̃z deladgarniſon toute groſſe artillerie et aut̂ que homme deguerre ne puiſſe porter et ſoy en aider deſaperſonne ſeullement et qui neſoit portative acheval et apie et en eſpecial arbaleſtes quilz ne

name of the king, within the day of Tuesday, fifteenth day of this present month of June, or, however, that between the said day, the people of the party of the abovenamed being in the said place of Fronsac may become, however, so strong that by power of arms, they can surmount my said lord, the count of Dunois, and those of his party, from the place before he can take the said castle of Fronsac, in which case that my said lord, the count of Dunois, will be by force removed from the said place by such a capture of him, and that the field remains to the English, my said lord, the count of Dunois, or his commissioners will be held to return to the said captain of Fronsac the hostages that he will have handed to him for this, free and quit. C Item and the above named of the said place of Fronsac cannot, however, aid those of their party, nor give any help, comfort, or aide to them, in whatever manner that it is, until the fifteenth day of this month. C Item and in delivering the said place by the above named on the said fifteenth day of this month, my said lord of Dunois will be held to release all those being in this place who want to go, whichever state or condition that they are, with good and sufficient safe conduct, in order to go safely with all theirs goods wherever in their party or it seems good to them. And for this to be done, they will be furnished with ships and vehicles at their expense, in delivering by them good caution to send them back where they had been taken and the men who will have conducted and taken them. C Item and the above named of this garrison will be able to take with them their horses, harneses, and all gear of war for which a man can carry on his body, with all their moveable goods whatsoever. C Item and the above named of the said garrison will leave in this place all the large artillery, and anything that a man of war cannot carry, and for which he cannot carry only on his person, and

perent bander aux Rains. C Item en cilya aucuns depreẽ eſtans oud chaſteau qui veuilleẽ demourer en party duRoy et faire leſerment deſtre bons et loẙaulx et vrays subgetz auRoy defrance nr̃e ſouverain ſ.r ſoient gens degliſe nobles bourgoiz et hâtans dequelq̂ eſtat ou condicion quilz ſoient faire lepouront et ẙ ſeront Receuz. et ence faiſant Ilz demoureront paiſibles en leurs benefices heritages Rentes et Revenus poceſſions quelzconques ou quilz ſoient ſituez et aſſis es party du Roy et en leurs biens meubles qui ſont en nature. Et auront abolicion deto⁹ cas. et ſeront bien traicties comme auẽs ſubgectz duparty duRoy. C Item et demoureroẽ doreſnavant en leurs franchiſes privilleges et libertez aeulx donnez par leurs predeceſſeurs Roys et ducz deguyenne Et promettra led ſeigneur conte dedunoiz de les faire Ratiffier par leRoy. C Item et cil ya aucuns en lad garniſons defronſſac qui veulleẽ faire leſerment deſtre bons etloyaulx ſubgectz et obaiſſans au Roynr̃edſ.r et leſervir en ſaguerres Ilz yſeront Receuz et ſeront ſouldoyez ſelon leurs eſtatz comme ſont les auẽs gens deguerre duRoy. C Item et par cepn̄t tractie ~~et adcorde~~ aeſte adcorde et promis aRaſſecharnoli priſonnier adaucuns francois et ſix deſes varletz nommez. Ceſt aſſavoir ~~p~~ olivier parker. guion debellet. guillaume defaingnac. pieretin gracie Remonnet pryre et Iehan deſaint pol auſſi to⁹ priſonniers dela prinſe deblaye ſeront et demourreront quictes et paiſſibles deleurs finances et auroẽ ſaufconduit depriſonniers pour eulx en aller. C Item et pa Reillement demourra quicte deſafinance et Ranſon Iehan ſtaffordin eſcuier angloiz delaprinſe dela Iournee deformygny et mis aplaine delivrance garny debon et loyal ſaufconduit. C Item et pend led temps

which is no longer portable by horse or on foot, and especially crossbows that one can sling onto the back. C Item and if there is anyone of those present in the said castle who want to enter into the party of the king and make the oath to him to be good and loyal and true subjects to the king of France, our soveriegn lord, being of the church, nobility, cityfolk, and inhabitants of whichever state or condition that they be, they can do it, and will be received there, and in making this, they will remain peacefully in the possession of their benefices, heritages, rents, and revenues, possessions, whatsoever, or where they are situated and seated in the party of the king, and in their goods that are by nature moveable. And they will have amnesty for all cases, and will be well treated as the other subjects of the party of the king. C Item and they will henceforth remain in their franchises, priviledges, and liberties given to them by the predecessor kings and dukes of Guyenne. And the said lord, count of Dunois, promises to make this ratified by the king. C Item and if anyone in the said garrisons of Fronsac who want to make the oath to be good and loyal subjects and vassals of the king, our lord, and serve him in his wars, they will be received there and will be paid according to their states, as the other men of war of the king. C Item and by this present treaty, it is agreed and promised to one named Cassicharnoly, prisoner of several Frenchmen, and six of his named servants—it is known, Oliver Parker, Guyon de Bellet, Guillaume de Sanignac, Pieretin Gracie, Raymonnet Pryre, and Jean de Saint-Pol, also all prisoners from the time of the capture of Blaye—will be and remain quit and free of their ransoms, and will have safe conduct of prisoners, in order for them to go. C Item and equally, Jean Stafford, an English squire, prisoner from the day of the battle of Formigny, will remain quit of his finance and ransom and will

ne ſera fait aucũe guerre dun coſte ne dauẽ ne ne feront aucunes approuches. Maiz chc̃n dedens leloges quil tient pourra fʳ et ordonner tout habillement deguerre et telle fortifficacion que bon lui ſemblera. C Item et pour faire et acomplir les choſes deſſſd depoint en point leſdeſſſd delad garniſon bailleront Re auement et defait. xviii. oſtages delad ville Leſquilz qui mond ſ.ʳ vouldra nommer. Ceſt aſſavoir ſix des gens deguerre eſtans en Icellui chaſteau et les xii. des hommes eſtans delad place. Toutes leſquelles choſ deſſſd laſdeſſſ nommez promettront et Iureront faire tenir et acomplir Ceſt aſſavoir. les commis delapart demonditſ.ʳ leconte dedunoiz par Icellui monſ.ʳ leconte. Et les auẽs par lecapⁿᵉ et auẽs hâtans delad ville par leurs ſeaulx et ſeingz manuelz cẙ mis le Cinquieſme Iour deIuing Lan mil CCCC Cinquante ⁊ung. Et pource pour venus aux fins et Intencions duRoy. comparureẽ en pſnnes les contes deNevers. de clermont. decaſtres etdevendoſme et depointievre. Et pluſſieurs auẽs barons chevalliers et eſcuiers et autres gens deguerre. Et fut terme par les francois lad Iournee haultement Richement etpuiſſammeẽ. Et furent en bataille led Iour prefix ⁊aſſignee pour actendre leurs ennemys qui ny vindrent en aucune maniere. Et la furent faiz chlr̃ leconte devendoſme. leviconte detouraine. le filz delaRochefoucault. lefilz duſire decômercy Iehan Rochecouart. leſire degomaulx. pierre deſbarois. pierre demontmorin. ſiroy degrancy Iehan debordelles. leſ.ʳ defontenilles. Iehan baſtard devendoſme. Iehan delahaye. triſtan lermitte. Iehan deſtrange. pierre louvain. Et pluſſieurs auẽs Iucques au nombre deCinquâte chevalliers et audeſſus. Apres laquelle Iôrnee actendue en belle ⁊Riche ordonnance. Les anglois

be completely and entirely released, [and] provided with good and loyal safe conduct. C Item and during the said time, there will be made no war on one side nor the other nor will there be any attacks. But each within the camps that he holds he may do and order all work of war, and such fortifications that seem good to him. C Item and in order to do and accomplish the abovesaid things point-by-point, the abovesaids of the said garrison will hand over in reality and by fact eighteen hostages of the said town, which my said lord will name—it is known: six of the men of war who are in this castle, and twelve others of the men inhabiting this place. All which abovesaid things the abovenamed promise and swear to do, hold, and accomplish—it is known: the commissioners and deputies on the part of my said lord, the count of Dunois, for this monseigneur, the count. And the others by the captain and the other inhabitants of the said town by their seals and signatures so placed, the fifteenth day of June, the year 1451. And, so, in order to come to the end and intentions of the king, the counts of Nevers, of Clermont, of Castres, of Vendôme, and of Penthièvre, and several other barons, knights, and squires, and other men of war, appeared in person. And the said battle was ended by the French, highly, richly, and powerfully. And the said day, they were in battalions, arranged and assigned to attend their enemies, who did not come in any manner. And the count of Vendôme, the viscount of Turenne, the son of Rochefoucaut, the son of the sire de Commercy, Jean Rochechouart, the sire de Goumaux, Pierre de Barois, Pierre de Montmorin, Sieroy de Grancy, Jean de Bordeilles, the seigneur de Fontenilles, Jean bastard of Vendôme, Jean de la Haye, Tristan the Hermit, Jean d'Estrange, Pierre Louvain, and several others, until the number was fifty knights and the above, were made knights there. After which

voyans et congnoiſſans leur Roy ne avoir aucune puiſſance deſtre fruſtrez dela Intencion. SeRendrent laveille demonſ.r Iehan baptiſte qui fut le xxiiire Iour deIuing. Et mirent lad place en lobbeiſſance duRoy defrance. Et auſſi leur fut tenu ce q̂ promis leur eſtoit ſi ~~lan~~ lecontenu des articles tant au Regard des xviii. oſtages côme autres que vouldronent demeurer en faiſant leſermens demourerent. Et lad place par mondſ.r le lieutenant duRoy fut bailler en garde a Iouchim Rouault.

Lecommencement. du traictie debordaulx.

LES. conqueſtes et acquiſicions faictes de partie des francois venues alacôgnoiſſ deceulx delacite debordeaulx tant angloiz que autres. Conſiderans lagrande et noble com paignie qui ſe diſpoſoit pour aller mettre le ſiege devant lad cite et ville envoyerent leur ambaxade aſaufconduit devers led lieutenant chancellier treſorier et autres affirmans eulx voulloir Rendre. Et en tant que touche les hâtans dicelle ville eulx mettre et Reddicion en lob beiſſance du Roy defrance et eſtre ſes bons et loyaulx ~~flog~~ ſubgectz. Et que leurd armee fuſt defferee dealler devant eulx. Aquoy led lieuten̑ general par meure delibéracion deconſeil et por pluſſieurs cauſes ace lemouvans leur donna c̑tain Iour preffix deceulx Rendre ou deulx deffend. Et ceRequeroient ileſdeſſſd debordeaulx tres Inſtamment et notairement affin defaire ſommer cependant leRoy dangleťre pour avoir delui ſecours et aide Car autrement nepouvoient ſauver leurs ſermens. Et fut mis

day they awaited in beautiful and rich order. The Englishmen, seeing and understanding their king had no power to be frustrated of their intention, rendered themselves on the eve of Saint John the Baptist, which was the 23rd day of June. And they put the said place into the obedience of the king of France. And so it was held that which had been promised to them, the contents of the articles, both in regard to the eighteen hostages and to the others, that those who wanted to remain in making the oaths would remain. And the said place was given by the said lieutenant of the king in guardianship to Joachim Rouault.

The beginning of the treaty of Bordeaux

THE conquests and acquisitions made by the party of the French came to the knowledge of those of the city of Bordeaux, both English and others. Considering the great and noble company who disposed themselves in order to go lay siege before the said city and town, they sent their ambassador with safe conduct to the said lieutenant, chancellor, treasurer, and others, affirming that they want to surrender to them. And regarding the inhabitants of this town, to put and reduce themselves into the obedience of the king of France, and to be his good and loyal subjects. And that their said army will stop its advancement against them. For which the said lieutenant general, by means of deliberations in council, and for several reasons moving toward this, gave a certain day prefixed for them to render or defend themselves. And this these said inhabitants of Bordeaux requested very insistently and notoriously in order to summon in some way the king of England to have from him rescue and aide, because otherwise they could not save their oaths. And it

leIour au dimanche [xxiv^m] deIuing oud an. Avecques laquelle ambaxade et aubon ſaufconduit des angloiz alla led maiſtre Iehan bureau treſoř. Et fut par lui entamee lamatiê pour parvenir aaucun bon tractie. Et quant Il ſceult la voullente deſd hâtans debordeaulx ſen Rtôurna pour narree aud lieutenant cequi avoit eſte pourparle entre les parties. Pourquoy allereť poſton deſaintrailles led treſorier defrance et agnus briquit pour traicter lamaniere les pointz les condicions dutraictie qui ſedevoit fř entre leſd parties. Leſquelz aRivez en lad ville fureť treſgrandement Receuz et honnourablemeť par les gouverneurs et habitans decelle. En faiſant le quil traictie furent faiz pluſſieurs argumens ouvertures diverſes matieres et dediverſes côdicions pour laReddicion dicelle eſtre ſeures pour toutes les deux parties duquel tractie et adcord la teneur ſenſuyt.

Traicte fait abordeaulx.

Traicte et appoinctement fait Enť poſton deſaintrailles bailly deberry eſcuier deſcuyerie du Roy defrance maiſtre Iehan bureau treſorier et ogier debrequit. Iuge demercent commis par monſr leconte dedunoiz et delongueville lieutenant general du Roy defrance ſur lefait deſaguerre pour et au nom dud charles dunep. Et les gens des trois eſtatz delaville et cite de bordeaulx et pays debourdellays. es noms deulx et des auťs pays deladuchie deguyenne qui de prt ſont en lobbeiſſance des angloiz dautrepart pour la Reddicion delad ville et cite debordeaulx et pays debordellays eſtans en lobbeiſſance deſd angloiz. Et pour Icelle cite

was done on the day of Sunday, the twenty-fourth day of June in the said year. With which ambassadors, and with good safe conduct by the English, went the said master Jean Bureau, treasurer. And it he who began the preparations to produce a good treaty. And when he learned the will of the said inhabitants of Bordeaux, he returned to report to the said lieutenant for that which he had been sent between the parties. For which Poton de Xaintrailles, the said treasure of France, and Ogier Bréquit went to negotiate the manner, points, conditions of the treaty, which ought to be made between the said parties. Who, arriving in the said town, were very favourably and honourably received by the leaders and inhabitants of this place. In making this treaty, there were made several arguments, overtures, diverse matters, and diverse conditions for the reduction of this place to have surety for both of the two parties, for which treaty and agreement the tenor followed.

Treaty made at Bordeaux

Treaty and agreement made between Poton de Xaintrailles, bailiff of Berry, squire of the squirerie of the king of France; master Jean Bureau, treasurer of France; and Ogier de Bréquit, judge of Mercent; commissioned by monseigneur the count of Dunois and Longueville, lieutenant general of the king of France for the conducting of his war, for and in the name of the said Charles, on one part, and the men of the three estates of the said town and city of Bordeaux and the lands of the Bordelais, in the names of those, and of the other lands of the duchy of Guyenne that are presently in the obedience of the English, on the other part, for the reduction of the

debordeaulx et pays deſſſd mettre et tenus en lobbeiſſance du Roy chr̃tn defrance.

Traicte fait par les francois avec ceulx. debordeaulx en lamaniere qui ſenſuyt.

ET POURCE. que apres pluſſieurs grandes ſommations faictes delapart dicellui Roy defrance aux gens des trois eſtatz des pays deguyenne et debordelloiz et aux habitans delaville debordeaulx et de eulx Rendre en ſon obbaiſſance. et de lui Rendre et mettre en ~~ſon obbaiff~~ ſes mains lad ville debor deaulx et toutes les autȓs villes et fortiſſes dupays eſtans en lobbeiſſance des angloiz. veu et en leur Remonſtrant que neleur eſtoit poſſible dendurer et ſouſtenir les faiz et charges delapuiſſance du Roy defrance qui Ia avoit conqueſte lepays delaRivrȇ dedordongne. voyans pas leſd trois eſtatz clairemeȓ latotalle deſtruction dupays ſe Remede ny eſtoit mis Iceulx gens deſd trois eſtatz ont fait Requerir amonſ.[r] leconte dedunoiz lieuten̑ general duRoy defrance q̂ par traictie Il leur voulſiſt donner ȓme et Reſpit ſuffiſ et convable pour envoyer devers leRoy dangleȓre lui ſigniffier les choſes deſſſd et avoir Reſponce delui. et prend Iour delabataille qui ſeroit leplus fort ſur les champs aIcellui Iour et autȓs pluſſieurs grans Requiſtes par eulx faictes et debatues par pluſſieurs Iournees. Ses quoy aeſte adcorde ce qui ſenſuyt. C Premierement que ceulx delapart duRoy defrance pour echever la totalle deſtruction dupays ſont conteŝ dedonner terme et

said town and city of Bordeaux and the lands of the Bordelais under the obedience of the said English, and for this city of Bordeaux and the lands abovesaid to be put and held in the obedience of the Christian king of France.

Treaty made by the French with those of Bordeaux in the manner that follows

AND FOR THIS, after several great summons made on the part of this king of France to the men of the said three estates of the lands of Guyenne and the Bordelais, and to the inhabitants of the town of Bordeaux and for them to submit into his obedience and to render to him and put into his hands the said town of Bordeaux and all the other towns and fortresses of the lands under the obedience of the English; seeing, and in their display that it was not possible for them to endure and sustain the actions and charges of the power of the king of France, who already had conquered the lands of the river Dordogne, seeing by the said three estates clearly the total destruction of the lands if remedy is not given, these men of the said three estates had made to request to my said lord, the count of Dunois, lieutenant general of the king, that by treaty, he would give to them terms and respite sufficient and suitable to send to the king of England, to signify to him the abovesaid things, and to have a response from him, and set the day of the battle, who was the stronger on the field of this day, and several other great requests by those made and debated by several days. Those that are agreed follow: C Firstly, that those of the party of the king of France, to avoid the total destruction of the lands, are content to give terms and delay to those of the said three estates in order to await the army

delay aceulx deſd trois eſtatz pour attend larmee du Roy dangleẗre qui eſperent venir en en brief. et latendent de-Iour en Iour Iucques au mercredy merquidy xxiiime Iour decepñt moys de Iuing. C Item et aucas que dedans led xxiiime Iour ceulx delapartie duRoy dangleẗre ne viendroit ſecourir ceulx dud pays debordellais et deguyenne en telle maniere que par puiſſance darmes Ilz puiſſent debouter les gens duRoy defrance du champ ou Ilz ſeront devant la-place defroſſac et en Icellui demourront les plus fors en cecas. Et tantoſt Icellui Iour paſſe les gens deſd trois eſtatz promettront et Iureront des apñt par leur foy et ſerment. et ſur lavraye croys baillr̃ et delivrer auRoy nr̃eſ.r aſaperſonne ſipoſſible lui eſt eſtre bonnement dy aeſtre auIour ainſſi qû on aeſperance quil yſera. Et aucas que a Icellui Iour ne leRoy me pouroit eſtre en pſon côme adcorde aeſtre ence cas. ceulx deſd trois eſtatz bailleront amondſ.r leconte de-dunoiz lieuteñ du Roy. et aauẗs ſrs conſeillr̃s et officers en ſacompaigne ainſſi que leRoy mandera par ſes lectres pat-entes dedens leſquelles ſeront ſes articles Incorporez. Et les promettra le Roy les enẗtenir depoint en point. lapoceſſ delad ville debordeaulx et apres conſequemmeẗ des villes chaſteaulx et fortreſſes deſd pays debordellaiz et deguy-enne. C Item et pour ſeurete defaire et acomplir les choſes deſſſd par leſd trois eſtatz debordelois et pays de guyenne. Aeſte adcorde quilz bailleront Rammeẗ et defait dedens demain qui ſera dimenche por tout leIour es mains de-mondſ.r leconte dedunoiz les villes et places devaires. de-Rioux. Saint marquaire. et deblangnac et es mains de-maiſtre Iehan bureau treſorier defrance laplace dechaſtillon en perigort. C Item et cil advenoit que dedens led xxiiim

of the king of England, that they hope to come soon, and they will wait for it day by day until Wednesday the twenty-third day of this present month of June. C Item and in the event that on the said twenty-third day, those of the party of the king of England do not come to rescue those of the said lands of the Bordelais and of Guyenne in such manner that by the force of armes they can defeat the men of the king of France on the field where they are before the place of Fronsac, and on this field remain as the stronger in this case. And when this day arrived, the men of the said three estates promised and swore at this moment by their faith and oath and on the true cross to hand over and deliver to the king, our lord, in his person, if it is possible for him to be there on this day, as one has hope that he will be there. And in the event that on this day the king cannot be there personally, as he agreed to be, in this case, those of the three estates will hand over to monseigneur the count of Dunois, lieutenant of the king, and to other lords, councillors, and officers in his company, as the king ordered by his letters patent, within which articles are incorporated, and the king promises to them and swears to maintain point-by-point the possession of the said town of Bordeaux and after consequently the towns, castles, and fortresses of the said lands of the Bordelais and of Guyenne. C Item and for surety to have done and to accomplish the abovesaid things by the said three estates of Bordelais and of Guyenne, it has been agreed that they will hand over in reality and by deed, by tomorrow, which will be Sunday, for the whole day, into the hands of my said lord, the count of Dunois, the towns and places of Vaires, Rioux, Saint-Macaire, and Blangnac; and into the hands of master Jean Bureau, treasurer of France, the place of Castillon in Périgord. C Item and if it happens that by the said twenty-third

Iour dece pn̂t moys deIuing larmee dangleťre viront pour ſecours led pays deguyenne Les porront ſecourir et aider en tout ce quilz pouront prend led temps. C Item et au cas que dedens led xxiii[m] Iour decepnt̂ moys deIuing leſd anglois et ceulx dud pays pouront par puiſſſ darmes debouter les francoiz hors deleur champ ou Ilz ſeront devant fronſſac et en Icellui demourer les plus fors en cecas. et tantoſt Icellui advenu led conte dedunoiz. et led maiſtre Iehan bureau delivreront leſd. cinq. places. Ceſt aſſavoir a monſ.[r] lecaptau. les places devaires blangnac et caſtillon. et les places deRioux. et ſaint macaire aux hâtans dud bordeaulx. Et auſſi Rendront les ſcellez que deſſſd ont pource baillez aud monſ.[r] leconte dedunoiz. C Item et cil advenoit q̂ aucunes citez villes ou places eſtans oud pays ne ſe voulleſſent Rend ne mettre en lobbeiſſance du Roy comme Icelle ville debordeaulx eulx ſurce deuement ſommez et Requis encecas le Roy les contraindra par puiſſance darmes alayde deſes ſubgetz. C Item et ſeront les hâtans deſd villes et chaſteaulx et fortreſes. Incontinent la poceſſion dicelles eues et prinſes leſerment au Roy ou aſes commis pour lui deſtre delors en avant bons vrays et loyaulx ſubgetz et obbaiſſans au Roy defrance et detenir ſon party envês et contre to⁹ atouſiourſmais perpetuellement. C Item et fera le Roy alentree delad ville debordeaulx auIour que baillr̂ ladoivet̂ ~~cel~~ cil yeſt pnt̂ ou mondſ.[r] leconte dedunoiz pour lui ſileRoy ny peult eſtre leſerment ſur lelivre et ſur lacroix ainſſi quil eſt acouſtume. detenir et maintenir. les habitans decelle ville et dupays et chcn̂ deulx pnt̂ et abſent qui demoureront ou demourer vould en ſon obbaiſſance en leurs franchiſes levirtez p̂ivileges ſtatuz

day of this present month of June the army of the king of England comes in order to the rescue the said lands of Guyenne, they will be able to rescue and aide them in every way that they can during the said time. C Item and in the case that by the said twenty-third day of this present month of June, the said English and those of the said lands can by force of arms push the French out of their camp where they are before Fronsac, and in this remain the strongest, in this case, and immediately, the said count of Dunois and the said master Jean Bureau will return the said five places, it is known, to monseigneur the captal, the places of Vaires, Blangnac, and Castillon, and the places of Rions and Saint-Macaire to the inhabitants of the said Bordelais, and also render the the seals that they earlier had handed over for this to the said monseigneur the count of Dunois. C Item and if it happens that any of the cities, towns, or places within the said land do not want to render themselves to be put into the obedience of the king as this town of Bordeaux, having been duly summoned and required in this case, the king will force them by force of arms with the aide of his subjects. C Item and the inhabitants of the said towns and castles will be immediately in possession of these and take the oath to the king or to his commissioners employed by him for this, to be henceforth good, true, and loyal subjects and vassals to the king of France and to hold to his party for all and against all always and forever. C Item and the king will be at the entrance of the said town of Bordeaux on the day they must hand it over, if he is present there, or my said lord, the count of Dunois, for him if the king cannot be there, the oath on the book and on the cross, as it is accustomed, to hold and maintain the inhabitants of the said town and lands, and each of them, present and absent, who remains or wants to remain in his

loyz couſtumes et eſtabliſſemens ſtilles obſervances et uſances dupays debordeaulx et debordellaiz. et des baſſadiz et dagenas en agenas. Et leur ſera le Roy bon p̂ince et droicturier ſeigneur. et les gardera detort et deforce deſoy meſme etdeto⁹ autŝ aſon pouvoir. Et leur fera ou fera faire droit Raiſ et acompliſſ deIuſtice et des choſes deſſſd et ch-c͡nes dicelles le Roy leur donnera et octroyera ſes lectres patentes ſcellees deſon grant ſcel en lameillr̂ forme que ſur ce devera et pourra faire quicter et franchement dece quil appartiendra auRoy. C Item et cil advenoit que leRoy ne pueſſe eſtre aud Iour delad entree mond ſ.r dedunoiz lieu-te͡n du Roy promettra et Iurera par leRoy faire Ratiffier toutes ces choſſ deſſſſd et deles lui faire Iurer etpromettre ainſſi que dit eſt. C Item et cil en ya aucuns qui ne veullet̂ demourer ne faire leſerment auRoy defrance aller ſen pourront quat̂ bon leur ſemblera et ou ~~bon~~ Illeur plaira. Et pourront emporter toutes marchandiſes ou argent et biens meubles nefz vaiſſeaulx et autres quelzconques. Et auront pource faire bon ſaufconduit et terme devvidange Iucques ademy acompter ladebte deces prn̂tes. Pourveu que quant Ilz ſeront oud party duRoy Ilz firont leſerment denon faire ou pourchaſſer enIcellui party aucun ~~de~~ dommaige tant quilz yſeront. Et cilz avoient aucuns heritages es pays. Iceulx demoureront aleurs plus prochains heritiers eſtans leſd pays et qui vouldront faire ~~et~~ leſerment auRoy et demourer en Icellui party. C Item et cil en ya aucuns dud pays deguyenne qui neſoiet̂ deliberez defaire leſerment et que veullet̂ allr̂ en aucuns lieux dece Royaulme ou dehors po[r] querir et pourchaſſer aucuns deleurs biens ou debtes faire lepourront et auront letemps et terme deulx deſclarer

obedience, in their franchises, virtues, priviledges, liberties, laws, customs, and establishments, styles, observances, and uses of the lands of Bordeaux and the Bordelais, and of Basas and the Basadois, and of the Agenois in Agen. And the king will be to them a good prince and rightful lord, and guard them from wrong and by his own force, and from all others in his power. And he will be to them and will make right, reason, and accomplish by justice, and of the abovesaid things and each of these, the king will give to them and grant his letters patent, sealed by his great seal, in the best form that he for this can and ought to make, quit and free of that which will belong to the king. C Item and if it happens that the king cannot attend on the said day of the said entrance, my said lord of Dunois, lieutenant of the king, promises and swears by the king to make to ratify by the king all the things abovesaid, and to make, swear, and promise to them, as if he were there. C Item and if there are any who do not want to remain nor make the oath to the king of france, they can go wherever it seems good to them or pleases them. And they can take all their merchandise, gold, silver, and moveable goods, ships, vessels, and other things whatsoever. And they will have for this good safe conduct and permission until midyear to account for the debts of these present, provided that while they are amongst those of the said party of the king, they will make the oath to not make or purchase from this party anything damaging, so long as they are there. And if they have any ancestral lands in the country, these will remain to their closest heirs who are in the said country, and who want to make the oath to the king and remain in this party. C Item and if there are any of the said lands of Guyenne who are undecided about making the said oath and who want to go into other places of this kingdom of France or

francois ſibon leur ſemble Iucques ademy an proch͡ ven͡. Et cil en ya aucuns embaſſadeurs ou auẗs qui depuis ſoieṫ abſens delad ville debordeaulx ou du pays deſſſd en veulleṫ Retourner et faire leſerment côme les auẗs faire lepourront et yſeront Receuz et auront to⁹ leurs biens et hêtx dedens demy an ainſſi que les auẗs deſſſ nommez. C Item et cil ya aucuns prend led temps dedemy qui ſen veullent aller hors delobbaiſſance duRoy. et laiſſer aucuns deleurs biens en garde en lad ville de bordeaulx ou ailleurs oud pays deguyenne faire lepourront et leur demoureront ſceurs pend led temps. Et auſſi les pourront envoyer querir en Icellui temps ſibon leur ſemble. et les faire emporter ou bon leur ſemblera. Et cil leur eſt deu aucune choſe en lad ville debordeaulx ou ailleurs oud pays deguyenne. Ilz lepourront pourſuivre et demander et leur en ſera fait Raiſ et bonne Iuſtice. C Item et cil yen a aucunes qui veullent avoir ſaufconduit pour eulx en aller avecques leurs biens meubles quelzconques chevaulx vaiſſeaulx et auẗs choſes Ilz auront bon ſaufconduit pource faire et ne leur couſtera chc͡n ſaufconduit que ung eſcu dor. C Item a eſte adorde et appoincte que en mettant par ceulx deſd trois eſtatz leſd villes citez chaſteaux fortreſſes des pays debordellays. deguyenne et degaſcogne. et en faiſant leſerment ainſſi que dit eſt deſſſ par les hâtans demourans eſd places to⁹ Iceulx hâtans avoient abolicion gn̂alle du Roy deto⁹ cas civilz et criminelz et detoutes paines encourues. Et leur en fera leRoy baillr̂ ſes lectres patentes ſeellees deſon grant ſeel en general ou en partiĉullr̂ ~~au~~ ou ainſſi que avoir levouldront quictement et franchement dece quil en appartiendra au Roy. C Item et demoureront to⁹ nobles non nobles et

within in order to seek and purchase any of their goods or debts, they can do it, and they will have the time and the term to declare themselves French if it seems good to them, until the following midyear. And if there are any ambassadors or otherwise there, who were absent from the said town of Bordeaux or of the abovesaid lands, who want to return and make the oath as the others, they can make it and they will be received there, and they will have all their goods and heritages within a year, as the others abovenamed. C Item and if there is anyone during the said time of the half year who wants to go out of the obedience of the king and leave any of their goods in guardianship in the said town of Bordeaux or elsewhere in the said lands of Guyenne, they can do it, and they will remain secure during the said time. And if anything is owed to them in the said town of Bordeaux or elsewhere in the said lands of Guyenne, they can pursue and demand it, and it will be done for them by reason and good justice. C Item and if there is anyone who wants to have safe conduct in order for them to go with their moveable goods whatsoever, horses, vessels, and other things, they will have good safe conduct in order to do this, and it will only cost each of them one *écu* of gold. C Item, it has been agreed and accorded that, in putting by those of the said three estates, the said towns, cities, castles, fortresses of the lands of the Bordelais, of Guyenne, and of Gascony, and in making the oath such as said above, by the inhabitants remaining in the said places, all these inhabitants will have a general abolition of the king for all cases civil and criminal, and of all penalties incurred. And the king will hand over to them his letters patent, sealed by his great seal in general or in particular, such that they will want to have them, quit and freely by that which it would belong to the king. C Item and all

hâtans deſd villes et pays gen demourer vouldront en Iceulx et avoient fait leſerment en leurs poceſſions duoctuas. et en leurs chaſteaulx villes fortereſſes et ſʳes et aut̂s heritaiges ou quilz ſorent ſratuez et aſſes. Et ainſſi en leurs biens meubles marchandiſes et autres quelzconques Sans ce que on leur en face aucun fort ou viollence ou que ~~leur~~ len leur ydonne ou aucun deceulx empeſcheret̂ ou deſtourbres. C Item et pareillement demouront les gens degliſe eſtans eſd pays en leurs benefices et dignitez biens meubles et Immeubles en leurs offices degliſe Iuridicions poceſſions ſpirituelles et temporelles ſeigneuries villes chaſteaulx et fortreſſes Revenus cens domaines et autres biens. aeulx appartenans et en Iceulx ſeront maintenuz et gardez. et auſſi et leurs franchiſes p̂ivileges et libertez quelzcôqz. Et dece auront bonnes lectres ſcellees duRoy deſon grant ſeel telles que aucas appartiendra quictement et franchement dece quelap̲p̲artiendra au Roy. C Item et ſe les Roys danglet̂re et ducz deguyenne ont donne parcy devant a aucuns des hâtans demourans eſd pays aucunes t̂res ſeigneuries chaſteaulx fortereſſes 7aut̂s quelzcôqz biens aeulx appartẽn acauſe delad duchie en quelque maniere que ceſoit Ilz ſeront et demoureront aceulx aqui Ilz auront eſte ainſſi donnes. Sauf et Reſerve lat̂re et ſʳie decurtan que le Roy adonnee. C Item et neſeront côtrains doreſnavant leſd hâtans dud pays ~~deconte~~ de paier aucunes tailles Impoſicions. gabelles. fouages cartages. Equeualent. ne aut̂s ſeredes quelzcôqz Et ne ſeront tenus doreſnavant q̂ depaier les droitz aucunes deuz et acouſtumez en lad ville debordeaulx. et es pays deſſſd. C Item et aeſte appoincte q̂ toꝰ marchans apporteront doreſnavat̂ marchandiſes et vivres

nobles, non nobles, and inhabitants of the said towns and lands will remain who want to remain in this place and have made the oath in their possessions and in their castles, towns, fortresses, and lordships, and other heritages where ever they are situated and seated, and also in their moveable goods, merchandise, and other things whatsoever, without which no force or violence will be done to them or given to them nor will any of them be hindered or disturbed. C Item and equally the men of the church being in the said lands will retain their benefices and dignities, moveable and immoveable goods in their offices of the church, jurisdictions, spiritual and temporal possessions, lordships, towns, castles and fortresses, revenues, taxes, domains, and other goods belonging to them; and in this they will maintain and guard, and also in their franchises, priviledges, and liberties whatsoever. And for this, they will have good letters sealed by the king with his great seal, such as in the case will belong quit and free of that which belongs to the king. C Item and if the king of England and dukes of Guyenne had given before any of the inhabitants remaining in the said lands any lands, lordships, castles, fortresses, and other goods whatsoever belonging to them from the said duchy, in whichever manner that it was, they will be and remain to those to whom they had been given, save and reserving the land and the lordship of Curton, that the king of France has given away. C Item and, henceforth, the said inhabitants of the said lands will not be constrained to pay any levies, impositions, salt taxes, harth taxes, transportation taxes, nor any subsidies whatsoever. And henceforth, no one will be held to pay any dues or customs in the said town of Bordeaux and in the lands abovesaid. C Item and it has been agreed that, henceforth, all merchants bringing merchandise and foodstuffs into the said

quelzconques en lad ville debordeaulx es pays debourdellaiz. Et pourrot̂ ſeurement venir par eaue doulce ou par terre en payant ſeullement les droitz et devoirs anciens deuz et acouſtumez daurvenete tant au Roy que aux autꝰ ſeigneurs aqui ſepourroit appartenir ſelon laforme deleurs p̊villeges franchiſes et libertez. ⁋ Item et ſera le Roy content que en lad ville debordeaulx yait Iuſtice ſou veraine pour ycongnoiſtre diſcetes ⁊deťminer diffinitivement detoutes les cauſes dappel qui ſeferont en Icellui pays. ſans pour Iceulx ap peaulx par ſimple querelle ou auťment eſtre traitz hors delad cite. ⁋ Item en oulť aeſte adcorde que doreſnavant le Roy neſes ſucceſſeurs Roys ne pourront tirer hors des pays deſſſd pour faire guerre. les nobles gens de guerre ne autꝰ gens dud pays ſans leur voulloir et conſentement. ſi non toute ſioys que le Roy les paye deleurs gages et ſouldoye. ⁋ Item et parce pnť tractie aeſte adcorde q̂ mond ſ.r leconte dedunoiz fera Rend et delivrer aceulx delad ville debordeaulx francs et quictes le maire delad ville. leſoubzmaire. Iehan de Roſtan et bertran daigas. Item et fera leRoy defrance batre monnoye en lad ville debordeaulx par ladvis et deliveracion deſes officiers et gens deſd trois eſtatz dud pays deguyenne ence congnoiſſans appellez avecquez eulx les gr̂aux maiſtres des monnoyes. Et promettra le Roy par ſes lectres patentes que les monnoyes qui apn̂t ont cours oud pays ypuiſſent encore avoir cours ung an ou deux ſebon leur ſemble. Et donnera leRoy en faiſant Icelle monnoye la pluſpart deſon droit ſeigneurial. Affin dy amender Icelle monnoye auprouffilt ~~deu~~ dupeuple dud pays. ⁋ Item et ſeleRoy laiſſe aucunes deſes gens darmes en lad cite debordeaulx

town of Bordeaux and in the lands of the Bordelais, and they can surely come by sea route or by land, will only pay the rights and ancient dues and customs, both to the king and to the other lords to whom this may belong, according to the form of their priviledges, franchises, and liberties. C Item and the king will be content that in the said town of Bordeaux he will have sovereign justice there, to know, discern, decide, and determine definitively for all causes of appeal which will be done in this land, without for this appealing for simple quarrels or otherwise to be drawn out of the said city. C Item and in addition, it has been agreed that, henceforth, the king or his successor kings cannot force out of the lands abovesaid to make war the noble, men of war, nor others from the said land against their will and consent except if the king pays them their wages and pension. C Item and and for this, it has been agreed by this present treaty that my said lord, the count of Dunois, will render and deliver to those of the said town of Bordeaux, freely and completely, the mayor of the said town and the submayor, Jean de Roustan and Bertrand Dagaz. Item and the king of France will create money in the said town of Bordeaux by the advice and deliberation of his officers and the men of the said three estates of the said land of Guyenne, in this knowledge, naming with them the general masters of finances. And the king will promise, by his letters patent, that the monies that at present have been used in the said lands can still be used for one or two years, if it seems good to them. And the king will give, in making this money, the majority of his seigneural right so that this money is improved to the profit of the people of the said lands. C Item and if the king leaves any of his men-at-arms in the said city of Bordeaux and the lands and duchy of Guyenne for the security and guardianship of this

et ſes pays et duchie deguyenne pour laſeurete et garde diceulx Il les paiera deleurs gaiges et fera gouv̂ner bien ⁊doulcement et paier ce quilz prendront. Et ceulx qui ſeront en lad ville debordeaulx ſeront logiez es hoſtelleries ou auꝰ̂s lieux moins grevables et dommagables pour les marchans et hâtans delad ville. C Item et aeſte appoincte que les officiers que leRoy cômettra oud pays promettront au Roy ou aſes commis et Iureront defaire bonne Iuſtice ſans faveaur et aupetit comme augrant. et quilz garderont les couſtumes et loys delad ville debordeaulx et des pays debordellaiz. et les maintiendront en leurs honneurs et p̊eminences. Et Ioyront ceulx delad ville debordeaulx ⁊auꝰ̂s quelzconques dud pays debordellaiz deleurs Iura decours temes ainſſi q̂ danciennete Ilz ont acouſtue͡. Item et deffendra leRoy ou fera deffend aſon procureur en lad ville debordeaulx quil ne vexe ou travaille aucuns des hâtans delad ville et du pays. ſans Requeſte departie ou quil y ait deue Informacion preudente. C Leſquelz tractiez adcordz appoinctemens promeſſes et con venances. Noꝰ pierre par lep̂miſſion divine arceveſque debordeaulx. bertran ſeigneur de montferant. gaulhart dedurefort ſeigneur deduras. gadifier chartreuſe. maire et conſ̂ debordeaulx. Iehan delalande ſeigneur de brande bernard angevin ſeigneur deRoſan et depuigraulx. guillemin andreiu ſeigneur de lauſſac promettons par les foy et ſerment de noz corps et ſur noz honneurs tenir et acomplir depoint en point ſelon leur forme et teneur ſans Icelles aucunement enffraindre. En Teſmoing dece noꝰ avons ſigners ces prn̂tes et ſcelles des ſceaulx denoz armes. leſamedy xii[m] Iour de Iuing. mille CCCC Cinquâte ⁊ung.

place, he will pay them from their wages and he will govern them well and carefully, and pay for that which they take. And those who are in the said town of Bordeaux will be lodged in boarding houses and other places less grevious and damaging for the merchants and inhabitants of the said town. C Item and it has been agreed that the officers that the king committed to the said lands promise to the king or to his commissioners and swear to make good justice, without favour, and to the small as to the large, and that they will guard the customs and laws of the said town of Bordeaux and of the lands of the Bordelais, and maintain them in their honours and preeminences. And those of the said town of Bordeaux and others wherever in the said lands of the Bordealais will enjoy their jurisdictions and uses, as they have been accustomed since ancient times. Item and the king will defend or make to defend by his procurator in the said town of Bordeaux, who will not vex or work any of the inhabitants of the said town and of the land, without request of the party or who has given him useful information. C Which treaties, accords, agreements, promises, and conventions we, Pierre, by the divine permission, archbishop of Bordeaux; Bertrand, seigneur de Monterrant; Gailard de Durefort, seigneur de Duras; Gadicr-Chartrcusc, mayor and count of Bordeaux; Jehan de la Lande, seigneur de Brande; Bernard Angevin, seigneur de Rosen and of Puigeaux; Guillemin Andreiu, seigneur de Lausac, promise by the faith and oath of our bodies, and to our honours, to hold and accomplish point-by-point, according to their form and tenor, without infracting on anything. In witness of this, we have signed, those present, and sealed with the seals of our arms, Saturday, twelfth day of June, in the year 1451.

Autre traicte pour lacaptau debuch.

LEdit appoinctement Ainſſi que dit eſt fait et conclude. venu alanotice et cognoiſſance. demonſr gaſton defouelz conte devenauges. et captau debuch. Icellui conte ceſte trait par devers led lieuteñ duRoy que tenoit les champs abelle et noble compaignie pour actend to⁹ venans ennemys du Roy coṁ deſſſ eſt dit. Et fiſt ung tractie et appoîtemeȇ touchant ſon fait et les ſiens. Et pource q̂ le captau eſtoit chevallier delordre delaIartre qui eſt lordre duRoy dangleȓe Il eſtoit en voullente deſoy Retraire et pour aucunes auȓs cauſes qui ace lout meu et meuvameȇ delaiſſer ſes hȓitages quil a eu pays deguyenne a aucuns deſes enffans ou enffans deſes enffâ qui demoureroient francois en lobbeiſſance du Roy defrance. deſtre adcorde par les parties ce qui ſenſſ. C Premierement q̂ mondſr le captau et ſes enffans et les enffans de ſes enffans leurs heritiers et ſucceſſeurs auront toutes les terres chaſteaulx ſeigneuries. fortreſſes hoſtelz et heritages que mond ſ.r lecaptau et monſ.r decandalle ſon filz tiennent et poſſedent en laduchie deguienne et qui lui competent et appartiennent par les ſucceſſions ~~eurs~~ deſes pere et mere et autres predeceſſeurs en toutes celles quilz ont acquiſes dequelque perſonne que ce ſoit. Et cil ya aucunes dicelles terres ⁊ſr ies chaſteaulx fortreſſes hoſtelz et hȓtages donc Ilz avent perdu lapoceſſion et ſr ie par lafortun delaguerre ou auȓment en quelq̂ manieȓ q̂ ſe ſoit Icelles ȓes ⁊ſr ies ſeront Rendues Reallemeȇ et defait aſeſd enffans et aſes heirs ⁊ſucceſſ.s par ceulx qui les tiennent qui ace ſȓ ſeront cotraints depar leRoy. C Item et

Another treaty regarding the Captal du Buch

THE said agreement thus said is made and concluded, having come to the notice and knowledge of monseigneur Gaston de Foix, count of Venauges and captal du Buch. This count made an agreement before the said lieutenant of the king, who held the field with a good and noble company in order to await the coming enemies of the king, as is said above. And he made a treaty and agreement regarding his fate and that of his possessions. And because the captal was a knight of the Order of the Garter, which was the order of the king of England, he had the desire to retreat, and for several other causes that moved and motivated him to leave his heritages, that which he held in the said land of Guyenne, to several of his children or to the children of his children, who would remain French in the obedience of the king of France, to be agreed by the parties that follow. C First, that seigneur the captal and his children, and the children of his children, their heirs and successors, will have all the lands, castles, lordships, fortresses, hotels, and heritages that my said lord, the captal, and monseigneur de Candale, his son, hold and possess in the duchy of Guyenne, and that are theirs and belong by the successions of their father and mother, and other predecessors, in all those that they had acquired, from whichever person that they be. And if there are any of these lands and lordships, castles, fortresses, hotels, and heritages which they have lost the possession and lordship of by the fortunes of war or otherwise, in whichever manner that it be, these lands and lordships will be rendered, in actuality and in fact, to his said children and his heirs and successors, by those who hold them, which to do this will be forced by the king.

ſiauront toutes les t̃res et ſ͛ies hoſtels ⁊hêtx. donc leſd monſ͛ lecaptau et monſ.ʳ decandalle ſon filz Ioyſſent ⁊poſſedẽt en lad duchie deguyenne qui leur ont eſte donnez et aleurs p̊decesſeurs par les Roys et duc deguyenne. Et ſeratenu leRoy ~~dangleẗre et ducz deguyenne~~ deRecompencer ceulx aqui Ilz ſont et doivent appartenir Iucques alavalle͛ dedeux mille livres touroſ deRente mônoye deRoy ſi tant montent. Et ſiplus montent les enffans ou enffans des enffans heritiers et ſucceſſeurs ſupleront et paieront leſurp⁹ aqui Il appartiendra. Et le Roy les fera Ioyz paiſiblement detoutes les t̃res ſ͛ies hoſtelz et heritages. C Item et ſimonſ͛ lecaptau et monſ.ʳ decandalle ſon filz ou ſes p̊deceſſeurs ont fait ou fait faire ou temps paſſe en quelq̃ maniere que ce ſoit par auctͥᵉ deIuſtice ou aut̃ment. Aucuns Reparacions neceſſaires et proffitables. chaſteaulx maiſons fortreſſes et aut̃s heritages aeulx donnez. par les Roys dangleẗre et ducz deguyenne. En ce cas Icelles Repparacions ſeront aloues ⁊Rabatues aceulx aqui devroient appartenir. leſd hr̃ts chaſteaulx et fortreſſes ſurce quil fauldra que leſd enffans hr̃tiers ⁊ſucceſſeurs Reſtituent ſiReſtituer fault out̃ leſd deux mille livres tournoſ deRente deſquelz leRoy doit acquicter leſd enffans leurs hoirs ſucceſſeurs ou ayans cauſe. Sans cequilz puiſſent Rabatre ou demander auſd meſſ͛ˢ captau. decandalle aucūe choſe des fruitz et Revenus dutemps paſſe deſquelz Ilz et leurſd enffans demoureront quictes pource quilz les ont fait lebourir et ſouſtenir. C Item et ſera content leRoy que led monſ.ʳ lecaptau emporte et face empoꝛ̃ dud pays deguyenne to⁹ ſes biens meubles et argent vaiſſelle ⁊aut̃s biens

C Item, and they will have all the lands and lordships, hotels and heritages for which the said monseigneur the captal and monseigneur of Kendal, his son, have enjoyed and possessed in the said duchy of Guyenne, which had been given to them and to their predecessors by the kings and the duke of Guyenne. And the king will be held to compensate those to whom they are and ought to belong until the value of 2,000 livres tournois of rent, money of the king, if not more. And if it is more, the said children or children of his children, heirs and successors, will supplement and pay the surplus to whom it will belong. And the king will allow them to enjoy peacefully all the said lands, lordships, hotels, and heritages. C Item and if monseigneur the captal and monseigneur of Kendal, his son, or their predecessors, had done or made to do in times past in whatever manner that was by authority of justice or otherwise—any reparations, necessaries, and proceeds, castles, houses, fortresses, and other heritages given to them by the kings of England and the dukes of Guyenne—in this case, these reparations will be allocated and reduced to them to whom the said heritages, castles, and fortresses ought to belong, on which it will be made that the said children, heirs, and successors are restored, other than the said 2,000 *livres tournois* of rent, for which the king ought to acquit the said children, their heirs, successors, of having cause, without which they can reduce or request to the said lords—Captal, Kendal—anything of the fruits and revenues of times passed, of which they and their said children request to leave, because they had to labour and sustain them. C Item and the king will be content that the said monseigneur the captal will take and make to take from the said land of Guyenne all his moveable goods and silver vessels and other goods whatsoever to wherever it seems good to him, and he will

quelzconq̃z quelque part que bon lui ſemblera et aura ſaufconduit et proudent pourcefaire. C Item et ſera leRoy content. que leſd ſ.[rs] captau et decandalle puiſſent delaiſſer leurſd tr̃es ſ[les] hr̃tages chaſteaulx fortreſſes et pouſſ quelzconques quilz ont aud pays deguyenne alaiſne filz dud monſ.[re] decandalle filz dud monſ.[r] captau et quil en puiſſe Iour et uſer par lui et ſes ſucceſſeurs hr̃tiers et ayans cauſe deulx atouſiours maiz perpetuellement. C Item et pource que led enffant monſ.[r] decandalle eſt en bas aage de ~~to~~ trois ans ou environ le Roy ſera contant q̂ monſ.[r] leconte defoulz ſon ~ couſin ait depar leRoy legarde ⁊gouvernemeȇ dicellui enffant et deſd tr̃es ſ[les] hr̃tages et biens quelzconques pour les Regir ⁊gouvr̃ner doreſnavant auproffilt dicellui enffant. Et quil nourrira led enffant soubz lobbeiſſance du Roy Iucques ace quil ſoit en aage ſuffiſ davoir ſon gouvr̃nement et deſeſd biens et hr̃tages. pource q̂ laRevenue deſd hr̃tages deceſte pr̃ſte annee ſera et demoura entieremeȇ auproffilt demonſ lecaptau. et demonſ[r] de candalle ou alun deulx lequel quil le[r] plaira. Et cepourront faire paier tant deſd Revenues que detoutes auȇs debtes et arerages quelzôqz aeux deus en leurſd tr̃es ⁊ſ[ries]. C Item aeſte adcorde que les officiers q̂ mond ſ[r] lecaptau et leſ[r] decandalle ont mis et mettre vould dedens trois moys proc͡h ve͡n eſd terres ⁊ſ[r]ies Ilz ſeront et demoureront doreſnavant po[r] Icelles Regir et gouvr̃ner pour led enffant en faiſ touteſſoys leſermeȇ defidelite et to⁹ auȇs quil appartiendra es mains des officiers du Roy demond ſ.[r] defoulz deſtre bons vrays ⁊loyaulx envers le Roy. et debien Regir et gouverner Icelles tr̃es ⁊ſ[r]ies auproffilt dud enffant. C Item et pource q̂ led enffe eſt ſoubzaage comme dit eſt.

have safe conduct and protection to do this. C Item and the king will be content that the said lords Captal and Kendal can be left with their said treasures, heritages, castles, fortresses, and possessions, whatsoever, that they have in the said lands of Guyenne to the eldest son of the said monseigneur of Kendal, son of the said monseigneur Captal, and that they can be held and used by him, his successors, heirs, and having cause always but perpetually. C Item and because the said son [of] monseigneur of Kendal is a minor of three years or thereabouts, the king will agree that monseigneur the count of Foix, his cousin, will have by the king the guardianship and government of this child, and of the said lands, lordships, heritages, and goods whatsoever, in order to rule and govern henceforth to the profit of this child. And that he will nourish the said child, under the obedience of the king, until he is of an age sufficient to have for himself the governance and his said goods and heritages himself, because the revenue of the said heritages for this present year will be and remain entirely to the profit of monseigneur the captal and to monseigneur of Kendal, or to one of them, whichever is pleasing to them. And it will be possible to pay, both the said revenues and all other debts and arrears whatsoever, to the two of them from their said lands and lordships. C Item to be agreed that the officers that my said lord, the captal de Buch, and the lord of Kendal, had put and want to put within the next three months coming into the said lands and lordships, they will be and remain henceforth in order to reign and govern for the said child, in making always the oath of fidelity and all others that he ought to make, into the hands of the officers of the king, of my said lord of Foix, to be good, true, and loyal to the king, and for good to reign and govern these lands and lordships to the profit of the said child. C Item and

Led monſ.[r] defoulx comme ayant lagarde et gouv̂nement dicelluy enffant fera auRoy les foy et hommage deuz et acouſtumez acauſe deſd hr̂tx. Et quant led enffant ſera en aage davoir ſon gouver nement Il en fera hommage auRoy comme ſon ſubget et vaſſal. et fera les aut̂s devoirs acouſtumez. C Item pareillement to⁹ les ſubgectz demourans es ſ[r]ies q̂ mond ſ[r.] lecaptau et monditſ[r] decandalle tiennent apret̂ et qui demoureront avecques led enffant feront le ſerment au Roy en lamain daucuns deſes officiers. deſtre bons ⁊loyaulx francoiz ſubgectz et obaiſſans auRoy defrance dainſſi quil eſt acouſtume en tel cas. C Item q̂ cil advenoit que led enffant venu en aage v̶ nevouſiſt demourer auparty du Roy nefaire leſermet̂ ou quil allaſt devie atreſpaſſerent ſans hoirs deſon corps. en ce cas toutes leſd t̂res ſ[r]ies chaſteaulx fortreſſes Rentes Revenues et poceſſions quelzconques ſeront et demôront auplus prochain heritier dud aiſne filz decel̅l̅ monſ.[r] decandalle ſoient maſles ou fumelles demourans ou venans au party duRoy. C Item et pource que mondit ſ.[r] decandalle neſt pas encore delibere deprand leparty francois leRoy ſera côtet̂ quil ait t̂me dun an deſoy deſclarer francois ſebon lui ſemble. et aura ſaufconduit bon et ſouffiſant daller ou bon lui ſemblera et dempot̂ ou faire emporter dupays deguyenne to⁹ ſes biens meubles or argent vaiſſelle et aut̂s biens quelzconques devant led temps dun an. C Item et cil advenoit que pend led temps dun an ou partie dicellui led monſ[r] lecaptau. et monſ[r] decandalle ſon filz voulſiſſent demourer ou lun deulx. et tenir en laduchie deguyenne quelque part q̂ bon leur ſemblera pour aucunes leurs beſongnes ou affaires faire lepourront. Pô̊urce quilz feront leſeranent ſolemnel.

because the said child is underage, it is said, the said Monseigneur of Foix, as having the guardianship and the government of this child, will make to the king the oath and homage due and accustomed on account of the said heritages. And when the said child is of an age to have his government, he will make homage to the king as his subject and vassal, and will do the other accustomed duties. C Item equally, all the subjects remaining in the lordships that my said lord, the captal, and my said lord of Kendal have held to the present, and which will remain with the said child, will make the oath to the king, into the hand of some of his officers, to be good and loyal French subjects and obedient vassals to the king of France, also as it is accustomed in such a case. C Item that if it happens that the said child, coming into his age, does not want to remain in the party of the king, nor make the oath, or that he dies without heirs of his body—in this case, all the said lands, lordships, castles, fortresses, rents, revenues, and possessions whatsoever will go and remain to the nearest heir of this eldest son of this, my lord of Kendal, males or females, remaining or coming into the party of the king. C Item and because my said lord of Kendal has not yet decided to take to the French party, the king will be content that he has a term of one year for him to declare himself French, if it seems good to him, and he will have good and sufficient safe conduct to go wherever it seems good to him, and to carry or make to carry from the land of Guyenne all his moveable goods, gold, silver, vessels, and other goods whatsoever before the said time of one year. C Item and if it happens that during the said time of a year or a part of this, the said monseigneur the captal and my lord of Kendal, his son, want to remain, or one of them, and to hold in the duchy of Guyenne, in which part seems good to them, in order to act in

quilz ne feront ou pourchaſſeront choſe qui ſoit audom mage du Roy ne deſes pays hommes ⁊ſubgetz tant côme Ilz feront et demoureront oud pays du Roy. C Item et cil advenoit q mond ſr de candalle ſevouſiſt faire francois dedens led temps dun an et eſtre vray ſubget ⁊obbaiſſſ au- Roy defrance. Et pource fr̂ delaiſſer les t̂res et ſ̂ies quil a en angleт̂re tant deſoy meſmes comme acauſe demadame ſa fême. leRoy por luy aider avivre et ſouſtenir ſon eſtat et ſon ſervice. luy donnera laſomme dedeux mille livres tourn depencion pour chcn an. C Item eſt adcorde q̂ leſd monſſ.r lecaptau ⁊decandalle pourront demander Requerir pourchaſſer envers et cont̂ to⁹ ainſſi que bon leur ſemblera toutes les debtes obligacions ypoteques Raiſons et accions quilz peuvent avoir envr̂s pluſſieurs perſonnes et ſur pluſſieurs lieux et places en eſpecial ſur laplace deleſpare. Et leur fera ou fera faire leRoy bonne ⁊briefve expedicion deIuſtice dedens ung an proch ven. C Item Leſquelz tractie adcords promeſſes et convenances No⁹ gaſton defoulz conte debenauges. captau debuch. promettrons par lafoy et ſermens de denoz corps et ſur nr̂ honneur tenir et faire tenir depoint en point ſelon leurs frome ⁊mannr̂ to⁹ les articles cy deſſus eſcripz ſans les enfraindre en aucune maniere. En teſmoing dece no⁹ avons ſigne ces pr̂etes denrê ſaing manuel et ſcelles dunoz armez. Ledimanche xiiime Ior deIuing. Lan mille CCCC Cinquante ⁊ung.

Autre traictie demonſr demontferrat̂.

EN. cemeſme temps et moment en perceverant eſd appoinctemens pour venir apaix et concorde fut fait ung

any of their needs and affairs, they can do it, [so long as] they not do nor purchase anything which will cause damage to the king or to his lands, people, and subjects, such that they are and remain in the said land of the king. C Item and if it happens that my said lord of Kendal wants to become French within the said time of a year, and to be a true subject and vassal to the king of France, and, in order to do this, to leave the lands and lordships that he had in England, both for himself and on behalf of madame, his wife, the king, in order to help support and sustain his estate and his service, will give him the sum of 2,000 *livres tournois* as a pension for each year. C Item it is agreed that the said lords, the captal and Kendal, can request, require, and purchase from all and against all, such as it seems good to them, all the debts, obligations, mortgages, means, and actions that they have toward several people and on several locations and places, especially in the place of Lesparre. And the king will or will make a good and brief expedition of justice within the following year. C Item, which treaties, aggreements, promises, and conventions we, Gaston de Foix, count of Benauges, captal de Buch, promise by the pledge and the oath of our body, and on our honour to hold and make to hold, point-by-point, according to their form and manner, all the articles abovesaid written, without infracting in any manner. In witness for this, we have signed these present [documents] with our manual signature and sealed by our arms. Sunday, thirtieth day of June, the year 1451.

Another treaty for monseigneur de Montferrant

IN this same time and moment, in perservering in the said agreements in order to come to a peace and concord, another

traicte et appoinctement Ent̃ monſ.r Iehan baſtard dorleans. conte dedunoiz et delongueville lieut̃ general duRoyun̄dſ.r ſur lefait deſaguerre poſton deſaintrailles bailly deberry eſcuier deſcuierie duRoy. et maiſtre Iehan bureau treſorier defrance dunepart. Et meſſſ.rs bertr̃ demonferrant et delagontran daulťpart en laforme et maniere cy ap̊s deſclaree. C Premierement aeſte adcorde ent̃ eulx q̃ led ſr demontferrant ſera comprins eutraicte fait par leſdeſſſd et auťs delapart du-Roy defrance avec ceulx deleville debordeaulx et les trois eſtatz dupays deguyenne et de bordellaiz. Et ſi Ioyra des privileges libertez preeminances et franchiſes donnees et octroyees par leRoy defrance aceulx delaville debordeaulx et du pays deguyenne et debordellaiz. C Item aeſte appoincte que eucas q̃ les angloiz par puiſſance darmes dedens lexxiiime Ior de ceprt̃ moys deIuing nemettront les francois hors deleur champ quilz ont prins et tiennent devant lechaſteau defronſſac et que ne demeurent en Icellui les pluſſors. En cecas led xxiiime Iour paſſe led ſeigneurs demontferrat̃ mettra toutes ſes places en lobbeiſſance du Roy defrance. C Item aeſte acorde et appointe q̃ ſededens led xxiiime Iour deIuing larmee des angloiz vient pour leſecours des gens dupays deguyenne ence cas led ſ.r demontferrant ſepourra armer avecques eulx et leur aider et ſecourir detout ſon pouvoir. Et eucas q̃ leſd angloiz nedemouret̃ les plus fors oud champ devant led lieu defronſſac dedens led xxiiime Iour deIuing en ce cas led ſ.r demontferrant acomplira ſond traicte cŏme dit eſt deſſſ. Et fera leſerment auRoy deſtre bon et loyal francois et mettra ſes places et les hommes deſes tr̃es 7ſſies en lobbeiſſance duRoy defrance. C Item et pource faire led Iour paſſe leRoy ſera contant que led

treaty and agreement was made between monseigneur Jean, bastard d'Orléans, count of Dunois and of Longueville, lieutenant general of the king, our lord, for the matter of his war; Poton de Xaintrailles, bailiff of Berry, squire of the squirerie of the king; and master Jean Bureau, treasurer of France, on one part. And monseigneurs Bertrand de Montferrant and of la Gontran, on the other part, in the form and manner so after declared. Firstly, it is agreed between them that the said seigneur de Montferrant will be included or treated by the abovesaid and others for the part of the king of France, with those of the town of Bordeaux and the three estates of the lands of Guyenne and of the Bordelais. And he will enjoy the privileges, freedoms, benefits, and franchises given and conveyed by the king of France to those of the said town of Bordeaux and of the lands of Guyenne and the Bordelais. Item it has been agreed that in case the English, by the power of arms, by the twenty-third day of this present month of June, push the French out from the camp that they have taken and held before the castle of Fronsac, and that they will not remain in this camp as the strongest. In this case, the said twenty-third day having passed, the said seigneur de Montferrant will put all his lands into the obedience of the king of France. Item, it has been acorded and agreed that if by the twenty-third day of June, the army of the English comes for the rescue of the people of the land of Guyenne, in this case the said seigneur de Montferrant can arm those with them and aid them and rescue them with all his power. And in case the said English do not remain the strongest in the said camp before the said place of Fronsac, by the twenty-third day of June, in this case the said seigneur of Montferrant will comply with his said treaty, as is said above. And he will make the oath to the king to be a good and loyal Frenchman, and put his places and the men of his lands and

ſeigne[r] demontferrant ſes hoirs ⁊ſucceſſeurs apres lui et auront toutes les tr̃es chaſteaulx fortreſſes ſ'ies. hoſtelz et heritages quelzconques q̂ led ſeigneurs demontferrant et ſes predeceſſeurs ont tenu et poſſde tiennent et poſſident en laduchie deguyenne et qui deuement lui competent et appartiennent par ſucceſſions deſon pere et deſes autŝ p̊-deceſſeurs. Et toutes celles q̂ lui et ſes predeceſſeurs ont acquiſes deuemens dequelque perſonne que ſeſoit et ſilui ou ſeſd predeceſſeurs ont perdu lapoceſſion daucunes deſd terres et ſ'ies par lafortune delaguerre ou aut̂ment. La Iouiſſance et poceſſion lui en ſera bail͡ depar leRoy Incontinent quil aura fait le ferment. C Item et ſi aeſte adcorde q̂ led ſeigneur demontferrant aura toutes les tr̃es ſ'ies hoſtelz et hêtages q̂ les Roy dangleŧ̂re et ducz deguyenne ont donne letemps paſſe aux predeceſſeurs dud ſ.[r] demontferrant et alui meſmes. et ſera tenu leRoy deRecomp̂ſer eulx aqui Ilz ſont et doivet̂ appartenir. cil en ya aucun ou aucuns Iucques alavallr̂ de cinq cens eſcuz dor vieulx deRente par ch͡cn an. Et ſiplus vallent q̂ lad ſomme de cinq cens eſcus dor vieulx led ſ.[r] demontferrant ſera tenu deRecompencer ceulx aqui ſont leſd hr̃tx decellui ſurplus aucuns en ya. Et Il ſera quicte envr̃s leRoy et to[s] autŝ des fruits et Revenus q̂ par cy devant lui et ſeſ pre deceſſeurs ont Receu des heritages deſſuſd. Item. aeſte adcorde et appoincte que des choſes deſſſd. LeRoy ~~octroya et donna~~ octroiera et donnera aud ſeigneur demontferrant ou aſes hoirs et ſucceſſeurs ſes lectres patentes en forme deue ⁊ſuffiſante. C Item et pour ſeurete des choſes deſſſd. led ſeigneur demoŧ̂ferrat̂ baillera es mains demondſ.[r] leconte dedunoiz dedens demain pour

lordships into the obedience of the king of France. Item and in order to do this, the said day having passed, the king will agree that the said seigneur de Montferrant, his heirs and successors after him, and they will have all the lands, castles, fortresses, lordships, hotels, and heritages whatsoever that the said seigneurs de Montferrant and their predecessors had held and possessed, hold and possess in the said duchy of Guyenne, and which duly is his and belongs by succession of his father and of his other predecessors. And all that which he and his predecessors had acquired duly by whatever person, that if he or his said predecessors had lost the possession of any of the said lands and lordships by the fortune of the war, or otherwise, the enjoyment and possession will be given to him by the king, so that he will make the oath. Item and it has been agreed that the said seigneur de Montferrant will have all the lands, lordships, hotels, and heritages that the king of England and dukes of Guyenne had given in times past to the predecessors of the said seigneur de Montferrant and to himself, and the king will hold to compensate those to whom they are and ought to belong, if there are any or several, up to the value of 500 écus of old gold in rent for each year. And if the value is more than the said sum of 500 écus of old gold, the said seigneur de Montferrant will be held to compensate those to whom the said heritages belong in surplus, if there is any. And he will be quit toward the king and all others of the fruits and revenues that heretofore he and his said predecessors had received from the abovesaid heritages. Item, it has been accorded and agreed that, of the abovesaid things, the king will deliver and give to the said seigneur de Montferrant, or to his heirs and successors, his letters patent in due and sufficient form. Item and for the surety of the abovesaid things, the said seigneur de Montferrant will deliver into the hands of my said lord, the count

tout leIour laplace de montferrant Laquelle ~~d~~ place mond ſ.r dedunoiz ſera tenu lui Rend tantoſt et Incontinent quil aura fait leſerment au Roy et mis toutes ſeſd tr̃es ⁊ſr̃ies en ſon obbeiſſ ou touteſſoys tantoſt apres q̂ dedens lexxiii.m Iour dece pr̂t moys deIuing les angloiz par puiſſance darmes auroient mis hors et boute leſd gens duRoy defrance duchamp quilz ont eſleu et tiennent devant dechaſteau defronſſac. C Toutes ſleſquelles choſes deſſſd et chacũe dicelle. No⁹ bertrand demontferrat̂ ſ.r dud lieu demontferrant ſeigneur dud lieu demontferrant promettons par lafoy et ſermet̂ den̂r corps et ſur n̂r honneur tenir et faire tenir et acomplir par no⁹ et les n̂r auRoy ~~de~~ n̂rd ſ.r depoint en point ſans les enffraindre en aucune maniê ſans fraulde barat ou mal engin Teſmoing n̂r ſeing manuel et ſeel denoz. armes cy mis lexxiiime Iour deJuing. Lan mil CCCC Cinquante ⁊ung.

Commet̂ ceulx debordeaulx Rendroit̂ la. ville dud bordeaulx au Roy defrance. et autre des francois.

ET tantoſt. apres que leſdeſſſdiz cômis aud tractie faire oulrent beſoigne avec ceulx debordeaulx. Retournerent par devers monſr lelieutenant general duRoy. lechancelr̂ defrance ⁊aut̂s duconſeil et leur Racomplirent et montferrant par eſcript les appoinctemens adcordz et convenances ſignez et ſcellez tant dun coſte que daut̂. lequel fut moult Ioyeulx et auſſi ſiroit̂ to⁹ les aut̂s ſeigneurs. Et auſſi fut la choſe delayee ~~apres led Iour~~ dehuit Iours apres led Iour dedimanche aceulx octroye par led lieutẽn. Auquel Iour ne leur vint ou comparont aucun ſecours. Et neantmoins oult̂

of Dunois, by tomorrow, the place of Montferrant, which place my said seigneur de Dunois will be held to render to him as soon as and immediately after he makes the oath to the king, and puts all his said lands and lordships into his obedience; or otherwise sometime after the twenty-third day of this present month of June, the English, by force of arms, will have pushed out and ejected the said men of the king of France from the field that they had chosen and held before the castle of Fronsac. All these things abovesaid and each of them we, Bertrand de Montferrand, lord of the said place of Montferrand, promise by the faith and the oath of our body and on our honour to hold and make held, and accomplish by us and ours to the king, our said lord, point-by-point, without infracting in any manner, without fraud, deception, or evil intention. Witnessed by our manual signature and seel of our arms so placed, the fourteenth day of June, the year 1451.

How those of Bordeaux rendered the town of the said Bordeaux to the king of France and otherwise to the French

AND soon after the abovesaid committed to the said treaty, having worked with those of Bordeaux, they returned to my said lord, the lieutenant general of the king, the chancellor of France, and others of the council, and they reported to them and Monterrant by writing the agreements, accords, and conventions, signed and sealed, both on one side and on the other, who were very joyous and so were all the other lords. And so the thing was delayed for eight days afterwards, the said day of Sunday, granted to them by the said lieutenant. On which day, nobody came or tried to rescue them. And nonetheless, over and again the promis-

et pardeſſſ les promeſſes faictes leſd debôdeaux ceulx confians touſiours deſecours avoir Rq̂uireȓ Iour debataille. lequel leur fut octroye par mond ſ.ʳ dedunoiz. aud xxiiiᵐᵉ Iour deIuing enſſ pour Illec eulx deffend ſiſecours leur venoit depar leRoy dangleȓre ou ſinon Ilz ſedevoieȓ Rend led Iour. Auquel Iour comparurent leſdeſſſ noȓz defrance pour cuider combatre les ennemis duRoy ou Redduire lad ville en ſon obbaiſſance comme alui appartenant deſon droit paternel Auquel lieu fureȓ expectans et actendans la bataille Iucques aſoleil couchant. Et acelle heure ceulx debordeaulx voyans avoir faulte deſecours firent faire ung hault cry par ung herault lequel croit ſecours deceux dangleterre pour Iceulx debordeaulx. Au quel cry ne fut aucunement Reſpondu ne donne ſecours. Pourquoy ſedepartirent Iceł̃ p̱tx et ſen allerent logier ſans auȓ choſe faire Icelle heure. Et lendemain Retourneȓeȓ meſd ſ.ʳˢ lechancellier et treſorier defrance avec pluſſʳˢ auȓs par devers Iceulx debordeaulx. Leſquelz appointerent q̂ amercredy enſ Ilz feroient tous preſtz. deRendre et baillȓ les clefz des tours ~~ha~~ chaſteaulx havre portes et des barrieres delad ville. et faire les ſermens deſtre bons et loyaulx doreſnavant et hommes naturelz duRoy defrance ſelon lappoinctement et promeſſes par eulx cy devant factes. Et fut ordonne led monſʳ le treſorier pour les grans dilligences quil avoit factes alapourſuite dicelle conqueſte. deguŷne maire delad cite debordeaulx. Et pareillemeȓ fut ainſſi ordonne Ioachim Rouault conneſtable dud lieu. Et fiſt leſerment led côneſtable led chancellȓ. et led maire es mains diceulx châ celler et côneſtable au merqredy enſ qui eſtoit pris pour Rendre lad ville furent preppares les ſʳˢ dupays avecques Iceulx debordeaulx poʳ plus

es abovesaid made, the said of Bordeaux, they always confident to have rescue, requested a day for battle, which was granted to them by my said lord of Dunois on the said twenty-third day the following June, in order to defend themselves, if rescue comes by the king of England, or, if not, they ought to render themselves the said day. On which day abovesaid, the said lords of France appeared in order to fight the enemies of the king or reduce the said town into his obedience, as it belonged to him by paternal right. At which place, they were expecting and awaiting the battle, until sunset. And at this hour, those of Bordeaux, seeing to have failed to be rescued, went to make a high cry by a herald, who cried: Rescue from those of England for those of Bordeaux! To which cry there was no response nor rescue given. For which these batallions departed this place and went to camp without anything else to do at this hour. And the next day, my said lords, the chancellor and treasurer of France, with several others, returned before those of Bordeaux, who agreed such that on the following Wednesday, they would render all present and hand over the keys of the towers, castles, harbours, ports, and barriers of the said town, and to make the oath to be henceforth good and loyal subjects and natural men of the king of France, according to the agreement and promises made by them as before. And the said monseigneur the treasurer was appointed, for the great effort that he had made in the pursuit of this conquest of Guyenne, mayor of the said city of Bordeaux. And at the same time, Joachim Rouault was appointed constable of the said place. And the said constable made the oath [to] the chancellor, and the said mayor in the hands of this chancellor and constable the following Wednesday, which was set for the rendering of the said town, the lords of the lands were prepared with those of Bordeaux to most honourably receive the said lieu-

honnorablement Recevoir led lieutenant general duRoy et laſeigneurie eſtant avecqẑ lui. Leſquelz firent lentree ced Iour. Et pour prendre lapoceſſion et ſaiſine dicelle cite entrereȇ premiers par lordonnance dud lieutenant meſſ.[r] thibault devalpergue bailly delyon. Et led ſire Iehan bureau conſeillȓ du Roy et maire de lad cite et ville. Et leur fureȇ baillees les clefz deto⁹ les lieux fors eſtans en Icelle cite. Alentree ne furent point les francs archiers et comme on diſoit alaRequeſte deceulx debordeaulx. Maiz furent envoyez logier autour delibourne aung port demer. Lad entree commenca aſoleil levant et fut faite par lehault dud lieu ou eſtoient les ſeigneurs deleſparre demoȋferaȃ et pluſſieurs auȇs nobles et notables perſonnes delad ville et du pays. Et aceſte Ioyeuſe entree furent to⁹ les gens degliſe Reveſtuz en chappes tant Religieux chanoines cures côme aultres. Et Receurent aproceſſion grandement et honorablement led lieutenant duRoy et ſa treſnoble ſeigneur. Et premierement cô mencerent aentrer les archiers delavaȃgȓde ceſt aſſavoir des mareſchaulx et autres ca[ne] eſtimez demil. axii.[C] donc eſtoient gouvȓneurs led Ioachim côneſtable dud bordeaulx et leſ[r] depananſac ſeneſchal dethouloуſe. Et apres les hommes darmes delad avantgarde to⁹ apie. q̂ gouvernoient leſd mareſchaulx de loheac et deIalongues trois cens hommes darmes. Et eſtoient leſd mareſchaulx bien montez. apres eulx venoient Les contes deNevers et darmagnac et leviconte delautrec frere duconte defourlz qui avoient trois cens hômes depie. Apres entrerent les archiers. duſ[r] labeſſiere lieutenant duconte du maine nôrez detrois aquatre cens. Apres entra labataille des archiers. nombrez trois mille. Et les gou vernoit led ſ.[r]

tenant general of the king and the lords who were with him, who were entering this said day. And, in order to take the possession of and seize this city, the first to enter, by order of the said lieutenant, was messire Théaulde de Valpergue, bailiff of Lyon, and the said sire Jean Bureau, councillor of the king and mayor of the said city and town. And to them was given the keys for all the strong places that were in this city. At the entrance were and could not be found the free archers, and this, it is said, [was] at the request of those of Bordeaux, but they were sent to camp near Libourne and at another seaport. The said entry began at sunrise and was made from the top of the said place, where the seigneurs of Lesparre, Montferrant, and several other noble and notable people of the said town and of the land were. And at this joyous entry, all the men of the church were vested in capes, both monks, chanters, curates, and others. And they received in grand procession and honourably the said lieutenant of the king and his very noble company. And firstly began to enter the archers of the avant-garde, it is known, of the marshals and other captains, estimated 1,000-1,200, of which the leaders were the said Joachim, constable of the said Bordeaux, and the seigneur de Panansac, seneschal of Toulouse. And after were the men-at-arms of the said avant-garde, all on foot, who were governed by the said marshals of Lohéac and Jallongnes—300 men-at-arms. And the said marshals were well-mounted on horseback, after whom came the counts of Nevers and of Armagnac, and the viscount of Lautrec, brother of the count of Foix, who had 300 men-at-arms on foot. Afterwards, the archers of the seigneur de la Bessière, lieutenant of the count of Maine, entered, numbering 300 to 400. After entered the batallion of the archers, numbering 3,000, and the leader was the said seigneur de la Bessière and the seigneur de la Rochefoucault. After

delabeſſiere et leſeigneur de laRoche foucault. Apres entrerent trois des ſ[rs] dugrant conſeil duRoy. Ceſt aſſavoir leveſque ~~labet~~ dalect Maiſtre guy bernard archediacre detours. apres leveſque et duc delangres et lechancellier de lamarche et aucuns des ſegretaires duRoy. Ainſſi enva meſſ.[r] triſtran lermite ꝑ̊voſt des mareſchaulx to⁹ acheval aveques les ſergens. Apres entrerẽt quatre trompettes du-Roy pourſuivans ⁊heraulx portans les cottes darmes du-Roy. et des ſ.[rs] aqui Ilz eſtoient. dapres entra une hacquenee la ſelle couverte develloux cramoiſy. et avoit ſur lacouppa ung drap develloux aſeur ſeme de fleurs deliz dor. et debroderie. Et ſur laſelle avoit ung petit coffret couvert develloux aſure ſeme defleurs deliz dor dorfavrerie. dedens leq̃l eſtoient les grant ſceaulx duRoy. et ung varlet apie menoit led hacquenee. Et ach̃n coſte dicelle avoit deux archiers veſtuz delivree. puis venoit lechancellr̃ defrance acheval qui eſtoit arme dun corſſet darchr̃. et par deſſus avoit une Iacquette develloux cramoiſy. Apres entra leſire deſantrailles bailly deberry et grãt eſcuier. deſcuierie du-Roy. monte ſur ung grant courſſier couvert deſoye. Et eſtoit led bailly arme tout aublanc ~~une lauce~~ tenant lune des banieres du Roy. et leſ[r] demontagu ſon nepveu tenant autr̃ aſeneſtre monte ſur ung autr̃ courſſier et chevauchoit ſans moyen. led lieutenant duRoy. Puis entra led conte dedunoiz lieutẽn general duRoy cõme dit eſt Lequel eſtoit seul monte ſur ung courſſier blanc couvert develloux bleu charge dorfavrerie et eſtoit tout arme deharnoiz blanc. Et apres lui venoient les cõtes dangouleſme et declermont armez ablanc et leurs chevaulx couverts et leurs pages apres eulx moult Richemẽt habillez. Puis entrerent les contes deven-

entered three of the lords of the grand council of the king—it is known the bishop of Alet, master Guy Bernard, archdeacon of Tours; afterwards, the bishop and duke of Langres and the chancellor of La Marche with him, and several of the secretaries of the king. Then, came messire Tristram the Hermit, provost of the marshals, all on horseback with the sargents. After entered four trumpeteers of the king, followers and heralds wearing the coats of arms of the king and of the lords, after whom entered a haquenée, the saddle covered with crimson velvet and it had on the rear a cloth of azure velvet sown with fleurs-de-lis of gold and embroidery. And on the saddle was a small box covered in azure velvet, sown with silver fleurs-de-lis, within which were the great seals of the king, and a servant on foot conducted the said haquenée. And on each side were two archers vested in livery. Then came the chancellor of France on horseback, who was dressed in a corset d'archier, and on top he had a jacket of crimson velvet. After, the sire de Xaintrailles, bailiff of Berry and grand squire of the squirie of the king, entered, mounted on a large courser covered in silk cloth. And the said bailiff was clothed all in black, holding one of the banners of the king, and the seigneur de Montagu, his nephew, holding the other banner, mounted on another courser, and he rode without assistance [before] the said lieutenant of the king. Then entered the count of Dunois, lieutenant general of the king, as it is said, who was all alone, mounted upon a white courser, covered in blue velvet interlaced with gold, and he was all clothed in white. And after him came the counts of Angoulême and of Clermont, wearing all white, having their horses covered, and their pages after them, very richly clothed. Then entered the counts of Vendôme and Castres, with them several noble barons and great lords, and each of them very richly clothed and dressed. And after

doſme et decaſtres. Avecques eulx pluſſieurs barons nobles et grans ſeigneurs et chc͡n deulx moult Richement parez et habillez. Et apres entra labataille des hommes darmes au nombre demille et cinq cens lances. Leſquilz gouvernoit meſſire Iacques dechabannes grant maiſtre doſtel duRoy. Et eſtoit acheval arme ablanc et ſon cheval couvert moult Richement. En apres les hômes darmes duconte du maine nombrez acent cinquante lances. Leſquelz gouverneroit geoffroy deſaint bellin bailly dechaumont en baſſigny. Puis entra larrieregarde que faiſoit Ioachim Roault avecques leſquilz eſtoient les gens darmes et les archiers duſ.[r] deſaintrailles. Et ainſſi allerent toutes les compaignies Iucques devant lagrant egliſe et ladeſcendit led lieute͡n general du Roy. et les contes dangloul leſire devendoſme darmagnac decaſtres Lechancelier et pluſſieurs auŝs deſſſd. Et adonc vint larchevеſque debordeaulx ala porte degliſe en pontifical Rueſtu de chanomes delad egliſe acompaigne. Et encenſſa led lieutenant et lui fiſt baiſer aucun Reliquaires avecques lacroix. Puis leprint par lamain et lemena dedens le ceur delad egliſe faire ſa priere et oraiſon devant legrant ~~hoſtel~~ autel. Avecques Led lieutenant entrerent deux heraulx du Roy veſtuz deleurs cottes darmes. Et apres entre leſ[r] deſſſ nomme et laiſſerent leſd banneres du Roy dedens legliſe. Et tantoſt apres ladeus con dud lieutenant et des auŝs ſeigne.[rs] faictes Led arceveſque print ung meſel et fiſt Iurer et promettre aud lieute͡n duRoy et auŝs ſeigne.[rs] le pr͡s q̂ leRoy les maintendroit et gardroit atouſiours en leurs franchiſes p̊elegez ⁊libertez accoumees ne quilz firent et q̂ bien ⁊loyalemeŝ en feroient leurs pouvoirs devers leRoy. Et pareillement led lieutên fiſt Iurer led arce veſque Leſei-

entered the batallion of the men-at-arms, until the number was 1,500 lances, which was governed by messire Jacques de Chabannes, grand master of the hotel of the king, and he was on horseback, clothed in white, and his horse very richly covered. Afterwards came the men-at-arms of the count of Maine, numbering 150 lances, which Geoffroi de Saint-Belin, balliff of Chaumont-en-Bassigny, led. Then entered the rear guard that Joachim Rouault created, with whom were the men-at-arms and the archers of the seigneur de Xaintrailles. And, thus, all these companies went until they reached the great church, and the said lieutenant general of the king, and the counts of Angoulême, the sire of Vendôme, Armagnac, Castres, the chancellor, and several others abovenamed descended. And then the archbishop of Bordeaux came to the gate of this church in a pontifical habit, accompanied by the chanters of the said church. And the said lieutenant was acclaimed, and he made to kiss several relics with the cross. Then he took him by the hand and escorted him into the choir of the said church to make his prayers and his meditations before the great altar. With the said lieutenant entered two of the heralds of the king, vested in their coats-of-arms. And after the above-named lords entered, they left the said banners of the king in the church. And soon after the devotions of the said lieutenant and the other lords was made, the said archbishop took a missal and made to swear and promise to the said lieutenant of the king and to the other lords present there that the king would maintain and guard them in all of their franchises, priviledges, and accustomed liberties that there were and that they would be good and loyal in doing whatever toward the king. And equally, the said lieutenant made to swear to the said archbishop, the seigneur de l'Esparre, and other lords assisting—nobles and men of authority of the said

gneur deleſparre 7auſ̃s ſeigne[rs] aſſiſtens nobles et gens ~~dau-troite~~ dautorite delad ville quilz ſeroient atouſiours bons vrays et loyaulx ſubgetz duRoy defrance. alui obbaiſſ et aſacouronne. Et meſmement toute lacômu naulte ce quilz firent et adcorderent to⁹ dune voix. les mains tendues aux ſains côm on aaccouſtue faire en tel cas. Ced ſermet̃ fut accepte led captau debuch. qui pour lors neſtoit point ad-viſe deceſ[r] pource quil eſtoit chlr̃ delaIartiere qui eſt delor-dre duRoy dangleſ̃re côme dit eſt. Apres ouyt led lieuten̄ et toute laſ[r]ie lameſſe bien 7devottemet̃ ~~lameſſe~~ q̃ chanta led arceveſq̃ davant laquelle fut chante. Veni creator ſpn̄s et tedeum laudam⁹. Et ſonna toutes les cloches ſollempnement tant en lad egliſe cathedralle côme en toutes les auſ̃s egliſes delad ville et cite. Et apres leſervice demy fait ſepartit led lieutenant et to⁹ les ſeigneurs degliſe et monterent to⁹ ache-val pour aller prend leur Refections et ſeRetrayt chcn̄ en ſon logis Re ſerve lechancellier defrance. Legrant maiſtre doſtel duRoy et lechancellr̃ delamarche. leſquelz demoure-rent pour Recevoir leſermet̃ demeſſ.[re] olivier decoitivi ſeneſchal deguyenne. lequel vint grandement acompaigne depluſſieurs des gens duRoy et des barons 7chevalliers dud pays deguyenne. Et auſſi des bourgois dud bourdeaulx. et lapn̄ta ſes lectres aud chancellr̃ defrance. Apres lalecture deſquelles led châ cellier lui fiſt faire leſerment q̃ bien et loyaulment Il tiendroit les Iourdicions et feroit Iuſtice egalle augrant côme aupetit aupauvre côme auRiche et tant en lad ville debordeaulx côme en laduchie deguyenne. Et commanda led chancellr̃ apres leſermet̃ tel q̃ dit eſt Receu dud ſey.[al] q̃ chcn̄ obbaiſt alui comme ala propre perſonne du

town—that they would always be good, true, and loyal subjects of the king of France, obedient to him and to his crown. And also all the community, which they did and agreed all in one voice, hands held to the saints, as one is accustomed to do in such cases. The said captal de Buch, who at this time had not yet been counciled, was exempt from this said oath, especially since he was a knight of the Garter, which was the order of the king of England, as it is said. Afterwards, the said lieutenant heard, with all the lordship, the mass very devotedly, which the said archbishop chanted, before which was chanted the veni creator spiritus and te deum laudamus. And one rang all the bells solemnly, both in the said cathedral as in all the other churches of the said town and city. And after the service was done, the said lieutenant and all the lords exited from this church and mounted all on horseback in order to take their reflection and each retreated into his lodging, except for the chancellor of France. The grand master of the hotel of the king and the chancellor of la Marche, who remained to receive the oath of messire Olivier de Coitivy, seneschal of Guyenne, who came very grandly accompanied by several of the men of the king and of the barons and knights of the said land of Guyenne. And also the cityfolk of the said Bordeaux, and he presented his letters to the said chancellor of France, after the words of which, the said chancellor made to make to him the oath that he would good and loyally hold the jurisdictions and make equal justice for both large and small, and to the poor as to the rich, and both in the said town of Bordeaux as in the duchy of Guyenne. And the said chancellor ordered, after the oath, such that it is said, received by the said seneschal, that each obey him as if he were the same person as the king in things touching and concerning his said office. And afterwards, the said lieutenant had sent men within the said castle of

Roy es chof touchans et confernans fond office. Et apres q̂ led lieuten̄ eult envoye gens dedens led chafteau delombriere chambre du Roy yfut mife une des bannieres duRoy puis alleret̂ ĉtains depputez depar led lieuten̄ es tours ⁊havres delad ville ou laut̂ banniere fut mife. Et apres fut fait ung cry folempnel afon detrompe en defend ato⁹ depar leRoy et depar led lieuten̄ q̂ nul ne print fus fon hofte ne ailleurs aucūe chofe fans paier. Et ce fait fen alla chc̄n logr̂ ainffi que par les fourriers eftoit appoincte pour faReĉ dedifgner prend. Maiz ꝺ ne demoura guares apres difgner que grant murmure eftoit en laville fus ung eftoit des gens duRoy le quel avoit tranfgreffe lecry fait depar leRoy et tantoft fut prins et amene aIuftice ou Il fut diligemment examine. Et ce venue alanotire et cognoiffance dud lieutenant quel fuft prendu et eftrangle et ainffi fut Iuftice acomplie qui moult fut plaifant et de bon exemple aceulx delad ville debordeaulx et dupays. Out̂plus fift led lieuten̄ fr̂ ung gibet tout neuf pour pendre cinq compaignies de hoft dud lieuten̄ qui en fauv[r] demeff.[re] guillê deflavy avoient navre meff.[re] pierre louvain chlr̂ lui eftant au fervice du Roy. Et lavoiet̂ efpie par pluffieurs Iournees lecuidans troier̂ pour tuer pour ĉtains debbat qui eftoit depierra ent̂ lefd delouvain et flavy. Et ainffi fut par led lieuten̄ bonne Iuftice faicte ⁊acomplie defd malfacteurs. donc to⁹ ceulx delad ville et cite furet̂ moult Ioyeulx davoir veu tel exploit Car dutemps quilz eftoient es mains defd angloiz Ilz eftoient to⁹ maiftres et ne couroit q̂ voye defait. Alaquelle leplus fage du monde ne favoit pas bien q̂ Refpondre. En lad ville et cite debourdeaulx feIourna led lieuten̄ par lefpace dexv. Iours ou environ pour en Icelle mettre pollice et bon gouvernement

Lambroise, room of the king, putting there one of the banners of the king, then certain people deputised by the said lieutenant went to the towers and harbours of the town, where another banner was put. And afterwards, a solemn cry was made, to the sound of trumpets, proclaiming defense to all, by the king and by the said lieutenant, that his army would take nothing, nor anyone or anything, without paying. And this done, each went to lodge so that by the quartermasters they were ordered to take a light meal for dinner, but it did not remain after dinner that a great murmuring was in the town by one [who] was of the men of the king, who had transgressed the cry above made by the king and soon was captured and handed before justice, where he was diligently examined. And this having come to the notice and knowledge of the said lieutenant, who hanged and strangled him, and so justice was accomplished, which was very pleasant and a good example to those of the said town of Bordeaux and of the land. Moreover, the said lieutenant erected an entirely new gibbet in order to hang five men of the army of the said lieutenant who, following messire Guillaume de Flavy, had wounded messire Pierre de Louvain, a knight, himself being in the service of the king. And he had spied on him for several days, thinking to kill him, because of certain debates that there had been between the said de Louvain and Flavy. And, thus, there was by the said lieutenant good justice made and accomplished upon the said malefactors, so all those of the said town and city were very joyous to see such exploits, because at the time that they were in the hands of the said English, they were all masters and could only be seen by acts, to which the wisest in the world could not know how to answer well. In the said town and city of Bordeaux, the said lieutenant remained for the space of fifteen days or therearound in order to put in this place manage-

et tellemet̂ fut par lui pourveu q̂ les gens deguerre ſe gouvñerent par ~~doumage en aucun grief~~ Raiſ gouvr̂nment qui pend led temps onques extorcion dommaige ne aucun grief ne fut fait. Aaucun delad ville et cite. Ainſſi fut côquiſe toute lad duchie deguyenne. Excepte laville debayonne. Alaquelle conqueſte faire en toutes les places fortes eſtans en Icelle duchie ſe gouvernerent haultement ⁊vaillement led conte dedunoiz lieuten̂ general duRoy. et toꝰ les aut̂s ſeigneurs conſeillers ⁊capitaines chcn̂ ſelon ſapuiſſance comme deſſſ eſt faicte mencion es lieux ou les biens faiz ont eſte mis acffect. Et demoura cap.^{ne} dud bordeaulx. leconte declermont et ſon lieutenant meſſire olivier decoitivi. qui avoit lacharge des gens deguerre demonſ^{r} ſon frere pregent decoitivi. en ſon vivant admiral defrâce.

Separacion degens darmes pour aucun temps.

Apres. laReddicion dud debordeaulx fut ordône que les contes de Nevers. declermont et decaſtres yroient devers leRoy eſtant en chaſteau detaillebourg et leurs armees yroiet̂ en leurs pays aſſignez pour vivre et les contes dangouleſme. darmaignac et depontievre eulx et leurs gens yroient en leurs maiſons et ſemblablement q̂ toꝰ les francs archiers q̂ avoit eſte en Icelle armee ſen yroient en le.^{rs} maiſons. Et eſoit larmee deſſſd qui fut alaconqueſte dud bordeaulx eſtime axx.^{m} combatans. Et ainſſi ſeRepoſa ung pou detp̂s lacôpaignie q̂ eſtoit euſervice duRoy en treſbelle etnoble ordonnâce comme dece deſſus eſt faicte mencion.

ment and good government, so much was done by him that the men of war governed themselves by reasonable governance that during the said time, they made no extortion, damage, nor any grief to any of the said town and city. Thus, all the said duchy of Guyenne was conquered except the town of Bayonne. For the completion of which conquest, in all the strong places in this duchy, the said count of Dunois, lieutenant general of the king, and all the other lords, councillors, and captains, governed themselves highly and valiantly, each according to his power, as has been made mention, where the good deeds had been put into effect. And the count of Clermont and his lieutenant, messire Oliver de Coitïvy, remained captains of the said Bordeaux, who had the charge of the men of war of monseigneur his brother, Prégent of Coitïvy, in his life admiral of France.

Separation of men at arms for some time

After the reduction of the said Bordeaux, it was ordered that the counts of Nevers, of Clermont, and of Castres go to the king, who was then at the castle of Taillebourg, and their armies would go into the lands assigned to them for supplies, and the counts of Angoûleme, Armagnac, and Penthièvre, they and their men, would go back to their homes and, similarly, that all the free archers who had been in this army would return to their homes. And the abovesaid army, which was for the conquest of the said Bordeaux, was estimated at 20,000 soldiers. And so, the company, being in the service of the king, rested for a little time, in very good and noble order, as has been above mentioned.

EN. brief temps et oud an ſedelibera leRoy par lemoyen deſon conſeil dealler mett̂. leſiege devat̂ lacite debayonne te͡n leparty des angloiz. Et pource ffr̂ ordonna euchaſteau de ~~cher bourg~~ taillebourg ſes lieutenans generaulx ſes contes defoix et dedunoiz. Leſquelz levi[me] Iour dumoys daouſt mirent leſiege devant lad cite. Et eſtoient en lacompaignie dud conte defoix legrant maiſtre doſtel duRoy. leſeigneur dela beſſiere lieute͡n ⁊gouverneur des gens darmes duconte dumaine. leſire delautrec frere legiti͡e dud conte defoix. meſſire bernard baſtard de burne. Leſ.[r] denouailles. meſſ.[re] theaulde de valpergue. meſſ.[re] bertrand deſpaigne. leſ.[r] de lavedan. meſſ.[re] martin gracian. Rouachin Roault Robinet petit lou leſpinette. et pluſſ.[rs] aut̂s ſ.[r] avecques leurs gens eſtimez avii.[c] lances avec les archiers et guiſarmiers. donc Il yen avoit iiii.[c] lances degens du Roy. et iiii.[c] lances des barons chlr̂s eſcuiers ſubgectz et hommes dud conte defoix. deſquelz Il faiſoit leamours les montures et harnoiz deteſtes avec led ſ.[r] eſtoit auſſi. led meſſ.[re] triſtan lermite chlr̂ ~ prevoſt deſd mareſchaulx. et Iaſpar bureau maiſtre ⁊gouvernet̂ delartillerie duRoy. Aced ſiege ſans porter blaſme aautruy ſeportreret̂ moult vaillammet̂. leſd maiſtre doſtel. meſſ.[re] bernard debearn et leſd Iaſpard bureau. car Ilz furet̂ leplus pres logez delamuraille etIucq͡z ſur les foſſez. Led conte defoix avoit aveq͡z lui deux mille arbaleſtriers paviſieux extraiz deſon pays. Quant led conte fut arive et quil ot poſe ſon ſiege Il fiſt pluſſieurs chlr̂s. Ceſt aſſavoir le filz dugrant maiſtre doſtel du Roy leſeigne[r] detreſſac frere duſ.[r] denouailles. bertrand deſpaigne ſen.[al] defoix. Rogier deſpaigne. le ſ.[r] debarac et pluſſieurs aut̂s Iucques au

In a brief time later and in the said year, the king decided, by the means of his council, to go lay siege before the city of Bayonne, holding to the party of the English. And for this, he made to order from the castle of Taillebourg his lieutenant generals, the counts of Foix and of Dunois, who, the sixth day of the month of August, laid siege before the said city. And in the company of the said count of Foix were the grand master of the hotel of the king; the seigneur de la Bessière, lieutenant and leader of the men-at-arms of the count of Maine; the sire de Lautrec, legitimate brother of the said count of Foix; messire Bernard, bastard of Bearn; the seigneur de Nouailles; messire Théaulde de Valpergue; messire Bertrand d'Espagne; the sire de Lavedan; messire Martin Gracie; Joachim Rouault; Robert Petit-Lou, Lespinette; and several other lords with their men, estimated at 700 lances with the archers and police, then there were 400 lances of the men of the king, and 400 lances of the barons, knights, squires, subjects, and men of the said count of Foix, for which it was wonderful to see the mounts and headgear, with the said lord was also the said messire Tristran the Hermit, a knight, provost of the said marshals, and Gaspar Bureau, master and governor of the artillery of the king. At the said siege, without blaming others, the said master of the hotel, messire Bernard de Béarn, and the said Gaspar Bureau comported themselves very bravely, because they were the most closely camped to the wall and up to the moat. The said count of Foix had with him 2,000 crossbowmen extracted from his land. When the said count arrived and had set his siege, he made several knights—it is known, the son of the said grand master of the hotel of the king; the seigneur de Tressac, brother of the seigneur de Nouailles; Bertrand d'Espagne, seneschal of Foix; Rogier d'Espagne; the seigneur de Barac; and sev-

nôbre dexv. chlr̃s. Et environ midy celui Iour aRiva led conte dedunoiz et delongueville lequel miſt ſon ſiege devant lacite ducoſte dedevers berne. ent̂ laRiviere deladour et delamue qui leſd ſieges ne pouvoient ſecourir laut̂. Et eſtoient en lacompaignie dud conte dedunoiz leſire deloheac mareſchal defrance. leſ.[r] dorval filz duconte dalbreth. et les gens duſ.[r] delalongnes mareſchal defrance. Leſquelz meſſ.[re] Iehan dachire gouvernoit pour led mareſchal et les gens duſ.[r] debeauvaiz du pays debôbonnoiz et les gens demeſſ.[re] pierre louvain. meſſ[re] bouſe deValpergue. Robert connigan. Iehan carbônel Les gens dud ſ.[r] deſaintrailles et pluſſieurs aut̂s Iucques au nombre de vi.[c] lances archiers et guiſarmiers. demettre led ſiege ſegouvêrnerent leſdeſſſ ſ.[rs] grandement et honorablement. Et lelendemain qui fut levii[me] Iour dud moys ceulx deddedens bayonne deſemparere t̂ les faulxbourgs deSains leon ducoſte dour eſtoit ledit conte defoix. leſquioz eſtoie t̂ treſſfort fermez defoſſez et grans paulx. Maiz lagrant mul titude des coullevrines ſerpentines ⁊Ribaudequins en Rompoient les palliz et tuoient les gens. deguerre qui yſſoient aladeffence leur firent labandonner et delaiſſer leſd faulxbourgs. Et adonc bouterent leſire aux egliſes qui de ceux eſtoient et maiſons. Et par eſpecial avant Ilz apreceure t̂ q̂ ceulx qui tenoient led ſiege ſemettoient appoint pour les aſſaillir. Et adonc entrerent Iceulx aſſallans alafille dedens Iceulx faulxbours et les pourſuivirent ſiaprement q̂ ~~cil~~ que cilz euſſent eſte cent hommes enſemble Ilz euſſent gagnie lad ville et yfuſſent entres par laporte peſlemeſle avecques ceulx dededens. Maiz Ilz nepovoie t̂ ſiacoup monter leſd foſſez pour venir haſti vement tant eſtoient parfons car Ilz

eral others until the number was fifteen knights. And around the middle of this day, the said count of Dunois and Longueville, who put his siege before the said city on the said side toward Berne, between the rivers Dour and Mue, which the said camps could not help one another, and there were in the company of the said count of Dunois the seigneur de Lohéac, marshal of France; the seigneur d'Orval, son of the seigneur d'Albret; and the men of the seigneur de Jallongnes, marshal of France. Which messire Jean d'Athire governed on behalf of the said marshal; and the men of the seigneur de Beauvais, of the lands of the Bourbonnais; and the men of messire Pierre de Louvain, messire Théode de Valpergue, Robert Cunningham, Jean Carbonel, the men of the said seigneur de Xaintrailles, and of several others, until the number was 600 lances, archers, and pikemen laid the said siege, the abovesaid lords governing themselves greatly and honourably. And the next day, which was the seventh day of the said month, those from within Bayonne decamped from the suburbs of Saint-Léon on the side where the said count of Foix was, these suburbs being very strongly [defended] by trenches and large spikes. But the greater multitude of the coulverines, cannon, and ribauldequins, which bombarded them and killed the men of war who had been there at the defense, abandoned them and left from the said suburbs. And so the sire set fire to the churches and homes that were there, and epecially before they perceived that those holding the said siege were at the point of assaulting them. And so these assailants entered at the slums within these suburbs and they pursued them so lively that, they having defeated one hundred men altogether, they had won the said town and had entered there pall mall via the gate with those within. But they could not mount the top of the said trench to come hastily, being

na voient nulles eſchelles. Et adonc ſeloge rent tous les aſſaillans en Iceulx faulxbourgs et eſtaingnirent lefeu es egliſes ⁊maiſons. Et ſeloga led conte defoulz aux auguſtins pource quilz neſtoient q̂ pou bruſlez. Et levi^{me} Iour enſ vint ducoſte debordeaulx leſ^{re} dalbreth. et leviconte detartas ſon filz et ſe logerent auſaint eſprit aubout dupont deboys par lequel ceulx delad ville pouvoient ſallir ſur leſiege lequel pont fut Rompu lanuyt enſ par les gens dud ſ.^{r} dalbreth. lequel avoit en ſacompaignie deux cens lances et les archiers et trois mille arbaleſtriers. Et lendemain ſaillirent ceulx debayonne par ung boullevert qui eſt ducoſte dedevers lamer pour prend et dommager ceulx eſtans oud ſiege aleſquere et lors meſſ^{re} bernard debearn et ſes gens vinrent aleſcarmouche et Iucques dedans leur ville. Et ainſſi q̂ led meſſire bernard ſen Retournoit deſcarmoche Il fut frappe dune ~~quarele~~ culevrine et ~~perca~~ laplombee ſon pas et entra en ſalambe en les deux oz qui depuis fut tenue et fut ſi bien gouverne par les ſeigneurs q̂ leperil deſue en fut hors. Puis lendemain matin fut p̂riſe forte fermee defoſſez et depaulx q̂ prindrent les gens dud meſſire bernard montie daſſault moutie damblee. Et quant ceulx ded dues virent quilz navoient pas du meilleur ſe Retrairent dedens laville et yen ot devoirs et deprins ł cinq ou ſix. et ainſſi fut aſſegee lad ville detoutes pars. Et furet̂ envoyez de deus leſ.^{r} deluce. meſſire martin gracien et leſpinace dedens lad egliſe. Et lors ducoſte dud couſte dedunoiz furet̂ faiz degrans aprou chemens detirer lamuraille ſans actendre lavenue des groſſes bombardes et qui les euſt voulu actendre ſans Remede lad ville en eut eſte prinſe daſſault veu les courage des aſſaillans. Touteffoiz

so low, because they had no ladders. And, thus, all the assailants camped in these suburbs and they extinguished the fire in the churches and houses. And the count of Foix lodged himself in the Augustinian monastery, because it was the only [church] not burned down. And the sixth day following the sire d'Albret and the viscount of Tartas came on the side of Bordeaux, who camped at Saint-Éprit, at the end of a wooden bridge, by which those of the said town could sally out of the said siege, which bridge was broken the following night by the men of the said seigneur d'Albret, who had in his company 200 lances and the archers, and 3,000 crossbowmen. And the next day those of Bayonne sallied out by a bulwerk that was on the side toward the sea, in order to take and damage those who were at the said siege in the space, and then Bernard de Béarn and his men came to the skirmish and went into their town. And when the said messire Bernard returned to the skirmish, he was struck by a coulevrine and fell from his feet, and the ball entered his shoulder into the two bones, which, since he held himself and was so well conditioned by the lords, the peril of death was put out. Then, the next morning, a strong church was taken, enclosed by trenches and stakes, which the men of the said messire Bernard captured, half by assault, half by pillaging. And when those of the said place saw that they did not have the best, they retreated into the town, and in this place the worked and took five or six, and thus the said town was besieged from all sides. And the sire de Lucé, messire Martin Gratien, and l'Espinette were sent within the said church. And then, from the side of the count of Dunois, great advances were made against the wall, without awaiting the arrival of the large bombards, and though he had wanted to wait for them, without waiting, the said town was captured by assault, seeing

quaῖ les aſſiegez ſceurent que les bombardes approuchoient Ilz comme ayans les ceurs faillez Requirent aparlamenter. Et fut lexviii^{me} Iour daouſt. Pourquoẙ Leſd contes defoiz et dedunoiz lieutẽn du Roy commitz en ceſte partie convindrent aparlamenter avec ceulx decite appellez avecquez leſd contes legrant maiſtre doſtel du Roy. meſſire pierre debeauvau ſ.^{r} de labouſſiere. meſſ.^{re} theaulde devalpergue bailly delion et meſſ^{re} Iehan lebourſſier gẽal defrance. leſquelz apres pluſſ.^{rs} choſ pourparlees traicterent en lamaniere qui ſenſ. Ceſt aſſavr̂ quilz bailleroient et mettroient en lamain du Roy daun Iehan debeaumont leur cap.^{ne} fre du conneſtable deNavarre delordre deſaint Iel̃ deIhrl̃m lequel demoureroit priſonnier et en avoullente duRoy. Et feroit mene devr̂s lui et to⁹ les gens deguerre eſtans en Icelle ville demeureroient to⁹ ſemblablement priſonniers alavoullente duRoy. Et ceulx delad ville ſeſoubz mettront aubon plaiſer du Roy. Et po^{r} loffence dedeſobbaiſſance quilz avoient fctẽ en xl.^{m} eſtuz dor. Et neIour Rendirent led damp Iehan leur cap.^{ne}. Lequel en lapr̂ce des aſſiſtans tant delaville côme auŝ bailla ſafoy aud grand maiſtre doſtel. Et ainſi fut fait ⁊concl̊ud Letratie delaville et cite de bayonne. Et tant q̂ led ſiege dura ceulx dupays debiſaye firent degroſſes dilligence defournir devivres led ſiege. Car le Roy leur en avoit eſcript. Et fut led ſiege fort advitaille tant pour gens darmes chevaulx q̂ auŝment Il venoit auſſi vivres debearn et deNavarre Maiz ceſtoit agrant paine pour lagrant multitude des p brigans qui eſtoient ſur lepays. Touteſſois Il oſt meult aucune faulte devivres. Leſd biſcayens vindrent atout xii. vaiſſeaulx darmes nommez ~~eſpua~~ eſpinaces et une grant

the great courage of the assailants. Suddenly, when the besieged learned that the bombards approached, they, having weak hearts, asked to talk. And it was the twenty-eighth day of August. For which the said counts of Foix and of Dunois, lieutenants of the king commissioned on this front, committed to speak with those of the city, named with the saids counts the grand master of the hotel of the king, messire Pierre de Beauvau, seigneur de la Bessière, messire Théaude de Valpergue, bailiff of Lyon, and messire Jean le Boursier, general of France, which after proposing several things, treated in the manner that follows: it is known that they will release and put into the hands of the king Sir Jean de Beaumont, their captain, brother of the constable of Navarre, of the order of Saint John of Jerusalem, who will remain a prisoner by the will of the king. And he will be brought before him, and all the men of war who were in this town will all similarly remain prisoners by the will of the king. And those of the said town will submit themselves at the good pleasure of the king. And for the offense of disobedience that they have made, [they will pay] 40,000 écus of gold. And the day, the said Sir Jean, their captain, will render himself, which, in the presence of all, he will assist those of both of the town and elsewhere to deliver his good faith to the said grand master of the hotel. And so was made and concluded the treaty of the town and city of Bayonne. And while the said siege remained, those of the lands of Biscay made great diligence to provide the said siege with supplies, because the king had written to them. And the siege was strongly supplied, both for men at arms, horses, and others; to them came also supplies from Bearn and from Navarre, but it was with great pain due to the great quantity of brigands who were in the lands. However, there was no default of supplies. The said Biscayans

nave. Leſquelz arriverent aune lieue debayonne affin q̂ ceulx qui eſtoient dedens laville neſen peuſſent fuir par eaue. Et eſtoient leſd biſcayens nombrez vi.[C] combatans et levendredi xx[me] Iour dud moys ung pou apres ſoleil levaȋ. Le Iour fut bel et cher et moult beau temps cy fut veu ~~v~~ en ciel par ceulx qui eſtoient en loſt du Roy. Et meſmement par les angloiz eſtans dedens bayonne une croix blanche laquelle fut veue pupliquement par leſpace dedemye heure. Et lors ceulx delad ville qui eſtoient duIour dedevant Rendez et leurs compoſicions faictes oſterent leurs bannieres et penons aux croix Rouges diſant quil plaiſoit adieu quilz fuſſent frñ et quilz portaſſent to⁹ lacroix blanche. Cette croix fut ~~vau~~ veue aung Iour devendredy qui eſt leIour q̂ nr̂e ſ.[r] Ihĉriſt fut crucifie. Et aheure dedix heures entra dedens la ville avecques leveſque dicelle leſeign[re] delabeſſiere pour prend lapoceſſ decelle ville et duchaſteau. Et lafureȋ portees les banr̂s du Roy auhault delatour duchaſteau par les heraulx du Roy. donc chĉn eult grant Ioye. Et aIcelle heure aRiva lenavire des biſcains dedens leport debayonne. Laquelle choſe Il faiſoit beau voir. Et leſamedy xxi[re] Iour daouſt entrerent les contes defoix et dedunoiz defrnd lad cite debayonne et entrerent avec led conte defoulz ~~led conte~~ legrant maiſtre doſtel du Roy. leſ[r] delautret frere dud dud conte. Leſ[r] denouailles. le ſ[r] delabeſſiere ⁊pluſſieurs autˆs et yavoit devant eulx. mille archers q̂ gouvernoit leſpinace. Et apres venoient les heraulx du Roy et autˆs portans leurs cottes darmes. Et apres meſſ.[re] bertrand deſpaigne ſen.[al] defoix. qui portoit labanniere duRoy et eſtoit armee tout aublanc et chevauchoit ung courſſier couvert develloux cramoiſy.

came with a dozen vessels in arms, called *espinaces*, and a massive navy, which arrived a league from Bayonne, so that those who were within the town could not flee by water. And the said Biscayans numbered 600 soldiers, and Friday, the twentieth day of the said month, a little after sunrise. The day appeared very beautiful and clear, and was a very good temperature, as it was seen in the sky by those who were in the army of the king. And similarly by the English who were in Bayonne, a white cross, which was seen publicly for the space of half an hour. And then those of the said town, who rendered themselves the previous day and who had made agreements to them, removed their banners and pennants in the red cross, saying that it pleased God that they were French, and that they would all carry the white cross. This cross was seen on a day of Friday, which was the day Our Lord was crucified. And at the hour of 10 o'clock, the seigneur de la Bessière entered within the town with the bishop of this place in order to take possession of this town and castle. And there were raised on the high point of the tower of the castle the banners of the king by the heralds of the king, for which each there was great joy. And at this hour, the navy of the Biscayans arrived within the port of Bayonne, which thing it was good to see. And Saturday, the twenty-first day of August, the counts of Foix and Dunois entered within the said city of Bayonne and with the said count of Foix entered the grand master of the hotel of the king; the sire de Lautrec, brother of the said count; the seigneur de Nouailles; the seigneur de la Bessière; and several others, and before them went 1,000 archers, who governed the *espinance*. And after came the heralds of the king and others carrying their coats of arms. And after, messire Bertrand d'Espaigne, seneschal of Foix, who carried the banner of the king and

Apres venoit led conte defoix armee ablanc monte ſur ung courſſier moult Richemẽt habille et eſtoit eupres lui ſon ſen.^{al} debearn auſſi bien monte ⁊Richemẽt habille et avoit aſon cheval ung chanfrain dachier garny dor et depierries p̊riceſs priſe axv.^{m} eſcuz dor et grant nombre deſ^{rs} apres lui. et ſans Intervalle venoient vii.^{c} lances apie. Et de laut͠ part entra led conte dedunoiz et avoit devant lui xii. archiers et apres deux des heraulx duRoy. et aut͠s portans diverſes armes. Apres venoit meſſ.^{re} Iamet deſa ſaveuſe monte ſur ung courſſier portant lune des bannieres duRoy. AIcelle entree Led dedunoiz fiſt chevalliers led Iamet leſ^{r} demontguyon. Iehan demômorin et lefilz de bouſſay. Apres lad banniere entra led conte dedunoiz tout arme aublanc et ſon cheval couvert develloux cramoiſy. Apres le ſ^{r} deloheac mareſchal defrance. leſ^{r} dorval et pluſſieurs aut͠s grans ſeigneurs et deſrê eulx. vi.^{c} lances. Ainſſi toſt ſe Rêcontrerent pres delagrant egliſe et alaporte decelle fut leveſque Reveſtu en pontifical les cha noines ⁊aut͠s gens degliſe Reveſtuz en chap͡pes qui les actendoient atout les Reliques et la deſſendirent apie leſd ſ.^{r} et baiſerent les Reliques et allerent faire leurs devocions dedens lad egliſe puis ſen allerent en le.^{rs} logis. Et envoya led conte defouilz la couverture deſon courſſier qui eſtoit dedrap dor. priſee iiii.^{c} eſcuz dor. devant nrê dame debayonne pour faire des chappes. Et lelendemain qui fut ledimanche leſd ſ.^{rs} vinrent ouir la meſſe en lad egliſe. et yeſtoit avecqẑ eulx leſire dalbreth. qui yeſtoit entre leſamedy auſoir. Et apres lameſſe prindrẽt leſermẽt de ceulx delaville. Et fut cômis maire en Icelle meſſ.^{r} Iehan lebourſſier general defrance et meſſ.^{re} martin gracian cap.^{ne} Leſquelz de moure-

was arrayed all in white, and he rode a courser covered in crimson velvet. Afterwards came the said count of Foix, arrayed all in white, mounted upon a courser very richly dressed, and after which came his seneschal of Béarn, equally well mounted and richly dressed, and he had atop his horse a chamfron of steel, complemented with gold and stones, priced at 15,000 écus of gold, and a great number of lords, after whom, and without break, came 700 lancers on foot. And for the other part entered the said count of Dunois, and he had before him twelve archers, and after which were two of the heralds of the king and others carrying various arms. Afterwards came messire Jamet de la Saveuses, mounted on a grand courser carrying one of the banners of the king. At this entry, the said count of Dunois made several knights: the said Jamet, the seigneur de Montguyon, Jean de Montmorin, and the son of Boussay. After the said banner, the said count of Dunois entered, all armed in white, and his horse covered in crimson velvet. After him, the seigneur de Lohéac, marshal of France; the seigneur d'Orval; and several other great lords, and behind them 600 lancers. So, soon, they met near the large church and at the door of this place was the bishop, clothed in a pontifical habit, the chanters and other men of the church wearing capes, who attended them with all the relics, and there, the said lords descended on foot and kissed the said relics, and they went to make their devotions within the said church, then each went into their lodgings. And the said count of Foix sent the covers of his courser, which was a cloth of gold, valued at 400 écus of gold, to Nôtre-Dame de Bayonne in order to make capes. And the next day, which was Sunday, the said lords came to hear mass in the said church, and there was with them the sire d'Albret, who had arrived Saturday night. And after the mass, they

rent pour garder ⁊govṽner lad ville. Et lelundy proc͡ſenſ leſd ſ.[rs] avecques leurs gens ſen allroint eu pays aeulx aſſigne po[r] vivre. Et tantoſt apres les barons chevallr̃s nobles bourgois et les trois eſtatz debordeaulx debourdellaiz. Debaionne. Brainnoiz. arcques et ceulx du pays environ allerent ataillebourc devr̃s leRoy pour confermer et Rattifier les articles et appoinctemens paſſez par eulx. Et pour faire pas les nobles hommaige auRoy deleurs ſ[r]ies. Et laleRoy donna xx.[m] eſcuz. aux bayonnoiz. dexl.[m] eſcuz quilz devoient paier ƀ pas lad comp.[on] deſſſ eſcrite ainſſi q̂ les hâtans ſupplieret̂ treſhumblemet̂ alabenignite du Roy. Et apres ſen Retôueret̂ chc͡n en leur ville tres contans du Roy et des ſeigneurs deſon grant conſeil ou ſervice du Roy ataillebourg eſtoient avecques lui les contes dumaine. deNevers. declermot̂ devendoſme. decaſtres detancarville et depluſſieurs autres grans ſeigneurs. Et lors vindront devers lui les contes defoix et dedunoiz. leſire dalbreth. leſire deloheac et pluſſieurs autres. Leſquelz tantoſt ſen Re tournerent en leurs pays eulx yverner et leRoy ſen alla paſſer ſon yver en ſon pays detouraine. Ainſſi par lagrace dedivine fut Redduite en lamain et lobbeiſſance du Roy defrance toute laduchie deguyêne et denormandie. Et generalement le le Royaulme defrance. Excepte ƚ ſeullemet̂ laville decalaiz qui eſt encoures demouree es mains des angloiz dune dont que bien brief puiſſe eſtre miſt et Redduite en lob beiſſance duRoy ſe ſera ce que dit eſt a couple. **Melioz. eſt. obbedientill. q[u] ſacriſumm**. Cen eſt adira en ſubſlare ſaraſire en vault par obbaiſſance ⁊cil.

took the oath of those of the town. And messire Jean le Boursier, general of France, was commissioned mayor in this place, and messire Martin Gracian, captain, who remained in order to guard and govern the said town. And on the following Monday, the said lords with their men went to the lands that were assigned to them to resupply. And soon afterwards, the barons, knights, nobles, cityfolk, and the three estates of Bordeaux, Bordelais, Bayonne, Brainnois, and Acqs, and those of the lands around them, went to Taillebourc to the king in order to confirm and ratify the articles and agreements passed by them. And in order for the nobles to make [oaths of] homage to the king for their lordships. And there, the king gave 20,000 écus to the Bayonnais of the 40,000 écus that they ought to pay by the said written agreement above, after which as the inhabitants begged very humbly for the benevolence of the king. And afterwards, they returned, each to their town, very happy with the king, and the lords of his grand council in the service of the king at Taillebourc with him were the counts of Maine, Nevers, Clermont, Vendôme, Castres, Tancarville, and several other great lords. And then the counts of Foix and Dunois, the sire d'Albret, the sire de Lohéac, and several others came before him, who soon returned into their lands to winter there, and the king went to pass his winter in his lands of Touraine. Thus, by the divine grace, were reduced into the hands and the obedience of the king of France all the duchy of Guyenne and of Normandy, and generally the kingdom of France, except only the town of Calais, which still remained in the hands of the English, though there is no doubt that it will briefly be put into and reduced into the obedience of the king; for then it will be, as it is said: '**Better is obedience than sacrifice.**' That is to say, in substance, obedience has more value more than sacrifice.

Commet̂ lempereur fredric fut couronne aRomme.

Oudit an. fut lempereur fredrich. duc dautriche couronne et eſpouſe aRomme par lepappe Nicollas. Alafille du Roy de portugal. Et yot grant feſte et ſollempnite côme aux partus appartenoit bien. Et apres pou detemps ſepartit deRomme et ſen Retourna led empereur en alemagne et ymena ſafemme. Et lafuret̂ grâdement et notablement Receuz ſelon luſage 7couſtu͡e dupays.

Laguerre degand faicte par monſ.ʳ Leduc debourgongnie.

EN. ce meſme an ſemeult grant di viſion et guerre. ent̂ en laconte deflandres Ent̂ monſʳ leduc debourgogne. et ceulx delaville degant. pource q̂ led duc côme leur ſeigneur voulloit mettre en lad ville gabelle deſel ce q̂ oncques navoit eſtre côme diſoient les hâtans dicelle ville. Et dura longuemet̂ lad guerre et yeut aloccaſion dece pluſſieurs gens mors des deux partis. Et meſmement feux bouttez et tellement que grant partie en eſt et aeſte bruſle.

Diviſion entre les princes dangletr̂e.

EN. cellee annee eult grant debbat et diſcord en angletr̂e Ent̂ leduc diorck et leduc deſombrecet pour legouvernemet̂ duRoyaulme. Et eſtoit lors leRoy poʳ led deſombrecet et tenoit les champs atoute ſa puiſſance en leur bataille bien

How the emperor Frederick was crowned at Rome

In the said year, the emperor Frederick, duke of Austria, was crowned at Rome by Pope Nicholas and married to the daughter of the king of Portugal. And there, a great feast and ceremony were held, as befitted such parties. And a little time afterwards, the said emperor left from Rome and returned to Germany, and he took his wife. And there they were greatly and notably received, according to the usage and custom of the land.

The war of Ghent made by monseigneur the duke of Burgundy

IN this same year, there moved great divisions and war within the county of Flanders between monseigneur the duke of Burgundy and those of the town of Ghent, because the said duke, as their lord, wanted to impose in the said town a salt tax, which had never been seen done, according to the inhabitants of this town. And the said war endured for a long time, and there had been on occasion several people killed of both parties. And even arson, and such that a great section in this place had been burned.

Division between the princes of England

IN this year, there moved great debate and discord in England between the duke of York and the duke of Somerset for the government of the kingdom. And the king of England at this time was in favour of the said of Somerset and he held the

ordonnee et led duc diorck en bataille pareillement et les ungz devant les auts̃ cuidas̑ côbatre maiz les prelatz et auts̃ avec les ſeigneurs du Royaulme. Conſiderans les grans maulx qui ſen pourroient enſuir les deſtournerent et trouverent maniere detractier. Et promiſt led duc diorck. ne faire Iamaiz aſſemblee et armee alencontre duſon Roy. Et ainſſi ſen Retourna chcn̑ en ſon lieu.

Legat envoye en France par lepappe Nichollas

EN celui an. lecardinal deſtouteville vint devers le-Roy comme legat et commis depar lepappe nichollas lui Reqerir quil vouſiſt faire paix avecques leRoy dan gletr̂e et q̂ laguerre qui yeſtoit portoit grat prudice alafoy catholique et plus pôroit faire ſibref aucun bon acord neſeſaiſoit entre les deux Royaumes Car on vroit deIour en Iour les meſcrans marchez et entreprendre et gaigner pays ſur les xpries̑. Et apres que led cardinal eult expoſe cedoc̑ lepappe lavoit charge. lui fut Reſpondu pour leRoy que le Roy avoit touſiours voulu et encore voulloit pour obvier aleffuſion deſangc et auſſi pour lebien delachoſe publique eſtoit preſt dy entendre en toutes bonnes voyes. et que par pluſſieurs foiz ceſt mis en ſon devoir pour Icelle paix trouver. Et encores eſtoit preſt de obtemeres a toute Raiſon et deſoy employer ſus leſd meſcroians en tout ce quil lui ſeroit poſſible. Et dy emploier grant part definances pour expulſer Iceulx ſaraſins. Et ce pendat̂ que led cardinal eſtoit encores devers. Lepappe ayant lachoſe ceur envoya larceveſque deRavenne qui eſt deceulz des urſins deRomme par devers le Roy dangletr̂e pour

field with all his power in a great battalion, well ordered, and the said York in a similar battalion, and one before the other, thinking to fight each other, but the prelates and others with the lords of the said kingdom, considering the great evil that could ensue, turned them and found means to negotiate. And the said duke of York promised to never make any assembly or army against the king. And so each returned to his place.

Legate sent into France by the Pope Nicholas

IN this year, the cardinal of Estouteville came to the king as legate and commissioned by Pope Nicholas, to ask of him that he desires to make peace with the English, and that the war brought great prejudice to the Catholic faith, and could do more, if a quick good agreement is not made between these two kingdoms, because one sees from day to day the heathens marching and working and winning new lands from the Christians. And after the said cardinal had exposed that which the pope had charged him, the king responded to him that the king had always wanted and still wanted to obviate the effusion of human blood, and also for the good of the public, he was ready to hear all good words, and that several times he had put himself in his duty to find this peace. And still he was ready to defer to all reason and employ himself against the said unbelievers in all that would be possible to him. And he would employ the greater part of finances to expel these Saracens. And while the said cardinal was still before [the king], the pope having the matter heavy on his heart, he sent the archbishop of Ravenna, who was of those Orsinis of Rome, to the king of England

lui monſtrer ſemblablemẽt quil voulſiſt faire paix avecques leRoy de France pour les meſmes et Raiſons devant touchees. Et que ladiviſion pourroit ẽgendr̃ content cont̃ laxpñte Combien que deſe Ilz conqueroient ſur les marches duhõgrie et des alemaignes treſſort. Se firent Reſ ponce pour leRoy dangleт̃re ceulx ace commis aud archeveſque que quant Ilz auroient autant conqueſte du paẙs duRoẙ defrance avoit conqueſte ſur eulx quil ſeroit temps deparler deceſte matiere qui eſt Reſponce demauvaiz ~ exemple. Car Il ſemble quilz avoient pluſchr̃ laloy dedieu eſtre perye et perdue q̃ce quilz ne conquiſtaſſent ne qui oncques me fut au Roẙ dangleterre et aſes predeceſſeurs Roys. Et ainſſi ſen Retourna led arceveſque dune part. Et led cardinal dautre pour porter leur Reſponce au pappe nicollas ne autre choſe par eulx ne fut faicte en ceſte matiere.

Comment lacques ceur argentr̃ du Roy defrance fut areſte priſonner

Lan. mil CCCC. Cinquante ⁊deux fut prins et areſte priſonnier par lecom mandement et ordonnance du Roẙ. lacques cuer ſon argentier et conſeillier pour aucuns cas touchant lafoy catholique et auſſi crime delezemageſte comme autrement. Et eſt vraẙ que led Iacques cuer eſtoit acauſe davoir baille adminiſtre et delivre aux ſarraſins ennemis delafoy xpnẽne armures detoutes ſortes auſa ige delaguerre. Et meſmement envoẙe pluſſ[rs] armuriers et ouvriers pour Icelles faire et Inſtruire les ſarraſins pour Icelles ſavoir fr̃e qui eſt au preudice et ~~do~~ grant dommaige. detoute xpẽnte. Et aeſte aiſſi areſte põrce que lui plus meu deſavoul-

in order to show him similarly that he wanted to make peace with the king of France for the same causes and reasons before touched upon. And that the division could engender contempt against Christianity, such that they could conquer up to the marches of Hungary and of Germany with force. Responding for the king of England, those who were commissioned to the said archibishop that when they had conquered from the lands of the king of France had conquered from them, then it would be time to speak on this matter, which was responded as a bad example because it seemed that it was more Christian the law of God to perish and be lost that they conquer that which never belonged to the king of England and to his predecessor kings. And so, the said archbishop returned on his part, and the said cardinal on the other, to carry their response to Pope Nicholas, nothing having been done for them in this matter.

How Jacques Cœur, treasurer of the king of France, was arrested and imprisoned

The year 1452, Jacques Cœur, the treasurer and councillor [of the king], was taken prisoner and arrested by the command and order of the king for several items touching on the Catholic faith and also certain crimes of lèse-majesté, and others. And it is true that the said Jacques Cœur caused to have released, administered, and delivered to the Saracens, enemies of the Christian faith, arms of all sorts to use in the war. And he had even sent several armourers and workers to do this and to instruct the Saracens in doing this, this being to the prejudice and great damage of all Christianity. And so he was arrested because of it, more moved and carried by his will than by reason,

lente que deRaiſon par linſtigacion delennemy deNature par convoitiſe ou autrement comme Infidelle. a Rendu par ſapuiſſance deſordonnee ou auťment ung xpen̄n qui eſtoit eſchappe des mains des ſarraſins ou Il avoit eſte priſonnier par longue eſpace detemps et ſouffert maint grant martere pour lafoy deIhû criſt et lavoit Renvoye defait et deforce au pays des ſarraſins en contemptnant lafoy deIhūs noſ̂ Redempteur. Aeſte auſſi fait priſonnier pource quil aeſte extorque prins et Rappine In duement pluſſieurs grans finances ſur les pays du Roy tant en languedoc languedouy comme ailleurs. Parquoy les hâtans deſd lieux ſeſont abſenter qui eſt eu grant dommaige du Roy et deſon Royaulme. Aeſte auſſi arreſte meſmemeť pourcece quil avoit pille et deſRobbie les finâces du Roy deſquelles Il avoit legouvernement et leſquelles paſſoient par ſes mains de Iour en Iour.

Comment madamoiſelle de Mortaigne fut auſſi areſtee.

Fut. auſſi arreſtee priſonnere madmoiſelle demortaigne pour ĉtaines offences quelle avoit faictes enṽs leRoy. et pource quelle avoit avoit occuppe led Iacques ceur daucunes choſes donc Il etoit Innocent. Et avecques ce avoit ocuppe ung nomme Iacques deboullongnes et ung auť nomme martin prandoulz et les avoit to⁹ trois ocuppez par laune ou aultremeť. Et pource que on donna ce quelle avoit donne aentend eſtre menterie fut miſe priſonniere pour Recevoir telle pugnicion que leſdeſſd euſſet̄ eu cilz euſſent eſte trouvez couppables et charges ducas. Lagrant miſericorde ence Reſervez.

by the instigation of the enemy of Nature, by lust or otherwise like an infidel, to render, by his disorderly power or otherwise, a Christian who had escaped from the hands of the Saracens, where he had been imprisoned for a long space of time, and suffered many great martyrdoms for the faith of Jesus Christ, and he had sent him for the deed and by force to the said lands of the Saracens in contempt of the law of Jesus, our redeemer. He was also taken prisoner because he had extorted, taken, and plundered unduely several great finances from the lands of the king, both from Languedoc, Languedoïl, as elsewhere. For which several of the inhabitants of the said places were absent, which was to the great damage of the king and to his kingdom. He was also arrested similarly because he had plundered and robbed the finances of the king, of which he had the governance, and which passed through his hands day-by-day.

How mademoiselle de Mortaigne was also arrested

Mademoiselle de Mortaigne was also arrested for certain offences that she had made toward the king and for this the said Jacques Cœur had accused her of several things for which he was innocent. And with this, he had accused one named Jacques of Boulogne, and another named Martin Prandoux, and all three were accused by one or another. And for this, when one asserted that that which she had given to hear was a lie, she was made prisoner in order to receive such punishment as the abovesaid would have had, if they were found culpable and charged for the case, the great mercy in this reserved.

Une deffiance du Roẙ auduc deSavoye

Aud an CCCC Cinquante deux Separtit le Roy deſa cite detours eu moys deMay et alla leRoy eu chaſteau detuce faire lafeſte et ſollempnite delapenthecoſte et fut laIucques au moys deIuillet. Et lors ſepartit et ala a mehun pres ſur yevre pres debourges et envoya deffier leduc deſavoye pour ĉtaines grandes extorcions quil avoit faites au Roy et alacourône defrance et en moys daouſt ſepartit avec ſon oſt ou Il yavoit moult belle et noble cō paignie deſeigneurs et autˆs gens deguerre et tant quil vint eu pays deforeſt pour paſſer et entrer aud pays deſavoye. Et ſceult led cardinal deſtouteville ſes nouvelles en allant aRomme. lequel meu decharite Retourna et alla devers led duc deſavoye puis apres devˆs leRoy. Apres quil eult ſceu lacauſe materelle. Et fiſt tant que en promettant đ auRoy de Remparer tout ce quil avoit eſte offence aubon plaiſir du Roy donc Il fut content et fut la paix faite afeurs en foreſt. Et ainſſi led cardinal ſen alla ſon chemin devers lepappe.

Comment bordeaulx Reſint angloiz ꝑ traiſon caſtillon et pluſſieurs autres places

Oudit an aucommencement du moys de ſeptembre leſire deleſparre et aucuns des bourgeois et hītans delaville debordeaulx par leconſeil demonſ[re] demontferrant du ſire de Roſan. duſ.[re] delanies. et duſ[re] danglade ſoubz ĉtaine faulce coulleur. trouverent facon et moyen daller en angletˆre et eulx aRrivez out pays tractierent deulx

A challenge by the king to the duke of Savoy

In the year 1452, the king left from the city of Tours in the month of May and the king went to the castle of Tuce to make the feast and ceremony of the Pentacost, and he was there until the month of July. And afterwards, he left and went to Mahun near to Yèvre near Bourges, and he sent the duke of Savoy a challenge for certain great exortions that he had made to his prejudice and to the crown of France, and in the month of August, he left with his army, where he had there a handsome and noble company of lords and other men of war, and he so went until the lands of the forest in order to pass and enter into the lands of Savoy. And the said cardinal of Estouteville learned this news while going to Rome, which, moved by charity to return, and he went to the said duke of Savoy, then from there afterwards to the king, after which he learned the true cause. And such that, in promising to the king to repair everything that had been offensive to the good pleasure of the king, he was happy and peace was made at Feurs-en-Forêt. And thus, the said cardinal went by his train to the pope.

How Bordeaux, Castillon, and several other places returned to the English by treason

In the said year, at the beginning of the month of September, the sire of Lesparre and several of the cityfolk and inhabitants of the town of Bordeaux, by the council of monseigneur de Montferrant, of the sire de Rosan, of the sire de Lanes, and of the sire of Langlade, under certain false colours, found a fashion and means to go into England, and having arrived in the said lands, agreed

Remettre en lobbeiſſance des angloiz cilz voulloient Retourner et pluſſieurs parolles baillorent auſd angloiz. et lafut machine et grant trayſon pour laquelle mettre aeffect fiſt leRoy danglet̂re aſſembler ſon conſeil et furet̂ evoques to^{9} les ſeigneurs et capitaines et la fut conclud denvoyer talleboth ou moys ~~doctobre~~ doctobre enſ eud pays debordellaiz. Et ce fait ſen Revint led ſ.^{re} deleſparre et ſes complices qui pouvoient bien eſtre acompaignies aIudas car Ilz avoient fait ſerment ſur les ſaincts evangilles dedieu deſtre bons et loyaulx au Roy defrance et alacouronne. Et Ilz avoiet̂ conſpire faulce et mauvaiſe traiſon qui eſtoit aller directement cont̂ les ſermens quilz avoiet̂ faiz. Et ainſſi en adherant âlad conſpiracion ſepartit lad talleboth dud pays danglet̂re lexvi^{me} Iour dumoys doctobre. acompagne de~~cinq~~ quatre acinq mille angloiz et aRriva en liſle demedoc ou Ilz prindrent deux petites places pour logier partie deleurs gens. Et adonc led talleboth commenca afaire courir lepays pour lemettre en ſubIection qui neſtoit pas fort affaire. Car Il ny avoit aucune Reſiſtance veu que larmee du Roẙ eſtoit Retraicte et ny eſtoit demoure que pou degens es garniſons des fortreſſes lavenue duquel ſceue par eulx delad ville de bordeaulx commencerent aparlamenter les ungz aux. aut̂s delamaniere deulx Remettre en lobbeiſſance deſd angloiz. Et voulloient les aucuns q̂ les francois eſtans dedens lad ville donc eſtoit cap.^{ne} pour leRoy. leſ.^{r} decoitie ſey.^{al} deguyenne dupuy et fou chevallr̂ ſoubz maire delad ville ſen allaſſent leurs corps et biens ſaufz. Maiz cepend aucuns dicelle ville al lerent ouvrir une porte aux angloiz et les boutterent dedens lexxiii^{me} Iour doctobre. parquoy furent to^{9} prins les francois qui eſtoient dedens lad ville ou au-

with them to return to the obedience of the English, if they wanted to return, and several words they gave to the said English, and there it was plotted, and a great treason, for which to put to effect, the king of England assembled his council, and there was convoked all the lords and captains, and it was concluded to send Talbot in the month of October following into the said lands of the Bordelais. And this being done, the said sire de Lesparre and his accomplices returned, who could well be compared to Judas because they had made oaths to the holy Apostles of God to be good and loyal to the king of France and to the Crown. And they had conspired a false and evil treason, which was directly against the oaths that they had made. And, thus, adhering to the said conspiracy, the said Talbot left from the said lands of England the sixteenth day of the month of October, accompanied by 4,000 to 5,000 Englishmen, and he arrived on the isle of Médoc, where they captured two small places in order to camp some of his men. And then the said Talbot began to make inroads into the lands in order to put it into subjection, which was not very difficult, because he had no resistance there, seeing that the army of the king had retreated and there remained there only a few men in the garrisons of the fortresses; his coming having been known by those of the said town of Bordeaux, they began to speak to one another on the manner of putting themselves back into the obedience of the said English. And several wanted the French who were in the said town, over whom was captain for the king the seigneur de Coitïvy, seneschal of Guyenne, du Puy-et-Fou, a knight, undermayor of the said town, to leave with their bodies and goods safely. But, however, several of this town went to open a gate to the English, and they came inside [on] the twenty-third day of October, for which all the French who were inside the said town were taken

moins laplusgrande partie tant gens deguerre côme officiers 7autr̃s et demourerent aprisonniers ausd angloiz. Ces nouvelles au Roy defrance venus Il fut moult dollent considerant que detraison nul ne se peult garder. Et pource envoya hastivemeẽt mess.[rs] les mareshaulx defrance les.[r] dorval Iouachim Rouault et plussieurs autr̃s capitaines Iucques au nombre devi[C] lances et les archr̃s pour Renforcer et garder les places dautour debourdeaulx. Ainssi q̂ monsr declermont lieuteñ general duRoy esd marches verroit estre ex pedient Iucques alasaison q̂ le Roy ymettroit et domeront plus ample provision. Neantmoĩs que avant que lesd gens du Roy defrance Led talleboth ses gens et barons et s.[rs] dud pais debordellaiz mirent laplus part des places decellui pars en lobbeissance du Roy dangleẽtre et par especial lachasteau decastillon en pie regort Laquelle estoit tenue par les gens du Roy defrance leur fut ~~leur~~ Rendue par faulte desecours et sen allerent les francois leurs corps et biens saufz. Combien q̂ led sr lieuteñ du Roy comme dit est se gouv̂na moult grandement et notablement aResiste aux angloiz avant lavenue desd francois puis vindrent dangleterre pour Renforcer larmee dud talleboth. Lesire decanuis le bastard desombrecet. lefilz dud talleboth s.[r] delisle. et les.[r] demoulins et yavoit iiii.[m] combatans en leur compaignie et ameneret̂ iiii.[xx] batraulx que grans et petz charges defarines et delars pour advitailler lad ville debordeaulx.

Commeẽt fronssac fut Redduit aux angloiz.

L'an mille CCCC. Cinquante trois. Ce partit leRoy desa cite detours et vint Logier en son chasteau delisignan.

prisoner, or at least the greater part, both men of war, officiers, and others, and they remained prisoners of the said English. This news coming to the king of France, he was very sad, considering the treason that nobody can guard against. And for this, he quickly sent messeigneurs the marshals of France, the seigneur d'Orval, Joachim Rouault, and several other captains until the number was 600 lancers and the archers, to reinforce and guard the places around Bordeaux. Also, monseigneur de Clermont, lieutenant general of the king for the said marches, would see to be expedient until the season that the king would give and put there the amplest provision. Nevertheless, the said men of the king of France having arrived, the said Talbot, his men, and the barons and lords of the said lands of Bordelais remitted the greater part of this part into the obedience of the king of England, and especially the castle of Châtillon in Périgord, which was held by the men of the king of France, rendered to them by lack of rescue, and from there, the French went with their bodies and goods safe, such that the said seigneur, lieutenant of the king, as it is said, govered himself very grandly and notably in resisting the English before the arrival of the said French; then came from England to reinforce the army of the said Talbot, the sire de Canuis, the bastard of Somerset, the son of the said Talbot, the lord of the Isle, and the lord of Molins, and there were around 4,000 soldiers in their company, and they brought eighty ships, both large and small, loaded with flour and meat to resupply the said town of Bordeaux.

How Fronsac was captured by the English

The year 1453, the king left from the city of Tours and went to lodge in his castle at Lusignan. And, however,

Et cepend led talleboth. mift lefiege devant lechafteau defronffac duquel eftoit cappitaine Ioachim Rouault pour le-Roy defrance et convint Rend lad place aux angloiz avant q̂ larmee du Roy fuft prefte. Et fen allerent les francois leurs corps et biens faufz.

Commet̂ challaiz fut francois.

LE fegond Iour deIuing enf. Cepartit. leRoy dud lieu delifignan. et alla afaint Iehan dangelẙ. et lexii[m] Iour enf. fut mis lefiege devant challaiz. Ceft affavoir par meff.[r] Iacqẑ dechabnes grant maiftre doftel du Roy et par leconte depointevre lef.[rs] defaincte fevere et deboucant Et levii[me] Iour enf fut lad challaiz prins daffault par les feigneurs deffſd ⁊autres deleur compaignie. nombres deiiii. av.[C] lances et les archiers. et ĉtains francs archiers combn que dedens lad ville yavoit en garnifon viii.[xx] combatans qui fe monftrerent bien avoir les ceurs failliz Car Il en fut tue al-aprinfe decelle ville. Delx. Aiiii.[xx] Et les autŝ fe Retrayrent en une tour ou Ilz furet̂ ĉtaine efpace detps Cuidans avoir aucun fecours deleurs gens. et parce quilz nen eurent point leur convint Rend alavoullente du Roy. Et eftoient dedens lad tour Iucques au nombre deiiii.[xx] hommes qui to⁹ furet̂ decappitez pour les fermens quilz avoient ~~fail~~ faulcez. et les trayfons donc Ilz eftoient complices. Et eftoit party debordeaulx lef.[r] danglas pour les cuider venir fecourir. Et quat̂ Il fceut les nouvell delaprinfe defd angloiz ⁊delad ville. Il fen Retourna haftivemet̂.

the said Lord Talbot laid siege before the castle of Fronsac, over which was captain for the king of France Joachim Rouault, and he convinced the said place to render itself to the English before the army of the king was ready. And the French left, their bodies and good safe.

How Chalais became French

THE second day of the following June, the king left from the said place of Lusignan and went to Saint-Jean-d'Angely, and the third day following, he went to lay siege before Chalais—it is known, by Jacques de Chabannes, grand master of the hotel of the king, and by the count of Penthièvre, the seigneurs de Saint-Sévère and de Boucan. And the seventh day following, the said Chalais was captured by assault by the abovesaid lords and others of their company, numbering 400 to 500 lancers, and the archers and certain free archers, such that within the said town were garrisoned 160 soldiers, who showed themselves well to have faint hearts, because from 60 to 80 [people] were killed in the capture of this town. And the others retreated into one tower, where they were for a certain period of time, thinking to receive some rescue from their men, and because they would not have any, they were convinced to render themselves to the will of the king. And there were in the said tower 80 men, who were all decapitated for their oaths that they had falsely made and the great treasons for which they were complicit. And the seigneur de Langlade left from Bordeaux thinking to come rescue them. And when he learned the news of the capture of the said Englishmen and of the said town, he returned quickly.

La Iournee decaſillon et connut̂ Il fut prins.

Oudit an et lexiii^me^ Jour du moys deIuillet fut mis caſtillon en perigort leſiege par les francois devant lechaſteau decaſtillon en perigort aſſis ſur laRiviere dedordonne ocuppe et tenu par les angloiz. Et yfurent envoyez pour mettre led ſiege. leſ^re^ deloheac et leſ^re^ deIalongnes mareſchaulx defrance. monſ.^r^ le grant maiſtre doſtel du Roy leſ^re^ debueil admiral defrance et meſſire loys debeaumoт̂ ſeneſchal depoitou. leconte depantievre maiſtre Iehan bureau treſorier defrance et pluſſieurs auт̂s grans ſ.^rs^ barons chevalliers eſcuiers et auт̂ grant nombre degens deguerre Iucques au nombre dexvi. axviii.^C^ hommes darmes et les archiers. enт̂ leſquelz eſtoient les gens demonſ.^r^ leconte du maine q̂ côduiſoit leſ.^r^ delabeſſiere nomme meſſ.^re^ pierre de beauvau. Et ſi yeſtoient les gens demonſ.^r^ leconte deNevers. q̂conduiſoit meſſ.^re^ ferry de fraucy. Et auſſi yeſtoient les gens demonſ^r^ leconte decaſtres filz duconte delamarche q̂ conduiſoit meſſ.^s^ loys dupuy ſen.^al^ delamarche et guillaume deluſach. et Iehan demeſſignac et les gens duduc debretaigne donc eſtoit ~~cheſt~~ chef ~~ſe~~ leconte deſtampes ſon nepveu et pour lui les conduiſoit leſ.^r^ delahunauld et leſ^re^ demontauban pource q̂ led conte eſtoit demoure devers leRoy. Et la eſtoit la groſſe et menue artillerie du Roy donc avoient lacharge maiſtre Iehan bureau et ſon frere Iaſpar bureau maiſtre delad artillerie. Et avoient en leur compaignie VII^C^ manouvriers leſquelz par lordonnance deſd treſorier et ſon frere firent haſtivement clorre defoſſez ung champ ou eſtoit toute lad artillerie. Et adonc poſerent et mirent leſiege

The campaign of Castillon and how it was captured

In the said year and the thirteenth day of the month of July, siege was lain by the French before the castle of Châtillon in Périgord, situated on the River Dordogne, occupied and held by the English. And the sire de Lohéac and the sire de Jallongnes, marshals of France; monseigneur the grand master of the hotel of the king; the sire de Bueil, admiral of France; and messire Louis de Beaumont, seneschal of Poitou; the count of Penthièvre; master Jean Bureau, treasurer of France; and several other great lords, barons, knights, squires, and others were sent there to lay the said siege [with] a great number of men of war, until the number was 1,600 to 1,800 men-at-arms, and the archers, amongst whom were the men of monseigneur the count of Maine, which was led by the seigneur de La Bessière, named messire Pierre de Beauvau. And then there were the men of monseigneur the count of Nevers, who were led by messire Ferry de Grancy. And also there were the men of monseigneur the count of Castres, son of the count of La Marche, who were led by messire Louis du Pays, seneschal of La Marche, and Guillaume de Lusach and Jean de Messignac, and the men of the duke of Brittany, over whom was leader the count of Étampes, his nephew, and for him the leaders were seigneur de La Hunaudaye and the sire de Montauban, because the said count remained with the king. And the great and small artillery of the king was there, for which master Jean Bureau and his brother, Jaspar Bureau, master of the said artillery, had charge. And they had in their company 700 workers who, by order of the said treasurer and of his brother, quickly enclosed a field with trenches, where

devant caſtillon et cevenue alacognoiſſance dud ſ.re detalleboth ſepartit Incontinet̂ et en haſte debordeaulx acompaigne dehuit cens amil combatans decheval. Ent̂ leſquelz eſtoit ſon filz. leſ.r deliſle leſ.r demoullins et pluſſ.rs autŝ des plus vaillans du Roy.me dangletr̂e tant ſ.rs chevalliers que eſcuiers et auſſi du pays debordellaiz. et apres venoient dequat̂ av.m angloiz apie. Et aRiva led talleboth et ſacompaignie devant led ſiege lemercredy xviime Iour deIuillet environ lepoint duIour. Et quat̂ les francois ſceuret̂ lavenue dud tal both. ſebouteret̂ auchamp qui eſtoit ferme de foſſez. Et trouva led talboth en ſon chemin aucuns francs archiers qui neſtoient pas encores Retraiz oud champ car Ilz eſtoient depie. En frapperent leſd angloiz ſur eulx et en tueret̂ decent avii.xx deceulx qui ne ſepeurent pas Retirer en temps en champ. Et lors commêceret̂ les francois atirer fort pour gagner led champ pource que leſd angloiz commencerent am̂rchr̂ pour approcher cuidans q̂ leſd angloiz fuiſſet̂ et levaſſent led ſiege et fiſt led telleboth en actendant partie deſes gens apie mettre une queue devin ſur bout pour leur donner aboire et les Refraiſchir. Et cepend les francois aRivoirent eu pars detoutes pars et ſe mirent en bonne ordonnance. Et auſſi les canonniers aſſortirent leurs coullevrines et Ribaudequins ſur les foſſez devant lavenue diceulx angloiz. Et trouverent maniere et facon ceulx dededens caſtillon demander aud talboth quil ſadvanchaſt legeremet̂ et q̂ les francois ſen fuyoient. Et quant Il fut venu Il fut moult eſbahy devoir lafortificacion q̂ avoient faicte leſd francois tant defoſſez artillerie q̂ aut̂ment. Et la eſtoient pour Reſiſter cont̂ leſd angloiz meſſ.rs les mareſ chaulx legrant maiſtre doſtel leconte de pantievre. leſeneſchal depoitou. leſ.r dela baiſſiere. ſire Iehan bureau ⁊cl. Leſquelz eſtoient commiſſaires pour laconduite

they stored all of the said artillery. And then they positioned and laid siege before Châtillon, and [when] this came to the knowledge of the said Lord Talbot, he left immediately and in great haste from Bordeaux, accompanied by 800 to 1,000 soldiers on horseback, amongst whom were his son, the lord of the Isle; the seigneur de Molins; and several others of the most valiant of the kingdom of England, both lords, knights, and squires, and also of the land of the Bordelais, and after him came from 4,000 to 5,000 Englishmen on foot. And the said Talbot and his company arrived before the said siege on Wednesday, the seventeenth day of July around daybreak. And when the French learned of the coming of the said Talbot, they retreated to the camp, which was well enclosed by trenches. And the said Talbot found in his train several free archers who had not yet retreated to the said camp, because they were on foot. The said English under him struck and killed from 100 to 120 of those who could not retreat into the camp. And then the French began to push strongly to win the said camp, for which the said English began strongly to approach, thinking that the English were fleeing and lifting the said siege, and the said Talbot, in attending partly to his footmen, put a glassful of wine on the rope to give them a drink and to refresh them. And, however, the French arrived from all parts, and they put themselves in good order. And also the cannoniers organised their coulevrines and ribaudequins in the trenches, before the coming of these Englishmen. And those who were within Châtillon found means and method to ask the said Talbot that he advance lightly and promptly, and that the French were fleeing. And when he came there, he was shocked to see the fortifications that the said French had, both the trenches, artillery, and other. And there to resist the said Englishmen were messeigneurs the marshals, the grand master of

dicelle armee. Et Icelle mettre en bonne ordre combien quil yavoit pluſſieurs auẗs grans ſ.rs en lacompaignie qui tindrent lechamp vail̂ et honnourablement alencontre des advr̂ſaires du Roy. or va venir led talleboth et ſacompai gne et aRivereť droit alabarriere cuidans entrer eu champ. Maiz Ilz trouvereť belle frontiere devaillans gens bien expers aufait delaguerre qui leurs firent bon viſage ⁊hardy donc leſd angloiz ſirent moult eſbahiz veu ceque leur avoit eſte mande. Led talleboth couduiſant les angloiz eſtoit monte ſur une petite hacquenee et ne deſcendit point apie pource quil eſtoit aucun homme. Maiz Il fiſt mettre apie ceulx deſacompaignie qui eſtoient venus acheval. Et alarmees avoient leſd angloiz huit bannieres deſployes tant duRoy dangleẗre deſaint george delatrinite et dud talboth avec pluſſieurs eſtendars ſciemment pourpenſez. Et adonc commenca laſſault et yot degrans vaillances et fort combatu aleur partie et delauẗ. dehaches guiſarmes lances et detrait moult vaillamment et dura le chaplis par leſpace dune groſſe heure. Et apres pour Rafraiſchir les francois qui avoieť moult travaille alagarde dicelle barriere furent envoyez querir les ſires demontauban et delahaynauldaye qui gouvr̂noit les gens deduc debretaigne quil avoit envoyes au Roy et deſquelz eſtoit chef led conte deſtampes. Et pour Renforcer lad aruiere et ceulx qui avoieť tout leIour garde lad labarriere. Leſquilz degrant et noble courage aleur venue Incontinêt quilz furent aRivez firent tant alaide dedieu et par leur proueſſe que leſd angloiz tournerent ledoz. Et fureť abbatues et Reves par tierre toutes le.rs bannieres par leſd bretons. Leſquelz en ſont bien aRecom mandes. Et yavoit dedens led champ til cliquertes decoullevrines et Rbaudequins que Iceulx angloiz furent contrains deulx en fuir. Touteffoiz pluſſieurs fureť mors en

the hotel, the count of Penthièvre, the seneschal of Poitou, the seigneur de La Bessière, the sire Jean Bureau, and others, who were appointed to lead this army. And this was put it in good order, such that there were several other great lords in the company, who held the field bravely and honourably against these adversaries of the king, where the said Talbot and his company went to come and arrived directly at the barrier, thinking to enter onto the field. But they found a good outwork of brave men, experts at the game of war, who had good sight and strength, for which the said English were very disconcerted seeing that which had been organised. The said Talbot, considering the English, was mounted on a small haquenée and he no longer descended on foot because he was not a man. But those of his company who were coming on horseback went on foot. And at the coming of the said English, eight banners were deployed, both of the king of England, of Saint George, of the Trinity, and of the said Talbot, with several standards maliciously invented. And then began the assault, and there were great deeds and strong combat there between their party and the other, with axes, polearms, lances, and and very brave conscripts, and the engagement lasted for the space of one long hour. And afterwards, to reinforce the French who had worked hard in guarding this barrier, the sires of Montauban and of la Hunaudaye, who led the men of the duke of Brittany, were sent, which he had sent to the king and over whom the said count of Étampes was leader, and this to reinforce the said barrier and those who had all day guarded the said barrier, who by great and noble courage came to them immediately, which [when] they arrived did such to the aid of God and by their prowess that the said English turned their backs, and all their banners were struck down and thrown to the ground by the said Bretons, for which they were well recommend-

laplace. Et pareſpecial fut ferue dune coullevrine lahacquenee dud talleboth ~ tellement quelle cheult toute morte et talboth deſſoubz Lequel fut tue darmes des francois. Pareillement auſſi furent mors ſon filz noſ̂ leſ.^{r} deliſle meſſire hedouel houl. thomas aurnigan. leſ.^{r} depuguillan. gaſcon. et trente chevalliers du Royaulme dangleſ̂re et des plus vaillans comme on diſoit et yfut prins leſire demoullins. Et pource que les francois eſtoient depie et fort allerez et travaillez ne pouorent pourvoir partout. ſeſchapperet̂ pluſſieurs angloiz et gaſtongs et Ribouterent dedens lad ville decaſtillon decinq. cens amille. Ent̂ leſquelz eſtoient lefilz du captau debuch. conte decandalle. leſ.^{r} demontferrant. leſ.^{re} deRoſan. leſ.^{re} adnglades. Et eſchappa leſire deleſparre car Il avoit eſte leprincipal detoute latrayſon. Et les auſ̂s qui ne ſepeurent ſa~~ceurs~~ prendrent les ~~che~~ clefz. des champs. les ungz par eaue les aut̂ par terre. Et quat̂ au Regard de ceulx qui allorent par eaue furet̂ noyez la pluſpart. Et pour auaucuns ceulx qui allont̂ parterre. mouteret̂ acheval leconte depoñteve lebailly detouraine et pluſſieurs auſ̂s deto^{9} eſtatz. eſtans delacompaigne des francois. Leſquelz ne ceſſerent oncques detuer angloiz en les pourſuivant Iucques pres deſaint milion. Et alabeſongne duchamp furet̂ enterres de quatre acinq cens angloiz. Et lendemain ordonnerent les ſeigneurs approuchr̂ canons veuglaires et bombardes devant lad ville pour feſtoier ceulx dededens. Leſquelz voyans et conſiderans lappareil q̂ on faiſoit ſecommeĉeret̂ ahumilier et abbaiſſer lorgueil donc Ilz eſtoiet̂ plus. Et ſeRendirent tous priſonniers ala voullente du Roy. eſtimez mil et cinq. cens du nombre deſquilz les ſeigneurs deſſſd furet̂ priſonniers duRoy.

ed. And there was on the said field such a barrage of coulevrines and ribaudequins that these Englishmen were convinced to flee. Suddenly, several were killed where they stood. And notably, the horse of the said Talbot was struck by one of the coulevrines such that it fell dead and Talbot under it, who was killed by the arms of the French. Similarly, his son, named the sire de l'Isle, messire Hedouel Houl, Thomas Aurnigan, the seigneur de Puguillan, a Gascon, and thirty knights of the kingdom of England were killed, and the bravest, it is said, and the sire de Moulins was captured there. And because the French who were on foot were very tired and overworked, they could not pursue and several Englishmen and Gascons escaped, and 500 to 1,000 of them retreated into the said town of Châtillon. Amongst whom were the son of the captal du Buch, count of Candale; the seigneur de Montferrand; the sire de Rosan; [and] the sire de Adnglades. And the sire de Lesparre escaped because he was the leader of all the treason. And the others who were not afraid took the keys from the field, one by water, the other by land. And when in regard to those who went by water, they drowned for the most part. And for any of those who went by land, the count of Penthièvre, the balliff of Touraine, and several others of all estates being in the company of the French mounted on horseback, who never stopped killing Englishmen in pursuing until near to Saint-Emilion. And at the field were interred from 400 to 500 Englishmen. And the next day, the lords ordered the cannons, veuglaires, and bombards before the said town in order to push out those inside, who, seeing and considering the weapons that one made there, they began to humble themselves and abase their pride, for which they were full. And they rendered themselves all as prisoners to the will of the king, estimated at 1,500 in number, of whom the lords abovesaid were prisoners of the king.

LaReddicion deSaint millon aux francois

DEpuis laReddicion dud caſtillon ſeparteret̂ leſd ſeigneurs conduiſeurs deloſt du Roy et commiſſaires en ceſte partie avec leur puiſſ canons et artillerie. Et vindrent devant la ville deSaint million. laquelle tantoſt ſe miſt en lobbeiſſance du Roy conſiderans quil ne leur eſtoit pas poſſible deReſiſter contre ſa puiſſance. et le Roy les Receult en ſamercy.

Lareddicion deliborne aux francois.

DE la ſetira toute larmee devant liborne Laquelle navoit pas eſte bailler des gens delad ville ne deleur gre ne miſe en lobbeiſſ des angloiz quant leſ.[re] detalleboth. ariva aud bordeaulx car on leur avoit baille francois po[r] les gardes. Et quant Ilz ſceurent lavenue dud tabboth. leſd francois deſemparent delad ville et lors comment auſd hâtains decelle obbair aud talboth. Parquoy par lad Reddicion mout eſte en Riens moleſtez. Et les aleRoy. Receuz en ſagrace

EN. ce meſme an temps et ſaiſon eſtoit lieut general du Roy eu pays deguyenne et debordeaulx leconte declermont lequel tenoit ſon armee dela laRiviere deguizonne es pays demadoc et eſtoient en ſacompaignie leconte defoix. leconte dalbreth. et leſ.[r] dorval ſon filz. meſſ.[re] theaulde devalpergue bailly delion Leſ.[r] deſaintrailles grant eſcuier deſcuierie. meſſ[re] bernard debearn leviconte

The reduction of Saint-Emilion to the French

Since the reduction of the said Châtillon, the said leading lords of the army of the king and commissioners in this part left with their strength, cannons, and artillery, and they went before the town of Saint-Emilion, which soon was put into the obedience of the king, considering that it was not possible for them to resist against his power, and the king received them into his mercy.

The reduction of Liborne to the French

From there, all the army went straight before Liborne, which had not been handed over by the people of the said town nor given to them nor put into the obedience by the English when Lord Talbot arrived at the said Bordeaux because one had given them to the French to guard them. And when they learned of the coming of the said Talbot, the said Frenchmen decamped from the said town and then some of the said inhabitants of this place abased themselves to the said Talbot, for which, due to the said submission, they were not molested. And the king received them in his grace.

In this same time and this season, the count of Clermont was lieutenant general of the king in the lands of Guyenne and of Bordeaux, who held his army on the River Garonne in the lands of Medoc, and there were in his company the count of Foix; the count of Albret and the sire d'Orval, his son; messire Théaude de Valpergue, bailiff of Lyon; the seigneur de Xaintrailles, grand squire of the squirie; messire Bernard de Béarn; the viscount of

detouranne lesſ.[re] de lauadan et pluſſieurs auťs capitaines nombrez viii.[c] lances et les archiers. leſquelz ſegouveñereť en telle maniẽe q̂ pour courſſe quilz fiſſent ſur lepais en prenant priſonniers diſipans et gaſtant les proviſions des angloiz tant vins foingz advoines blez q̂ auťment oncques les angloiz debordeaulx qui eſtoient huit mil combatans ne ſenbaterent ne nepraticquereť ſur eulx en maniere quilz ſoſaſſent trouver ſur les champs

Commeť leſeigne ſur mis p̲ les francois devant madoc blanquefort cadillac Sa maranie langon et villendras.

LE xiii Iour dud moys deIuillet. les contes declermont et defoix et dalbreth allerent mettre leſiege devant chaſteau neuf demedoc et furent devant par leſpace dexv. Iours et tenoit laplace pour leRoy dangleťre leſire deliſle chevallier gaſcon lequel voyans eſtre aliu choſe Impoſſible delatems laRendit auſd ſeigneurs. Et yfut mis pour capitaine alagarde dicelle place Robinet petit lot puis ſepartirent leſd contes declermont et dalbreth et pluſſieurs autres deleur compaignie et allerent mettre leſiege devant blanque fort. Et ſedepartit larmee car monſ.[r] le conte defoix et leviconte delautrec ſon frere allerent mettre leſiege devant lechaſteau decadillac. Et leſire des autrailles alla devant ſaint macaire et ſemiſt en lobbeiſſ du Roy. Et led ſ.[r] dalbreth ſepartit dedevať blanquefort et alla devant langon et villandras Leſquilz Il miſt pareill̅ en lobbeiſſance du Roy eſtans encores devant blanquefort et tenoient deux ou trois ſieges alafoiz. po[r] leſq̅lz maintenir avoieť leſd

Turenne; the sire de Lavedan; and several other captains, numbering 800 lances, and the archers, who governed themselves in such manner that for battles that they made on the lands, in taking prisoners, dispersing and wearing out the provisions of the English, both in wine, hay, oats, fruits, and others, until the Englishmen of Bordeaux, who were around 8,000 soldiers, never fought nor practiced by themselves in a manner that they exposed themselves to discovery on the field.

How the seigneur undertook by the French before Médoc, Blancafort, Cadillac, Saint-Macaire, Langon, and Villendras

The fourteenth day of the said month of July, the counts of Clermont and Foix and d'Albret went to lay siege before Châteauneuf-de-Médoc and they were before it for the space of fifteen days, and the Lord of the Isles, a Gascon knight, held the the place for the king of England, who, seeing that it would be impossible to hold, rendered it to the abovesaid lords. And Robinet Petit-Lot was installed there as captain for the guardianship of this place; then the said counts of Clermont and Albret deprted, and several others in their company, and they went to lay siege before Blancafort. And the army left because monseigneur the count of Foix and the viscount of Lautrec, his son, went to lay siege before the castle of Cadillac. And the sire de Xaintrailles went before Saint-Macaire and put it into the obedience of the king. And the said seigneur d'Albret left from before Blancafort and went before Langon and Villandras, which he equally put into the obedience of the king, who was still before Blancafort, and they maintained two or three seiges at the same time, for

conqueurs en le[r] cõpaignie mille lances et les archiers. Ence comprins les gens duconte darmaignac q̂ conduiſoit ung eſcuier nõme laſne delange ſen.[al] de Rouergue. Et en lacompaignie audela de Riviere degueroune eſtoient lapluſpart chevalliers et eſcuiers. Et ce pend q̂ leſiege eſtoit devant cadillac mond ſ.[r] leconte de clermont tenoit touſiours leſiege devant blanquefort et Iucques ace quil ſeRendiſt alui. Et y laiſſa lecompte de dampmãtin po[r] capitaine ~~et~~ pour leRoy.

Dune baſtille miſe devant bordeaulx par les francois et lap̊nſe decadillac

LE. xvii[m] Iour deIuillet et emeſme an Separtit leRoy delacite dangoleſme pour aller aupays debordellaiz pour conforter et aider loſt. et en ſacompaignere eſtoient Meſſeigneurs les contes dangouleſme du maine. deſtampes. deNevers. decaſtres. et devendoſme et pluſſieurs auſ̂s grans ſeigne[r] barons eſcuiers et chevalliers. Et vint an laville deliborne. Et fut ſon oſt devant fronſſac q̂ tenoiet̂ les angloiz. leſquelz ſe Rendirent et ſen allerent par compoſicion en angletr̂e chun̑ ung baſton en ſamain puis paſſa ſon oſt laRiviere dedordonne po[r] cõqueſter et mettre en lobbeiſſance duRoy lepais dent̂ deux mers et ymirent pluſſieurs petites villes et chaſteaulx q̂ tenoient leſd angloiz et leRoy vint amontferant et fiſt mettre une baſtille q̂ tint partie deſon oſt devant la ville debordeaulx ou lieu dit loremot̂. Et laut̂ partie deſon oſt mirent leſiege devant laville et chaſteau decadillac. Et dautre coſte eſtoient monſ.[r] leconte declermont lors lieutenant du Roy et pays

which sieges to maintain the said conquerers had in their company 1,000 lancers and the archers. In this included the men of the count of Armagnac, who were led by a squire named Lasne de Lauge, seneschal of Rouergue. And in the company at the River Garonne was the majority of the knights and squires. And regardless of the siege before Cadillac, my said lord, the count of Clermont, always held the said siege before Blancafort and until this place rendered itself to him. And he left there the count of Dammartin as captain for the king.

Of a bastide made before Bordeaux by the French and the capture of Cadillac

The seventeenth of July and in this same year, the king left from the city of Angoulême in order to go into the land of the Bordelais to comfort and aid his army, and in his company messeigneurs the counts of Angoulême, of Maine, of Étampes, of Nevers, of Castres, and of Vendôme, and several other great lords, barons, squires, and knights. And he went into the town of Lisborne. And his army was before Fronsac, which the English held, which they rendered themselves and they went by agreement into England, each a stick in his hand, then his army crossed the River Dordogne in order to conquer and put into the obedience of the king the lands between the two seas, and they captured there several small towns and castles that the said English held, and the king went to Montferrand and made to construct a bastide that held part of his army before the town of Bordeaux in a place called Lormont. And the other part of his army laid siege before the town and the castle of Cadillac. And from the other side were monseigneur the count of Clermont, then lieutenant general of the king

deguyenne et debordellaiz comme dit eſt. Les contes de foix et dalbreth. leſ.ʳ dorval. leſ.ʳ deſantrailles lebailly delion et pluſſieurs autꝭ Iucques au nombre demil lances et les archiers eſtoieꝭ ~~deb~~ devant bordeaulx ducoſte dedevers les laynes pour faire legaſt et mengꝛ les blez foingz et autres proviſions qui eſtoient ſur lepays. affin que ceulx debordeaulx ne ſen peuſſent aider. Le xviiiᵐ Iour deIuillet leRoy en perſonne et ſon oſt aſſaillirent laplace et ville decadillac et fut prinſe et emportee daſſault. Et entra le premier dedens ung eſcuier nommee guiffroy deſaint bellin bailly dechaumont en baſſigny. Et lors les ſeRetrahirent leſd angloiz oud chaſteau qui eſt moult fort. Car neceſſite les contraignoit ace veu q̂ auᵐent Ilz eſtoient to⁹ perduz. Et combien quilz fuſſent Retrais et bien enfermes. Ne autmoins lapuiſſance duRoy et lebon gouvn̂emeꝭ et police quil avoit mis en ſond oſt qui eſtoit de mil lances et les archiers. Il convint leſd angloiz dire lemot. Et pource ſeRendirent au moys doctl enſ to⁹ priſonniers duRoy et lecapitaine dud lieu nomme gaillardet fut decappett.

Commeꝭ bordeaulx Refut gaigne par les francois.

DEdens labaſtille delormont eſtoient monſ.ʳ deloheac mareſchal defrance monſ.ʳ debueil admiral defrance meſſ.ʳᵉ loys debeaumont ſeneſhal depoitou. meſſ.ʳᵉ Iacques dechabanes grant maiſtre doſtel duRoy. Monſ.ʳ leconte depointievre. monſ.ʳ delahunaudaye monſ.ʳ demontauban et pluſſieurs autꝭ ſ.ʳˢ et cappitaines Iucques au nombre dexv axvi.ᶜ lances avecques les gens detrait bien garnis dartil-

and lands of Guyenne and the Bordelais, as it is said; the counts of Foix and Albret, the seigneur d'Orval, the seigneur de Xaintrailles, the bailiff of Lyon, and several others, until the number was 1,000 lancers and the archers; they were before Bordeaux on the side toward Lannes in order to damage it and eat the wheat, hay, and other provisions that were in the lands, so that those of Bordeaux would not benefit. The eighteenth day of July, the king in person and his army assailed the place and town of Cadillac and they captured and carried it by assault. And the first within was a squire named Geoffroi de Saint-Belin, baliff of Chaumont in Bassigny. And then the said Englishmen retreated into the said castle, which was very strong, because necessity constrained them to this, seeing that otherwise they would all be lost. And so they had retreated and were well locked up. Nonetheless, by the power of the king and the good government and order that he had put into his said army, which was 1,000 lances and the archers, he convinced the said Englishmen to say the word. And for this, they rendered themselves in following the month of October, all as prisoners of the king, and the captain of the said place, named Gaillardet, was decapitated.

How Bordeaux was won by the French

Within the bastide of Lormont were monseigneur de Lohéac, marshall of France; monseigneur de Bueil, admiral of France; messire Louis de Beaumont, seneschal de Poitou; messire Jacques de Chabannes, grand master of the hotel of the king; monseigneur the count of Penthièvre; monseigneur de la Hunaudaye; monseigneur de Montauban; and several other lords and captains until the number was 1,500 to 1,600 lancers, with the conscripts,

lerie delaquelle eſtoit gouverneur maiſtre ~~delor~~ Iehan bureau treſorier defrance lequel fait bien aRecommander pour ſes grans diligens Iaſpar bureau ſon frere maiſtre delad artillerie et meſſ.re triſtan lermitte prevoſt des mareſchaulx. Lequel eſt bon Iuſticier aufait des gens de guerre et leſquelz conduiſoient et eulx trois ordonnanent lefait deloſt des vivres et dela Iuſtice aud lieu. Et aupres dicelle baſtille eſtoient les vaiſſeaulx delarmee duRoy par mer. Ceſt aſſavoir debretaigne depoitou deſ pagne dehollande. dezelande et deflandres armez et advitaillez. Et lafuret dedens la Riviere degeronde Iucques ace q̂ laville de bordeaulx fut miſe en lobbeiſſance du Roy du party des angloiz pareillement eſtoient leurs bateaulx et navires venus du pays dangletre. Et Incontinet eulx aRivez fiſt le ſire decamus mettre les cordaiges dedens lad ville debordeaulx affin quilz ne ſes peuſſet aller hoſpite en ſalutato ceſt adire ſans prendre congie firent auſſi faire leſd angloiz une baſtille contrariant celle des francois. Et audeſſus decelle combien q̂ ce leur prouffita bien peu. Neantmoins quilz fuſſent dedens lad ville pour leRoy dangletre grans gens. Ceſt aſſavoir leſire decamus. le ſire decliton. lebaſtard deſombrecet. leſire deleſparre gaſton. leſire deRoſan. leſire du ſa. leſire de liſle lebaſtard deſalbry et avoiet en leur compaignie detrois aquat mille angloiz dangletre. Et autant ~~dupays~~ ou plus du pais degaſcongne donc lune des parties fut leur des parties fut dedens Icelle ville. et laut fut dedens leur baſtille pour garder leur naivres et lafuret leurs puiſſances les ungs devant les auts et chcn en ſabaſtille pour garder les naivres depuis. lepremier Iour daouſt. Iucques au xviim Iour doctobre en endommageant et grevat chcn Iour lun laut en toutes les manieres quilz povoient. Et quant leſd angloiz et

well supported by artillery, over whom was leader master Jean Bureau, treasurer of France, who was well-recommended for his great diligence; Jaspar Bureau, his brother, master of the artillery; and Tristan the Hermit, provost of the merchants, who was a good justiciar of the men of war, and which men led and the three ordered the deeds of the army, for the supplies and for the justice at the said place. And after this bastide were the vessels of the army of the king by sea—it is known, of Brittany, of Poitou, of Spain, of Holland, of Zealand, and of Flanders, armed and supplied. And they held themselves in the River Garonde until this town of Bordeaux was put into the obedience of the king; the party of the English equally were in their boats and ships coming from the land of England. And immediately when they arrived, the sire de Camus put all the ropes within the said town of Bordeaux, since they could not go hospite en salutato, which is to say without taking leave; they were also to make the said English a bastide against that of the French. And as above by this such that they profitted very little. Nonetheless, there was within the said town for the king of England many men—it is known, the sire de Camus, the sire de Clifton, the bastard of Somerset, the sire de Lesparre, Gaston; the sire de Rosan, the sire du Sa, the sire of the Isle, the bastard of Salisbury, and they had in their company 3,000 to 4,000 Englismen of England and about or more from the lands of Gascony, for which one of their parts was of the parties within this town, and the other was within their bastide, in order to guard their ships, and their powers were there, one against the other, each in his battalion, in order to guard the ships, since the first day of August until the seventeenth day of October, in damaging and wounding each day one another, in all the manners that they could. And when the said English and Gascons were overwhelmed and had run out of

gaſcons ſeverent oppreſſez et avoir faultes devivres furent bien eſbahis et auſſi lecas leRequeroit bien quilz veoient toutes les places ⁊forthereſſes dicellui pays miſes par forc-es darmes en pleiẽ obbeiſſance du Royaume defrance Re-quiront q̂ on leur fiſt amiable compoſicion. Aquoy le Roy eult Reſgard adeux choſes. lap̊miere quil eſtoit preſt defaire et Rend lebien cont̂ lemal Et ſeconduirent conſidera lamor-talite qui eſtoit aſon oſt qui eſtoit fort adoubter. Affin dechan-gr̂ air fut content decompoſer auſd angloiz en la maniere qui ſenſuyt. Ceſt aſſavoir q̂ lad ville et cite debordeaulx ſeroient Renduz au Roy defrance. et en demoureroient to⁹ les hâtans ſes vrays ⁊loyaulx ſubgetz. Et feroient leſermet̂ denom Ia-maiz Rebeller cont̂ lacouronne de france Recognoiſſans et affermans leRoy eſtre leur ſouverain ſ^r. Et les angloiz ouboit̂ congie deulx en allr̂ en leurs navires en pays dangletr̂e ou acallaiz ſebon leur ſembloit Et pource que aucuns des ſeigneurs du pays et delad cite avoient eſte frauduleuſement traitreu ſement ⁊malicieuſement querir en angletr̂e leſd an-gloiz en Rompant lieu foẙ promeſſe et ſerment quilz avoient fait lannee precedente au Roy qui deforce et agrant peine fraiz ⁊meſſous les avoit conquis les avoit ~~biens~~ furent bannis du pays debordellaiz. xx perſonnes qtilz quil plaiſoit auRoy deceulx qui avoient eſte querir leſd angloiz en angleterre du nombre deſquelz eſtoit leſire deduras et leſire deleſparre ⁊rl. Et fut faicte lad compoſicion lexvii^m Io^r doctl oud an iiii^c liii. Et en verte leRoy ſitravaille et peina grandement decorps et debiens etde ſon ſens car apres laide et grace dedens la-bonne conduicte qui aeſte en liu. ledoulx acueil deſes gens et leReconfortement et allant deplace en aut̂ lui afait eſtre ſ.^r dud pays paiſiblement. Tous ſes vaſſaulx pareill̂ et allyez

supplies, they were well shocked and so, in the case, he asked it well that they see all the places and fortresses of this land put by force of arms in full and entire obedience of the king of France, he asked that one make with them an amenable agreement, to which the king considered them for two things: the first, that he was ready to make and render the good against the bad, and, considering the mortality that was in his camp, which was a strong thing to fear; so, changing his attitude, he was happy to compose to the said English in the manner that follows: it is known, that the said town and city of Bordeaux will be rendered to the king of France and all the inhabitants will remain true and loyal subjects. And they will make the oath by name never to rebel against the crown of France, recognising and affirming the king of France to be their sovereign lord. And the English will leave from them to go in their ships into the land of England or Calais, if it seems good to them. And despite this, several of the lords of the said lands and of the said city have been fraudulent, traitorously making oaths and maliciously sought in England the said Englishmen, breaking the faith, the promise, and the oath that they had made the preceding year to the king, who by force and with great effort and expenses, had conquered, having banished from the lands of the Bordelais, twenty people, such that it was pleasing to the king of those who had sought the said Englishmen in England, amongst whom were the sire de Duras and the sire d'Éparre, and others. And the said agreement was made the seventeenth day of October of the said year 1453. And in truth, the king worked and struggled greatly by body, by deed, and by his sense, because after the help and grace within the good conduct which had been in place of the gentle acceptance of his men, and the comfort and going from one place to another, he had made to be lord of the said land peacefully. All

deſſ nommez. ont ſervy leRoy deleur puiſſance comme ſi ce euſt eſte leur propre fait. Et en ce fort granement alouer. et po^r lamo^r deulx leurs ſucceſſeurs. Meſſire pierre debeauvau ſ.^r delabeſſiere mourut environ trois Iours apr^s labaſtaille decaſtillon. Auſſi mourut meſſire Iacques dechabanes grant maiſtre doſtel qui fut moult plaint car Il eſtoit moult vaill chevallier. led pays ainſſi adelivre ſedelibera leRoy ſen Retourner en ſacite detours. Et po^r laiſſa pour laproviſion et garde decellui pays monſ.^r leconte declermont ſon lieuten geñal Avecques lui meſſire theaulde devalpergue. ſire Iehan bureau treſorier defrance et maire delad cite. Et pluſſieurs gens darmes archiers et arbaleſtriers avecques eulx aladeffence dud pays. Car dece eſtoit grant beſoing et urgente neceſſite veu lagrant traiſon qui par eulx avoit eſte commiſe et perpetree. Et ainſſi que dit laloy Semel. maſus. ſemper. preſumitur. maſus. pôquoy eſt expediant deleur tenir lefer audos affin quilz furent en grangeous ſubgection. et telle quilz ne ſe puiſſent plus Rebeller.

Informacion. envoye par franceſque de trave atreſReverend pere en dieu monſ.^r lecardinal davignon et une par Iehan blanchin deIacques cetaldy. marchant florentin. lequel eſtl pnt alaprinſe decoſtan noble. coſtantin noble

Comment. morbeſan. turc. huitenant. dugrant. empereur. duoganie a ſiega. lacite decoſtantnople.

Audit. an mille CCCC Cinquante trois leiiii.^m Iour demarl. avant paſques. Morbeſan filz deoreſte ſeigneur

his vassals, too, and allies abovenamed, had served the king with their power as if it was their rightful duty, and in this great desire to praise and for the love of them, their successors. Messire Pierre de Beauvau, seigneur de la Bessière, died around three days after the battle of Châtillon. Also died messire Jacques de Chabannes, grand master of the hotel, which was very tragic, because he was a brave knight; the said land thus delivered, the king debated to return to his city of Tours. And for the provision and guardianship of this land, he left monseigneur the count of Clermont, his lieutenant general. With him messire Théaulde de Valpergue, [and] Sir Jean Bureau, treasurer of France and mayor of the said city, and several men-at-arms, archers, and crossbowmen, with those in the defence of the said land, because this was a great need and urgent necessity, seeing the great treason which had been committed and perpetrated by them. And thus the law says evil once is always presumed to be evil, for which it was expedient to hold iron on the back so that they would be in certain subjection, and such that they would no longer rebel.

Information sent by Francisco de Trévè to the very reverend father in God, monseigneur the cardinal of Avignon and one by Jean Blanchin and Jacques Cetaldy, Florentine merchant, who was present at the capture of Constantinople.

How Morbesan, a Turk, lieutenant of the great emperor of Turkey besieged the city of Constantinople

In the said year 1453, the fourth day of May, before Easter, Morbesan, son of Oreste, lord in the parts of Acheaia, cam-

es parties dachaye courut aupres decoſtan noble. Cinq.m Iour dud moys poſa ſon ſiege devant lad cite. C Item oud ſiege avoit entours deux cens mille hommes. deſquilz Il pouvoit bien avoir. Lx.m defait donc Il en yavoit dexxx. alx. mille acheval. et eſtoit armes lequart deux dehaubergons. deIacques et aucuns en yavoit armez alaguiſe defrance aucuns alaguiſe deburgarie aucuns en autres facons. aucuns avoient chapeaulx defer et avoient aucuns arcs et cranequins. Les autȇs gens defait pour laplus part eſtoient ſans armes Sauf quilz avoient targes et ſauvetarres qui ſoȇt eſpees deturque. C Item et leſurplus. Delx.m eſtoieȇt gaſteurs Robeurs marchans archiſans et autres ſuivans leſiege pour gaigner. C Item aud ſiege avoit pluſſieurs bombardes et treſgrant nombre decoullevrines et autȇs Inſtrumens pour offendre Et enȇt les autȇs une groſſe bombarde demetal toute dune piece tirant pierre dexii. eſpaulz et quatre doiz detour. et peſant mil. huit cens livres. leſquelles bombardes tiroient chcn Iour decens avi.xx coupz et dura cinquante et cinq Iours. parquoy fuit on compte quilz emploierent chûn Iour mil leurs depould debombarde ainſſi en lv. Iours eſpauderent ~~mil~~. lv. ~~leurs~~ mille livres depould. Et par ainſſi ſefait Raiſ quil yavoit. x.m coullevrines. C Item larmee du turc en mer eſtoit tant auport q̂ dehors de xvi. axviii. gallees. lx. ou iiii.xx galliottes de xviii. axx. Vaucheres. et dexvi. axx. barques petites comme pour porter chevaulx quilz ap pelloient pallandins et aſſez dautȇs fuſtes. C Item leſiege poſe et mis par terre Sangobaſa conſeiller deturcq. et celui qui aplus decry et dactorite entour lui fiſt porter delamer par deſſſ terre leſpace dedeux atrois mille. lx. a iiii.xx gallees q̂ autȇs fuſtes armees Iucques dedans lapulſe

paigning around Constantinople, the fifth day of the said month laid his siege before the said city. C Item at the said siege, there were around 200,000 men, of which he could well have 60,000 in fact, of which he had there 3,000 to 4,000 on horseback, and a quarter of them were armed with hauberks, and several there were armoured in the style of France, several in the style of Bulgaria, others in other fashions; several had capes of fur, and several had bows and crossbow cranks. The other men by deed were for the most part without armour, except that they had small shields and scimitars, which is a manner of sword to the Turk. C Item and the surplus of the said 60,000 were drapers, merchants, artisans, and others, following the siege in order to win. C Item at the said siege, there were several bombards and a very great number of culverins and other instruments of attack. And amongst the others was a great bombard of metal all of one piece, launching stones of twelve inches, and four fingers around, and weighing 1,800 pounds, which bombards launched each day from 100 to 120 rounds, and it endured for fifty-five days 1,000 pounds of powder in their bombards; thus, in fifty-five days there was 55,000 pounds of powder. And so it is correct that they had 10,000 culverins. C Item the army of the Turk at sea, both at the port and outside it was sixteen to eighteen galleys or 60 or 80 galliots of eighteen to twenty benches, and sixteen to twenty small barques so as to carry horses that they called pallandins, and there were also others. C Item the siege being assembled and laid by land, Sango Bassa, councillor of the Turk, and he who was the most frightening and of authority around him carried by the sea as above the land, the space of two or three miles, 60 to 80 galleys as other feats of arms, until within the gulf of Mandagaran, which was afterwards Père, between the two cities, at

mandagaran qui eſt aupres pere entre les deux citez. Auquel port nepouvoient auſ̂ment Les navires duturcq. ~~po~~ pour larmee des xpiens̑ entire eſtant aung pont debarque q̂ les xpiens̑ avoient fait ſur latr̂e dupar pour allr̂ deconſtinople apere pour ſoy entre ſecourer. et deceſte armee deturcqs fut cap.ne ung nôme albitangoth. lequel Rompit quatre nefz genevoiſes. Et lors leturcq. fiſt ung aut̂ capitaine. Et auſſi fut ſon ſiege ferme par mer et par terre. C Item conſtaninople eſt treſſorte en figure ⁊triangulaire et axx.m detour devers terre cinq devers lamer et cinq devr̂s leport et goulfe cinq. Et les murs dedevers laterre ſont treſgros ⁊hautx et deſſus ya barbacanes et machicolis et audehors faulx murs et foſſez. et ſont eſtimez largres haulx les murs principaux. dexx. a xxii. braches et eſtimez larges en aucuns lieux. ſix. et en aut̂s lieux huit braches. Les faulx murs dedehors ont leterrain hault dexxii. braches. lemur dedeſſſ hault dexxiiii. braches et gros detrois braches. Les foſſez ſont larges de xxv. braches et parfons dex. braches. C Item en Icelle cite avoit en tout de xxv. axxx.m hômes et devi avii.m combatans. C Item auport pour deffend lachayne yavoit dexpiens̑ xxx. nefs et neuf gallees. ceſt aſſavoir deux ſubtilles et trois marchands veniciennes trois delempereur et une demeſſ.re Iehan Iuſtinian bon genevois au gaiges delempereur. C Item conſtantinople donc ainſſi aſſiegee par mer et par terre et ainſſi combatu dehors et dedans debombardes et detrait ſedeffendit cinquante Iours. C Item parmy cetemps advint aucunes particullaritez ſemblant aux xpieńs eſtre leger abrullez Les navires aux turz. Lacappitaine delagallee nommee treppiſonde monta ſur une gallee ſubtille pource faire avecques ĉtains aut̂s

which port the navy of the Turk could not otherwise enter since the entire army of the Christians was near to a bridge of boats that the Christians had made in order to enter the part in order to go from Constantinople to Père to rescue each other, and over this army of the Turks was a captain named Albitangoth, who destroyed four Genoese ships. And then the Turk made another captain. And so his siege was enclosed by sea and by land. C Item Constantinople is very strong in design, and triangular, with twenty towers on the land side, five on the sea, and five on the port, and five on the gulf. And the walls on the land side are very large and high, and above there are barbicans and machicolations, and outside are false walls and moats, and the principal walls are from twenty to twenty-two armlengths and estimated as think in several places as [twenty]six [armlengths], and in other places [twenty]eight armlengths. The false walls outside have the high terrain of twenty-two armlengths, the abovesaid wall a height of twenty-four armlengths and as thick as [twenty]three armlengths. The moats are twenty-five armlengths wide and ten armlengths deep. C Item in this city there were in all 25,000 to 30,000 armed men, and 6,000 to 7,000 soldiers. C Item at the port, in order to defend the chain, there were thirty Christian ships and nine galleys, it is known two stealth and three Venetian merchants, three of the emperor, and one of messire Jean Justinian, a good Genoese in the employ of the emperor. C Item Constantinople was thus besieged by sea and by land, and thus strongly bombarded outside and inside by bombards and siege weapons; it defended itself for fifty days. C Item about this time, some particular people came to the Christians to help set fire to the ships of the Turk; the captain of the galley named Trebizond rode out on a quiet galley in order to do this, with certain others

ace ordonnez. Maiz lagallee fut effondree dune bombarde des turcqz qui furet̂ par lefondement affichez aux paulx aguz devant ceulx qui faiſoiet̂ lagarde ſur lamer. C Item ducoſte delaterre eſtoit Sangobaſa albanoys Roy qui en ſon ſiege avoit pluſſieurs acouſtumez deminer lor ⁊larget̂ et myna en xiiii. lieux ſoubz les murs delaville pour les tailler. Et commenca ſes mynes bien loingz des murs. les xpienŝ contminerent et en obſcouant leRbout et par diverſes foiz eſtoit firent les turcqz en leurs mynes par fumees et en aucuns foiz acombatre main amain. C Item led Sangobaſa fiſt une chaſteau deboys ſigrat̂ ſi hault et ſi fort quil ſeiguouroit lemur. C Item fiſt faire ſur bateaulx ung pont longc demil braches. et large devii. pour paſſer lamer atravers dupont Iucqẑ aupie du mur. C Item fiſt et pluſſieurs autŝ Inſtrumens deboys et treſhaultes et grands eſtables et legeres. C Item et auſſi faiſoient chun̂ Iours grands eſcar mouches ou Ie mouroult degens deca et dela Maiz pour ung qui en mouroult deceulx dede dens. Il en mouroult cent dedehors. C Item au ſiege dutourq. avoit pluſſieurs xpienŝ degrece et autŝ nacions q̂ combien quilz ſoient duturcq ſubgetz. toutefuoys cy neſont Ilz pas par lui contraints deRegnouir lafoy xprien̂. Ains a dorent et prent aleur plaiſir. En oult̂ yavoit autres capitaines et autŝ puiſſans turcqz qui par deſpit deSangaubaſa qui trop les oppreſſoit ad veſoient ceulx dededans par lectres quilz tiroiet̂ dedans laville et en toutes autŝ maniere poſſibles detout ce qui ſefaiſoit auſiege. Et ent̂ les autŝ choſes furent les xpienŝ advertiz côme leturcq avecques ſes barons princes ſeigneurs et conſeillr̂s avoit tenu conſeil quat̂ Iours ent̂ leſquelz eſtoit capitaine nôme coulombaſa qui conſeilloit a

in this order. But the galley was sunk by a bombard of the Turks, which were affixed at the stern to sharp stakes, before those who were guarding the sea. C Item on the side of the land was Sango Bassa, an Albanian king, who in his siege had several men accustomed to mining the gold and the silver, and he mined in fourteen places under the walls of the town in order to cause its collapse. And he began his mines well away from the walls; the Christians countermined and by listening, they recognized them, and several times they choked the Turks in their mines by smoke, and several times by hand-to-hand combat. C Item the said Sango Bassa made a castle out of wood so high and so strong that he overcame the wall. C Item he had made a bridge out of boats one-thousand armlengths long and seven armlengths wide to cross the sea from the port to the foot of the wall. C Item he made several other instruments of wood and very high and great lightweight ladders. C Item and also each day, they made great skirmishes where [people] were killed by men of one place and the other, but for one of those who died within, a hundred died outside. C Item at the siege by the Turk, there were several Christians of Greece and other nations, who, even though they were subjects of the Turk, nevertheless were not forced by them to renounce the Christian faith. Thus, they worshipped and prayed as they wished. In addition, there were other captains and other powerful Turks, who out of spite of Sango-Bassa, who was very oppressive, would warn those within by letters that they would go straight into the town, and in all other manner possible, of everything that was happening at the siege. And amongst the other things, they warned the Christians how the Turk, with his barons, princes, lords, and councillors, had held council for four continuous days, amongst whom was a captain named Coulom-

lever leſiege en alleguant auturcq. Tu as fait ton devoir tu leur as Ia donne pluſſieurs grans batailles et atant deIours en ont eſte mors grant quantite detes gens. Tu vois lacite deffenſable et Imexpregnable et en maniere que quant plus va degens alaſſault plus en demeurene ceulx qui ont eſte ſur lemur ont eſte Rebbouttez et tuez. Et tes anceſſeurs Iamais ne vindrent ne vouldrent venir ſe avant ceteſt grant gloire dy avoir eſte et te doit ſouffire ſans voulloir deſtruire toutes tes gens. Et tant fut dit que leturq. ſe deliberoit ſoy leurs et ſon Retourner. et deficher la aucuns coulompnes pour notiffier aIamaiz quil avoit fait ce q̂ oncques nil deſes ~~fuceff.~~[rs] anceſſeurs navoit fait et q̂ plus mil turcq ne ſeoſa approuchr̂ decoſtantinople. Sangaubaſa eſtoit doppinion contraire et diſoit auturcq Tu as fait leplus fort Tu as Rue Iuz une grant partie des mur. No[9] en Ruerons delautre donnons oncques oncques ung aſpre aſſault et ſi nous faillons no[s] prendrons apres tel party. que bon te ſemblera tant ſceult dire que leturcq ſeconſentit detout furent advertiz ceulx dededans et confortez et quilz ſefeiſſent vaillans deux ou trois Iours. Car puis ſeroient touſiours ſceurs que le ſiege ſen yroit ſans nil Retours. C Item leturcq delibera tout ainſſi aſſailler trois Iours devant laſſault commanda ſolepnel Ieune en honneur et Reizence du dieu duciel leql̂ ſeul Ilz aovaent. Ieunerent lui et ſes gens trois Iours to[9] continuelz par ainſſis q̂ tout leIour nemangerent Rien Maiz ſeullemet̂ denuyt pour leurs une ſouſtimer. denuyt firent Infini lu minere dechandelles deboys qui brulloit deſoy meſme en mer et en t̂re tant quil ſembloit q̂ mur et t̂re bruilloit avecques treſgrans ſous detabours et autŝ Inſtrumens car detromppettes nont Ilz qui bien peu. C Item

basa, who advised him to lift the siege, in alleging to the Turk: "You have made your effort, you have given them several great battles, and over so many days, where there is a great quantity of your dead men. You see the city defended and impregnable in such manner that when more men go to the battle, of the dead those who had been under the wall have been defeated and killed. And your ancestors never came nor wanted to come there before the head of such great glory to have been, and you ought to be satisfied, without wanting to destroy all your men." And so it is said that the Turk pondered this, and upon his return, he wrote on several columns to record forever that what he had done none of his ancestors had done, and that no Turk from now on would dare to approach Constantinople. Sango-Bassa was of the opposite opinion and said to the Turk: "You have the most strength. You have collapsed by land a great part of the wall, we fighting from the other. We give still have hope to assault and if we fail, we will accept such advice that seems good to you; hearing thus what was said, the Turk contented himself that all this was advised [regarding] those outside, and he was comforted, and that they would work bravely for two or three days, because they were always aware that the seige would proceed without turning back. C Item the Turk considered attacking again; three days before the assault he ordered a solemn fast in honour and respect of the God of the sky, whom they adored. They fasted, he and his men, for three continuous days, until nobody could eat on one day, but only by night, for to sustain them by night were an infinite number of lights from candles of wood which burned by itself on the sea and on land, such that they seemed that wall and land burned with very great sounds of drums and other instruments, because they only had a few trumpets. C Item having the things in these

eſtans les choſſ en ces t̂mes et leturcq delibere daſſaillir quil̂ oppinion ouIntencion quil euſt devaincre et ceulx dededans deliberez deulx bien deffend. leturcq commenca ſon aſſault bien lentement lexxviii.ᵐ Iour deMay auſoir. et avoit ordonne leturcq ſes gens en lamaniere qui ſenſ. Ceſt aſſavoir ſuglardy capitaine gñal deturquie. Xx.ᵐ honn̂s alaporte depichy ou eſtoit lagrant bataille Et Sangobaſſa auſſi conſeillr̂ duturcq. avec pres delaturce partie des gens duſiege ala porte deſaint Romain loing depichy entour ung mille. Ebbigabeth. Cap.ⁿᵉ gñal degrece fut mis aucoſte degaligaria alendroit du pallaiz alempereur Et eſtoit lapluſgrant des mynes loingtz deſaint Romain deux mille ~ Sangobaſſa albanois Regnye eſtoit oult̂ leau devr̂s pera avec pluſſieurs xpien̂s Renyez. Car dece pais ſen Renoye moult tous les Iours. C Item laſſault commence ceulx dededens ſedeffendirent par tout vaillamment aSaint Romain eſt lelieu plus legier aprend. et lamuraille plus foible delaquelle avoit Iaeſte abatu par les Iours paſſez. La eſtoient les bombardes qui boutere t̂ Iuz une barbaqcuene et lamoitie du murs du milieu duquel en cheult bien deux cens braches. la auſſi avoit decoullevrines et de traict q̂ apaue veoit on leciel. Touteſſoiz ceulx dededens Releurent les braches du murs de groſſes tounes et boys en t̂re ⁊aut̂s choſes et ſedeffendoient lemeulx quilz povoient. C item ence lieu deffendoit meſſr.ʳᵉ Iehan Iuſtinian bon genevois qui eſtoit aux gaiges delempereur et ſeporta baillement auſſi toute lacite avoit grant eſpoir en lui et en ſavaillance. C Item en celieu pour faire ſon deſrnier effort ſeapprocha leturcq adeux banieres avec x.ᵐ hommes eſleuz pour lagarde deſaperſonne et aut̂s Iufuir nôble deturcqz avecques

terms, and the Turk debated attacking, that his opinion or intention that he would conquer, and those within discussed amongst themselves well to defend; the Turk began his assault the next day, the twenty-eighth day of May, in the evening, and the Turk ordered his men in the manner that follows: it is known, Suglardy, captain general of Turkey, had 20,000 men at the Gate of Pischy, where there was a great bastide. And Sango-Bassa, also councillor to the Turk, with nearly a third part of men of the siege, went to the gate of Saint-Romain, about one mile from Pischy. Ebbigabeth, captain general of Greece, was put on the side of, Galigaria, at the location of the palace of the emperor. And the great quantity of mines was about two miles from Saint-Romain. Sango-Bassa, a former Albanian, was on the other side of the water toward Péra with several renounced Christians. Because in this country, more renounced every day. C Item the assault began, those within defending themselves very bravely at Saint-Romain, which was the easiest place to capture and the wall was the weakest, which had already partially been destroyed in the days before. The bombards were there, which cast down a barbican and the part of the wall in the middle, where there were shot at least 200 armsmen; also there were the culverins and the arrows such that one could not see the sky. However, those within pushed back the holes in the wall with great bundles of wood and earth and other things, and they defended themselves the best that they could. C Item in this place, messire Jean-Justinian Long, a good Genoiese, who was in the pay of the emperor, defended and carried himself there bravely; also the whole city had a great hope in him and in his bravery. C Item in this place, in order to make his last effort, he approached the Turk with two banners with 10,000 men elected for the guardianship of his per-

ceulx dechaſteau deboys par eſcholles et autš Inſtrumens commencerent a remplir les foſſez et monter ſus lemur. C Item lafut meſſr.e Iehan Iuſtinian bleche dune coul levrine et ſen partie pour ſoy faire mediciner et bailla ſagarde adeux ~~hier~~ gentlz hômes genevoys. Les turcqz monterent ſur lemur. Et adonc les xpiens eulx voyans ſe oppreſſez et que leſd turcqz eſtoient. Ja ſur lamuraille côme dit eſt. Et auſſi q̂ meſſire Iehan Iuſtinian ſen eſtoit alle cuidans quil ſen fuyſt habandônereť leur garde et ſen fuyrent. Auſſi les turcqz entrerent en coſtantinople alaube duIour lexxviii^e Iour demay defrain paſſe mettans tout aleſpire quantquil leur faiſoit Reſiſtence. C Item perra navoit encore eu nul aſſault et eſtoient aplluſgrand part des xereciens en conſtantinople pour deffend ceulx qui eſtoient apere qui navoient Riens oſte deleurs biens deliberans denvoyer leurs clefz auturcq. et ſoy Recommander alui et lui offres lacite en laquelle Il yavoit vi.^c hômes. et ainſſi la miſericorde dedieu actendroient. Touteſſoiz une grant partie des hommes et des fêmes môtereť ſur une nef degenevoys pour eulx en aller. Et ſemble aud Iacques tetaldy q̂ une nef aucontrains chargee defemmes depira fut prinſe des turcqz. C Item lempereur de coſtantinople mourult alad prinſe et aucus duret quil eult lateſte tranchee ⁊autš duť quil mourult alaporte et en lapreſſe ſen voullant yſſir. lun ⁊lauť peult eſtre vray ceſt aſſavoir quil fuſt mort en lapreſſe et q̂ de puis les turs lui euſſent tranche lateſte. C Item lad entre fut moult pretemſe et doulloureuſe pour les xpiens car apres q̂ leſd turcs oulrent poceſſon paiſble delad cite ~~ſe~~ tranſportant aux egliſes decelle et par eſpl en lamaiſtreſſe appeller Sancte ſophie qui eſt belle large grande ⁊ſpacueuſe. Et la trouvereť

son and others, and the fair nobility of the Turks, with those of the wooden castles, by ladders and other instruments, began to fill the trenches and climb upon the wall. C Item there was messire Jean-Justinian wounded by a coulevrin and he left to get medical treatment and handed the guardianship to two Genoiese gentlemen. The Turks mounted upon the wall. And then the Christians, seeing them, were crushed and the said Turks were already on the wall, as is said. And so those of messire Jean-Justinian left, thinking that he had fled, abandoning their guardianship and they fled. Thus, the Turks entered within Constantinople at the break of day, the twenty-eighth day of May, putting everything to the torch, whoever made resistance to them. C Item Pera had still not been attacked and the greater part of the Christians in Constantinople to defend those who were at Pera, who did not want to risk their goods, debated sending their keys to the Turk and to recommend to him and offer him the city, in which there were around 600,000 men, and so await the mercy of God. However, a great part of the men and women climbed aboard a Genoese ship in order to go. And it seemed to the said Jacques de Taldy that one ship trying to take women from Pera was captured by the Turks. C Item the emperor of Constantinople died during the said capture and several said that he was beheaded, and others that he died at the gate and in the press, wanting to go out, one and the other could be true: it is known that he died in the press and that then the Turks had removed his head. C Item the said entrance was overwhelming and sorrowful for the Christians, because after the said Turks had peaceful possession of the said city, they transformed the churches of this place and especially the mistress named Hagia Sophia, which was a beautifully large, tall, and spacious. And they found several dames, damsels, and women of

pluſſieurs dames damoiſelles et femmes degrant auctorite et pluſſ.[rs] autŝ filles pucelles auvierges leſquelles conguirent aux unes adultaire et aux autŝ eurent leur compaignie charnelle deforce et oultˆ leurs grez et voullentez et eu contend dedieu nor̂ treateur et delafoy catholicque. Et meſmes led turcq. violla en Icelle egliſe lafemme delempereur et latant pour ſaconcubine et lamiera avecques lui quatˆ Il partit delad cite. Pluſſieurs auſſi deſes gens cômerent lepechie deNature luixure contˆ nature en pluſſieurs et diverſes manieres. C Item les gallees groſſes venconnes du voyage deRômenie cappezande demourerent laIucques aundi. actêd yfaimes aucuns xpriens donc Il yen ung bien iiii[c]. Entˆ leſquelz fut led Iacques cetaldy qui eſtoit en ſagarde bien longtz delapart ou ĉteratˆ les turcqs. et ſcetit bien leur entree bien deux harnois en murs. Auſſi gaigna lamur et ~~def~~ ſedeſpulla et naga Iucques aux gallees qui leReceurent. C Item ſelaſmur devinſe qui memort meſſire Iehan leRandous fuſt aRiver ung Iour avant quil fuſt prins ĉtes Il ny avoit nulle doubte quelle euſt moult ſecouru. En laquelle armee eſtoient neuf gallees veniſſiennes et xx. naves atout le moins Il nevint pas atemps. Maiz ſeullemetˆ aRriva anigrepont aung Iour apres quil fut p̊rs. C Item on eſtime que les biens decoſtantinople ont vaille aux turcqs quatre mille millions deducas laperte deveniſſe ſe eſtime cinquatˆ mille ducas. Car en ceſte gallee ceſt ſauve environ xx.[m] ducas des genevois Il ya perte grande et Infinie de~~flobre~~ florentins. xx[m] ducas deceulx delamarche dancone plus dexv.[m] ducas. Ancone eſt lameilleure cite delamr̂che anncone. C Item on treuve pas ceulx qui ont converſe avec leturc et qui ont congneu ſes faitz ſacondicion et ſapuiſſance

great authority, and several other virgins, which they violated, to some adulterously and to others they had their carnal company by force, and others they hurt and wounded and had to contend with God our creator and by the Catholic faith. And even the said Turk violated in this church the wife of the emperor and treated her like his concubine and took her with him when he left from the said city. Several others of his men began the sin against nature in several places and in the same manner. C Item the large Roman galleys voyaging from Trebizond remained until midday, waiting to save any Christians, of which there were around 400, amongst whom was the said Jacques de Taldi, who had under his guardianship the section furthest from where the Turks entered, and they discovered their entry by around two harnesses in walls. Thus, he went over the wall and undressed himself and swam to the gallies, which received him. C Item what has been told to me, had messire Jean Le Randous arrived one day before the capture, there is no doubt that he would have been very helpful. In which army were nine Venetian galleys and twenty ships, all for nothing since he did not come in time. But they only arrived at Nigrepont one day after the it was captured. C Item one estimates that the value of the goods of Constantinople seized by the Turks at four million ducats; the loss to Venice is estimated 50,000 ducats, because in this galley was saved around 20,000 ducats; of the Genoese, they lost there a great and infinite amount; the Florentines, 20,000 ducats; of those of the march of Ancône, more than 25,000 ducats—Ancône is the best city of the march of Ancône. C Item one finds those who had conversed with the Turk and who had knowledge of his deeds, his conditions, and his power, that he was twenty-three or twenty-four years old, crueller than Nero, delighting himself in spilling human blood, a courageous

quil eſt dexxiii. axxiiii. ans cruel plus que noron delictant auſpandre ſangr courageulx et ardant deſ[r]ie et triumpher tout lemonde voire plus q̂ alixand ne ceſar ne autres vaillans qui avent eſte. Et allegnie quil aplus grant ſ[r]ie ⁊puiſſance plus que nul deulx navoit. Et touſiours ſefait lire hiſtoires devant lui et demande ou et commet̂ par nez et tient q̂ legier et bien aiſee choſe ſeroit aavoir fait ung pont ~~demur~~ durant demegara aveniſe pour pouvoir paſſer laſes gens darmes. Et pareillement demanda deRomme ou elle eſt aſſiſe. et auſſi duduc ~~demil~~ demillan et de ſes vaillances et daut̂ choſe fors q̂ deguerre Il ne parle. Et dit quil veult fixer ſon ſiege acoſtantinople. car la Ilpeult et veult faire mr̃veilleux navire. Ainſſi eſtime quil neſera nul en mer ne en t̂re quil nelui portent les avant quilz lactendent conſiderant quil a prins par force coſtantinople laplus forte cite deuroppa et ſi puiſſant que on ne cuidoit que Iamaiz armee pour grand quelle fuſt ladeuſt ſurmonter. Et conſiderant que lui et les ſiens ſont hardiz et Ingenieulx en armes tant que plus ne peult et ne ſont eſtime deleur vie. C Item on eſtime que pour ceſt eſte leturc meſera nul aut̂ fait darmes. Maiz entiendra aſes faiz po.[r] lavenir demourer. aconſtantinople ſinon q̂ ~~au leur~~ aucun lieu devollonte ſans guerre ſe vouſiſt Rend. Ses gens vouldront Retourner chc͡n en leurs maiſons pour Recueillir leurs biens et eulx Repoſer. Maiz on peult tenir pour ĉtain q̂ merveilleuſement leturcq ſa preſte par mer et par terre pour ſemettre ſus autemps nouvel. Maiz ſexpien͡s yamouroit preſtement on tient fermement con les chaſſera du pays et conqueſtera lui ſur eulx du pays po[r] Iamaiz et les maniers dy pourvoir ſerot̂ ceſtes. C Premierement Il fouldroit fr̃ paix ent̂ les xpien͡s.

and ardent lord, and triumphing over the world, seeing more than Alexander or Caesar or any other brave man who had been before, and allegedly he had the greatest lordship and power than any of them ever had. And he always had histories read to him and asked where and how things happened, and he held that it is a simple and easy thing to build a bridge from Megara to Venice so that he can cross his men-at-arms. And similarly, he asked of Rome, where it was situated and also of the duke of Milan and of his brave people and of other things strengthened for war that he could not speak. And he said that he wanted to fix his seat at Constantinople, because there he could and wanted to prepare a marvellous navy. So, predicting that there will be no one on the sea nor the land that he would not carry, they waited, confident that he had taken by force Constantinople, the strongest city in Europe and so powerful that no one thought that any army was large enough to surmount it, and considering that he and his people were hardy and ingenious in arms such that no one could predict their deeds. C Item one predicts that, although the Turk did not make another great feat of arms, but he understood by his deeds that in the future in order to remain at Constantinople, notwithstanding any place of will, without war it would render itself. His men would return each to their house in order to receive their goods and rest themselves. But one can hold for certain that marvellously the Turk captured by sea and by land to put himself under at a new time. But the Christians killed and captured there, one holds firmly to chase them from the land and conquer it from under those of the land so never and the manners it can be done are these: C Firstly, he would make peace between the Christians. C Item, it would be necessary that the Venetians, the duke of Milan, the Florentines, and other lords of Italy make an army

C Item. fauldroit q̂ les veniciens leduc de millan les florentins 7autr̂ s.rs dytalle fassent une armee dexx.m chevaulx bien en point et bons capitaines. Laquelle fut conduite devers pera par lalbanye Iucques aux secours des xpiens et la seposast en lieu habondant de vivres car la Ilz sont et seroient sceurs. Et Incontinent augmentez dalbanoiz. sclavons et autrs nacions xpiens que voullentiers viêdroiet pour deffend lafoy catholique. C Item par mer oultr̂ larmee Ia sange en Icelle fauldroit adioindre une autr̂ armee duRoy daragon des venissiens des genevois. des florentins. docozaire et autrs gens qui sont en lamarine qui souffiroit avaincre celle duturcq. celle nestoit pl.9 grosse quelle mest depnt. Laquelle avoir sen allast auport denygrepont pour prend sagripoli et por prend autrs lieux du turcq. et obvier aupassage delestroit q̂ leturcq. veult faire deturquie en grece et en contre. C Item fauldroit q̂ lempere r les hongres. les bohesme. les poullonois. les vaisie et autrs nacions dicellui avecques Iehan ~ vvayvvada en ceste partie tresRedoubte des turcs feissent une armee qui entrast en grece pour prend andripol et autrs lieux ocuppez des turcs. Et fauldroit tenir maniere q̂ en toutes as armes fussent toutes en ung temps esd lieux ~~lieu delat~~. Et eussent bonne Intelligence lune delautr̂ decefaire firant cest effect. C Item leturc qui afait tout son effort et toute sapuissance na q̂ deux cens mille hommes tat̂ en bons q̂ en meschans ent̂ lesquilz ya grant quantite dexpiens et autrs ses subgetz qui le serent mal voullentiers. lesquilz sentans larmee des xpiens habandonneroiet̂ leturc et seadioingurent aux autrs xpiens. C Item le turcq. par nature et usage naturel point la guerre en cite men chasteau. Maiz setient continuellement aux champs

of 20,000 horses, well-organised and with good captains, who would lead toward Zara by Albania to the rescue of the Christians, and it would position itself in a place abundant in supplies because there they would be and would help. And immediately Albanians, Slavs, and other Christian nations would augment them, which willingly would come to defend the Catholic faith. C Item, by sea, another army already active in which would be joined another army of the king of Aragon, of the Venetians, of the Genoese, of the Florentines, of corsairs, and other men who were of the sea, which suffered to defeat those of the Turk, so it was not as large as it is at present, which has to go to the port of Negrepont in order to take Sarrapoli and to take other places from the Turk and obviate the passage of the strait that the Turk wants to make from Turkey to Greece and everywhere else. C Item, it will be necessary that the Emperor, the Hungarians, the Bohemians, the Poles, the Vaisies, and other nations of this place, with John Voivode, very redoubtable of the Turks in this part, will make an army, which will enter in Greece in order to capture Adrianople and other places occupied by the Turks. And it will be necessary to hold in a manner that in all arms will make all in a time in the said places. And they all will have good intelligence, one with another, for putting this into effect. C Item the Turk, who has put all his effort and all his power, only has in total 200,000 men, both good and bad, amongst whom there is a great quantity of Christians and others of his subjects who follow him with ill will, who feel that the army of the Christians will freely abandon the Turk and will join themselves to the other Christians. C Item, the Turk naturally and natural usage no longer awaits the war in any city or castle, but holds the field continuously, he and all his power, for which it will diminish him and his

lui et toutes ſa puiſſance. Pourquoy ſediminuera lui et les ſiens. C Item en oult̂ les xpiēns deRuſſiye et deſes autŝ pays viendroient to⁹ alarmee des xpiēns. C Item en oult̂ letaramain qui eſt grant seigne.[r] en turquie eſt ennemy capital duturc cil eſt adinſe q̂ xpiēns guerroient leturc Il lopprefferoit moult grandement en turquie et liu feroit guerre et apou dechoſe ſeferoit xpiēn. C Item en grece ny aura ſepuiſſant ou laboureur qui neportaſt armes aux xpiēns les vivres fauldronent auturc en grece. lepays deturqie lui ſera empeſche par mer. les xpiēns degrece vouldront Recouvrer aleſpee leurs terres et lieux duturcq. Ainſſi maiz que les armees ſaprouchent pou apou lune delaut̂. Il neſt nulle doubte q̂ brief q̂ leturcq. et ſon excercite neſoit affamer et deffaicte. Maiz ſeon ny pourvoit dilligemmet̂ et que on donne temps et loiſir auturcq. deſoy mettre en point par mer et par terre Il neſt nulle doubte quil neface grande eſrlande aux ~~paniers~~ xpiēns donc dieu no⁹ gard. C Item en ceſte gallee ſont Revenus huit citadins veniciens decoſtantinople et ſont la demourez. xxxv. gentilz hommes et dautŝ gens debien pres dequarante dieu leur vueille aidier. quoy qui le[r] couſte pour eulx ~~deſpa~~ deſpeſcher.

Lectre en francois envoyee dud. grant turcq. au Saint pere Nicollas cinq.[me] decenom. appelle par led turcq. legrat̂ preſte Rommain.

Oudit an et tantoſt apres led turcq. voyant ſaproſperite Iudice ſur lui. Meu depre ſumption et grant orgueil envoya aupappe ni colas deux lectres ~~done~~ tout dune meſme matiere lune en latin et laut̂ en francois. duquel francois late-

own. C Item in addition, the Christians of Russia and of the other lands would come all to the army of the Christians. C Item in addition, the Taramain [Crimean], who is a great lord in Turkey, is the mortal enemy of the Turk, so if it happened that the Christians waged war [against] the Turk, he would oppress him very greatly in Turkey and would make war against him, and with little thing he would be Christian. C Item in Greece, there was no peasant or labourer who did not carry arms to the Christians, the supplies would be needed to the Turk in Greece, the land of Turkey he would stop him by sea, the Christians of Greece would want to recover with the sword their lands and places from the Turk. Thus, but only the armies will approach each other step-by-step, one against the other, there will have no doubt that shortly, the Turk and his followers are not hungry and defeated, but if one does not diligently provide for it and we give time and leisure to the Turk to collect himself both by sea and by land, there is no doubt that he will do great harm to the Christians, for which God protects us. C Item in this galley, eight Venetian citizens returned from Constantinople, and there remained thirty-five men and other people, around forty in all. May God help them, whatever the cost to them, for them to safely escape.

Letter in French sent from the said Great Turk to the holy father Nicholas, fifth of this name, called by the said Turk the great Roman priest.

In the said year and soon afterwards, the said Turk, seeing such prosperity shine before him, moved by arrogance and swelling with great pride, sent to the pope Nicholas two letters, both of the same matter, one in Latin and the other in French, for which

neur ſenſ. Morboſan ſeigneʳ es parties dachaye. filz deoreſtes avecques les freres doĉ lun eſt collabullabre collactereus aux bellateurs deuganeus Imperateur augrant preſtre Romain Iouxſte nr̂ ſes merites ſalut. Il eſt nagueres parvenu anoz oreilles q̂ aux prieres et Requeſtes dupeuple des veniciens vo⁹ faictes publiq̂meт̂ divulguer en voz egliſes q̂ quiconque prendra hommes conт̂ no⁹ aura en ce ciecle. Remiſſion deſes pechez et leurs promeſtez benoiſte vie au temps advenir. Delaquelle choſe nous avons congnie laĉtaine vratie par lavenue daucuns pietons portans croix. Leſquelz ont nagueres tranſnage et paſſe lamer es na vires des venitiens Pour laquelle choſe no⁹ ſômes vechement eſmr̂veillez. Car Iaſoit ce q̂ dugrant dieu tonnant vo⁹ fuſt donne lapuiſſance de abſouldre et deſlier les ames tant devriez pl⁹ meurement ace proced. Ne ne devriez Induire les xpiens encontre no⁹ eſpcialemeт̂ les ytallens car no⁹ ſavons depuis nagueres q̂ noz peres dirent q̂ nrê peuple des turcqs avoit eſte Innocent et quictes delamort devr̂e criſt cruxifie. Et commeт̂ quil ſoit ainſſi q̂ les lieux et les т̂res ou ſont voz choſes ſainctes ne poceſſ ſions ne no⁹ ne noz gens Maiz touſio.ʳˢ ayons eu et ayons en hayne lepeuple des Iuifz. Car ſelon ce q̂ no⁹ liſons en noz hiſtoires et croniques bail lerent proditoirement et par envye Icellui ciſt au Iuge des Romains en Ihlem et lefirent mourir augibet delacroix. No⁹ eſmr̂veillons auſſi ⁊doullos q̂ les ytaliens ſeſont mis conт̂ no⁹ côme Il ſoit ainſſi q̂ no⁹ avons Inclinacion naturelle ales aymer. car Ilz ſont yſſus du ſang detroye et en ont leur premiere nobleſſe et ſ.ⁱᵉ duquel ſange et lignee no⁹ ſommez anciens hoirs et les noes. avoir eſte augmentateurs et accroiſſeurs leſquelz eſtoient iyſſus dugrant Roy priamus et deſalignee en laquelle no⁹ ſômes

the French is in the following tenor: Morbezan, lord of the parts of Achaeia, son of Orestes, with his brothers, of whom one is Collabullabre, cousin to the belligerents, Uganeus, emperor, to the great Roman priest, we, adjoining his merits, greetings. It has recently come to our ears that, at the prayers and requests of the Venetian people, you made publicly to disclose in your churches that whoever takes arms against us will be in this instance remitted of his sins, and you promise them a blessed life in the future. For which thing we have learned by certain truth by the coming of several pedestrians carrying the cross, who had navigated across and crossed the sea on the ships of the Venetians. For which thing we greatly marvelled, because I know that by the great thundering God you are given the power to absolve and detach souls, for which you would kill to do this. And you would induce the Christians against us, especially the Italians, because we know that not long ago our fathers said that our people, of the Turks, had been innocent and unblemished by the death of your crucified Christ. And how is it also that the places and the lands where your holy things and possessions are, neither ours nor our men's, but always having had and having in hatred the Jewish people. Because, according to what we read in our histories and chronicles, they handed over jealously and by envy this Christ to the judge of the Romans in Jerusalem, and killed him on the gibet of the cross. We also marvel and regret that the Italians have put themselves against us, as it is thus that we have a natural inclination to love them, because they are issued out of the blood of Troy and there have their first nobles and lords, from which blood and lineage we are ancient heirs and named to have been augmenters and aggrandisers, who were issued out of the great king Priam and of his lineage, in which we are born and intend to rebuild

nez et avons Intencion deRepparer troye lagrant et devengr̃ lesange dehector. et Ruyne dillion en subguant ano⁹ lempire degrece et en lunissant alestat de nrê dieu pallas. et pugnirons les hoirs des transgresseurs. No⁹ avons aussi Intencion de soubzmettre totallement anoʳ empire ⁊ſſie Crete ⁊auts̃ Isles delamer. lesquelles lepeuple des venissiens devantdiz no⁹ ont viollentment ostens et no⁹ promis q̂ vo⁹ Imposez silence avoz messagers par laterre ditalie alaRequeste desdessusd venissiens en ne provoquant plus lepeuple xpiẽns soubz espoir depuissance comme no⁹ meayons mille guerre vers lui pour lacraiance et difference qui est ent̂ no⁹ comme Il ne vo⁹ appartient en Rien si no⁹ necroions point en vr̃e crist. lequel nous Repputtons avoir este tresgrant prophette. Et aussi selon ce q̂ no⁹ avons entendu selon laloy dicellui ne no⁹ devriez point compellr̃ asa croiance. Et si aucune controversite est meue ent̂ no⁹ et mille coulleur delustice. Sans laucteʳᵉ decesar ne daut̂ prince Maiz pour leʳᵉ orgueil et temerite Ilz ont subugue et occupe aucẽs Isles delamer et auts̃ lieux qui sont commis en nr̃e empire. Lesquelles desormaiz no⁹ ne povons nedevons souffrir car letemps denr̃e. Repromession approuche. Parlesquelles choses vo⁹ povez et devez par Raison desister devoz entrep̊ises et dece vo⁹ taire. Especiallement côme no⁹ con gnoissons Icellui peuple devniciens estre estrâge delavie et murs des Romains. Car Ilz nevi vinet̂ pas selon les loys et selon les meurs des auts̃. Maiz secuident estre milleurs deto⁹ les auts̃ peuples adiacens desquelz alaide denr̃e. grant dieu Ioupr̃t. no⁹ mettrons lorgueil et force nevie affin. ou autr̃ment si vr̃e proudence nese desiste deses ent̃prises no⁹ no⁹ efforcerons cont̂ vo⁹ alaide des orgauielx Imperateurs ⁊auts̃ Roys dorient. Lesquelz feignent ago aulourduy dormir. et

Troy the Great and avenge the blood of Hector and the ruin of Ilium by subjugating to us the Empire of Greece and by uniting it to the state of our God Allah and we will punish the heirs of the transgressors. We have also the intention to totally submit to our empire and lordship Crete and the other islands of the sea, which the abovesaid people of the Venetians have violently taken from us, and was promised to us, having imposed silence upon your messengers in the land of Italy at the request of the abovesaid Venetians, by no longer provoking the Christian people, under the hope of power, since we mean no war against it; for the belief and difference that is between us, how it is never a concern of yours if we no longer believe in your Christ, who we repute to have been a very great prophet. And also, according to what we have heard, following the law of this [religion], you should no longer compel us to its belief. And if there is any controversy moving between us and thousand colour of Justice without the authority of Caesar nor any other prince, but by their pride and temerity, they had subjugated and occupied several islands of the sea, and other places that had existed within our empire, which from now on we cannot nor ought to suffer, because the time for our vengeance approaches. For which things you can and should by reason desist from your enterprises and be quiet, especially because you know these people of Venice to be very strange from the life and customs of the Romans, because they do not live according to the laws and according to the customs of others, but hold themselves to be better than all the other adjacent peoples, for which, at the aide of our great God, we put the work and the pride and force to an end, or otherwise, if your prudence does not desist from these enterprises, we will reinforce ourselves against you, with the aid of the natural emperors and other kings of the East, who pretend

denoz. contrees feront venir aides darmes et nefz coppeuſes et artifficieuſes par leſquelles no⁹ avons Intencion deReſter bellerqueueſemet̂ non pas ſeullemet̂ cont̂ voz pietons portans croix. Maiz auſſi cont̂ gr̂manie Rommanie et france ſi cont̂ no⁹ les Incitez. Et avec laide deneptunes devie delamer. Nous avons Intencion depaſſer aloſepont et dalmarine avec Innombrable navires navire par voilles et par advirons. Et avons auſſi Intencion depaſſer. par laRegion ſeptentrionalle et viſiter eſpeciallement vers damacie et croyce donne en lan. demahommet huit cens quarante en Iuing en nr̂e pallaiz triumphal ſcellee et en Regiſtree.

Entrep̊inſe de xpien͡s ſur les turcs.

MEmoire que ung chevallier nomme le chevallier blanc mareſchal dehongrie. Lequel neſtoit pas noble car Il eſtoit mareſchal eu paravant quil ſemiſt alaguerre capitaine ſoubz leRoy dehongrie. Semiſt ſur les champs pour combatre les turqz. et avoit en ſacô paignie. dexx. axxiiii.[m] combatans. leſquelz avoient Ia gaigne leport deſambrime et avoit bien. ~~et~~ iiii.[xx] led turc. Auquel port furet̂. xv. Iours pour actend toute puiſſ̄ qui pourroit venir ſus lui et ſes gens. Ece venu alacognoiſſance dud chlr̂. blanc. Se partit demorienne et vint se Ioindre aud ~~due~~ turcq. environ deux heures. devant leIour et tellement fut combatu ſur ceulx qui eſtoiet̂ ſur terre que tout fut mort Iuques au nôbre dexxiiii[m]. Et ceulx delamer voyans ledeliege ⁊fortune eſtre tournee ſur leurs gens ſen fuyrent et ne peuret̂ eſtre pourſuis. p̊rce q̂led chevallr̂ blanc navoit aucuns navires. Touteffoiz leſd turqs ſe combatiret̂ baill͡l

to sleep today, and from our countries we will come to aide by arms and ships, cutters, and siege engines, by which we have the intention to resist courageously, not only against your pedestrians carrying crosses, but also against Germany, Rome, and France, if we are incited against them. And with the aid of Neptune, god of the sea, we have the intention to cross the Hellespont and of the Sea of Marmara with an innumerable navy of ships by sails and oars. And we have also the intention to cross by the northern region and visit, especially to Dalmatia and Croatia. Given in the year of Muhammed 840, in June, in our triumphal palace, sealed and registered.

Assault by Christians against the Turks

Remember a knight named the white knight, marshal of Hungary, who was not noble, because he was marshal before he put himself in the war, captain under the king of Hungary. He put himself on the field in order to fight the Turks, and he had in his company 20,000 to 24,000 soldiers, who had already won the port of Sambrime, and the said Turk at that time had around 80,000 men. At which port they were for fifteen days in order to await all the power that could come under him and his men. When this came to the knowledge of the said white knight, he left from Maurienne and came to join himself to the said Turk around two hours before daybreak, and there was such combat between those who were on the land that all were killed, until the number was 24,000. And those on the sea, seeing the disaster and fortune turning against their men, they fled and they were not afraid of being followed because the said white knight had no ships. Nevertheless, the said Turks fought hard and such that the said white knight

et tant que led chevallier blanc fut fort navre et pluſſieurs deſes gens. Et ainſſi ſen Retourna et yfurent prins cinquante turcqs ou environ. deſquelz lechlr̃ blanc en envoya ſix. aupappe nicollas. ſix au Roy defrac̃e et ſix. amonſ^r^ debourgongne. Et lepropre couſin du turcq. yfut prins et par ainſſi demeura led port auchlr̃ blanc.

Commet̂ ung auguſton docteur en theologie fut preſche publicquemet̂ pource quil ceſtoit donne alcememy

Audit. an mil cccc. cinquante trois lexviii. Iour deMay fut prononcee ĉtaine Sentence prt̂ leRoy par monſ.^r^ lechâcellr̃ defrance cont̂ Iaques ceur devat̂ nomme côme convaincu des cas pour leſquilz Il eſtoit emp̂ſône en lamanr̃e qui ſenſuyt. Combien q̂ led Iacq̃z ceur pour les criſmes par lui commis ⁊p̲petrez euſt confiſque euſt confiſque corps ⁊biens. Touteſſoiz leRoy qui touſiours degrant equite en preferant miſericorde audevant deIuſtice deſirant auſſi lamendement et convertiſſement dun chc̃n pecheur et non lamort. lui Remet degrace eſpecialle. lamort et lui ſauve lavie ⁊leꝯdampne aRachatr̃ des mains des ſarraſins lexpien̂ quil a Rendu ſe Il eſt en lieu quil ſe puiſſe faire ~~quil~~ quelque ſomme dargent quil doive couſter ou ſinon aRachater des mains deſd ſarraſins ung aut̂ xpien̂s. C Item pour les ſommes dedeniers par lui Indeuement prinſes ⁊extorquees ſur les ſubgetz duRoy montans aſommes Ineſtimables Il eſt ꝯdampne alaſomme decent mille eſcus. C Item et pour les offences par lui commiſes apluſſieurs et diverſes foiz leRoy leꝯdampne en laſomme detrois mille eſcuz. C Item. leſur-

was badly wounded and several of his men. And so he returned and there were captured fifty Turks or therearound, to which this white knight only wanted to give life, for which the white knight sent six to the pope Nicholas, six to the king of France, and six to the duke of Burgundy. And the full cousin of the Turk was captured and by so the said port remained with the white knight.

How an Augustinian, doctor in theology, was publically preached again because he had given himself over to Alchemy

In the said year 1453, the twenty-eighth day of May, certain sentence was pronounced, the king being present, by monseigneur the chancellor of France against Jacques Cœur, before named, as convicted for the case for which he was imprisoned in the manner which follows. How the said Jacques Cœur, for the crimes committed and perpetrated by him, had confiscated his body and goods. However, the king, who always of great equity in preferring mercy before justice, desiring also the amendment and conversion of each sinful person and not his death, remitted to him by special grace death and saved his life, and condemned him to redeem by the hands of the Saracens the Christian that he had rendered to them, if he is still in a place that he can do this, whatever sum of money that it ought to cost, or if not, to redeem from the hands of the said Saracens another Christian. C Item, for the sums of money unjustly taken and extorted by him from the subjects of the king, totalling near-inestimable sums, he is condemned to the sum of 10,000 écus. C Item, and for the offences committed by him at several and different times, the king condemns him with the sum of 3,000 écus. C Item, the surplus of all

pl⁹ detous et chcn͡s ſes biens quelq̂ part quilz ſoient ſont et demoureront confiſques aud ſ^r. C Item Il eſt prive det-outes offices Royaulx ſecretz ⁊publiques et deſclare eſtre ~~Inabiller~~ Inhabille aIamaiz les tenir. C Item et avecques ce eſt banny atouſiours du Royaulme defrance. C Item ſera tenu faire amende au Roy honnorable alaperſonne deſon procureur ſans chappron ⁊deſchaint une torche dedix livres peſant en ſes mains en diſant que faulcement ⁊mauvaiſe-ment Il aRendu led xpien͡ auſd ſaraſins et auſſi led harnois et armures en Requerant adieu mercy ⁊aIuſtice. C Item eſt deſclare les ſcellez des ſeigneurs delafaiete et et decadil-lac eſtre nulz ⁊denulle valleur. et q̂ led Iacques ceur ne ſes hr̂tiers ne ſen pourront aider alencontre deulx. Et comme nulz et denulle valleur caſſez ⁊adnullez leur furent Ren-duz. C Apres lequel arreſt prononce leRoy fiſt dire par ſond chancellier ces parolles Reſerve auRoy touchant led ban-niſſemet̂ ⁊autŝ choſes labonne grace ⁊plaiſir duRoy.

Grace et amende hônourable et prammelle.

ET. au Regard deladamoiſelle demortaigne combi-en quelle ait confixque corps et biens touteſſoiz en conſideracion degrans ſervices q̂ les predeceſſeurs deliu ⁊ſon mary ont faiz auRoy. led ſeigneur lui Remet lamort et lui Reſtitue ſes biens comme non confiſques. Et lui eſt deffendu en paine deconfixcacion de corps et debiens de-Non approcher laperſonne du Roy ne delaRyne dedix lieues pres et auſſi aeſte ꝯdampnee affaire amende hônorable au

and each of his goods, whatever portion they were, are and will remain confiscated to the said lord. C Item, he is deprived of all royal offices, secret and public, and declared to be unable to ever hold them. C Item, and with this, he is banished forever from the kingdom of France. C Item, he will be held to make amends to the king honourably, in the person of his representative, without hood and chains, a bundle of sticks weighing ten pounds in his hands, saying that falsely and maliciously, he rendered the said Christian to the said Sarrasins, and also the said harness and armors, requesting from God mercy and justice. C Item, the seals of the seigneurs de Lafayette and de Cadillac are declared to be void and of no value, and that of the said Jacques Cœur and his heirs cannot aide against them. And as void and of no value, broken and cancelled, they were rendered to them. C After which arrest was pronounced, the king made to say by his said chancellor these words, except to the king, touching upon the said banishment and other things, the good grace and pleasure of the king.

Thanks and honourable amends and reparation

And in regard to the damsel of Mortagne, such that he had confiscated her body and goods, always in consideration of the great services that his predecessors and his wife had made to the king, the said lord remitted to him the death penalty and restored to him his goods as if they were not confiscated. And he forced him, on pain of confiscation of body and goods, to not come within ten leagues of the person of the king nor of the queen, and also he is condemned to make honourable amends to the king in the person of his representative. In saying that

Roy alaperſonne deſon procureur. En diſaĩ que faulcement ⁊deſloyaument elle avoit occupe et accuſe led Iacques ceur. Iacques coulompne et martin prandoulz. en Requerant dece adieu et au Roy et alaIuſtice pardon et mercy. Et envrs̃ les deſſſd. ceſt aſſavoir envrs̃ led martin aeſte ꝯdampnee en laſomme deiiii.c livres tourñ. Et envrs̃ lafemme et les deux filles dud Iacques coulompne envrs̃ chacũe decent livres tl. qui môteĩ iii.c livres tournoiz.

Sentence prononce prt̃ leRoy. contre. Iacques. ceur.

Audit an ledimanche ſourveille fut eſ charfaude et preſche publiquement en lacite devreulx ⁊ꝯdamne ppetuellemeĩ es priſons deleveſque dicelle cite maiſtre guil̃le endeline docteur en theologie prieur deſaint germain en laye et audavant auguſtin ⁊deĉtaines auſ̃ ordres. lequel par temptacion et exortacion delennemy denfer Auquel Il ceſtoit donne pour acomplir ſes delitz mondains. et par eſpãl pour faire ſon plaiſir et voullente dune dam̃ chevallereſſe comme on diſoit. Et ſemiſt en telle ſervitute delennemy quil lui convenoit eſtre en certain lieu. Touteſſoiz quil eſtoit Innuite par led ennemy ouquel lieu Ilz avoient acouſtume faire leur conſiſtoire. Et ne lui failloit q̂ monter ſur ung ballay que Il eſtoit preſtement tranſporte la ou led conſiſtoire ſefaiſoit. Et confeſſa led me guillaume deſabonne voullente avoir fait hôage aud ennemy en ſemblance et eſpace dun mouton en lebaiſant par lefondement. Et perſevera led maiſtre guillaume par pluſſieurs et diverſes annees en ſon dampnable propos. et avoit touſiors aide ⁊confort

falsely and disloyally she had occupied and accused the said Jacques Cœur, Jacques de Coulonne, and Martin Prandoux, in asking for this pardon and mercy to God, and to the king and to the justice, pardon and mercy. And toward the abovesaid, it is known toward the said Martin to be condemned and the sum of 400 livres tournais. And toward the wife and two daughters of the said Jacques de Coulonne, toward each, of 100 livres tournais, which totals 300 livres tournais.

Sentence pronounced by the king against Jacques Cœur

In the said year, the Sunday two days before [Christmas], was condemned perpetually to the prisons of the bishop of this city master Guillaume Edeline, doctor in theology, prior of Saint-Germain-en-Laye, and before an Augustinian monk and of certain other orders, who devised and preached publicly in the city of Évreux, by the temptation and exortation of the enemy from Hell, which he was given to accomplish his mundane delights and especially to make his pleasure and will of a knight's wife, it is said. And he put himself in such servitude of the enemy that it suited him to be in a certain place. Every time that he was mentioned by the said enemy, at which place they were accustomed to making their consistory. And all he had to do was climb on a broomstick that he was presently transported there where the said consistory had been made. And the said messire Guillaume confessed by his good will to have made homage to the said enemy in the form and semblance of a sheep, kissing him by the feet. And the said master Guillaume perservered for several and many years in his damnable purpose, and he always had aide and comfort from the

dud ennemy ence q̂ Il le boulloit Requerir. Et Iucques ace quil fut accuſe ⁊actant dud mallefice parquoy fut areſte ⁊determe priſonnier. depuis lequel empriſonnement fait par Iuſtice. lapuiſſance delennemy fut denul effect. Et demoura led maiſtre guillaume en lafoſſe aupain et aleaue par lacondampnacion que deteſt. Et lui Remonſtra Inquiſiteur delafoy moult haul tement ⁊ſollempnellement les haultes p̂dicacions et enſeignemens quil avoit faiz ⁊enſſeignez au peuple en temps paſſe quant Il alloit par lepays preſchr̂ lafoy deIhus̄ et pluſſieurs autŝ Remonſtrances lui furent faictes p̲hd Inquiſiteurs. Et fut metter en lap̄nce degrant multitude de peuple devant lad predicacion dud Inquiſite[r]. Apres laquelle Remonſtrance led maiſtre guil̄le ſachant et conſiderant quil avoit deluigue moult grandement envr̂s dieu nor̂ createur et Redempteur. commenca agemir et doullour et deſon meffait en criant mercy adieu. Alevesq̂ et alaIuſtice et en ſoy Recommandant aux prieres des aſſiſtans. En apres fut enferre et mene en lafoſſe pour faire penitence du treſornible cas quil lui eſtoit advenu.

Ambaſſade defrance en eſpaigne.

Lan. mil cccc. cinquantre quatre. Se partit treſReverend pere en dieu. maiſtre Iehan bernard arceveſque detour. et meſſ.[re] guillot deſtan chlr̂ ſeneſchal deRouargue pour allr̂ en ambaxade depar leRoy defrance devr̂s leRoy de caſtille pour confirmer les aliances des Roys de france et deſpaigne.

said enemy in that which he required. And until that which he was accused and attained for the said maleficence, for which he was arrested and detained as a prisoner, for which imprisonment made by justice, the power of the enemy was of no effect. And the said master Guillaume remained in a low pit with bread and water by the condemnation that he hated. And an inquisitor of the faith very highly and solemnly showed him the high predications and teachings that he had done and taught to the people in times passed, when he went by the lands to preach the faith of Jesus Christ, and several other remonstrations which were made to him by this inquisitor. And it was put in the presence of a great quantity of people before the said preaching of the said inquisitor. After which remonstrations, the said master Guillaume, knowing and considering that he had transgressed very strongly toward God, our creator and Redeemer, began to groan and suffer, and, for his misdeeds, crying mercy to God, to the bishop, and to justice, and recommending himself to the good prayers of the assistants. Afterwards, he was locked up and led to the pit in order to make penance for the very enormous crime that he had done.

Ambassador of France in Spain

In the year 1454, the very reverend father in God, master John Bernard, archbishop of Tours, and messire Guillot d'Étaing, a knight, seneschal of Rouergue, left as ambassadors for the king of France to the king of Castile to confirm the alliances of the kings of France and of Spain.

Garifon degens darmes abourdeaulx.

Oudit an envoya leRoy grant nombre de gens darmes et defrancs archiers dedans laville et cite debordeaulx. et ordonna faire deux chafteaulx en Icelle cite pour leur lexample en fubection. donc lun eftoit fcitue fur lebord dela Riviere et laut̂ alaut̂ bout delaville ducofte devers bierne. Et eftoient pour lafortificacion deceulx faire fr̃ ordonnez et commis monf.[r] le conte declermont lefeigneur defantrailles lebailly delion. legouverneur delaRochelle fire Iahan bureau maier delad ville. meffire guifchard lebouffier. lefquilz firent groffe dilligence defaire befongner deIour en Iour efd deux chafteaulx qui feront fors mr̃veilleuf aRefifter cont̂ to.[9] Et mefmement atenir les hâtans et demourans en Icelle ville ⁊cite deb[r] deaulx en fubuctôn pl·
[9] conquis maiz navoiet̂ efte

EN. ce mefmes temps et an print leduc diorck legouvernement du Royaulme dangleterre et fift mettre en prifon les ducz defombrecet et declocefter. Ceft affavoir le duc defombrecet en lagroffe tour delondres. et celui declocefter eu chafteau deproufort.

Mariage demonf.[r] decharolois

EN cemefme temps et an. monf.[r] leconte decharolloiz filz duduc debourgogne efpoufa lafille duduc debourbon. Et mourult leRoy defpagne en liage decinquante ans qui fut grant dommage car Il eftoit bon saige et beau prince.

Garrison of men-at-arms at Bourdeaux

In the said year 1454, the king sent a great number of men-at-arms and free archers into the said town and city of Bourdeaux, and he ordered to build two castles in this city as an example of subjugation to them; thus, one was situated on the bank of the river, and the other on the other side of the town, on the side toward Béarn. And for the fortification of these were commissioned and ordained monseigneur the count of Clermont; the seigneur de Xaintrailles; the bailiff of Lyon; the governor of La Rochelle; Jean Bureau, master of the said city; [and] messire Guichard le Boursier, who made great diligence to do what was needed from day to day in the said two castles, which were marvellously strong to resist against everything, and even to hold the inhabitants and remain in this town and city of Bourdeaux for those in subjugation, more conquered as it had not been.

IN this same time and year, the duke of York took the government of the kingdom of England and put in prison the dukes of Somerset and Gloucester—it is known, the duke of Somerset in the large tower of London and that of Gloucester in the castle of Pomfret.

Marriage of the monseigneur de Charolais

IN this same time and year, monseigneur the count of Charolais, son of the duke of Burgundy, married the daughter of the duke of Bourbon. And the king of Spain died at the age of fifty years, which was a great tragedy, because he was a very good, wise, and handsome prince.

Lamort dupappe. nicollas.

EN. Icellui an mourult lepape nicollas qui eſtoit encores en ſa force. Mais Il fut empoiſonne comme Il fut trouve quant Il fut ouvert par les phiſiciens et fut eſleu pappe calixte.

Jehenoanic depriſonniers en angleťre

EN. Icellui an meſmes eu moys defevrier leRoy henry dangleťre manda aucuns des ſeigneurs deſon pays. et leur Remonſtra commeť leduc deſombrecet et leduc decloceſter ſes propres parens et deſon sange eſtoient priſonniers. Si voulloit que ſeIlz neſtoient trouves bien gran dement charges des cas criminelz touchant la mageſte Royalle quilz fuſſent delivrez. Aquoy furent dacord aucuns ſeigneurs et meſmemeť lemaire et gouverneur delondres en baillant bonne et ſeure caupcion deſter adroit. Et tantoſt apres ladelivrance deſd ſeigneurs vint led duc deſombrecet en poious et aucte.[e] et telle que Il eult leRegnie et gouvernement du Roy. Et ce voyant led duc diorck. ſedepartit delacoť et ſen alla laplus ſecrettement quil peult en ſon pays doubtant q̂ led duc deſombrecet nelui furſt deſplaiſir.

Comment leſire deleſparre. fut decappette apoitiers.

EN ce meſme temps et an fut prins leſ.[r] deleſparre. lequel autreffoiz en allant conť ſon ferment avoit eſte querir les angloiz pour Remettre en leur main lepays debordellaiz

The death of Pope Nicholas

IN this year, the pope Nicholas, who was still in full strength, died. But he was poisoned, as it was found when he was opened by the surgeons, and Pope Calixtus was elected.

Release of prisoners in England

IN this same year, in the month of February, the king Henry of England ordered several of the lords of his country and showed them how the duke of Somerset and the duke of Gloucester, his rightful relatives and of his blood, were prisoners. If he wanted that, if they were not found very greatly charged of a criminal case touching the royal magesty, they would be released. For which it was agreed by several lords and even the mayor and governor of London, releasing fully and surely, cautious of their rights. And soon after the deliverance of the said lords, the said duke of Somerset returned in credit and authority, and such that he had the kingdom and government of the king. And the said duke of York seeing this, he left from the court and went as secretly as he could into his lands, fearing that the said duke of Somerset was displeased with him.

How the sire de Lesparre was decapitated at Poitiers

IN this same time and year, the sire de Lesparre was taken, who otherwise, in going against his oath, had asked the English to return into their hands the lands of the Bordelais, and in this,

et ence fut traicte aſon ſouverain ſeigneur Roy defrance. Et combien que lad traiſon euſt eſte annexer et magnifiſtre. Neantmains leRoy aladeſerniere prinſe debordeaulx ſoy monſtraẗ touſiours begnin et miſericordz. lui Remiſt la vie et fut ſeullement bany des pays deguyenne et debordellaiz. Et depuis par linſtigacion de lennemy denature ſoubz dun ſaufconduit Il cuidoit encores de~~Recheſt~~ Rechef Remettre led pays debordellaiz es mains deceulx angloiz comme plus faulx et deſloyal traictre que paravant. Et pource que leſcripture dit q millum. abſconditrum. q. non. fratir nec occullum. qd. non. renellatur. Cen eſt adire que mille choſe tant ſoit ſegrettemeẗ et mechement faicte ne peult eſtre celui quelle ne ſoit ſceue me pour demourer lôguemeẗ choſe mal faite Impugnie. Et venu alacognoiſſ du Roy fut prins mene en laville depoitiers et ſurce queſtionne. Et apres lachoſe par lui confeſſee Iuridicuement ꝯademne amourir. Et fut baille au bourreau. lequel lui oſta lamoulle deſon chapperon. ceſt aſſavoir lateſte. Et puis fut eſcartelle et mis en ſix pieces et pendu en divers lieux comme on acouſtume defr̂ en tel cas. Et fut ꝯdampnie et abon droit qui eſt et peult eſta exemple atous autres.

Commeẗ toute laconte darmignac Fut miſe en lamain du Roy

Lan mil cccc. cent cinquante cinq. en moys demay le-Roy envoya monſ.[r] leconte de clermont. monſ.[r] de-loheac mareſchal defrance et pluſſieurs auẗs capitaines en laconte darmaignac. Et pareillement envoya leconte dedampmâtin lebailly devreulx et pluſſieurs auẗs dupays

he committed treason to his sovereign lord, the king of France, and such that the said treason had been ajoined and manifested. Nonetheless, at the last capture of Bourdeaux, the king, showing himself always benign and merciful, remitted to him life and he was only banished from the lands of Guyenne and the Bordelais. And since, by the instigation of the enemy of nature, under the shadow of a safe conduct, he thought again to return the said lands of the Bordelais into the hands of these Englishmen, he is a more false and disloyal traitor than before. And on this matter the scripture says: there is nothing hidden that was at one time found. This is to say that a thousand things done secretly and malevolently cannot remain without someday being known nor a wrongdoing remain for long unpunished. And coming to the knowledge of the king, he was captured in the town of Poitiers and questioned about this. And after the thing was confessed by him, he was legally condemned to death. And he was delivered to the executioner, who cut him from the groin to the hairline, that is to say the head. And then he was quartered and made into six pieces, and taken into different places, as one is accustomed to do in such a case. And he was condemned and by rightful law, which was and could be an example to all others.

How all the county of Armagnac was put into the hand of the king

In the year 1455, in the month of May, the king sent monseigneur the count of Clermont; monseigneur de Lohéac, marshal of France; and several other captains into the county of Armagnac; and at the same time, he sent the count of Dammartin, the bailiff of Évreux, and several others into the lands of Rouergue against

de Rouarge. Alencontre dud conte darmaignac pource quil navoit point voullu obbair amettre larceveſque daux en poceſſion et ſaiſine de larceveſche lequel eſtoit eſleu abon droit et dece avoit ſes bulles dupappe. Et voulloit led conte q̂ ung nomme deleſcun contre tout ordre dedroit leſuſt. et lavoit boute en ſad cite et fait prend ſapoceſſion oult̂ legre et voullons duRoy. Et pource que led conte avoit poſe led deſtun defait et deforce. leRoy moult Indigne ſurce envoya gens darmes devaт̂ lacite deleſtore pour ymettre leſiege. laquelle ſe Rendit aux gens du Roy. Et ~~pareillement~~ toutes les places delad conte et celles deRouargue et celle duvaldore. Et ainſſi perdit led conte toutes ſes teres par leRebellion quil avoit faicte au Roy. Car forte choſe ceſt deRegiber contre leſguillon. Et ainſſi ſe fait ſen les Retournerent leſd ſeigneurs et cappitaines.

Comment leduc diorck oult le. govn̂mement duRoy.^{me} dangleт̂re.

Oudit an et meſme temps henry Roy dan gleт̂re par leconſeil duduc deſombrecet manda to^{9} les grands ſeigneurs deſon Royaume venir devers lui atout leur ſimple eſtat pour ordonnoit comme Il diſoit deto^{9} les haulx affaires deſon Royaulme donc en une une grant partie alondres. Se ſepenca leduc diorck. q̂ Il ſe trou veroit et defait ſemiſt en chemin et ſepartit deſon pays atout mil combatans. Et apres lui venoient dequatre acinq mille auт̂s combatâs deſquilz mil combatans fut leRoy et ceulx de londres biens advêtiz et non des auт̂s qui venoieт̂ apres. Si ſedelibera leRoy et leduc deſombrecet acompaignez. duconte denantaubellan

the said count of Armagnac, because he no longer wanted to obey to put the archbishop of Auch in possession and seisen of the archbishopric, who was elected by good right and for this he had obtained his bulls from the pope. And the said count wanted one named Lescun against all order of right, and he had pushed him from his said city and made him take his other possession against the desire and the will of the king. And because the said count had positioned the said de Lescun by deed and by force, the king, very indignant for this, sent men-at-arms before the city of Lectoure in order to lay siege to it, which place rendered itself immediately to these men of the king, and all the places of the said count and those of Rouergue and those of Valdore. And thus the said count lost all his lands by this rebellion that he had made to the king, because it is a hard thing to push against the quillons. And this deed being so done, the said lords and captains returned.

How the duke of York had the government of the king of England

In the said year and same time, Henry, king of England, by the council of the duke of Somerset, ordered all the great lords of his kingdom to come before him with their simple estate to order, as it is said, all the high business of his kingdom; so, a large part of them came to London. The duke of York thought to himself that he would go there, and by deed, he set out and left from his lands with around 1,000 soldiers. And after him came from 4,000 to 5,000 other soldiers, of which 1,000 soldiers was [from] the king, and those of London were well advised and not all the others who came afterwards. So, the king and the duke of Somerset, accompanied by the count of Northumberland and by several oth-

et de pluſſieurs auſ̃s ſeigneurs et dece quilz peureẽ finer haſtivement degens dedens londres. Et eſtoit leRoy tout eſbahy decequil venoit en armes ſur les champs et ne ſavoit Rien dela groſſe compaignie qui ſuyvoit led duc diorck. delongtz. pourquoy leRoy ſemiſt ſur les chap̃s et chevaucha lui. et ſon oſt tellement q̃l Rencôtra Icellui duc. Et tantoſt ſans quelque proces commencerent leſd parties afrapper les ungtz ſur les auſ̃s. Et la fut ſifort combatu quil yen eult grant foiſſon demors dun coſte ⁊dauſ̃. tou teſſois lavictoire delaIournee demoura aud duc diorck. Et furent tuez leſd duc deſombrecet et leconte deNotoubellan et pluſſieurs autres grans ſeigneurs que auſ̃s Iucques au nombre dequatre acinq. cens hommes. Et meſmemeẽ fut leRoy navoir et perce dune fleche parmy lecol. et fut en grant admentire deſon corps. Et fut pas led duc diorck prins pluſſieurs p̊ſ tant ſ.[rs] nobles que auſ̃s. Leſquelz Il mena alondres avecques leRoy. Et lafureẽ les ungz delivrez et les auſ̃s pugniz ſelon leurs demeurtes. et deceſte heure fut tout legouv̂ne ment du Roy Renverſſe. Et demoura led duc diorck. gouverneur du Roy dangleſ̂re et du Royaume ſeul et pour letout.

Commeẽ leRoy miſt ledaulphine en ſa main

Lan mil CCCC Cinquante Six leRoy ſachant mondit ſ[r] ledaulphin ſon filz aiſne eſtre party deſon pays dedaulphine et ſen eſtre alle es pays demonſ[r] leduc debourgogne deſraẽ parler aud duc fut mal content dece quil ne lui en avoit Rien fait ſavoir. Et pource q̃l doubtoit quil ne creuſt mauvaiz conſeil et quil neſegouvênaſt auſ̃ment q̃

er lords, deliberated, and for that which they could gather hastily from men within London. And the king was very amazed for that which came in arms on the field, and he did not yet know of the large company which followed the said duke of York from afar, for which the king put himself in the field and rode, he and his army, such that he encountered this duke. And soon, without any forewarning, the said parties struck, one against the other. And there was so strong combat that there was a great many killed, on one side and the other; however, the victory remained at the end of the day with the said duke of York. And the said dukes of Somerset and the count of Northumberland were killed, and several others, great lords and others, until the number reached 400 to 500 men. And even the king was wounded and pierced by an arrow through the collar, and he was in great danger to his person. And the said duke of York took several prisoners, both lords, nobles, and others, which he took to London with the king. And some were released there, and others punished according to their merits, and at this hour all the government of the king was thrown out. And the said duke of York remained governor of the king of England and of the kingdom in all and for all.

How the king put Dauphiné into his hand

In the year 1456, the king, knowing the said monseigneur le Dauphin, his eldest son, to have gone from his land of Dauphiné and to have gone into the lands of monseigneur the duke of Burgundy in order to speak to the said duke, was very discontent since he had not let him know anything. And since he feared that he would believe bad advice and that he could not govern himself

par Raiſon. pour entrez ato[9] Inconveniens qui par faulte deſes ~~gouv~~ gouverneurs ſepouroient enſuir. Affin quil fuſt plus enclin aſoy Redduire et venir en ſon obbeiſſ devers lui comme vray filz doit eſtre aſon pere. Se tranſporta eu pays du daulphine atout noble compagnie degens darmes et leprint et ſaiſit et miſt en ſamain toutes ſes Rentes et Revenus enſemble toutes les villes chaſteaulx et fortereſſes decellui pays. Affin que ſond filz ne peuſt deRiens Iour eſperant deletrana par cemoyen. Et envoya gens darmes en pluſſ.[rs] et divers lieux pour garder les paſſages côme aponthoiſe acompiegne en labrye et aille[rs] en Reſcripvant aux bonnes villes con nebaillaſt aucun paſſage aud daulphin ne entree ~~aux~~ en bonne ville ne aſes gens auſſi Sans eſtre les plus fors. Et meſmement pource quil lui ſembloit trop vollage et plein deſavoullête comme leRoy lapercevoit et avoit aperceva clerement en tant que quant Il ſe partiſt davec leRoy ſon pere Il ne demanda conge que pour. Iiii. Moys. et Il demoura aſagrant deſplaiſaire bien pres dedix ans

Commet̂ monſ.[r] dalencon fut. areſte priſonnier aparis.

Oudit an fut prins et areſte priſonnier aparis. leduc dalencon couſin duRoy. Le Iour defeſte du Sainct Sacrement. Et lefiſt priſonnier duRoy demain miſe. Leconte dedunoiz et delongueville. Par vertu dun mandemet̂ Royal appellez avecques lui. leprevoſt delad ville deparis et deux ou trois autŝ duconſeil du Roy. et fut mene amelun ou monſeigne.[r] Leconneſtable alla pour lequeſtionner ſur aucun cas touch-

otherwise, that, in order to avoid all inconveniences which by fault of his governors could have ensued, so that he was more inclined to reduce and return into his obedience, as a true son ought to be towards his father, he went to the said lands of Dauphiné with a noble company of men-at-arms, and he captured and seized and put into his hands all his rents and revenues, together with all the towns, castles, and fortresses of this land, so that his said son could not enjoy anything anymore, hoping by this means to come back to him. And he sent men-at-arms into several and different places in order to guard the passages, such as at Pontoise, at Compiègne in Brie, and elsewhere, writing to the good towns that one should not permit any passage to the said Dauphin, nor entry into a good town, nor to his men as well, without being the stronger. And similarly, because it seemed to him that he was very flighty and clear of his will, as the king perceived it, and he had perceived clearly in such that when he departed from the king, his father, he did not request leave for four months, and he remained, to his great displeasure, for well near ten years.

How monseigneur d'Alençon was taken prisoner at Paris

In the said year, the duke of Alencon, cousin of the king, was captured and arrested at Paris the day of the feast of the Holy Sacrament. And he was made prisoner by the king by the hand of the count of Dunois and Longueville by virtue of a royal mandate, named with him the provost of the said town of Paris, and two or three others of the council of the king, and he was then taken to Melun, where monseigneur the constable went in order to question him on whether the case touched on

ant criſme delezemajeſte. Et dela led conte dedunoiz porta nouvelle deſa prinſe au Roy devers lequel Il fut mene tantoſt apres. Pource quil diſoit tout plainement quil diroit au Roy ſon fait et non aautre.

Certains articles envoyez au Roy depar monſ^r deboupgogne touc͡h monſ^r ledaulphin

APRES. que mondſeigneur ledaulphin eult eſtre par certain eſpace detemps avec led duc debourgogne ſans lecongie et aucte^r deſon pere et quil avoit envoye depuis c̃taines lectres faiſans et portans en ſoy Requeſte doubtat̂ eſtre en lamalveuillance deſon pere. pour. cauſe dece quil ceſtoit ainſſi abſente ſoudaine ment delui deſquelles Requeſtes Icellui daulphin navoit Riens obtenu. Icellui duc debourgogne ſoubz umbre debien envoya ſes ambaſſadeurs devers leRoy. Ceſt aſſavoir. meſſ.^re Iacques decroy. ſimon delaing et auſ̂ et prêteren au Roy Icelles lectres touchant led daulphin portat̂ credance. leſquelles eſtoient Redduites en. Iiii. pointz et furent baillers par eſcript agrengne^r memoire en lamaniere qui ſenſ. Lepremier eſt q̂ laRemonſtrance demond ſ.^r debourgogne frê au Roy. quil nedoit point eſtre mal content delaRecepcion qui aeſte frtê amond ſ.^r ledaulphin en ſes pays et ſ^ries. Car Il aeſt meu afaire Icelle Recepcion pour lonneur duRoy duquel Il eſt aiſne filz et quil eſtoit venu par devers lui deloingtain pays. et que ſans charge deſon honneur envers toutes nacions xp͡iens Il ne leuſt peu Reffuſez en ſes t̂res et ſ^ries et lui faire honneur ⁊ſervice tel quil lui appartient. C Leſecond eſt cône led duc debour-

the crime of lèsé majesté. And from there, the said count of Dunois newly carried by his capture to the king, toward whom he was handed soon afterwards. For which he said plainly that he would tell the king the facts and none other.

Certain articles sent to the king by monseigneur de Burgundy touching on monseigneur the Dauphin

AFTER my said lord, the Dauphin, had stayed for a certain space of time with the said duke of Burgundy, without the leave and authority of his father, and he had sent to him since certain letters making and carrying within his request, suspecting to be in the ill-will of his father because he had absented himself so suddenly from him, from which requests this dauphin had obtained nothing at all. This duke of Burgundy, under the shadow of goodness, sent his ambassadors to the king—it is known: messire Jacques de Croy, Simon de Lalaing, and others—and they presented to the king these letters touching the said Dauphin, carrying promises, which were reduced to four points, and these delivered in writing, for greater memory, in the manner that follows: The first is the remonstration that my said lord of Burgundy made to the king, that he no would no longer be discontented at the reception that he made to my said lord the Dauphin in his lands and lordships, because he had been moved to make this reception for the honour of the king, for whom he is eldest son, and he came to him from a distant land and that, without damaging his honour towards all Christian nations, he would not have refused him in his lands and lordships, and he made honour and service such as belonged to him. C The second is that the said duke of

gogne quant Il eſt aRrive a brucelles devr̃s mond ſ.[r] ledaulphin en parlant enſemble Il letrouva fort eſpouvente. Et lui diſt entre autres choſes comment Il avoit envoye devers le Roẙ. Et lui avoit fait faire pluſſieurs offres et Requeſtes. Et que le Roy avoit bien accepte les offres. Maiz au Regard des Requeſtes Il ne lui en avoit Rien adcorde. C Letiers com ment mond ſ.[r] ledaulphin lui avoit dit lavoulête quil avoit deſoy emploier cont̂ leturcq. Et quat̂ Il plairoit au Roy lui donner chr̃ge deceff̃ et baillr̃ gens pour lacompagner ainſſi q̂ a aiſne filz defrance appartient. led duc ſoffre deſoy mettre ſoubz liu et de lacompaigner oud voyaige et ſervice. C Lequart quil plaiſe au Roy Recepvoir mond ſ.[r] ledaulphin en ſa bonne grace et le Redduire et actirer alui. Et ace ſoffre led ce ceſt lebon plaiſir du Roy. et en tant quil touche lepays du dauphine ſetenir atant ſans plus avant proceder. C Sur leſquels quatre pointz aeſte Reſpondu auſd ambaſſadeurs en lamaniere qui ſenſuyt.

Reſponce du Roy ſus leſd articles.

Et. premierement quant alaRecepcion de mond ſ.[r] ledaulphin. leRoy abien côgnoiſſ que alui eſt bien deu lui eſtre fait honneur et bon Recueil par led ſ.[r] debourgogne et autres princes dece Royaulme quant Ilz ſauroient et con gnoiſtroient que mond ſ.[r] ledaulphin ſe maintiêdroit envr̃s leRoy ſon pere comme bon et obbeiſſant filz eſt tenu defaire et aut̂ment ne ſe doit f̃ par Raiſon car lonneur qui lui eſt deu deppend duRoy. C Quant ace que led duc debourgogne a trouve mond ſ.[r] ledaulphin fort eſpouvente deſirat̂ atout ſon ceur eſtre et demourer en labonne grace duRoy et

Burgundy, when he arrived at Brussels to my said lord the Dauphin, in speaking together, he found him very scared, and he said to him amongst other things how he had sent to the king and had tried to make to him several offers and the requests, and that the king had well accept the offers. But in regard to the requests, he had accorded him nothing. C The third article explained how my said lord the Dauphin had said to him the desire that he had to go against the Turk, and that he pleaded to the king to give him charge to do this and release men to accompany him, as belonged to the eldest son of France, the said duke offered to put him under him and to accompany and serve him on the said voyage. C The fourth, that it is pleasing to the king to receive my said lord the Dauphin in his good grace and to reduce him and entice him, and to this, the said offers that it is the good pleasure of the king and such that touching the lands of Dauphiné, to hold onto it without having proceeded further. C Upon which four points he responded to the said ambassadors in the manner that follows:

Response of the king to the said articles

And firstly, when at the reception of my said lord, the Dauphin, the king knew well that to him it is well owed to make honour and receive well by the said duke of Burgundy and other princes of this kingdom, when they learned and knew that my said lord, the Dauphin, maintained himself toward the king, his father, as a good and obedient son is held to do, and otherwise, it must not be done by reason, because the honour which is due to him derives from the king. C When the said duke of Burgundy found that my said lord, the Dauphin, was terrified, desiring with all his heart to be and remain in the good grace of the king, and that he

quil lui octroye ſes humbles Re queſtes et que le Roy ne lui avoulu adcorder. le Roy eſt fort eſmr̃veille decellui eſpouventement. Et ne ſoit congnoiſtre cauſe pourquoy. Car Il atouſiours trouve leRoy enclin aleRecpevoir en ſa bonne grace. Et en lannee paſſee q̂mond ſ.r le daulphin aenvoye devers leRoy par pluſſieurs foiz. et encores deſrnierement gabriel vernes et leprieur des celeſtins davignon Il ler adit debouche en lapr̃ce ducardinal dadvignon envoye depas noſ̃ ſaint pere lepappa et autŝ ſeigneurs duſangt et notables hômes en grant nombre quil eſtoit ~~a~~ content q̂ mond ſ.r ledaulphin vinſtſt devers lui et deleRecpevoir et traicter comme Bon ſeigneur doit Recevoir et traicter ſon bon ⁊obeiſſant filz. lui pardonner et oublier quilzconques choſe paſſers. Et pource que leſdeſſd devernes et prieur des celeſtins diſoient q̂ mond ſ.r avoit de grans craintes. LeRoy leur diſt q̂ quat̂ Il lui fera ſavoir cedouc ceſte crainte lui print Il lui en feroit telle et ſi bonne Reſponce quil ſeroit bien content et nauroit cauſe deRien doubter. Ainſſi na pas tenu au Roy ne ne tient q̂ mond ſ.r ne ſoit en ſa bonne grace et hors deſes doubtes et craintes. Maiz au Regard des Requeſtes quil lui fiſt faire. Ceſt affavoir de non venir devers lui ~~mil~~r deſes ſerviteurs qui touſiours ont eſte dela part demond ſ.r miſes et couchees cõme cõdiciõnelles en faiſant les offres par lui faictes Iamaiz leRoy neuſt eſte meu neconſeille deles lui adcorder. Car ceuſt eſte alle directement contra ledeſir deto⁹ ceulx du Royaulme. et meſmement cont̂ leconſeil demonſ.r debourgongne et des autŝ ſeigneurs duſangc et notables ſeigne.rs deceRoyaulme qui lui ont conſeille et Requis deRedduire mond ſ.r ledaulphin et ſeſervir de lui. Avecques ce lepourvoir deſerviteurs et conſeillers prudes hômes et notables

convey to him his humble requests, and that the king did not want to grant to him, the king was very amazed for this terror, and he did not know the cause for it, because he had always found and been inclined to receive the king in his good grace. And so the year passed, which my said lord, the Dauphin, send to the king several times and Gabriel Vernes and the prior of the Celestines of Avignon still remained, the prince said to them by word of mouth via the cardinal of Avignon, sent to the feet of our Holy Father, the pope and other lords of the blood and notable men in great number, that he would be happy if my said lord the Dauphin would come to him and to receive him and negotiate as a good lord ought to receive and negotiate his good and obedient son, pardoning and forgiving him whatever thing passed. And since the abovesaid de Vernes and the prior of the Celestines had said that, my said lord had great fears. The king said to them that he would know where these fears came from, he made to let him know such and so good a response that he would be very contant and have no reason to doubt. Thus, he had not held to the king nor held that my said lord was not in his good grace and beyond his fears. But in regard to the requests that he made to him—it is known, not to come to him from his servants, who had always been on the side of my said lord, putting and laying down as conditions, in making the offers to him, the king would never be moved nor councilled to agree to them for him, because it would go directly against the desire of those of the kingdom and even against the council of monseigneur of Burgundy and of the other lords of the blood, and notable lords of this kingdom, who had given him council and requested that my said lord the Dauphin abase himself and serve him. With this, the power of servants and councillors, prudent and notable men, who have regard to his honour and goodness, and guided him to

qui aiet̂ Regard aſon honneur et bien. et leduire aſoy employer au ſervice et bien du Roy et deſon Royaulme ainſſi quil yeſt tenu et oblige deſâ par Raiſon. Et quant le Roy lui eult adcorde leſd Requeſtes meſd ſ.[rs] deſon ſangt et meſme ment to⁹ ceulx du Royaulme. euſſent eu grat̂ cauſe depencer q̂ lalongue abſence demond ſ.[r] ledaulphin euſt eſte par le Roy et deſon voulloir ce quil neſt pas. Car quat̂ mond ſ[r] partit deluy Il meult conge dedemeurer q̂ quatre moys. ou Il ademoure plus de x. ans augrat̂ Regret et deſplaiſir du Roy qui euſt eſte moult Ioyeaulx que durant letemps deſon abſence Il ſefuſt trouve es victorieuſes beſongnes qui ſeſont faictes en le Recouvrance duRoyaume. Car lagloire dupere eſt quant lefilz fait ouvres louables. Et quant aſes ſerviteurs le Roy euſt bien deſire en temps paſſe et encores deſireroit q̂ mond ſ.[r] ſeſerviſt degens notables qui touſio[r]s leconſeillaſſent et Induiſſent atoutes choſes qui fuſſent pour ſon bien et honneur. Et en lui laiſſant entour lui gens qui aut̂ment lecôſeilla ſſent ne me ſeroit pas pour Radraces ceſte matr̂e ainſſi que leRoy ledeſire et que pour lebien et honneur demond ſ.[r] Il fuſt expediant et neccеſ ſaire. C Letiers touchant lavoullête q̂ mondſ.[r] dit aavoir deſoy amployer auvoage deturquie quant leRoy aveu les lectres q̂ mond ſ.[r] lui a Reſcriptes deſaint glaude faiſantes mencion dud voyage. Il aeſte moult eſmr̂veille qui a meu mond ſ.[r] aſi ſouldainement prend ceſte nouvelle ymaginacion. delaquelle Il navoit par avant Rien fait ſavoir au Roy. Et ſemble bien q̂ ceſte une nouvelle coulleur prinſe pour touſiours eſloigner aſoy Redduire et venir devr̂s leRoy leſervir et obbair ainſſi quil doit. Et quat̂ Il euſt eu deſire defaire led voẙage Il deuſt ~ p̊ealablement avoir mis peine deſoy Redduire au Roy et

employ himself to the service and good of the king and of his kingdom, as he is held and obliged to do by reason. And when the king had granted him the said requests, my said lords of his blood, and even all those of his kingdom, would have had great cause to think that the long absence of my said lord, the Dauphin, would have been by the king and of his will, which it was not, because when my said lord left from him, he did not have leave to remain for four months and he had remained more than ten years, to the great regret and displeasure of the king, who had been very happy that during the time of his absence, he had found in the victorious needs that he had made in the recovery of the kingdom, because the glory of the father is when the son does loudable deeds. And when to his servants, the king had well desired in times passed—and still desired—that my said lord served himself with notable men, who always councilled him and induced him toward all things that were for his good and honour. And in him, he left still around him some men who otherwise councilled him, it would not be to address this matter, as the king desired, and therefore, for the good and the honour of my said lord, it is expedient and necessary for him to do. C The third, touching upon the will that my said lord was said to have endeavoured to voyage to Turkey, when the king saw the letters that my said lord had written to him, from Saint-Glaude, making mention of the said voyage, he was very surprised that my said lord was moved so suddenly to take this new imagination, for which he had not before done anything to make known to the king. And it seemed well that this was a new colour taken to always move away from being reduced and come to the king, to serve and obey him as he ought to do. And when he had had desire to make the said voyage, he ought first to have taken pains to submit himself to the king and to obey him, and so

de lui obbair ainſſi q̂ ſelon dieu et Raiſ Il doit deſirer lefaire. Et apres lui euſt peu dire et Remonſtrer laffection quil avoit aud voyage pour ſavoir pource lebon plaiſir duRoy. Sans lauctê et conſentement duquel Il nepeult ne nedoit faire telles entreprinſes. Et meſmemet̂ en ſi grands matiere. Et actendu q̂les angloiz anciens ennemys dece Royaulme chu͡n Ioʳ cefforcet̂ et mettent leurs ententes plus q̂ Iamaiz aIuinade les pays ſeigneuries et ſubgetz du Roy. Et que puis aucun temps par exquſicions degrans et ſubtilz moiens ont pourchaſſe dy avoir entrer et fait degrans entrepriſes. deſquelles ſe celles euſſent ſorti effect ſefuſſent enſuire dauſſi grans maulx et perilleux Inconveniens ace Royaulme quil y eult longc temps a. conſidere auſſi que leſd angloiz ont fait Reſponce au legat q̂ nor̂ Saint pere envoye par devers eulx quilz neveullet̂ entend aguilĝ paix. Maiz ſont en continuelle voullente deguerouer ~ cont̂ leRoy et ſon Royaulme. Il appert bien q̂mond ſ.ʳ napas grandement pence aleſtat et ſeurete deced Royaulme car ſeſeroit metlt̂ Icellui Royaulme entrop cuident peril que den vuyder lachevallerie et nobleſſe. Et demôur en guerre avecques ſes anciens ennemis qui continuellement mettre leur entente dy avoir entree par divers et ſubtilz moens côme dit eſt. Aquoy leRoy abien pourveu Iucques acy et a Intencion detouſiours ~~pource~~ pourvoir alaide denor̂ ſeigneur. Et quant leRoy par paix lôgues treves ou aut̂ment euſt veu et ꝑ verroit ſeurete en ſon Royaulme ainſſi quil afait dire et Remonſtr̂ anor̂ ſainct pere lepappe Il nya prince ne Roy xpie͡n qui plus avant ſevouſiſt emploier au ſecours delaxpiête quil euſt fait et feroit. Lequart quil pleuſt auRoy Retenir mond ſ.ʳ en ſabonne grace et touchant lepays dudaphine ſe te-

according to God and reason he ought to desire to do it. And after he had little to say to him and to show the affection that he had toward the said voyage, in order to know for the good pleasure of the king, without the authority and consent of whom he could not nor ought to do such enterprises, and even in such great matters. And awaiting the English, ancient enemy of this kingdom, each day striving and putting their desires more than ever to appeal to the lands, lordships, and subjects of the king. And that then, several times, by executions of great and subtle means, they had purchased, had entered into, and made great battles, through which they had fortified themselves, ensuring also great evils and perils, inconveniencing this kingdom that that it had for a long time, considering also that the said English had made a response to the legat of our Holy Father, sent to those that they did not want to hear of any peace, but they are of a continuous will to fight against the king and his kingdom. It appears well that my said lord had not greatly thought about the state and security of this said kingdom, because he would put this kingdom in too much peril by removing the knights and the nobility, and they would remain at war with his ancient enemies, who continuously put their agreement aside to have entered by various and subtle means, as it is said. To which the king had done well until now and had the intention to always do well, with the aide of Our Lord. And when the king, by peace, long treaties, or otherwise, had seen and would see security in his kingdom, so that he made to say and show to our holy father, the pope, there was no Christian king who ever before wanted to employ himself to the rescue of the Christians than he had and would do. The fourth that he would plead to the king to retain my said lord in his good grace and touching the lands of Dauphiné, to hold himself as before without proceeding further. The

nir atant ſans plus avant proceder. Le Roy atouſiours ~~eſtre~~ eſte preſt et encores eſt de Recevoir mondit ſ.[r] benignement quant deſapart Il ſe mettra en ſon devoir ainſſi que leRoy atouſio.[r] dit et fait dire aux gens demondſ.[r] quant Ilz ſont venus devers lui. Et au Regard du pays du daulphine quant le Roy aveu lamaniere demondſ.[r] et côme Il aeſte conſeille aſoy departir et abſenter ainſſi ſoudainement dud pays. Nonobſtant les doulces et gracieuſes Reſponces quil lui avoit faites. LeRoy pour obvier aux Inconveniens que pas leurmortement deceulx qui ont ainſſi cô ſeille mond ſ.[r] fuſſent peu venir leſquelz puis quilz ont ainſſi adventure ſaperſonne ꝑvoyes perilleuſes et dangereuſes ainſſi q̂ leſd ambaſ ſadeurs meſmes lont dit et propoſe eſtoit adouter que par lemoien dud pays et des places et fortereſſes dicellui Ilz euſſent peu faire et entreprend des choſes audeſplaiſir du Roy et p̊udice demond ſ.[r] et dupays le Roy aceſte conſeille deſoy tranſporter aud pays pour ydonner proviſion et mettre ſeurete en lamaniere q̂ aucun Inconvenient ny puiſſe advenir. En quoy touteſſoiz Il atellement procede q̂ to⁹ ceulx dupays quant Ilz ont aꝑceu lebon voulloir du Roy en ceſte matiere en ont eſte treſioyeulx et conſollez. Et eſtoit leRoy content quilz envoyaſſent devers monſ.[r] po[r] lui Remonſtrer ſon cas. Ladoulceur que leRoy atenue et eſſayant aleRedduire. Et abien leRoy eſperance que ouyes les Remonſtrances deceulx dud pays et par lebon conſeil et emortement demondſ.[r] de bourgongne mond ſ.[r] ſeRedduira et fera ſon debvoir envers lui ainſſi quil doir et ence faiſant leRoy oubliera toutes ſes deſplaiſances dutemps paſſe leRecevra en ſabonne grace et leRecueillera benignement comme bon ſeigneur et pere doit ſon bon et obbaiſſant filz

king had always been ready and still is to receive benignly my said lord, when on his part he put himself in his duty, so that the king had always said and made to say to the men of my said lord when they had come before him. And in regard to the lands of Dauphiné, when the king had seen the manner of my said lord and how he had been counciled at his departure and absence so suddenly from the said lands, notwithstanding the sweet and gracious responses that he had made to him, the king to obviate the inconveniences that, at the persuasion of those who had thus counciled my said lord, would little come, which then that they had so adventured his person by sights perilous and dangerous so that the said ambassadors even had said and proposed he would doubt that by the means of the said county and of the places and fortresses of this place, they would have little to do and undertake of the things to the displeasure of the king and prejudice of my said lord and of the country, the king, in his council to him, to go to the said lands in order to give them provision and secure it in such manner that any inconvenience cannot happen there. In what ways, however, he has so proceeded that all those of the lands, when they had perceived the good will of the king in this manner, they had been very joyous and consoled. And the king was content that they would send to my said lord in order to disapprove of his case. the sweeter that the king had held and tried to reduce him. And the king had good hope that, hearing the disapproval of those of the said lands and by the good council and exortation of my said lord of Burgundy, my said lord would submit himself and do his duty to him, as he ought to do and in this the king would make him obey all his displeasures of times passed, receive him in his good grace, and take him on benignly, as a good lord and father ought to toward his good and obedient son.

Deſtruction deturcs fête par les hongres.

EN. ce meſme temps firent les hongrois eu pays dehongrie une grande deſtraictōn ſur les ennemys delafoy delhûcriſt. et par le conſeil defrere Iehan capeſtran diſciple Iadiz de ſaint bernadin. Et par leconſeil deſaige et puiſſant chlr̂. appelle meſſ.[re] guillê blanc furent boutez hors et expellez delacite debeldrage En laquelle yavoit grant peuple deturcqs Leſquilz furet̂ to⁹ mors Iucques au nombre de xv.[m] et nen eſchappa homme q̂ tout ne fuſt oave et mis amort. Et vindrent grans oſtz et compaignie deturcqs leſquilz furet̂ lendemain vaillamment combatus par les xpiēns ⁊tellemet̂ quil mourult deRechef cent mille turcqs. ent̂ leſolleil levant et ſolleil couche. Et la eſtoit en perſonne leſoubdanc deperſe p̊incipal cappitaine detous les turqs. luy voyant telle deſconfiture eſtre ſur ſes gens ſen foyt avecq̄z peu deſes gens en lacite nôme boibe et dela en lat̂re degrece. Apres ſetranſporterent led chevallier nôme lechlr̂ blanc et toute ſacompaignie devant lad cite deboẙbe. Laquelle fut par eulx gaignee et ymirent amort deux mille turcqs. Apres en enſuivant leur bonne for tune par lagrace dedieu gaignerent pluſſieurs citez et chaſteaulx. ceſt aſſavoir lacite debaſtili ane vigara. faſtigia emere. et une aut̂ cite nômee auguſta qui eſt moult belle cite en la quelle mouront et furent deſtruitz. xv.[m] turcqs et alaIournees moroult cinq mille xpiēns q̂ dieu muble leurs ames en parades. **gma. dugn.⁹ eſt. operarms. mercede. ſua.** Depuis. prindrent leſd xpiēns Saint vincent et laville devallence avecques lechaſteau. Et tellemet̂ procuderoient que tout fut convr̂ty alafoy catholicq̄. Se fait ſen

Destruction of the Turks made by the Hungarians

IN this same time, the Hungarians of the land of Hungary made a great destruction of the enemies of the faith of Jesus Christ, and by the council of brother Juan Capistrano, former disciple of Saint Bernard. And by the council of a wise and powerful knight named messire Guillaume Blanc, they were pushed out and chased from the city of Belgrade, in which place was a great number of Turks, who were killed until the number was 15,000, and no man escaped but all were killed or put to death. And a great host and company of the Turks came, who the next day fought bravely against the Christians, and such that another 100,000 Turks died between sunrise and sunset. And there were in person the sultan of Persia, principle captain of all the Turks, who seeing such defeat to be upon his people, fled with few of his men into the city named Boibe and from there into the land of Greece. Afterwards, the said knight, named the white knight, and all his company went before the said city of Boibe, which was won by them, and they put to death there 2,000 Turks. Afterwards, in following their good fortune, by the Grace of God they won several cities and castles—it is known the city of Bâtiliane, Vigra, Fastigia, Emère, and another city named Augusta, which was a very beautiful city, in which were killed or were destroyed 15,000 Turks, and on these campaigns 5,000 Christians died, whom God absolves their souls in Paradise, **for a worker is worthy of his wage**. After this, the said Christians took Saint-Vincent and the town of Valence, with the castle, and in such a way that they were all converted to the Catholic faith. This being done, the said Christians went in order to win more and

allerent leſd xpiens̄ pour gaigner deplus en plus. et prindrent laville ⁊chaſteau deflagis. Puis prindrent gamadalo. apres prindrent porrus. Apres prindrent ſtauenger et chaſconen et lafuret̂ deſtruitz quatre mille turcqs et lacite gaignee. Maiz Il ymoront cent xpiens̄ q̂ dieu abſoille. Et tantoſt apres entra toute lacompagnee diceulx xpiens̄ en laître degrece et lagaignerent une grant cite nômee glotuaſe ou Ilz tuerent dix mille turcqs. Et de la ſen fuyrent et delaiſſant toꝰ les chaſteaulx villages villes cloſes et murres et autŝ forteresſes eſtans eſd marches et ſen allerent en laprovince decalde qui eſt empres conſtantinople. Et ainſſi leur demeura laître peuple et grant partie du pays docident degrece. Apres furet̂ prins ſur leſd turcqs lacite delatheres. celle deglan.ꝰ et lachaſteau avec pluſſieurs autŝ places for tereſſes et villages. Apres leſquelz allerent atoute puiſſance les xpiens̄ eſtans aſſemblez en ceſte partie. Et lafuret̂ nombres toꝰ les turcqs qui avoient eſte detruetz deux cens mille et huit[xx] citez et villes murees ⁊quat̂ cens chaſteaulx et autŝ fortereſſes. Ceſted conqueſte Relatee pour mettre es croniques et affirmee ſur les ſaincts evangilles dedieu et ſur leveu depreſtriſe. par venerables et eccleſiaſtiques perſonnes. meſ.[re] Ieh̄ valade pbrê meſſ.[re] patrix tournalle auſſi pbr̄e. et andry valati. hôme lay toꝰ trois eſtans eu dioceſe dumblam. en dachye. Et fut navre led chevallier blanc dune lance treſgriefvemet̂ en ladeſrniere bataille. Et tant q̂ neceſſite lecontraignit ſoy Retraire en lacite dauguſte. Alaquelle Il alla devie atreſpas dieu lui face mercy alame côme choſe bien deſire. Et pareillement fut fort navre leturcq et ſe Retrait en coſtantinoble treſfort malade par ĉtain temps. Interrogez par moy croniqueur les deſſnoiz̄ par leſerment q̂ dit

more, and they took the town and the castle of Flagis. Then they captured Gamadalo, after which they took Porrus. After they captured Stauenger and Chasconen, and 4,000 Turks were destroyed there and the city was won, but 100 Christians died there—may God absolve them! And soon afterwards, the entire company of these Christians entered into the land of Greece and won there a great city named Glotuase, where there were killed 10,000 turks. And from there they fled and abandoned all the castles, villages, towns, paddocks, and walls, and other fortresses located in the said marches, and they went into the province of Calde, which was near Constantinople. And so the land, the people, and the greater part of the lands of Greece remained theirs. After which, the city of Cutheris, that of Glannus, and the castle with several other places, fortresses, and villages were captured from under the said Turks. After which the Christians who were assembled in this country went out with all power. And all the Turks who had been killed were numbered to be 200,000, and 160 cities and walled towns and the 400 castles and other fortresses [were captured]. This conquest was related in order to put in chronicles and was affirmed by the holy Apostles of God, and in the sight of the priesthood by venerable and ecclesiastical people, messire Jean Valade, priest; messire Patrix Tournalle, another priest; and Andé Valati, a layman, all three being of the diocese of Dinublamini in Achaea. And the said white knight was wounded by a lance very grievously in the final battle, and such that he was constrained by necessity to retreat into the city of Augusta, at which place he died, God have mercy on his soul, as is a good thing to say. And at the same time, the Turk was wounded, and he retreated into the town of Constantinople, where he was very ill for a period of time. I, chronicler, did the questioning myself—the abovespoken

eſt commeт̂ Ilz ſavoient les choſes deſſſd eſtre vrayes dep poſerent quilz avoient eſte et aſſiſte perſonen̄ en toutes les batailles en armes a~~compa~~ côbatre. Et pour les grans perilz demort ou Ilz avoieт̂ eſte ceſtoient vouez amonſ.r ſaint denis et a pluſſieurs aultres pellerinages quilz avoieт̂ Intencion dacomplir avant q̂ Iamaiz Re tournaſſent en leur pays. Et ſemonſtroieт̂ comme Il ſembloit bien affectez aufait dela xpiens̄. Et depuis ſe partit led turcq. deconſtantinoble pour Retourner en ſon pays.

Ung terremote fait es partus. du Royaulme denapples.

Oudit. an leſamedy iiii Iour dedecembre environ trois heures devant le Iour. ſoul dainement ſe meult ung terremote. Le Roy darragon eſtant en lacite defogia et tel quil neſt homme qui peuſt pencer cil nelavoit veu Iaſoit ce q̂ en lad cite ced terremote nait pas fait treſgrant dommaige. Maiz eſt bien vray que par aucunes contrees dud Royaulme et par les lieux ou led terremote aeſte ſeſont enſuis grans maulx et Innombrables telz et ne lamaniere qui ſenſ. Tout přmieremeт̂ eſt fondue et perie une cite oud Royaulme nômee ariano. en laquelle fut mort huit mille pſoēs. C Item une auт̂ cite nômee padulle ou demouroient trois mille perſonnes qui ont eſte to⁹ mors ſans en eſchapper. C Item une auт̂ cite nômee bochery et en maniere quil neſt homme qui ſceuſt donc que oncques euſt une auſd lieux citez villes chaſtaulx ⁊fortereſſes excepte ceulx qui les ont veulx au paravaт̂ quelles fuſſent fondues ou peries. C Item eſt alle en Ruyne par led terremote lemoitie du pais depouille ceſt aſſavoir lamoitie dune cite nômee troye en laquelle eſt mort grant peuple. C Item eſt alle par

oaths that were said, how they knew the things abovesaid to be true, because they had been present, that they had been at the assaults personally in all the battles being in arms to fight. And due the great peril of death where they had been, they were visiting monseigneur Saint Denis and several other pilgrimages that they had the intention to accomplish before ever returning into their countries. And they would show, as it seems, good affection toward the fate of the Christians. And since the said Turk left from Constantinople to return into his lands.

An earthquake occured in parts of the kingdom of Naples

In the said year, Saturday, the fourteenth day of December, around three hours before dawn, suddenly there was a great earthquake, the king of Aragón being in the city of Foggia, and such that no man could imagine it if he had not seen it, realising that in the said city, the said earthquake did not make very great damage. But it is very true for several countries of the said kingdom and at the places where the said earthquake occurred, there ensued great and innumerable bad things, such and in the manner that follows. First of all, a city of the said kingdom named Ariano sunk and perished, in which around 8,000 people were killed. C Item, another city named Padule, where there had been 3,000 people, who were all dead, without anyone escaping. C Item, another land named Bocheri, in a manner that no man who knew it thus one day had one of the said places, cities, towns, castles, and fortresses except those who had seen them before, that they dimished or perished. C Item, half of the land of Pouille went into ruin by the said earthquake—it is known, the half of a city named Troye, in which was killed a

terre lapl⁹grāt partie des ville et chaſteau decanoſſe par led terremote. ℂ Item les citez daſcolly et deſainte agathe. lechaſteau darpti et pluſſieurs autres. ℂ Item en laconte demoleſſe ſont fondues en abuſme lacite decampobaſſo. lacite delauſtino Lechaſteau deſaint deSaint Iulian. lacite demizcona et lechaſteau deSaint lou. Les chaſte aulx decaſtime et delaRippe. Et auſſi pluſſi.[rs] terres delaconte de alteville fondues comme deſſ. Et eſquelles ſont bien mors. xxviii.[m] perſonnes. ℂ Item en lacite denapples aeu par led terremote aucun dommaige. Et par eſpecial plus aux egliſes q̃ aux ediffices delad cite. Et dura led terremote par leſpace dedetrois Iours et en aucunes parties plus longuement. Et eſt aſſavoir que depuis le[r] iiii[m] Iour dud ~~mie~~ moys deſſuſd. Iucques au vii.[m] Incluz ſoῑ mors cent mille perſonnes cōme Il aeſte Relacte par gens dediverſes contrees qui ſcavoῑt lachoſe eſtre vraye. ℂ Item aeſte mis en Ruyne par led terremote en une nuyt lechaſteau ſangtrinie. Lechaſteau deperſſolle. et laRoche decappra et ny eſt demeure muraille ne maiſon. ℂ Item amis en Ruyne led terremote lamoitie de lacite deſcerone et lechaſteau dolineto eſquilz ſont mors cinq cens perſonnes. et euchaſteau preſolle Six cens. Et pareillemēt eu chaſteau detogur eſt mort leſ.[r] et toutes les perſonnes qui eſtoient dedans. ℂ Item en une nuyt miſt en Ruyne led terremote laprimſe du mur danconne devers laporte dalmonte. ℂ Item aeu grant dommaige en ediffices de capra de adverſa debenivento. et lechaſteau deluſano qui eſt choſe bien forte et difficile acroire qui ne lavoit veu. Ceſte grande et pitiable ꝑte envoyee au marquis deferare par eſcript par meſſire herculez ſon frere qui eſtoit eu Royaume denapples avecques leRoy darragon. Et eſcript aRogea le Septieſme Iour de decembre mil CCCC. Cinquante. Six.

great number of people. C Item it went by land, the greater part of the castle of Canossa by the said earthquake. C Item, the cities of Ascoli and of Saint-Agatha, the castle of Arpino, and several others. C Item in the county of Molesse were dimished in the abyss the city of Campobasso, the city of Laurentinol, the castle of Saint Julian, the city of Miscona, and the castle of Saint Lou, the castles of Castime and of the Rippe, and also several lands of the county of Alteville, dimished as above, and in which about 28,000 people were killed. C Item, in the city of Naples there was, due to the said earthquake, some damage, and especially to the churches and other edifaces of the said city. And the said earthquake endured for the space of three days, and in several parts much longer. And it is known that since the fourteenth day of the said month abovesaid until the seventeenth inclusive, there were about 100,000 people killed, as it was reported by men of many countries who learned the thing to be true. C Item, the castle Sangtrinie, the castle of Persolle, and the rock of Capra have been put into ruin by the said earthquake in one night and there remains no wall nor house. C Item, the said earthquake put into ruin half of the city of Scerone and castle of Dolineto, in which were killed 500 people, and at the castle of Presolle 600. And equally at the castle of Togur was killed the lord and all the people who were inside. C Item, in one night, the said foremost section of the wall of Anconne, toward the gate of Amonte, was put into ruin by the earthquake. C Item, there had been great damage to the edifaces of Capra, Adversa, Benevento, and the castle of Lusano, which was a very shocking and difficult thing to believe to those who have not seen it. This great and pityable report was sent by writing to the marquis de Ferrara by messire Hercule, his son, who was in the kingdom of Naples with the king of Aragón. And he wrote from Rogea the seventeenth day of December 1456.

Commeť ofto caftellan argentier defrance et guillaume gouffier fireť areftez. prifonniers. alion

Oudit. an mille CCCC. Cinquante Six le premier Iour de lan. LeRoy eftant afaint prier en daulphinie pres lion octoraftellan florêtin argentier du Roy fut prins fur lepont delyon par Iehan delagardette p̊voft deloftel duRoy pource que leRoy avoit efte Informe que Icellui otho avoit faictes ĉtaines caractres. alenconť et au preiudice defaperfonne. Car Il avoit fait ĉtains ymages par lefquilz par art diabolique Il devoit avoir longuement legouvernement duRoy tel lement q̂ leRoy feroit ~~tel~~ tout ce quil plaifoit aud otho. Et auffi eftoit fon complice guille gouffier. longuement tenans en prifon pour avoir et favoir laverete dufait. Et fut led otho mene prifonnier athouloufe auparlement la ou Il avoit demoure longuement treforier pour le Roy. Et led gouffier fut mene atours et en lan ~~le.~~ lvi. fut condampne par lechâcellr̂ eu grant confeil duRoy aperdre tout ce quil avoit et eftre bany. Maiz leRoy lui fift grace quil ne perdit fors les officers quil tenoit duRoy. Et fut Remis afes biens autres et banẙ axx. lieues pres du Roy. Et fut condampne amil efcuz pour les fraiz et defpens qui avoient efte faiz pour lui. C Item auffi avoit led otho com̂ lepecher defodomye. Pourquoy Il fut Ramene atours. lan. lvii. pour eftre fententie 7Il. combn quil fuft depuis mene aparis es prifons dupallaiz pource que pluffieurs difoient quil avoit appelle en parlement. Et au Regard delacôclu fon Irmen Rapporte ace qui fait en acefte car Il aefte tramporte deprifon en autre parquoy mift Incongnue ladiffucion.

How Otto Câtillon, treasurer of France, and Guillaume Gouffier were arrested as prisoners at Lyon

In the said year 1456, the first day of the year, the king being at Saint-Priest in Dauphiné, near Lyon, Otto Câtillon, a Florentine, treasurer of the king, was captured on the bridge of Lyon by Jean de la Gardète, provost of the hotel of the king, because the king had been informed that this Otto had made certain signs against him and to the great prejudice of his person, because he had made certain images by which by diabolical arts he must have for a long time the government of the king, such that the king would do everything that would be pleasing to the said Otto. And also there was his accomplice, Guillaume Gouffier, held in prison for a long time in order to have and know the truth of the deed. And the said Otto was taken prisoner to Toulouse to the parlement there, where he had remained treasurer for a long time for the king. And the said Gouffier was taken to Tours, and in the year 1456, he was condemned by the chancellor in the great council of the king to lose everything that he had and be banished. But the king showed him grace in that he only lost the offices that he held by the king, and he was remitted in his other goods and banished to thirty leagues distance from the king, and he was condemned 1,000 écus for the costs and expenses that had been made by him. C Item, also, the said Otto had committed the sin of sodomy, for which he was brought to Tours in the year 1457 in order to be sentenced, and such that he was then brought to Paris into the prisons of the palace, for which several said that he had been called to parlement. And in regard to the conclusion, his brother reports that he had been transported from prison into another, for which his final fate is unknown.

Commet̃. maiſtre. blaize. Regnier. dit. greſſe. fut. côſacr. aſait̃. denis. en frâce en. arceveſque. debordeaulx.

Lan. mil CCCC Cinquante ſept lelundi Iour deRogacions en moys deMay fut beney et conſacre en ceur deleglife et mô naſtere deSaint denis en france en arceveſq̃ debordeaulx. Maiſtre bleze Regnier autremet̃ dit greſſe prt maiſtre milles dilliers arche diacre dechartres et pluſſieurs aut̃s et lecôſacra monſ.[r] larceveſque deRains nomme monſ.[r] Iôh Iuvenal des urſſins deRomme Et furet̃ cond ucteurs affaire lemiſtere. meſſ.[r] les eveſques deNoyon et deparis. Et fut led archeveſq̃ avat̃ ſad conſacracion en prieres et oraiſons durant leſervice cothidien fait en lad egliſe ⁊môaſtere. Et apres lameſſe faicte et dicte leſd prelatz et pluſſieurs notables gens tant clerc deglife que laiz allerent diſgner en lagrant ſalle bien tendue et paree detapiſſerie. Et la furent grandement et haultement ſervis et dediverſes viandes. Et eſt bien cechappitre anotter veu letemps que les angloiz avoiet̃ pocede et occuppe tout lepays debordellaiz. Et auſſi conſidere latreſnoble conqueſte denouvel faicte par treſhault xpien et ſouverain pnce Le Roy charles vii.[m] dece nom qui Recouvra en ung an tout led pays.

La mort depierre duc de bretai[gne].

Oudit an termina devie atrespas treſpuiſſ prince monſ.[re] le pierre duc debretaigne Auquel ſucceda leconte deRichemont ſ.[r] par tenay et conneſtable defrance. lequel

How master Blaize Régnier, called Grêle, was consecrated at Saint-Denis-en-France by the Archbishop of Bourdeaux

The year 1457, Monday, day of the prayers in the month of May, was blessed and consecrated in the choir of the church and monastery of Saint-Denis-en-France as archbishop of Bordeaux master Blèze Régnier, otherwise called Grêle, those present being master Milles d'Illiers, archdeacon of Chartres, and several others, and he was consecrated by monseigneur the archbishop of Reims, named monseigneur Jean Juvénal des Ursins of Rome. And messeigneurs the bishops of Noyon and of Paris were conductors to make the mystery. And the said archbishop, before his said consecration, was three days in prayers and orations before the daily service made in the said church and monastery. And after the mass was made and said, the said prelates and several notable men, both clerics of the church and laiety, went to dine in the great hall, well decorated and adorned by tapestry. And there were great and high services and different meats. And this chapter is good to note, seeing the times that the English had possessed and occupied all the lands of the Bordelais, and also considering the very noble conquest newly made by the very high Christian and sovereign prince, the king Charles, seventh of this name, who recovered in one year all the said lands.

The death of Pierre, duke of Brittany

At the said end of the year, monseigneur Pierre, duke of Brittany, passed from life to death, to whom succeeded the earl of Richmond, seigneur de Partenay, and constable of

vint devers leRoy faire ſes hommages telz q̂ de Raiſon. et comme en telz cas ſes p̊deceſſeurs ducz debretaigne ont acouſtume defaire.

Lambaxade dehôgrie au Roy. defrance.

Oudit an letreſxpieñ Roy defrance affectat̂ deInſulter ſes ennemys et par eſpecial Leturcq. ſaraſins et aut̂s eſtans cont̂ lafoy. xpien̂ fiſt aliance avecques leRoy dehôgrie qui eſt treſpuiſſant prince et Roy detrois Roy.mes ceſt aſſavoir dud hongrie depoullaine et de boeſme. Par lemoien deſquelles Ildevoit avr̂ en mariage madame magdeleine fille duRoy defrance. Et pour Icelle fiancer furet̂ envoyez par led Roy dehongr̊e pluſſieurs grans ſ.rs dechun̂ diceulx Royaulmes comme barons et aut̂s. et meſmement des gens degliſe côme larceveſque decalonme et leveſque depara menſe et des ſeculliers yeſtoient monſ.r de la ſela depoullaine baron monſ.r deſtr̂nebenere deboeſme auſſi baron. Monſ.r demichonſp̱t deboeſme monſ.r debourger auſſi deboeſme meſſ.re Iehan ſcambert baron et pluſſieurs aut̂s tant nobles q̂ aut̂s Iucques au nombre de cinq. aſix cens chevaulx. leſquelz alleret̂ devers leRoy veſtuz dedevers habitz ſelon lacouſtu͡e deleurs pays. Et aRiverent en laville deto.rs leRoy eſtant au montiz et laRoyne et lad fille eſtoient atours et laprêterent alaRoyne une Robe dedrap dor ſemee deperles et depierreries moult Riche et alafille une aut̂ pareille. Et avoient amene ung chariot branlat̂ moult ſumptueulx et Riche audevant deſd ambaſſadeurs allerent Iucques aune lieue ou environ pluſſieurs grans ſ.rs Ceſt aſſavr̂ monſ.r dorleans. Monſ.r dangouleſme. Monſ.r

France, who went to the king to make his homage according to reason, and as in such case his predecessor dukes of Brittany were accustomed to make.

The embassy of Hungary to the king of France

In the said year, the very Christian king of France, hoping to insult his enemies and especially the Turks, Sarasins, and others who were against the Christian faith, made an alliance with the king of Hungary, who was a very powerful prince and king of three kingdoms—it is known of the said Hungary, of Poland, and of Bohemia. By the means of which he ought to have in marriage madame Magdeleine, daughter of the king of France. And to finance this, several great lords of each of these kingdoms, such as barons and others and even those of the church, such as the archbishop of Coulonne and the bishop of Paramense, and of the secular [lords] there were monseigneur Ladislas of Poland, a baron; monseigneur de Sternberg of Bohemia, also a baron; monseigneur de Michelsperg of Bohemia; monseigneur de Burger, also of Bohemia; messire Johan de Starkemberg, a baron; and several others, both nobles and others, until the number was 500 to 600 knights, were sent by the said king of Hungary, who went to the king vested in different clothes, according to the custom of their lands. And they arrived in the town of Tours, the king being at Montiz, and the queen and the said daughter were at Tours, and there they presented to the queen a robe of golden cloth embroidered with pearls and very valuable gems, and to the daughter a similar one. And they brought a very sumptuous and richly-adorned sword chariot, before the said ambassadors went to a place where there were around several great lords—it

dumaine. Monſ.r defoix. Monſ.r devendoſme. Monſ.r delamarche. Monſ.r lechancellier et pluſſieurs auťs et quant Ilz fureť aRivez Ilz fureť moult haultement et Reallemeť Receuz par le Roy. et detoute ſaſeignourie en grans chieres deboire et demenĝr. Et par eſpecial leconte defoix les feſtoya moult grandement leIeuſdi. devant noel en labbaye deSaint Iulien detours la ou eſtoient tous les ſeigneurs et princes eſtans en lacourt La oulrent leſd ſeigneurs tres grant habundance deviandes. les plus pre cieuſes et dillicieuſes qui ſepeuveť trouvȓ côme. faiſans perdrilz. ouſtardes. grues et oupes ſauvaiges. connis ſans nombre ſchappons dehaulte greſſe. Six.xx quartes dypocras tant blanc que Rouge. entremeſtz. moriſques denffans ſauvaiges ſaillans dune Roche chantres trompettes et clairons. et pluſſieurs auťs choſes moult nobles tant q̂ en ſôme lediſgner couſta xviii.c eſcuz. et en grans et Riches dons. Et firent touſiours grande et bonne chiere. eſperant lun deſd ſeigne.rs defiancer apres noel par procuracion dud Roy dehongrie Icelle fille. Et pource quil eſt eſcript q̂ ſouvent ce que homme propoſe contraire dieu en diſpoſte. Car lendemain denoel vindrent au Roy defrance treſpiteuſes nouvelles delamort et treſpas detreſhault et treſpuiſſant prince leRoy dehongrie. Parquoy lui et toute ſa ſ'ie fut fort troublee et firent grant dueil. Et adonc leRoy ordôna ſon ſervice et funerailles eſtre faiz en laville detours. Ceſt aſſavoir en la~~mortals~~metropo litaine egliſe demonſ.r ſaint gacian tant en ſonnerie ~~laura~~ luminaire detorches ⁊cierges en grant et exceſſif nombre et côme aung tel prince appartenoit. Et adoncques le ~~premier~~ Iour delan Revolu prindrent côge du Roy pour eulx en Retourner en leurs pays et vindrent

is known, monseigneur d'Orléans; monseigneur d'Angoulême; monseigneur du Maine; monseigneur de Foix; monseigneur de Vendôme; monseigneur de la Marche; monseigneur the chancellor; and several others, and when they arrived, they were very highly and personally received by the king and by all of his lordship, and there was great amounts to drink and to eat. And especially the count of Foix feasted them very grandly the Friday before Christmas in the abbey of Saint-Julien-de-Tours, where there were all the lords and princes who were at court; there the said lords saw a very great abundance of meats, the most precious and delicious that they could find, such as feasants, partridges, bustards, cranes, and wild geese, rabbits beyond number, very fatty capons, 120 quarts of hippocras, both white and red, desserts, Morish dances of wild children leaping from a rock, singers, trumpeters, and clarioners, and several other very noble things, such that in sum the dinner cost 1,800 écus, plus great and rich gifts. And always there was great and good cheer, hoping one of the said lords to finance him after Christmas, by procuration of the said king, this girl. And for this he wrote, often that which the man proposed, against God in disposition, because the next day of Christmas, there came to the king of France very tragic news of the death and passing of the very high and very powerful prince, the king of Hungary, for which he and all his lordship was greatly troubled, and they mourned greatly. And then the king ordered his service and funerals to be made in the town of Tours—it is known in the metropolitan church of monseigneur Saint-Gacian, with ringing, lighting of torches, and candles in great and excessive number, and as belongs to such a prince. And then the first day of the year, they took leave of the king in order to return to their countries, and they came amidst the town of Paris, where

parmy laville deparis ou Ilz furent grandement Receuz et allerent audevant deulx Iucques au moullin avent hors delaporte Saint Iacques. Monſ.[r] leconte deu. Monſ.[r] delangres. Monſ.[r] deparis. Monſ.[r] denerbonne. Monſ.[r] denoyon. Monſ.[r] deRodes. Monſ.[r] demeaulx. Monſ.[r] debeſiers. Monſ[r] deſaint brieu en bretaigne. Leconte darmi gnac. leprevoſt deparis. lepremier p̊ſideт̂ delacour deparlement acompaigne depluſſ.[rs] deſd ſeigneurs. des comptes. des generaulx eſleuz. et eſchevins et auт̂s notables bourgois delad ville. Et le Recteur acompaigne deluniversite vint Iucques aux Iacopins Apres furent logiez en laRue ſaint Iacques partie en laRue delaharpe. et partie en laporte baudet. en laRue ſaint anthoine et leurs chariotz to⁹ chargez deleurs biens de mourerent par chacūe nuyt tant quilz fureт̂ aparis parmy les Rues. Et yavoit gens eſtabliz acouchr̂ deſſus to⁹ enchaines degroſſes chains quelq̂ froidure quil feiſt qui eſtoit bien exceſſive. Et eſtoient fermeres aſerures et aclef que lun des gouverneurs emportoit auſoir quant Il ſen alloit couchr̂. En legliê nrêdame fut fait ung notable ſervice et yot grant luminaire. tant en torches ſierges côme auт̂ment tant et ſilonguement q̂ Icelle ſeigneurie dehongrie fut aparis Leur fut pn̂te chcn̄ Iour livroiſon depain et devin. Et tant quilz fureт̂ treſbien contes̄ deceulx delaville et des hâtans. et en firêt Remercier leRoy par maiſtre georges de ſacramville dit havart maiſtre des Requeſtes duRoy. lequel par lordonnance du Roy vint avecques eulx aud lieu deparis. leſd hongres eſtans aparis faiſoit degrans gelles glaces et verglas parmy paris pour les eaues q̂ on gectoit devant les huys des maiſons. Pourquoy les ſ.[rs] noſoient allr̂ parmy laville ne apie ne acheval. Maiz ſe ~ faiſoient tray-

they were greatly received, and monseigneur the count of Eu, monseigneur de Langres, monseigneur de Paris, monseigneur de Narbonne, monseigneur de Noyon, monseigneur de Rodez, monseigneur de Meaux, monseigneur de Bésiers, monseigneur de Saint-Brieu in Brittany, the count of Armagnac, the provost of Paris, the first president of the court of parlement, accompanied by several of the said lords of the chamber of accounts, of the general elected and aldermen, and other notable citizens of the said town, went before them until the windmill at the gate of Saint-Jacques. And the rector, accompanied by the University, went as far as the Jacobins. Afterwards, they were lodged partly on the Rue Saint-Jacques, partly on the Rue de la Harpe, and partly in the Baudet gatehouse on the Rue Saint-Antoine, and their chariots all loaded with their goods, they remained such each night that they were in Paris, amongst the streets. And they had there people established to deliver above all enchained by large chains whatever freezing that he had, which was very excessive. And they were closed with lock and key, that one of the governors took away in the evening, when he wanted to sleep. In the church of Notre-Dame there was made a very notable service and a great candle [service], made of torches, candles, and other things, such and so long was this lordship of Hungary at Paris, it was presented each day to them a delivery of bread and wine. And such that they were very happy for those of the town and of the inhabitants, and in making thanks, the king via master George de Saccamville, called Havart, master of the requests of the king, who, by order of the king, went with them to the said place of Paris, the said Hungarians being in Paris, making frosts, ice, and black ice throughout Paris, for the waters one threw before the doors of the houses, because the lords did not dare to

ner aung cheval ou adeulx eulx aſſis dedens. partout ou Ilz avoient abeſongner tant aviſiter laville et lacite comme auſ̂ment. et eulx partis deparis ſen tirerent droit en leurs pays et furet̂ Receuz par toutes les citez et bonnes villes en paſſant pource q̂ chc͡n ſavoit q̂ ceſtoit lavoullête duRoy q̂ ainſſi fuſt fait. Et meſmement eulx eſtans aparis vindrent viſiter lanoble et Royalle egliſe demonſ.r Saint denis ou Ilz furent moult notablement Receuz. ducouvent monſ.r labbe abſent et eſtoit led couvent en chappes. et furent Receuz alaporte delad egliſe. et leur fut porte abayſier une croix dor plaine ⁊ſemee depierreries et deperles en laquelle ya une partie dufuſt delavraye croix. furent auſſi porter letexſte delevangille. Aſperges deaue beniſte et encêſſies. Et fut laRe cepcion telle q̂on peu faire au deffunct Roy dehongrie cil yfuſt venu deſon vivant. En Icelle egliſe leur fut monſtre tout le treſor. les veſtemens duſacre. les corps ſains qui ſont en lad egliſe en chacun͡ chapelle. Et auſſi les ſepultures des Roys et Roynes en Icelle egliſe Inhumez. dequoy Ilz furent bien Ioyeaulx. Et depuis leur fut pn̂te pain vin et eſpices donc les aucuns en prindrent et les autres non. Et yavoit ung des pour ſuivans du Roy qui eſtoit leur trucheman et ordonne depar leRoy pource quil ſavoit leur langaige. Puis ſen Retourneret̂ aud lieu deparis et delaen leur pays.

Entree faicte. agand par. monſeigneur. debourgogne.

Ceſt lentree detreſhault ⁊puiſſat̂ prince. monſr leduc debourgongne faite en laville degant. ledymanche xxiiim

go amongst the town either on foot or horseback, but they made sleds with a horse where two of them sat inside, wherever they needed, both to visit the town and the city, and elsewhere, and those parts of Paris, they went straight to their country, and were received by all the cities and good towns in passing, because each knew that it was the will of the king to do so. And even those who were in Paris went to visit the noble and royal church of monseigneur Saint-Denis, where they were very notably received at the convent by monseigneur the abbot, and the said convent were in cloaks, and they were received at the gate of the said church and were taken to kiss a cross of solid gold decorated with gemstones and pearls, in which there was a part of the true cross, also carrying the text of the Apostles, sprinkled with holy water and incense. And the reception was such that one did little at the dead king of Hungary, that he had come from his lifetime. In this church he showed them all the treasure, the clothing of the sacrament, the bodies of saints who were in the said church in each chapel. And also the sepulchres of the kings and queens inhumed in this church, for which they were very joyous. And then they were presented with bread, wine, and spices, of which several took some and others none. And there was one of the messengers of the king, who was their interpreter and ordained on behalf of the king, because he knew their language. Then they returned to the said place of Paris and from there into their lands.

Entry made at Ghent by monseigneur of Burgundy

This is the entry of the very high and powerful prince, monseigneur the duke of Burgundy, made in the town of Ghent,

Io^r davril apres pafques. Lan mil CCCC. Cinquâte huit. environ dequatre acinq heures apres midi. laquelle fut faicte en trefgrant et puiffant eftat côme fera defclar̂ cy apres. Premierement. fe mirent en ordonnance toutes les gens deglife par maniere deproceff audehors delaville en faifant Reverence chcn̂ en fon endroit. laplus humble et devotte q̂l povoit. C Item lebailli et les efchevins en partie avecques les bourgois dud lieu furent audevant demond f.^r acheval veftuz de noir et le Receurent leplus humblement et obbaiffanment q̂ plus peurent. Laut̂ ptie defd efchevins furent alaporte. Et latierce en loftel demond f.^r et en chcn̂ defd lieux lui firent Reverence en mettant par chcn̂ deulx lun des genoulx par terre en lui prêtant corps et biens. C Item et les doiens des meftiers et les Iurez furent auffi audehors delaporte chcn̂ une torche en famain. honneftement veftuz et en bonne ordonnance. Ceft affavoir deux. cens ou plus veftuz demanteaulx pers. et autant veftuz demanteaulx blancs traynans Iucques en terre. C Item audehors delad porte oult̂ leaue oult perfonnages dechcn̂ cofte delarue ung en maniere deprophettes. lun faifant maniere de Regarder en famain ung Rollet auquel avoit en efcript. Ecte. nomen. domini. venit. de longaco. yfaye. XXX. Et lautre perfonnage fut Regardant les trompettes qui furent fur la porte et ot en fon Rollet efcript. Canite. tuba. parentur. omnez. ⁊cil. C Item au dehors et aupie delad porte oult fait ung Iardin ou vergier ouquel avoit une Ieune fille pucelle delaage denviron. x. ans Les chevaulx pend veftue trefsimplement dedrap dedamas blanc en fourme demanteau. laquelle femettoit adeux genoulx et Ioinges mains et ot ung efcripteau difant. Inveni. quen. diligit anima. mea. cantic. iij°. C Item lavat̂ porte et auffi laporte furent tendues dedrap noir gris et

Sunday, the twenty-third day of April after Easter, the year 1458, around four or five hours after midday, which was made in a very great and powerful state, as it will be revealed afterwards. Firstly, all the men of the church showed themselves in order by manner of processions outside of the town, making reverence each in his place, the most humble and devoted that he could. C Item, the bailiff and part of the aldermen, with the citizens of the said place, were in front of my said lord, on horseback, vested in black, and they received him very humbly and obediently the best that they could. The other part of the said aldermen were at the gate. And the third in the hotel of my said lord, and in each of the said places they received him reverently by each one of them kneeling to the earth while presenting to him their body and goods. C Item, and the deans of the trades and the jurors were also in front of the gate, each a torch in his hand, honestly dressed and in good order—it is known 200 or more wearing blue-green coats and the other wearing black coats, trailing on the ground. C Item, outside of the said gate, beside the water, there were characters on each side of the road; one in the manner of a prophet, the one making gestures as if he had a scroll in his hand, upon which was written: Here a name comes from a distant land (Isaiah 30). And another character looked as if he held the trumpets which were at the gate, and had written on his roll: The sound of the trumpet provides all, etc. C Item, outside and at the foot of the said gate there was made a garden, or orchard, in which was a young virgin girl aged around ten years, leading the horses, wearing very simple cloth of Damascus white in the form of a coat, who was kneeling and joining hands, and had one sign that said: I found him whom my soul loves (Song of Solomon 3). C Item, in front of the gate and also at the gate were cloths of dark gray

vermeil. et en drap delavant porte ou barriere fut eſcript en lectre dor. Venit nobis. pacificus. dominus. utere. ſer vicio. nr̃. ſicut. placuerit. tibi. Iudic. iij°. Et ſur ledrap delagrant porte eult les armes demond ſ.r atymbre. C Item depuis lad porte Iucques alacour demond ſ.r furent les Rues tendues dun coſte ⁊daut̂ dedrap deſd coulleurs. ceſt aſſavoir noir gris et vermeil Et au noir drap eult en eſcript en groſſes lectre dargent. venit. nobis. pacificus. domin.⁹ en gris. utere. ſervicio. nrê. Et en vermeil ſicut. placint. tibi. Et audeſſus deſd draps eult torches. v. ou. vi. Sur chc̃n drap ainſſi Som̂ deſd torches comprinſes celles qui furent devat̂ les maiſons et ſur les bateaulx dedens la Riviere de xv. axvi[m]. torches. C Item dedens lad ville aſſes pres delad porte eult ung perſonnage delenffant prodigue que lepere apres lacongnoeſſance deſon meffait Receuſt en grace et euſt en eſcript. Pater. pectam in. celum. et coram. te. ſeri. luce xv°. C Item aſſes pres dela eult ung perſonnage en maniere deprophette qui tenoit ung Rollet Euquel avoit en eſcript. lex. clemencie. in. linga. eius. Proverb[s]. xxx°. C Item en apres eult ung eſchauffault ſur lequel fut leperſonnage delempereur gai.⁹ en melieu de xii. ſenateurs et devant lui eult leperſonnage demarcus. tullius qui en louant laclemence dud empereur en laliberacion depluſſieurs priſonniers quil avoit prins quant Il gaigna Romme conmenchant diuturny. ſilentii en la quelle oraiſon ent̂ aut̂s choſes eſt couche. nulla. devirtutibus. tuis. maior clementia. eſt. Lequel mot fut en Rabat des courtines delad figure. C Item en enſ eult une figure ou Il yavoit ung lion noir qui tenoit en ſapate ung eſtandart des armes demondſ.r et devant une lyonne blanche hû blement couchee aterre. et enmelieu des deux eult trois petitz lionneaulx. amoitie mors Leſquelz par lecry dud lion Reprindrent vie et conſolacion et

and vermillion, and on the cloth in front of the gate or barrier was written in letters of gold: We came to our services and deal as you please (Judges 3). And on the cloth of the large gate were the arms of my said lord with timbrels. C Item, from the said gate to the court of my said lord, on either side of the roads were cloths of the said colours—it is known, black, grey, and vermillion. And on the black cloth was written in large letters of silver: For we are the peaceful; in grey: Use our service. And in vermillion: As you please. And the abovesaid cloths had five or six torches on each cloth, thus counting the said torches, comprising those which were before the houses and on the boats on the river, 50,000 to 60,000 torches. C Item, within the said town close to the said gate, there was a character of the prodigal child that the father after learning of his misdeeds received in grace, and there was written: Father, I have sinned against heaven and before you (Luke 15). C Item, seated near to this, there was a character dressed in the manner of a prophet who held a roll upon which he had written: In her tongue is the law of kindness (Proverbs 3[1]). C Item, and after there was a scaffold, on which was the character of the emperor Gaius in the middle of twelve senators, and before him was the character of Marcus Tullius, who praised the clemency of the said emperor in the liberation of several prisonners that he had taken when he won Rome, beginning, 'a long silence', in which words amongst other things was hidden: There is no greater virtue than mercy, which word was in the folds of the robes of the said figure. C Item, next, there was a figure where there was a black lion which held in its paw a coat of arms of my said lord, and before, a white lioness, humbly resting on the earth, and in the middle of the two, there were three small lions half dead, which by the cry of the said lion, retook life and con-

eult en eſcript. Quaſi. leo. Pugiet. et. formidabunt. filii. os. et. xi. C Item encores dela eult ung prophette qui en Regardant mondſ.r tint ung Rollet enquel eult en eſcript. Ecte. venit. deſi-deratus. cunctis. gentibus. et. Re plebitur. gloria. eius. domus. domini agez. ii°. C Item pres dela eult une figure dedavid. lequel delingdignacion quil eult contre Nabal fut Rappaiſie alumble priere delafẽme dud nabal par ſagrant humilite et eult en eſcript. Benedictus. dominus. deus. Iſrael. qui. te. miſit. p̊. Regum. xx̊ cap̊. Item laut̂ porte fut couverte dedrap noir et gris en laquelle oult les armes demondſ.r a tymbre et auſſi les armes dun chcn̄. demeſſ.rs delordre delatoiſon. C Item dedens lad porte eult ung aut̂ eſchaffault et ou melieu avoit une fontaīe et alenviron leſtat deleglife triũphat̂. Item aſſez pres dela eult ung paſteur qui eult Retourne ſes brebis eſgarees. lequel tenoit ung Rollet ou Il yavoit en eſcript Congratulamini. mihi. quia. inve-ni ovem quam. perdideram. luce xv°. C Item en apres aupont eult une figure de pompee cappitaine deRomme qui avoit p̊ins leRoy darmenye pour les Rebellions par lui commis contre les Rommains. Sevoyant ſon obbaiſſance et humilite eult pitie delui et ſeRemiſt en ſapremiere liberte parce quil lui ſembloit choſe dauſſi grant gloire et louenge depardonner comme de-vaincre. Et yot en effect. Eque. pulchrum. eſt vince re. Reges. extere. valerii. libro. quinto. capp°. C Item et oult̂ eult ung aut̂ prophette pres delaut̂ porte qui monſtroit dudoy vers leaue et tenoit ung Roullet enquel Il yavoit en eſcript Reſpice. domine. In. ſervos. tuos. pſalmo. lxxxix°. C Item en laRiviere ot v. ou vi. apoſtres ent̂ leſquelz eſtoit Saint Iehan qui diſoit par eſcript. aSaint pierre voullant venir devers norſ.r qui eſtoit cheminant ſur leaue et ſoy voyant en dangier denoier diſt par. eſcript. Domine. ſalvum. me. fac mathieu. xx iii°. C Et noſ̂ ſeigneur

solation, and it was written: The lion roars and so shall the children (Hosea 11). C Item, again, there was a prophet who, looking at my said lord, held a roll on which there was written: Here comes all nations, which will be filled with the glory of his house (Haggai 2). C Item, near to there was a figure of David, who by the indignation that he held against Nabal was recalled with a humble prayer of the wife of the said Nabal by his great humility, and there was written: Lord God of Israel, who came today to meet me (1 Kings 20). Item, the other gate was covered in black and grey cloth, on which were the arms of my said lord, with timbrel and also the arms of each of the lords of the Order of the Fleece. C Item, within the said gate there was another scaffold, and in the middle there was a fountain and around it the state of the triumphant Church. Item, soon afterwards, there was a pastor who had returned his lost sheep, who held a roll on which was written: I am glad that I discovered that I had lost a sheep (Luke 15). C Item, and after, at the bridge, there was the figure of Pompey, captain of Rome, who had captured the king of Armenia because of the rebellions committed by him against the Romans. Seeing his obaissance and humility, he had pity on him and returned to him his first liberty, because it seemed to him a thing also of great glory and praise to pardon as to vanquish. And there was written: It is equally fair to conquer kingdoms and to do so (Valeri Maximi – Book 5, Chapter [1]). C Item, and there was another prophet, near to the other gate, who showed himself to the water and held a roll on which was written: Look down at your slaves (Psalm 89). C Item, in the river, there were five or six apostles, among whom was Saint John, who said by writing to Saint Peter, wanting to come to Our Lord, who was walking along on the water, and seeing that he was in danger of drowning,

avoit ung Rollet qui dift C Modici. fidei. quare. dubitafti. eod cap̊. Et en Icelle mefmes Riviere ot ~~cinq ou fex apoftres~~ ung grant bateau charge de torches ardans et femblablemet̂ en lad Rivê. C Item encores ung perfonnage en guife de prophette qui tenoit ung Roullet en famain et monftroit une grant. figure devant lui en dif par efcript. Exultabunt. omnia. ligna. filvarum. afacie. domini. quoniam venit pfalm. xv°. C Item devant led pphê avoit ung grant efchauffault fur lequel et au ~~quel~~ bout dicellui eult une forterefſe adeux tournelles adeux carreaulx. delaquelle forterefſe furent penduz les efcuz armoyez des armes detous les pays demond f.ͬ Alaporte dicelle forterefſe avoit ung perfonnage en maniere degeant qui fut nomme mars et fut int̂prete l~~eveu~~ victorieulx en armes et eult empres lui ung lion. Et devant lad forterefſe eult ung boys ~~oul~~ ouquel oulrent divêfes manr̂es debeftes comme dragons loups Regnars et aut̂s beftes fauvages qui furent femblans devoulloir envahir et voulloir entrer en lad forterefſe qui toutes furet̂ deboutees. Et eftoit devant lad porte ung homme Reprefentant les trois eftatz demondf.ͬ ceft affavoir fur latefte côme homme deglife. ducofte dextre dune Robbe longue dedrap defoye. lecofte fenextre côme laboureur des champs. Si yeult en efcript audeffus dicellui. dilligam te domine fortitudo. mea ⁊cl. Et nifi cuftodi eris. civitatem. fruftra. vigillat. qui cuftodit. eam pfalmo xxv°. C Item en avat̂ fut ung perfonnage duRoy pfalmon et dela Royne fabba devant lequel perfonnage fut efcript ~~Majr~~ maior eft. gloria. quam Rumor. quem. audivi. iiį. Regnum x̊. C Item apres fut une figure degedeon. enquel puis quil eult obtenu victoire les enffans difrael vindrent humblement alui endifant dominare. noftri. tu. et. filius. tuus et. filius. filii. tui. quia. liberafti noz. Iudes viį. C Item en apres fut ung

said by writing: Lord save me! (Matthew 13). C And our lord had a roll which said: You of little faith, why did you doubt? ([Matthew 14]). And in this same river there was a great boat full of burning torches, and they seemed in the said river. C Item, still a character in the guise of a prophet, who held a roll in his hand and showed a great figure before him, saying by writing: All of the trees of the woods shall rejoice before the face of the Lord, because he is coming (Psalm 15). C Item, before the said prophet, there was a great scaffold upon which and at the end of it there was a fortress with two small towers with two windpanes, from which fortress were hung the coats of arms of all the lands of my said lord. At the gate of this fortress, there was a character dressed in the manner of a giant, who was named Mars, and he represented victory-in-arms, and after him there was a lion. And in front of the said fortress was a forest in which there were different types of beasts, such as dragons, wolves, foxes, and other savage beasts, which seemed to want to invade and want to enter into the said fortress, all of which were kept away. And before the said gate was a man representing the three estates of my said lord—it is known, on the head a man of the church, on the right side a long robe of silk cloth, on the left side like a labourer of the fields. There was in writing above this: I will love thee, O Lord, my strength, etc. And lest he keep the city, in vain shall he work who keeps watch over it. (Psalm 25). C Item, ahead there was a character of King Solomon and the Queen of Sheba, before which character was written: thy glory exceeds the fame which I heard (Kings 10). C Item, after, there was a figure of Gideon in which then, having obtained victory, the children of Israel came humbly to him saying: Rule over us, you and your son and your son's son, for you have delivered us (Judges 7). C Item, after which,

ori phamp. portant ung chaſteau ſur lequel furent deux hommes et quatre enffans qui chanterent une nouvelle et Ioyeuſe chancon donc les moz ſen ſuyvent

Vive bourguongne eſt noſ̃ cry
Gardons le en fait et pencee
Autre nairons bien noꝰ agree
Noꝰ levoullons touſiours ainſſi.
Vive bourguongne.

De ceur chancons Ie vous en pry.
En ſa haulte Ioyeuſe entree
Vive bourguongne

Reſiouiſſons noꝰ pour celui
Qui eſt venu en ſacontree
Par qui noz triſteſſe eſt finee
En criant decourage uny.
Vive bourguongne

CElle entre fut moult haulte et excellente et laplus que prince feiſt ~~oncques~~ longc temps a. Car acoſte delui eſtoit acheval lechap peron ſur leſpaulle lebaſtard darmaignac ma reſchal demond ſ.r ledaulphin et devant lui eſtoiẽt les huiſſiers darmes ſon premier eſcuier deſ cuierie portant lespee devant lui et ſes Roys darmes heraulx et pourſuivans veſtuz deleurs cottes darmes en grant nombre. C Item devãt leſd heraultx eſtoient les trompettes et clairons environ xii. ou xiiii. C Item devant eulx lecôte deſtampe et meſſire thibault deneufchaſtel ſ.r deblancmont mareſchal debour-

there was an elephant carrying a castle on which were two men and four children, who chanted a new and joyous song, of which the words follow:

Vive Burgundy, it is cried by us!
Let us keep it in fact and thought.
Others will not go, we well agree,
We always want it thus.
Vive Burgundy!

For heartfelt singing, I beg of you,
At his very joyous entry:
Vive Burgundy!

We rejoice for this man
Who is coming into his country,
By which our sadness is ended.
In crying with united courage:
Vive Burgundy!

This entry was very great and excellent, and the most that a prince has done for a long time, because at the side of him was on horseback, the cape on the shoulder, the bastard of Armagnac, marshal of my said lord the Dauphin, and before him were the bailiffs-at-arms, his first squire of the squirerie, carrying the sword before him, and his kings-at-arms, heralds, and runners, vested in their coats-of-arms in great number. C Item, before the said heralds were the trumpeteers and buglers, totalling twelve or fourteen. C Item, before them [were] the count of Étampes and messire Thibaut de Neufchâtel, seigneur de Blancmont, marshal

gogne. C Item devant eulx les ſeigneurs et gentilz hommes demonſr ledaulphin. les deux filz demonſ.r de crouy et les deux filz dud neufchaſtel debôgone. C Item devant eulx eſtoient monſ.r lof decleves monſ.r lebaſtard debourgongne et meſſ.re phlê pot. Richement habillez eulx et leurs chevaulx. Item devant eulx eſtoient to9 les grans ſeigneurs delacourt et devant leſd ſeigneurs les gentilz hommes deux adeux ſans varlet ne page. Et devant leſd gentilz hommes eſtl. ceulx dela ville en grant nombre veſtuz. C Item empres mondſ.r eſtoient cinquante archiers deſon corps apie veſtuz deleur hucques et chcn ayant ung vouge en ſamain. Et deſriere lui eſtoient xv. pages et pluſſieurs gentilz hommes. Et furet̂ les chevaulx eſtimez qui eſtoient en lad entree ſans les varletz et les pages qui eſtoient Ia dedens laville deux mille chevaulx ou plus. C Item en concluſion cefut leplus grant triûphe qui fut fait au pays paſſe. v.c ans por venue deſeigneur. Car lendemain auſoir toutes les ~~choſes~~ torches furet̂ alumees. ceſt aſſavoir nouvelles torches et fallotz. ceulx delaville Iouerent pluſſieurs perſonnages. Par leſquelz en laprêce demondſ.r Iucques en loſtel dela ville Ilz firent expoſer les figures 7pſonnages deſſuſd en priant louant leprince et en côfeſſat̂ leur meffait. C Item ſemblablement firent lemardi auſoir. Maiz pour Icellui ſoir ne firent point tant detorches alumees côme les deux Iours preced. car aucuns dient q̂ mond ſ.r ne levoulloit pas. C Item en lad ville yavoit ung bourgoiz qui avoit fait couvrir ſamaiſon dargent et deſſoubz dor et devant Icelle treſgrant quantite de torches et delanternes. C Item ſemblabemet̂ en pluſſieurs et diverſes Rues pluſſieurs des bourgoiz avoient fait parer et aourner leurs maiſons dedraps et deluminaires treſRichemet̂ et

of Burgundy. C Item, before them [were] the lords and gentleman of monseigneur the Dauphin, the two sons of monseigneur de Crouy, and the two sons of the said Neufchâtel, marshal of Burgundy. C Item, before them were monseigneur of Cleves, monseigneur the bastard of Burgundy, and messire Philippe Pot, richly dressed, they and their horses. Item, before them were all the great lords of the court, and before the said lords, the gentlemen, two by two, without attendant nor page. And before the said gentlemen were those of the town in great number, clothed [in black]. C Item, after my said lord were fifty archers of his body on foot, vested in their robes, and each having a poleax in his hand. And behind him were fifteen pages and several gentlemen. And the horses, which were in the said entry, without the attendants and the pages who were there within the town, totalled 2,000 horses or more. C Item, in conclusion, this was the greatest triumph that had been made in the land for 500 years, since the coming of lords, because the next day in the evening, all the torches were rekindled—it is known, new torches and lanterns, those of the town enjoyed several characters, by whom in the presence of my said lord, until the hotel of the town, they were exposed to the figures and characters abovesaid, in praising the prince and in confessing their misdeeds. C Item, similarly, they did this on Tuesday evening, but for that evening they no longer lit torches as with the two previous nights, because several said that my said lord did not want it. C Item, in the said town there was a citizen who had worked to cover his house in silver and gold underneath, and before it was a very great quantity of torches and lanterns. C Item, similarly, on several and different roads, several of the citizens had dressed up and adorned their homes with cloth and very rich lighting and with large plants,

agrant fraiz. et dura trois Iours ceſte feſte. C Item ced mardi les officiers et bourgois de lad ville vindrent devers mond ſʳ en ſon hoſtel. Et Illec leRem̂cierent treſhumblement dece quil eſtoit venu en ſabonne ville en lui offrat̂ corps et biens donc Il les mercia. Et lors les genoulx at̂re lui ſupplierent quil lui pleuſt ſoupper par maniere debanquet en lamaiſon delad ville ledimenche enſ deſr̃ Iour davril. lequel leur octroya. Et diſoit on que leblancquet ſeroit fait ato⁹ venans et comme court ouverte et quil couſteroit pl.⁹ dedix mille eſcuz. dor Car lendemain ceulx degand envoyerent querir par toutes contrees ahuit aneuf lieues alaRonde toutes les viandes dillicieuſes quilz peurent finer tellement q̂ lon vendoit ung petit poucin deux patars

Lit deluſtice. tenu. par. le Roy. appelle. Les. douze. pers. deſon. Royaulme. et. autres. ſes. conſeillers.

Lan mil CCCC. Cinquante huit manda leRoy aux xii. ~~partes~~ pers defrance tant degliſe que lays et aceulx deſacourt deparlement q̂ ung chc͡n ſeRendiſt en la ville demontargis. Le viiiᵐᵉ Iour deIuing Auquel lieu Il avoit Intencion detenir ſon lit deIuſtice ou convencions pour aucuns affaires touchans lefait deſon Royaulme moult grandement ce quilz firent en lapluſpart. Et lafurent par leſpace dedeux moys pour traicter delexpedicion abolicion et condampnacion ~~de~~ duduc da lencon couſin germain du Roy et lun des pers defrance Lequel eſtoit priſonnier po⁹ĉtains criſmes delezemajeſte qui lui eſtoient Im putez et donc on diſoit quil eſtoit couppable Et eſtoient en ceſted convencion. Meſſ.ʳ le-

and this feast lasted three days. C Item, the said Tuesday, the officers and citizens of the said town came to my said lord in his hotel, and they received him there very humbly because he had come into his good town, offering to him servants and goods, for which he showed them mercy. And then, kneeling on the ground, they begged him that he would eat by manner of a banquet in the house of the said town on the following Sunday, the last day of April, which he granted them. And one said that the banquet would be made so all came and as an open court, and that it would cost more than 10,000 écus of gold. But the next day, those of Ghent sent to find in all countries from eight to nine leagues around, all the delicious meats that they could find, such that one sold a little chick for two clams.

The *lit de justice* made by the king, calling the dozen peers of his kingdom and others of his councillors

The said year 1458, the king ordered the dozen peers of France, both of the church and the laiety, and those of his court of parlement, that each render himself in the town of Montargis [on] the eighth day of June, at which place he had the intention to hold his *lit de justice* or conventions for several affairs touching very greatly on the fate of his kingdom, which most of them did. And they were there for the space of two months in order to negotiate the expedition, abolition, and condemnation of the duke of Alençon, agnatic cousin of the king and one of the peers of France, who was imprisoned for certain crimes of lésè-majesté that they had ascribed to him and for which one said he was culpable. And there was in this said convention messeigneurs the count

conte dedunoiz et delongueville. Le chancellier defrance. Maiſtre pierre du Re fuge general defrance et pluſſieurs autꝭ ſeigneurs et officiers aceſtedite convencion ne comparut aucunement leduc debourgongne qui eſt lepremier per defrance Combien quil fut admoneſte dy venir cil yvoulloit aſſiſter et comparoir. Maiz ce non obſtat̃ Il ny vint point pource que par letraicte fait arras ent̃ leRoy et lui Il neſtoitne ne povoit eſtre contraint aquelq̃ aſſẽblee ou convencion. ſinon deſon bon gre et voullẽte. Leſd deux moys deſſſd durans ſetenoit le Roy abaugency eſperant touſiôs allr̃ aud lieu demontargis. Maiz lui doubtat̃ lamortalite et mauvaiz air ſedeppartit et donna congie aung chcn̄ de ſen Retourner ſur ſon lieu. Et fut tranſmuee lad convenſion au xvme Iour dud moys proch̃ enſ enlaville de vendoſme. Et oud an mil cccc cinquâte huit. Leiiii[m] Iour daouſt mourut lepappe pius. Et oud an xvme Iour daouſt vindret̃ audit vendoſme par mandement to⁹ les conſeilliers pour leRoy en ſacourt de parlement tant lays que degliſe. Et meſ mement leveſque deparis et labbe deSaint denis qui navoiet̃ point eſte amontargis.

Areſt. pronn̂ce. leRoy. pnt̂ avêdoſme. contre. lehan. duc. dalencon.

Charles par lagrace dedieu Roy defrâce Atous pres̄ et advenir Salut et dillecton̄ comme no⁹ duement Informez que Iehan duc dalencon per defrance avoit conduit et demene et fait conduire et demener pluſſ.[rs] traictez et appoinctemens avec noz anciens ennemys et adverſaires les angloiz. Et pource faire avoit envoye en angletr̃e et ailleurs es pays deſd angloiz. pluſſieurs meſſages ſans noz congie et

of Dunois and of Longueville; the chancellor of France; master Pierre du Refuge, general of France; and several other lords and officers, at this said convention, the duke of Burgundy, who was the first peer of France, did not appear at all, although he was admonished to come there so he could assist and contribute there. But this notwithstanding, he did not come, because, by the treaty made at Arras between the king and him, he could not be constrained in any way to [come to] an assembly or convention, if not of his own free will and desire. The two months abovesaid, while the king based himself at Baugency, hoping always to go to the said place of Montargis, but he feared the death and bad air if he left and he gave leave to each one to return themselves to his place. And the said convention was transmuted to the fifteenth day of the following said month in the town of Vendôme. And in the said year 1458, the fourteenth day of August, the pope Pius died. And the said fifteenth day of August, all of the councillors came to the said Vendôme by order for the king in his court of parlement, both of the laiety and the church. And even the bishop of Paris and the abbot of Saint-Denis, which was no longer to be at Montargis.

Arrest pronounced, the king present, at Vendôme against Jean, duke of Alençon

Charles, by the grace of God, king of France, to all present and here, welcome and love, as we have been duly informed that Jean, duke of Alençon, peer of France, had conducted and led and made to conduct and lead several treaties and agreements with our ancient enemies and adversaries, the English. And to do this he had sent into England and others of the places of the said English several messages without our leave and licence, and without let-

licence et ſans aucune choſe nous en faire ſavoir. En grant preiudice deno⁹ et delachoſe publicque denoſ̃e Royaulme en tant que ano⁹ touche. Et pour ceſte cauſe et pour obvier aux Incôvenies̑ qui ſen euſſent peu enſuir ſe par no⁹ neuſt eſte donne Remede ſurce. Noſ̃ treſchier et ame couſin leconte dedunoiz et delongueville et noz amez et feaulx conſeilliers et chambellains pierre debrez ſeigneur delavarenne et grand ſeneſchal denormendie. Iehan lebourſſier general ſur le fait denoz finances. guillaume couſinot bailly deRouen chevallier et oud daydie bailly decoſtâce euſſent par noſ̃ commandement et par vertu denoz lectres patentes donnees auchaſtellier pres eſbruille Le xiiiime Iour deMay Lan mil CCCC. lvi. prins et arreſte led dalencon noſ̃ nepveu. Et pour proceder aupê lexpedicion deſon proces. par ladvis et deliberacion des gens denoſ̃ conſeil euſſions ordône par noz autres lectres donnees aumontRichard. lexxiiii^me Iour dud moys deMay deſrain paſſe que noſ̃ court deparlement lors ſceant aparis ſeroit et ſetendroit en noſ̃ ville demontargis. Et commenchant le premier Iour deIuing deſrain paſſe et Iucques alaperfection dicellui proces. Et pour Icelle côt tenir euſſions mande et ordonne venir aud lieu demontargis denoz preſidens et conſeilliers en noſ̃d court en bon et ſouffiſant nombre. et mandez pour yeſtre les pers et ſeigneurs denoſ̃ ſange et lignage tenans en parrye et auſ̃s. Et auſſi yeſtre noſ̃ ame ⁊feal chancellier et aucuns des maiſtres des Requeſtes denoſ̃ oſtel et autres gens denoſ̃ conſeil. En enſ^t laquelle noſ̃ ordonnance noſ̃d chancellier et noz amez et feaulx conſeilliers. Larceveſque et duc de Rains. Les eveſques et ducz delaon et delangres Les eveſques et contes debeauvoiz. challons et noyon pers defrance et nozd

ting us known anything, to the great prejudice of us and to the public [good] of our kingdom, and for this reason, and to obviate the inconveniences which would have ensued if by us we had not been given notice of this, our very dear and loved cousin, the count of Dunois and of Longueville, and our loved and faithful councillors and chamberlains, Pierre de Brézè, seigneur de la Varenne and grand seneschal of Normandy; Jehan le Bourssier, general for the sake of our finances; Guillaume Cousinot, bailiff of Rouen, knight; and Odet d'Aydie, bailiff of Constance, had by our command and by virtue of our letters patent given to the castellan, near Ébruille, the fourteenth day of May, in the 1456, taken and arrested the said of Alençon, our nephew, and to proceed on the expedition of his trial, by the advice and deliberation of the men of our council, we would have given, by our letters given at Montrichard the twenty-fourth day of the said month of May recently passed, that our court of parlement, then seated at Paris, would be and would render in our town of Montargis, and beginning the first day of June recently passed and until the completion of this trial. And in order to hold this court, we would have mandated and ordered to come to the said place of Montargis to our presidents and councillors in our said court in good and sufficient number, and ordered there to be the peers and lords of our blood and lineage holding in peerage and others. And also to be there our beloved and faithful chancellor, and others of the masters of requests of our house, and other men of our council. In following which of our orders, our said chancellor and our beloved and faithful councillors, the archbishop and duke of Rheims, the bishops and dukes of Laon and Langres, the bishops and counts of Beauvais, Chalons, and Noyon, peers of France, our said presidents and some of our said masters of requests and of our said councillors of our said court of parlem-

preſidens et aucuns de noſd maiſtres des Requeſtes et denoſd conſeilliers denoſ̃d court deparlement et auſſi denoſ̃d conſeil ſeſont trouvez auſd Iours et lieu. Et Illec aient beſongne aux preparations dud proces par aucuns temps. Et aux Intͬogatos daucuns adherens facteurs et complices dud dalêcon. Et Iucques environ lexv Iour deIuillet deſr̃ paſſe actendans laller denous pardella et des ſeigneu.[rs] denoſ̃ ſangc et dautres gens denoſ̃ conſeil eſtans par devers no.⁹ En Intencion deproceder alaffin dud proces. Laquelle allee nous euſſions differee acauſe delamortallite qui pend led temps ~ ſurvint en laville dorleans. ſully et autͬs lieux circonvoiſins dud lieu demontargis eſquelz no⁹ convenoit paſſer pour yaller. Et tant acauſe delad mortalite et pour obvier aux Inconvenies qui acauſe dece ſen euſſent peu enſuir. Et auſſi que nouvelles nous ſurvindrent depluſſieurs pays que noz ennemys qui avoient fait ĉtaine groſſe armee ſur lamer en Intencion defaire deſcente en noſ̃ Royaulme et marches denoz pays de xaîtonage et depoitou ou delabaſſe normendie. Et effin q̂ peuſſion eſtre en lieu demarche plus propice et convenable pour ſecourir aux lieux delentͬprinſe denoſd ennemys euſſions par ladviz et deliberacion denoſ̃d conſeil voulu ordonner et eſtablir noſ̃d court deparlement eſtre côtinuee et eſtre tenue en ceſte ville de vendoſme. Et auſſi les gens denoſ̃d court garnie des pers et ceulx denoſ̃ ſangc ⁊lignage et autͬs par nous mandez yeſtre et comparoir au xiime Iour dumoys daouſt. deſr̃ paſſe. Et ſemblablement euſſions mande et ordonne y eſtre leſurplus denoz preſidens. maiſtres des Requeſtes denoſ̃d hoſtel et autͬs noz conſeilliers en noſ̃d court deparlement. Leſquelz pour lors eſtoient encores demourans en noſ̃ bonne ville et cite deparis pour

ent, and also of our said council, found themselves at the said day and place, and here they attended to the preparations of the said trial for some time, and at the interrogations of several adherants, agents, and accomplices of the said of Alençon. And until around the fifteenth day of July recently passed, they attended the journey of us from there and of the lords of our blood and of other men of our council being for us, with the intention to proceed to the end of the said trial. Which journey we had deferred because of the mortality which, during the said time, occurred in the town of Orléans, Sully, and other places around the said place of Montargis, in which it suited us to go. And thus, because of the said mortality and to obviate the inconveniences that, because of this, would ensue, and also due to news we received from several lands that our enemies had made a certain large army on the sea in anticipation of making a descent into our kingdom and marches of our lands of Saintonage and Poitou or Lower Normandy, and so that it may be in a place on the march more favourable and convenient to secure from the attacks of our said enemies, we have, by the advice and deliberation of our said council, want to order and establish our said court of parlement to be continued and be held in this town of Vendôme, and also the men of our said court, supported by the peers and those of our blood and lineage and others, by our order to be there and appear on the twelfth day of the month of August recently passed. And similarly, we had mandated and ordered there to be a surplus of our presidents, masters of the requests of our said hotel, and others of our councillors in our said court of parlement, who for this will then remain in our said good town and city of Paris in order to proceed otherwise and to proceed with the said process until its conclusion, as it belongs by reason. And since we knew to come to the said place of Vendôme

proceder oulṫ et beſongner oud proces Iucques alaperfection dicellui ainſſi quil appartiendroit par Raiſon. Et depuis ſoyons venins aud lieu devendoſme. et auſſi pluſſieurs des ſeigneurs denoȓ faingc et lignage pers de france et tenans en paryie. Et les arceveſque et eveſque deſſuſnommez auſſi pers defrance et pluſſieurs auṫs prelatz. contes barons et chevallȓs en grant nombre denoȓd court deparlement et auṫs denoȓ conſeil. Et pardevant no⁹ ſcans en noȓd court garnie depers et auṫs aceappellez ait eſte aucune led dalencon. Lequel apres le ſerment par lui fait dedire verite. Inṫroge ſur les cas et criſmes donc Il aeſte trouve chȓge par Informacion adit et confeſſe deliberalle ⁊franche vollente ce quil ſenſuyt. QUE. apres q̂ leſ.[r] detalleboth oult prins bordeaulx ung nomme Iacques haye angloiz ſerviteur dun nôme Richard vvideville chlȓ auſſi angloiz vint aſaufconduit A alencon. Et parla aud dalencon ꝑ en ſegret du fait du mariage delafille deduc dalencon avec ~~leſ~~ lefilz du duc diork. Et que tant pour le fait dud mariage q̂ auſſi pour toutes auṫs choſ quilz vouldroient faire ſavoir les ungz aux autres lui et led Iacques haye eſlirent enſaigne de prend lepoulce delamain dicellui auquel le message de lune des parties ſadreſſoit. Et environ lemoys daouſt q̂ on diſoit mil CCCC Cinquante cinq. Led dalencon envoya querir ung nomme thomas gillet pbrê demourant adampfront et lui fiſt faire leſerment deſtre ſegret. Et apres lui diſt quil levoulloit êvoyer en angleterre et letint par aucun temps aceſte cauſe. Et lemena avecques lui alafleſche en eſperant ledeſpeſcher Illecc. Et que lors ſurviṫ aud lieu delafleſche ung nomme hotinton angloiz herault dangleṫre auquel Il ſedeſcouvrit et lui bailla charge daller en angleṫre po[r] admoeſtȓ et ~~exto~~ exorter de-

and also several lords of our blood and lingeage, peers of France and landholders, and the archbishops and bishops abovenamed, also peers of France, and several other prelates, counts, barons, and knights, in great number of our said court of Parlement, and others of our council. And before us, enunciated in our said court, filled with peers and others, anybody who knows the said d'Alençon, who, after the oath made by him to uphold the truth, interrogated on the case and crimes for which he has been found charged by information, to say and confess deliberately and of free will that which follows: THAT after the said Lord Talbot had captured Bordeaux, one named Jaques Haye, an Englishman, servant of one named Richard Woodville, a knight, also English, came with safe conduct to Alençon. And he spoke to the said of Alençon in secret about the act of marriage of the daughter of the duke of Alençon with the son of the duke of York. And that in order to do the deed of the said marriage, that also for everything they would want to do to know one another, he and the said Jacques Haye elected as a sign to take the thumb of their hand to which the message of the one of the parties addressed. And around the month of August—that one said 1455—the said of Alençon sent to fetch one named Thomas Gillet, a priest, remaining at Damfront, and he made the oath to be secret. And after that he said that he would send him into England, and he held him for some time for this reason. And he went with him to La Flêche, hoping to dispatch him from there. And then one named Huntington, an Englishman, herald of England, came to the said place of La Flêche, at which place he discovered and released his charge to go into England in order to admonish and urge through him our said enemies to come and descend into our lands of Normandy, ordering them that they agreed by God or by the devil, and that they thought in other things

parlui noſd ennemis avenir et deſſend en noȓ pays denormendie. En leur mandant quilz fuſſent dacord depardieu oude par lediable et quilz pencaſſent en auȋ choſe et quil ſeroit heure deſoy bouter avant et que oncques Ilz navoient eu ſi beau faire côme Ilz avoient lors et quil eſtoit temps ou Iamaiz et q̂ no⁹ eſtions loingtz et noȓ armee en armignat. Lautre en guyenne et lauȋ pour aller conȋ noȓ treſchȓ et treſame filz ledaulphin deviennoiz. Et que ~~lors~~ les nobles. les bonnes villes et lepeupple en to⁹ eſtatz eſtoient ſi mal contens q̂ plus ne povoient. Et q̂ led dalencon meſmement eſtoit mal content et q̂ ſe noz ennemys ſevoulloient aider Il leur aideroit deplaces dartillerie et detout ſon povoir. et quil avoit aſſez dartillerie pour combatre dix mille hômes aux champs pour ung Iour. Et noſd ennemis amenaſſent le-Roy dangleȋre et xxx. ou xl.ᵐ hommes pô côbatre dumoins. Et quil ny avoit en noȓd pays de normendie que ung denoz chiefz deguerre et iiiiᶜ· lances. Et quilz auroient conqueſte partie du pays avant que ypeuſſions mettre Remede. Et quil conſeilloit anoſd ennemys q̂ leRoy dan gleȋre apres ſadeſſente feiſt crier aſon detrompe et ſur paine delahart q̂ nul ne fuſt ſi hardy de prendre aucune choſe ſur les laboureurs ⁊gens du plat pays. Et que chc͡n peuſt demourer paiſiblet͡ en ſes biens et heritaiges. Et ſaucun faiſoit le contraire q̂ Incontineȇ pugnicion en fuſt faicte. Auſſi que leRoy dangleȋre Revocaſt les dons faitz par ſon pere et par lui et pardonnaſt atout lemonde tout letemps paſſe et procedaſt comme en conqueſte nouvelle. Auſſi q̂ noſd ennemys feiſſent leur deſcente en pluſſieurs pays. Ceſt aſſavoir leRoy dangleȋre et leduc diorck en labaſſe normandie. Et leduc debougangan acallaiz pour venir par picardie et lepays de

and that it would be the time to throw himself before and that one day they would not have had such beauty to make as they had then and that it was now or never, and that we would be far away, and our army in Armagnac, the other in Guyenne, and the other in order to go against our very dear and very beloved son, the dauphin of Viennois, and that the nobles, the good towns and the people, in all estates, would be so discontented that they could not be moreso. And that the said of Alençon even was discontent and that if our enemies wanted to aide him, he would aide them with pieces of artillery, and with all his power, and that he had enough artillery to fight 10,000 men on the fields for a day, and our said enemies will bring the king of England and at least 30,000 to 40,000 men to fight. And that there will be in our said land of Normandy only one of our generals and 400 lancers. And that they will have conquered part of the land before they could counterattack. And that he would council our said enemies that the king of England, after descending, would pronounce by trumpet and on pain of death that none would be so hardy to take anything from the labourers or men of the flat country, and that each could remain peacefully with their goods and heritage, and if anyone acted against him, that a punishment would be made immediately. Also, that the king of England would revoke his gifts made by his father and by him, and pardon to all the world all the times passed, and proceed as a new conquest. Also, that our said enemies would make their descent into several lands—it is known, the king of England and the duke of York into Lower Normandy, and the duke of Buckingham at Calais, in order to go via Picardy and into the lands of Cauz. And that we would want to go into the said marches in order to defend the said lands, those of Guyenne, as the said duke of Alençon said, being discontent, if our said enemies wanted to give

caulz. Et q̂ ſeno⁹ voullions allr̂ eſd marches pour deffend led pays. ceulx deguyenne coê diſoit leduc dalencon eſtoient malcontens ſe noſd ennemys leur voulloient donner ung pou dayde ſe pourroient mettre ſus et Rebeller conť no⁹ et q̂ en brief no⁹ perdrions tout le pays depardella. En oulť q̂ noſd ennemys feiſſent ſavoir aud dalencon leur deſcente trois moys devant Icelle deſcente affin quil peuſt pourveoir aſes places. et q̂ nen peuſſions faire anoȓ plaiſir. Et q̂ apres leur deſcente Ilz envoy aſſent led hotinton pour lui dire quelz gens Ilz avoient et leur Intencion Affin quil adviſaſt quil auroit affaire pour ſoy conduire avec eulx. Et oulť plus leur mandoit par led hotinton quilz admenaſſent leplus dordonnance quilz pôroient et lui feiſſent delivrer abruges ou ailleurs xx.ᵐ eſcuz ou atout lemoins promptement x.ᵐ eſcuz et ung moys apres leſurplus pour lui aider apaier partie des gens quil mettroit en ſes places et pour parfaire ſon artillerie. Et auſſi donna charge aud hotinton dedire anoſd ennemys quilz trouveroient apres leur deſcente aalencon ou adompfront partie deſon artillerie. Et promiſt et Iura led dalencon es mains dud hotinton herault ~~doſt~~ deſdeſſuſd quil tendroit anoſd ennemys tout ce quil leur prommettoit. Et auſſi ꝑ fiſt Iurer et promettre aud hotinton dedire les choſes deſſſd aud duc diorck. Richard Wideville et Iacques haye et quil ne lediroit ne ne Reveleroit aautre q̂ aeulx. Et pour certiffier et approuver tout ce quil avoit donne en charge aud hotinton dedire anoſd ennemys et q̂ aupartement dud hotinton led dalencon lui bailla lectre decreance adrecans aud duc diorck. ſignee dune. N. trenchee conten̂ ceſte forme. Seigneur vieullez croire ceporteʳ dece quil vo⁹ dira

to them a little aide, they could put themselves under and rebel against us, and in brief we would lose all the lands beyond. In addition, our said enemies would know due to the said Alençon to descend three months before this descent, so that he could provide for these places, and that we would not do to our pleasure. And that after their descent, they would send the said Huntington by them to say that men they had and their intention, so that he would advise what he would have to do for him to conduct with them. And also additionally, he ordered them by the said Huntington, that they bring most of the supplies that they could, and make to deliver to him at Bruges or around 20,000 écus, or at least 10,000 promptly, and one month after the surplus, in order to aide with paying part of the men who he put in his places, and to acquire his artillery. And also he gave charge to the said Huntington to say to oursaid enemies that they would find after their descent, at Alençon or at Dampfront, part of his artillery. And the said Alençon promised and swore to the hands of the said Huntington, herald of the abovesaid, that he would hold to our said enemies all that which he promised them. And also he swore and promised to the said Huntington to say the abovesaid things to the said duke of York, Richard Woodville, and Jacques Haye, and that he would not say it nor reveal it to anyone but them. And in order to certify and approve all that which he had placed in charge to the said Huntington, to say to our said enemies, and at the departure of the said Huntington, the said Alençon gave him a letter of credence addressed to the said duke of York, signed by one N., split into three parts, containing the following: 'Lord, desiring you to believe this bearer of that which I said to him, and your mercy on the side of good will, because I have a good desire to meet with you.' Saying with this, oursaid nephew, which he has well recorded in general,

demoy et vo⁹ mercye. deceȓ bon voulloir car Iay bonne voullente ſe ~~aven~~ avo⁹ netient. diſant avec ce noȓd nepveu quil eſtoit bien Recors en gñral quil avoit baille aud hotiton toutes les perſuaſions et coulleurs tant dartillerie que dauts choſes quil avoit peu pour parvenir aſes fins. Et apres pour executer ce q̂ d eſt avoit envoye led hotinton et pouence en angletre diſant auſſi led dalencon q̂ ĉtain temps apres Il avoit envoye led thonmas gillet pbrê en angletre et lui avoit donne chȓge dedire au duc diorck. ou aud Richard ~~ou~~ Wideville de par lui auſd enſaignes du poulce leſtat dupays et les charges denoȓ peuple. Et de amener noſd ennemys Leplus toſt quilz pourroient pô deſcend en ce Royaulme en laplus grant compaignie quilz pourroient et quilz eſtoient bien meſchas quilz ne ſavancoient devenir. Et quilz navoiet oncques eu ſibeau finer neconquerir lepays quilz avoient. Et que cilz avoient xx.ᵐ hômes pardera Ilz auroient conqueſte grant partie dud pays avant q̂ ypeuſſions pourveoir. Et auſſi q̂no⁹ eſtions loingtz. partis deberry pour aller ſur noȓd filz ledaulphin. Et que aupays navoit aucuns gens darmes et tout lepeuple mal côtet. Et que aIcelle heure eſtoit temps quilz veniſſent ou Iamaiz. Et avecques ce que quat Ilz vendroiet quilz amenaſſent leplus quilz pourroient et q̂ Il leur diſt q̂ led dalencon eſtoit fort eſbahy quil navoit eu aucunes nouvelles deulx nede ſond pourſ. Et quilz lui ~~Remoyffa~~ Renvoyaſſet et feiſſent ſavoir deleurs nouvelles et quil leʳ diſt franchement q̂ ce neſtoit Rien deleur fait ne deleur entreprinſe cilz ne monſtroient autment quilz vouſiſſent beſongner. Auſſi quil leur parlaſt deſd. xx.ᵐ eſcuz donc Il avoit donne charge aud hotinton. Et avecques ce quil charga aud thonmas gillet dedire aud duc diorck. q̂de-

that he had released to the said Huntington all the persuasions and colours, both of the artillery and of other things that he has little to achieve on his end. And afterwards, to execute that which he said, he had sent the said Huntington and Pouencé into England, saying also the said Alençon that, a certain time after, he had sent the said Thomas Gilley, a priest, into England, and he had given him charge to say to the duke of York or to Richard Woodville, on his behalf, the abovesaid gestures, the state of the land and the charges of our people. And to lead our said enemies the best that they could to descend into this kingdom in the greatest company that they could, and that they were quite wicked that they were not planning to come. And that they had never had so great a chance to conquer the country that they had. And that if they had 20,000 men on this side, they would have conquered the greater part of the said land before we could do it. And also that we were a long time gone in Berry in order to go against our said son, the Dauphin. And that in the lands there were no men-at-arms, and all the people were discontent, and that at this hour it was time that they came, or never. And with this, that when they came, they should bring as much as they could, and that he said to them that the said Alençon was very dumbfounded that he had had no news from them nor from his said messenger, and that they would send him and make known their news, and that he said freely to them that it was nothing for them to do nor for them to try, if they did not otherwise show that they wanted to go. Also that he spoke to them of the abovesaid 20,000 écus, for which he had given charge to the said Huntington. And with this, that he ordered the said Thomas Gillet to say to the said duke of York that of all his possessions on this side, he was best loved in Normandy. And this is why the men of the land would be greater. And he also ordered the said Gillet

tous les ſiens depar deca Il eſte lemieulx ayme en normendie. Et eſtoit celui pour qui les gens du pays ſeroient leplꝰ Et charga en oulſ̂ aud gillet quil diſt auſd angloiz q̂ apres leur deſcente Ilz feiſſent leurs ordonnances crys et publicacions telles quil avoit dictes et deſclairees aud hotinton. Et que ſe on parloit aud gillet du mariage de lafille denoſ̃d nepveu avec lefilz aiſne dud duc diorck. Il diſt delad fille ce quil en ſavoit et avoit veu. Et quil bailla aud gillet pour porter aud duc diorck. ĉtaines lectres conten͡ laforme qui ſenſuyt. Seigneur etcl. Ieme Recommande avous. et voꝰ prie q̂ en toute haſte mefacez ſavoir devoz nouvelles et pencez demoy car Il eſt temps. pourdieu metes diligence en voſ̃ fait et vous acquitez ceſte foiz car trop ennuye aqui actent. Et en toute haſte envoyez argent car voſ̃ fait machier couſte. Et adieu ſoyez qui voꝰ doint ce que deſires. Eſcript ubi ſupra. Et deſſoubz letout voſ̃. N. diſant oulſ̂ q̂ ung peu devant noel enſuivant Il envoya ung ~~hôme p~~ nomme pierre fortin et lui donna charge deparler auſd enſeignes dupoulce. auſd Wideville et Iacques haye et ſavoir aeulx cilz avoient eu aucunes nouvell͡ deſd pouence et thonmas gillet. Oulſ̂ diſt et confeſſa q̂ ~~oulſ̂~~ entre lad feſte denoel et la typhanie oud an leſd pouence et gillet Revindreſ̂ dangleſ̂re par devers lui. Et lui fiſt ſon Rapport led pouence appart dud gillet par lequel Il lui diſt q̂ led duc diorck et lechancellier dâ gleterre lemercioient deſon bon voulloir. Et q̂ leparlement dangleſ̂re neſtoit point encores aſſemble ne le Roy dangleſ̂re en leſtat delui en faire Reſponce finalle. Maiz que briefen tendroit parlemêt et beſongneroit len ſibien q̂ led duc dalencon en ſeroit content et q̂ noſd lui en feroient ſavoir deleurs nouvelles par led Wideville dedens kareſme lors apres enſ et

that he say to the said English that, after their descent, they would make their orders, crying and publishing such as he had said and declared to the said Huntington. And that if one spoke to the said Gillet of the marriage of the daughter of our said nephew with the eldest son of the said duke of York, he said of the said girl that he knew and had seen, and that he gave to the said Gillet, in order to take to the said duke of York, certain letters containing the form that follows: Lord, etc., I recommend myself to you and it pleases you that in all haste you know me for your news and thoughts by me, because it is time, for God puts diligence into your deed and aquits you this time, because he is annoyed at what is happening. And in all haste you sent money, because your deed has cost me dearly. And through God you will be that which you desire. Written as above. And below: All yours N saying in addition that a little before the following Christmas, he sent a man named Pierre Fortin and gave him charge to speak with the said signs to the said Woodville and Jacques Haye, and to know from them if they had had any news of the said Pouencé and Thomas Gillet. Otherwise, he said and confessed that between the said feast of Christmas and of Epiphany in the said year, the said Pouencé and Gillet returned into England on his behalf. And the said Pouencé made his report to him on behalf of the said Gillet, by which he said to him that the said duke of York and the chancellor of England thanked him for his good will. And that they told him that England was no longer unified, nor was the king of England in the state of making a final response to him. But that briefly he would hold parlement and he would work in it so well that the said duke of Alençon would be content and that oursaid [enemies] he would make to know of their news by the said Woodville within Lent then afterwards following, and that our said enemies or others of them would have

que noſd ennemys au aucuns deulx avoieṫ baiſie les armes ou lenſaigne les lectres dud duc dalencon. leſquelles portoit led pouence ſon pourſuivant pour lonneur dud dalencon. diſoit auſſi que led gillet par ſon Rapport lui avoit d q̂ led duc diorck ſe Recommandoit alui et leRemercioit deſon bon voulloir et auſſi lui prioit q̂ touſiours levouſiſt cȏtinuer et q̂ avant quil fuſt lemoys deſeptembre enſ led duc acompaigne des plus grans ſ.[rs] dangleṫre deſcendroit en noȓd pays deNormend aſi grande et bonne puiſſance q̂ led dalencon en devroit eſtre content. Auſſi q̂ noȓd nepveu trouvaſt maneȓ deRecouvrer aucue place ou port demer pour ladeſcente denoſd ennemys et quil leur fiſt ſavoir ſe noȓd filz ~~les~~ le daulphin yroit point ennormendie. Et autelles et ſemble Reſponce avoit fait led thonmas gillet duchancellȓ dangleṫre pour ladire et faire ſavoir aud dalencon. Et oulṫ pl⁹ confeſſa q̂ Incontineṫ apres leRetour deſd pouence et thonmas gillet Il envoya en angleṫre ung nomme maiſtre emond gallet apres cequil oult prins delui leſerment ſur lelivre detenir les choſes ſegrettes et quil bailla aud gallet unes lectres adrecans aud duc diorck. ſignees deſon vray ſaing et deſon nom Iehan. Lequel Il avoit trenche en quaṫ et le bailla aud gallet pour legarder appart deſd lettres deſquelles Il diſoit leffect eſtre tel Seigneur Ieme Recommande avous. Iay ouy ce que mavez fait ſavoir. et vo⁹ prie q̂ Iaye devous auṫs nouvelles leplus toſt q̂ vo⁹ pourrez ſe vo⁹ voullees entendre aux matieres donc ce porteur vous parlera. Il en eſt temps Ie. ẙ entendray voullentiers et ſiray tant q̂ vous ſerez content. et lecroies dece quil vo⁹ dira demapart. Auſſi diſoit quil avoit donne charge aud gallet deſavoir laReſponce dud mariage et des auṫs choſes quil

kissed the arms or the sign of the letters of the said duke of Alençon, which the said Pouencé, his messenger, carried in honour of the said Alençon, saying also that the said Gillet, by his report, had said to him that the said duke of York recommended himself to him and thanked him for his good will and also prayed to him that always it would continue, and that after it was the month of September following, the said duke, accompanied by the majority of the great lords of England, would descend into our lands of Normandy with so great and good power that the said of Alençon ought to be happy. Also that our said nephew would find the manner of recovering any place or port of the sea for the descent of our said enemies, and that he made known to them if our said son, the Dauphin, would go into Normandy. And the said Thomas Gillet made other such and similar responses to the chancellor of England in order to say to him and make known to the said of Alençon. And in addition, he confessed that immediately after the return of the said Pouencé and Thomas Gillet, he sent into England one named master Emond Gallet, after which he had taken the oath on the book to hold the things secret, and that he gave to the said Gallet letters addressed to the said duke of York, signed by his true sign and by his name Jean, which he had cut into quarters, and he gave it to the said Gallet to guard with part of the said letters, of which it said the effect was such: Lord, I recommend myself to you. I have heard that you have made to know me, and I pray to you that I have for you other news as quickly as you can, if you want to understand the matters of which this porter speaks to you. It is time I hear about it willingly, and I will such that you will be happy, and I will believe that he says to you for my part. Also he said that he had given charge to the said Gallet to know the response of the said marriage and of the other things that he

leur avoit fait ſavoir par led hotinton pouence et gillet. Et deleur dire quil eſtoit temps debeſongner cilz voulloient Riens bien faire. Et quil vouldroit quilz fuſſent deſſenduz auſſi eſpes q̂ mouches ou greſle et quil eſtoit aſ̂tene q̂ no⁹ alions ſur noſ̂ filz ledaulphin et quil ſetenoit ſceur davoir du Retour des nopces. Et que ceilz venoieτ̂ et prenoient appoinctement avecques lui led dalencon leur aidroit deſes places deſon artillerie. Et detout ce que en monde lui ſeroit poſſible et quil ne failliſſent pource avenir. Et auſſi quil ny euſt point defaulte q̂ ne lui fuſſent delivrez leſd xx.m eſcuz. diſant oulſ̂ q̂ environ paſques lors procĥ enſ pource quil ſeſmerveilloit q̂ led gallet neſtoit Retourne dangleterre Il Renvoya led fortin aud lieu decallaiz. Et lui donna charge deparler auſd angloiz aux enſaignes q̂ deſſ. Et leur demander cilz voulloient Rien ou non. Et oulſ̂ plus diſt et confeſſa q̂ environ quaſimodo enſ led gallet Retourna dangleſ̂re par devers lui et lui apporta lectres duRoy dan gleſ̂re ſignees comme diſoit led gallet dela main dicellui Roy dangleſ̂re ceſt aſſavoir henry. Et q̂ les lectres contenoient en effect ce quil ſenſ. Treſchier couſin no⁹ vo⁹ ~~envoyons~~ m̂cions du bon voulloir q̂ avez en no⁹. No⁹ envoyerons noz facteurs aupremier Iour daouſt abruges pour lefait des treves denτ̂ nous et beaucouſin debourgongne et que la ſetienneτ̂ voz facteurs pour appoincter detoutes choſes et ferons tant ſedieu plaiſt q̂ vo⁹ ſerez bien content. Et oulẑ diſoit q̂ led gallet avoit d que le Roy dangleſ̂re avoit Recuilly legouvſ̂mment. Et que led duc diork. eſtant alle en galles et q̂ aceſte cauſe led gallet ceſtoit adieu aud Roy dangleterre et lui avoit d levoulloir et Intencion dud duc dalencon. donc Il ceRemeuroit et faiſoit ſañ par lui quil envoyeroit ſes ambaſſadeurs aud lieu

had made known to them by the said Huntington, Pouené, and Gillet, and to tell them that it was time to work if they wanted to do anything, and that he would like that they descend also as quickly as flies or hail, and that he ascertained whether we would ally with our said son, the Dauphin, and that he make himself certain to have in return the wedding. And that if they would come and make an agreement with him, the said of Alençon would help him with his places, of his artillery, and of all that which in the world was possible to him, and that they would not fail for this to come. And also that they would no longer default on delivering to him the said 20,000 écus, saying otherwise that, around Easter then following next, for that which he would marvel that the said Gallet did not return from England. He resent the said Fortin to the said place of Calais, and gave him charge to speak to the said English with the signs as above, and to ask them whether they would do it or not. And in addition, he said and confessed that around the following Quasimodo, the said Gallet returned from England to him and delivered to him letters from the king of England, signed, as the said Gallet said, by the hand of this king of England, it is known Henry, and that the letters contained in effect that which follows: 'Very dear cousin, we thank you for the good will that you have toward us. We have sent our representatives on the first day of August to Bruges to make treaties between us and our good cousin of Burgundy, and that they will hold your representatives there to arrange for all things, and we do such, if it pleases God, that you will be very happy'. And otherwise he said that the said Gallet had said that the king of England had received the government, and that the said duke of York having gone to Wales and that for which cause, the said Gallet, it is with God to the said king of England, and he had said to him the will and intention of the said

debruges ſelon les conten eſd lectres. Et q̂ led duc dalencon yenvoyaſt ſemblablet̂ ~~yevre~~. Et que leſd ambaſſadeurs appointeroiet̂ en ſemble deſd. xx.m eſtuz. et auſſi debaillez Reallez detoutes aut̂s choſes. diſt auſſi ⁊confeſſa led dalencon q̂ tant pource q̂ lelieu deſſſd auquel noſd ennemys lui devoient envoyez leſd xx.m eſcuz lui eſtoit long. que auſſi po^r^ce quil deſiroit ſavoir liſſue deſon appoinctemet̂ avec noſd ennemys Il Renvoya deRechief led gallet en angleterre affin dadvancer led argent. Et auſſi pour Recouvrer ung ſaufcôduit pour ung deſes gens duquel ſaufconduit lenom devoit eſtre en blanc affin quil peuſt envoyez aucû homme pour beſongner avec leſd angloiz la ou meſtr̂ euſt eſte et paſſer ſes appoinctemens. Et que en oult̂ Il deiſt aud gallet quil ne ſavoit quelles les fortunes delaguerre ſeroient et quil vouldroit bien avoir quelq̂ Retrait en anglet̂re ſelecas advenoit affin quil ſetraiſt par della. Et quil lui parlaſt deladuchie debethford de laduchie decloceſtre et des terres q̂ les ducz deſd duchiez tenoient en ~~ſon~~ leur vivant affin quilen fuſt parle au Roy dangleterre. Et q̂ aupartement dud gallet Il luy bailla unes lectres adreſans aud duc diorck. conten̂ ceſte forme. Seigne.rs Ie me Recommande avo⁹ et me donne grant mêveille q̂ aut̂ment Ie nay eu nouvelles devo⁹ parce porte^r^. Et vo⁹ prie q̂ men facez ſavoir debrief. et le vueillez croire dece quil ~~vo⁹~~ dira depar moy Et oult̂ eſcrivy aut̂s lectres amaiſtre loys gallet demourant en anglet̂re et pere dud maiſtre emond conten̂ q̂ led dalencon lemercioit deſa bonne voullente quil avoit vue alui ainſſi quil avoit ſceu par ſon filz. et quil adrecaſt touſiours les matieres. diſoit oult̂ q̂ ainſſi q̂lui et led maiſtre emond deviſoient des matierese led maiſtre emond lui diſt q̂ lefilz duſire de talboth deſcen-

duke of Alençon, thus he remembered and made sane by him, that he sent his ambassadors to the said place of Bruges according to the contents in the said letters. And that the said of Alençon would similarly send there. And that the said ambassadors would appoint together of the said 20,000 écus and also for the actual release of all other things said also, and the said of Alençon would confess that, due to the fact that the abovesaid place to which our said enemies must send to him the said 20,000 écus was far away from him; also, because he desired to know the issue of his agreement with our said enemies, he sent again the said Gallet into England in order to advance the said money and also to recover a safeconduct for one of his men, of which safeconduct the name ought to be blank, for which he could send any man to work with the said English, whatever occupation he be, and pass his agreements. And that in addition, he said to the said Gallet that he did not know what the fortunes of war would be, and that he may well have to at some point retreat into England if the case arose, which he pulled out for this. And that he spoke to him of the duchy of Bedford, of the duchy of Gloucester, and of the lands that the dukes of the abovesaid duchies held in their lives, for which he had spoken to the king of England. And that at the departure of the said Gallet, he gave him letters addressed to the said duke of York containing this form: 'Lord, I recommend myself to you, and it gives me great wonder that so far I have had no news from you by this messenger, and I beg to you that you know me shortly, and you believe that which he says on my behalf,' and also he wrote other letters to master Louis Gallet, remaining in England, and father of the said master Edmond, happy that the said Alençon thanked him for his goodwill that he had shown to him; also that he had learned by his son and that he addressed always the matters, saying otherwise

droient en guyenne atout x. ou xx.m combatans. Et que le Roy dangleẗre et leduc diorck. 7auẗs deſcendroient en ~ nôd pays. denormendie. Et leduc debouquîghan et leconte devillechet et duncheſte deſſendroieẗ acallaiz et vendroient par picardie. x. ou. xiim combatans. Oulẗ plus diſt et confeſſa led ~~da~~ dalencon avoir parle afortin ſon varlet dechâbre affin q̂ led fortin fuſt deſon aliance touchaẗ lefait deſd angloiz ~~commeẗ Il eſperoit quil fuſt~~. Et en oulẗ lui avoit donne charage de ſavoir commeẗ noẗ place degrantville eſtoit emparee et celle eſtoit bien fortiffiee et quelles Repparacions on yavoit faictes et en eſpecial ducoſte ou elle avoit eſte auẗffoiz prinſe. Et que ce Il ſefuſt Ioinct avec leſd angloiz commeẗ Il eſperoit quil feiſt Il euſt bien voulu trouver maniere par quelque moien que ce euſt eſte debaillẗ lad place degrantville et toutes les autres places quil lui euſt eſte poſſible auſd angloiz Et faire tout lepovoir et dilligence quil euſt peu. diſoit oulẗ led dalencon quil aeſt meu defaire exciter et eſmouvoir leſd angloiz avenir deſcend enced Royaulme par leſd meſſagiers. Alaſubgeſcion dun nomme mathieu pbrê. duquel Il ne ſavoir lenom qui ſediſoit eſtre dupays delion et ſerviteur dubaſtard darmignac duquel Il ſedeſoit Lequel côme diſoit Icellui dalêcon lui avoit apporte lẗs decreance ſur leporteur dicelles. et par noẗd filz ledaulphin et auſſi depar lebaſtard darmignac. Et eſquell lectres denoẗ filz lui avoit acouſtume lui eſcripre Led alencon ainſſi quil diſoit faiſoit doubte pource quelles neſtoient pas en la forme ſelon laquelle noẗ filz lui avoit acouſtume eſcripre. Et auſſi faiſoit doubte en laſignature deſd lectres. Sur laquelle choſe et aſaRequeſte euſſent eſte examiez par aucuns noz cômiſſaires pluſſieurs teſies nommez par led

also that he and the said master Edmond would devise the materials. The said master Edmond told him that the son of Lord Talbot would descend into Guyenne with about 10,000 or 20,000 soldiers. And that the king of England and the said of York and others would descend into our said lands of Normandy, and the duke of Buckingham, and the earl of Wiltshire and Worchester would descend on Calais and would come via Picardy with 10,000 to 12,000 soldiers. In addition, the said Alençon said and confessed to have spoken to Fortin, his chamber servant, after which the said Fortin was by his alliance touching upon the deed of the said English. And in addition, he had given charge to know how our place of Grantville could be seized and it was well fortified and which repairs one had made there, and especially on the side where it had been previously captured. And that if he was to join with the said English as he hoped that he would, he would have liked to find the manner by which means that this could be, to release the said place of Grantville and all the other places that it had been possible to him with the said English, and to exert the power and diligence that he should have; the said of Alençon also saying that he had been moved to excite and move the said English to come to descend into this said kingdom by the said messengers at the suggestion of one named Matthew, a priest, of whom the surname is not known, who said of himself to be from the land of Lyon and a servant to the bastard of Armagnac, who, as this of Alençon says, had given letters of credence to him on the carrier of these, and by our said son the Dauphin and also by the bastard of Armagnac. And to which letters of our son, the said of Alençon, as he says, were doubted, because they were not in the form according to which our son had been accustomed to writing to him. And also it was doubted in the signature of the said letters. On which thing

dalencon ſes ſerviteurs de ſon hoſtel. Et leſquelz affermerent côme Ilz avoient veu led preſtre et auſſi euſt eſte examine led maiſtre emond gallet avecques lequel led dalencon ſediſoit aû bien amplement communique touc̅h lefait dud preſtre. Et led gallet euſt eſte ſurce confronte avec led dalencon. Auſſi euſſet̂ eſte Interrogez ſurce leſd meſſagiers ⁊autŝ complices dud dalencon. leſquelz côme Il eſtoit acroire devoiet̂ ſavoir delad maniere ou cas q̂ ceſuſt choſe vraye. Par to⁹ leſquelz Teſmoings nont eſte trouvez aucu̅e choſe dece q̂ diſt eſt en ceſtepartie par led dalêcon. Ainſſoiz aient deſpoſe pluſſieurs choſes qui donnet̂ preſumption aucontraire. Et en oult̂ diſoit led dalencon q̂ oncques neult lectres denor̂d filz et ne ouyt parler delad matrê a aut̂ q̂ aud mathieu et neſavoir encores cil lediſoit delui meſme ou par qui Il le diſoit. Et q̂ led dalencon navoit oncques veu povoir ne Inſtruction denor̂d filz touĉh telle matiere. Et ſurce et autŝ choſes euſſent eſte faictes aud dalencon. pluſſ.rs Remonſtrances parleſquelles euſt apparu q̂ ceſtoit choſe controuvee par lui pour ſoy cuider couvrir et donner coulleur aſacharge. Auſquelles Remonſtrances ou alaplus part dicelles led dalencon euſt dit quil ny ſavoit que Reſpondre. ou autŝ parolles dautre effect. Et oult̂ plus Icellui dalencon en parlant dud preſtre et en Reſpondant auſd Remonſtrances. et auſſi aux Interrogacions qui ſurce lui avoient eſte faictes euſt eſte vaxillant et variant en pluſſieurs pointz et articles comme tout ce appert pluſapplain par led proces. Parquoy nepar choſe qui ait eſte dicte par led dalencon ne deppoſee par leſd teſmoings ſurce examinez et aſa Requeſte et aut̂ment parchoſe contenue oud proces. Na eſte trouve par choſe ꝑquoy no⁹ et nor̂d court devions tenir ne tenons

and at his request they had been examined by several of our commissioners, several witnesses named by the said Alençon, his servants of his hotel, and who affirmed as they had seen the said priest; and also the said master Edmond Gallet had been examined, with whom the said Alençon said had been in ample communication regarding the deed of the said priest, and the said Gallet had been for this compared with the said Alençon. Also the said messengers and other accomplices of the said Alençon had been interrogated on this matter, who, as it is believed, ought to know of the said matter or case that this was a true thing. By all which witnesses nothing had been found of that which is said in this party by the said of Alençon. So they had desposed several things that gave presumption to the contrary. And in addition, the said Alençon said that he never had letters of our said son, and he only heard the matter spoken with another to the said Matthew, and he still did not know if he said it himself or by whom he said it. And that the said Alençon never had wanted to be able to nor instructed our said son regarding this matter. And on this and other things there had been made with the said Alençon several remonstrations by which it had appeared that this thing was contrived by him in order to consider himself covered and given colour to his charge. To which remonstrations, or at the most part of them, the said Alençon had said that he knew only the response, or other words to other effect. And in addition, this Alençon, in speaking of the said priest and in responding to the said remonstrations and also to the interrogations which for this had been made to him, had been vacillating and varying on several points and articles, as this became more clear through the trial. For which nothing which had been said by the said of Alençon, nor revealed by the said witnesses under this examination and at his request, and otherwise by things contained

noȓd filz ne auſſi led baſtard darmignac aucunement charges envȓs no⁹ et Iuſtice. Et depuis eult eſte conclud et delibere q̂ led proces eſtoit en eſtat aIuger. Savoir faiſons. que veues et viſitees par no⁹ et noȓd court garnye des pers et dautres côme Il appartient ~~des~~les charges Informacons et confrontacions des teſmoings faictes a lencontre dud dalencon enſemble les confeſſions et auťs choſes contenues oud proces bien aulong et atreſgrande et menue deliberacion denoȓd court garnye côme deſſus. Avons dit et deſclaire diſons ⁊deſclairos par arreſt led dalencon eſtre criminel deleze maieſte et comme tel eſtre prive et deboute delonneur et dignite deparrye defrance et auťs dignitez et prerogatives. Et lavons condampne et condampnons. aRecevoir mort et eſtre execute par Iuſtice. Et avecques ce avons deſclaire et deſclairons to⁹ ſes biens quelzconques eſtre confiſquez et ano⁹ compectez et appartenir. Touteffoiz no⁹ avons Reſerve et Reſervons defaire et ordonner ſur letout noȓ bon plaiſir. Lequel no⁹ deſclairons eſtre tel. Ceſt aſſavoir que auRegard delapſonne dud dalencon no⁹ plaiſt q̂ lexecucion dicelle ſoit differee Iucques anoȓ bon plaiſir. Et quât aux biens qui furet̂ et appartindret̂ aud dalencon. Ia ſoit ce q̂ veu lenormite des cas ⁊ crimes deſſ deſclares. Les enffans dicell dalencon ſelon droit et uſages gardez en tel cas deuſſent eſtre privez et deboutez deto⁹ bies honneurs et preRogatives et vivre en telle povrete et mendicite que ce fuſt exemple ato⁹ auťs. Neantmoins en Remenbrance des ſervices des predeceſſeurs dud dalencon faiz anoſd predeceſſeurs et alachoſe publicq̂ denoȓ Royaulme. Eſperant auſſi q̂ led enffs ſegouvȓneront et conduiront envȓs no⁹ côme bons vrays et loyaulx ſubgetz doivet̂ faire envȓs leur ſouverains

in the said process, nothing had been found by which we and our said court should hold nor hold our said son, nor also the said bastard of Armagnac, in any way charged by us and justice. And since it had been concluded and decided that the said process was in a state to be judged, to know making that, seeing and visiting by us and our said court, garnished by peers and others, as they belong to it, the charges, informations, and confrontations of the said witnesses made against the said of Alençon, together with the confessions and other things contained in the said process well long and very large and small deliberations of our said court garnished as above. Having said and declared, saying and declaring by proclaimation the said of Alençon to be guilty of the crime of lèsé-majesté, and as such to be deprived and rejected of the honour and dignity of peer of France, and other dignities and prerogatives. And having condemned and we condemn him to receive death and to be executed by justice. And with this, having declared and declaring all his goods whatsoever to be confiscated and counted and belonging to us. However, we have reserved and reserve to make and order for him all at our good pleasure, which we declare to be such—it is known, that, in regard to the person of the said of Alençon, it pleases us that the execution of this will be deferred at our good pleasure. And in regard to the goods that were and belonged to the said of Alençon, already it was this that, viewing the enormity of the case and crimes above declared, the children of the said of Alençon, according to right and usages maintained in such a case, should be deprived and disallowed all of the goods, honours, and prerogatives, and live in such poverty and mendicancy that it is an example to all others. Nonetheless, in remembrance of the services of the predecessors of the said of Alençon, made to our said predecessors and to the public good of our kingdom, hop-

ſeigneurs. Et en faveʳ et ~~com~~ contemplacion des Requeſtes ano⁹ ſurce fctes par noſ treſchier et treſame couſin leduc debretaigne oncle dud dalencon. No⁹ de grace en moderant laconfiſcacion ⁊forfaiture deſſſ deſclaſ ~~vous~~ voullons deſclairer et no⁹ plaiſt en tant q̂ touche les biens meubl qui fureẽ aud dalencon quilz ſoient ⁊demeureẽ aſes femme et enffans Reſerve ano⁹ lartil lerie harnoiz et auſs habillemens deguerre. Et auRegard des ſeigneuries et biens Immeubles. No⁹ en moderant côme deſſſ Retenons ano⁹ les ville chaſteau chaſtellenie et viconte dalençon. Les ville chaſteau chaſtellenie et viconte dedampfront. Les ville chaſteau chaſtellenie et viconte de vernoil tant deca q̂ delaRiviere darne avecques les apparten deppend deſd villes chaſteaulx chaſtellenies ⁊vicontes. Leſquelz des aprẽ no⁹ uniſſons adioingnons et Incor porons aupatrimoine et domaine denoſ cou ronne. Et avecques ce avons Retenu et et Retenons ano⁹ leſurplus des chaſteaulx chaſtellenies terres vicontez ſᵉies. Rentes Reve nues poceſſions et bien Immeubles qui fureẽ deladuchie dalencon adiacente ⁊apparten dicelle duchie. enſemble to⁹ droitz noms Raiſons et accions qui fureẽ et pourroient eſcheoir compecter et appartenir aud dalêcon. Acauſe delad duchie tant en propriete poceſſion q̂ autrement et tous auſs droitz et ſeigneuries qui ſont parties denoſ courône et appanage defrance ou quilz ſoient Reſve leconte duperche donc cy apres ſera faicte mencion pour en faire et ordonner noſ bon plaiſir. Et auſſi avons Retenu ⁊Retenoſ ano⁹ les chaſteau chaſtellenie terre ⁊ſᵉie deblancay en touraine enſemble ceque led dalencon avoit et prenoit ſur les pontz denoſ ville detours et autres Rentes fiefz et Reve nues que Icellui dalencon avoit et prenoit en

ing also that the said children govern and conduct themselves towards us as good, true, and loyal subjects ought to do toward their sovereign lords, and in favour and contemplation of the requests to us on this fact made by our very dear and very beloved cousin, the duke of Brittany, uncle of the said of Alençon, we, by grace, in moderating the confiscation and forfeiture above declared, wanting to declare and please us, in such that touches the moveable goods that were with the said Alençon, that they will be and remain to his wife and children, reserving to us the artillery, equipment, and other material of war. And in regard to the lordships and immoveable goods, we, in moderating as above, retain to us the town, castle, castelleny, and viscounty of Alençon; the town, castle, castelleny, and viscounty of Dampfront; the town, castle, castelleny, and viscounty of Vernuil, both here and across the River Orne, with the appurtenances, dependences of the said towns, castles, castellanies, and viscounties, which at the present are united to us, adjoining and incorporated into the patrimony and domain of our crown. And with this, we have retained and retain to us the surplus of the castles, castellanies, lands, viscounties, seigneuries, rents, revenues, possessions, and immoveable goods that were in the duchy of Alençon, adjacent, or belonging to this duchy, together with all rights, names, reasons, and actions that were and could scheat, correspond and belong to the said Alençon because of the said duchy, both in propriety, possession, and otherwise, and all other rights and lordships which were a part of our crown and apanage of France, or which would be, reserving the county of Perche, which will be made mention afterwards, in order to make and ordain at our good pleasure. And also we have retained and retain to us the castle, castelleny, land, and fief of Saint-Blançay in Touraine, together with that which the said Alençon had and took

noȓd ville et chaſtellenie detours pour en faire et ordonner comme deſſſ. Et ſem blablement avons Reſerve ano⁹ les foys et hommages droitz et Recognoeſſances qui compectoient et appartenoient aud dalêcon acauſe delad conte duperche. Sur et pour Raiſon des tȓes ⁊ſˀies. deNogent le Rotrou. ſes appartenances et appendences et auȓs terres apparteñ anoȓ treſchȓ ⁊treſame couſin leconte du maine. Acauſe denoȓ treſchiê et treſamee couſine ſafemme. Et au Regard des auȓs terres ſˀies et biens Immeubles qui furent ~~et app~~ appartindrent aud dalencon. No⁹ les laiſſons ⁊voullons quilz ſoient et demeurent auſd enffans dud dalêcon ainſſi et par lamaniere qui ſenſuyt. Ceſt aſſavoir laconte tȓe ſˀie duperche pour en Ioir par pierre ſeul filz. dud Iehan dalencon et par ſes heritiers maſles deſcend deſon corps en loyal mariage. Sans touteſvoẏe Aucune dignite ou preRogative deparrie. Et quant auſurplus des terres et ſeigneuries qui furent et appartindrent aud Iehan dalencon No⁹ les laiſſons et voullons quelles ſoient et demeurent aux enffans dud dalencon tant maſles que fumelles pour en Iouir par leſd enffans ſoubz noȓ main Iucques ace quilz et chcñ deulx ſoient en aage. Et apres cequilz ſeront aagiez par leurs mains comme deleur propre choſe etpar les hȓtiers deſcendans deleurs propres corps en loyal ~ mariages et tout ſelon les couſtumes des pays ou leſd terres et ſeigneuries ſont cituees et aſſiſes. En teſmoing dece ⁊l. donne. avendoſme Lexᵐ Iour doctobre Lan mil ~ CCCC. Cinquante. huit. Et denoȓ Regne le xxxviiᵐ.

ICelle. ſentence donnee ⁊prononcee en labſence dud Iehan dalencon et apres alui notiffie et fait aſſavoir en

from the bridge of our town of Tours, and other rents, fiefs, and revenues that this of Alençon had and took in our said town and castelleny of Tours, in order to make and order as above. And similarly, we have reserved to us the oaths and homages, rights and recognitions that fall and belong to the said Alençon because of the said county of Perche, for and by reason of the lands and lordships of Nogent-le-Rotrou, its apputrements and appendices, and other lands belonging to our very dear and very beloved cousin, the count of Maine, because of our very dear and very beloved cousin, his wife. And in regard to the other lands, lordships, and immoveable goods that were and belong to the said of Alençon, we leave them and want that they be and remain with the said children of the said Alençon, thus and by the means that follow—it is known, the county, land, and lordship of Perche, to be enjoyed by Pierre, only son of the said Jean d'Alençon, and by his male heirs, descending from his body in loyal marriage, without any dignity or prerogative as peer. And regarding the surplus of lands and lordships that were and belong to the said Jean d'Alençon, we leave them and want that they will be and remain to the children of the said Alençon, both males and females, to be enjoyed by the said children under our hand until each of them comes of age. And after they are of age, by their hands as is their right, and by the heirs, descending from their rightful bodies in loyal marriage, and all according to the customs of the countries where the said lands and lordships are situated and seated. In witness of this, etc. Given at Vendôme the tenth day of October in the year 1458 and of our reign the thirty-seventh.

This sentence given and pronounced in the absence of the said Jean d'Alençon, and afterwards to him notified and made

laprifon ou Il eftoit par monf.ʳ legrant prefident dethorete Maiftre Iehan leboullengier confeillr̃ duRoẙ en facourt de-parlement Maiftre Iehan bureau treforier defrance et au-cuns autres dugrant confeil du Roy. donc led dalencon fut bien efbahy et defconforte et non fans caufe.

Oudit an mil CCCC. Cinquante huit en moy deIanvier ter-mina devie a trefpas trefhault et puiffant prince. Monf.ʳ art.⁹ debretaigne et en paravant et en apres fa vie devant conftable defrance. Apres la mort duquel fucceda alad duch-ie. Monf.ʳ francois filz demadame deftampes feur de madame dorleans. Laquelle en perfonne le mena. ⁊t̂.

Commet̂ le Roẙ alita. aulit delamort.

Lan. mil. ᶜ CCCC Soixante ⁊ ung. environ lecommence-ment du moys deIuillet fut feme c̃tain langage par gens plains dezizanie et difoit on que on voulloit empoifonner. LeRoy trefxpi͡en charles viiᵉ dece nom. luy eftant ameun fur yevre. delaquelle chofe apres quil fut Informe ficha tellemet̂ led empoifonnement en fon ceur que oncques puis neult Ioye ne fante. Maiz pource quil fut advr̃ti par ung capitaine qui moult laymoit y adioufta telle foy et fedefconforta telle ment quil delaiffa lemengier par lefpace dehuit Iours ou environ pource quil ne fofoit fier anul defes gens. Ne pour chofe que fes phificiens lui diffent Il ne voulloit menger ne prendre au-cune Refection. Et Iucques ace que fes fuficiens lui dirent que cil ne mangoit Il eftoit mort. Et adonc mift paine demengr̃ Maiz nepeult. Car fes conduits eftoient Ia to⁹ Rettraitz. Et adonc feconfeffa et ordonna co͡m bon catholicque tel quil eftoit

known in the prison where he was, by monseigneur the grand president of Thorette, master Jean le Boullenger, councillor of the king in his court of parlement; master Jean Bureau, treasurer of France; and several others of the grand council of the king, for which the said Alençon was well amazed and discomforted, and not without cause.

In the said year 1458, in the month of January, the very high and powerful prince Monseigneur Arthur of Brittany, and before and after his life before constable of France, went from life to death. After the death of the said man, Monseigneur François, son of Madame d'Étampes, sister of Madame d'Orléans, succeeded to the said duchy, who in person handed it to him, etc.

How the king settled into the death bed

The year 1461, around the beginning of the month of July, certain language was sown by men full of discord, and one said that one wanted to poison the very Christian king Charles, seventh of this name, he being at Meun-sur-Yèvre, for which reason after he was informed, the said poison in his heart was such that he no longer had joy nor health. But because it was noticed by a captain who greatly loved him, he expressed such faith there and despaired such that he did not eat for the space of eight hours or more, because he did not dare to trust any of his men nor anything that his physicians said to him. He would not eat nor take any meal. And [this continued] until his physicians told him that if he would not eat, he would die. And so he tried to eat, but he could not, because his throat was already all sealed up. And thus he confessed and was ordained as a good catholic such as he ought to do. And then, seeing his illness

doit fr̃. Et depuis lui voyant ſamalladie engregr̃ et ſes Iours abregier Receult bien 7devotemet̃ to⁹ ſes ſacremens et fiſt ſes deſrenieres ordon̄n et laiz telz que bon lui ſembla. Et ordonna aſes executeurs quil voulloit eſtre ſa ſepulture en legliſe monſ.ʳ Saint denis en france en lachapelle ou ſon pere et ſon grant pere ſont enterres. Ainſſi finerent ſes deſreniers Iours. Le Iour delamagdeleine oud an et moys en lad ville demeun ſur yevre.

La piteuſe. et doulloureuſe. mort du Roẙ. et ſon. entr̃emet̃.

LE. Iour delamagdeleine mil CCCC Soixante 7ung. Treſpaſſa lebon Roẙ charles. Sept.ᵐᵉ dece nom. treſvictorieulx p̊nce en chaſteau demeun ſur yevre aqui dieu face pardon et mercy alame. Le mardi enſuivat̃ fut fait ſon ſervice en legliſe monſ.ʳ ſaint denis en france moult ſolempnellement tout ainſſi q̂ on aacouſtume faire tous les ans pour leRoy loys legros. Iadiz Roy defrance. C Lemerquedi v.ᵐᵉ Iour daouſt enſuivant adix heures denuyt fut apporte lecorps dud Roy charles aparis et laiſſe hors laville en legliſe nor̃dame de paris. Et yot quatre ſeigneurs delacourt de parlement qui tenoient les quatre cornieres du pouelle veſtuz en manteaulx deſcarlache et pluſſieurs autres ſeigneurs delad court veſtuz devermeil tenant led pouelle. C Item apres lecorps dud Roy. lequel eſtoit couvert dun pouelle dedrap dor bien Riche en une littiere. laquelle portoient v.ˣˣ henouars. Et yeſtoient monſ.ʳ dorleans Monſ.ʳ dangouleſme Monſ.ʳ deu et Monſ.ʳ dedunoiz faiſans ledueil acheval tous quatre. C Item apres ung chariot ouquel avoit eſte led corps demeun Iucques aparis couvert dun pouelle

progress and his days shortened, he received well and devotedly all his sacrements and made his last orders and laws such as it seemed good to him. And he ordered to his executors that he would be entombed in the church of monseigneur Saint-Denis-en-France, in the chapel where his father and grandfather were interred. So ended his last days, the day of the Magdeline in the said year and month in the said town of Meun-sur-Yèvre.

The piteous and sad death of the king, and his interrment

THE day of the Magdeleine 1461, the good king Charles, seventh of this name, a very victorious prince, died in the castle of Meun-sur-Yèvre, to which God has pardon and mercy for the soul. The following Tuesday, his service was held very solemnly in the church of monseigneur Saint-Denis-en-France, all according to what one was accustomed to do all the years since the king Louis the Fat, late king of France. C Wednesday, the fifth day of the following August, at ten at night, the body of the said king Charles was brought to Paris and left outside the town in the church of Nôtre-Dame-de-Paris. And there were four lords of the court of parlement who took the four corners of the covering, vested in coats of scarlet, and several other lords of the said court vested in vermillion holding the said covering. C Item, after the body of the said king, which was covered by a covering of very rich gold cloth on a litter, which was carried by 120 salt porters. And monseigneur d'Orléans, monseigneur d'Angoulême, monseigneur d'Eu, and monseigneur de Dunois were there, feeling the loss, all four on horseback. C Item, after, a chariot on which had been the said body from Mahun until

develloux noir tout atravers couvert dune grant croix blanche dedrap develloux figure moult Riche. C Item aud chariot avoit. v. chevaulx qui lemenoient couvers Iucq̃z aterre develloux noir figure et ne veoit on que les yeulx deſd chevaulx. C Item apres led chariot avoit vi. pages veſtuz develloux noir en chapperonnes demeſmes ſur vi. chevaulx donc les harnoiz eſtoient develloux noir C Item devant lecorps eſtoient monſ.[r] le patriarche lors evſque debayeulx lequel fiſt leſervice tant anoſ̃ dame deparis que aSaint denis comme Il ſera dit cy apres. Et eſtoient ceulx denoſ̃dame deparis et ceulx dupallaiz avec les parroiſſes. C Item devant eſtoit monſ[r] leRecteur deluniverſite deparis. C Item eſtoient devant meſſ.[rs] des comptes to⁹ veſtus denoir. C Item meſſeigneurs des Requeſtes. C Item devant eſtoit monſ.[r] leprevoſt deparis lacourt dechaſtelet et lepeuple deparis chc̃n par ordonnance. C Item devant eſtoieẽ pluſſ.[rs] ordres deReligion dud paris. C Item devant les quatre ordres mendians delad ville. C Item et tout deſriere toutes ſes gens et led corps eſtoit Innumerable peuple tant deparis cõme dailleurs. C Item yavoit deux cens torches chc̃ne dequatre livres q̃ portoient deux cens hommes veſtuz denoir. C Item en legliſe noſ̃ dame deparis laquelle eſtoit tendue doublemeẽ detoille perce en ſon largetoute ſemee defle[rs] deliz. C Item et fut porte lecorps dud Roy en mellieu duceur denoſ̃dame deparis et la furent chantees vegilles demors pour led Roy et lendemain lameſſe Laquelle chanta monſ.[r] lepatriarche. Et fut levendredi. Vi.[me] Iour daouſt lan que deſſus. C Ced vendredi environ trois heures apres midi. les ſeigneurs deſſus nommez Leſquelz avoient eſte auſervice duRoy. apporterent ſon corps depar-

Paris, covered by a covering entirely of black velvet, covered by a great white cross of velvet cloth very richly designed. C Item, the said chariot had five horses which led it, covered to the ground in black decorated velvet, and one could only see the eyes of the said horses. C Item, after the said chariot were six pages wearing black velvet, wearing the same hoods, on six horses that the harneses were made of black velvet. C Item, before the body was monseigneur the patriarch, then bishop of Bayeux, who made the service both at Nôtre-Dame-de-Paris and at Saint-Denis, as will be said afterwards. And those of Nôtre-Dame-de-Paris and those of the palace were with the Parisians. C Item, before was monseigneur the rector of the university of Paris. C Item, before, monseigneurs the accounts were all vested in black. C Item, monseigneurs of requests. C Item, before was monseigneur the provost of Paris, the court of the Châtelet, and the people of Paris, each by order. C Item, before were several orders of religion of the said town. C Item, before, the four orders of mendicants of the said town. C Item, and behind all these men and the said body were innumeral people, both of Paris and elsewhere. C Item, there were 200 torches, each of four pounds, which 200 men vested in black carried. C Item, in the church of Nôtre-Dame-de-Paris, which was covered twice in fabric because of its size, all decorated with fleurs-de-lis. C Item, and the body of the said king was carried to the middle of the heart of Nôtre-Dame-de-Paris, and there were sung vigils of death for the said king, and the next day the mass, which monseigneur the patriarch sung. And it was Friday, the sixth day of August in the abovesaid year. C The said Friday, around three hours after noon, the abovenamed lords, who had been at the service of the king, brought his body from Paris until

is Iucques alacroiz au fiens Laquelle eſt entre lachap pelle ſaint denis et lelendit en ordonnance comme deſſ. Et la eult groſſe contradicion pour porter led corps Iucques alegliſe et demoura en celieu par longue eſpace detp̃s. Et tellement que les bourgoiz delaville deſaint denis prindrent labierre ainſſi cōe elle eſtoit et vouldrent porter led corps aSaint denis. pource q̂ les henouars le laiſſerent ſur lechemin pour laſomme dedix livres q̂ Ilz demandoient pour leporter. Et dicelle ſomme dedix livres led eſcuier ~ deſcuierie duRoy leur en Reſpondit. Et lors leporterent Iucques dedens leceur delegliſe monſ.ʳ ſaint denis. et fut bien huit heures denuyt avant que led corps aud lieu deſaint denis. C Item acelle heure furent chantees veſpres demors pour led Roy ſeullement et lendemain matines. ceſt aſſavoir dirige environ ſix heures dematin. Et yeſtoient Monſ.ʳ dangouleſme. Monſ.ʳ dedunoiz Monſ.ʳ debreſſes. Monſ.ʳ dechaſteau bruyant Monſ.ʳ legrant eſcuier. Leveſque deparis et lacourt deparlement Leveſque debayeulx fiſt leſervice. les eveſques detroye et de chartres loffice. Leveſque dorleans. leveſq̂ dangiers. leveſque debeſiers. leveſque de ſenliz. leveſque demeaulx. labbe deſaint germain. Labbe deſaint magloire. Labbe deſaint eſtienne dedion. Labbe deſaint victor. Tous les deſſſ nommez furet̂ en la meſſe. et Icy ny eult q̂ une grant meſſe pour le roy Monſeigneur dorleans et ma dame dorleans yfurent. Monſ.ʳ deu ny fut point. Maiz ſen alla lematin. C Item apres lad meſſe fut le Roy mis en terre en lachap pelle deſon grant pere entre led grant pere et ſon pere. C Item fut leceur delad egliſe tendu tout autour dedrap develloux noir et une chappelle laquelle fut moult belle en melieu duceur ſoubz laquelle eſtoit led Roẙ

the Croix-au-Fiens, which was between the chapel of Saint-Denis and the Lendit, in order as above. And there was a great contradiction to carry the said body to the church and remain in this place for a long space of time. And such that the citizens of the town of Saint-Denis took the bier as it was, and wanted to take the said body to Saint-Denis, because the salt porters left it on the procession, for the sum of 10 *livres parisis* that they requested to carry it. And for this sum of ten livres, the said squire of the squirerie of the king responded to them. And then they carried it until within the heart of the church of monseigneur Saint-Denis, and it was about eight at night before the said body arrived at the said place of Saint-Denis. C Item, at this hour were chanted vespers of death only for the said king, and the next day, matins—it is known, Dirige, around six in the morning. And at this place were monseigneur d'Angoulême, monseigneur de Dunois, monseigneur de Brézé, monseigneur de Château-Bruyant, monseigneur the grand squire, the bishop of Paris, and the court of parlement. The bishop of Bayeux did the service; the bishops of Troyes and Chartres the office; the bishop of Orléans, the bishop of Angiers, the bishop of Besiers, the bishop of Senlis, the bishop of Meaux, the abbot of Saint-Germain, the abbot of Saint-Magloire, the abbot of Saint-Étienne-de-Dijon, [and] the abbot of Saint-Victor—all of the above-named were in the mass and here there was held a great mass for the king. Monseigneur d'Orléans and madame d'Orléans were there. Monseigneur d'Eu was no longer there, but he went in the morning. C Item, after the said mass, the king was interred in the chapel of his grandfather, between the said grandfather and his father. C Item, the heart of the said church was decorated all in black velvet cloth and a cape which was very beautiful, in the

tendue pareillement develloux et par deſſus tant decierges queon yen peult mettre. C Item eſtoit leRoy dedans ung coffre decypres enchaſſe et en ung deplomb. deſon longc leſ quelz eſtoient enfermez dedens une bierre de boys. C Item eſtoit leRoy par deſſus en figure ſur ung matheras une paire dedraps delin Lapouelle deſſſd et eſtoit lad figure decuir veſtue dune tunique et ung manteau de velloux. afleurs deliz fourre dermines. en une deſes mains une main côme ung ſeptre et ung anneau dor. Et en laut̂ main ung grat̂ ſceptre une couronne ſur lateſte. et ung orillier develloux deſſoubz. C Item avoient les gens du Roy apporte ung ~~drap~~ ciel dedrap dor auql̂ avoit huit lances pour leporter et alad croix auſiens ſur lechemin deparis vindrent huit des Religieux de paris Saint denis prend led ciel pour leporter deſſus lecorps du Roy Iucques aud Saint denis. Maiz le grant eſcuier leur Refuſa abailler en diſant que ce neſtoit point lacouſtume et q̂ led ciel ne ſedevoit point porter ſur led corps parmy les champs. Maiz ſedevoit portr̂ parmy les villes ſeullement. Et quant lecorps fut alaporte delad ville Saint denis fut faicte ſtacion et lafuret̂ chantees trois oroiſons leſquelles ſechantoient achacue̅ ſtacion. Et lafut baille led ciel auſd huit Religl Leſquelz leporterent Iucques alegliſe par deſſus led corps en telle maniere queon ne povoit veoir Icellui ~~cop~~ corps tout applain. ceſt aſſavoir lad figure. C Item apres lent̂remet̂ dud Roy eult groſſe contradicion Entre le grant eſcuier deſcuierie du Roy. et les Religl dud Saint denis pour lapouelle qui eſtoit ſoubz lad figure pource que led eſcuier diſoit que aeulx ne appartenoit et tellement que Il convint que led drap fuſt mis en lamain demonſ.r dedunoiz et demonſ.r lechancel-

middle of the heart, under which was the said king, covered equally by velvet, and above as many candles as someone could place there. C Item, the king was in a coffin of cypress, encased in one of lead of his length, which was enclosed within a bier of wood. C Item, above the king was a figure on a mattress, a pair of linen sheets, and the abovesaid covering, and the said leather figure, clothed in a tunic and a coat of velvet with fleurs-de-lis, stuffed with ermine, in one of his hands, one hand as a septer and a gold ring and in the other hand a large septer, a crown on the head and a pillow of velvet underneath. C Item, the men of the king brought a canopy of gold cloth that had eight lances to carry it, and at the said Croix-au-Fiens, on the road to Paris came eight of the monks of Saint-Denis taking the said canopy to carry it above the body of the king until the said Saint-Denis. But the grand squire refused to release them, saying that it was no longer the custom and that the said canopy ought to no longer be carried over the said body upon the fields, but ought to be carried only within the towns. And when the body was at the gate of the said town of Saint-Denis, a station was made, and there were chanted three songs that they chanted at each station. And the said canopy was handed over to the said eight monks there, who carried the said body until the abovesaid church in such manner that one could not see this body completely—it is known, the said figure. C Item, after the interment of the said king, there was a great debate between the grand squire of the squirerie of the king and the monks of the said Saint-Denis for the sheet that was under the said figure, because the said squire said that it belonged to him, and such that he agreed that the said cloth was put into the hand of monseigneur de Dunois and monseigneur the chancellor of France. Finally, it was agreed that the

lier defrance. Finablement fut appoincte q̂ led pouelle lequel eſtoit dedrap dor. vermeil moult bel demourroit en lad egliſe Saint denis en diſant par led grant eſcuier q̂ ſe aucun droit yavoit Il le donnoit alad egliſe deSaint denis en france. C Item au Regard duciel Il demoura alad egliſe Saint denis Sans contradicion. avec velloux cendaulx cires et auт̂s choſes. Maiz Ilz Rem porterent ledrap develloux noir alacroix blanche. lequel couvroit ledchariot et toutes auт̂s choſes. C Item allerent mondſ[r] dedunoiz et led ~~conte~~ grant eſcuier par toutes les chappelles ou Il yavoit corps ſains et donnerent aladecoracion des autelz du drap develloux et deſatin acouvrir deux tables dautel hault et bas. C Item en melieu delagrant meſſe yot une p̊dicac̅on que fiſt maiſtre thonmas decourcelles docte[r] en theologie Alaquelle avoit grant peuple gemiſſant et priant pour led deffunct. lequel fut tiltre le Roy charles. Sept.[me] decenom treſvictorieulx. C Item apres lenterremet̂ fut crie vive loys. Roy defrance. Et dieu ait lame decharles. Sept.[me] treſvictorieulx comme dit eſt. Et adonc Iecterent leurs verges ſur lafoſſe les huiſſiers et autres ſergens. C Item apres tout leſervice fait allerent diſgner en lagrant ſalle delabbe et yot court plainiere et ouverte atous venans. Et dicelle heure lediſgner et graces dictes. monſ.[r] leconte dedunoiz et delongueville diſt ahaulte voix q̂lui et to⁹ les auт̂s ſerviteurs avoient perdu leur maiſtre et que ung chc̅n penſaſt aſoy° ~ pouvoir. Aquoy furent moult doullens chc̅n en ſon cuidoit et non ſans cauſe. Et par eſpecial commencerent les pages ~~tros~~ treſſort apleurer ⁊cl. mil. lxv. ⁊cl.

said sheet, which was of very beautiful vermillion gold cloth, remain in the said church [of] Saint-Denis, the said grand squire saying that any right that he had to it he gave to the said church of Saint-Denis-en-France. C Item, in regard to the canopy, it remained at the said church [of] Saint-Denis without debate, with the velvet, candles, wax, and other things, but they took back the black velvet cloth with the white cross, which covered the said chariot, and all other things. C Item, my said lord of Dunois and the said grand squire went to all the chapels where there were holy bodies, and gave the decorations of the altar of velvet and satin cloth to cover the two tables of the high and lower altar. C Item, in the middle of the great mass there was a sermon that was made by master Thomas de Courcelles, doctor in theology, with which he had great people moan and pray for the said deceased, who was titled king Charles, seventh of this name, very victorious. C Item, after the internment, it was cried over the grave: Vive Louis, king of France. And God have love for Charles the seventh, very victorious, it is said. And then the court officers and other sergeants threw their rods of office into the pit. C Item, after all the service was done, they went to dine in the great hall of the abbey, and there court was held plain and open to all who came. And at this hour the dinner was made and the graces said, monseigneur the count of Dunois and of Longueville said with a high voice that he and all the other servants had lost their master, and that each should think to himself what to do. To which each was very sorrowful in thinking of himself, and not without reason. And especially the pages began to cry very strongly, etcetera, 1465, etcetera.

www.ingramcontent.com/pod-product-compliance
Lightning Source LLC
LaVergne TN
LVHW020052110826
845155LV00022B/72